Dr Ambedkar and the
Revival of Buddhism 1

THE COMPLETE WORKS OF SANGHARAKSHITA
include all his previously published work, as well as talks,
seminars, and writings published here for the first time. The
collection represents the definitive edition of his life's work as
Buddhist writer and teacher. For further details, including the
contents of each volume, please turn to the 'Guide' on pp.593–602.

FOUNDATION

1   A Survey of Buddhism / The Buddha's Noble Eightfold Path
2   The Three Jewels I
3   The Three Jewels II
4   The Bodhisattva Ideal
5   The Purpose and Practice of Buddhist Meditation
6   The Essential Sangharakshita

INDIA

7   Crossing the Stream: India Writings I
8   Beating the Dharma Drum: India Writings II
9   Dr Ambedkar and the Revival of Buddhism I
10   Dr Ambedkar and the Revival of Buddhism II

THE WEST

11   A New Buddhist Movement I
12   A New Buddhist Movement II
13   Eastern and Western Traditions

COMMENTARY

14 The Eternal Legacy / Wisdom Beyond Words
15 Pāli Canon Teachings and Translations
16 Mahayana Myths and Stories
17 Wisdom Teachings of the Mahayana
18 Milarepa and the Art of Discipleship 1
19 Milarepa and the Art of Discipleship 11

MEMOIRS

20 The Rainbow Road from Tooting Broadway to Kalimpong
21 Facing Mount Kanchenjunga
22 In the Sign of the Golden Wheel
23 Moving Against the Stream
24 Through Buddhist Eyes

POETRY AND THE ARTS

25 Poems and Stories
26 Aphorisms and the Arts

27 Concordance and Appendices

COMPLETE WORKS *9* **INDIA**

Sangharakshita
Dr Ambedkar and the
Revival of Buddhism 1

EDITED BY KALYANAPRABHA AND VIDYADEVI

Windhorse Publications
169 Mill Road
Cambridge
CB1 3AN
UK

info@windhorsepublications.com
www.windhorsepublications.com

Cover design by Dhammarati
Cover images © Clear Vision Trust Picture Archive
Typesetting and layout by Ruth Rudd
Printed by Bell & Bain Ltd, Glasgow

**British Library Cataloguing
in Publication Data:**
A catalogue record for this book is
available from the British Library.

ISBN 978-1-909314-78-8 (paperback)
ISBN 978-1-909314-82-5 (hardback)

CONTENTS

Foreword, Subhuti   xi

AMBEDKAR AND BUDDHISM

Preface   1
1   The Significance of Ambedkar   3
2   Three Meetings   13
3   The Hell of Caste   25
4   Milestones on the Road to Conversion   45
5   The Search for Roots   74
6   Thinking about Buddhism   92
7   The Great Mass Conversion   120
8   'The Buddha and His Dhamma'   136
9   After Ambedkar   150

LECTURE TOUR IN INDIA
December 1981 – March 1982

Notes from the Editors   163
Map   167
1   Ambedkar Housing Society Welcoming Programme   169
2   The Buddha's Religion is Morality   178
3   Being a Buddhist Means Changing Your Life   189

4   The Seed of the Dhamma Revolution: *Samādhi*   197

5   The Five Spiritual Faculties   207

6   Turning Points in the Lives of the Buddha
      and Dr Ambedkar   219

7   Seeing the True Nature of Existence: *Prajñā*   226

8   Has the Dhamma Revolution Failed?   235

9   Going for Refuge   244

10 Losing and Finding the Jewel of the Dhamma   260

11 How to Distinguish Between the True
      and the False Buddhist   270

12 My Life and Mission and the Teaching
      of Dr Ambedkar   277

13 The Seven *Bodhyaṅgas*   291

14 Working Together for the Dhamma   302

15 The *Sanantana-Dhamma*   312

16 Reason and Emotion in Spiritual Life:
      Dr Ambedkar's Great Example   321

17 Questions and Answers at Milind College   327

18 Religion and the Secular State   347

19 Getting Out of the Burning House – Together   356

20 The Four Animals of Aśoka and What They Represent   363

21 Things That Can Help Us to Change   370

22 The Five Mudrās of the Buddha   379

23 Why Buddhism Disappeared from India and How
      It Can Be Prevented from Disappearing Again   387

24 Aspects of the Middle Way   396

25 Dr Ambedkar's Dhamma Revolution and its
      Importance in the Scientific Age of Today   404

26 A New Vihara Means a New Life   415

27 Buddhism is the Only Alternative   422

28 Buddhism and Education   435

29 Entering the Stream of the Dhamma   449

30 The Meaning of the Buddha Puja
      and the Function of a Vihara   459

31 Why Choose Buddhism?   466

32 Words and Meanings   476

33 Why People in the West Have Become Buddhists   486

34 Buddhism in India and Buddhism in England – A Parallel   499

35   Questions and Answers in Bombay   513

36   Questions and Answers with Order Members   530

Appendix
Dr Ambedkar's Twenty-Two Conversion Vows   541

Glossary   543
Notes   549
Index   579

A Guide to *The Complete Works of Sangharakshita*   593

A NOTE ON PLACE NAMES

The names of a number of Indian cities that appear in this volume changed in the years between 1978 and 2001. In consultation with the author, the editors have kept Sangharakshita's use of the older forms throughout. Thus in both *Ambedkar and Buddhism* and the India lectures you will find 'Poona', 'Bombay', and 'Calcutta' (rather than Pune, Mumbai, and Kolkata). In the notes, however, as well as in the Foreword, the modern names are used.

A NOTE ON THE USE OF PĀLI AND SANSKRIT

Pāli and Sanskrit terms appear with their full complement of diacritics throughout this volume except where they have become accepted as part of the English language. It should be noted, however, that the editors have not attempted to standardize Sangharakshita's use of Buddhist terms. He uses Pāli or Sanskrit depending on the context. In his India talks he moved fluidly between the the two. Some Pāli terms were familiar to his audiences but Sanskrit forms were often preferred as being closer to their own languages. There are also some hybrid terms such as 'Dhammamitra' which use both Pāli and Sanskrit. For further explanation see the Glossary (p.543) and the editors' notes to the India talks (p.163).

FOREWORD

In this volume of the *Complete Works* of Urgyen Sangharakshita, we are able to witness one of the most far-reaching of his contributions to modern Buddhism. Here we see him in the act of giving shape to the Buddhist conversion movement begun by the great Indian statesman and reformer, Dr B. R. Ambedkar.

Until recently, Dr Ambedkar was little known outside India, quite eclipsed by the charisma of Mr Gandhi and other luminaries of the Independence struggle. Even in India, though he has always been the revered hero of the hundreds of millions of those coming from castes formerly considered 'untouchable', he was not a widely acknowledged figure until thirty or so years after his death in 1956. Now he is one of the most important icons of India, his image adorning the platforms of political parties of every hue, whether their policies agree with his or not – in some cases being even diametrically opposed! Yet his conversion to Buddhism, the work that gave him the greatest satisfaction of all his many achievements, is still understood by very few and is often dismissed as a mere political stunt taken in a fit of pique at the failure of his ministerial ambitions.

This was far from being the case. His conversion was a deeply serious act undertaken with the utmost sincerity in a mood of intense devotion. It was truly the culmination of his life's work. In the first place, he himself had long been drawn to the Buddha and he embraced him as his teacher and ideal, as he said, for 'reasons spiritual'.[1] However, he also saw conversion as the best way for his fellow 'untouchables' to transform themselves. By quitting Hinduism, from which their outcaste status was derived, they would leave behind the 'hell of caste' and, by becoming Buddhists, take on their true status as equal human beings. Finally, he recognized that, however necessary and significant was the new constitution of the Republic of India, of which he had been the principal author, without a widespread change in fundamental attitudes throughout India, the oppressions of caste would continue. If India was to be a genuine *political* democracy, *social* democracy must be established first – and that could only come from a new moral outlook on the part of the majority of citizens. The best basis for such a renewal was, he urged, the Buddha-Dhamma.

These were the high hopes that Dr Ambedkar had for conversion. Besides its power to give spiritual fulfilment to those feeling that call, he believed the Buddha-Dhamma could liberate millions from the stigma of Untouchability and be the basis for a new India, imbued with the principles of liberty, equality, fraternity, and justice, principles he had insisted were written into the Preamble to the Constitution – and which he says he derived, not from the French Revolution, but from, 'my master, the Buddha'.[2] But within weeks of the great mass conversion in Nagpur, he was dead.

Sangharakshita's life intersected with Dr Ambedkar's at a crucial stage for both men. In the first text in this volume, Sangharakshita describes their three meetings. The third of these is especially significant, for by then Dr Ambedkar was but days from his end. Sangharakshita had gone to visit him in Delhi with a party of 'Eminent Buddhists from the Border Areas' to felicitate him on his entry into Buddhism, just a month before. In Sangharakshita's words, we hear Dr Ambedkar speaking to the gathering of his 'hopes and fears – mostly fears' for the movement of conversion to Buddhism that he had inaugurated. And then, as he grows more and more weary in the burning midday sun, we glimpse him whispering for Sangharakshita's ears alone: 'There was still so much to be done, the sad, tired voice was saying ... so much to be done.' Sangharakshita 'had the distinct impression that he somehow knew we would not be meeting again and that he wanted to transfer to my shoulders some of the weight that he was no longer able to bear himself'.[3]

Sangharakshita did try to shoulder some of that weight once Dr Ambedkar was gone, most notably in Nagpur in the days following his death. He then made regular preaching tours among the new Buddhists, doing his best to educate them in the religion they had espoused. He has said that so great was the faith of these largely illiterate masses, rightly guided many of them could have attained Stream Entry. However, over the next few years, politics and faction began to dominate the movement and he encountered increasing difficulties in his own work. When, in 1962, he received an invitation to visit the UK to help the nascent Buddhist movement there, he therefore felt able to accept. He soon saw the potential for the spread of the Dhamma in the West and, at the same time, the need for a completely new start. In 1967, he therefore initiated a new Buddhist movement, the Friends of the Western Buddhist Order – now the Triratna Buddhist Community. Although he has never explicitly stated so, perhaps he also saw that this new Buddhist movement offered the means by which that burden transferred to him by Dr Ambedkar could more effectively be shouldered.

Dr Ambedkar had indeed himself initiated a widespread movement of conversion and had given its broad outlines. He had founded the Buddhist Society of India as a vehicle for the work and had published *The Buddha and His Dhamma* as a manageable account of the basic teachings, drawing mainly on Pāli sources, but also on Mahāyāna scriptures and commentaries. He had hoped that international Buddhist help would come pouring in and that guidance would be given by missionaries from Buddhist countries.

However, he had not had time to establish that movement in depth and what help came from the Buddhist world was, at best, not very effective. Above all, he had had no chance to establish a *sangha*: a living community, both lay and monastic, of men and women actively practising the Dhamma together. Indeed, without a *sangha* there could be no practicable path of practice, beyond the most basic following of the precepts and performance of social ceremonies according to Buddhist forms. He had founded an organization, but without a true *sangha* that organization was bound to have limited success and to be subject to factionalism and the dominance of powerful personalities.

Dr Ambedkar saw no way forward with the *bhikṣu sangha* and was very critical of the forms of it he had experienced in Sri Lanka and Burma.[4] Indeed, so great was his suspicion of the *bhikṣu sangha* that he at first wanted to convert only by Going for Refuge to the Buddha and Dhamma, without the Sangha. He only consented to do so once it had been explained to him that the 'Sangha', *as Refuge*, did not refer to the *bhikṣus* but to the Āryasaṅgha: those who have attained Stream Entry and beyond, who may not necessarily be monks – indeed, it could include women!

Beyond his doubts about the *bhikṣu saṅgha* as he had experienced it, he had not had the opportunity to do more than envisage a new kind of Dhamma-worker, who would not necessarily be a monastic. He spoke of founding Dhamma training centres for such workers in the main cities of India. But he was dead before he could put that vision into effect or even supply more detail as to what it constituted, and the conversion movement gradually stalled.

Meanwhile, in the unusually propitious environment of 1960s Britain, Sangharakshita was forging a new kind of *saṅgha*, very much along the lines that Dr Ambedkar had envisaged: rejecting the identification of *saṅgha* with the *bhikṣus* and opening it to all, regardless of gender, culture, social background, or whether one was celibate or living a household life, emphasizing the primacy of commitment over lifestyle, and encouraging an active spreading of the Dhamma and the creation of a 'new society'. As this new kind of *saṅgha* developed, at first as the Western Buddhist Order and later as the Triratna Buddhist Order, so a praxis evolved: teachings and practices that suited the times and which arose from the needs of his disciples.

Sangharakshita had, however, never forgotten the conversion movement in India, often speaking of it to his Western disciples, and in 1978, he found an opportunity to re-engage directly with it. One of his senior disciples, Dhammachari Lokamitra, wanted to visit India to practise hatha yoga, so Sangharakshita, ever resourceful, gave him the addresses of his main Indian disciples. Lokamitra very quickly found that there was great potential for the new Buddhist movement Sangharakshita had founded amongst the many followers of Dr Ambedkar in India. When he visited the Diksha Bhumi in Nagpur, on the anniversary of the conversion ceremony that had taken place there in 1956, he saw a million or so people crowded into the grounds in their overwhelming devotion to their great leader. It became clear to him that he must move to India and start activities of what is now the Triratna Buddhist Community.

Over the next few years, in close consultation with Sangharakshita, Lokamitra, with astonishing energy and determination, established a flourishing branch of the Order and Community, with centres and groups in several key places, especially in Maharashtra, Dr Ambedkar's own state. Sangharakshita himself guided this emerging movement, albeit largely through what now seems the cumbersome processes of airmail.

In 1979, Sangharakshita visited India again after an absence of twelve years. He conducted the first ordinations of Indians into the Order, made key decisions about the future of the work, and gave a number of talks. He was back again in 1981, consolidating further the Indian branch of the Movement, and conducting a far more extensive tour, giving talks at many of the main places of the conversion movement. These talks are published here, many appearing for the first time, and give a flavour of what he was doing – although they can never, in this form, capture the extraordinary sights and sounds of the occasions on which they were given – wide-eyed children, gazing up at the orange-clad speaker, lines of women in gorgeous saris, flower garlands by the score, and crackling loudspeakers ringing on the evening air. Above all they cannot convey the mood, the intense joy and faith they awakened in their audiences: the shining faces, the soaring spirits. For a taste of that I can only recommend Dhammachari Nagabodhi's *Jai Bhim! Dispatches from a Peaceful Revolution.*[5]

In the course of these talks, often addressing thousands of people in the open air through a translator, he very carefully, clearly, and skilfully laid out the principles for the continuance of Dr Ambedkar's conversion movement, especially through the Triratna Buddhist Order and Community. He was, first and foremost, educating them in the depths of the Buddha's teaching, just as he was his Western disciples in the UK, expounding such essential themes as the three fetters, the power of *mettā*, how one should test the Buddha's words as gold is tested by the goldsmith in the fire, entering the stream of the Dhamma, important verses from the *Dhammapada*, and so on. Indeed, it is striking that though many in his audience would have been far less educated than their Western counterparts at that time, the Dhammic content is the same and just as pure and deep – indeed, in some way more so because he could count on the open hearts of those he was addressing. He took his audience very seriously.

At the same time as teaching the core messages of the Dhamma, Sangharakshita had to address the situation of Dr Ambedkar's movement. Twenty-five years after his conversion and death, there was a great deal of unclarity among his followers about the meaning and significance of becoming a Buddhist. Many problems had emerged and these Sangharakshita analysed for his audiences who, though often very poorly educated, if educated at all, were intelligent and perceptive:

> These problems are of various kinds, e.g. problems of disunity, of lack of enthusiasm, of partial failure, but the root cause of all of them is threefold. They are due to (a) lack of a clear understanding of why Dr Ambedkar chose Buddhism, (b) failure to understand the significance of the movement of mass conversion, (c) failure to discover a right way of working.[6]

So he proceeded to show, in talk after talk, how those problems could be faced, especially pointing out how the Triratna Buddhist Order and Community offered their solution.

Sangharakshita made several more lengthy visits to India, each time taking the understanding of his Indian disciples further and deeper. But it was clear that something more was needed if the movement of conversion was to be established on a firm footing. His Indian followers still needed to understand Dr Ambedkar's conversion more clearly if they were truly to fulfil it. At the same time, Sangharakshita's Western disciples needed to understand the perspective of their Indian brothers and sisters. He decided, therefore, to write a book, published in 1986 as *Ambedkar and Buddhism* and included here as the first work in this volume.

Ambedkar and Buddhism was the only one of his books, apart from his memoirs, that began life as a book – all the others emerged from talks or, in the case of *The Three Jewels* and *The Eternal Legacy*, encyclopaedia entries. This is deeply significant. It was written to perform a vital task for which no other work was available – and is still not, to this day: showing how Dr Ambedkar's conversion to Buddhism was the fulfilment of his whole life and mission and clarifying what it signified for the future. More than ephemeral talks could do, this met the first two reasons given above for why the conversion movement had become bemired in problems: '(a) lack of a clear understanding of why Dr Ambedkar chose Buddhism, (b) failure to understand the significance of the movement of mass conversion'.

We see here at work one of Sangharakshita's key contributions, discernible in many fields: drawing out and expounding, in terms of sparkling lucidity, the essential principles on which the Buddhist life is to be lived today. He is especially gifted at drawing those principles out of existing cultural circumstances and linking them to the fundamentals of the Dhamma. This is what he did for my generation in the UK: taking our 'hippie' idealism, naive and muddy as it was, and channelling it into the clearer and purer ocean of the Buddha's teaching. In this volume we can witness him applying that clarity of principle to the conversion movement and showing how Dr Ambedkar's deep inspiration and understanding can be fulfilled through a new kind of *sangha* and a fresh presentation of the Dhamma.

Those who read this volume in India will better understand the origins and basis of the Triratna Buddhist Order and Community there and therefore what has made them what they are today. This will also be important for people connected with our movement elsewhere, and enable them to connect more deeply with their Indian brothers and sisters and to identify with their perspective. However, it also will help all modern Buddhists and others to recognize the significance of Dr Ambedkar and his distinctive contribution to the development of a modern Buddhist political understanding. He is the first significant individual to apply the principles of the Dhamma to modern democratic society and to show how they are indispensable to the creation of a just, free, equal, and harmonious society anywhere in the world. As such he deserves to be far more widely known and honoured, and Sangharakshita's writing and speeches offer us an excellent basis for that to come about.

This volume is published in the 125th year of Dr Ambedkar's birth and the 60th of his conversion and death, and thirty years or more after the book and the talks it contains first appeared. Much has changed: in India, in the Buddhist movement there, and in the Triratna Buddhist Community itself worldwide. The grandchildren of many in Sangharakshita's audiences from the slums of Nagpur or Mumbai now may have had the university education and be gaining the professional positions that were unimaginable then. A whole section of the Buddhist community in Maharashtra has entered the middle classes, largely because of the opportunities opened up for them by Dr Ambedkar and the courage and self-confidence derived from conversion. Yet caste-based prejudice is still evident, even for them, and countless others, especially in certain parts of the subcontinent, suffer the same oppression, exclusion, and violence as of old.

The seismic shock of Dr Ambedkar's mission, and especially of his conversion, still reverberates and continues to shake down old barriers and stimulate yet more people to free themselves from the shackles of caste. He is the chief hero and hope for hundreds of millions of Indians. It is striking how much his influence has grown in India since his death and how many more people there are who are open to his Buddhist message, if they are fortunate enough to hear it. In the prevailing political conditions it is evident that his vision of Indian democracy is needed more than ever.

The Triratna Buddhist Community also has continued to grow and is gradually reaching beyond Maharashtra, encompassing more people from different states and different communities. From that point of view, it has certainly become far more diverse. And now, thirty years later, it is Indians who are leading the Movement in their own country and increasingly participating in the leadership of the Movement worldwide. And women are playing an ever more equal part in that leadership. Modest though the Triratna Buddhist Community in India is in size, it is influential and that influence is growing, the work that we see bearing greater and more bountiful fruit.

Subhuti

Ambedkar and Buddhism

No volcano bursting up through peaceful pastures is a greater
   revolution than this;
No vast mountain chain thrown out from ocean depths to form the
   primitive streak of a new continent looks further down the future;
For this is lava springing out of the very heart of Man;
This is the upheaval of heaven-kissing summits whose streams shall
   feed the farthest generations,
This is the draft and outline of a new creature,
The forming of the wings of Man beneath the outer husk –
The outspread pinions of Equality, whereon arising he shall at last lift
   himself over the Earth and launch forth to sail through Heaven.

Edward Carpenter, *Towards Democracy*[7]

PREFACE TO THE FIRST EDITION 1986

There are at present 100,000,000 Untouchables in India, the vast majority of whom are underprivileged in every sense of the term. Each year between four and five hundred of them are murdered by their caste Hindu compatriots, while thousands more are beaten, raped, and tortured and their homes looted and burned. An incalculable number of them are not only subject to social, economic, and religious discrimination but daily suffer personal harassment and humiliation.

In the course of the last thousand or so years saints and reformers have sought to ameliorate the lot of the Untouchables – none of them with any great success. The latest and most heroic of these attempts was made by Dr Bhimrao Ramji Ambedkar, himself an Untouchable by birth, who came to the conclusion that there was no salvation for the Untouchables within Hinduism and that they would have to change their religion. In October 1956 he and half a million of his followers therefore became Buddhists, thus bringing about the renaissance of Buddhism in India and initiating a religious and social revolution of major significance.

Though the sufferings of the Jews in Nazi Germany and of the blacks in white supremacist South Africa are well known and widely discussed, the no less horrifying sufferings of the Untouchables at the hands of the caste Hindus, as well as Ambedkar's heroic efforts to emancipate his people from their age-old slavery, have remained virtually unknown outside India. Thirty years after his death, the West has yet to see a biography of the great Untouchable leader, while there is still no sign of a book-length study of the movement of mass conversion to Buddhism which he inaugurated. The present work cannot be considered as remedying these deficiencies, but only as taking a small step in that direction. In the following pages I have given a brief account of Ambedkar's career, described why and how he became a Buddhist, and explained what Buddhism meant to him.

Sangharakshita

I

THE SIGNIFICANCE OF AMBEDKAR

In the grounds of the parliament building in Delhi stands a statue of a stout, elderly man clad in a business suit and wearing spectacles. The statue is about fifteen feet high, and stands with right foot slightly advanced on the square top of a pedestal of much the same height. Underneath the left arm of the statue is a large book, while its right arm is outstretched practically to its full extent, index finger pointing in the direction of the parliament building. The statue represents Bhimrao Ramji Ambedkar, Law Minister in the Government of India from 1947 to 1951; the book underneath his arm is the Indian Constitution, and his finger points to the parliament building because it was there that in 1948 he presented his draft Constitution to the Constituent Assembly, there that it was accepted a year later, and there that the legislation based on its provisions has ever since been passed.

Bhimrao Ramji Ambedkar was one of the most remarkable men of his time, and the story of his life is the story of how exceptional talent and outstanding force of character succeeded in overcoming some of the most formidable obstacles that an unjust and oppressive society has ever placed in the way of the individual. Born in Mhow in central India in 1891, he was the fourteenth child of parents who belonged to the very lowest stratum of Hindu society. According to orthodox Hindu tradition, he was not entitled to receive education or to acquire property, he could engage only in the most menial and degrading work, and he could not come into physical contact with members of the higher castes. In short, Bhimrao Ramji Ambedkar was born an outcaste or Untouchable. He was expected to wear cast-off clothes, to eat the leavings of his higher caste masters, to be humble and obedient, and to accept his lot as the well-deserved punishment for sins committed in a former existence.

Fortunately for him, however, his father had served in the Indian army and there acquired a certain amount of formal education in both Marathi and English. This enabled him to teach his children, especially Bhimrao Ramji, and to encourage them in their own pursuit of knowledge. In 1908 the young Ambedkar passed the matriculation examination of Bombay University, and so uncommon was such an achievement on the part of an Untouchable boy that the event was celebrated with a public meeting. Four years later he graduated from the same university with Politics and Economics as subjects and soon afterwards entered the service of the Baroda State, the ruler of which had awarded him a scholarship. At this point his father died (his mother had died when he was five) and four months later the bereaved son left India to continue his studies at Columbia University (USA) on a further scholarship from the same liberal-minded ruler. Though he had climbed higher up the ladder of academic achievement than any other Untouchable, Ambedkar was far from being satisfied. Convinced as he was that knowledge is power, he knew that without that power in full measure he had little hope of breaking the bonds that kept millions of Untouchables in a state of virtual slavery – and how strong those bonds were his own bitter personal experience had already taught him.

From 1913 to 1917, and again from 1920 to 1923, Ambedkar was in the West, and when at the age of thirty-two he finally returned to the country of his birth it was as one of the most highly qualified men in public life. During his three years at Columbia University he studied Economics, Sociology, History, Philosophy, Anthropology, and Politics, and was awarded a PhD for the thesis which he eventually published in book form as *The Evolution of Provincial Finance in British India*.[8] His first published work, however, was a paper on 'Castes in India: Their Mechanism, Genesis and Development'[9] which he had originally read at an Anthropology seminar conducted by one of his professors. After completing his studies in America, Ambedkar left New York for London, where he was admitted to the London School of Economics and Political Science and to Gray's Inn. A year later his scholarship came to an end and it was only in 1920 that, having taught in a Bombay college and started a Marathi weekly called *Mooknayak* or 'Leader of the Dumb', he was able to return to London and resume his studies there. In the course of the next three years he completed his thesis on *The Problem of the Rupee*,[10] for which the University of London awarded him a D.Sc., and was called to the Bar. Before leaving England he spent three months in Germany, where he engaged in further studies in Economics at the University of Bonn.

Thus the man who returned to India in April 1923 to continue his fight on behalf of the Untouchables and, indeed, all the Depressed Classes, was uniquely well equipped for the task, and from this time onwards it becomes increasingly difficult to separate the biography of Bhimrao Ramji Ambedkar from the history of modern India. During his three year absence in London the Indian political scene had changed dramatically. The demand for independence from Britain had grown louder than ever: Mahatma Gandhi had started advocating a policy of non-cooperation with the Government and only a year before Ambedkar's return had launched the first of his campaigns for mass civil disobedience. But though Ambedkar was a staunch patriot, and though initially he was of the opinion that only political independence would bring social equality within the reach of the Depressed Classes, he was emphatic that if – as Gandhi and the Congress Party maintained – no country was good enough to rule over another it was equally true that no class was good enough to rule over another class. Certainly the caste Hindus were not good enough to lord it over the Depressed Classes, and while Ambedkar remained sharply critical of British rule it was to the removal of the social, economic, educational, and legal disabilities of the Depressed Classes that he devoted the major part of his energies. As early as 1920 he had realized, however, that the interests of the Depressed Classes would have to be safeguarded by means of separate electorates, at least for a period, and it was his increasing insistence on this point that eventually brought him into open conflict with Mahatma Gandhi and the Congress Party, as well as with practically the whole of orthodox Hindu India.

This conflict did not come to a head until 1932. In the meantime Ambedkar established himself in Bombay, built up his legal practice, taught in college, gave evidence before various official bodies, started a newspaper, and was nominated to the Bombay Legislative Council, in whose proceedings he at once took a leading part. He also attended the three Round Table Conferences that were held in London to enable representatives of the various Indian communities and the three British political parties to consider proposals for the future constitution of India. One of his most significant achievements during the years immediately following his return to India in 1923 was the formation of the Bahishkrit Hitakarini Sabha or Depressed Classes Welfare Association, the objects of which were to promote the spread of education and culture among the Depressed Classes, to improve their economic condition, and to represent their grievances.

These grievances were serious enough. Untouchables were not allowed to enter Hindu temples, they could not draw water from public tanks or wells, they were denied admittance to schools, and prevented from moving about freely in public places – and so on. Between 1927 and 1932 Ambedkar therefore led his followers in a series of non-violent campaigns to assert the right of the Untouchables to enter Hindu places of worship and to draw water from public tanks and wells. Two of these campaigns were of special importance. These were the campaigns against the exclusion of Untouchables from the Kalaram Temple, Nasik, and from the Chowdar Tank, Mahad, both of which involved tens of thousands of Untouchable *satyagrahi*s or 'passive resisters', provoked a violently hostile reaction from the caste Hindus and, in the case of the Chowdar Tank campaign, resulted in a legal as well as a moral victory for the Depressed Classes only after years of litigation. The Chowdar Tank campaign also saw the ceremonial burning of the *Manusmṛti* or 'Institutes of Manu', the ancient Hindu law book that bore much of the responsibility for the cruel and degrading treatment that the Untouchables had hitherto suffered at the hands of the caste Hindus. By committing the much-revered volume to the flames the Depressed Classes were serving notice to the orthodox Hindu community that in future they intended to be treated as human beings.

Unpopular as Ambedkar's activities had already made him with the caste Hindus, during 1931 and 1932 he became more unpopular still. In his own words, he became the most hated man in India[11] – hated, that is, by the caste Hindus and by the Congress Party, which they dominated. The cause of the trouble was Ambedkar's continued insistence on the necessity of separate electorates for the Depressed Classes. Mahatma Gandhi and the Congress Party were opposed to separate electorates for the Depressed Classes (though not for the Muslims, Sikhs, Christians, and Europeans), and Ambedkar and Gandhi had clashed on the subject at the Second Round Table Conference, when the Mahatma went so far as to challenge the right of Ambedkar to represent the Untouchables. Ambedkar's arguments did, however, convince the British Government, and when Ramsay MacDonald published his Communal Award the following year the Depressed Classes were given the separate electorates for which they had asked. Gandhi's response was to go on a fast to the death for the abolition of separate electorates for the Depressed Classes. Since he was the acknowledged leader of the Independence movement his action created consternation throughout India. Ambedkar was reviled as a traitor and threats were made against his life. But though unmoved by the pressure that was brought to bear on him Ambedkar was not unwilling to negotiate and eventually agreed to exchange separate electorates for joint electorates and a greatly increased number of reserved seats. This agreement was embodied in a document that became known as the Poona Pact, the signing of which by Ambedkar marked his emergence as the undisputed leader of the Depressed Classes.

In the mood of relief that swept the country when the weak and ailing Mahatma ended his fast there was even a little sympathy to spare for the wretched Untouchables, but it did not last long, and soon Ambedkar was as much hated as ever. Partly as a result of the opposition he had encountered over the question of separate electorates, partly because of the continued exclusion of Untouchables from Hindu temples, Ambedkar now began to think that the caste Hindus were not going to mend their ways. He therefore changed his tactics – though not his strategy – and started exhorting his followers to concentrate on raising their standard of living and gaining political power. He also began to think that there was no future for the Untouchables within Hinduism and that they should change their religion. These thoughts found dramatic expression at the 1935 Depressed Classes Conference, when he made his famous declaration that though he had been born a Hindu he did not intend to die one – a declaration that sent shock waves through Hindu India. In the same year Ambedkar was appointed principal of the Government Law College, Bombay, built a house for himself and his books, and lost his wife Ramabai. They had been married in 1908, when he was sixteen and she was nine and she had borne him five children, of whom only one survived. Though the demands of public life had left him with little time for his own domestic affairs, Ambedkar was deeply attached to the gentle and self-effacing woman and mourned her bitterly.

When he had recovered from his grief he plunged back into his customary activities and soon was busier than ever. In the course of the next few years he founded the Independent Labour Party, took part in the provincial elections that were held under the Government of India Act, 1935, was elected to the Bombay Legislative Assembly, pressed for the abolition of agricultural serfdom, defended the right of industrial workers to strike, advocated the promotion of birth control, and addressed meetings and conferences all over the Bombay Presidency. In 1939 the Second World War broke out in Europe and the fact that Britain was locked in a life-and-death struggle with Nazi Germany soon had its effect on the political situation in India. According to Gandhi and the Congress Party, Britain's difficulty was India's opportunity, and from 1940 they adopted a policy of non-cooperation with the Government war effort. Ambedkar did not agree with this attitude. Not only was he not a pacifist but he regarded Nazi ideology as a direct threat to the liberties of the Indian people. He therefore exhorted them to help defeat Nazism by supporting the Government, and himself encouraged the Untouchables to join the Indian army. In 1941 he was appointed to the Defence Advisory Committee and in the following year joined the Viceroy's Executive Council as Labour Member, a post he occupied for the next four years. During the same period he transformed the Independent Labour Party into the All-India Scheduled Caste Federation, founded the People's Education Society, and published a number of highly controversial books and pamphlets. Among the latter were *Thoughts on Pakistan, What Congress and Gandhi have Done to the Untouchables*, and *Who Were the Shudras?*

In 1947 India achieved independence and Ambedkar, who had already been elected a member of the Constituent Assembly, was invited by Pandit Nehru, the first prime minister of the country, to join the Cabinet as Minister for Law. A few weeks later the Assembly entrusted the task of framing the Constitution to a Draft Committee, and this committee elected Ambedkar as its chairman. For the next two years he was hard at work on the Draft Constitution, hammering it out article by article and clause by clause practically single-handed. While he was thus engaged the country was passing through a period of turmoil. Independence had been won only at the cost of partition, partition had led to the wholesale slaughter of Hindus by Muslims and Muslims by Hindus, and at the beginning of 1948 Mahatma Gandhi was assassinated. Besides being deeply concerned about the fate of the Untouchables living in what was now Pakistan, Ambedkar had troubles of his own to face. His health had been deteriorating for some time, and now gave him cause for such grave concern that on the day following his fifty-eighth birthday he married a Brahmin woman doctor whom he had met in hospital and who would, he hoped, be able to provide him with the care he needed.

Despite his ill health Ambedkar managed to complete the Draft Constitution by the beginning of 1948 and later that year, when it had been before the country for six months, had the satisfaction of introducing it in the Constituent Assembly. Thereafter he piloted it through its three readings with his usual competence and in November 1949 it was adopted by the Assembly with very few amendments. The new Constitution gave general satisfaction and Ambedkar was warmly congratulated by friend and foe alike. Never had he been so popular. The press hailed him as the Modern Manu, and the irony of the fact that it was an Untouchable who had given Free India its Constitution was widely commented upon. Though he lived for seven more years, it was as the Architect of the Constitution and the Modern Manu that he was destined to pass into official history. When his statue came to be erected outside the parliament building after his death it was therefore as the Modern Manu that he was depicted, holding the Constitution underneath his arm and pointing in the direction of the parliament building. But though by 1948 Ambedkar had achieved so much, and though today he is most widely remembered as the author of the Indian Constitution, his greatest achievement was in fact still to come.

This achievement was an essentially spiritual one, and it came only at the very end of his life, when he had spent several years in the political wilderness after failing to secure the passage of the Hindu Code Bill. The Bill represented a putting into shape by Ambedkar of work accomplished during the previous decade by a number of eminent Hindu lawyers and dealt with such matters as marriage and divorce, adoption, joint family property, women's property, and succession. Though it was a reforming rather than a revolutionary measure, the Bill met with violent opposition both inside and outside the Assembly, and even within the Cabinet. Ambedkar was accused of trying to destroy Hinduism and there were angry exchanges on the Assembly floor between him and his orthodox opponents. In the end the Bill was dropped after only four clauses had been passed and in September 1951, tired and disgusted, Ambedkar resigned from the Cabinet. In his resignation statement (which he was prevented from making in the Assembly itself) he explained that he had left the Cabinet for five reasons. The second of these was that it was apathetic to the uplift of the Scheduled Castes, the fifth that Pandit Nehru had failed to give adequate support to the Hindu Code Bill.

Ambedkar's resignation from the Cabinet marked the virtual end of his political career. In the general elections of January 1952 he failed to win a seat in the Lok Sabha or House of Representatives, and was equally unsuccessful when he contested a by-election the following year. Towards the end of March 1952 he was, however, elected to the Rajya Sabha or Council of States as one of the seventeen representatives of the State of Bombay, and was soon vigorously attacking the Government. But while he continued to participate in the proceedings of the Rajya Sabha, and was to do so until the end of his life, from now onwards Ambedkar's energies were increasingly devoted to more important things. Ever since the 1935 Depressed Classes Conference, when he had shocked Hindu India with the declaration that though he had been born a Hindu he did not intend to die one, he had been giving earnest consideration to the question of conversion. The longer he thought about it the more he was convinced that there was no future for the Untouchables within Hinduism, that they would have to adopt another religion, and that the best religion for them to adopt was Buddhism. During his years in office it had been hardly possible for him to bring about so momentous a change, but he had lost no opportunity of educating his followers in the issues involved, and it became increasingly apparent in which direction he – and they – were moving. In 1950 he not only praised the Buddha at the expense of Krishna, Christ, and Mohammed but also visited Ceylon at the invitation of the Young Men's Buddhist Association, Colombo, addressed a meeting of the World Fellowship of Buddhists in Kandy, and appealed to the Untouchables of Ceylon to embrace Buddhism. In 1951 he defended the Buddha against the charge that he had been responsible for the downfall of the Indian woman and compiled the *Bauddha Upasana Patha*, a small collection of Buddhist devotional texts. Thus when his resignation from the Cabinet, and his failure to secure election to the Lok Sabha, finally left Ambedkar with the time and energy for his greatest achievement, the ground was already well prepared.

In 1954 he twice visited Burma, the second time in order to attend the third conference of the World Fellowship of Buddhists in Rangoon. In May 1955 he founded the Bharatiya Bauddha Mahasabha or Indian Buddhist Society, less than half a year after installing an image of the Buddha in a temple that had been built at Dehu Road, near Poona. Addressing the thousands of Untouchables who had assembled for the occasion, he declared that henceforth he would devote himself to the propagation of Buddhism in India. He also announced that he was writing a book explaining the tenets of Buddhism in simple language for the benefit of the common man. It might take him a year to complete the book, but when it was finished he would embrace Buddhism. The work in question was *The Buddha and His Dhamma*, on which he had been working since November 1951 and which he completed in February 1956. Not long afterwards Ambedkar, true to his word, announced that he would be embracing Buddhism in October of that year. Arrangements were accordingly made for the ceremony to be held in Nagpur, and on 14 October 1956 the Untouchable leader took the Three Refuges and Five Precepts from a Buddhist monk in the traditional manner and then in his turn administered them to the 380,000 men, women, and children who had come to Nagpur in response to his call.[12] After further conversion ceremonies in Nagpur and Chanda, Ambedkar returned to Delhi knowing that the Wheel of the Dharma had again been set in motion in India. A few weeks later he travelled to Kathmandu in Nepal for the fourth conference of the World Fellowship of Buddhists and addressed the delegates on 'The Buddha or Karl Marx'. On his way back to Delhi he made two speeches in Benares and visited Kusinara, where the Buddha had died. In Delhi he took part in various Buddhist functions, attended the Rajya Sabha, and completed the last chapter of his book *Buddha or Karl Marx*.[13] On the evening of 5 December he asked for the Preface and Introduction to *The Buddha and His Dhamma* to be brought to his bedside, so that he could work on them during the night, and the following morning he was found dead. It was 6 December, he was sixty-four years and seven months old, and he had been a Buddhist for only seven weeks.

But though Bhimrao Ramji Ambedkar had been a Buddhist for only seven weeks, during that period he had probably done more for the promotion of Buddhism than any other Indian since Aśoka. At the time of his death three quarters of a million Untouchables had become Buddhists, and in the months that followed hundreds of thousands more took the same step – despite the uncertainty and confusion that had been created by the sudden loss of their great leader. So much was this the case that when the results of the 1961 census were published it was found that in the course of the previous decade the number of Buddhists in India had risen by a staggering 1,671 per cent and that they now numbered 3,250,227, more than three quarters of whom lived in the state of Maharashtra. This was Ambedkar's last and greatest achievement, so that even though it was as the Architect of the Constitution of Free India and the Modern Manu that he passed into official history and is today most widely remembered, his real significance consists in the fact that it was he who established a revived Indian Buddhism on a firm foundation. It is therefore as the Modern Aśoka that he really deserves to be known, and the statue standing outside the parliament building in Delhi should really depict him holding *The Buddha and His Dhamma* underneath his arm and pointing – not for the benefit of the Untouchables only, but for the benefit of all mankind – in the direction of the Three Jewels.

In order to appreciate the nature of Ambedkar's achievement, and thus the real significance of the man himself, it will, however, be necessary for us to take a look at the diabolical system from which he sought to deliver the Untouchables, as well as to trace the successive stages of the road by which he – and his followers – travelled from Hinduism to Buddhism. We shall also have to see the way in which Ambedkar discovered his spiritual roots, explore his thoughts on the subject of the Buddha and the future of his religion, survey the historic occasion on which he and 380,000 Untouchables were spiritually reborn, study his posthumously published *magnum opus* and, finally, see what happened after his death.

But before that, a few personal recollections may not be out of place.

2

THREE MEETINGS

I knew Ambedkar only during the latter part of his life, when he was in his early sixties and I was in my late twenties and early thirties. Our three meetings may not have been very important to him, but they were certainly important to me, and after his death they were to be of considerable importance for the movement of conversion to Buddhism which he had inaugurated. In both background and temperament we were very different, and had it not been for our common allegiance to Buddhism it is doubtful if our paths would ever have crossed. I had been born in London in 1925, two years after Ambedkar had returned to India on the completion of his studies in the West. At the age of sixteen I read *The Diamond Sūtra* and *The Sūtra of Wei Lang* and thereupon realized that I was a Buddhist and had, in fact, always been one. Two years later, the Second World War having broken out, I was conscripted into the British army and posted first to India, then to Ceylon, and finally to Singapore. At the end of 1946 I left the army and after spending two years in South India as a wandering ascetic visited the Buddhist sacred places of north-east India and was ordained as a *śrāmaṇera* or novice monk. 1949 was spent mainly in Benares, studying Pāli and Buddhist Philosophy, and early in 1950 my teacher took me up to Kalimpong, in the foothills of the eastern Himalayas, and told me to stay there and work for the good of Buddhism.[14]

In obedience to these instructions I founded the Young Men's Buddhist Association (Kalimpong) and started publishing a monthly magazine of Himalayan Buddhism called *Stepping-Stones*. Shortly afterwards I wrote to Ambedkar telling him what I had done and received from him a friendly and encouraging reply in the course of which he said, 'Great responsibility lies on the shoulders of the Bhikkhus if this attempt at the revival of Buddhism is to be a success. They must be more active than they have been. They must come out of their shell and be in the front rank of the fighting forces.' His name had been familiar to me since 1949, when I heard it in connection with the controversy that was beginning to rage over the proposed Hindu Code Bill, but it was only after reading his article on 'The Buddha and the Future of His Religion' in the April–May 1950 issue of the *Maha Bodhi*, the monthly journal of the Maha Bodhi Society of India, that I came to understand how deep was his interest in Buddhism and decided to get in touch with him. Towards the end of 1952 I was in Calcutta, writing a Biographical Sketch of Anagarika Dharmapala, the founder of the Maha Bodhi Society of India, for the Society's *Diamond Jubilee Souvenir*,[15] and the successful conclusion of this work led to my being invited to take part in the re-enshrinement of the relics of the Buddha's two chief disciples, Sāriputta and Moggallāna, in the brand new temple the Society had built for them at Sanchi, near Bhopal, not far from the stupa from which they had been removed a hundred years earlier by a British archaeologist. From Sanchi I went to Bombay, where I had been asked to advise on the production of a Buddhist film, and on coming to know that Ambedkar was in the city decided to go and see him.[16]

Five years after Independence Bombay was still a fine city. That is, it was a fine city if one confined oneself to the Esplanade and Marine Drive. Beyond these favoured regions stretched the densely populated working class districts of Bombay's industrial hinterland. Prominent among these districts was Dadar, and it was at the house that he had built for himself in Dadar that Ambedkar and I had our first meeting. On my arrival I was shown into a large, rather bare room that in the case of a modern British politician would have been called his surgery. A number of people were already present. After we had exchanged salutations and I had introduced myself (it was in any case obvious from my garb that I was a Buddhist monk) Ambedkar asked me to take a seat while he attended to some people who had come to see him. The people in question were the ten or twelve members of what seemed to be a deputation of some kind. As Ambedkar advanced towards them, a frown on his face, the three or four men in Western-style reach-me-downs, who appeared to be the leaders of the deputation, produced an enormous marigold-and-tinsel garland which they attempted to place round his neck. This token of homage Ambedkar thrust roughly aside with every mark of impatience, not to say irritation. Far from resenting this display of apparent rudeness the leaders of the deputation stood clutching the garland and gazing at their leader with an expression of utter devotion as, still frowning, he addressed to them (in Marathi) a few short, sharp sentences of what seemed to be rebuke. Evidently they had done something wrong, and he was scolding them. But they no more resented this than they had resented his refusal of the garland, the expression on their faces plainly saying that if instead of scolding them he was to beat them with a stick they would count it the greatest of blessings. This was my first experience of the devotion with which Ambedkar was regarded by his followers, and I never forgot that scene in the surgery. Indeed four years later it helped me to understand the readiness with which those same followers responded to his call to embrace Buddhism.

While Ambedkar was talking with the delegation (and eventually something seemed to be settled between them) I not only observed their reactions but also studied the great man himself. Ambedkar was of above average height, brown complexioned, and heavily built, with a distinct inclination to corpulence. His Western-style suit was well cut, but hung on him rather loosely, like the wrinkled hide on an elephant. As for his head, this matched his body, being large and well formed, while the pear-shaped face revealed an exceptionally lofty brow, very full jowls, a slightly aquiline nose, and a mouth the corners of which were turned down to a remarkable degree. More noticeable still was Ambedkar's expression, which was grim and lowering, as of a man who rarely smiled. So grim and so lowering was it, indeed, that watching him I had the impression of a great black storm cloud – a storm cloud that might discharge thunder and lightning at any minute.

This impression proved to be not without foundation. When the delegation had departed Ambedkar seated himself behind his desk and, after we had exchanged the usual amenities, fixed me with an unfriendly stare, and demanded belligerently, 'Why does your Maha Bodhi Society have a Bengali Brahmin for its President?' The word Brahmin was not only emphasized but pronounced with such contempt and scorn that the whole Brahmin caste, as well as any organization so misguided as to have a Brahmin for its president, was at once consigned to a kind of moral dustbin. Realizing that Ambedkar took me for one of the *bhikkhus* (mostly Sinhalese) who ran the Maha Bodhi Society's various pilgrim-centres, I hastened to make my position clear. It was not *my* Maha Bodhi Society, I explained. Though I was happy to help the Society in whatever way I could, I did not actually belong to it, and one of the reasons I did not belong to it was that it had a Brahmin for its President, as well as a Governing Body that was dominated by caste Hindus who had no real interest in Buddhism. Some of the Buddhist members of the Society, I added, were no more satisfied with the present state of affairs than he was and both they and I hoped that before long we would be able to do something about it. This explanation appeared to mollify Ambedkar, and the fixed stare became less unfriendly. For my part, I not only sympathized with his question but knew why he had asked it with so much feeling. Not only was the President of the Maha Bodhi Society a Bengali Brahmin, but that Brahmin was also a former President of the Hindu Mahasabha, a right-wing caste Hindu organization. What I did not know at the time, however, was that Prasad Mookerjee – the Brahmin in question – had been one of the leading opponents of Ambedkar's Hindu Code Bill.[17]

The air having been cleared between us, the conversation must have turned to Buddhism, for presently I asked him (probably with his article on 'The Buddha and the Future of His Religion' in mind) whether he thought that Buddhism really had a future in India. His answer to this question was an indirect one. '*I* have no future in India!' he exclaimed bitterly, his grim and lowering expression giving way to one so gloomy and despondent as to be akin to despair. But whatever he may have thought at the time (he had then been out of office for more than a year) fortunately there was, after all, a future in India for both Ambedkar and Buddhism, and when we met three years later this fact was already beginning to be obvious.[18]

This second meeting also took place in Bombay, though not in Dadar but in the Fort area, at the Siddharth College of Arts and Sciences, an institution started by Ambedkar in 1946 mainly for the benefit of untouchable students.[19] We met in his office on the top floor of Buddha Bhuvan, and on entering the book-lined room I found him seated behind his desk, with Mrs Ambedkar standing beside him. He did not look very well and apologized for receiving me sitting down. He was suffering from arthritis, he explained, and this made standing up difficult. Whether because he was in pain, or for some other reason, he was much quieter and more subdued than he had been on the occasion of our first meeting, and seemed to have lost much of his belligerence. In the course of our discussion, in which Mrs Ambedkar also joined from time to time, mainly in order to reinforce a point made by her husband, Ambedkar explained to me at length his plans for the revival of Buddhism in India, adding that he intended to devote the rest of his life to Buddhism. But though he had, as it seemed, made up his mind that he and his followers should embrace Buddhism, he appeared to be uncertain as to exactly how this was to be done. At any rate, he questioned me closely on the subject and I explained that formal conversion to Buddhism consisted in 'Going for Refuge', as it was called, to the Three Jewels, i.e. the Buddha, the Dharma, and the Sangha, and in undertaking to observe what were known as the five precepts, or five basic principles of ethical behaviour. It was as simple as that. One could 'take' the Refuges and Precepts from any Buddhist monk.

By this time Ambedkar and I had been talking a good while, and a feeling of warmth and confidence had sprung up between us, as though we were members of the same family. I was therefore not surprised when he asked me if I would be willing to administer the Three Refuges and Five Precepts to him and his followers. To this I replied that I would certainly be willing to administer them, but that their conversion would probably be taken more seriously by the Buddhist world if it took place at the hands of the oldest and seniormost monk in India, who to the best of my knowledge was U Chandramani of Kusinara, from whom I had received my own *śrāmaṇera* ordination. At the time Ambedkar seemed not to pay much attention to this suggestion, but he must have given it further thought, for it was from U Chandramani that, ten months later, he took the Three Refuges and Five Precepts. Before we parted he did, however, ask me to write to him recapitulating everything I had said on the subject of conversion. He also asked me to speak to his followers and explain to them what conversion to Buddhism really meant. To both these requests I gladly acceded, and it was settled between us that I would write to him from Poona (where I was planning to spend a few weeks) and that a talk would be organized for me by his lieutenants in the city.[20]

On New Year's Day 1956 I accordingly addressed 3,000 Untouchables, most of whom (I was told) were desirous of being converted to Buddhism, on 'What it Means to Become a Buddhist'. The meeting took place at Worli, a working-class district situated south of Dadar, on a piece of waste ground adjoining some chawls or tenement blocks.[21] Since many of Ambedkar's followers in the area were factory workers, and did not get home much before eight o'clock, the meeting did not start until quite late, and by the time I rose to speak there was a cold wind blowing, so that I shivered in my thin cotton robes. With the President of the Scheduled Caste Federation of Bombay for my interpreter, I addressed the gathering for over an hour, speaking as simply as I could and confining myself to fundamentals. Becoming a Buddhist meant Going for Refuge to the Buddha, the Dharma, and the Sangha, I declared, as well as undertaking to observe the Five Precepts, but one could do this only if one understood what the terms Buddha, Dharma, and Sangha actually meant and in what the observance of the five precepts consisted. The Buddha was a human being who, by virtue of his own efforts, had gained the state of supreme spiritual perfection known as Enlightenment or Nirvāṇa. He was not God, or the messenger of God, and he was certainly not an *avatāra* of Vishnu as the Hindus believed. Going for Refuge to the Buddha meant resolving to attain Enlightenment as he had done, for inasmuch as one was, like the Buddha, a human being, one was capable of attaining what he had attained. The Dharma was the Teaching of the Buddha: the Teaching of the Way to Enlightenment – especially as embodied in such formulas as the 'three trainings', or Morality, Meditation, and Wisdom, and the Noble Eightfold Path. Thus for Buddhism the word '*dharma*' had a very different meaning from what it had for Hinduism. In Buddhism there was no place for the caste system, or for Untouchability – which for orthodox Hindus were an integral part of their '*dharma*' or religious duty. Going for Refuge to the Dharma meant studying the teaching of the Buddha, understanding it, and practising it. In Buddhism there was no place for blind belief. A non-practising Buddhist was a contradiction in terms. The Sangha was the spiritual community of the Buddha's disciples, past and present, monk and lay, Enlightened and unenlightened. Going for Refuge to the Sangha meant being receptive to the spiritual influence of those who were further advanced upon the path than oneself: it meant being inspired by their example and guided by their advice. As for the observance of the five precepts, this consisted in abstention from harming living beings, from taking the not-given, from sexual misconduct, from false speech, and from indulgence in intoxicating drinks and drugs.

Such was the gist of my remarks, as it was to be the gist of hundreds of other speeches I was to deliver to untouchable converts to Buddhism in the course of the next ten years. I did, however, seek to clothe the bare bones of my subject in a certain amount of living flesh in the form of illustrations and anecdotes. My poorly clad and predominantly illiterate audience followed everything I said with the closest attention and in a silence that was broken only by the applause that greeted any remark of which they particularly approved. Not unnaturally, the biggest applause was reserved for my comments on the subject of caste and Untouchability.

The third and last meeting between Ambedkar and myself took place eleven months later, about a month after the Nagpur conversions. Unfortunately, I had had to miss this historic ceremony, since the Indian Buddhist Society's invitation reached me rather late, when I had already accepted an invitation to give some lectures in Gangtok, the capital of Sikkim, and all I could therefore do was send a message of congratulation. Not long after giving my Gangtok lectures I went down to Calcutta, and from there left on a tour of the principal Buddhist sacred places with some fifty other 'Eminent Buddhists from the Border Areas' (as we were officially described) as guests of the Government of India. After visiting Bodh Gaya, Rajgir, Nalanda, Sarnath, Kusinara, Lumbini, Sanchi, and Āgra, as well as various dams and other industrial projects that the Government wanted us to see, we were taken to Delhi in time to participate in the 2500th Buddha Jayanti celebrations. On our arrival in Delhi I lost no time in going to see Ambedkar. Indeed, I not only went to see him but took with me as many other 'Eminent Buddhists from the Border Areas' as I could persuade to go. Most of them had not heard of Ambedkar before, but when I explained who he was, and how he had been responsible for the conversion of hundreds of thousands of people to Buddhism, they agreed that it was our duty to go and personally congratulate him on his great and historic achievement.

It was therefore with some two or three dozen colourfully clad monks, nuns, and laymen from Tibet, Sikkim, Bhutan, Kashmir, Ladakh, Himāchal Pradesh, Darjeeling, North-East Frontier Agency (NEFA), and Assam that I descended on Ambedkar's house in Alipore Road one morning in the second week of November. The sky was an unbroken expanse of brilliant blue from which the sun shone down with steadily increasing warmth. Since there were so many of us it was difficult for Ambedkar to receive us indoors, and chairs were therefore set out in the compound. Here the Eminent Buddhists from the Border Areas sat facing Ambedkar in a semicircle, with the sunlight falling on the vivid magentas, oranges, and yellows of their robes. Ambedkar himself sat behind a small table, Mrs Ambedkar beside him. He wore a light tropical suit and a pith helmet and looked so old and so ill that I felt obliged to apologize for our troubling him, explaining that we had come simply to pay our respects and to congratulate him on his conversion to Buddhism. Despite the poor state of his health Ambedkar was obviously glad to see me again and glad to meet the representatives of so many different forms of Buddhism. When he spoke, however, it was in so low a voice that I had to come quite close to him in order to catch what he was saying.

In this way we talked for some ten or fifteen minutes. I then rose to say goodbye, the rest of the party rising with me. The purpose of our visit had been achieved, and in the circumstances it would have been inconsiderate for us to stay any longer than was strictly necessary. But Ambedkar would not hear of our going. Or rather, he would not hear of *my* going, for he had made no attempt to enter into conversation with any of the other Eminent Buddhists from the Border Areas. There was evidently much that was weighing on his mind, much that he wanted to speak to me about, and he had no intention of allowing bodily weakness and suffering to prevent him from continuing the conversation. The longer he spoke, though, the more concerned about him I became, for his head gradually sank until it almost touched his outstretched arms, which were resting on the surface of the table. Sitting there in that way, like an Atlas for whom the globe had at last become almost too heavy for him to bear, he spoke of his hopes and fears – mostly fears – for the movement of conversion to Buddhism that he had inaugurated. Once more, twice more, I attempted to bring the meeting to an end, especially as I could see that Mrs Ambedkar was becoming uneasy and that some of the Eminent Buddhists, not understanding what Ambedkar was saying, were beginning to show signs of restlessness. It was now the hottest part of the day, I expostulated; he had been sitting out in the sun for longer than was perhaps good for him, and we really ought not to trouble him any further. But the figure in the light tropical suit and the pith helmet refused to take any notice, though his head was now frankly resting on his arms and though the broken sentences came with increasing difficulty and at ever longer intervals. As I sat there, torn between my desire to let Ambedkar have his say and my fear that the continued exertion might do him serious harm, I had the distinct impression that he somehow knew we would not be meeting again and that he wanted to transfer to my shoulders some of the weight that he was no longer able to bear himself. There was still so much to be done, the sad, tired voice was saying ... so much to be done.... Eventually the great leader's eyes closed in sheer weariness and, seeing from Mrs Ambedkar's expression that it was time for us to go, I and my two or three dozen colourfully clad companions quietly filed out of the compound. My third and final meeting with Ambedkar had lasted exactly two hours.[22]

From his appearance as he sat there in the blazing sunshine of that November morning I doubted if Ambedkar would ever set foot outside his house again, but a few days later he left for Kathmandu, where the delegates to the fourth conference of the World Fellowship of Buddhists gave him a tremendous ovation. For my part, having spent two weeks participating in the 2500th Buddha Jayanti celebrations I left Delhi for Bombay on 29 November – the day before Ambedkar returned from Kathmandu, as I afterwards discovered. In Bombay I stayed for only a few days, for though my friends there were hoping for a longer visit I was in a hurry to return to Calcutta, and on 5 December I accordingly caught the overnight train to Nagpur. Since I had been unable to attend the conversion ceremony on 14 October I was eager to make the acquaintance of the newly converted Buddhists there who had, in fact, already invited me to spend a few days with them on my way back to Calcutta and give some lectures. On my arrival in Nagpur the following day, at one o'clock in the afternoon, I found a crowd of some 2,000 excited ex-Untouchables waiting on the platform to receive me. After being profusely garlanded I was escorted to the house of the friend with whom I had arranged to stay and then left to rest there and recover from my journey. Less than an hour later, when I was still settling into my new quarters, there was a sudden disturbance outside and three or four members of the Indian Buddhist Society burst into my room with the news that 'Baba Saheb' – as Ambedkar's followers respectfully and affectionately called him – had died in Delhi the previous night. The speakers seemed utterly demoralized. What was more, they reported that the Society's downtown office was being besieged by thousands of grief-stricken people who, knowing that I had arrived in Nagpur, were demanding that I should come and speak to them. Pointing out that it would be impossible for me to address so many people without a microphone and loudspeakers, I told my visitors to organize a proper condolence meeting for seven o'clock that evening. I would address it and do my best to console people, who from the accounts that now started coming in were frantic with grief and anxiety at the sudden loss of their great leader.

A condolence meeting was therefore held in the Kasturchand Park at the time indicated. When I arrived it was quite dark and the long columns of mourners were still converging on the place from all directions. They came clad in white – the same white that they had worn for the conversion ceremony only seven weeks earlier – and every man, woman, and child carried a lighted candle, so that the Park was the dark hub of a wheel with a score of golden spokes. Partly because of their demoralized state, partly because there had been so little time, the organizers of the meeting had been able to do little more than rig up a microphone and loudspeakers. There was no stage and, apart from a petromax or two, no lighting other than that provided by the thousands of candles. By the time I rose to speak – standing on the seat of a rickshaw, and with someone holding a microphone in front of me – about 100,000 people had assembled. By rights I should have been the last speaker but as things turned out I was the first. In fact I was the only speaker. Not that there were not others who wanted to pay tribute to the memory of the departed leader. One by one, some five or six of Ambedkar's most prominent local supporters attempted to speak, and one by one they were forced to sit down again as, overcome by emotion, they burst into tears after uttering only a few words. Their example proved to be contagious. When I started to speak the whole of the vast gathering was weeping, and sobs and groans rent the air. In the light cast by the petromax I could see grey haired men in convulsions of grief at my feet.

It would have been strange if I had remained unaffected by the sight of so much anguish and so much despair, and I was indeed deeply moved. But though I felt the tears coming to my eyes I realized that for me, at least, there was no time to indulge in emotion. Ambedkar's followers had received a terrible shock. They had been Buddhists for only seven weeks, and now their leader, in whom their trust was total, and on whose guidance in the difficult days ahead they had been relying, had been snatched away. Poor and illiterate as the vast majority of them were, and faced by the unrelenting hostility of the caste Hindus, they did not know which way to turn and there was a possibility that the whole movement of conversion to Buddhism would come to a halt or even collapse. At all costs something had to be done. I therefore delivered a vigorous and stirring speech in which, after extolling the greatness of Ambedkar's achievement, I exhorted my audience to continue the work he had so gloriously begun and bring it to a successful conclusion. 'Baba Saheb' was not dead but alive. He lived on in them, and he lived on in them to the extent to which they were faithful to the ideals for which he stood and for which he had, quite literally, sacrificed himself. This speech, which lasted for an hour or more, was not without effect. Ambedkar's stricken followers began to realize that it was not the end of the world, that there was a future for them even after their beloved 'Baba Saheb's' death, and that the future was not devoid of hope. While I was speaking I had an extraordinary experience. Above the crowd there hung an enormous Presence. Whether that Presence was Ambedkar's own departed consciousness still hovering over his followers, or whether it was the collective product of their thoughts at that time of trial and crisis, I do not know, but it was as real to me as the people I was addressing.

In the course of the next four days I visited practically all the ex-untouchable 'localities' of Nagpur and made more than forty speeches, besides initiating about 30,000 people into Buddhism and delivering lectures at Nagpur University and at the local branch of the Ramakrishna Mission. Wherever I went I repeated, in one form or another, the message that I had given in Kasturchand Park: Ambedkar was not dead and his work – especially the work of conversion – must continue. When I left Nagpur I had addressed altogether 200,000 people and the members of the Indian Buddhist Society assured me that my presence at such a critical juncture was a miracle and that I had saved Nagpur for Buddhism. Whether or not I had saved Nagpur for Buddhism it was difficult to tell, but there was no doubt that during those five memorable days I had forged a very special link with the Buddhists of Nagpur and, indeed, with all Ambedkar's followers.

It was a link that was destined to endure. During the decade that followed I spent much of my time with the ex-Untouchable Buddhists of Nagpur, Bombay, Poona, Jabalpur, and Ahmedabad, as well as with those who lived in the small towns and the villages of central and western India. I learned to admire their cheerfulness, their friendliness, their intelligence, and their loyalty to the memory of their great emancipator. I also learned to appreciate how terrible were the conditions under which, for so many centuries, they had been compelled to live.

3
THE HELL OF CASTE

Apologists of the caste system try to represent it in terms of a division of labour, as a force making for social stability and cohesion, and as a framework within which a rich and varied religious and cultural life can flourish. For the Untouchables, who occupied the very lowest place within that system, the reality was far otherwise. Speaking at the time of his conversion to Buddhism, Ambedkar declared that he felt as though he had been delivered from hell, and there is no doubt that the hundreds of thousands of Untouchables who followed his example felt similarly. The hell from which they had been delivered was the hell of caste, to which they had been condemned for centuries and which had inflicted on them, in the most systematic manner, what Ambedkar himself characterized as torment.

A clue to the nature of that hell is provided by the word 'Untouchable' itself. An Untouchable is one who cannot be touched, and he cannot be touched because his touch automatically pollutes the one who touches him or whom he touches. Such 'touch' is not limited to direct physical contact. Pollution can be transmitted indirectly, through the medium of an article with which Touchable and Untouchable are in direct physical contact, as when both stand on different parts of the same carpet, as well as through anything previously touched by an Untouchable. In particular, pollution is transmitted through food and drink. Contact is also held to take place, and therefore pollution to be transmitted, when the shadow, or even the glance, of an Untouchable falls on the Touchable's person or possessions. Indeed, contact with certain Untouchable castes is so polluting that they are not permitted to approach within a certain distance of higher-caste Hindus (say thirty feet in the case of a Brahmin) or even to be seen by them. Thus the connotation of the term 'Untouchable' includes 'unapproachable' and even 'unseeable'. Since contact with an Untouchable pollutes, it is not surprising that such contact should be shunned and that to the Touchable or caste Hindu the Untouchable should normally be an object of horror, disgust, contempt, and loathing. It is also not surprising that to the Untouchable the caste Hindu, particularly the Brahmin, should be an object of fear and hatred.

But why is it that contact with the Untouchable pollutes? The traditional answer is that contact with him pollutes because he is a creature of filthy personal habits and low morals who moreover engages in unclean occupations such as the removal of faeces and the disposal of the carcasses of cows and other animals. Should it be further asked why the Untouchable engages in these occupations the answer is that according to the Hindu scriptures it is his God-given *dharma* or religious duty to engage in them and in no others. But what is it that makes him an Untouchable in the first place? To this most fundamental question the Hindu tradition makes an emphatic and unambiguous reply. The Untouchable is an Untouchable because he has been born of untouchable parents, i.e. of parents belonging to an untouchable caste, just as a Brahmin is a Brahmin because he has been born of Brahmin parents, a Rajput a Rajput because he is of Rajput parentage, and so on. Having been born of untouchable-caste parents the Untouchable must live as an Untouchable and die as an Untouchable. Nothing can alter his position within the caste system. Even if his personal habits are immaculate and his morals irreproachable and he does not engage in any unclean occupation, he is still an Untouchable and contact with him continues to pollute. Similarly, even if a Brahmin is of filthy personal habits and low morals and forsakes his God-given *dharma* of studying the Vedas he is still a Brahmin and his touch continues to purify. In the well-known words of the sixteenth-century poet Tulsidas, whose *Rāmacarita-mānasa* has been described as the Bible of the Hindi-speaking peoples of North India, 'a Brahmin possessed of all the vices is to be worshipped, and a Shudra endowed with all the virtues is to be despised.'[23]

From the fact that one is an Untouchable because one has been born of untouchable parents it follows that according to Hinduism Untouchability is something that is inherited. The Hindu Untouchable is a hereditary Untouchable, and because he is a hereditary Untouchable he is polluted and polluting not at certain times of his life and under certain special conditions but permanently and under all conditions. He is Untouchable in his very nature, and not only inherits his Untouchability from his parents but transmits it unimpaired to his offspring. But even though he himself is an Untouchable, could he not (it might be asked) at least marry a Touchable and thus ensure that his offspring were Untouchable to a lesser degree, much as a black man might marry a white woman in order to produce lighter-coloured offspring? And could not those offspring in turn marry Touchables, so that in the course of a few generations the taint of Untouchability would be bred out of his descendants altogether?

Within the context of the caste system such a proceeding is quite impossible, even unthinkable. Though the definition of 'caste' (from the Portuguese *casta* meaning 'breed', 'race', or 'class') has been the subject of a good deal of discussion, and though it has been suggested that the word should be used as an adjective rather than a noun, there is a general agreement that the most distinctive feature of the caste, or caste group, is that its members marry and give in marriage only among themselves. In the language of anthropology, the caste (*jāti*) is endogamous, though the clans (*gotra*) of which it is composed are exogamous in that they intermarry, and must intermarry, with other clans within the same caste. A caste thus represents a combination of endogamy and exogamy. It is endogamous in respect to its relations with other castes, exogamous in respect of the relation of its constituent clans to one another. If one regards the exogamy as being more fundamental than the endogamy, and even prior to it, then one can speak of a superimposition of endogamy on exogamy.

Not only is there agreement that the most characteristic feature of the caste, or caste group, is that it is endogamous; there is also agreement that castes exist, and can exist, only in the plural number. Caste in the singular number is an unreality, even a contradiction in terms. This is because a caste defines itself, so to speak, through the relations in which it stands to other castes and in which they stand to it. A caste, or caste group, is a social unit whose members may or may not touch, may or may not intermarry with, may or may not eat with, members of other units within the same Hindu society. Above all, it is a social unit whose members think of themselves as being, both collectively and individually, superior to the members of some other social units and inferior to all the rest. This is why Ambedkar characterized the caste system as a system of graded inequality – though he might well have added that it was a system in which, while all were unequal, some were a lot more unequal than others. It was a system that comprised a congeries of hereditary groups, each adhering to its own God-given *dharma* or religious duty, whether that of a priest, a trader, an oil-presser, a potter, a weaver, a thief, and so on; each excluding the lower castes and in its turn being excluded by the higher castes, and each doing its utmost to protect and, if possible, extend its own social and economic interests at the expense of the interests of all the other hereditary groups. Thus the Hindus are not merely an assortment of castes but 'so many warring groups each living for itself and for its selfish ideal'.[24]

How many of these warring groups there are it is difficult to say. Some authorities speak of 2,000, some of 4,000, and some of 20,000, the discrepancy being mainly due to disagreements as to whether certain groups are castes or sub-castes. Whatever the actual number may be, in principle it should be possible to organize all the different castes into a single, completely unified hierarchy wherein no two castes occupied any one grade, for in principle each caste is necessarily either higher or lower than every other caste. In practice it is not so easy to do this, since there are castes whose exact position in the caste system is a matter of dispute either between them and their immediate neighbours in the system or, as in the case of Shudras claiming to be Rajputs, between them and those supreme authorities in such matters, the Brahmins. But even though there is no completely unified hierarchy, the lines of demarcation between the different castes are generally clear enough, and in the case of the major caste groupings they are very clear indeed. The thickest and blackest line of demarcation, perhaps, is that separating the Savarnas or so-called 'caste Hindus' from the Avarnas or 'non-caste Hindus'. The caste Hindus, who are above the line, are those Hindus who belong to castes traditionally regarded as falling within one or another of the classical four Varnas or 'classes' (literally 'colours'), the four Varnas being those of the Brahmin or priest, the Kshatriya or warrior, the Vaishya or trader, and the Shudra or menial. The non-caste

Hindus, who are below the line, are all those Hindus who belong to castes other than the ones falling within the four Varnas. The caste Hindus are synonymous with the Touchables, the non-caste Hindus with the Untouchables.

Almost as thick and almost as black as the line of demarcation separating the Savarnas or caste Hindus from the Avarnas or non-caste Hindus are the lines which, among the Savarnas themselves, separate first the Brahmins from the non-Brahmins and then the Dvijas or 'twice-born ones' from the Ekajas or 'once-born ones'. The Brahmins are separated from the other Varnas, and indeed from all other Hindus, by virtue of the fact that theirs is the highest caste – or group of castes – and that, as the custodians of the Vedas and other scriptures, they are not only the teachers of the other castes but their ultimate authority in all matters relating to their social and religious life. The Dvijas or twice-born ones are separated from the Ekajas or once-born ones by virtue of the fact that they have been invested with the sacrificial thread. Investiture with this thread constitutes a second, initiatic birth and confers certain important privileges. Only those belonging to castes falling within the first three Varnas are also Dvijas, for only they are entitled to the sacrificial thread. Shudras, not being entitled to the sacrificial thread, are not Dvijas. The position of the Shudras within the caste system is therefore somewhat anomalous, since as Savarnas or caste Hindus they belong with the Brahmins, Kshatriyas, and Vaishyas, while as Ekajas or once-born ones they belong with the Untouchables. According to Ambedkar the anomaly is due to the fact that the Shudras are the descendants of Kshatriyas who, as a result of their conflicts with the Brahmins, were deprived of their right to be invested with the sacrificial thread and degraded to a fourth Varna. The Brahmins were able to do this, Ambedkar points out, because they alone could officiate at the ceremony at which investiture with the sacred thread took place. Deprived of the sacrificial thread, the erstwhile Kshatriyas sank lower and lower in the caste hierarchy and eventually lost all their privileges. In modern times the Shudras, especially the so-called 'unclean Shudras', are virtually indistinguishable from the Untouchables.

From the lines of demarcation separating the Touchables from the Untouchables, the caste Hindus from the non-caste Hindus, and the twice-born caste Hindus from the once-born Hindus, it is obvious that the caste system comprises four major caste groupings: the Brahmins, the non-Brahmin Dvijas, i.e. the Kshatriyas and Vaishyas, the Shudras, and the Untouchables. It is also obvious that, since the caste system is a system of graded inequality, the greatest inequalities will be those between the castes at the very top and the castes at the very bottom of the system, that is, between the Brahmins and the Untouchables. The Brahmins are the Bhudevas or 'terrestrial gods' and as such enjoy numerous privileges. According to the texts cited from various Hindu scriptures by the great nineteenth-century social reformer Jyotirao Phooley, whom Ambedkar regarded as one of his three 'gurus' (the others being the Buddha and Kabir),

The Brahmin is styled the Lord of the universe, even equal to God Himself. He is to be worshipped, served, and respected by all. A Brahmin can do no wrong. Never shall the king slay a Brahmin, though he has committed all possible crimes. To save the life of a Brahmin any falsehood may be told. There is no sin in it. No one is to take away anything belonging to a Brahmin. A king though dying from want, must not receive any tax from a Brahmin, nor suffer him to be afflicted with hunger, or the whole kingdom will be afflicted with famine. The feet of a Brahmin are holy. In his right foot reside the holy waters of all places of pilgrimage, and by dipping it into water he makes it [i.e. the water] as holy as the waters at the holiest of shrines.[25]

And so on. So holy is the water into which a Brahmin has dipped his right foot that the other castes can actually purify themselves by drinking it.

Thus according to the Hindu scriptures – scriptures composed by the Brahmins themselves – the Brahmin occupy an extremely exalted position. The position occupied by the Untouchables is one of corresponding degradation. If the Brahmins are the terrestrial gods and enjoy numerous privileges, the Untouchables are the terrestrial devils and enjoy no privileges and hardly any rights. If the touch of a Brahmin purifies, contact with an Untouchable automatically pollutes, as the term Asprashya or '(hereditary) Untouchable' itself suggests, for it is because contact with him pollutes that he is an Untouchable and is so designated. Other designations for the Untouchables are hardly less opprobrious and hardly less indicative of the extreme lowliness of their position. They are Panchamas or 'fifth-class people', since they constitute a fifth class outside of, and separate from, the classical four Varnas; they are Antyajas or 'those born at the end', since they were born at the end of creation, after the four Varnas (the traditional account) or at the end of the village (Ambedkar's explanation); they are Atishudras or Shudras (menials) par excellence, and they are Pariahs and Outcastes – designations that are self-explanatory. From about the middle of the nineteenth century the Untouchables were referred to in Government literature as the Depressed Classes, which is what in the most literal sense they were, and from 1935 onwards as the Scheduled Castes. 1935 was the year of the India Act. In this Act provision was made for reserved seats for the Untouchables in the central and provincial legislatures, and the Government of India therefore attached to the Orders-in-Council issued under the Act a schedule or list of all those castes that were treated as Untouchable. Thus the castes included in the schedule came to be known as 'Scheduled Castes' and their members are Scheduled caste Hindus as distinct from caste Hindus.

Another modern designation for the Untouchables is Harijans or 'Children of God'. This rather sentimental and patronizing term seems to have been coined by Mahatma Gandhi, but although enshrined in legislation it has found little favour with the Untouchables themselves, especially when used by caste Hindus who, in practice, continue to treat them as Untouchables. On the same principle as that on which

a rose
By any other name would smell as sweet

Untouchability stinks in the nostrils of the Untouchables, as well as in the nostrils of all those who possess even the slightest vestige of human feeling, regardless of whether they are known as the Depressed Classes or the Scheduled Castes or even the Children of God. Whatever they may be called they are still Untouchables in the eyes of the orthodox caste Hindus and contact with them continues to pollute.

But although Untouchability was the principal and, in a sense, the basic disability suffered by the untold millions of human beings who, down the centuries, occupied a position at the very bottom of the Hindu caste system, it was by no means the only one. The fact that they were Untouchables resulted in their being burdened, either directly or indirectly, with a wide variety of other disabilities as well. By the time Ambedkar was born some of the worst of these disabilities had, of course, been removed, though enough of them remained to cause him and his immediate followers serious hardship and suffering throughout their lives. Even today, thirty-eight years after the Constituent Assembly adopted clause 17 of the Constitution, the clause abolishing Untouchability, and thirty-two years after the Untouchability (Offences) Bill became law, the Untouchables continue to suffer at the hands of the caste Hindus many of the disabilities imposed upon them by the Hindu scriptures. What is hardly less disturbing, even the small number of caste Hindus who are inclined to be critical of the caste system, and who believe that the Untouchables should be treated in a more humane fashion, continue to revere the very scriptures which uphold the caste system and which prescribe for the Shudras and Untouchables the most systematically inhumane treatment that one section of a religious community has ever inflicted upon another.

The disabilities imposed on the Untouchables were mainly social, religious, economic, political, and educational in character. Many of their social disabilities, in particular, stemmed directly from the fact of their Untouchability, for since contact with them automatically polluted there could be no question of social intercourse between them and the caste Hindus and no question, therefore, of the two groups living together. In Ambedkar's own forthright words,

> The Hindu society insists on segregation of the Untouchables. The Hindu will not live in the quarters of the Untouchables and will not allow the Untouchables to live inside Hindu quarters. This is a fundamental feature of Untouchability as it is practised by the Hindus. It is not a case of social separation, a mere stoppage of social intercourse for a temporary period. It is a case of territorial segregation and of a *cordon sanitaire* putting the impure people inside a barbed wire into a sort of cage. Every Hindu village has a ghetto. The Hindus live in the village and the Untouchables in the ghetto.[26]

The location of the ghetto was often highly insalubrious. In the case of a village near Poona, which I visited in the early sixties, it was situated not only outside the mud wall of the village but on the very spot where the drainage pipes of the village discharged their effluent, so that the wretched inmates of the ghetto lived surrounded by streams of filth.

Since the village depended on the Untouchables for various services, such as the removal of faeces and the disposal of dead animals, it was impracticable to keep them permanently confined to the ghetto. Their freedom of movement was, however, restricted in various ways, so as to minimize the possibility of their coming into contact with the caste Hindus. They were not permitted to use certain paths, or to pass through the village at certain hours, especially at those times of day when the sun was low in the sky and when the shadow of an Untouchable could be thrown a long way. In some parts of India they were not allowed to enter the village at all during the daytime. What was more, they were not permitted to bathe in the public bathing-tank or to draw water from the public well. They were also prohibited from using metal cooking utensils, from wearing decent clothes, and from wearing gold or silver ornaments, all of which were the prerogatives of the caste Hindus. They were not even permitted to use proper Hindu names, for Hindu names generally incorporated the name of a god or goddess and for an Untouchable to be called by such a name would bring pollution on the deity concerned and thus be tantamount to sacrilege. The Untouchables were therefore known by derisive nicknames or, in some parts of India, by the names of birds and animals.

The religious disabilities of the Untouchables related mainly to what became known, in modern times, as 'temple entry'. Untouchables were not permitted to enter Hindu temples or even, in some cases, to walk along the street in which a Hindu temple was situated. Some untouchable communities possessed small, insignificant temples of their own in which they worshipped either the popular Hindu gods and goddesses or quasi-tribal divinities peculiar to themselves. Brahmins did not, of course, officiate in these temples. Indeed, the Brahmins and other caste Hindus could no more think of entering the temples of the Untouchables than they could think of allowing the Untouchables to enter theirs. Thus the Untouchables were segregated from the caste Hindus not only in the social but in the religious sense. There was a temple – or temples – in the village and there was a temple in the ghetto. The Untouchables were not permitted, in fact, to participate in the religious life of the Hindu community in any way. They were prohibited from studying the scriptures, especially the Vedas, and from engaging in the practice of asceticism (*tapasya*). In this respect they were in much the same position as the Shudras. According to scriptures like the *Bṛhaspati-smṛti* and the *Gautama-dharmasūtra* a Shudra may not listen to the recitation of the divinely inspired words of the Vedas, he may not recite them, and he may not learn them by heart. If he listens to them his ears are to be filled with molten tin or lac, if he recites them his tongue is to be cut out, and if he learns them by heart his body is to be split in two.[27] As for the Shudra who engages in the practice of asceticism, the punishment that awaits him is sufficiently illustrated by the famous episode in the *Rāmāyaṇa* in which king Rāma, the divine embodiment of all the virtues, cuts off Śambūka's head for daring to engage in a practice reserved for the higher castes.[28] The Shudras were, however, allowed to participate in the religious life of the Hindu community to a limited extent, even though their real religious duty (*dharma*) was to serve the three higher castes in various menial ways. They could, for instance, invite Brahmins to perform certain ceremonies for them and they could make offerings to the Brahmins. The Untouchables were denied even these doubtful privileges. Many of them, however, found consolation in the devotional mysticism of the great teachers of the Bhakti school, some of whom were themselves of low-caste origin and who were, more often than not, critical of the caste system and of the pretensions of the Brahmins. Among those who found consolation in this way were Ambedkar's own senior relations, for both his father's and his mother's family belonged by tradition to the Kabir sect, one of his father's uncles having in fact been a sadhu or wandering holy man.

The economic and political disabilities of the Untouchables were no less crippling than the social and religious ones. To an even greater extent than was the case with the Shudras, their condition was, in effect, one of economic and political slavery. The only reason they were not actually bought and sold in the market place was that they were, so to speak, public property and the caste Hindus were free to make use of their services for whatever low and degrading purpose they pleased. As Ambedkar reminded an organization of caste Hindu social reformers in a famous undelivered speech,

For slavery does not merely mean a legalized form of subjection.
It means a state of society in which some men are forced to
accept from other[s] the purposes which control their conduct.

This condition obtains even where there is no slavery in the legal sense. It is found where, as in the Caste System, some persons are compelled to carry on certain prescribed callings which are not of their choice.[29]

The state of society referred to by Ambedkar certainly obtained in the case of the Untouchables. They were compelled to follow callings which were not of their own choice but laid down for them by the Hindu scriptures on account of their having been born in a particular caste. Besides being compelled to follow callings which they had not themselves chosen the Untouchables were also compelled to follow them on terms dictated by the caste Hindus. Whether working as sweepers and scavengers or, as did the more fortunate among them, as landless labourers and tenant farmers, they were obliged to accept from their caste Hindu masters whatever meagre recompense the latter were prepared to give them. The condition of the Untouchables was thus one of very real economic slavery and that slavery, bad as it was, was made even worse in modern times by the evil of hereditary indebtedness – indebtedness, that is, to the caste Hindu moneylender. The caste Hindus were able to keep the Untouchables in a condition of economic slavery mainly because the latter had no civic or political rights and because, being at the same time totally devoid of political power, they had no means of wresting those rights from the caste Hindus. The condition of the Untouchables was thus one of political slavery, and because it was one of political slavery it was one of economic slavery too. Political slavery led to economic slavery, and economic slavery in turn reinforced political slavery, both these forms of subjection being sanctioned and, indeed, prescribed by the Hindu scriptures.

The educational disabilities of the Untouchables were the direct consequence of their social and religious disabilities. Contact with an Untouchable brought pollution, and for this reason the Untouchables were not allowed into the Hindu schools, which in any case were in effect Brahmin schools, being run by Brahmins – who were the learned class – mainly for the benefit of Brahmins. Another reason why the Untouchables were not allowed into Hindu schools was that the principal subjects taught in those schools were the Vedas and the subjects ancillary to the Vedas, such as grammar and prosody, and an Untouchable was not permitted even to hear the divinely inspired words of the Vedas being recited. The study of the Vedas was for the twice-born who, having been invested with the sacred thread, were alone eligible for such study. An Untouchable was not even permitted to learn Sanskrit, which was as much a key to knowledge in ancient and medieval India as Latin was in medieval and Renaissance Europe. Sanskrit was the language of the Vedas; it was the language of the gods (*devabhāṣā*), just as the script in which it was normally written was the script of the city of the gods (*devanāgarī*), and the very idea of an Untouchable speaking, reading, and writing Sanskrit was therefore an abomination.

The result of this policy was that for centuries together the Untouchables were kept in a state of ignorance and illiteracy that has lasted, for the majority of them, right down to the present day. In the Bombay Presidency Untouchables were first admitted into Government schools only about ten years before Ambedkar was born, and even then only in the face of strong opposition from the Brahmin teachers, who treated their untouchable pupils in the most humiliating fashion. They could not sit with the caste Hindu children, they could not take water from the school water pot, and their teachers refused to mark their exercise books from fear of pollution. Some teachers even refused to cane their untouchable pupils, for caning them would mean coming into contact with them, even if only for a moment. They therefore hurled clods of earth at the untouchable children whenever they misbehaved.

Burdened as the Untouchables were with disabilities of this kind, it is hardly surprising that on the occasion of his conversion to Buddhism Ambedkar should have felt as though he had been delivered from hell – from the hell of caste, Untouchability, and subjection. It was also hardly surprising that, immediately after embracing Buddhism by taking the Three Refuges and Five Precepts, he should have formally abjured the Hindu religion, declaring, among other things,

> I renounce Hinduism which is harmful for humanity, and the
> advancement and benefit of humanity, because it is based on
> inequality, and adopt Buddhism as my religion.[30]

It is interesting and significant that, at a time when Hinduism was not being exported to the West to the extent that it is today, Ambedkar should have renounced it because it was *harmful to humanity*. It was certainly harmful to the Untouchables. Just how harmful it had been for how many people and over how long a period it is impossible to tell, but writing in 1948 and referring to the schedule attached to the Orders-in-Council issued under the India Act 1935, Ambedkar comments,

> This is a very terrifying list. It includes 429 communities. Reduced to numbers it means that today there exist in India 50–60 millions of people whose mere touch causes pollution to the Hindus. Surely, the phenomenon of Untouchability among primitive and ancient society pales into insignificance before this phenomenon of hereditary Untouchability for so many millions of people which we find in India. This type of Untouchability among Hindus stands in a class by itself. It has no parallel in the history of the world. It is unparalleled not merely by reason of the colossal numbers involved which exceed the number of [a] great many nations in Asia and in Europe but also on other grounds.[31]

These 'other grounds' are the disabilities imposed on the Untouchables by the caste Hindus and the sufferings that those disabilities entailed. At the time of Ambedkar's conversion to Buddhism in 1956 the population of (divided) India numbered about 400 million of whom at least one eighth were Untouchables. Assuming the proportion of Untouchables to caste Hindus to have remained unchanged for the last thousand or so years, that is, from the time of the decline and disappearance of Buddhism, then the total number of Untouchables who have been forced to live in the hell of caste must run into several hundreds of millions. This represents a truly appalling mass of human suffering, compared with which the sufferings of the blacks under white majority rule in America and South Africa, and even the frightful sufferings of the Jews under the Nazis, assume a temporary and local significance. Ambedkar himself spoke of the Untouchables as having undergone a holocaust, and a holocaust it indeed was in the metaphorical, if not in the literal, sense of the term. It was a holocaust that lasted for at least ten centuries, claimed several hundreds of millions of victims, and was conducted under the auspices of a religion that professes to see the Divine in every man.

Among the 429 untouchable communities enumerated by the schedule of 1935 there were many differences, including differences of size. One of the biggest of these communities was that of the Mahars, who were one of the two principal untouchable castes of the Bombay Presidency, the other being that of the Mangs. Though there were so many of them, and though in the Marathi-speaking parts of central and western India they constituted one tenth of the population, the Mahars were not concentrated in any particular place but scattered throughout the area now occupied by the State of Maharashtra. Every Hindu village had its colony of Mahars, who of course lived in the ghetto, and who besides serving the caste Hindus in the usual way acted as watchmen and messengers. In return for these services they were given cast-off clothing and leavings of food, as well as being allowed to cultivate certain lands. These lands were known as *watan*. They had been granted to the Mahars by the Government in ancient times, and were exempt from taxation, but the fact that they held them by right of their services to the village meant, in practice, that there was no limit to the services they could be called upon to perform. Thus in addition to all the usual disabilities suffered by the Untouchables the Mahars lived in a state of actual serfdom. They were at the beck and call of their caste Hindu masters at all hours of the day and night, they were not entitled to wages, and regardless of the amount of work they did they could ask only for a few rounds of unleavened bread or a few handfuls of grain by way of recompense. This state of affairs lasted well into the twentieth century, the Mahar *watans* being abolished only in 1958, by which time comparatively few Mahars still followed their traditional calling.

The sufferings of the Mahars were especially severe under the Chitpavan Brahmin dynasty that ruled the Maratha empire during the eighteenth and early nineteenth centuries, first as Peshwas or prime ministers of the weaker descendants of Shivaji and afterwards in their own right. During this period the *watan* lands were taxed, the tax being payable in kind, and the Mahars themselves were compelled to go about with a broom tied to the end of their loincloth and an earthenware pot hanging from their neck. The broom was for covering up their footprints and the pot for spitting in, so that the feet of the caste Hindus using the same road might not come into contact with anything polluting. Those Mahars who dared to rebel against the restrictions imposed on them, or even to raise their voices in protest, were liable to be trampled to death by elephants in the courtyard of the Peshwa's palace. Mahars could also be buried alive in the foundations of caste Hindu buildings. Though the Peshwas were deposed after the Third Maratha War of

1817–19, the horrors of Brahmin rule were not easily forgotten. In the early 1850s a fourteen-year-old untouchable girl (not a Mahar but a Mang) who was attending Jyotirao Phooley's school for low-caste girls in Poona wrote an essay on the condition of the Mahars and Mangs. In this essay she observed, *inter alia*:

> Formerly we were buried alive in the foundations of buildings. We were not allowed to pass by the Talimkhana. If any man was found to do so, his head was cut off playfully. We were not allowed to read and write. If [Peshwa] Bajirao II came to know about such a case, he would indignantly cry: 'What! If Mahars and Mangs learn to read and write, are the Brahmins to hand over their writing work to them and to go round shaving widows [i.e. working as barbers, who were of Shudra caste] with their bags hanging from their shoulders?' God has bestowed on us the rule of the British and our grievances are redressed. Nobody harasses us now. Nobody hangs us. Nobody buries us alive. Our progeny can live now. We can now wear clothes, can put on cloth around our body. Everybody is at liberty to live according to his means. No bars, no taboos, no restrictions. Even the bazaar at the Gultekadi is open to us.[32]

But severely as the Mahars suffered under Peshwa rule, there were signs that a new day was about to dawn for them and, indeed, for all the Untouchables of India. One such sign was the recruitment of Mahars as soldiers by the East India Company. Mahars continued to be recruited in this way even after 1858, when the Government of India passed from the East India Company to the Crown, and the practice did not come to an end until 1892. Whether under the Company or the Crown, service with the army made a tremendous difference to the lives of thousands of Mahar men, as well as to the lives of their dependants. They were liberated from the ghetto, they were provided with proper food and clothing, they were paid wages, they could even learn to read and write. Indeed, during the latter part of the century education was made compulsory for the children and other relations, both male and female, of all those in military service.

Among the Mahar families to benefit from these changes was that from which Ambedkar sprang. His father, his two grandfathers, and his six maternal great-uncles, were all military men, his father in fact being the headmaster of an army school for a number of years. Ambedkar was therefore born not in a ghetto outside a mud-walled village but in the midst of the garrison town of Mhow, where his father's regiment was then stationed. Since the family lived in the cantonment the young Bhimrao Ramji had little contact with the world outside the military area, and it was not until he was five years old that he had any personal experience of Untouchability. By this time his headmaster father had retired from the army and the family had moved first to Dapoli, in the Konkan, and then to Satara, where his mother died shortly after their arrival. In Satara they found that no barber was prepared to cut their hair (contact with Mahars brought pollution even to the 'clean' Shudra caste to which the barbers belonged), and Ambedkar's own hair used to be cut by his elder sister. He could not understand why, despite the presence of so many barbers in the town, not one of them was prepared to cut their hair. Questions of this sort disturbed him more and more deeply as time went on, and as one humiliating incident after another burned into his brain the consciousness that he was a Mahar and that for his caste Hindu co-religionists contact with a Mahar brought pollution.

Years later, in a speech on 'Reasons for Conversion', Ambedkar declared that there were four or five incidents which had left a deep impression on his mind and led him to decide in favour of the renunciation of Hinduism and the adoption of some other religion. One of these was the haircutting incident. Another, which he also described, took place at about the same time, and may be called the bullock cart incident. Ambedkar's father had gone to work as a cashier in Goregaon, leaving the children in Satara. One day he wrote inviting them to pay him a visit. The idea that they would be travelling by train to Goregaon thrilled the young Ambedkar greatly, since he had never seen a train before. With the money sent by his father they bought new clothes, and with his elder brother and sister he set off for Goregaon. On their arrival at Badali, the railhead for Goregaon, they found to their dismay that there was no one there to meet them, their father not having received the letter they had sent. Ambedkar's own affecting words best describe what then happened.

> Soon everybody departed and there were no passengers, excepting us, left on the platform. We waited in vain for some three quarters of an hour. The Station Master enquired who we were meeting, what caste

we belonged to, and where we wanted to go. We told him we belonged to the Mahar caste. This gave him a shock and he retreated some five steps backwards. But seeing us well dressed, he presumed that we belonged to some well-to-do family. He assured us that he would try to get a cart for us. But owing to our being members of the Mahar caste, no bullock cart driver was willing to drive us. Evening was approaching and till 6 or 7 p.m. we did not succeed in getting a cart. Finally a cart-man agreed to take us in his cart. But he made it clear at the outset that he would not drive the cart for us.

I had been living in the military area and driving a cart was not difficult for me. As soon as we agreed to this condition, he came with his cart and we, all of us children, started for Goregaon.

At a short distance outside the village we came across a brook. The cart driver asked us to eat our food there for [since we were Untouchables] no water was available elsewhere on the way. Accordingly, we got down from the cart and ate our food. The water was murky and mixed with dung. In the meantime, the driver also returned after having his dinner.

As the evening grew darker, the driver quietly boarded the cart and sat beside us. It became so dark soon, that neither any flickering lamp nor any human being was visible for miles. Fear, darkness, and loneliness made us cry. It was well past midnight and we were frightened. So scared were we that we thought we should never reach Goregaon. When we reached a toll post we jumped out of the cart. We made enquiries from the toll-collector whether we could get anything to eat in the vicinity. I spoke to him in Persian. I knew how to speak in Persian and had no difficulty in speaking to him. He replied in a very curt manner and pointed towards the hills. Somehow, we spent the night near the ravine and early in the morning we set off again on our journey to Goregaon. At last we reached Goregaon on the following day in the afternoon, utterly exhausted and almost half dead.[33]

But though the children had reached Goregaon, their troubles were far from over. A few days after their arrival the young Ambedkar, his throat parched with thirst, surreptitiously drank some water from a public watercourse. Unfortunately, he was discovered, and the enraged caste Hindus gave him a severe beating.

By this time he had been admitted to the Government Middle School at Satara, and the reason for his being able to speak to the toll-collector in Persian was that he had been compelled to take that language instead of Sanskrit. Even in their high school days neither Bhimrao Ramji nor his elder brother were ever allowed to study 'the language of the gods'. They were Untouchables, and the Brahmin pundits simply refused to teach them. This was not the only bitter pill he had to swallow during his student days. He and his brother were usually made to squat in a corner of the classroom on a piece of sacking that they carried with them to school each day. The teachers refused to touch their exercise books, and some of them would not even ask the two boys to recite poems or put questions to them for fear of being polluted. Even when the family moved to Bombay, and Bhimrao was attending a leading government high school, the same cruel persecution continued. One day the teacher asked him to come to the blackboard and solve a problem. Instantly the class was in an uproar. The reason was that the caste Hindu boys were in the habit of keeping their lunch boxes behind the blackboard, and the presence of an Untouchable so near the blackboard would have polluted the food and made it unfit to eat. Before Bhimrao Ramji could reach the blackboard and touch it, therefore, they darted across the room and threw the lunch boxes to one side. As though incidents of this sort did not make life hard enough for the sensitive boy, his teachers did their best to discourage him. One of them went so far as to tell him that education was of no use to him. After all, he was a Mahar, and what did a Mahar want with education? But the young Ambedkar, who was already beginning to have a mind of his own, angrily told the man to mind his own business.

Despite all difficulties, however, Bhimrao Ambedkar persevered with his studies. He passed the matriculation examination. He became a graduate. He went abroad. He attended two of the most prestigious seats of learning in the West and eventually, in 1917, he returned with a master's degree in arts and a doctorate in philosophy from Columbia University. But his difficulties were by no means over. In the eyes of the caste Hindus he was still a Mahar and contact with him continued to pollute. Only a month after his return there occurred an incident that reminded him, in the most brutal fashion, that his position in Hindu society was exactly the same as it had always been. This incident took place in Baroda, and was another of those four or five incidents that left a deep impression on his mind and led him to decide in favour of the renunciation of Hinduism and the adoption of some other faith. It may be called the Parsi *dharamsala* incident, and Ambedkar described it in the same speech on 'Reasons for Conversion' in which he described the haircutting incident and the bullock cart incident.

With a scholarship granted by Baroda State, I had gone for education abroad. After returning from England, in accord with the terms of the agreement, I came to serve under the Baroda Durbar. I could not get a house to live in at Baroda. Neither a Hindu nor any Moslem was prepared to rent out a house to me in the city of Baroda. Failing to get a house in any locality, I decided to get accommodation in a Parsi *Dharamsala*. After having stayed in America and England, I had developed a fair complexion and an impressive personality. Giving myself a Parsi name, 'Adalji Sorabji', I began to live in the Parsi Dharamsala. The Parsi manager agreed to accommodate me at Rs. 2 per diem. But soon the people got wind of the fact that His Highness the Maharaja Gaekwad of Baroda had appointed a Mahar boy as an officer in his Durbar. My living in the Parsi Dharamsala under an assumed name gave rise to suspicion and my secret was soon out.

On the second day of my stay, when I was just leaving for my office after taking breakfast, a mob of some fifteen or twenty Parsis, armed with *lathis*, accosted me, threatening to kill me, and demanded who I was. I replied, 'I am a Hindu.' But they were not to be satisfied with this answer. Exasperated, they began to shower abuses on me and bade me vacate the room immediately. My presence of mind and knowledge gave me the strength to face the situation boldly. Politely I asked for permission to stay for eight hours more. Throughout the day I searched for a house to live in, but miserably failed to get any place to hide my head. I approached my friends but all turned me down on some plea or the other, expressing their inability to accommodate me. I was utterly disappointed and exhausted. What to do next? I just could not decide. Frustrated and exhausted, I quietly sat down at one place, with tears flowing out of my eyes. Seeing no hope of getting a house, and no alternative but to quit, I tendered my resignation and left for Bombay by the night train.[34]

One of the the strangest features of this incident was that Ambedkar should have been driven from a Parsi *dharamsala* by Parsis. The Parsis were not Hindus but Zoroastrians of Iranian descent, but owing to their long residence in India they had become deeply infected by the poison of the Hindu caste system. Though he did not mention the fact in his speech, during his brief stay in Baroda Ambedkar was not only driven from the Parsi *dharamsala* but, virtually, from his own office as well. His staff, including the peons, were all caste Hindus, and even though they were his subordinates they treated him like a leper. Fearful that contact with him would bring pollution, the peons threw files and papers on to his desk from a safe distance. Drinking water was not available to him in the office. Thoroughly mortified by the caste-ridden atmosphere of the place, Ambedkar was forced to seek refuge in the Baroda public library.

Incidents of this kind having led him to decide in favour of the renunciation of Hinduism and conversion to some other religion, Ambedkar naturally devoted much thought to the question of which religion would be the best for the Untouchables to adopt. Should it be Christianity? Or Islam? Or Sikhism? Or should it be a new religion, founded by Ambedkar himself? In the event he and his followers adopted Buddhism, but they did not do so until twenty years after his 'Reasons for Conversion' speech and twenty years after his description of the haircutting incident, the bullock cart incident, and the Parsi *dharamsala* incident. The road to Conversion was not always an easy one, nor was it always clear. Yet looking back one can make out what seem, at least in retrospect, to have been milestones, some of them indeed going back to an early period of Ambedkar's life. These milestones were not all of the same kind, nor were they distributed along the road at exactly equal intervals. Some were not even very plainly marked, while others indicated the greatness of the distance that Ambedkar had travelled from Hinduism rather than the smallness of the distance that separated him from Buddhism. But all of them – and there may well have been others of which we have no knowledge – are important as illustrating the stages through which Ambedkar passed on the long journey that ended only when, on 14 October 1956, he went for Refuge to the Buddha, Dharma, and Sangha.

4
MILESTONES ON THE ROAD
TO CONVERSION

Ambedkar's first recorded contact with Buddhism occurred in 1908, when he was sixteen. He had just passed the matriculation examination of Bombay University, and so extraordinary an achievement was this for an untouchable boy that the Mahars celebrated the occasion with a public meeting in his honour. The meeting was held in Bombay under the presidency of S. K. Bole, a well-known social reformer from the Bhandari community who, some two decades later, was to cooperate with Ambedkar in the Chowdar Tank campaign. Among the speakers at the meeting was a local high school teacher called Krishnaji Arjun Keluskar. Though a Maharashtrian Brahmin by birth Keluskar was a man of liberal views and an admirer of the Buddha. He had, in fact, recently published a life of the Buddha in Marathi, and a copy of this work he now presented to the young Ambedkar. Being nothing if not an avid reader, the new matriculate lost no time in devouring the book, and there is no doubt that the sublime story of the Buddha's renunciation of all earthly ties, his search for truth, his eventual attainment of Enlightenment, and his compassionate activity on behalf of his fellow men, left an indelible impression on his mind. Keluskar, for his part, continued to take a keen interest in the brilliant untouchable boy, and it was through his good offices that, three years later, the Maharaja Gaekwad of Baroda granted Ambedkar the scholarship that enabled him to continue his education.

That a liberal-minded Brahmin like Keluskar should have written and published a life of the Buddha was a sign of the times. For at least seven or eight centuries Buddhism had been unknown in India, the land of its birth, and the name of the Buddha himself had lingered on only as that of an alleged incarnation of the god Vishnu who had taken birth for the express purpose of misleading the *asuras* or anti-gods with a false teaching. But the darkness was lifting. Thanks to the labours of orientalists like James Prinsep and archaeologists like Alexander Cunningham, as well as to the more popular activities of the Theosophists, by the end of the nineteenth century the main events of the Buddha's career and the general nature of his teaching had begun to penetrate the consciousness of English-educated Hindus and, by their means, to percolate through the rest of society. In eastern India the founding of the Buddhist Text Society in Calcutta in 1892 gave an impetus to the scholarly study of Buddhism, while Anagarika Dharmapala's work for the resuscitation of Bodh Gaya, where the Buddha had gained Enlightenment, helped to remind people of the greatness of India's Buddhist heritage. The precise nature of Keluskar's relation to all these developments is difficult to ascertain, but it is clear that the worthy Brahmin was one of those who had come under the influence of the movement of Buddhist revival and that the book he presented to the sixteen-year-old Ambedkar was a product of that influence. Thus the book represented not only Ambedkar's first contact with Buddhism; it also represented his first contact with the movement of which he himself was to be the brightest ornament.

From 1908 to 1917 the future leader of the Untouchables was fully absorbed in his studies, first in India itself and afterwards in America and England, and during this period there was nothing to indicate that he was moving in the direction of Buddhism or even that he was giving any special thought to the Buddha's teaching. It was only in his middle and late twenties, after his second sojourn in England and his re-emergence into Indian public life, that there occurred any more of those incidents which, as we can now see, were milestones in his – and his community's – progress to Buddhism. But though Ambedkar may not have been moving in the direction of Buddhism during the period of his graduate and post-graduate studies he was nevertheless developing an outlook and even a philosophy that was, in certain essential respects, thoroughly Buddhistic. This was evident as early as 1918, when he wrote a review article on Bertrand Russell's *The Principles of Social Reconstruction*, published the previous year. Since the article was written for a journal of economics Ambedkar was obliged to confine himself to Russell's analysis of Property, but before dealing with this topic he discussed the question of how the philosophy of war was related to the principles of growth as expounded by the English philosopher. Characteristically, Ambedkar agreed with Russell that there is more hope for a nation that has the impulses that lead to war than for a nation in which all impulse is dead, observing,

> The gist of it all is that *activity is the condition of growth*.
> Mr. Russell, it must be emphasized, is against war but is not for
> quieticism [*sic*]; for, according to him, activity leads to growth
> and quieticism is but another name for death. To express it in the
> language of Professor Dewey he is only against 'force as violence'
> but is all for 'force as energy'. It must be remembered by those who
> are opposed to force [as such] that without the use of it all ideals will
> remain empty just as without some ideal or purpose (conscious or
> otherwise) all activity will be no more than mere fruitless fooling.[35]

This is very reminiscent of Buddhism's emphasis on *vīrya*, energy or vigour, as being indispensable at every stage of spiritual life. It is also interesting to find the youthful Ambedkar lamenting the prevalence of the 'philosophy of quieticism' among Indians, and rejecting the stock contrasts between the East and the West, bluntly declaring, 'Materialist we all are; even the East in spite of itself.'[36] He concluded this part of his article by quoting Bertrand Russell to the effect that every man needs some kind of contest, some sense of resistance overcome, in order to feel that he is exercising his faculties, adding, 'in other words to feel that he is growing.'[37] Once again, this is reminiscent of Buddhism.

If contest and a sense of resistance overcome are necessary to human growth, then 1927 was certainly a year of growth for Ambedkar and his followers. This was the year of the Chowdar Tank campaign, which at least in its opening phases was a complete success. The background of the campaign was what was known as the Bole resolution. This was a resolution moved in the Bombay Legislative Council by S. K. Bole, the social reformer, to the effect that the untouchable classes be allowed to use all watering places, wells, and *dharamsalas* which were built and maintained by the Government or created by statute, as well as public schools, courts, offices, and dispensaries. After being adopted by the Council the resolution was accepted, with some reluctance, by the Bombay Government. Heads of departments were directed to give effect to the resolution so far as it related to public places and institutions belonging to and maintained by the Government, and Collectors were requested to advise the local public bodies in their jurisdiction to consider the desirability of accepting the recommendation made in the resolution so far as it related to them.

One of the local public bodies thus advised was the Mahad Municipality, and one of the amenities administered by the Mahad Municipality was the Chowdar Tank. This tank was a rectangular artificial lake of the traditional type, and the caste Hindus were accustomed to draw water from it for household purposes. Untouchables were not allowed anywhere near the tank. Even when the Mahad Municipality, in compliance with the Bole resolution, threw the tank open to the Untouchables the latter were unable to exercise their moral and legal right to draw water from the tank owing to the hostility of the caste Hindus. This state of affairs lasted for three years. Then in March the Depressed Classes of Kolaba district, in which Mahad was situated, decided to call a two-day conference to deal with the situation. The conference was held on the outskirts of Mahad, 3,000 untouchable representatives from all over the Bombay Presidency attended, Ambedkar delivered a stirring speech, resolutions were passed, and on the second day the conference formed itself into a procession which marched four abreast through the streets of Mahad to the Chowdar Tank. There Ambedkar, who was in the forefront of the procession, took water from the tank and drank it and the rest followed his example. Having thus demonstrated their right the processionists returned to the conference venue in the same peaceful manner that they had set out and started making preparations to leave for home.

They were not allowed to enjoy their victory for long. A rumour having gone round the town to the effect that the Untouchables were planning to enter the Vireshwar temple, a crowd of infuriated caste Hindus burst into the conference venue and proceeded to belabour the delegates who still remained there with heavy bamboo sticks. Soon the whole town was in an uproar, and had Ambedkar not succeeded in restraining his more militant supporters a full-scale riot would probably have ensued. As it was, twenty Untouchables were seriously injured, and numerous others were assaulted by gangs of orthodox caste Hindus as they made their way out of the town. Belatedly, the police arrested nine of the troublemakers and three months later five of these were sentenced to four months rigorous imprisonment. Ambedkar remarked that had the principal officers of the district not been non-caste Hindus justice would not have been done to the Untouchables, adding that under Peshwa rule he himself would have been trampled to death by an elephant.

But the caste Hindus of Mahad were still far from having learned their lesson. In their eyes, as in the eyes of the vast majority of caste Hindus throughout India, the action of the Untouchables in taking water from the Chowdar Tank had polluted the tank and rendered its water unfit for consumption. What had been polluted could, however, be purified, and what more effective means of purification was there than the five products of the cow, that is, milk, curds, clarified butter, urine, and dung? One hundred and eight earthenware pots of water having been drawn from the tank, a corresponding number of pots containing a mixture of these five products were therefore emptied into it to the recitation of mantras by Brahmins and the water of the tank was declared to be again fit for caste Hindu consumption.

This so-called purification of the Chowdar Tank was deeply offensive to the Untouchables, and Ambedkar decided to continue the struggle and establish their right to draw water from the tank once and for all. In December of that year, after extensive preparations, a second conference was therefore called at Mahad. On this occasion 15,000 people attended, 3,884 of whom, in response to Ambedkar's appeal, declared their readiness to take water from the tank regardless of consequences. By this time, however, a group of caste Hindus had filed a suit claiming that the Chowdar Tank was private property, an injunction had been issued restraining Ambedkar and his principal lieutenants from approaching the tank or drawing water from it, and the town was bristling with police. Ambedkar was in a quandary. On the one hand, he wanted to demonstrate the right of the Untouchables to draw water from the tank; on the other, he had no wish to break the law or antagonize the Government. In the end, after much anxious debate, a compromise was reached. On Ambedkar's recommendation the conference decided to postpone the struggle until the courts had settled the question of whether or not the Chowdar Tank was private property, but it also decided to go in procession to the tank and to march round it carrying banners and placards. The authorities having been notified, this was accordingly done and after Ambedkar had addressed a meeting of the town's Chamar or cobbler community the conference came to an end.

The right of the Untouchables to draw water from the Chowdar Tank was not finally established until 1937, when the Bombay High Court gave judgement in their favour. By that time the Mahad campaign had been overshadowed by other events. Even in 1927 itself, the first conference's action in taking water from the Chowdar Tank had been overshadowed, before the year was out, by the still more revolutionary proceedings of the second conference. That conference having repudiated those Hindu scriptures which preached the gospel of social inequality, and reaffirmed its opposition to applying them to the present social order, on the night of 25 December Ambedkar and his followers publicly and ceremonially burned one of the most celebrated of all such scriptures, the notorious *Manusmṛti* or 'Institutes of Manu', which had governed the life of the Hindu community for 1,500 years and which, in the words of the conference,

> decried the Shudras, stunted their growth, impaired their self-respect, and perpetuated their social, economic, religious and political slavery.[38]

It was one of the great iconoclastic acts of history, and the greatest blow orthodox Hinduism had suffered for more than a thousand years. So far-reaching were the consequences that Ambedkar's burning of the *Manusmṛti* has been likened, by some of his admirers, to Luther's burning of the Pope's bull of excommunication against him. The comparison would have been still more apt if what Luther had burned at Wittenberg had been not the Pope's bull of excommunication but the Bible, for the *Manusmṛti* was as much loved and revered by the caste Hindus as it was hated by the Untouchables. Ambedkar himself, interviewed in 1938, emphasized the essentially symbolic nature of the burning of the *Manusmṛti*.

> It was a very cautious and drastic step, but [it] was taken with a view to forcing the attention of caste Hindus. At intervals such drastic remedies are a necessity. If you do not knock at the door,

none opens it. It is not that all the parts of the *Manusmriti* are condemnable, that it does not contain [any] good principles and that Manu himself was not a sociologist and was a mere fool. We made a bonfire of it because we view it as a symbol of injustice under which we have been crushed across centuries.[39]

If the burning of the *Manusmṛti* indicated how far Ambedkar had travelled from Hinduism, other incidents occurring in connection with the Chowdar Tank campaign showed how near he was beginning to draw to Buddhism. These incidents, which were three in number, were of a much less dramatic character than the burning of the *Manusmṛti* and their significance was probably not appreciated at the time. Addressing the opening session of the first Mahad conference, Ambedkar told his poorly clad and illiterate audience,

> No lasting progress can be achieved unless we put ourselves
> through a threefold process of purification. We must improve the
> general tone of our demeanour, re-tone our pronunciations, and
> revitalise our thoughts.[40]

The threefold purification of which Ambedkar spoke was, of course, the purification of the three principles of body, speech, and mind, which between them make up the individual human being. What is especially noteworthy about Ambedkar's insistence on the need for a threefold purification is that whereas references to a threefold purification, corresponding to a threefold division of the individual human being, are found throughout Buddhist literature, they appear to be unknown to the Vedic and post-Vedic literature of Hinduism.[41] This suggests that even before the time of the Chowdar Tank campaign Ambedkar had not only familiarized himself with the Buddhist scriptures but had started thinking in specifically Buddhist terms. It also suggests that he saw progress not as simply material but as having a moral and spiritual basis. As the Buddhist scriptures make clear, the threefold purification is effected by abstention from the ten modes of 'unskilful' (i.e. ethically disastrous) action. Body is purified by abstention from killing, stealing, and sexual misconduct; speech by abstention from falsehood, abuse, idle chatter, and backbiting; and mind by abstention from covetousness, hatred, and wrong views. These ten constitute what are traditionally known as the 'ten precepts' (*dasa-sīla*), in their negative rather than their positive form, and it is not surprising that when, towards the end of his life, Ambedkar came to compile *The Buddha and His Dhamma*, he should have included in that work a number of passages from the Pāli scriptures dealing with the threefold purification and the ten precepts. In the light of these facts one cannot help thinking that when Ambedkar told the first Mahad conference that no lasting progress could be achieved unless they put themselves through a threefold process of purification he was, in effect, telling them that no lasting progress could be achieved without Buddhism.

The two remaining incidents occurred in connection with the second Mahad conference. Two prominent non-Brahmin leaders of Maharashtra offered to support Ambedkar in his campaign on certain conditions. One condition was that no Brahmins, i.e. no liberal-minded Brahmins sympathetic to the cause of the Untouchables, should be allowed to participate in the campaign. Ambedkar flatly rejected the two leaders' offer. The view that all Brahmins were enemies of the Untouchables was erroneous, he declared. What he hated was the *spirit* of Brahmanism, that is, the idea that some were high caste and others low caste – an idea that implanted such notions as the pollutability of one human being by another, social privilege, and inequality. A non-Brahmin filled with ideas of superiority and inferiority was as repellent to him as a Brahmin free from the spirit of Brahmanism was welcome. This noble and truly humanistic declaration showed that much as he and his fellow Untouchables had suffered at the hands of the caste Hindus in general, and the Brahmins in particular, Ambedkar believed in seeing people not simply as members of this or that community but as individuals. In his eyes what counted was not birth but worth, and it was in accordance with the latter that men should really be judged. This was, of course, a basic Buddhist principle, and the fact that Ambedkar should have stated it so unequivocally shows how close he was, even at that time, to Buddhism.

But Ambedkar's closeness to Buddhism was not just in respect of certain principles; it was also a closeness of personal sympathy. In other words, the closeness was not only intellectual but emotional. Two days after the burning of the *Manusmṛti* Ambedkar and his entourage went on an expedition to a place in the neighbourhood of Mahad in order to see the excavations of some ruins that were believed to date from the time of the Buddha. Deeply moved by the sight of the sculptures that had been unearthed, Ambedkar described to the members of his entourage how the Buddha's disciples had lived lives of poverty and chastity and selflessly devoted themselves to the service of the community. In a reverential mood, he asked them not to sit on the ancient stone benches that formed part of the ruins since these may have been the seats of Buddhist monks. It was almost as though he felt himself to be back in the days when Buddhism flourished in India and when Buddhist monks and monasteries were to be seen in every part of his beloved Maharashtra.

The six years that followed the Chowdar Tank campaign were years of vacillation. Sometimes it seemed that Ambedkar had travelled a long way from Hinduism, whether or not in the direction of some other religion, and sometimes it seemed that he had not. Sometimes he even appeared to be retracing his steps. Speaking at Jalgaon in May 1929, at a conference called by the Depressed Classes of the Central Provinces and Berar, he bluntly told his hearers that it was quite impossible for them to get rid of their disabilities so long as they remained in the Hindu fold and a resolution was passed to that effect. Fifteen months later, however, addressing the All-India Depressed Classes Congress in Nagpur, he declared that whatever hardships the caste Hindus inflicted on him he would not abjure the Hindu religion. By 1933 the question of his abjuring Hinduism had become rather an academic one, for in February of that year he told Mahatma Gandhi that he could not honestly call himself a Hindu. Why, he demanded, should he be proud of that religion which condemned him to a position of degradation?

The truth of the matter was that for Ambedkar and his followers the question of their renouncing Hinduism was a difficult and complex one, with all kinds of social, economic, and political implications, and the untouchable leader tended to move nearer to, or farther away from, the taking of so drastic a step according to whether a change of heart on the part of the caste Hindus seemed more, or less, likely. In the end, after years of unsuccessful struggle for the basic human rights of his people, he was forced to recognize that there was going to be no change of heart on the part of the caste Hindus, and that the casteless, 'Protestant' Hinduism of which he had sometimes spoken so enthusiastically was only a dream. Indeed, it was a contradiction in terms. Hinduism and the caste system were inseparable, and since the outcaste was a by-product of the caste system – for where there were castes there were outcastes – it followed that there could be no emancipation for the Untouchables within the caste system and, therefore, no emancipation for them within Hinduism. If they wanted to rid themselves of their age-old disabilities they had no alternative but to renounce the religion into which they had been born.

As Ambedkar became increasingly convinced that renunciation of Hinduism was the way forward for him and his people the rumours began to spread, and in the summer of 1933 he had to assure an anxious correspondent that he was not about to become a convert to Islam. Writing from London, where he had gone as a delegate to the parliamentary select committee on Indian constitutional reform, he made it clear that while he was determined to leave the fold of Hinduism and embrace some other religion he would never embrace Islam and was at that juncture inclined to Buddhism. A year later he was still inclined to Buddhism, for on the completion of the house that he had been building for himself and his books at Dadar he called it Rajagriha, after the ancient capital of King Bimbisāra of Magadha, on the outskirts of which the Buddha had often stayed and where he had delivered some of his most important discourses. But much as Ambedkar was inclined to Buddhism, even at that stage, there could be no real movement in the direction of Buddhism or any other religion until he had definitely severed his connections with Hinduism. This dramatic step he was now about to take. The caste Hindus having refused to change their attitude towards the Untouchables, the immovable object that was orthodox Hinduism was about to meet the irresistible force that was Ambedkar's determination to emancipate himself and his people, and when an immovable object meets an irresistible force there is bound to be an explosion.

The explosion took place at Yeola on 13 October 1935, and it rocked Hindu India in a way that even the burning of the *Manusmṛti* had not done. The occasion was a conference which, it was announced, the leaders of the Depressed Classes had convened to review the social and political situation in the light of their ten-year-old struggle and the coming constitutional reforms. Ten thousand Untouchables of all shades of opinion attended, including representatives from the Central Provinces and the adjoining princely states, and Ambedkar delivered a powerful and impassioned speech in which he described the hardships suffered by the Depressed Classes in all spheres of life, whether social, economic, educational, or political, and spoke bitterly of the failure of their attempts to secure their basic human rights as members of the Hindu community. The Kalaram Temple campaign, for example, had been a complete failure and a waste of time and energy. The time had therefore come for them to settle the matter once and for all. Since the disabilities under which they laboured were the direct result of their membership of the Hindu community, they should sever their connections with Hinduism and seek solace and self-respect in another religion. As for himself, it was his misfortune that he had been born an untouchable Hindu. *That* was beyond his power to prevent, but it was certainly within his power to refuse to live under ignoble and humiliating conditions. 'I solemnly assure you,' he declared, 'that I will not die a Hindu.'[42]

The effects of Ambedkar's declaration were immediate and far-reaching. Meetings were held up and down the country by various interested parties, statements and counter-statements were made, and Ambedkar himself was approached by all kinds of organizations and individuals in all kinds of ways. Not surprisingly, the most enthusiastic response to his speech came from the Untouchables themselves, for many of whom his promise that he would not die a Hindu carried a message of hope and deliverance. A few of them, indeed, acting on what they thought was a hint, at once became converts to Christianity, or Islam, or Sikhism, which was not Ambedkar's intention at all. The response of the existing followers of those religions was hardly less enthusiastic than the Untouchables' own. In some cases, it was even more enthusiastic. K. L. Gauba, a Muslim leader, telegraphed Ambedkar saying that the whole of Muslim India was ready to welcome and honour him and the Untouchables and promising full political, social, economic, and religious rights. Other Muslim leaders were no less pressing, and one of them – later reported to have been the Nizam of Hyderabad, 'the Richest Man in the World' – offered Ambedkar the sum of 40 or 50 million rupees if he would undertake to convert the whole untouchable community to Islam. The Christians, who since the beginning of the nineteenth century had converted hundreds of thousands of Untouchables to their own faith, were not quite so straightforward. Asked what he thought of Ambedkar's declaration, Bishop Badley of the Methodist Episcopal Church, Bombay, replied that communities consisting of millions of people could become Christian only if their members experienced a real change of heart. It was a change of heart that constituted conversion. All the same, he added, Ambedkar's statement would be welcomed by the Christian church, since it indicated that the Depressed Classes were ambitious for the better things of life and that a new era was about to dawn for them. On behalf of the Sikhs, Sardar D. S. Doabia, the Vice-President of the Golden Temple Managing Committee, telegraphed Ambedkar saying that the Sikh religion met the requirements of the Depressed Classes with regard to conversion. 'The Sikh religion', he added, 'is monotheistic and all-loving, and provides for equal treatment of all its adherents.'[43]

A response to Ambedkar's declaration also came from the Buddhists, though unfortunately it was rather a mixed one. While the Burmese monk U Ottama, who was one of the leaders of the Hindu Mahasabha, condemned the renunciation of Hinduism by the Untouchables, representatives of the Buddhists of Burma, Siam, Tibet, and China who were assembled in Calcutta after the Yeola conference welcomed Ambedkar's decision and sent him a telegram inviting him to join the Buddhist community. The secretary of the Maha Bodhi Society, Sarnath, also sent a telegram. This read,

> Shocked very much to read your decision to renounce Hindu
> religion. Very sorry to read your resolution that Depressed Classes
> should break away completely from Hindu fold. Please reconsider
> your decision. I see Untouchability is being brought to an end by
> thoughtful Sanatanists [i.e. orthodox Hindus] themselves. But
> if you still persist in embracing another religion, you with your
> community are most cordially welcome to embrace Buddhism
> which is professed by the greater part of Asia. Among Buddhists
> there are no religious or social disabilities. We grant equal status
> to all converts. There are no caste distinctions amongst us. We are
> willing to send workers.[44]

This rather ambivalent communication probably represented a compromise between the views of the Society's Bengali Brahmin president (not Shyama Prasad Mookerjee but his predecessor) and those of its Sinhalese Buddhist secretary. What Ambedkar thought of the telegram is not known, but he could hardly be blamed for thinking that the Maha Bodhi Society would not be sorry if he did not 'persist' in embracing another religion.

The least enthusiastic response to Ambedkar's declaration naturally came from the caste Hindus. Indeed the very idea that the most despised section of the Hindu community should have the effrontery even to think of renouncing Hinduism shocked and outraged them, and they at once took steps to ensure that the Untouchables remained within the Hindu fold. These steps consisted mainly in showering Ambedkar with abuse and his followers with promises that could be kept only by abolishing Hinduism – which the caste Hindus of course had no intention of doing. The caste Hindus were, in fact, as unwilling to allow the Untouchables to renounce Hinduism as Pharaoh was to allow the Israelites to leave Egypt, and for much the same reasons. If the Untouchables renounced Hinduism, and gave up their traditional occupations, the caste Hindus would have no one to sweep and scavenge for them and would, moreover, be deprived of a valuable source of cheap and even unpaid labour. What was more, the renunciation of Hinduism by the Untouchables would drastically reduce the numerical strength and, therefore, the political power, of the Hindu community, and this would result in a corresponding increase in the political power of the Muslims, the Christians, or the Sikhs. Such a possibility the vast majority of caste Hindus refused to contemplate. The only caste Hindus to give even qualified approval to Ambedkar's decision to renounce Hinduism were some of the more far-sighted leaders of the Hindu Mahasabha, but even they gave their approval only on condition that Ambedkar and his followers embraced Sikhism, which according to them was a sect of Hinduism. As a matter of fact, Ambedkar was far more attracted to Sikhism than to either Islam or Christianity, and for a time seemed to be considering the possibility of adopting that religion.

Prominent among the opponents of conversion – even to Sikhism – were Mahatma Gandhi and other caste Hindu leaders of the Congress Party. In a statement to the press, the Mahatma said,

> The speech attributed to Dr. Ambedkar seems unbelievable. If
> however, he has made such a speech and the Conference has
> adopted a resolution of a complete severance [of connection with
> Hinduism] and acceptance of any faith that would guarantee
> equality, I regard both as unfortunate events, especially when one

sees that in spite of isolated events to the contrary 'Untouchability' is on its last legs. I can understand the anger of a high-souled and highly educated person like Dr. Ambedkar over atrocities such as were committed in Kavitha and other villages. But religion is not like a house or a cloak which can be changed at will. It is a more integral part of one's self than that of one's body.... I would urge [Dr Ambedkar] to assuage his wrath and to reconsider the position and examine his ancestral religion on its own merits, and not through the weakness of its unfaithful followers.[45]

Ambedkar was as far from thinking that religion was like a house or cloak as Gandhi himself. When shown the Mahatma's comments he replied,

What religion we shall belong to we have not yet decided. What ways and means we shall adopt we have not thought out. But we have decided one thing, and that after due deliberation and with deep conviction, that the Hindu religion is not good for us. Inequality is the very basis of that religion and its ethics are such that the Depressed Classes can never acquire their full manhood. Let none think that I have done this in a huff or as a matter of wrath against the treatment meted out to the Depressed Classes at the village of Kavitha or any other place. It is a deeply deliberate decision. I agree with Mr. Gandhi that religion is necessary, but I do not agree that man must keep to his ancestral religion if he finds that religion repugnant to his notions of the sort of religion he needs, as the standard for the regulation of his own conduct, and as the source of inspiration for his advancement and well-being.[46]

The atrocities to which Gandhi and Ambedkar referred had taken place shortly before the Yeola conference. The Untouchables of Kavitha, a village in Gujerat, had decided to send their children to the local school. This was unacceptable to the caste Hindus, who objected to untouchable children attending the same school as their own children and sitting next to them in class, and they vowed before the image of Mahādeva that unless the Untouchables withdrew their children from school they would enforce a strict boycott against them. The Untouchables did not withdraw their children, and the caste Hindus proceeded to carry out their threat. Untouchables were denied work as agricultural labourers, their cattle were prevented from grazing, and paraffin was poured into their wells so as to deprive them of drinking water at one of the hottest times of the year. In the end the entire untouchable community had to leave Kavitha. Neither the Government nor the Congress Party made the slightest attempt to intervene, though Mahatma Gandhi was ready enough with words of advice. Writing in his weekly paper *Harijan*, he observed,

> There is no help like self-help. God helps those who help themselves. If the Harijans concerned will carry out the resolve to wipe the dust of Kavitha off their feet, they will not only be happy themselves, but they will pave the way for others.[47]

As a recent commentator caustically observes,

> Migration of Untouchables from Kavitha did not affect Hinduism or Gandhi's politics, so he advised them to quit Kavitha, but he dare not advise renunciation of Hinduism, because he loved Hinduism more than the poor helpless Untouchables.[48]

Although according to Gandhi Untouchability was on its last legs, this was by no means the case for, as Ambedkar grimly observed, 'Kavitha does not represent an isolated incident.'[49] Disregarding the opposition of the caste Hindus and the objections of certain non-Mahar untouchable leaders, the great champion of the Depressed Classes therefore continued to follow his chosen path and reaffirmed his determination to renounce Hinduism from a number of platforms. Addressing the Maharashtra Untouchable Youths' Conference at Poona in January 1936, he declared that even if God himself was produced before him to dissuade him from leaving the Hindu fold, he would not go back on his resolution. Similarly, in his 'Reasons for Conversion' speech in Bombay three months later, in which he related some incidents from his own life which had led him to decide in favour of the renunciation of Hinduism and conversion to some other religion, he told his audience,

> If you continue to remain in the fold of Hinduism, you cannot attain a status higher than that of a slave. For me, personally, there

is no bar. If I continue to remain an Untouchable I can attain any position that a Hindu can.... But it is for your emancipation and advancement that conversion appears to be very necessary to me.... To change this degraded and disgraceful existence into a golden life conversion is absolutely necessary. I have to start conversion to improve your lot. I am not at all worried about the question of my personal interest or progress. Whatever I am doing today, it is for your betterment and in your interest.

Then, in words reminiscent of the vows taken by the bodhisattvas in the great Mahāyāna *sutras*, he concluded,

You look upon me as a 'God' but I am not a god. I am a human being like you all. Whatever help you want from me, I am prepared to give you. I have decided to liberate you from your present hopeless and degrading condition. I am not doing anything for my personal gain. I will continue to struggle for your upliftment and to make your life useful and meaningful. You must realise your responsibility and follow the path which I am showing you. If you follow it earnestly, it would not be difficult to achieve your goal.[50]

The most important of the meetings addressed by Ambedkar at this time was, however, the Bombay Presidency Mahar Conference that was held at Dadar, Bombay, on the last two days of May. The object of this conference was to decide how to implement the resolution that the Yeola Conference, following the lead given by Ambedkar, had passed seven months earlier – the resolution that the Untouchables should leave the fold of Hinduism. As Ambedkar himself explained at the outset of his address, he had called a conference of the Mahars rather than a conference of all the Untouchables for two reasons. Firstly, the question of what they should do for the betterment of their life was one that had to be solved by the different castes separately, through their respective conferences. Secondly, the time having come to assess the response of the untouchable masses to his Yeola declaration, the simplest and most reliable way of doing this was through separate meetings of each caste. Having thus cleared up any possible misunderstanding with regard to why he had called a conference of the Mahars, Ambedkar devoted the remainder of his 12,000-word address to an elaborate and well-considered statement of the case for conversion and, after urging the 500 delegates to discharge their responsibility and decide whether or not to abandon Hinduism, concluded by giving them the message that the Buddha had given to his disciples shortly before his *mahāparinirvāṇa* or 'great decease':

> I have preached the truth without making any distinction between exoteric and esoteric doctrine; for in respect of the truths, Ānanda, the Tathāgata has no such thing as the closed fist of a teacher, who keeps something back.... Therefore, O Ānanda, be ye lamps unto yourselves. Be ye a refuge to yourselves. Betake yourselves to no external refuge. Hold fast to the Truth as a lamp. Hold fast as a refuge to the Truth. Look not for refuge to anyone besides yourselves.[51]

If they kept in mind these words of the Lord Buddha, Ambedkar told the delegates, he was sure their decision would not be wrong.[52]

So great an effect did Ambedkar's address have on the conference that the delegates passed a resolution declaring that they were ready to change their religion *en masse* and that the Mahar community should, as a preliminary step in this direction, refrain from worshipping Hindu deities, from observing Hindu festivals, and from visiting Hindu places of pilgrimage. Nor was this all. Immediately after the conference Ambedkar addressed a meeting of Mahar ascetics at the same venue and these too decided to renounce the Hindu religion and, as though to demonstrate their determination, actually made a bonfire of the insignia of Hindu asceticism. Thus on that day – the second day of the Mahar Conference – there began the great movement of 'de-Sanskritization' whereby the Mahar community gradually severed its connections with Hinduism by discontinuing many of the traditional Hindu religious observances. On that day Ambedkar and his followers actually started travelling away from Hinduism. On that day they began the great march which, with every year that passed, put a greater distance between them and the religion that had inflicted on them such unparalleled suffering.

But despite the fact that Ambedkar had now started travelling away from Hinduism, and despite the fact that he had concluded his address to the Mahar Conference by quoting the words of the Buddha, he had apparently still not made up his mind which religion to embrace. When the flamboyant and eccentric Italian Buddhist monk

Lokanatha interviewed Ambedkar in Bombay early in June, with the object of persuading him to become a Buddhist, all he could tell the press afterwards was that he believed he had succeeded in convincing Dr Ambedkar that if the Harijans agreed to their conversion to the Buddhist faith they would raise themselves morally, spiritually, and socially and attain a higher status in society. Dr Ambedkar had seemed to be impressed with the Buddhist faith, the monk added, and had promised to consider the question carefully. He had not, however, given any definite reply. Nevertheless, even though the untouchable leader had not yet decided which religion to embrace, and was not to give 'a definite reply' to questions on the subject for some years to come, there were signs that he continued to be mentally preoccupied with Buddhism and was, perhaps, inclining more and more to that religion. Addressing a meeting of the Depressed Classes at Bandra, Bombay, in August 1937, he again quoted from the words of the Buddha, telling his hearers that they should adopt another religion only after testing it as gold is tested in the fire. Similarly, speaking to the Christians of Sholapur in January 1938 he declared that he could say from his study of comparative religion that only two personalities had been able to captivate him: the Buddha and Christ. In South India, however, the caste system was observed in the Christian churches, and the Christians as a community had never fought for the removal of social injustice.

On 1–3 September 1939 the Second World War broke out in Europe and soon involved India, and on 15 August 1947 a truncated India achieved Independence. During the eight years spanned by these events Ambedkar reached the zenith of his political career, first as Labour Member of the Viceroy's Executive Council, then as a member of the Constituent Assembly, and finally as Minister for Law in the first government of free India. Since he also continued to play a leading part in the affairs of the Depressed Classes and to work for the social, economic, political, and educational advancement of its members, there was no question of his being able to move very far in the direction of conversion, which he of course saw as concerning not just himself personally, but the whole untouchable community. Even during this period, however, there were indications that he remained preoccupied with Buddhism. In February 1940 he told the representative of a Bombay newspaper that Untouchability was originally imposed as a punishment for sticking to Buddhism when others had deserted it – a thesis he was to develop in his book *The Untouchables*, published in 1948. The villains of the piece were, of course, the Brahmins. In September 1944, speaking in a similar vein, he told a public meeting held under the auspices of the Madras Rationalist Society that the fundamental fact of ancient Indian history was that there had been a great struggle between Buddhism, which had ushered in a revolution, and Brahmanism, which had launched a counter-revolution. The quarrel was over a single issue: 'What is Truth?' According to the Buddha, Truth was something that was borne witness to by one's own human faculties, physical and mental, whereas according to Brahmanism it was something that was declared by the divinely revealed Vedas. In November 1945 the pandal in which Ambedkar addressed the Provincial Conference of the Scheduled Caste Federation, held in Ahmedabad on the banks of the Sabarmati River, was called Buddhanagar or 'City of the Buddha', while in June the following year he himself gave the college that the People's Education Society had started in Bombay the name of Siddharth College, Siddhārtha (or Siddhattha) being the personal name of the Buddha.[53] What was perhaps of greater significance, in 1948 he brought out a new edition of P. Lakshmi Narasu's *The Essence of Buddhism*, originally published in 1907. In the preface he wrote for it he praised the author for his unflagging faith in the Buddha and recommended his book as 'the best book on Buddhism that has appeared so far'.[54] He also revealed that he was himself working on a Life of the Buddha, in which he intended to deal with some of the criticisms that had been levelled against the teachings of the Buddha by his adversaries – past and present.

This Life of the Buddha must have been the work that was eventually published under the title of *The Buddha and His Dhamma*, and the fact that Ambedkar engaged on it while still a member of the Cabinet showed that he was more preoccupied with Buddhism than ever. So preoccupied was he, indeed, that speaking in the Constituent Assembly in November 1949 he could not forbear observing,

> It is not that India did not know Parliaments or Parliamentary Procedure. A study of the Buddhist Bhikshu Sanghas discloses that not only there were Parliaments – for the Sanghas were nothing but Parliaments – but [that] the Sanghas knew and observed all the rules of Parliamentary Procedure known to modern times. They had rules regarding seating arrangements, rules regarding Motions,

Resolutions, Quorum, Whip, Counting of Votes, Voting by Ballot, Censure Motion, Regularization, Res Judicata etc. Although these rules of Parliamentary Procedure were applied by the Buddha to the meetings of the Bhikshu Sanghas, he must have borrowed them from the rules of the political Assemblies functioning in the country in his time.[55]

Out of the abundance of the heart the mouth speaketh! Ambedkar had clearly been making a close study of the Vinaya Piṭaka or 'Book of the Discipline' (a study the fruits of which are visible in *The Buddha and His Dhamma*, Books I and IV), and it was no doubt partly as a result of his study of the Buddhist scriptures that he was now definitely inclined to Buddhism and had, in fact, more or less made up his mind to embrace that religion.

It was therefore not surprising that on 2 May 1950 he should have delivered at the Buddha Vihara, New Delhi, a speech that the press, at least, took to be a call to India's 70,000,000 'Harijans' to embrace Buddhism and which it therefore described as 'a Dramatic development of great national importance and interest throughout South-East Asia'.[56] In the course of this speech, given on the occasion of the anniversary of the Buddha's attainment of Enlightenment, Ambedkar declared that neither Rama nor Krishna could be compared to the Buddha, that it was impossible for the Untouchables to love Hinduism, which had deprived them of all their rights, that a religion should be examined rationally before acceptance, and that without religion society would perish. Later he told a reporter that he was 'on his way to embrace Buddhism' – a statement that defined his position with lawyer-like precision. The following day, in Bombay, he was somewhat more forthcoming. He had been a student of Buddhism for several years, he told the *Times of India*, though it might not be entirely correct to describe him as a Buddhist. As for his having called on the Scheduled Caste community to embrace Buddhism, he had not done so. Again his statement defined his position with lawyer-like precision, for if it was not entirely correct to describe him as a Buddhist it followed that it was not entirely correct to describe him as not a Buddhist. As he had said the day before, he was on his way to embracing Buddhism.

Thus Ambedkar's position with respect to Buddhism was quite clear. A week later, however, P. N. Rajbhoj, the General Secretary of the All-India

Scheduled Caste Federation, issued a statement to the press saying that following certain controversies regarding Dr Ambedkar's advice to the Scheduled Caste community to embrace Buddhism he had had a long talk with Dr Ambedkar and that it appeared to him that Dr Ambedkar was of the opinion that the entire Hindu community should adopt Buddhism and not just the Scheduled Castes, since Hinduism

> tended to perpetuate vested interests, and was utterly unsuitable in the present set up when all people demanded equality, opportunity and freedom.[57]

This statement only served to create fresh confusion, and the press complained that it was a mystery why India's Law Minister should allow his followers to interpret his views on important subjects instead of openly expressing his attitude. Yet in reality there was no mystery, for there was no inconsistency between Rajbhoj's statement and Ambedkar's declared position. Ambedkar was on his way to embracing Buddhism, and Rajbhoj's statement amounted to no more than saying that the great leader wanted to take with him as many people as possible. That such was indeed the case was evident from an article on 'The Buddha and the Future of His Religion' which Ambedkar contributed to the April-May issue of the *Maha Bodhi*, the journal of the Maha Bodhi Society. In this important article, which showed how deeply he had been thinking about Buddhism, Ambedkar even went so far as to declare that Buddhism was the only religion which the world could have.

> If the new world – which be it realised is very different from the old – must have a religion – and the new world needs religion far more than the old world did – then it can only be [the] religion of the Buddha.[58]

But whatever 'mystery' there might be about whether or not Ambedkar was on his way to Buddhism, there could be no doubt, even in the minds of newspaper editors, that he was on his way to Ceylon (Sri Lanka). On 25 May he arrived in Colombo by air with his wife and Rajbhoj and the same day attended the inaugural meeting of the World Fellowship of Buddhists at the Temple of the Tooth in Kandy. Since he was not attending the meeting as a delegate (for that would have implied that he considered himself a Buddhist), he declined to speak at the official session and, instead, addressed the delegates after they had adopted the resolution inaugurating the Fellowship. There were people in India, he told them, who thought that the time had come when the effort might be made to revive Buddhism, and one of the objects of his visit was to observe Buddhist ceremonies and rituals, which the people of India had no means of witnessing. Another object was to find out to what extent Buddhism was practised in its pristine purity and to what extent its teachings had been encrusted with beliefs incompatible with its basic principles. He was also interested in finding out to what extent the religion of the Buddha was 'a live thing' and whether it existed merely because the people of Ceylon happened to be Buddhists in the traditional sense of the word. Having thus explained the purpose of his visit, Ambedkar turned to the conference itself. He was not fully satisfied, he said, with the resolution that had been passed calling for a World *Fellowship* of Buddhists. What was wanted was a declaration on the part of all the Buddhist countries that they were determined not merely to have a Fellowship but that they would propagate the religion and make sacrifices for it. Whether the delegates realized it or not, what Ambedkar was really saying was that the Buddhist countries of Asia should be less inward-looking and more outward-looking.

He himself was, as usual, sufficiently outward-looking. After the conclusion of the conference he not only saw as much as he could of the ceremonies and rituals of Ceylon Buddhism but found time to address the Young Men's Buddhist Association, Colombo, on 'The Rise and Fall of Buddhism in India'. Buddhism had not disappeared from India, he asserted. Though its material form had disappeared, as a spiritual force it still existed. What had led to the decline of Buddhism in India was not clear. He himself was still studying the subject, but he believed that Buddhism had faded away in India because of the rise of Vaishnavism and Shaivism and because of the Muslim invasion of India.

> When Allauddin marched into Bihar, he killed over 5,000 *bhikkhus*. The remaining *Buddhist* monks fled to neighbouring countries like China, Nepal and Tibet. Efforts were subsequently made by *Buddhists* of India to raise another priesthood in order to revive *Buddhism*. But these failed as by then 90 per cent of Buddhists had embraced *Hinduism*.[59]

Answering the question why Hinduism had survived in India and Buddhism had died, Ambedkar observed, 'This religion [i.e. Buddhism] is difficult to practise while Hinduism is not.'[60] Shortly afterwards he addressed a meeting in Colombo Town Hall and appealed to the Untouchables there to embrace Buddhism, saying that there was no need for them to have a separate organization. He also urged the Buddhists of Ceylon to accept the Untouchables and look after their interests with paternal care.

Ambedkar's visit to Ceylon naturally attracted a good deal of attention, and on his return to India some of his opponents accused him of being an opportunist. Replying to the charge in the course of a speech delivered under the auspices of the Bombay Branch of the Royal Asiatick Society on 25 July he denied that he was an opportunist with regard to his views on Buddhism and said that he had been interested in Buddhism since his boyhood. Later in the year, on 29 September, he returned to the question of conversion in a way that showed how broad was his vision and how much he had the welfare of the whole country at heart. Speaking at the Japanese Buddhist Temple, Worli (Bombay), he deprecated the idea that political independence meant the end of all the country's ills. So long as there was no purity, wrongdoing and utter disregard of morals would continue in everyday life; and as long as man did not know how to behave with man, India could never be prosperous.

> To end all these troubles, India must embrace *Buddhism. Buddhism* is the only religion based upon ethical principles and teaches how to work for the good and well-being of the common man.[61]

As if to underline the urgency of the situation, he concluded his speech by declaring that he would devote the rest of his life to the revival and spread of Buddhism.

This was more easily said than done. As Minister for Law, Ambedkar was responsible for piloting the Hindu Code Bill through Parliament, besides which the poor state of his health was giving increasing cause for concern. But though he was not, as yet, able to devote himself to the revival and spread of Buddhism his mind was made up, and speaking at the Buddha Vihara, New Delhi, in May 1951, he declared,

If the rest of the Hindu Society does not co-operate, then we, the members of the Scheduled Castes, will go on our own and try once again to bring back Buddhism to its former glory and prestige in this country.[62]

Buddhism could not be restored to its former glory, however, whether by the members of the Scheduled Castes or anyone else, so long as the charges that were often levelled against it were allowed to remain unanswered. A Hindu author writing in *Eve's Weekly* having claimed that it was the Buddhist theory that had first thrust women into the background and that the Buddha was ever exhorting men to beware of women, Ambedkar therefore contributed to the April-May issue of the *Maha Bodhi* a pungent and scholarly article entitled 'The Rise and Fall of the Hindu Woman. Who was Responsible for it?' In this article he showed conclusively that it was not the Buddha who was responsible for the downfall of the Hindu woman but the Hindu law-giver Manu, the author of the *Manusmṛti*. According to Ambedkar, the Buddha endeavoured to ennoble woman and raise her to the level of man.

July saw the formation of the Indian Buddhist Society, and in September Ambedkar told Parliament, in the course of a speech on the Hindu Code Bill,

The Buddha preached equality. He was the greatest opponent of the chaturvarnya;[63] he was the greatest opponent of belief in the Vedas because he believed in reason and did not believe in the infallibility of any book. He believed in Ahimsa. Brahmanic society accepted [only] the most innocuous dogma of ahimsa. They were never able to accept, in fact they opposed, his belief in equality. That is why Hindu society has remained what it has always been.[64]

A week later, on 29 September 1951, the Hindu Code Bill was killed even in the truncated form of a Marriage and Divorce Bill and Ambedkar resigned from the Nehru Cabinet.

But though he was no longer a member of the Government, Ambedkar continued to play a prominent role in the political life of the country, both inside and outside Parliament, and continued to express unpopular opinions from a variety of platforms. In February 1953, speaking at a reception given in honour of M. R. Murti, the

Vice-President of the Indo-Japanese Cultural Association in Japan, he declared,

> In the present condition of the world, so far as I have been able to study the situation, I have come to the conclusion that the conflict, whatever form it may take, will ultimately be between the Gospel of the *Buddha* and the Gospel of *Karl Marx*.[65]

It was from that point of view, he added, that he had been attracted by Japan, by China, and by other Eastern countries. Two months later, on the occasion of his sixty-second birthday, when a mile-long procession was taken out through the streets of Bombay in his honour, he told journalists that he would devote the rest of his life to the welfare of the Scheduled Castes people and the study of Buddhism. This assurance he repeated the following month, when presiding over a meeting organized by the Scheduled Caste Federation to celebrate the anniversary of the Buddha's attainment of Enlightenment. There would be no progress in the country, he told his 5,000-strong audience, unless a classless and casteless society was created. There would be no improvement in the lot of the Depressed Classes so long as they remained within the Hindu fold. He was glad to note that (Caste) Hindus, too, were participating in the celebration in large numbers. Buddhism would spread rapidly in India, and he was going to devote the rest of his life to propagating its teachings.

By this time India's first general election had come and gone, the Congress Party had swept the polls, and Ambedkar had failed to gain a seat in the Lok Sabha.[66] Though he subsequently became a member of the Rajya Sabha, and took an active part in its proceedings for the rest of his life, his political career was now virtually over and he was at last free to devote himself to spreading Buddhism. In May 1954 he spent two weeks in Burma, attending the annual Vaiśākha celebrations, in June he announced that he was starting a seminary in Bangalore to train preachers for the propagation of Buddhism in India, and in August, in the course of an important speech on India's foreign policy, he not only warned the Government of the possibility of Chinese aggression but criticized Chairman Mao for the way in which he treated the Buddhists of China. October saw Ambedkar in the role of broadcaster. Speaking on All-India Radio in the series 'My Personal Philosophy', he declared,

Positively, my social philosophy may be said to be enshrined in three words: liberty, equality and fraternity. Let no one however say that I have borrowed my philosophy from the French Revolution. I have not. My philosophy has roots in religion and not in political science. I have derived them from the teachings of my master, the Buddha.[67]

In December he was again in Burma, this time in connection with the Third Conference of the World Fellowship of Buddhists which was being held in Rangoon. Addressing the Conference, he said,

I have to say this with great anguish that in the land where the Great Buddha was born, his religion has declined. How such a thing happened is beyond anyone's comprehension.[68]

As he spoke, his eyes filled with tears and for a few minutes he was unable to proceed with his speech. Later, he gave a résumé of his plans for the revival of Buddhism in India, adding that the enormous sums of money that the Buddhists of Ceylon and Burma spent on decorating their shrines on the occasion of religious festivals could be more usefully devoted to the propagation of Buddhism in other countries. After the Conference the delegates were taken to see Mandalay, formerly the capital of Upper Burma. Here Ambedkar stayed for a week and here, according to one account, he decided that he and his followers would formally embrace Buddhism in the 2500th year of the Buddhist era, i.e. in 1956–7. Even if such a decision actually was taken, however, no announcement of the fact was made either then or after Ambedkar's return to India, though an article by Dr R. L. Soni, an Indian medical man with whom Ambedkar had stayed in Mandalay, appeared in a Burmese newspaper under the heading 'An Open Invitation to the Scheduled Caste Indians'. In this article the doctor, who was himself a Buddhist, called upon his outcaste fellow countrymen to embrace Buddhism.

The moment you come under the benevolent refuge of the All-Compassionate Buddha, your eyes shall twinkle with a new brilliance, your heart shall register the first throb of an experience of real social freedom and your mind shall know the impulse of a joy that is beyond the ken of words.[69]

Immediately after his visit to Burma, on 25 December 1954, he installed an image of the Buddha with which he had been presented in Rangoon in a temple built by members of the Scheduled Caste community at Dehu Road, near Poona. Twelve hundred years after the fall of Buddhism – he told the 4,000 men, women, and children who had gathered to hear him – the honour of establishing the image of the Lord Buddha had fallen to his people. It was a great event, and would undoubtedly go down in history. As for his personal intentions, he would dedicate himself to the propagation of the Buddhist faith in India. At present he was writing a book explaining the tenets of Buddhism in simple language for the benefit of the common man. It might take him a year to complete the work, but when it was finished he would embrace Buddhism.

This was the first time Ambedkar had actually declared that he would embrace Buddhism, as distinct from declaring that he was on his way to embracing it, and the first time that he had given anything like a definite date for that much-heralded event. But now, twenty years after the Yeola declaration had rocked Hindu India, the long journey from Hinduism to Buddhism was beginning to come to an end, and on his return to Bombay Ambedkar not only continued working on his book but started making arrangements for the holding of the actual conversion ceremony. He also started giving serious thought to the question of how one became a Buddhist, in the formal sense, and what becoming a Buddhist really meant. This was, in fact, the principal subject of the discussion I had with him in December 1955, as well as the subject of the lecture which, at his request, I delivered to 3,000 of his followers on New Year's Day 1956. The question of how one became a Buddhist was also, apparently, the subject of correspondence between Ambedkar and Devapriya Valisinha, the General Secretary of the Maha Bodhi Society. Ambedkar was particularly concerned that the conversion of the so-called laity to Buddhism should be a real conversion, and that their membership of the Buddhist religion should not be merely nominal – as had been the case in India and was often the case in Buddhist countries at the present day. It was this concern that led him to publish, at about this time, his *Bauddha Puja Path* or 'Buddhist Worship', a little anthology of devotional texts in Pāli (with Marathi translation) which he had started compiling as early as 1950, shortly after his return from Ceylon. The booklet began with the Three Refuges and Five Precepts and ended with the *Ratana Sutta* or

'Jewel Discourse', and also included verses to be recited when offering flowers to the Buddha and three of the most important verses of the *Dhammapada*. In his preface Ambedkar wrote,

> Consequent on the [recent] spreading of Buddhism, people became anxious to know about Buddhism, its literature and where it was available. In this regard, there appears to be great eagerness among the people in India. Certain classes appear to have gone beyond the limits of eagerness. They became mad [to know] the methods of worship in Buddhist religion [as distinct from] its teachings. They demanded the literature about worship in [the] Buddhist religion. Owing to my physical indisposition, I could not meet their demands [until now].[70]

Years of physical indisposition had also delayed the completion of a much more important work, but by February 1956 the last chapters of *The Buddha and His Dhamma* had been written and on 15 March Ambedkar was able to write – or dictate – the preface. From this time onwards he and his followers travelled along the road to conversion with increasing rapidity, and incidents that show in which direction they were moving occurred more and more frequently. In May a talk by Ambedkar on 'Why I Like Buddhism' was broadcast by the BBC, London, and in the same month he gave the manuscript of *The Buddha and His Dhamma* to the press for printing. May 24 was the anniversary of the Buddha's attainment of Enlightenment and, according to the Sinhalese Buddhist calendar, the 2500th anniversary of his *parinirvāṇa* or final passing away. On that day Ambedkar addressed a meeting in Nare Park, Bombay, and declared that he would embrace Buddhism in October. He also took the opportunity of making clear the difference between Hinduism and Buddhism. Hinduism believed in God and the (permanent unchanging) soul, whereas in Buddhism there was neither God nor soul. Similarly, Hinduism believed in the *chaturvarnya* and the caste system, whereas Buddhism had no place for them. He added that his book on Buddhism would be published soon, that he had closed all the breaches in the organization of Buddhism and would consolidate it so that the tide of Buddhism would never recede in India. The Communists should study Buddhism, so as to know how to remove the ills of humanity. It was the great leader's last speech in Bombay.

On 23 September Ambedkar issued a press note announcing that his conversion to Buddhism would take place on 14 October in Nagpur. U Chandramani of Kusinara was invited to initiate him into the religion. 'It is our great wish,' Ambedkar wrote to the seventy-nine-year-old Burmese *bhikkhu*, 'that you should officiate at the ceremony. You being the oldest monk in India we think it would be appropriate to have the ceremony performed by you.'[71]

He also wrote to Devapriya Valisinha expressing his desire that the Maha Bodhi Society should participate in the function. On the morning of 11 October he flew from Delhi to Nagpur accompanied by his wife and N. C. Rattu, his private secretary. On the evening of 13 October he gave two press conferences, among other things telling the assembled newsmen that his Buddhism would adhere to the tenets of the faith as preached by the Buddha himself, without involving his people in the differences which had arisen with regard to the Hīnayāna and Mahāyāna. His Buddhism would be a sort of neo-Buddhism or Navayāna. At 9.15 the following morning he ascended the dais that had been erected at one end of the Diksha Bhumi or 'Initiation Ground', as the spot afterwards came to be called; fifteen minutes later he and his wife took the Three Refuges and Five Precepts from U Chandramani, and fifteen or twenty minutes after that Ambedkar himself administered the same Three Refuges and Five Precepts – together with twenty-two supporting vows of his own devising[72] – to the 380,000 men, women, and children who had assembled there in response to his call. They had reached the end of their long journey. They had now not only renounced Hinduism but embraced Buddhism. In the words of one of the twenty-two vows, they felt that they were being reborn. No longer were they Untouchables. They were human beings. They were Buddhists. After centuries of separation, they had re-established contact with their spiritual roots and could start producing flowers.

5

THE SEARCH FOR ROOTS

The search for roots is one of the preoccupations of our time. The white American tries to find out from which part of England or Ireland his forefathers emigrated to the New World, and under what circumstances, while the black American tries to discover from which part of West Africa his ancestors were sold into slavery and shipped to the cotton plantations on the other side of the Atlantic. For much of his life Bhimrao Ramji Ambedkar was preoccupied with a similar quest, though in his case it was largely confined to books and did not take him beyond the confines of his own land. Moreover, what he as an Untouchable was engaged in was not so much a sentimental search for roots as a scientific investigation into origins – though it was an investigation that proved to be not without important religious implications. Who were the Untouchables, and why had they become Untouchables? Why did the caste Hindus treat them in the inhuman fashion that had persisted right down to the present day and threatened to go on for ever unless something was done about it?

Questions like these had tormented Ambedkar for many years, but it was not until 1938 that he was able to take time off from his work for the Depressed Classes and start committing the results of his investigations to paper. In March that year, when it seems there was speculation as to why Dr Ambedkar had been less conspicuous on public platforms of late and why he was not devoting as much time as usual to the work of the Bombay Legislative Assembly, there appeared in the

Bombay Chronicle an article that showed that the rising untouchable leader had not been passing his time in idleness:

VOLUME THAT WILL CREATE CONSTERNATION AMONG ORTHODOX AND ROUSE REFORMER, ran the headline, DR AMBEDKAR'S FORTHCOMING 'MAGNUM OPUS'.[73]

The article went on to reveal that a well-known British publishing house had commissioned Ambedkar to prepare a comprehensive work on the Depressed Classes which would trace the origin of Untouchability, the various stages through which it had passed in the course of history, and the nature of the effect it had had on Hindu society and on Indian social, political, and cultural life during all those centuries. The article also revealed that the work would consist of seven chapters, beginning with an autobiographical chapter describing the author's own experience of Untouchability. Other chapters would explain the social, religious, and philosophical background of Untouchability, show the various means by which the caste Hindu ruling class had kept the Untouchables down, and demonstrate the British Government's failure to do anything substantial to eradicate the evil. There would also be a chapter on the work of the Christian missionaries, and a chapter on the activities of the social reformers, both ancient and modern, and how Hindu society had reacted to these activities. This last chapter would bring the story up to date with an analysis of the activities of Mahatma Gandhi and Pandit Nehru. Concluding its account, the article said that the work would cover well over 600 pages and that its exposure of the systematic manner in which art, literature, and philosophy – in fact the entire cultural system – had been harnessed to maintain the domination of the ruling class was such that its publication would be bound to create a first class sensation in Indian politics and consternation in the ranks of the orthodox.

To what extent this prediction would have been fulfilled we have no means of telling. The *magnum opus* was never completed, and we do not even know the name of the enterprising British publishing house that commissioned it. But though the work was never completed, Ambedkar remained deeply preoccupied with the various questions with which it was to deal, and in the course of the following decade published two important books which, though complete in themselves, covered much the same ground as certain chapters of the projected *hauptwerk*.

These two books were *What Congress and Gandhi Have Done to the Untouchables* (1945), a well documented exposure of the Congress Party's claim to represent the Untouchables, and *The Untouchables* (1948), a pioneering exploration of who the Untouchables were and how they became Untouchables. The first corresponded to the latter part of the seventh and last chapter of the unfinished *magnum opus*, while the second corresponded to the second and perhaps the third chapters. Unpublished writings by Ambedkar that cover much the same ground as other parts of the unfinished *magnum opus* include *Revolution and Counter-revolution* (the revolution being that of the Buddha and the counter-revolution that of the Brahmins), which at the time of Ambedkar's death was complete except for a few chapters, and the unfinished *Riddles of Hinduism*.

Two years after the appearance of the *Bombay Chronicle's* article Ambedkar again took its representative into his confidence, as it would seem, and there appeared in the same newspaper a report that showed not only that the untouchable scholar-politician was preoccupied with the same questions as in 1938 but that he thought he had found the answer to at least one of them, that is, the question of the origin of Untouchability. This time the headline ran,

DR AMBEDKAR SAYS 'UNTOUCHABILITY WAS PUNISHMENT FOR STICKING TO BUDDHISM.' BRAHMINS' ADAPTABILITY – WHEN BUDDHA STOPPED ANIMAL SACRIFICES, COWS WERE SANCTIFIED BY THEM.[74]

These were, in fact, the main points of Ambedkar's 'novel theory', as the *Chronicle's* representative called it, and the 1,200-word report was little more than a summary of *The Untouchables*, which did not appear until five years later. The delay was due partly to the fact that for Ambedkar the forties were years of high political office, first as Labour Member in the Viceroy's Executive Council and then as Minister for Law in the Nehru Government, and partly to the fact that during this period he was busy with several other literary projects.

One of these projects was *Who Were the Shudras?* (1946), which was published one year after *What Congress and Gandhi Have Done to the Untouchables* and two years before *The Untouchables*. This work did not cover any of the ground covered by the unfinished *magnum opus*, and did on a lesser but still very substantial scale for the Shudras what that work was to have done for the Depressed Classes and what *The Untouchables* actually did do in a more concentrated fashion. In each case there was a problem to be solved. In the case of the Untouchables it was the problem of who they were and how they had become Untouchables. In the case of the Shudras it was the problem of who they were and how they had come to be the fourth Varna in the Indo-Aryan society. Until the fifth Varna of the Untouchables came into being the Shudras were in the eyes of the Hindus the lowest of the low. How was it that under the *chaturvarnya* system – the system of graded inequality – the Shudra was

> not only placed at the bottom of the gradation but ... subjected to
> innumerable ignominies and disabilities so as to prevent him from
> rising above the condition fixed for him by law?[75]

According to Ambedkar, the Shudras were not a dark-skinned non-Aryan race that had been conquered and enslaved by the fair-skinned Aryan invaders in prehistoric times, as some Western scholars believed. Nor had they been Shudras from the very beginning, as the Brahmins maintained on the basis of the cosmogonic myth set forth in the famous Puruṣa Sūkta of the *Rig Veda* – the myth that describes the Brahmin or priest as originating from the mouth of the Cosmic Man, the Rajanya (i.e. Kshatriya) or warrior from his arms, the Vaishya or trader from his thighs, and the Shudra or menial from his feet. The truth was that the Shudras were Aryans, being one of the Aryan communities of the 'solar line', and thus belonged to the same race as the three other Varnas or classes. They did not form a separate Varna (originally there were only three Varnas) but ranked as part of the Kshatriya Varna or warrior class. In the course of the continuous violent conflict that took place between the Shudra kings and the Brahmins the latter were subjected to many tyrannies and indignities. As a result of this, they conceived a great hatred for the Shudras and out of this hatred refused to perform the *upanayāna* ceremony for members of the Shudra community, that is, refused to perform for them the time-honoured ceremony of initiation into full membership of Indo-Aryan society. Deprived of the *upanayāna*, which only the Brahmins had the right to perform, the Shudras who were Kshatriyas became socially degraded, fell below the rank of the *Vaishyas* and thus came to form the fourth *Varna*.[76]

Such were the terms in which Ambedkar himself summarized his answers to the twin questions of who were the Shudras and how they came to be the fourth Varna of the Indo-Aryan society. But no summary can do justice to the skill with which he organized his material (most of it drawn from the ancient Brahmanical literature), to the closeness and cogency of his reasoning, or to the sleuth-like persistence with which he pursued his enquiry until, one clue having led to another, the problem he had set himself was eventually solved. *Who Were the Shudras?* does, in fact, read very much like a detective story or a murder mystery, and could well be described as a sociological whodunit. There is, so to speak, a dead body, in the form of the Shudras in their traditional state of degradation as described by Ambedkar in the third chapter of the book, entitled 'The Brahmanic Theory of the Status of the Shudra'. Who is responsible for the crime? How was it carried out? And is the victim really dead or only so badly injured as to appear dead?[77] These are the questions confronting the sociological detective, and Ambedkar brings to bear on them a combination of scholarship, logic, and a determination to get at the truth despite threats from interested parties that, in the end, enables him to track down the criminal and find out exactly how he committed his crime and for what reason.

The Untouchables, which Ambedkar described as a sequel to *Who Were the Shudras?*, also reads like a sociological whodunit. This time there is an even more cruelly mutilated body, in the shape of the still worse state of degradation of the 50,000,000 Untouchables produced by Hindu civilization, and Ambedkar brings to the solution of this even darker mystery the same combination of qualities that is so conspicuous in the earlier book. In the case of *The Untouchables*, however, he has

to use his imagination and intuition to bridge the gaps left in the chain of facts by links not yet discovered and to propound a working hypothesis suggesting how facts which cannot be connected by known facts might have been interconnected.[78]

Such a procedure is quite permissible. The origin of Untouchability is lost in antiquity, and the attempt to explain it is not the same as writing history from texts. It is a case of gathering survivals of the past, placing them together, and making them tell the story of their birth. One's task is analogous to that of an archaeologist who reconstructs a city from broken stones, of a palaeontologist who conceives a new animal from scattered bones and teeth, or of a painter who reads the lines of the horizon and the smallest vestiges on the slopes of the hill to make up a scene.

> In this sense the book is a work of art even more than of history. The origin of Untouchability lies buried in a dead past which nobody knows. To make it alive is like an attempt to reclaim to history a city which has been dead since ages past and present it as it was in its original condition.[79]

In setting out to clear up the mystery of who the Untouchables were and how they came to be Untouchables Ambedkar is very conscious of the fact that there is, so to speak, a dead body (corresponding to the buried city of his own analogy). He is very conscious that a crime has been committed. But he is no less conscious of the fact that nobody else is aware that there is a dead body in the house and that it is important to find out who is responsible. The reason nobody else notices that there is a dead body in the house of Hindu civilization (in fact, three dead bodies, if one includes the Criminal Tribes and the Aboriginal Tribes) is that for the orthodox Hindu the observance of Untouchability is a normal and natural thing and as such calls for neither expiation nor explanation. For Ambedkar, however, Untouchability is by no means either a normal or a natural thing and he is, therefore, very conscious of the fact that there is a dead body and that a crime has been committed. He is also very conscious of the fact that this crime is unique for, as he proceeds to show in the first two chapters of the book, Untouchability among Hindus is a very different thing from Untouchability among non-Hindus. Untouchability is based on the notion of pollution or defilement, and pollution can be caused by the occurrence of certain events (for example death), by contact with certain things, and by contact with certain persons, just as it can be removed with the help of certain purificatory agents and purificatory ceremonies. So far there is little difference between the notion of pollution obtaining in primitive societies like those of the Polynesians and East Africans, or in ancient societies like those of the Egyptians, Greeks, and Romans, on the one hand, and the notion of pollution prevalent among the Hindus on the other. Among Hindus, however, there is another form of Untouchability: the hereditary Untouchability of 429 different communities amounting to 50–60,000,000 people. These people are held to be impure, and contact with them polluting, not because of anything they have done in their individual capacity but simply because they have been born into a certain caste. Moreover, their impurity is not temporary but permanent, and instead of being isolated for a limited period they are permanently segregated in separate quarters. What is the reason for the existence of this unique form of Untouchability among Hindus? In particular, why do the Untouchables live outside the village and what made their Untouchability permanent and ineradicable? The remaining chapters of the book are devoted to finding the answers to these two questions.

Ambedkar begins by pointing out that there are only two possibilities. Either the Untouchables originally lived in the village together with the caste Hindus and were subsequently declared Untouchables and made to live outside it, or else they lived outside the village from the very beginning. Of these two possibilities he finds the second more acceptable, since the phenomenon under discussion is not confined to a single village or area but exists all over India and it is inconceivable that at some time in the past all the Untouchables in the country should have been transplanted from within the village to outside the village. The Untouchables therefore must have lived outside the village from the very beginning. Here too there are only two possibilities. Either the Untouchables lived outside the village from the very beginning and also were Untouchables from the very beginning, or else they lived outside the village even before they became Untouchables and continued to live outside it because of the supervention of Untouchability at a later stage. Ambedkar believes that only the latter possibility is worth consideration. But this raises a very difficult question. Why did the (future) Untouchables live outside the village? What forced them to do so?

In order to answer this further question Ambedkar invokes the help of sociology, explaining that it is necessary to bear in mind that modern society differs from primitive society in two respects. Firstly, primitive society consisted of nomadic communities while modern society consists of settled communities; secondly, primitive society consisted of tribal communities based on blood relationship whereas modern society consists of local communities based on territorial affiliation. Thus in the transformation of primitive society into modern society there are two lines of evolution, one leading from the nomadic community to the settled community, the other leading from the tribal community to the territorial community. Confining the enquiry to the first line of evolution, one has to understand what made primitive society nomadic and what happened in the course of the transition from nomadic to settled life. Primitive society was nomadic, in the sense of migratory, because its wealth was in cattle and its cattle needed fresh pastures. It became fixed in one spot, or in other words became a settled community, only when its wealth changed from cattle to land and this happened when man discovered the art of agriculture. For an understanding of what happened in the course of the transition from nomadic life to settled life, one has to bear in mind two facts. Firstly, all the tribes did not become fixed in one spot at one and the same time: some became settled and some remained nomadic. Secondly, in their nomadic state the tribes were always at war with one another. When some tribes became settled the tribes that remained nomadic soon found that organizing raids on the wealthy and comparatively defenceless settled tribes was a more profitable business than fighting one another. This created a problem for the settled tribes. Fortunately for them, however, the constant warfare between the nomadic tribes had brought into existence a third group of people. These were the Broken Men, as sociologists call them, or the scattered remnants of defeated tribes, who, unable to join another tribe (for tribal organization was based on community of blood), lived in constant danger of attack. Thus the Broken Men needed shelter and protection no less than the settled tribes needed a body of men to keep watch and ward against the raids of the nomadic tribes. In the end a bargain was struck between the two groups. The Broken Men agreed to do the work of watch and ward for the settled tribes, and in return the settled tribes agreed to give the Broken Men food and shelter. Only one thing remained to be decided. Where were the Broken Men to stay? They could not stay in the midst of the settled community because according to primitive notions only persons of the same tribe, i.e. the same blood, could live together, and the Broken Men were aliens. For this reason, and because it was in any case desirable that they should be in a position to meet the raids of any hostile nomadic tribe, the Broken Men were assigned quarters outside the village.

Having cleared the ground by explaining what made primitive society nomadic and what happened in the course of the transition from nomadic life to settled life, Ambedkar returns to the main question, namely, why do the Untouchables live outside the village? According to him, the Untouchables were originally only Broken Men and it was because they were originally only Broken Men that they lived outside the village. As Hindu society passed from nomadic life to the life of the settled village community, the same process must have taken place in India as took place elsewhere. In primitive Hindu society there must have been both settled tribes and Broken Men. It is therefore natural to suppose that, since the (future) Untouchables were originally only Broken Men they lived outside the village from the very beginning and that Untouchability had nothing to do with the matter.

Ambedkar is, of course, conscious that his theory is a novel one and that he will be asked to produce evidence in its support. Direct evidence, he admits, has yet to be collected, but there are two pointers on account of which it can be said that the Untouchables were Broken Men. The first of these pointers is the fact that the name Antya and its derivatives was given to certain communities by the ancient Hindu law books. Orthodox Hindu scholarship maintains that *antya* means '(born) last' or '(born) at the end' and that since, in the order of creation, the Untouchable was born last, Antya means an Untouchable. Ambedkar points out that this explanation contradicts the Vedic theory of creation, according to which it was the Shudra who was born last, the Untouchable not being mentioned at all. In his view the word *antya* means not '(born) at the end' of creation but '(born) at the end' of the village and dates from the time when some people lived inside the village while others lived outside it. Those who lived outside the village must have done so because they were Broken Men. The second pointer on account of which it can be said that the Untouchables were Broken Men is the position occupied by the Mahars – the single largest Untouchable community in Maharashtra – in relation to the caste Hindus. It is noteworthy that Mahars are to be found in every village, that every village in Maharashtra is surrounded by a wall and that the Mahars have their quarters outside the wall, that the Mahars keep watch and ward on behalf of the village, and that the Mahars claim no less than fifty-two rights against the caste Hindus, the most important of them being the right to collect food from the villagers, the right to collect corn from them in harvest time, and the right to appropriate their dead domestic animals. If the case of the Mahars is typical of Untouchables throughout India (and Ambedkar admits that the matter awaits investigation) then it follows that, in his own words,

> there was a stage in the history of India when Broken Men belonging to other tribes came to the Settled tribes and made a bargain whereby the Broken Men were allowed to settle on the border of the village, were required to do certain duties and in return were given certain rights.[80]

Thus there is some evidence in support of Ambedkar's theory that the Untouchables were originally only Broken Men and that it was because they were only Broken Men that they lived outside the village. This evidence would be stronger if there were any other cases known to history of Broken Men living outside the village, and if it could be shown that what was said to have occurred in India had actually occurred elsewhere. Fortunately Ambedkar is able to cite the parallel cases of the Fuidhirs or 'Stranger-tenants' of ancient Ireland, as revealed in the Brehon Laws as summarized by Sir Henry Maine, and of the Alltudes or 'Unfree-tenants' of ancient Wales, as described by Frederic Seebohm.[81] Both the Fuidhirs and the Alltudes were made to live outside the village and both were made to live outside it for the same reason, namely, that they belonged to different tribes and were of different blood. Thus the case of the Untouchables was not the only case of a people living outside the village. Indeed, it illustrated a phenomenon that was universal and marked by the same distinctive features everywhere.

There was, however, one important respect in which the case of the Untouchables differed from that of the Broken Men in other parts of the world. In other parts of the world the separate quarters of the Broken Men eventually disappeared and, as common territory rather than common blood became the bond of union, the Broken Men themselves became part of the settled tribe and were absorbed into it. The only place where this development did not occur was India, and according to Ambedkar the reason it did not occur in India was that here the notion of Untouchability supervened and perpetuated the difference between kindred and non-kindred, tribesmen and non-tribesmen, in another form, namely, in the form of the difference between Touchable and Untouchable. But why did this new factor enter into the situation? *What was the origin of Untouchability?* With this crucial question we come to the very heart of the book, and to the point where Ambedkar's scientific investigation into origins starts becoming indistinguishable from a spiritual search for roots. Before giving his own answer to the question, however, Ambedkar considers two earlier theories of the origin of Untouchability. According to the first theory the origin of Untouchability is racial, the Untouchables being non-Aryan, non-Dravidian aboriginals who had been conquered and subjugated by the Dravidians. According to the second theory the origin of Untouchability is occupational, being found in the filthy and unclean nature of the occupations in which the Untouchables engaged. Ambedkar has no difficulty in disproving both these theories. In the case of the first he shows, on anthropometric and ethnological grounds, that the Aryans, the Dravidians, and the allegedly aboriginal Untouchables all belonged to the same race. In the course of the second he shows that under certain circumstances Brahmins, Kshatriyas, Vaishyas, and Shudras alike could engage in even the filthiest of occupations without thereby becoming Untouchables. The earlier theories having been disproved in this manner the way is now clear for Ambedkar to put forward his own theory of the origin of Untouchability.

He begins by drawing attention to the census reports. Since 1910 these had divided the Hindus into three categories: Hindus, Animists and Tribals, and Depressed Classes or Untouchables. The division was made in accordance with ten criteria, out of which the first five served to differentiate the Hindus from the Animists and Tribals and the second five to divide the Hindus from the Untouchables. The replies received by the Census Commissioner to questions based on the second five criteria revealed that the Untouchables did not receive mantra-initiation from a Brahmin; that they were not served by good Brahmins as family priests; that they had, in fact, no Brahmin priests at all; and that they ate beef and did not reverence the cow. These facts were important, especially the fact that the Untouchables had no Brahmin priests, for they showed that the Brahmins shunned the Untouchables. Owing to the one-sidedness of the questions put by the Census Commissioner, however, what the replies did not reveal was that the Untouchables also shunned the Brahmins. If the Untouchables did not have Brahmin priests, and instead had priests drawn from their own community, this was not only because the Brahmins refused to be employed as priests by the Untouchables; it was also because the Untouchables were reluctant to employ them as priests. Surprising though it may seem, in much the same way that the Brahmins regarded the Untouchables as impure and inauspicious the Untouchables regarded the Brahmins as impure and inauspicious – a fact for which there was ample evidence. The reason for this strange state of affairs, Ambedkar says, is more important than the state of affairs itself, for behind it is hidden the clue to the origin of Untouchability. This clue consists in the fact that the mutual antipathy that existed between the Brahmins and the Untouchables can be explained only on the basis of the hypothesis that the Broken Men (as the Untouchables originally were) were Buddhists. Because they were Buddhists they did not revere the Brahmins, did not employ them as their priests, and regarded them as impure, and because the Broken Men were Buddhists the Brahmins, for their part, preached hatred and contempt against them with the result that the Broken Men came to be regarded as Untouchables.

Ambedkar is well aware that there is no direct evidence for his hypothesis that the Broken Men were Buddhists, but in his opinion no evidence is necessary. The majority of Hindus, he declares, were Buddhists (in this connection he appears to be using the term Hindu in its American sense of 'Indian') and we may take it that the Broken Men were Buddhists too. But though there is no direct evidence that the Broken Men were Buddhists, there is certainly evidence that there existed hatred and abhorrence against the Buddhists in the minds of the Hindus and that this feeling was created by the Brahmins. (Though Ambedkar does not mention the fact, the reason the Brahmins as a class were so hostile to Buddhism was that its critique of the notion of hereditary superiority had the effect of undermining their privileged position in society.) How widespread the spirit of hatred and contempt against the followers of the Buddha had become can be observed, Ambedkar points out, from certain scenes of classical Sanskrit drama. In the well known *Mṛcchakaṭikā* or 'Little Clay Cart', for instance, an inoffensive Buddhist monk is not only avoided as inauspicious by the hero of the play but also abused and beaten by one of the other characters. Even in the absence of any direct evidence for his hypothesis, therefore, Ambedkar has no difficulty in believing that the Broken Men were Buddhists who, when

Brahmanism triumphed over Buddhism, did not return to it as easily as others did. If we accept this, he says, we can see why the Untouchables shunned the Brahmins. We can also see why the Broken Men came to be regarded as Untouchables.

> The Broken Men hated the Brahmins because the Brahmins were
> the enemies of Buddhism and the Brahmin imposed untouchability
> upon the Broken Men because they would not leave Buddhism.
> On this reasoning it is possible to conclude that one of the roots of
> untouchability lies in the hatred and contempt which the Brahmins
> created against those who were Buddhist.[82]

In the blunt words of the *Bombay Chronicle's* headline ten years earlier, Untouchability was a punishment for sticking to Buddhism.

Awareness that India had once been a Buddhist country, and that many of their own ancestors must have been Buddhists, had, of course, been growing among educated Indians for some time. Ambedkar fully shared this awareness. Indeed, he shared it to a greater degree than any of his contemporaries. For him Buddhism was not just an object of archaeological interest, much less still an excuse for indulgence in chauvinistic self-congratulation. For him – especially after the Yeola declaration – Buddhism represented a spiritual possibility, even a religious alternative, and though it was an alternative which he did not, at first, consider as seriously as Sikhism, it was the one for which he eventually opted and towards which, by the time *The Untouchables* was published, he was already moving. To what extent his decision in favour of Buddhism was influenced by the fact that the Untouchables were originally Buddhists, and Untouchability itself a punishment for sticking to Buddhism, it is difficult to say. At the very least, his discovery of the hidden connection between the Untouchables and Buddhism must have enabled him, as an Untouchable himself, to identify with Buddhism in a way that he had not done before and to feel that, in embracing Buddhism, he and his followers would not be converting to a new religion so much as returning to the old one. In other words, Ambedkar's discovery that the Untouchables were originally Buddhists represented a discovery of his own spiritual roots, and the fact that those roots were Buddhist roots must have made it easier for him to establish an emotional as well as an intellectual connection with

Buddhism than would otherwise have been the case. It is even possible that, without that emotional connection, he may not have been able to take the final step and actually go for Refuge to the Buddha, Dharma, and Sangha.

Be that as it may, though Ambedkar has shown that the Untouchables were originally Buddhists, and that they became Untouchables because they stuck to Buddhism, he has yet to show why only the Broken Men (as the Untouchables then were) became Untouchables. After all, the hatred and contempt preached by the Brahmins was directed against Buddhists in general and not against the Broken Men in particular. What, then, was the additional circumstance on account of which Untouchability was imposed on the Broken Men? In order to answer this question and thus complete his solution of the mystery of Untouchability by showing not only why but how it originated, Ambedkar refers to the fifth and last of the five criteria in accordance with which the census reports from 1910 onwards had divided the Hindus from the Untouchables. The criterion related to beef-eating, and Ambedkar has no hesitation in affirming that the Broken Men came to be treated as Untouchables because they ate beef. In the first place, only the Untouchables eat dead cows and it is *only* those who eat dead cows who are tainted with Untouchability. In the second place, even those Hindus who are non-vegetarians never eat cow's flesh, with the result that the Touchables, who are united in their objection to the eating of cow's flesh, are completely marked off from the Untouchables, who eat it without compunction and as a matter of course. It is therefore not too far-fetched to suggest that those who are nauseated by beef-eating should treat those who eat beef as Untouchables.

Not that speculation as to whether beef-eating was or was not the principal reason for the rise of Untouchability is really necessary. Ambedkar has no difficulty in showing that the authors of the ancient Hindu law books knew very well that the origin of Untouchability was to be found in the eating of beef. He therefore concludes that his new approach to the origin of Untouchability has revealed that the latter had two sources, one being the general atmosphere of scorn and contempt spread by the Brahmins against those who were Buddhists and the other the habit of beef-eating kept on by the Broken Men. The first of these circumstances alone, he believes, cannot account for the stigma of Untouchability attaching itself to the Broken Men, for the scorn and contempt for Buddhists that was spread by the Brahmins was of a general kind and affected all Buddhists, not only the Broken Men.

> The reason why Broken Men only became Untouchables was because in addition to being Buddhists they retained their habit of beef-eating which gave additional ground for offence to the Brahmins to carry their new-found love and reverence to the cow to its logical conclusion. We may therefore conclude that [though] the Broken Men were exposed to scorn and contempt on the ground that they were Buddhist the main cause of their Untouchability was beef-eating.[83]

The theory that beef-eating was the cause of Untouchability naturally gives rise to a number of questions, and Ambedkar is well aware that unless these questions are answered the theory will remain 'under a cloud' and that it will be regarded as plausible but may not be accepted as conclusive. He therefore devotes the remaining chapters of *The Untouchables* not just to dealing with the questions which, he says, critics are sure to ask, but to dealing with them in such a way as to demonstrate the exact nature of the process whereby beef-eating came to be the cause of Untouchability. Thus he shows that, contrary to popular belief, there was a time when Hindus – both Brahmins and non-Brahmins – ate not only flesh but also beef; that the non-Brahmins gave up beef-eating (though not necessarily the eating of meat) in imitation of the Brahmins, and that the Brahmins themselves gave up beef-eating and started worshipping the cow as part of their strategy for establishing the supremacy of Brahmanism over Buddhism. Here Ambedkar points out that the strife between Buddhism and Brahmanism is a crucial fact of Indian history, and that unless this is realized it is impossible to explain some of the features of Hinduism. Since the struggle in which the two creeds were engaged lasted for 400 years, and left indelible marks on the religion, society, and politics of India, the present book is not the place for describing the full story of the struggle. All he can do is mention a few salient points.

The most important of the points mentioned by Ambedkar is the fact that Buddhism had taken such a strong hold on the minds of the masses that, in order to regain their lost power and prestige, the Brahmins had no alternative but to adopt certain features of Buddhism. Thus the Buddhists having set up images of the Buddha and built stupas, the

Brahmins, in their turn, built temples and installed in them the images of Hindu gods – all with the object of drawing people away from the worship of the Buddha. Similarly, the Buddhists having rejected the Brahmanical religion, which consisted of *yajña* or animal sacrifice, particularly sacrifice of the cow, the Brahmins sought to improve their position by abandoning *yajña* as a form of worship. What was more, they not only gave up the eating of beef, of which they were notoriously fond, but actually became vegetarian, the reason for this being

> that without becoming vegetarian the Brahmins could not have recovered the ground they had lost [to their rival], namely, Buddhism. In this connection it must be remembered that there was one aspect in which Brahmanism suffered in public esteem as compared to Buddhism. That was the practice of animal sacrifice which was the essence of Brahmanism and to which Buddhism was deadly opposed. That in an agricultural population there should be respect for Buddhism and revulsion against Brahmanism which involved slaughter of animals including cows and bullocks is only natural. What could the Brahmins do to recover the lost ground? To go one better than the Buddhist Bhikshus – not only to give up meat-eating [i.e. beef-eating] but to become vegetarians – which they did.[84]

The reason Ambedkar speaks of the Brahmins as going one better than the *bhikṣus* and giving up meat-eating and becoming vegetarian is that, as he proceeds to show, the *bhikṣus* were permitted to eat meat that was 'pure' in the sense of being from an animal the slaughter of which had not been seen or heard or suspected by them as having been on their account. It is worth noting, however, that the *bhikṣus* were not all agreed in thinking that the eating of 'pure' meat was permitted to them and that the permission had come from the Buddha himself. Those *bhikṣus* who were Mahāyānists (that is, who studied the Mahāyāna *sūtras* and worshipped the bodhisattvas) certainly did not think that 'pure' meat was permitted to them, and there is some evidence that those who belonged to the prominent and influential Sarvāstivāda school did not think so either. In becoming vegetarians, therefore, the Brahmins went one better than some Buddhist *bhikṣus* but not better than all. Not that this really affects the main thrust of Ambedkar's argument, for if, in becoming vegetarians, the Brahmins only went one better than some *bhikṣus* they undoubtedly went one better than all *bhikṣus* – indeed, than all Buddhists – in making the cow a sacred animal and inducing the Gupta kings to treat cow-slaughter as a capital offence.

Having demonstrated the exact nature of the process whereby beef-eating came to be the cause of Untouchability, thus showing the convincingness of his theory, Ambedkar has only to explain why, when the non-Brahmins gave up beef-eating in imitation of the Brahmins, the Broken Men did not do likewise. The reason was twofold.

> In the first place, imitation was too costly. They could not afford it. The flesh of the dead cow was their principal sustenance. Without it they would starve. In the second place, carrying [away] the dead cow had become an obligation though originally it was a privilege. As they could not escape carrying [away] the dead cow they did not mind using the flesh as food in the manner in which they were doing previously.[85]

Thus the Broken Men, who in any case were exposed to scorn and contempt on the ground that they were Buddhist, continued to eat beef when everyone else had given it up, and because they ate beef – as well as because they stuck to Buddhism – they were treated as Untouchables. This did not, of course, happen all at once, and it is therefore not possible to fix an exact date when the seed of Untouchability could be said to have been sown. But it is possible to give an approximate date. Since the root of Untouchability is beef-eating, it follows that the date of the birth of Untouchability must be intimately connected with the ban on cow-slaughter and on eating beef. Cow-slaughter was made a capital offence by the Gupta kings in the fourth century.

> We can, therefore, say with some confidence that Untouchability was born some time about 400AD. It is born out of the struggle for supremacy between Buddhism and Brahmanism which has so completely moulded the history of India and the study of which is so woefully neglected by students of Indian history.[86]

With these sombre words the book concludes. Ambedkar has solved the mystery of who the Untouchables were and how they became

Untouchables. He has discovered his own spiritual roots and, in this way, established an emotional as well as an intellectual connection with Buddhism – a connection without which he may not have been able to go for Refuge to the Buddha, Dharma, and Sangha. But the fact that Ambedkar had established an emotional connection with Buddhism certainly did not mean that he had stopped thinking about it. He was thinking about it more vigorously than ever, and his thought was to be of significance not only to his own followers but to Buddhists throughout the world.

6

THINKING ABOUT BUDDHISM

Between the publication of *The Untouchables* and the organizing of the Nagpur conversion ceremony there elapsed eight years. Surveying this crucial period of Ambedkar's life one cannot help wishing that there had been someone at hand to perform for him the service that Boswell performed for Johnson (whom Ambedkar resembled in a number of respects) and that H. N. Coleridge performed for Coleridge (whom Ambedkar did not resemble at all), for we should then have possessed a record of Ambedkar's table-talk, and if we had possessed a record of his table-talk we would have been in a better position to follow his thinking at the time – especially his thinking about Buddhism. As things are, we have to rely for our knowledge of his thoughts on this subject mainly on the glimpses of them that he gives us in his speeches in and out of Parliament, in newspaper interviews, in letters, and in his published writings. Of these the writings are naturally the most important, though they are by no means as extensive as one might wish and show the nature of Ambedkar's thoughts on Buddhism only to a limited degree. Leaving aside the polemical article entitled 'The Rise And Fall of the Hindu Woman. Who was Responsible for It?', which in the present context is only of peripheral interest, we find that Ambedkar's thoughts on Buddhism are contained in his article on 'The Buddha and the Future of His Religion' and in certain sections of *The Buddha and His Dhamma*. Since the latter was not published until nearly a year after Ambedkar's death, and since these sections will in any case fall to be considered when the book is dealt with as a whole, this leaves us with 'The Buddha and the Future of His Religion' as the principal evidence for the way in which Ambedkar was thinking about Buddhism during the years immediately preceding his conversion.

The article appeared in the April-May 1950 issue of the *Maha Bodhi*. This was not without significance. Founded by Anagarika Dharmapala in 1892 as the official organ of the Maha Bodhi Society, the *Maha Bodhi* was at that time the leading English-language Buddhist magazine and enjoyed an extensive, even if numerically small, circulation among English-speaking Buddhists throughout the world. On account of its president being a Bengali Brahmin the Society itself was anathema to Ambedkar (as I was to discover on the occasion of our first meeting), and he therefore must have allowed 'The Buddha and the Future of His Religion' to appear in the pages of the *Maha Bodhi* only because he wanted to share his thoughts on Buddhism with Buddhists outside India and, in fact, with students of religion and philosophy everywhere. Moreover, the April-May issue of the *Maha Bodhi* was always a Vaiśākha number, that is, a special double issue in commemoration of the Buddha's attainment of Enlightenment, and reached more people than any other issue of the magazine.

But though 'The Buddha and the Future of His Religion' made its appearance in the *Maha Bodhi* it bore very little resemblance to the dry, academic disquisitions on Buddhist history and doctrine by scholarly Hindus, or the pompous pronouncements by Buddhist dignitaries, that the magazine only too often featured. Ambedkar's 6,500-word article was the work of a man who was in deadly earnest. It was the work of a man who was as yet only 'on his way to embrace Buddhism' and who knew that, when he did finally take that momentous step, it would bring about a radical change in the lives of millions of his fellow countrymen and alter, perhaps, the entire course of Indian history. It was the work of a man who was not afraid to think for himself and who was not afraid to say what he thought. At the same time, the article was the work of a man who was in a hurry and had no time to revise and polish. From a literary point of view 'The Buddha and the Future of His Religion' is therefore distinctly rough in texture, reminding one of a stream of lava that, issuing white-hot from the depths of a volcano, has set in bold and jagged shapes, or of a lump of gold that has come from the furnace with fragments of rock still adhering to it and which has yet to be wrought into ornaments.

The fact that 'The Buddha and the Future of His Religion' is rough in texture does not, however, mean that Ambedkar's thinking about Buddhism is not fully defined or that the article itself is unsystematic. Though short, the article is in fact divided into five numbered sections, each with its own distinctive subject matter. In the first section Ambedkar shows what distinguishes the Buddha from the founders of three other major religions; in the second – which is the longest section – he compares Buddhism with Hinduism; in the third he expresses his faith in the revival of Buddhism in India; in the fourth he summarizes his conclusions with regard to how Buddhism stands in comparison with other, non-Hindu religions, and in the fifth he outlines the three steps that have to be taken if the ideal of spreading Buddhism is to be realized. Thus in the course of some sixteen pages a great deal of ground is covered, and Ambedkar manages to make a number of points of enormous significance and value. At the same time, he makes them in so condensed a manner that, as with the aphorisms in which the sages of old summarized their knowledge of the different arts and sciences, a certain amount of commentary is needed if their meaning is to be fully appreciated.

This is very much the case with the first section of the article, where Ambedkar boldly declares that what distinguishes the Buddha from Jesus, Mohammed, and Krishna – the founders of the three other major religions – is his self-abnegation. By the Buddha's self-abnegation Ambedkar means his refusal to claim for himself the kind of position that Jesus, Mohammed, and Krishna claimed for themselves, and it is not without significance that in enumerating these three founders he should enumerate them in the order of the increasing largeness of their claims, and, therefore, in the order of their increasing distance from the Buddha. Thus throughout the Bible (that is, throughout the Four Gospels) Jesus insists that he is the son of God and that those who wish to enter the kingdom of God will fail to do so if they do not recognize him as such. Mohammed went a step further. Like Jesus he claimed that he was a messenger of God on earth (here Ambedkar is apparently treating Jesus's claim to be the son of God as equivalent to his claim to be the messenger of God), but he further insisted that he was the last messenger. On this footing he declared that those who wanted salvation must not only accept that he was a messenger of God but also accept that he was the last messenger. Krishna went a step beyond both Jesus and Mohammed, refusing to be satisfied with being merely the son or the messenger of God, or even with being the last messenger of God. According to Ambedkar, Krishna was not even satisfied with calling himself God.

> He claimed that he was 'Parameshwar' [God Supreme] or as his followers describe him 'Devadhideva', God of Gods.[87]

In representing Krishna as claiming to be *Parameshwar*, Ambedkar is regarding him, for the purpose of his article, as a historical figure and regarding that figure as having actually made that claim – a claim that the *Bhagavad Gītā* or 'Song Celestial' and other Hindu scriptures do in fact represent him as making. There is no doubt, however, that Ambedkar was well aware that for the majority of Western scholars the blue-complexioned charioteer of Arjuna and lover of the Gopis belongs to Hindu myth and legend and that he can be regarded as the founder of Hinduism only in a strictly symbolic sense.

Having described the claims made by Jesus, Mohammed, and Krishna, Ambedkar proceeds to emphasize the very different attitude assumed by the Buddha who, he says, never arrogated to himself any such status as they did. In striking contrast to all three of them,

> He was born as a son of man and was content to remain a common man and preached his gospel as a common man. He never claimed any supernatural origin or supernatural powers nor did he perform miracles to prove his supernatural powers.[88]

In speaking of the Buddha as a common man Ambedkar does not, of course, mean to deny that there is any difference between the Buddha and ordinary humanity. The Buddha is, after all, the Enlightened One, and between the Enlightened One and those who are not Enlightened Ones – who are not even Stream Entrants – the difference is so great as to be virtually unimaginable. What Ambedkar is really saying, therefore, is that the difference between the Buddha and ordinary humanity consists not in the fact that the Buddha occupies an inherently privileged position or status, so to speak, but rather in the fact that he has attained a higher level of spiritual development. No one can be the son and messenger of God in the sense that Jesus was, or the last messenger of God in the sense that Mohammed was, and certainly no one can be *Parameshwar* or 'God Supreme' as Krishna was, for there is by definition only one son of God, one last messenger of God, one *Parameshwar*. But anyone can become a Buddha, that is, anyone who makes the effort that the Buddha made and attains the level of spiritual development that the Buddha attained, and it is for this reason that Ambedkar speaks of the Buddha as a common man. The Buddha is a common man in the sense that he has achieved nothing that a common man (that is, one born a common man) cannot achieve likewise. Similarly, in saying that the Buddha 'never claimed any supernatural origin or supernatural powers nor did he perform miracles to prove his supernatural powers' Ambedkar does not mean to deny the difference between supernatural powers, such as those possessed by Jesus by virtue of his status as the son and messenger of God, and supernormal powers, such as those acquired by the Buddha in the course of his experience of concentration and meditation. Supernormal powers are extensions of ordinary human faculties and can be acquired by anyone who practises the necessary disciplines. They do not constitute evidence for the attainment of wisdom or insight – and it is wisdom or insight alone that leads to Enlightenment.

Because the Buddha never claimed any supernatural origin or supernatural powers for himself it naturally followed that he never claimed any supernatural sanction, or divine authority, for his teaching, in the way that Jesus, Mohammed, and Krishna did. All he claimed for it was that it was a reasonable teaching, and that it was possible for a sincere and open-minded person to experience the truth of it for himself, in this very existence. In Ambedkar's words, the Buddha 'preached his gospel as a common man', that is, he preached it not as something thundered by God in the ears of a reluctant humanity but simply as something communicated by a man to his fellow men – by a man who was an Enlightened One to men who were not, as yet, Enlightened Ones – and which the latter were free to accept or reject as they saw fit. The Buddha did not issue orders, but only advised, encouraged, and inspired. He did not pick men up and carry them bodily to the goal of the spiritual life, as it were, but only showed them the way by which they could reach it on their own two feet. Ambedkar is therefore able to say,

The Buddha made a clear distinction between a *Margadata* [Giver of the Way] and a *Mokshadata* [Giver of Salvation]. Jesus, Mahommed and Krishna claimed for themselves the role of *Mokshadata*. The Buddha was satisfied with playing the role of a *Margadata*.[89]

To this one can only add that the Buddha was not satisfied with the role of *Margadata* in the sense of being content with an inferior role, for according to Buddhism there is in fact no such role as that of *Mokshadata* and to think so is a delusion.

Besides being distinguished from the three other founders of religions by his self-abnegation the Buddha is distinguished from them by the fact that he did not claim infallibility for his teaching. This was the natural consequence of his preaching his gospel 'as a common man', for infallibility can be claimed only for the word of God and for it to be the word of God a teaching must come either from a messenger of God, as in the case of Jesus and Mohammed, or directly from God himself, as in the case of Krishna, and the Buddha claimed to be neither God nor a messenger of God. Nor is that all. From the fact that the Buddha did not claim infallibility for his teaching there follow certain consequences of great practical significance – consequences which Ambedkar is not afraid to draw.

In the *Mahaparinibbana Sutta* [the Buddha] told Ananda that His religion was based on reason and experience and that His followers should not accept his teaching as correct and binding merely because it emanated from Him. Being based on reason and experience they were free to modify or even to abandon any of his teachings if it was found that at a given time and in given circumstances they did not apply.[90]

In other words, that which is not infallible is capable of revision. The passage of the *Mahāparinibbāna Sutta* or 'Book of the Great Decease' to which Ambedkar refers is probably the well known one where the Buddha, on the eve of his departure from the world, tells his faithful attendant,

When I am gone, Ānanda, let the Order, if it should so wish, abolish all the lesser and minor precepts.[91]

As it happened, the Order did not so wish. On considering the matter shortly after the Buddha's death, they declined to avail themselves of his permission, maintaining – according to tradition – that he had given it simply in order to test the *bhikkhus*,

> to try whether, if leave were granted them, they would, after His death, revoke the lesser and minor regulations, or still adhere to them.[92]

To this Ambedkar would doubtless have replied that if there was any question of a test the Order had failed it, for obviously the Buddha

> wished His religion not to be encumbered with the dead wood of the past. He wanted that it should remain evergreen and serviceable at all times. That is why He gave liberty to His followers to chip and chop as the necessities of the case required.[93]

In drawing such a conclusion Ambedkar must have been aware that, nearly 2,500 years after the Buddha's death, Buddhism as practised in the Buddhist countries of Asia was by no means unencumbered with dead wood and that if it was to be made serviceable to him and his followers a good deal of chipping and chopping would have to be done. Not that Ambedkar saw such chipping and chopping as a negative thing. For him the fact that the Buddha had given liberty to his followers to 'chip and chop' was nothing less than a direct expression of his teaching and a triumphant affirmation of the nature of Buddhism as a religion based not on authority but on reason and experience. It demonstrated the Buddha's faith in his teaching and in his followers. Indeed, it demonstrated his courage – a courage that, Ambedkar believes, no other religious teacher had shown.

> They were afraid of permitting repair. As the liberty to repair may be used to demolish the structure they had reared. Buddha had no such fear. He was sure of His foundation. He knew that even the most violent iconoclast will not be able to destroy the core of His religion.[94]

With this insight into the psychology of the founders of religion Ambedkar brings the first section of his article to a close. He has shown that what distinguishes the Buddha from Jesus, Mohammed, and Krishna is his self-abnegation and the fact that he did not claim infallibility for what he taught, as well as his courage in giving his followers the freedom to revise his teaching. Having done this, and having declared the Buddha's position to be unique, Ambedkar proceeds, in the second section of his article, to compare Buddhism and Hinduism. In so doing, he limits himself to two points: one regarding the position of morality and the meaning of the word *dhamma* (or *dharma*) and the other regarding the question of equality versus inequality.

With regard to the position of morality Ambedkar exhibits the contrast between the two religions in the boldest and starkest terms. 'Hinduism', he says bluntly, 'is a religion which is not founded on morality.'[95] This is not to say that in Hinduism there is no morality at all but rather that whatever morality Hinduism has is not an integral part of it, but a separate force which is sustained by social necessities and not by injunctions of the Hindu religion. With Buddhism the exact opposite is the case.

> The religion of the Buddha is morality. It is imbedded in religion. Buddhist religion is nothing if not morality. It is true that in Buddhism there is no God. In place of God there is morality. What God is to other religions morality is to Buddhism.[96]

This could hardly have been better or more strongly put, though it is important to understand that Ambedkar is not using the word morality in a narrow, legalistic sense but as representing the whole ethical and spiritual dimension of human existence. The fact that in Buddhism morality takes the place of God means that in Buddhism God is subordinated to morality, not morality to God. It means that actions are to be performed or not performed, not according to whether they are, or are not, commanded by God, but according to whether they are, or are not, right or wrong or, in Buddhist terms, skilful or unskilful. God's commands are, of course, contained in the infallible scriptures which constitute his 'word'. The fact that in Buddhism morality takes the place of God therefore also means that in Buddhism the infallible scriptures too are subordinated to morality, as well as God, and that one is perfectly free to reject those scriptures if their injunctions conflict with the requirements of morality. Indeed, it is one's duty to reject them. In the case of Hinduism it is the Vedas that are the infallible scriptures, and the Buddha rejected the Vedas because they enjoin the performance of rituals involving animal sacrifice and because animal sacrifice contravenes the principle of non-violence or reverence for life.

Not only did the Vedas enjoin the performance of rituals involving animal sacrifice, but according to the Brahmins the performance of such rituals constituted *Dharma* (or Dhamma), that is, constituted religion. As Ambedkar observes,

> The *Dharma* as enunciated by the Brahmins and as propounded in the *Purvamimamsa* of Jaimini meant nothing more than the performance of certain *karmas* or to use terminology of the Roman religion, observances. *Dharma* to Brahmins meant keeping up of observances, i.e. *yajnas*, *yagas*, and sacrifices to Gods. This was the essence of the Brahmanic or Vedic Religion. It had nothing to do with morality.[97]

For the Buddha, of course, the performance of Vedic rituals was far from constituting Dharma. According to him, the essence of Dharma or religion was not *yāgas* or *yajñas* but morality. Thus,

> Although the word *Dhamma* was used by Brahmanic teachers as well as by the Buddha, the content of both is radically and fundamentally different.[98]

The Buddha in fact gave the word *Dhamma* what Ambedkar has earlier called 'a most revolutionary meaning', and the latter therefore concludes that

> the Buddha was the first teacher in the world who made morality the essence and foundation of religion.[99]

Be that as it may (for the transition from ethnic to universal religion was everywhere accompanied by a redefinition of key terms), there is no doubt that in Buddhism the word *Dhamma* (or Dharma) has a totally different meaning from what it has in Hinduism and that unless this is understood the contrast between the two religions will not be fully appreciated.

With regard to the question of equality versus inequality, the second of the two points to which Ambedkar limits his comparison of Buddhism and Hinduism, the contrast between the two religions is exhibited no less boldly and starkly than it was in the case of the first point. Going straight to the heart of the matter, Ambedkar declares that 'the official gospel of Hinduism is inequality',[100] and that the concrete embodiment of this gospel of inequality is the doctrine of *chaturvarna* or the doctrine that (Indian) humanity is divided into four divinely ordained hereditary classes in accordance with their innate superiority or inferiority to one another. These four classes are, of course, those of the Brahmin or priest, the Kshatriya or warrior, the Vaishya or trader, and the Shudra or menial, that is, the four classes of which the 2,000 or more hereditary castes of Hindu society are at least theoretically the subdivisions, so that the doctrine of *chaturvarna* is in principle the doctrine of the caste system. As against the gospel of inequality and its concrete embodiment the doctrine of *chaturvarna* the Buddha stood for equality and was, in fact, the greatest opponent of *chaturvarna*.

> He not only preached against it, fought against it, but did
> everything to uproot it. According to Hinduism neither a *Shudra*
> nor a woman could become a teacher of religion nor could they
> take *sannyasa* [initiation into the ascetic life] and reach God.
> Buddha on the other hand admitted *Shudras* to the *Bhikkhu
> Sangha*. He also admitted women to become *Bhikkhunis*. Why did
> he do so? Few people seem to realise the importance of this step.
> The answer is that Buddha wanted to take concrete steps to destroy
> the gospel of inequality.[101]

But though Ambedkar rightly represents the Buddha as standing for equality and opposing the gospel of inequality and taking concrete steps to destroy it, he certainly does not think that the Buddha believed that all men are equal in the sense of believing that they are identical in all respects and, therefore, interchangeable. Ambedkar himself did not believe any such thing. As he had made clear as far back as 1936, in his undelivered address on 'Annihilation of Caste', even though the objections to equality are sound, and even though all men are not equal, one must still accept equality as the governing principle of social life. Standing for equality, therefore, means treating men as equal even though they are in fact not equal. If they are treated as equal even though they are not equal society will get more out of them – which obviously will be to society's advantage. Moreover, since people are unequal in so many ways it is not possible to classify them and since they cannot be classified it is impossible to treat them according to their need or capacity. For this reason the statesman, who is concerned with vast numbers of people, has no alternative but to follow the rough and ready rule of treating everyone alike.[102]

It is noteworthy that both in connection with the position of morality and in connection with the question of equality versus inequality – the two points of contrast between Buddhism and Hinduism to which he limited himself – Ambedkar makes reference to the *Bhagavad Gītā* or 'Song Celestial', probably the most popular of the Hindu scriptures. Unlike the Buddha, Krishna, the preacher of the *Bhagavad Gītā*,

> was not able to extricate himself from the old conception of religion being [the] equivalent of rituals and observances.[103]

Even his doctrine of *niṣkāma-karma* or 'disinterested action', which was wrongly understood to mean the doing of good without thought of reward, really means the disinterested performance not of actions in general but of ritual actions which, according to the Brahmanic Vedic religion, were to be performed regularly as a matter of religious duty. Thus

> even for Krishna religion did not consist of morality. It consisted of *Karmas*, i.e. of *Yajnas* and *Yagas* though of the *Nishkama Karma* category.[104]

Krishna was also unable to extricate himself from the doctrine of *chaturvarna*. Indeed, in the *Bhagavad Gītā* he develops 'a new justification of *chaturvarna*' and

> says that he as God created the system of *Chaturvarna* and he constructed it on the basis of the theory of *Guna-Karma* – which means that he prescribed the status and occupation of every individual in accordance with his innate *gunas* (or qualities).[105]

Though Ambedkar has no quarrel with the Sāṃkhya philosophy from which the theory of the *guṇas* is taken, and no quarrel with the theory of the *guṇas* itself, he is far from agreeing that the theory can in fact be used, as Krishna uses it, to justify *chaturvarna*. Neither in the Sāṃkhya philosophy nor in actual experience, he points out, is there any ground for Krishna's assumption that a particular *guṇa* will dominate an individual throughout his life and, therefore, determine both his Varna and his occupation. Unfortunately, in its eagerness to find a better foundation for *chaturvarna* than the authority of the Vedas Hinduism did not see this. To most Hindus Krishna's justification of *chaturvarna* – which is the parent of the caste system – seems quite convincing, even irrefutable, with the result that Hinduism continues to uphold the Varna system and its gospel of social inequality.

Since Buddhism is free from the evil of not being founded on morality and from the evil of inequality it is hardly surprising that, in modern times, some people should believe that only the acceptance of the Gospel of the Buddha can save the Hindus. Some of them are filled with sorrow, however, because they do not see much prospect of the return of Buddhism to India or its revival there. Ambedkar does not share this pessimism, and in the third section of 'The Buddha and the Future of His Religion' he not only says that he does not share it but explains why. He does not share it for two reasons. In the first place, though there are some Hindus for whom Hinduism is true because all religions are true (a thesis than which, according to Ambedkar, no thesis can be more false) there are other Hindus who have come to realize that there is something wrong with their religion. For one reason or another, however, they are not ready either to denounce Hinduism openly or to abandon it; nor are they ready openly to embrace Buddhism. In some cases they console themselves with the thought that since all religions are wrong there is no point in bothering about religion anyway. Such an attitude on the part of the Hindus, Ambedkar believes, can only have one result.

Hinduism will lapse and cease to be a force governing life. There
will be [a] void, which will have the effect of disintegrating the
Hindu Society. Hindus then will be forced to take a more positive
attitude. When they do so, they can turn to nothing except
Buddhism.[106]

In the second place, Hinduism gives no mental or moral relief to the millions of people belonging to the so-called Backward Classes or Scheduled Castes, and it is therefore futile for the Hindus to expect these people to go on living under Hinduism. The truth is that Hinduism is sitting on a volcano which, though today it appears to be extinct, will become active once

> these mighty millions have become conscious of their degradation and know that it is largely due to the social philosophy of the Hindu religion.[107]

Ambedkar is reminded of the overthrow of Paganism by Christianity in the days of the Roman Empire.

> When the masses realized that Paganism could give them no mental and moral relief they gave it up and adopted Christianity. What happened in Rome is sure to happen in India. The Hindu masses when they are enlightened are sure to turn to Buddhism.[108]

It is perhaps because he is optimistic rather than pessimistic about the prospect of the return of Buddhism to India, as well as for other reasons, that in the fourth section of his article Ambedkar does not take the other non-Hindu religions and compare them with Buddhism but, instead, puts his conclusions in summary form. This he does by stating the three requirements which a religion must fulfil and the extent to which, in his opinion, the existing religions fulfil them. Before he can state his three requirements, though, Ambedkar has to show that religion is necessary. In doing this he takes for his point of departure the fact that society must have something to hold it together. What holds it together, he maintains, is 'either the sanction of law or the sanction of morality,'[109] for deprived of either of these society is sure to fall to pieces. In all societies, however, law plays a very small part, being intended to keep the antisocial minority under control and prevent it from disrupting the social order. The majority is necessarily left to sustain its social life by means of what Ambedkar calls 'the postulates and sanction of morality'.[110] It is for this reason that religion, in the sense of morality, must remain the governing principle of any society, and it is because it is the governing principle of every society that it is necessary. Having shown this, Ambedkar is in a position to state the three requirements which religion – in the sense in which he has defined it – must fulfil. It must be in accord with science, it must recognize the fundamental tenets of liberty, equality, and fraternity, and it must not sanctify and ennoble poverty.

Ambedkar's character and personal background being what they were, it is not difficult to see why he should have thought it necessary for religion to fulfil these three requirements, and in his brief comments on them he does in fact provide us with a few clues to his thinking. As one who had spent seven of the most impressionable years of his life in the West, and indeed had received his higher education there, he was well aware how immense was the prestige of science and how great the extent of its influence in the modern world. Having declared that religion must be in accord with science, he therefore goes on to explain that unless religion accords with science

> [it] is bound to lose its respect and therefore become the subject
> of ridicule and thereby not merely lose its force as a governing
> principle of [social] life but might in course of time disintegrate and
> lapse.[111]

In saying that religion must be in accord with science Ambedkar does not, of course, mean that it is possible to demonstrate the truth of religion scientifically, or that there is nothing in religion which is not susceptible to scientific investigation. (In Buddhism the Dharma is said to be *atakkāvacarā* or 'beyond reason' and for Ambedkar science and reason are synonymous.) What he means is that what does not accord with science, in the sense that it can be actually disproved on scientific grounds, cannot be accepted as religion even though it may traditionally be regarded as such.

Recognition of the tenets of liberty, equality, and fraternity is a requirement of religion because the three are fundamental principles of social life and 'unless a religion recognises these three fundamental principles of social life, religion will be doomed'.[112] These are strong words indeed, but there is no doubt that Ambedkar realized – as many people have come to realize in this century, especially in the West – that unless religion can show that it has a social conscience and that it is actively involved in the struggle for social justice it will not be taken seriously by thinking men and women. Ambedkar's own commitment to the principles of liberty, equality, and fraternity seems to have gone back a long way, even though he at first saw in them only 'the slogan of the French Revolution'. Later in life, when he had immersed himself in the study of Buddhism for some years, he came to see that their roots were in fact religious rather than political and that they could be derived from the teachings of the Buddha. His most detailed treatment of them is to be found, however, in his undelivered address on 'Annihilation of Caste', to which reference has already been made. Halfway through this address, having told 'the tiresome tale of the sad effects that caste has produced' he turns to the constructive side of the problem to consider the ideal society. His own ideal society, he says, would be a society based on liberty, equality, and fraternity. Taking the three in reverse order, he declares he cannot imagine any objection to fraternity, for an ideal society should be mobile, should be full of channels for conveying changes taking place in one part of society to other parts.

> In an ideal society there should be many interests consciously communicated and shared. There should be varied and free points of contact with other modes of association. In other words there must be social endosmosis.[113]

This is fraternity, which Ambedkar believes is only another name for democracy, for democracy is not merely a form of government but is primarily a mode of associated living, of conjoint communicated experience. In fact democracy 'is essentially an attitude of respect and reverence towards [one's] fellow men'.[114] As for liberty, there can surely be no objection to that either. But liberty does not mean only the right to life and limb, or the right to property, tools, and materials as being necessary to the earning of one's living. There must also be the right to make full use of one's powers, and this must include the right to choose one's profession – a right which the caste system denies. In the case of equality there may indeed be objections, and these objections may be sound, but – as we saw in connection with the question of equality versus inequality – Ambedkar believes that for a variety of practical reasons equality has to be accepted as a governing principle of social life.

Poverty is one of the curses of humanity, and in declaring that religion must not sanctify or ennoble poverty Ambedkar gives full recognition to this fact. By poverty he does not mean voluntary poverty of the kind exemplified by the Buddha, Milarepa, and St Francis of Assisi, for he is prepared to recognize that 'renunciation of riches by those who have it, may be a blessed state'.[115] In requiring of religion that it must not sanctify and ennoble poverty what Ambedkar has in mind is the bitter, grinding poverty that is imposed on people against their will either by force of circumstances or by the greed and selfishness of their so-called fellow men. Poverty of this degrading and demoralizing kind – such as he had studied at first hand and in which the vast majority of Untouchables still lived – in his opinion can never be a blessed state and to declare it to be a blessed state 'is to pervert religion, to perpetuate vice and crime, to consent to make earth a living hell'.[116] Hinduism had certainly perverted religion in this way, for in its view both Shudras and Untouchables had no right to wealth and the caste Hindus were performing a religious duty, so to speak, in depriving them of the little they were able to acquire. Even today, thirty years after Ambedkar's death, reports appearing in the Indian press testify to the fact that Untouchable prosperity is still regarded as an affront by the caste Hindus and still visited, on occasion, with condign punishment.

Such, then, are the requirements that religion as a code of social morality must fulfil. It must be in accord with science, it must recognize the fundamental tenets of liberty, equality, and fraternity, and it must not sanctify or ennoble poverty. Having stated these requirements, Ambedkar has only to consider the question of which religion fulfils all the tests he has proposed. In so doing, he confines himself to existing religions, for in his opinion,

the days of the Mahatmas are gone and the world cannot have a new Religion. It will have to make its choice from those that exist.[117]

Not surprisingly, he believes that the only religion that the world can have is Buddhism. Some religions may satisfy one of the tests, some may even satisfy two, but so far as he knows, Ambedkar declares, only Buddhism satisfies them all, so that if the new world – which is very different from the old world – is to have a religion – and it needs a religion far more than the old world did – then it can only be the religion of the Buddha. The claim is a big one, and Ambedkar is conscious that 'all this may sound very strange'.[118] However, he attributes the strangeness to the fact that most of those who had written about the Buddha had propagated the mistaken idea that the only thing that he taught was *ahiṃsā* or non-violence. Though it is true that the Buddha did teach *ahiṃsā* – and Ambedkar does not want to minimize its importance, for it is a great doctrine and the world cannot be saved unless it follows it – he nonetheless wishes to emphasize that the Buddha taught many other things besides *ahiṃsā*.

> He taught as part of his religion, social freedom, intellectual freedom, economic freedom and political freedom. He taught equality, equality not between man and man only but between man and woman.[119]

In short,

> It would be difficult to find a religious teacher to compare with Buddha whose teachings embrace so many aspects of the social life of people, whose doctrines are so modern and [whose] main concern [is] to give salvation to man in his life on earth and not to promise it in heaven after he is dead![120]

With this enthusiastic tribute the fourth section of 'The Buddha and the Future of His Religion' concludes.

If only Buddhism fulfils all the requirements of religion, and if only Buddhism can therefore be the religion of the new world, then obviously Buddhism must be spread as widely as possible. But how can it be spread? In the fifth and last section of his article Ambedkar addresses himself to this question. Believing as he did that the Buddha wished his religion not to be encumbered with the dead wood of the past and that he had given his followers the liberty to chip and chop as the necessities of the case required, it is not surprising that the future convert to Buddhism should suggest some radical changes. If the ideal of spreading Buddhism is to be realized, then in his opinion three steps are 'quite necessary'.[121] These are: to produce a Buddhist Bible; to make changes in the organization, aims, and objects of the *bhikṣu saṅgha*, and to set up a world Buddhist Mission.

The foremost of these needs is the production of a Bible of Buddhism. As Ambedkar says, Buddhist literature is a vast literature and it is impossible to expect a person who wants to know the essence of Buddhism to 'wade through the sea of literature'.[122] He is also of the opinion that the greatest advantage that the other religions have over Buddhism is that each has a gospel which everyone can carry with him and read wherever he goes, that Buddhism suffers from not having such a 'handy gospel', and that the Indian *Dhammapada* has failed to perform the function which such a gospel is expected to perform. While it may indeed be impossible for even the greatest scholar to have an intimate acquaintance with the entire extent of Buddhist canonical literature in Pāli, Sanskrit, Tibetan, and Chinese one must not overlook the fact that the essence of Buddhism – in the sense of the fundamental principles of the Dharma – can be known from a number of works, and even chapters of works, both canonical and non-canonical, such as the *Sutta-Nipāta*, the *Diamond Sūtra*, Śāntideva's *Bodhicaryāvatāra* or 'Entry into the Life of Enlightenment', the *Milarepa Kah Bum* or 'Hundred Thousand Songs of Milarepa', and Hakuin's 'Song of Meditation'. One must also not forget that Buddhism spread throughout the whole of Asia without the help of any 'handy gospel' of the Christian or Islamic type, and that its success may not have been unconnected with the fact that in place of a single gospel it had a variety of gospels (in the literary not the doctrinal sense), some of which appealed to one kind of devotee and some to another. But regardless of whether or not Buddhism suffers from not having a handy gospel – and it cannot be denied that fresh compilations from the Buddha's teaching may be needed from time to time – such a gospel can never be regarded as authoritative for all Buddhists in the way that the Bible is authoritative for all Christians. The Bible is the Word of God. It is a divinely inspired and hence infallible guide to human belief and conduct which, on account of its supernatural origin, reason is powerless to question. Buddhist canonical literature, on the other hand, is the record of the life and teaching of a 'common man' who, after attaining Enlightenment by his own human efforts, 'preached his gospel as a common man'. As Ambedkar has already shown, since the Buddha did not claim to be either the son or the messenger of God, much less still God himself, he never claimed any supernatural sanction, or divine authority, for his teaching, and since he never claimed any supernatural sanction for his teaching, that teaching was not to be regarded as infallible. Not being infallible it did not have to be accepted unquestioningly and could even be revised or, in Ambedkar's language, chipped and chopped as the necessities of the case required. Thus between the Bible or Word of God and Buddhist canonical literature or the record of the Buddha's life and teaching there is an enormous difference, and for this reason it would be inappropriate, and perhaps misleading, to describe a gospel culled from the latter as a Buddhist Bible. The connotations of the term 'Bible' and the connotations of 'Buddhist canonical literature' belong, in fact, to two completely different systems of ideas, or worlds of thought, and strictly speaking it is no more possible for us to have a Buddhist Bible than it is possible for us to have a Buddhist Veda or a Buddhist Koran.

Though in the previous section of his article Ambedkar has insisted that religion must be in accord with science or reason, he is far from thinking that religion should therefore be devoid of emotional appeal. Explaining why, in his opinion, the Indian *Dhammapada* fails to perform the function of a handy gospel, he makes the interesting and important point that 'Every great religion has been built on faith', by faith apparently meaning not simply blind belief but the emotional-devotional as distinct from the rational component in human nature or, in more concrete terms, the heart as distinct from the head. Nor is that all. Not only has every great religion been built on faith, but 'faith cannot be assimilated if presented in the form of creeds and abstract dogmas',[123] that is, cannot be assimilated if presented in conceptual terms which, by their very nature, appeal to the reason rather than to the emotions. Hence faith

> needs something on which the imagination can fasten – some myth or epic or gospel – what is called in journalism, a story.[124]

It is because the (Indian) *Dhammapada* 'is not fastened around a story' and seeks, according to Ambedkar, to build faith on abstract dogma, that it fails to perform the function of a handy gospel. From this it is clear that what Ambedkar means by a handy gospel is, in principle, simply the essence of Buddhism presented in imaginative form or in a form that appeals to the deeper, non-rational element in human nature. It is therefore not surprising that in his opinion the proposed gospel of Buddhism should contain a short life of the Buddha, the 'Chinese' *Dhammapada*, some of the important dialogues of the Buddha, and Buddhist ceremonies for birth, initiation, marriage, and death. Of these the life of the Buddha would appeal to the imagination, while the 'Chinese' *Dhammapada* – which as translated by Beal comprises both stories and moral precepts – would appeal to both imagination and reason. Thus a considerable portion of the proposed gospel of Buddhism is in a form that imagination can grasp and in a form, therefore, that makes possible the 'assimilation' or development of faith.

But if faith 'needs something on which the imagination can fasten', it is no less true that the 'myth or epic or gospel' on which imagination fastens has to find expression in an appropriate and aesthetically satisfying form. Having indicated what the proposed gospel of Buddhism should contain, Ambedkar therefore insists that, in preparing such a gospel, the linguistic side of it must not be neglected.

> It must make the language in which it is produced live. It must become an incantation instead of being read as narrative or an ethical exposition. Its style must be lucid, moving and must produce an hypnotic effect.[125]

In laying down these requirements Ambedkar may have had in mind the majestic rhythms of the Authorized Version of the Bible (a moving passage from which heads the dedication to *What Congress and Gandhi have done to the Untouchables*) or the refined imagery and exquisite diction of Aśvaghoṣa's *Buddhacarita* or poetic 'Life of the Buddha', extracts from which he was to include in *The Buddha and His Dhamma*. He may even have had in mind the noble eloquence of those episodes from the *Rāmāyaṇa* and the *Mahābhārata* which, as a boy, he had heard his intensely religious father reading and reciting every evening. Whatever the case may have been, Ambedkar's insistence that the language of his proposed gospel should be living and incantatory shows that, despite his own rather unadorned manner of writing, he was sensitive to the magic of style and fully aware of its importance. It might even be said that for Ambedkar a gospel is not really a gospel unless it is, at the same time, literature in the most exalted sense of the term. The beauty of the casket must correspond to the value of the jewels it contains.

Though the production of a Buddhist Bible – in the sense of a presentation of the essence of Buddhism in imaginative form – is the foremost need it does not follow that it represents the most radical change. The most radical change is represented by the second of the three steps which, in Ambedkar's opinion, are quite necessary if the ideal of spreading Buddhism is to be realized, namely, to make changes in the organization, aims, and objects of the *bhikṣu saṅgha* or Monastic Order. For many 'born Buddhists' in the Buddhist countries of Asia the idea of making even the slightest change in the constitution of the *bhikṣu saṅgha* is unthinkable. Popular belief, both monastic and lay, insists that the Vinaya or Monastic Code was laid down, in all its details, by the Buddha himself, and that it has been preserved complete and unaltered down to the present day. As a scholarly student of Buddhism, Ambedkar knew that this was not really the case and that, even in the Theravāda countries of South-east Asia, the Vinaya had been altered from time to time, at least in actual practice. With his customary boldness he has, therefore, no hesitation in declaring that changes in the organization, aims, and objects of the *bhikṣu saṅgha* are needed – the more especially since he also believes that the Buddha gave full liberty to his followers to chip and chop as the necessities of the case required.

Before saying what kind of changes in the *bhikṣu saṅgha* he thinks necessary Ambedkar has something to say about the Buddhist *bhikṣu* and the Buddha's purpose in creating a separate society of *bhikṣus*. Proceeding from the known to the unknown, he declares that there is the world of difference between a Hindu sannyasi and a Buddhist *bhikṣu*.

> A Hindu *Sannyasi* has nothing to do with the world. He is dead to the world. A *Bhikkhu* has everything to do with the world.[126]

In saying that a Hindu sannyasi was dead to the world Ambedkar probably had in mind the fact that on the occasion of his initiation into the ascetic life an orthodox sannyasi performed his own obsequies, which meant that he was thereafter considered civilly dead and his property passed to his heirs. The *bhikṣu* performed no such obsequies for himself – though this certainly did not mean that in having 'everything to do with the world' he was involved with it in the same way, or for the same reasons, as the ordinary 'worldly' person. The *bhikṣu* had everything to do with the world in the sense that he was concerned with people's material and spiritual welfare, and it was possible for him to be concerned with people's material and spiritual welfare because though he was not civilly dead to the world, like the Hindu sannyasi, he was spiritually dead to it in that he was devoid of any mundane interest or ambition. In other words, the *bhikṣu* had 'everything to do with the world' *out of compassion* – a compassion that was the fruit of wisdom or insight. But though Ambedkar must have realized this he does not dwell upon the point and, having briefly described the difference between the Hindu sannyasi and the Buddhist *bhikṣu*, he moves straight on to the question of the Buddha's purpose in creating a separate society of *bhikṣus*.

According to Ambedkar, the Buddha established the *bhikṣu saṅgha* for three reasons: To provide a model of the ideal society, to create an intellectual elite, and to create a society whose members were free to render service to the people. Though the untouchable leader was 'on his way to embrace Buddhism' he was, at the same time, acutely conscious that it was 'a religion very difficult to practise' and that if its followers were to live up to the ideals embodied in the principles of Buddhism they would need all the help they could get, both personal and institutional. In particular, they would need a model of the ideal society, that is, a model of a society in which people actually practised Buddhism. That model was the *bhikṣu saṅgha*.

> Buddha knew that it was not possible for a common man to
> realize the Buddhist ideal. But He also wanted that the common
> man should know what the ideal was and also wanted [that] there
> should be placed before the common man a society of men who
> were bound to practise His ideals. That is why He created the
> *Bhikkhu Sangha* and bound it down by the rules of *Vinaya*.[127]

In saying that it is impossible for a common man to realize the Buddhist ideal Ambedkar no doubt means that it is *difficult* for him to realize it, or that it is impossible for him to realize it while still adhering to his old attitudes and beliefs. If it were literally impossible for a common man to realize the Buddhist ideal, even to a limited extent, then there would be no point in placing the model of an ideal society before him, for a model is meant not simply to be admired but to be imitated. What this in fact implies is that there are degrees in the realization of the ideal, and that those members of the Buddhist community who have realized it to a greater extent provide a model for those who have realized it to a lesser extent. The difference between those who provide a model and those for whom they provide it does not, however, necessarily correspond to the formal difference between the *bhikṣus* and those who Ambedkar designates 'the laymen'.

About the Buddha's two other reasons for establishing the *bhikṣu saṅgha* Ambedkar has little to say, though that little is of considerable interest. The function of the *bhikṣu saṅgha* as an intellectual elite being, apparently, 'to give the laymen true and impartial guidance'[128] he is of the opinion that it was for this reason that the Buddha prohibited the (individual) *bhikṣu* from owning property (other than his three robes, bowl, etc.).

> Ownership of property is one of the greatest obstacles in free
> thinking and application of free thought.[129]

This is, perhaps, an oversimplification of a complex issue or even a half-truth. Members of the wealthy, property-owning 'Siamese' subdivision of the Sinhalese branch of the *bhikṣu saṅgha* have been known to argue that they have greater freedom of thought and action than their poorer 'Burmese' brethren because the latter, being economically dependent on the laity, are subject to pressure from that quarter and are, in consequence, often unable to speak their minds even on matters directly concerning the Dhamma. Thus Ambedkar's pronouncement is not altogether beyond dispute, even though it may be granted that it is essential that whatever guidance is given by an intellectual elite such as the *bhikṣu saṅgha* should be true and impartial and that, therefore, steps ought to be taken to create the conditions necessary to ensure its truth and impartiality. With regard to the Buddha's third reason for establishing a *bhikṣu saṅgha*, Ambedkar is of the opinion that it was because he wanted to create 'a society the members of which would be free to do service to the people' that the Buddha 'did not want the *Bhikṣus* to marry',[130] presumably on the principle that no man can serve two masters, or because, in the well known words of Sir Francis Bacon, he that has wife and children has 'given hostages to fortune'.[131] But though it was because the Buddha wanted him to be free to serve the people that he did not want the *bhikṣu* to marry, this was not the only reason. 'Not marrying' also meant leading a life of chastity, and chastity was an important part of the spiritual life – so much so, indeed, that in Sanskrit and Pāli the word *brahmacarya* or *brahmacariya* connotes both chastity and the spiritual life itself. This aspect of 'not marrying' Ambedkar does not, however, pursue.

The *bhikṣu saṅgha* thus having been established to provide a model of the ideal society, to create an intellectual elite, and to create a society whose members were free to render service to the people, there arises an important question, a question Ambedkar is not afraid to ask – and to answer.

> Is the *Bhikkhu Sangha* of today living up to these ideals? The answer is emphatically in the negative. It neither guides the people nor does it serve them.[132]

This is, of course, rather sweeping, but Ambedkar has his reasons. Casting his eye over the Buddhist countries of South-east Asia, in particular, the first thing that strikes him is how many *bhikṣus* there actually are. In fact, in his opinion there are too many *bhikṣus* and of these, he says,

> a very large majority are merely *Sadhus* and *Sannyasis* spending their time in meditation or idleness. There is in them neither learning nor service. When the idea of service to suffering humanity comes to one's mind everyone thinks of the Ramakrishna Mission. No one thinks of the Buddhist *Sangha*. Who should regard service as its pious duty? The *Sangha* or the Mission? There can be no doubt about the answer. Yet the *Sangha* is a huge army of idlers.[133]

Thus in Ambedkar's view the *bhikṣu saṅgha* of today is not living up to its ideals because its members have, to all intents and purposes, ceased to be Buddhist *bhikṣus* and become Hindu sadhus and sannyasis – a sadhu being a kind of freelance sannyasi who often is no better than an ordinary beggar. In strictly Buddhist terms, the *bhikṣus* have given up the altruistic bodhisattva ideal and adopted the individualistic Arahant ideal, by which is meant not the Arahant ideal taught by the Buddha (which in principle does not differ from the bodhisattva ideal) but its later 'Hīnayāna' distortion. It is no doubt for this reason that Ambedkar describes the majority of *bhikṣus* as spending their time in 'meditation or idleness', leaving it unclear whether these are alternative occupations or the same thing. By meditation he means, in this context, not the development of calm and insight (*śamatha* and *vipaśyanā*), which between them constitute the royal road to the attainment of Supreme Enlightenment for the benefit of all sentient beings, but rather the subtly individualistic enjoyment of higher states of consciousness for their own sake regardless of the sufferings of the world.

The Ramakrishna Mission, to which Ambedkar so unfavourably compares today's *bhikṣu saṅgha*, was established in 1897 by the famous Hindu preacher Swami Vivekananda with the aim of spreading the teachings of his master, the Bengali mystic Shri Ramakrishna, and the organization was well known in India for its social, educational, and medical work. Ironically enough, Vivekananda had modelled the Order of Sannyasins of Ramakrishna, the ascetic confraternity that conducted the Mission's activities, partly on the ancient *bhikṣu saṅgha* as known to him from the writings of Western orientalists. Ambedkar may not have been aware of this fact. Aware of it or not, when it came to remodelling the ineffective *bhikṣu saṅgha* of today he looked, despite his appreciation of the Ramakrishna Mission's 'service to suffering humanity', not to the Mission but to the Roman Catholic church. Declaring that what was wanted, in place of the 'huge army of idlers', was fewer *bhikṣus* and *bhikṣus* who were highly educated, he observed:

> *Bhikkhu Sangha* must borrow some of the features of the Christian priesthood particularly the Jesuits. Christianity has spread in Asia through service – educational and medical. This is possible because the Christian priest is not merely versed in religious lore but because he is also versed in Arts and Science.[134]

The reference to the Jesuits is interesting. They were the missionaries to Asia *par excellence*, and the fully fledged Jesuit was, in the words of a source with which Ambedkar is known to have been familiar,

> a man well over thirty, who for at least a dozen years had been going through a process of formation under strict control, a large part of the time having been spent in study, three years in purely spiritual discipline, and, ordinarily speaking, another long period in the teaching or moral supervision of youth.[135]

The same source goes on to point out that the Jesuit system of training stood in acute contrast to the haste with which the earlier monastic and mendicant Orders often bound their members by solemn and irrevocable vows before they were well out of their teens.[136]

Reading these lines Ambedkar would have been reminded of the speed with which the *bhikṣu saṅgha* ordained its own youthful recruits, even though, in the case of *śrāmaṇeras* and *bhikṣus*, the vows taken were technically not irrevocable. He would also have known that unlike the *bhikṣu* the Jesuit was not obliged to wear a special clerical dress on all occasions, so that it was much easier for him to work with and among people and to be accepted by them as one of themselves.

But though Ambedkar believed that inasmuch as the *bhikṣu saṅgha* of today neither guided nor served it could, in its present condition, 'be of no use for the spread of Buddhism', and though he believed that it 'must borrow some features of the Christian priesthood particularly the Jesuits', he was, at the same time, well aware that things had not always been thus. There had been a period when the Buddhist *bhikṣu*, too, was versed not merely in religious lore but in the arts and sciences.

> This was really the ideal of the *Bhikkhus* of olden times. As is well known the Universities of Nalanda and Taxila were run and manned by *Bhikkhus*. Evidently they must have been very learned men and knew that social service was essential for the propagation of their faith.[137]

Here Ambedkar clearly sees the ancient Buddhist *saṅgha* as the precursor of both the Ramakrishna Mission and the Jesuits, and he continues with the moving words:

> The *Bhikkhus* of today must return to the old ideal. The *Sangha* as [it] is composed cannot render this [social] service to the laity and cannot therefore attract people to itself.[138]

This need for the *bhikṣu* of today to return to the old ideal is closely connected with the third of the three steps which, in Ambedkar's opinion, are necessary if the ideal of spreading Buddhism is to be realized, namely, the setting up a world Buddhist Mission.

Without a Mission Buddhism can hardly spread. As education requires to be given, religion requires to be propagated.[139]

Though Ambedkar does not go into the question, it is evident from the whole trend of his thinking that his world Buddhist Mission must be either a reformed or revitalized *bhikṣu saṅgha*, or, if the *bhikṣu saṅgha* is incapable of reforming itself, an entirely new body that will re-create the ancient Buddhist ideal of *saṅgha* or Spiritual Community in a form appropriate to modern conditions. Ambedkar is, of course, fully aware of the practical difficulties that the immense task of setting up a world Buddhist Mission would involve.

Propagation [or propaganda] cannot be undertaken without men and money. Who can supply these? Obviously countries where Buddhism is a living religion. It is these countries which must find the men and money at least in its initial stages. Will these? There does not seem to be much enthusiasm in these countries for the spread of Buddhism.[140]

Unfortunately, Ambedkar's impression proved to be justified, and during the thirty years that have passed since his death the Buddhist countries of Asia have found few men and little money for propaganda. Least of all have they found either men or money for propaganda in India. Typical of their attitude was the reply of a Thai *bhikṣu* who, when asked if he and his friends would come and work in India among the newly converted ex-Untouchable Buddhists, replied, 'Why should we work in India? We are quite comfortable in our own country.'

Yet despite the Buddhist countries' seeming lack of enthusiasm for the spread of Buddhism Ambedkar believes that, paradoxically, '[the] time seems quite propitious for the spread of Buddhism'.[141] The reason for this state of affairs is that nowadays religion is no longer simply part of one's inheritance, and one is free to examine its (supposed) merit and virtues. One is even free to reject religion altogether, as many throughout the world have had the unprecedented courage to do, either as the result of the influence of scientific enquiry or as a result of Marxist teaching. Whatever the causes may be, the fact is that people have developed an enquiring mind in respect of religion and the question of whether religion is at all worth having and, if so, which religion is worth having, are questions which according to Ambedkar are uppermost in the minds of those who dare to think about the subject. He is therefore convinced that so far as the spreading of Buddhism is concerned the time has come.

> What is wanted is will. If the countries which are Buddhist can develop the will to spread Buddhism the task of spreading Buddhism will not be difficult. They must realize that the duty of a Buddhist is not merely to be a good Buddhist, his duty is to spread Buddhism. They must believe that to spread Buddhism is to serve mankind.[142]

Shortly after sharing his thoughts on 'The Buddha and the Future of His Religion' with the readers of the *Maha Bodhi* and, through them, with Buddhists of the world, Ambedkar left for Ceylon (Sri Lanka), where he attended the inaugural meeting of the World Fellowship of Buddhists, observed Buddhist ceremonies and rituals, and tried to find out to what extent Buddhism was a living religion in Ceylon. In May 1954, and again in December 1954, he visited Burma. From these two Buddhist countries he returned not with the men and the money that were needed for the propagation of Buddhism in India but only with promises of help and (in the case of Burma) an image of the Buddha, which was duly installed in a newly constructed temple at Dehu Road, near Poona. Nonetheless, the great untouchable leader continued to be on his way to embrace Buddhism, and continued to think about Buddhism until, six years after the appearance of his article, the day dawned when he was no longer on his way but had arrived and when thinking about Buddhism was transformed into the reality of Buddhism itself.

7

THE GREAT MASS CONVERSION

Ambedkar arrived at his spiritual destination, along with nearly 400,000 of his followers, on 14 October 1956, the place being Nagpur. Neither the time nor the place of the great mass conversion, as it came to be called, had been decided upon without a good deal of deliberation. October marked the end of the rainy season, when the weather would neither be very hot (by Indian standards) nor particularly cold, and when it would be easy for people to travel, while that year 14 October happened to be the day of the great Hindu festival of Dussehra. According to Hindu tradition Dussehra, also known as Vijaya Dashami or 'Victory Tenth', was the anniversary of Rama's triumphant return to his capital after slaying Ravana, the ten-headed demon king of Lanka. It was a festival of lights, for in honour of the hero's return his loyal subjects had illuminated the city with thousands of oil lamps, and on Dussehra night devout Hindus still placed rows of oil lamps before their houses. So far as Ambedkar and his followers were concerned, however, Ashok Vijaya Dashmi (as they termed it) commemorated not Rama's return from Lanka but the emperor Aśoka's return from subduing the people of Kalinga and his subsequent conversion from belief in conquest by means of war (*yuddhavijaya*) to belief in conquest by means of righteousness (*dharmavijaya*). Thus for Ambedkar and his followers, even more than for the Hindus, the festival of Dussehra symbolized the victory of the forces of light over the forces of darkness – symbolized, in fact, the victory of Buddhism over Brahmanism.

The place of the great mass conversion was no less significant than its time. The city of Nagpur, then the capital of the State of Madhya Pradesh, was situated exactly in the centre of (divided) India, and in the very region associated – according to some scholars – with the great Buddhist sage Nāgārjuna, sometimes called the second founder of Buddhism. Moreover Nagpur, as its name suggested, was the city of the Nagas, and it was the Nagas who, Ambedkar believed, had worked in the beginning for the propagation of Buddhism. As he explained when he addressed the vast gathering on the day following the conversion, the Nagas were non-Āryans, and between the Āryans and the Nagas there existed fierce enmity.

> Many a battle was fought between the Aryans and the non-Aryans. Aryans wanted to completely annihilate the Nagas. There are many legends to be found in the Puranas in this connection. Aryans had burned Nagas [alive]. The Sage 'Agastya' saved one Naga and we are supposed to be the descendants of that Naga.

Nor was that all.

> [The Nagas] needed a great man to liberate them and they found that great man in the person of Lord Buddha. Bhagwan Buddha saved them from decay and extinction. It was the Nagas who spread the religion of the Buddha throughout the world.... This is mainly the reason for selecting Nagpur for this great occasion.[143]

Thus Nagpur was selected instead of Bombay or Sarnath (which at one stage were also under consideration) not just on geographical and historical grounds but for very much deeper reasons. It was selected because Ambedkar believed that he and his followers had their spiritual roots in Nagpur. *'We are supposed to be the descendants of that Naga.'* In these words, at once both humble and proud, we see Ambedkar identifying himself and his followers with the Nagas, and through them with Buddhism, in much the same way as in *The Untouchables* he had identified the Untouchables with those Broken Men who had refused to give up Buddhism and who had been punished by the Brahmins for their refusal. In both cases he was seeking to establish an emotional connection with Buddhism. He was trying to convince himself, and trying to convince his followers, that in embracing Buddhism they were not adopting an alien creed but were simply reclaiming a spiritual heritage of which they had been unjustly deprived and whose existence they had forgotten for centuries.

From this it is obvious how little foundation there was for the accusation that Ambedkar had chosen Nagpur as the venue of the conversion ceremony because it was the headquarters of the Rashtriya Swayamsevak Sangh, a right-wing Hindu organization, and because he wanted to annoy them by doing something spectacular right in front of their eyes. As he himself said, this was not true. He had no desire to irritate or provoke anybody by 'scratching his nose' nor did he have any time for such childish pranks. When selecting Nagpur for the historic ceremony he had not had even the remotest idea of the RSS in his mind, and the city had been selected for a reason very different from the one alleged. Ambedkar had, in fact, chosen Nagpur for basically spiritual reasons and these reasons were no more a matter of party politics than the conversion itself was 'only a political stunt' as his opponents afterwards tried to make out.

There was certainly no thought of politics in the minds of the tens of thousands of men, women, and children who, in response to their Baba Saheb's call, left home in the course of the week prior to the ceremony and made their way to Nagpur by train, by motorbus, and by bullock cart from all over the Marathi-speaking areas of central and western India. Those who were unable to find transport travelled the entire distance on foot, with parents and others carrying children who were too young to walk. By whatsoever means they came, all of them, even the poorest, clad in the spotless white shirts and saris that had been prescribed for the occasion by their beloved leader. Some families had had to sell trinkets in order to buy their new clothes and meet the expenses of the journey, but they had made the sacrifice gladly, and set out for Nagpur with songs on their lips and the hope of a new life in their hearts. Those who were making the journey on foot formed themselves into companies of a hundred or more and marched seven or eight abreast behind men carrying banners inscribed with such slogans as, 'Baba Saheb gives the call: Embrace Buddhism one and all!' and 'Move the heavens, move the earth! Turn to Buddhism and have a new birth!' Every now and then one of the more brazen-throated members of the group would raise a cry of 'Victory to the Lord Buddha! Victory to Baba Saheb Ambedkar!' to which the deep voices of the men and the shrill voices of the women and children would respond with an exultant 'Victory!' that could be heard several miles away. On their arrival at Nagpur railway station, at the motorbus depots, or at the reception posts that had been set up on the roads into the city, the pilgrims – for such they were – were met by members of the Indian Buddhist Society's volunteer corps and given whatever help they needed. Some stayed with relations in the Mahar ghettoes, of which there were three or four dozen in and around Nagpur, while others were accommodated in school buildings that had been taken over for the purpose. Many simply camped on any patch of waste ground they could find and cooked, ate, and slept either in improvised shelters or in the open air. By the end of the week 400,000 men, women, and children had poured into Nagpur, with the result that the population had nearly doubled and the white-clad Untouchables had virtually taken over the city. The caste Hindus, who were accustomed to think of the Untouchables as dirty and undisciplined, gazed with astonishment at the spectacle of tens upon tens of thousands of clean, decently dressed, well behaved and well organized people in whom they had difficulty in recognizing their former slaves and serfs.

Ambedkar himself arrived by air from Delhi on 11 October accompanied by his wife and N. C. Rattu, his private secretary, and was accommodated in a hotel in the heart of the city. Two days later, on the eve of Vijaya Dashami, he held a press conference at the hotel and made clear his position on a number of issues. The most important of these, from a Buddhist point of view, was the question of which form of Buddhism he would be adopting when he embraced Buddhism. The caste Hindu press, quick to seize upon any opportunity of sowing dissension among the Buddhists and creating confusion in the minds of Ambedkar's followers, had professed great concern about this matter, but with a few straightforward words the great leader cut through the net in which they were trying to entangle him. His Buddhism would adhere to the tenets of the faith as taught by the Buddha himself, he told the assembled reporters, without involving his people in differences which had arisen on account of Hīnayāna and Mahāyāna. His Buddhism would be a sort of neo-Buddhism or Navayāna. By this Ambedkar did not mean that his Buddhism would be an entirely different form of Buddhism, as distinct from Hīnayāna and Mahāyāna as they were distinct from each other, but rather that it would be a Buddhism stripped of the 'dead wood' referred to in 'The Buddha and the Future of His Religion' and based on principles which, having been taught by the Buddha, were the common foundation of Hīnayāna and Mahāyāna and, in fact, the foundation of any form of Buddhism deserving of the name. Thus when he and his followers came to embrace Buddhism the next day they would literally be embracing just Buddhism and would, therefore, be becoming neither Hīnayānists nor Mahāyānists but simply Buddhists. Far from wanting to establish a separate sect in the name of Buddhism they would be joining the world-wide Buddhist spiritual community – though joining it only to the extent that that community was faithful to the teaching of the Buddha.

At his press conference Ambedkar had no time to make all this clear. Most of the reporters not only represented caste Hindu-controlled newspapers but were themselves caste Hindus of one kind or another and they wanted to know – or pretended to want to know – why Ambedkar was embracing Buddhism, as though there was a great mystery surrounding the matter which he was unwilling to allow them to penetrate. Provoked by their insincerity, as well as by the hostile manner in which they raised the question of his motives, Ambedkar angrily demanded,

Why cannot you [put] this question to yourself and to your
forefathers as to why I am getting out of the Hindu fold and
embracing Buddhism?[144]

By this he meant that he was renouncing Hinduism and adopting another religion on account of the inhuman treatment he and his fellow Untouchables had for generations suffered at the hands of the caste Hindus, as the reporters knew perfectly well was the case, though like the vast majority of caste Hindus they feigned ignorance of the fact. To have admitted that they knew why Ambedkar was embracing Buddhism would have meant admitting that they knew that the responsibility for his departure from the Hindu fold rested fairly and squarely on their own shoulders and on the shoulders of their forefathers and this they could not bring themselves to do. Shifting their ground, the reporters therefore raised the issue of the reserved seats and other concessions to which, as Scheduled Caste Hindus, Ambedkar's followers were legally entitled. Would it not be a disaster if they lost these as a result of giving up Hinduism and embracing Buddhism? But once again Ambedkar answered their question with one of his own. Did they want his people to remain Untouchables, he asked the reporters, simply in order to go on enjoying such 'benefits' as those of reservation? If the latter were, in fact, so highly desirable were the Brahmins, for example, prepared to be Untouchables in order to enjoy them? What the Untouchables were really doing, he added in a more conciliatory tone, was making an effort to achieve manhood, which meant learning to stand on their own feet without the help of concessions. As for their embracing Buddhism, he had once told Mahatma Gandhi that though he differed from him on the issue of Untouchability when the time came he would choose only the least harmful way for the country. 'And that is the greatest benefit I am conferring on the country by embracing Buddhism,' he continued proudly, 'for Buddhism is a part and parcel of Bharatiya culture. I have taken care that my conversion will not harm the tradition of the culture and history of this land.'[145]

This was no more than the truth, and the reporters were therefore obliged to listen in silence as Ambedkar, warming to his theme, went on to predict that within the next ten or fifteen years the wave of mass conversion would spread all over the country, and India would become a Buddhist country. The Brahmins would be the last to follow, and let them be the last! If mass conversion on such a scale seemed impossible, he told his silent but obviously sceptical audience, then let them remember how in the days of the Roman Empire the most despised sections of the population had embraced the Christian faith and how Christianity had eventually taken over the mighty Roman Empire itself. Admittedly his followers were at present ignorant, but through his writings and speeches he would educate them in the principles of Buddhism. Poor and ignorant though they were, they at least preferred honour to bread, as their readiness to embrace Buddhism and lose their concessions showed. Yet though prepared to sacrifice their concessions if necessary, his followers were not indifferent to material things and would make every effort to improve their economic condition.

From economics to politics was only a short step, and soon Ambedkar was having to answer questions about the forthcoming general elections, the second to be held since Independence, and about his own political position. He wanted to form a new political party, he declared, and he wanted to form it before the elections took place. The new party would be called the Republican Party, and it would be open to all who accepted its three guiding principles of liberty, equality, and fraternity. He himself would be contesting election to the Lok Sabha from a suitable constituency on the Republican Party ticket and he would be fighting for – among other things – the abolition of the newly created bilingual State of Bombay which combined Gujarat and Maharashtra. With this end in view he extended his wholehearted support to the Samyukta Maharashtra Samiti, which was fighting for a united Maharashtra with the city of Bombay as its capital.

But even when the press conference was over and the largely unsympathetic reporters had left, Ambedkar, tired though he was, had still not finished with politics – or rather, politics had still not finished with him. Some of the younger and more ambitious of his lieutenants, afraid that conversion to Buddhism would spoil their chances of getting into the Lok Sabha, did their utmost to prevail upon their sixty-four-year-old leader to postpone the conversion ceremony until after the elections. For Ambedkar this was absolutely out of the question. There were upwards of half a million Untouchables in Nagpur, all eagerly looking forward to the following day as the greatest day of their lives, and it was unthinkable that he should disappoint them. Moreover, he was a very sick man, and if the conversion ceremony was not held as planned it would perhaps not be held at all. To these and other arguments the lieutenants in question turned a deaf ear and in the end a deeply distressed Ambedkar had no alternative but to assert his authority. He had made up his mind once and for all, he told them as he dismissed them from his presence, and no power on earth was going to stop him embracing Buddhism the following day. They could embrace it or not embrace it with him as they pleased, but if they decided not to embrace it they would have to take the consequences. Overawed, they withdrew their objections and took leave of their great leader with assurances of their unqualified support.

Wednesday 14 October dawned calm and bright, with a sky of unbroken blue. Having awoken early, Ambedkar asked Rattu to arrange for a hot bath and then to go and see if arrangements for the forthcoming ceremony were complete. On his return the faithful secretary reported that all was well and that vast crowds of white-clad people could be seen streaming towards the Diksha Bhumi or Initiation Ground from every part of the city. They had, in fact, been on the move for several hours, though early as they were the sweepers had been up even earlier, sweeping the road at daybreak and making sure that not a speck of dirt would be visible when their great emancipator passed that way. What was more, as an increasingly brilliant sun rose higher in an increasingly blue sky, and as the vast crowds slowly converged on the Diksha Bhumi in a solid mass of white-clad humanity, the shouts of 'Victory to the Lord Buddha!' and 'Victory to Baba Saheb Ambedkar!' became so loud that they could be heard even in the remotest parts of the city.

At exactly 8.30 a.m. Ambedkar, wearing a white silk dhoti and knee-length coat, left by car for the Diksha Bhumi with his wife, who was wearing a white sari, and Rattu. The Diksha Bhumi was a fourteen-acre enclosure situated on an expanse of open ground near the Vaccine Institute at Shraddhanand Peth. At the northern end of the enclosure stood a roofed-in stage hung on three of its sides with white cloth and surmounted by the hemispherical form of a replica of the Sanchi Stupa, so that it looked like a great white marquee open down one of its longer sides. On Ambedkar's arrival at the Diksha Bhumi, which was gaily decorated with bunting and with the five-hued international Buddhist flag, a wave of excitement passed through the vast gathering, and so eager were those nearest the gangway to get a glimpse of their hero, or even to touch his feet, that his progress to the stage was seriously delayed. Having at length reached it, and having been assisted up the steps, he stood facing his people with bowed head and half-closed eyes, one hand grasping a bamboo staff while the other rested on Rattu's shoulder – the very picture of a pilgrim who has well-nigh reached the end of his journey. For an instant the crowd was silent, then broke into thunderous applause. It was now 9.15 a.m. Silently acknowledging the ovation, Ambedkar took his seat near the centre of the stage in between his wife and the wrinkled, russet-robed U Chandramani, the oldest and seniormost *bhikṣu* in India, whom he had invited specially to Nagpur to officiate at the ceremony. To the right of U Chandramani stood a small table, and on the table there was a gleaming brass Buddha-image flanked by two bronze-gilt *chinthes*.[146] In front of this improvised shrine incense was burning. Seated behind Ambedkar and U Chandramani were Devapriya Valisinha, the Sinhalese General Secretary of the Maha Bodhi Society, in white Indian shirt and lungi, together with Venerable Sangharatana and three other Sinhalese *bhikṣus* belonging to the Society, all of them resplendent in bright yellow robes. To the rear of the stage, as well as to the right of the Buddha-image and the left of Mrs Ambedkar, sat and stood leading members of the Scheduled Caste Federation and the Indian Buddhist Society – among them some of the young politicians who had wanted Ambedkar to postpone the conversion ceremony until after the general elections.

In accordance with Indian custom, the proceedings opened with a song, and on this occasion the song was, not unnaturally, in praise of Ambedkar. When it was over the entire gathering stood for a minute's silence in memory of Ambedkar's father, who had died more than forty-three years earlier and without whose constant encouragement the gifted young Bhimrao Ramji might never have grown up to be the leader and emancipator of his people – might never have led them to the promised land of Buddhism. Honour having been paid where honour was due, the actual conversion ceremony could now begin. As 400,000 pairs of eyes followed their every movement, the white-clad Ambedkar and his wife rose and stood before U Chandramani with their hands joined in the traditional 'lotus bud' and heads slightly bowed. U Chandramani, who was seated cross-legged on his chair, then recited the time-honoured formula of 'Going for Refuge' to the Buddha, the Dharma, and the Sangha. '*Buddham saranam gacchāmi,*' the old man intoned in his impeccable Pāli, from which more than fifty years of residence in India had removed all trace of a Burmese accent, '*Dhammam saranam gacchāmi, sangham saranam gacchāmi*'; and Ambedkar and his wife, their heads turned in the direction of the gleaming brass Buddha image, repeated the formula three times after him. Though the vast gathering was not aware of the fact, it had originally been Ambedkar's intention to take only the first and second Refuges, since in his view the present day *bhikṣu sangha* was part of the 'dead wood' that would have to be removed if Buddhism was to spread and taking refuge in it was therefore a waste of time. Devapriya Valisinha, who at Ambedkar's suggestion had arrived in Nagpur early, had however pointed out to him that if he and his followers did not take refuge in the Sangha, as well as in the Buddha and the Dharma, they would not be recognized as Buddhists by the rest of the Buddhist world and the great leader had therefore eventually changed his mind. Besides this more practical consideration there was also the point that – as Ambedkar may have known – the *sangha* to which one goes for Refuge is not the *bhikṣu saṅgha* or Monastic Order as such but the *Āryasaṅgha* or 'Spiritual Community' of all those who, whether in the past, the present, or the future, and whether as monks or nuns or as laymen or laywomen, have attained one or another of the stages of the transcendental path. Thus it was that when U Chandramani recited '*Saṅghaṃ saraṇaṃ gacchāmi*,' Ambedkar and his wife repeated it after him and Valisinha, who was seated only a few yards away, breathed a sigh of relief. After the Refuges came the precepts, and repeating the formula for these, too, after U Chandramani, the pair undertook to abstain from harming living beings, from taking the not-given, from sexual misconduct, from false speech, and from indulgence in intoxicating drinks and drugs. Twenty-one years after his declaration that though he had been born a Hindu he would not die a Hindu, Ambedkar had redeemed his pledge. He was now a Buddhist, and as he and Savita Ambedkar bowed three times before the image of the Buddha and offered white lotus flowers the great assembly gave expression to its feelings on the occasion with full throated cries of 'Victory to the Lord Buddha!' and 'Victory to Baba Saheb Ambedkar!' The time was 9.45 a.m.

But though he had gone for Refuge to the Three Jewels in the traditional manner and was now a Buddhist, Ambedkar had one thing more to do before the ceremony was, for him, complete. As soon as his closest supporters had garlanded him and Valisinha had presented him with a Sarnath-style image of the Buddha, he therefore again rose to his feet and repeated a series of twenty-two vows which he had drawn up specially for the occasion. In these vows he pledged himself not to believe in the gods and goddesses of Hinduism or to worship them, not to regard the Buddha as an incarnation of Vishnu, not to perform the traditional Hindu rites for the dead, and not to employ Brahmins to conduct religious ceremonies, as well as – more positively – to believe in and seek to establish the equality of men (which amounted to a repudiation of the caste system), to follow the path shown by the Buddha, and to observe the Buddhist precepts. The twenty-two vows were, perhaps, summed up in the last four, in which Ambedkar declared,

I renounce Hinduism which is harmful for humanity and the
advancement and development of humanity because it is based on
inequality, and adopt Buddhism as my religion. I firmly believe that
the Dhamma of the Buddha is the only true religion. I believe that I

am having a [spiritual] rebirth. I solemnly declare and affirm that I shall hereafter lead my life according to the principles and teachings of the Buddha and his Dhamma.[147]

Once or twice in the course of repeating his vows, especially when abjuring the worship of the Hindu gods and goddesses and pronouncing the fateful words 'I renounce Hinduism' the great leader seemed greatly moved, his voice choking slightly as he spoke. At such moments he was, no doubt, experiencing a variety of conflicting emotions, from joy and thankfulness at his liberation from Hinduism to bitter regret and even resentment at the thought of all the misery and degradation that he and his people had had to endure at the hands of the followers of that religion.

These emotions did not, however, last very long. His conversion to Buddhism having been completed to his own satisfaction, Ambedkar turned to the 400,000 white-clad figures sitting below him in the enclosure, men on the right and women and children on the left, and in a voice that boomed and crackled from the loudspeakers called upon all those who wanted to embrace Buddhism to stand up. In response to his call the whole vast gathering rose as one man, hands joined in the traditional 'lotus bud' in readiness, whereupon Ambedkar repeated first the Three Refuges, then the Five Precepts, and finally the twenty-two vows, and as one man the whole vast assembly repeated them after him in loud and joyous tones. Thus in the space of half an hour 400,000 people became Buddhists. Ambedkar had made Buddhist history. Indeed, he had made it in more ways than one. Quite apart from the unprecedented number of people he had brought with him into the Buddhist fold (and he was to bring many more the following day and the day after), thus making possible the revival of Buddhism in India on a scale that the pessimists had thought impossible, he had made Buddhist history by himself administering the Three Refuges and Five Precepts to his followers and by making the twenty-two vows an integral part of the conversion ceremony.

In making Buddhist history in these two ways Ambedkar was not, of course, simply making Buddhist history but also, at the same time, breaking with tradition – or with what had come to be regarded as tradition. In the Buddhist countries of South-east Asia, at least, it was – and still is – unthinkable for a mere layman to administer the Refuges and Precepts in the presence of *bhikṣus*. Such a proceeding would have been considered as showing gross disrespect not only to those *bhikṣus* who were actually present but to the whole *bhikṣu saṅgha* and would not have been tolerated for an instant. The reason for this was not far to seek. What had originally been no more than a difference between those followers of the Buddha who lived as *bhikṣus* or monks (or as *bhikṣunīs* or nuns) and those followers of the Buddha who lived as *upāsakas* or laymen (or as *upāsikās* or laywomen) had in the course of centuries hardened into an actual division between the two groups, with the result that the *bhikṣus* had come to be regarded as the real Buddhists (the *bhikṣunīs* had by that time dropped out of the picture) and the laity as simply their humble supporters. It was, therefore, the *bhikṣus* who took the lead in all religious – and sometimes even in political and social – matters and who officiated at all ceremonies. In particular it was the *bhikṣus* – generally the seniormost one present – who administered the Refuges and Precepts to the laity whenever the latter wished to 'take' them, that is, when they wished to repeat them after a *bhikṣu* as an act of piety or as a means of affirming their membership of a particular ethnic group. Ambedkar's action in administering the Refuges and Precepts to his followers himself, instead of allowing U Chandramani to administer them, therefore represented a bold and dramatic departure from existing South-east Asian Buddhist praxis and, indirectly, a return to something more in accordance with the spirit of the Buddha's teaching. Indeed, by demonstrating that an *upāsaka* no less than a *bhikṣu* could administer the Refuges and Precepts, Ambedkar was reminding both the old Buddhists and the new that the difference between those who lived as *bhikṣus* and those who lived as *upāsakas* and *upāsikās* was only a difference, not a division, since all alike went for Refuge to the Buddha, the Dharma, and the Sangha. Thus he was, in effect, asserting the fundamental unity of the whole Buddhist spiritual community, male and female, monastic and lay.

Ambedkar's other break with tradition, namely, making the twenty-two vows an integral part of the conversion ceremony, had much the same kind of significance. That too was, in effect, an assertion of the fundamental unity of the whole Buddhist spiritual community. One of the main reasons for the eventual disappearance of Buddhism from India was the fact that although there was an initiation ceremony for monks, whereby they were formally received into the monastic order, there was no really-corresponding ceremony for lay people, with the result that many of the latter were unable to identify themselves with the Buddhist spiritual community and the Buddhist spiritual tradition in the way the monks did. The result of this state of affairs was twofold. Not only was the division – as distinct from the difference – between the monks and the lay people exacerbated but the loyalties of the lay people became increasingly divided between Buddhism on the one hand and the various cults of a resurgent Brahmanism on the other. A high proportion of the monks had, moreover, tended to congregate in large monasteries which were economically dependent not – as the monks had been before – on the good will of the local lay Buddhist population but on royal patronage. When these monasteries were destroyed by the Muslim invaders, therefore, and their occupants either killed or dispersed, an already half-Hinduized Buddhist laity fell increasingly under the influence of the Brahmins until, having lost their separate religious identity, they were eventually absorbed into the Hindu community (in the case of the Buddhist Broken Men, as Untouchables) and little or nothing remained to show that there had ever been such a thing as Buddhism in India. Knowing all this as he did, Ambedkar was determined to make sure that history did not repeat itself. Having converted his followers to Buddhism he was determined to make sure that they would remain Buddhists and that they would not, when he was no longer there to guide them, revert to their old ways and be reabsorbed into Hinduism.

Obviously, the only way in which he could do this was to make sure that they actually practised Buddhism (and gave up practising Hinduism). But they could hardly be expected to practise Buddhism unless they felt that they were real Buddhists, not merely supporters of the real Buddhists, and they could hardly be expected to feel that they were real Buddhists unless they felt that they were full members of the Buddhist spiritual community. This meant that they had to be formally received into the Buddhist spiritual community, just as a monk was formally received into the monastic order, and that they had to undertake to live as lay followers of the Buddha with the same seriousness as a monk undertook to live as a monk follower. In other words, it meant that in addition to taking the Three Refuges and the Five Precepts they also had to take the twenty-two vows, wherein the implication of taking the Three Refuges and the Five Precepts – that is, the implications of being a Buddhist and a member of the Buddhist spiritual community – were spelled out in some detail. It was this taking of the Three Refuges and the Five Precepts *and* the twenty-two vows that constituted conversion to Buddhism in the full sense, or what Ambedkar termed *Dhammadiksha* – Initiation into the Dharma.

Thus by making the twenty-two vows an integral part of the conversion ceremony Ambedkar did three things. He made it clear that embracing Buddhism meant repudiating Hinduism, he made it clear that a lay Buddhist was a full member of the Buddhist spiritual community (thereby asserting the fundamental unity of that community), and he made it clear that the lay Buddhist, no less than the monk, was expected actually to practise Buddhism. By the time the historic ceremony came to an end at 10.50 a.m. a tired but triumphant Ambedkar was therefore able to leave the Diksha Bhumi knowing that there were now 400,000 more Buddhists in the world than when he arrived there, and that he had placed the revival of Buddhism in modern India on a firm foundation.

What Ambedkar and his followers were doing in Nagpur did not pass altogether unnoticed by the rest of the Buddhist world. Messages of congratulation were received from U Ba Swe, the Prime Minister of Burma, and from U Nu, the former Prime Minister, as well as from a handful of prominent Indian, Sinhalese, and British Buddhists. No such message was received from any of the leading figures of either religious or secular India – not even from Ambedkar's former colleagues in the Cabinet, despite the fact that the Government of India was currently sponsoring the celebration of the 2500th Buddha Jayanti. Eulogizing the Buddha and his teaching from public platforms, and extolling the glories of India's ancient Buddhist heritage, was one thing. Declaring oneself a follower of the Buddha, and actually practising his teaching, was, it seemed, quite another.

The following day, Thursday 15 October, Ambedkar held a second conversion ceremony at the Diksha Bhumi and administered the Three Refuges, the Five Precepts, and the twenty-two vows to more than a 100,000 people who had arrived too late for the main ceremony, thus bringing the total number of converts to a round half million. The movement of mass conversion to Buddhism that he had so courageously inaugurated was beginning to gain momentum. He was also presented with an address of welcome by the Nagpur Municipal Corporation at the town hall. On both these occasions Ambedkar spoke at some length, though on rather different topics. Replying to the address of welcome, which gave expression to the Corporation's pleasure at receiving a 'social reformer, philosopher, and erudite constitutionalist like Baba Saheb', he denounced the ruling Congress Party in general, and its leader Pandit Nehru, the Prime Minister, in particular, in the most scathing terms, declaring that the Congress had made a mess of politics and that if it remained in power for long the country would be in flames. At the conversion ceremony he explained to the gathering why he had selected Nagpur as the place of the *Dhammadiksha*, replied in some detail to the critics who had accused him of misleading his downtrodden, poverty-stricken followers by choosing the path of conversion, declared that self-respect was more important than material gains, warned people that they would have to make sacrifices for Buddhism, recalled his Yeola declaration of 1935, and spoke of the 'enormous satisfaction' and 'unimaginable pleasure' that his conversion had given him. He felt, he said, as though he had been liberated from hell, and he wanted all those who were initiated into Buddhism to have the same experience. But, he added sharply,

> I do not want any blind followers. I do not like sheep mentality. Those who wish to come under the refuge of Buddha should do so [only] after counting the cost, for [Buddhism] is a religion very difficult to practise.[148]

Among the other subjects on which Ambedkar, out of the fullness of his heart, spoke on that occasion, was the subject of enthusiasm or inspiration. Without enthusiasm, he told the gathering, life became a mere drudgery, a mere burden to be borne. Without enthusiasm, nothing could be achieved, and the reason for the lack of enthusiasm was the loss of all hope of getting an opportunity to elevate oneself. It was the hopelessness that led to lack of enthusiasm, in which the mind became diseased. In the words of the Maharashtrian poet-saint, 'If a man lacks enthusiasm, either his mind or body is in a diseased condition'.[149] One who saw no hope of ever escaping from his present misery lacked enthusiasm and was always cheerless. Enthusiasm was created when one breathed an atmosphere in which one was sure of getting the legitimate reward for one's labours. Only then did one feel enriched by enthusiasm and inspiration. Hinduism, which was founded on the twin ideologies of inequality and injustice, unfortunately left no room for the development of enthusiasm. So long as the Untouchables continued to slave under the yoke of Hinduism, which was a diabolical creed, they could have no hope, no inspiration, no enthusiasm for a better life. They might produce a few hundred poor clerks who would do nothing except fill their own bellies but that would be all. The Untouchable masses would not gain anything. Consequently the Scheduled Castes could never feel enthusiasm about Hinduism or derive inspiration from it, for 'man derives inspiration [only] if his mind is free to develop.'[150]

In these few words Ambedkar gave expression to the real significance of the great mass conversion for his followers. By embracing Buddhism they had become free to develop, and since they had become free to develop – socially, economically, culturally, and spiritually – they were able to derive inspiration and to generate enthusiasm. As Buddhists, the ultimate source of their inspiration was, of course, the Three Jewels, but for the vast majority of them its immediate source was the great leader under whose guidance they had gone for Refuge to those Three Jewels. During the seven weeks of life that still remained to him they continued to derive inspiration mainly from his actual physical presence among them. After his death they derived inspiration from the memory of his noble example, from the record of his words, and from his published writings. Above all, perhaps, they derived inspiration from the book on which he had worked for a number of years and which was in the press at the time of his death: the famous and controversial *The Buddha and His Dhamma*.

8

'THE BUDDHA AND HIS DHAMMA'

The work which has been described as Ambedkar's *magnum opus* was written during the years 1951–6 and published by the People's Education Society in November 1957, almost a year after the great leader's death. In the preface he wrote for it in March 1956, but which did not appear in print until September 1980, Ambedkar traced the origin of the work to his article on 'The Buddha and the Future of His Religion'. In that article, he recalls, he had argued that the Buddha's religion was the only religion which a society awakened by science could accept and without which it would perish. He had also pointed out that in the modern world Buddhism was the only religion which it must have, if it was to save itself. But Buddhism made only a slow advance, and this was

> due to the fact that its literature is so vast and no one can read it [all] and it has no such thing as a Bible as the Christians have. On the publication of ['The Buddha and the Future of His Religion'] I received so many calls, written and oral, to write such a book. It is in response to these calls that I have undertaken the task.[151]

The writing of *The Buddha and His Dhamma* was thus an attempt on Ambedkar's part to produce the Buddhist Bible which he had, in his 1950 article, pronounced 'quite necessary' if the ideal of spreading Buddhism was to be realized. Despite his use of the inappropriate term 'Bible', however, Ambedkar was far from regarding *The Buddha and His*

Dhamma as possessing any special authority. As he wrote of the work in the (recently published) preface,

> How good it is I must leave it to readers to judge. As for myself, I claim no originality. I am only a compiler. All I hope is that the reader will like the presentation. I have made it simple and clear.[152]

Ambedkar was not, of course, the first person to be impressed by the vast extent of Buddhist literature, nor even the first to compile a volume of selections for the benefit of the common reader. As early as the ninth century CE the poet-sage Śāntideva had compiled – mainly from earlier Mahāyāna *sūtras* – his *Śikṣāsamuccaya* or 'Compendium of Instruction', and in modern times American and British scholars, in particular, have produced a number of such works. By far the most popular of these was Paul Carus's *The Gospel of Buddha*, published in 1894, which apart from Sir Edwin Arnold's *The Light of Asia* (1879) did more to promote the wider dissemination of Buddhism than any other book. Two years after Carus's best-seller came Henry Clarke Warren's *Buddhism in Translations*, a scholarly work which had a much more limited circulation. After an interval of several decades these pioneering efforts were followed by such well-known anthologies as F. L. Woodward's *Some Sayings of the Buddha* (1925), Dwight Goddard's *A Buddhist Bible* (1932), E. J. Thomas's *Early Buddhist Scriptures* (1935), J. G. Jennings' *The Vedantic Buddhism of the Buddha* (1947), E. Conze's *Buddhist Texts Through the Ages* (1954), and E. A. Burtt's *The Teachings of the Compassionate Buddha* (1955). These works, with most of which Ambedkar was familiar, fall into two groups. There are those anthologies which have been compiled from the Buddhist literature of one particular language and even of one particular school of Buddhism and those which have been compiled from the Buddhist literature of more than one language and of more than one school. A good example of the first kind is Woodward's *Some Sayings of the Buddha*, which consists entirely of translations from the Pāli scriptures of the Theravāda school, while a good example of the second is Conze's *Buddhist Texts Through the Ages*, which contains translations from the Pāli, Sanskrit, Chinese, Tibetan, Japanese, and Apabhraṃśa scriptures of the Hīnayāna, Mahāyāna, and Vajrayāna traditions. Each of these two groups of anthologies falls in its turn into two sub-groups, one consisting of anthologies containing only doctrinal material, the other of anthologies in which material illustrative of the Buddha's actual teaching is interwoven with material illustrative of the story of his life. Probably the best example of an anthology belonging to the first of these two sub-groups is Goddard's *Buddhist Bible*, which consists mainly of (sometimes shortened) versions of a limited number of major Pāli, Sanskrit, Chinese, and Tibetan doctrinal and spiritual texts. In terms of popularity, at least, no doubt the best example of an anthology belonging to the second sub-group is Carus's *The Gospel of Buddha*, which, as its title suggests, attempts to do for the founder of Buddhism what the fourth evangelist, in particular, did for the founder of Christianity.

It is not difficult to see to which group of anthologies, and which sub-group within that group, *The Buddha and His Dhamma* belongs. In the first place, it has been compiled from Buddhist canonical and non-canonical literature, in Pāli, Sanskrit, and Chinese, and from texts belonging to the Theravāda, Sarvastivāda, and Mahāyāna schools of Buddhism. In the second, it interweaves material illustrative of the Buddha's actual teaching with material illustrative of the story of his life, both of these being further interwoven with what Carus, in the case of *The Gospel of Buddha*, terms 'Explanatory Additions', the Explanatory Additions to *The Buddha and His Dhamma* being of course by Ambedkar himself. Between the work of the American scholar-scientist and the work of the Indian scholar-statesman there is, in fact, a closer resemblance than there is between *The Buddha and His Dhamma* and any of the other anthologies which have been mentioned. Both *The Gospel of Buddha* and *The Buddha and His Dhamma* are divided into eight books (as Ambedkar styles them), each book being subdivided into chapters and verses. More remarkable still, in the case of both works the verses are all numbered, the numbering being separate for each chapter.

But though there are resemblances between *The Buddha and His Dhamma* and *The Gospel of Buddha* there are also differences. On the whole, the material contained in *The Buddha and His Dhamma* is more systematically organized, and Ambedkar's Explanatory Additions are not only much more numerous than Carus's but more substantial in character. The biggest difference between the two anthologies, however, consists in the fact that they were intended for two very different audiences. Whereas Carus compiled *The Gospel of Buddha* mainly, though not exclusively, for the benefit of relatively affluent and well-educated Americans and Europeans, Ambedkar compiled *The Buddha and His Dhamma* mainly, though not exclusively, for the benefit of desperately poor ex-Untouchable Indian Buddhists, many of whom were illiterate and would need to have his words orally explained to them in their own vernacular. Moreover, though in his Preface Carus speaks of Christianity in appreciative rather than in critical terms, *The Gospel of Buddha* was in fact meant for those who were disillusioned with Christianity, or who did not consider themselves Christians in the orthodox sense. *The Buddha and His Dhamma*, on the other hand, was meant for those who were disillusioned with Hinduism, or who were even in active revolt against it, and the terms in which Ambedkar speaks of Hinduism are definitely critical rather than appreciative. What is perhaps more important still, whereas Carus presents data of the Buddha's life in the light of what he terms its religio-philosophical importance, Ambedkar presents them in the light of what may be termed its socio-political importance. Ambedkar's approach to Buddhism thus is social and ethical rather than philosophical and mystical, as even a short account of *The Buddha and His Dhamma* will be sufficient to reveal.

As we have already seen, *The Buddha and His Dhamma* is divided into eight books, the last four of which are only half the length of the first four. Six of the books are further divided into parts (that is, chapters), subsections, and verses, the remaining two books being divided into parts, sections, subsections, and verses. Altogether there are 40 parts, 14 sections, 248 subsections, and 5013 verses, which between them cover 430 pages. At a rough estimate, three-quarters of the work consists of extracts from – or adaptations of – Buddhist literature both canonical and non-canonical, while the remaining quarter consists of Ambedkar's own Explanatory Additions. In the vast majority of cases, the extracts from the canonical literature are taken from the Sutta and Vinaya Piṭakas of the Theravāda Pāli Tipiṭaka or 'Three Collections' (Ambedkar apparently regarded the Abhidhamma Piṭaka as a later addition), only a few of them being taken from the Mahāyāna *sūtras*. As for the extracts from the non-canonical literature, most of these are taken from Aśvaghoṣa's celebrated epic poem the *Buddhacarita* or 'Life of the Buddha', though the Pāli commentaries, the *Milinda-pañha* or 'Questions of [King] Milinda', and even a Chinese translation of a prayer to Amitābha, the Buddha of Infinite Light, are also laid under contribution.

Book I of *The Buddha and His Dhamma*, entitled 'Siddarth Gautam – How a Bodhisatta became the Buddha', is mainly, though not exclusively, biographical in character. In the first five parts Ambedkar tells the story of the Buddha's life from his birth to his leaving home and from his leaving home to his attainment of Enlightenment, while in the last three parts he compares the Buddha with his predecessors and contemporaries and explains which of their ideas he rejected, which he modified, and which he accepted in formulating his own teaching. But though Ambedkar tells the story of the Buddha's life from his birth to his leaving home, and from his leaving home to his attainment of Enlightenment, he does not tell it quite in the traditional way. Indeed, he tells it in a very untraditional way. The main reason for this is that he finds it impossible to accept the traditional answer to the question of why the Buddha (or rather the Bodhisattva, as he then was) left home, namely, that he left it as a result of seeing, for the first time, an old man, a sick man, a corpse, and a wandering ascetic. Taking a hint from an apparently autobiographical passage in the *Sutta-Nipāta*, an ancient text belonging to the fifth division of the Sutta Piṭaka, and combining this with an antedated version of the conflict between the Śākyas, to whom the Buddha was related through his father, and the Koliyas, to whom he was related through his mother, he therefore represents the Buddha-to-be as leaving home as a result of his opposition to the Śākya clan's decision to go to war with the Koliya clan. As told by Ambedkar, the story of this 'crisis in the life of Siddharth', as he calls it, is both consistent and psychologically convincing, as well as of great human interest, especially as his own Explanatory Additions are interwoven with some of the most affecting episodes from Aśvaghoṣa's *Buddhacarita*. Yet despite its essential truth (for was not the Bodhisattva's preoccupation with the problem of human suffering a preoccupation, at the same time, with the problem of human conflict?) Ambedkar's retelling of the story of the Buddha's early life is an imaginative reconstruction rather than the product of strictly scientific research. Though accepted by many of his followers it has not, therefore, been taken seriously by Buddhist scholars.

The Buddha's attainment of Enlightenment having been followed by his decision to preach, in Book II of *The Buddha and His Dhamma* Ambedkar describes the preaching of the First Sermon and the conversion of the five *parivrājakas* or wandering ascetics, as well as the conversion of 'the High and the Holy', of the Buddha's own relations, of 'the Low and the Lowly', of women, and of 'the Fallen and the Criminals'. This book is therefore entitled 'Campaign of Conversion'. Before describing the Buddha's 'First Sermon' and the conversion of the five *parivrājakas*, however, Ambedkar devotes a short section to the subject of the two types of conversion. In the Buddha's scheme of things, he says, conversion has two meanings. There is conversion to the Order of *bhikkhus* and there is a householder's conversion as an *upāsaka* or lay follower, though 'except on four points there is no difference in the way of life of the Bhikkhu and the Upasaka'.[153] One of these points is that 'to become an Upasaka there is no ceremony'[154] – a deficiency which Ambedkar sought to remedy by drawing up his list of twenty-two vows and administering these to his followers at the time of the great mass conversion. By emphasizing that there are two kinds of conversion and that, therefore, conversion does not (necessarily) mean becoming a monk, as well as by emphasizing that except on four points there is no difference in the way of life of the *bhikkhu* and the way of life of the *upāsaka*, Ambedkar in effect asserts the fundamental unity of the whole Buddhist spiritual community, just as he did by administering the Three Refuges and Five Precepts to his followers himself and making the twenty-two vows an integral part of the conversion ceremony.

According to tradition the Buddha's First Sermon, delivered to the five *parivrājakas* in the Deer Park at Sarnath, near Benares, consisted in a brief statement of the Middle Way, the Four Noble Truths, and the Noble Eightfold Path. Ambedkar regards this as quite inadequate. Indeed, besides being doubtful whether the Four Noble Truths formed part of the original teaching of the Buddha he is of the opinion that they are 'a great stumbling block in the way of non-Buddhists accepting the gospel of Buddhism'.[155] In describing the events leading up to the conversion of the five *parivrājakas* he therefore represents the Buddha as speaking of the Dharma he had discovered not just in terms of the Middle Way and in terms of what is, in effect, a 'revised version' of the Four Noble Truths, but also in terms of the Path of Purity, the Path of Righteousness, and the Path of Virtue, which he seems to regard as three successive stages of spiritual development. The Path of Purity consists in recognizing the five precepts as principles of life, the Path of Righteousness in following the Noble Eightfold Path, and the Path of Virtue in observing the ten *pāramitās* or 'States of Perfection' (as he calls them), these last being enumerated according to the Theravāda tradition.

(In Book I they are enumerated according to the Mahāyāna tradition, and the Buddha-to-be is represented as practising them seriatim for ten successive lifetimes, whereas the traditional teaching is that he practises them simultaneously over a period of three successive *kalpas* or aeons.) The preaching of the (revised and enlarged) First Sermon having led the five *parivrājakas* to realize that 'this was really a new Dhamma',[156] the Buddha's campaign of conversion proceeds apace. Among 'the High and the Holy' to be converted are Yasa, the nobleman's son, the three fire-worshipping Kassapa brothers, the young Brahmin seekers Sāriputta and Moggallāna, subsequently to become the Buddha's chief disciples, King Bimbisāra of Magadha, the royal treasurer Anāthapindika, and the royal doctor Jīvaka, while 'the Low and the Lowly' are represented by Upāli the barber, Sunīta the sweeper, Sopāka and Suppiya, the Untouchables, Sumaṅgala the peasant, Dhaniya the potter, Kappaṭakura the grass-seller, and Suppabuddha the leper, all of whom are received into the Order. The Buddha also converts women like his aunt and foster mother Mahāpajāpatī Gotami and his former wife Yasodharā, as well as the low-caste girl Prakṛti, vagabonds like the unnamed man of Rājagaha, and robbers like the ferocious Aṅgulimāla. Not that the Buddha had converted only those whose stories Ambedkar actually relates. As the latter is careful to explain:

> The instances are chosen only to show that he did not observe any distinction as to caste or sex in admitting persons to his Sangh or preaching his Dhamma.[157]

That the Buddha did not observe distinctions of this kind was, of course, one of the principal reasons why Ambedkar and his followers decided to embrace Buddhism and it is therefore natural that he should want to draw particular attention to this feature of the Buddha's teaching.

Book III, entitled 'What the Buddha Taught', and Parts I and II of Book IV, entitled 'Religion and Dhamma', are mainly philosophical in character. Parts III and IV of Book IV, on the other hand, are mainly ethical and psychological. Conscious that there is an astonishing divergence of views regarding Buddhism, Ambedkar is concerned to establish the real nature of the Buddha's teaching. This he does with the help of a classification which the Buddha himself (he believes) had adopted, namely, the classification of Dhamma into the three categories of

Dhamma, Not-Dhamma (*Adhamma*), 'though it [goes] by the name of Dhamma',[158] and *Saddhamma* which is another name for the philosophy of Dhamma. Dhamma consists in maintaining purity of life (including purity of body, speech, and mind), in reaching perfection in this life (here Ambedkar includes a dialogue between Subhūti and the Buddha taken from the *Pañcaviṃśati-sāhasrikā* or Perfection of Wisdom 'in 25,000 lines'), in living in Nirvāṇa or living free from greed, hatred, and delusion, in giving up craving, in believing that all compound things are impermanent, and in believing that the law of karma is the instrument of the moral order. Not-Dhamma consists in belief in the supernatural as the cause of events, in the belief that the world was created by God, in the belief that Dhamma is based on union with Brahmā, in the belief that sacrifices – including animal sacrifices – are a part of religion, in the belief that speculations regarding the origin of the self and the universe are a part of religion, in the belief that the reading of books is Dhamma, and in belief in the infallibility of sacred books like the Vedas. Finally, the functions of *Saddhamma* are in the first place to cleanse the mind of its impurities and in the second to make the world a kingdom of righteousness. In order to be *Saddhamma*, however, Dhamma must promote *prajñā* or insight, and this it does by making learning open to all, by teaching that mere learning is not enough, as it may lead to pedantry, and by teaching that what is needed is *prajñā* or right thinking. Moreover, Dhamma is *Saddhamma* only when it teaches that *prajñā* must be accompanied by *śīla* or right action, as well as by *karuṇā* or compassion for the poor and helpless and by *maitrī* or love for all living beings. From this it follows that, in order to be *Saddhamma*, Dhamma must break down the barriers between man and man, must teach that worth and not birth is the measure of man, and must promote equality between man and man. Thus Ambedkar establishes the real nature of the Buddha's teaching by, in effect, replacing the traditional triad of *śīla*, *samādhi*, and *prajñā* by his own triad of *śīla*, *prajñā*, and *karuṇā-maitrī*. This enables him to bring out the social implications of the Buddha's teaching more fully and clearly than they had been brought out before and to answer in the affirmative the question, 'Did the Buddha have [a] Social Message?'

Since much of the divergence of views regarding Buddhism is semantic in origin, Ambedkar also explores the nature of the difference between religion and Dhamma, and between their respective purposes, as well as the way in which similarities in terminology with regard to such questions as rebirth, karma, and *ahiṃsā* or non-killing, may conceal a fundamental difference of outlook. Perhaps the most valuable and important part of his exploration is that in which, having dealt with the relation between Dhamma and religion, he asserts that mere Morality is not enough, but that it must be 'sacred and universal'.[159] Here we encounter some of Ambedkar's deepest thinking. Morality, he asserts, has no place in religion, for religion is concerned with the relation between man and God, morality with the relation between man and man. Though every religion preaches morality, morality comes into religion only in order to help maintain peace and order, and is not the root of religion. '[Morality] is a wagon attached to [religion]. It is attached and detached as the occasion requires.' (If 'God' tells you to do something, morality can be disregarded.)

> The action of morality in the functioning of religion is therefore casual and occasional. Morality in religion is therefore not effective.[160]

So far as Dhamma is concerned the exact opposite is the case. We cannot even say what place morality has in Dhamma, for 'Morality is Dhamma and Dhamma is Morality'.[161] Morality is the essence of Dhamma; without it there is no Dhamma, and 'Morality in Dhamma arises from the direct necessity for man to love man.'[162] Such morality does not require divine sanction.

'It is not to please God that man has to be moral. It is for his own good that man has to love man.'[163] This morality which is Dhamma is not, however, the anti-social morality that serves to protect the interests of a particular group. On the contrary, it is that sacred and universal morality which protects the weak from the strong, which provides common models, standards, and rules, and which safeguards the growth of the individual. It is what makes liberty and equality effective, for if there is liberty for some but not for all, and equality for a few but not for the majority, what is the remedy?

> The only remedy lies in making fraternity universally effective. What is fraternity? It is nothing but another name for brotherhood of men which is another name for morality. This is why the Buddha

preached that Dhamma is morality and as Dhamma is sacred so is morality.[164]

Parts III and IV of Book IV, which are respectively entitled 'The Buddhist Way of Life' and 'His Sermons', besides being mainly ethical and psychological in character, contain hardly any Explanatory Additions. The first of the two parts is about a third of the length of the second and consists almost entirely of verses from the Pāli *Dhammapada* arranged under such headings as 'On Craving and Lust', 'On Anger and Enmity', 'On Man, Mind and Impurities', 'On Self and Self-Conquest', 'On Wisdom, Justice and Good Company', and 'On Thoughtfulness and Mindfulness'. The sermons (as Ambedkar insists on calling the Buddha's discourses) are organized in accordance with the type of person or persons to whom they are addressed and in accordance with their subject matter. Thus there are sermons for householders, sermons on the need for maintaining character, sermons on righteousness, sermons on Nirvāṇa, sermons on Dhamma, and sermons on socio-political questions. Among the sermons organized in accordance with their subject matter are some of the best known short discourses in the Sutta and Vinaya Piṭakas, such as the Buddha's explanation of what constitutes the downfall of man, his reminder of the (spiritual) futility of outward washing, and his enumeration of what have been called the conditions of communal stability.

Book V of *The Buddha and His Dhamma* is entitled 'The Sangh', Book VI 'He and His Contemporaries', Book VII 'The Wanderer's Last Testament', and Book VIII 'The Man who was Siddharth Gautama'. These four books are only half the length of the first four, the last two of them being only half the length of the previous two. From this it would appear that, as the work progressed, Ambedkar became increasingly unsure whether he would live to finish it, and therefore included less and less material in each successive book in order to reach the end of his labours as quickly as possible. But short though the last four books of *The Buddha and His Dhamma* may be their material is as well organized as ever and the points which Ambedkar is concerned to make, whether indirectly through excerpts from the Buddhist scriptures or directly through his own Explanatory Additions, stand out all the more clearly for the succinctness with which he makes them. In Part I of 'The Sangh' Ambedkar gives a brief outline of the organizational structure of the monastic order, including a summary of the rules governing admission (he emphasizes that there was no bar of caste, sex, or social status), of the vows taken by the *bhikkhu*, and of the procedure to be followed with regard to the trial and punishment of offences. He also has something to say on the subject of 'Confession, called Uposatha', which he describes as

> the most original and unique institution created by the Blessed Lord in connection with the organization of the Bhikkhus.[165]

The Buddha introduced confession, Ambedkar believes, because he could find no effective way of enforcing certain restrictions which were not offences.

> He therefore thought of Confession in open as a means of organizing [mobilizing?] the Bhikkhu's conscience and making it act as a sentinel to guard him against taking a wrong or false step.[166]

In Part II, 'The Bhikkhu – the Buddha's Conception of Him', Ambedkar outlines, with the help of verses from the Pāli *Dhammapada*, the Buddha's conception of what a *bhikkhu* should be, answers the question of whether the *bhikkhu* is an ascetic, or whether he is the same as the Brahmin, in the negative, and explains the true nature of the distinction between the *bhikkhu* and the *upāsaka*. Part III deals with the *bhikkhu*'s duty to convert – though not by means of miracles or by force, Part IV with the relations between the *bhikkhu* and the laity, and Part V with the Vinaya for the laity, that is, the particular Vinaya or discipline to be observed by the wealthy, by the householder, by children, by a pupil, by husband and wife, by master and servant, and by girls. Book VI, entitled 'The Buddha and His Contemporaries', deals with the Buddha's benefactors, with his enemies, with the critics of his doctrines, and with his friends and admirers. Book VII, entitled 'The Wanderer's Last Journey', describes the Buddha's last meetings with those near and dear to him, his departure from Vesāli and arrival in Kusinārā, and some of the principal events leading up to his *parinirvāṇa* or final passing away. Much of the material is taken straight from the Pāli *Mahāparinibbāna Sutta*, and Ambedkar on the whole allows the text's simple and sublime narrative to speak for itself and make its own impression. When the

Buddha has breathed his last his only comment is, 'He was beyond question the light of the world.'[167]

From a practical point of view the most important part of the last four books of *The Buddha and His Dhamma* are perhaps those sections of Book V in which, while doing justice to the historical distinction between the *bhikkhus* and the *upāsakas* or 'lay followers' of the Buddha, Ambedkar at the same time emphasizes the fundamental unity of the Buddhist spiritual community. To him it is obvious that in principle 'the Dhamma was the same for both'.[168] The *bhikkhu* and the *upāsaka* alike observe the five precepts, the only difference being (according to Ambedkar) that the *bhikkhu*'s observance of them is compulsory whereas the *upāsaka*'s is voluntary. Moreover compassion, which is the essence of the Dhamma, requires that everyone shall love and serve, 'and the Bhikkhu is not exempt from it', as some Buddhists thought. Indeed,

> A Bhikkhu who is indifferent to the woes of mankind, however perfect in self-culture, is not at all a Bhikkhu. He may be something else but he is not a Bhikkhu.[169]

Ambedkar also points out that it must not be supposed that, because the Buddha's sermons were addressed to the gathering of the *bhikkhus*, what was preached was intended to apply to them only. It applied to both the *bhikkhu* and the *upāsaka*. That the Buddha had the laity in mind when he preached the five precepts, the Noble Eightfold Path, and the ten *pāramitās* or Perfections,

> is quite clear from the very nature of things and no argument, really speaking, is necessary. It is to those who have not left their homes and who are engaged in active life that Panchasila, Ashtanga Marga, and Paramitas are essential. It is they who are likely to transgress them and not the Bhikkhu who has left home, who is not engaged in active life and who is not likely to transgress them. When the Buddha, therefore, started preaching his Dhamma it must be principally for the laity.[170]

But though the Dhamma was the same for the *bhikkhu* and the *upāsaka*, and though it had been preached more for the benefit of the laity, Ambedkar was very conscious that there was no separate ceremony of

Dhammadiksha for those who wanted to be initiated into Buddhism but did not wish to become monks and go forth from home into homelessness.

> This was a grave omission. It was one of the causes which ultimately led to the downfall of Buddhism in India. For this absence of the initiation ceremony left the laity free to wander from one religion to another and, worse still, follow [two or more religions] at one and the same time.[171]

Probably it was in order to make good this omission, at least to some extent, that Ambedkar included in Book V of *The Buddha and His Dhamma* a separate part dealing with the Vinaya for the laity, thus making it clear that the laity, too, had an ethical and spiritual discipline to observe and that they were not merely the supporters of the monks.

With Book VIII, which is little more than a quarter of the length of Book I, *The Buddha and His Dhamma* ends where it had begun: with the Buddha. Here we are given a thumbnail sketch of 'the Man who was Siddharth Gautama' – as the title of the book significantly styles him – which tells us almost as much about Ambedkar himself as it does about the Buddha. The Buddha's physical appearance was highly pleasing, and the fascination of his personality was such that he exercised an unequalled influence over the hearts and minds of men and women alike. He therefore had the 'capacity to lead', and was respected by his disciples more than the other religious teachers of the day were respected by theirs. Yet his humanity was such that he was full of compassion, a consummate healer of sorrow, concerned for the sick, tolerant of the intolerant, and possessed of a sense of equality and equal treatment, claiming no special privileges for himself. He also had his likes and dislikes. He disliked poverty and the acquisitive instinct, and 'was so fond of the beautiful that he might well bear an *alias* and be called Buddha, the Lover of the Beautiful.'[172]

In his short Epilogue to the work Ambedkar quotes from the tributes which nine modern 'scientists and thinkers', both Indian and Western, have paid to the greatness and uniqueness of the Buddha and his Dhamma, besides reproducing what he calls 'A Vow to Spread His Dhamma' and 'A Prayer for His Return to His Native Land'. The Vow is taken from the Mahāyāna *sūtras* and is none other than the bodhisattva's famous fourfold vow, that is, his vow to deliver all beings from suffering, to eradicate all passions, to master all teachings of the Buddha, and to attain Supreme Enlightenment. As for the Prayer, this is taken from the invocation to Amitābha, the Buddha of Infinite Light, with which the great Indian master Vasubandhu opens his commentary on the *Sukhāvatī-vyūha* or 'Array of the Happy Land' *Sūtra*. Patriotically (and perhaps rationalistically) identifying the Happy Land not with Amitābha's Western Pure Land of that name but with India, Ambedkar quotes it in such a way that Vasubandhu's aspiration to attain rebirth there with all his fellow beings and to proclaim the Truth like Amitābha himself becomes his own heartfelt aspiration to be reborn in his native land and to continue his work for the revival of Buddhism in India.

By appropriating Vasubandhu's invocation in this manner Ambedkar shows his deep feeling for his own country and, what is more, his intense concern for what would happen to the movement of mass conversion after his death.

9

AFTER AMBEDKAR

Bhimrao Ramji Ambedkar died in the early hours of 6 December 1956 and at 7.30 p.m. the following day his body was cremated in Bombay, which had been his headquarters for the greater part of his career and where he still had the greatest number of followers. Five hundred thousand people joined the two-mile long funeral procession, which took four hours to make its way from 'Rajagriha', Ambedkar's residence in Dadar, to the local burning ghat, and was the biggest such procession the city had ever seen. Afterwards more than 100,000 of those who had witnessed the cremation escorted the great leader's ashes back to 'Rajagriha'. Before leaving the burning ghat, however, they insisted on fulfilling 'Baba Saheb's' wishes and embracing Buddhism. An impromptu conversion ceremony was accordingly held, and one of the *bhikkhus* who was present administered the Three Refuges and Five Precepts to all 100,000 of them on the spot.

From Bombay a portion of the ashes was taken to Delhi where, a week later, a conversion ceremony was held at which 30,000 people were initiated into Buddhism. These same ashes having been divided in their turn and a portion handed over to Ambedkar's followers in Agra, a similar ceremony was held in that city too. This time 200,000 people were initiated into Buddhism. Thus the great movement of mass conversion that had been inaugurated in Nagpur only seven weeks earlier continued unabated. Between 7 December 1956 and 10 February 1957 conversion ceremonies were in fact held not only in Bombay, Delhi, and Agra but in more than twenty different towns and cities, most of them within the boundaries of the present-day state of Maharashtra, with the result that by the end of that period the number of ex-Untouchable Buddhists had risen from 750,000 – the number converted by Ambedkar himself in Nagpur and Chanda – to well over 4,000,000.[173] Most of the ceremonies were organized by branches of the Indian Buddhist Society, the body re-founded by Ambedkar in 1955, and the new converts were received into the Buddhist fold either by a leading member of the Republican Party (some of whose office-bearers doubled as office-bearers of the Indian Buddhist Society) or by a Sinhalese or Indian *bhikkhu* from the Maha Bodhi Society. Sometimes the new converts would be received into the Buddhist fold by the politician and the *bhikkhu* jointly, with the *bhikkhu* administering the Three Refuges and Five Precepts and the politician administering the twenty-two vows.

After 10 February 1957, however, the conversion movement was suspended until after the March general elections – the same elections on account of which some of Ambedkar's lieutenants had wanted him to postpone the original mass conversion ceremony. The expectation was that when the elections were over the conversion movement would be not only continued but intensified. This did not, unfortunately, prove to be the case. Though conversion ceremonies indeed continued to be held all over central and western India, and even further afield, with the exception of that held at Aligarh on 13 April, when 200,000 people embraced Buddhism, they were on the whole smaller and less spectacular affairs than before. This may have been due to the fact that the conversion movement, having been virtually suspended for two crucial months, had now lost much of its original impetus and that what had been lost could not easily be regained. It may equally have been due to the fact that the movement had reached what were, for the time being, its natural limits. Though Ambedkar was held in the highest esteem by all the untouchable communities of India, his influence was greatest within his own Mahar community, and it was the Mahars who had responded most enthusiastically to his call to embrace Buddhism. Once the Mahars had been converted, therefore, the conversion movement naturally slowed down, the more especially since Ambedkar himself was no longer present to convince the other untouchable communities of the rightness of the step he had taken and persuade them to do likewise.

The fact that the conversion movement had reached its natural limits by the beginning of 1957 was reflected in the official statistics. According to the 1961 census returns there were 3,250,227 Buddhists in India (an increase of 1,671 per cent over the 1951 figure), of whom 2,789,501 were to be found in Maharashtra as compared with 2,489 ten years earlier. The increase in the number of Buddhists in Maharashtra was thus out of all proportion to the increase in the rest of the country. By 1971, however, the figures had risen only very slightly and there were altogether 3,812,325 registered Buddhists in India, from which fact it was clear that even though a number of conversion ceremonies had been held outside Maharashtra the movement of mass conversion among the Mahars had not been followed by any corresponding movement among the other untouchable communities.

Not that the statistics in question were completely accurate. The newly converted Buddhists themselves were convinced that they were very inaccurate indeed and that the number of Buddhists in India was actually far greater than the census returns showed, and in this they were undoubtedly right, though perhaps not quite to the extent that some of them believed. (According to one source, by March 1959 'nearly 15 to 20 million Untouchables had embraced Buddhism'.)[174] There were two reasons for the discrepancy between the official figures, on the one hand, and the facts as known to the Buddhists themselves on the other. In the first place, the census-takers, most of whom were caste Hindus, in some cases deliberately enumerated Buddhists as Hindus in order to minimize the extent, and therefore the significance, of the conversion movement. (In 1951, at the time of the first post-independence census, I had myself been enumerated, despite my vigorous protests, as 'Hindu by religion and Buddhist by caste'.) In the second place, many of those who had embraced Buddhism at one or another of the conversion ceremonies, and who therefore appeared in the Buddhists' own statistics, did not officially declare themselves as Buddhists, and hence were not included as such in the census returns. Some of those who thus remained suspended in a kind of limbo, able neither really to leave the hell of Hinduism and caste nor really to enter the heaven of Buddhism and equality, were unwilling to declare themselves Buddhists because they were afraid that, if they did so, they would be subject to harassment by the more militant caste Hindus, who in some places were actually attacking and killing the newly converted Buddhists for daring to renounce their ancestral religion. Others, and these were the more numerous, were unwilling to declare themselves as Buddhists because they did not want to forgo the scholarships and stipends and other benefits to which they were entitled as members of the Scheduled Castes and which, they believed, were essential to their advancement.

These social and educational 'concessions', as they were significantly termed, were given by the central government and by the various state governments, and they were given not on account of the recipient's religion but solely because of the extreme poverty, as well as the social and educational backwardness, of the community to which he happened to belong. Nonetheless, a few weeks after the general elections both the central government and the State Government of Bombay, of which Maharashtra was then a part and in which the majority of newly converted Buddhists were to be found, stopped giving scholarships and stipends to those students who had declared themselves Buddhists, or whose parents had declared themselves Buddhists, even though change of religion had not made the slightest difference to their economic position. Despite appeals from the Maha Bodhi Society and other Buddhist organizations, as well as from various humanitarian groups, the Government of India refused to rescind its decision, ostensibly on constitutional grounds, so that the ex-untouchable Buddhist students lost their central scholarships and stipends for good. The State Government of Bombay fortunately adopted a more generous and far-sighted policy and, early in 1958, restored to the untouchable Buddhist students the scholarships and stipends which formerly they had enjoyed as members of the Scheduled Castes. Thus a situation was created in which ex-untouchable Buddhist students were not entitled to their former central government concessions anywhere in India, including the state of Bombay, and in which they were entitled to the corresponding state government concessions only in the state of Bombay. This meant that the ex-untouchable Buddhist students in the state of Bombay had a decided advantage over their opposite numbers in other states and that they – and their parents – had, therefore, less inducement *not* to declare themselves as Buddhists.

Some twenty years later, ex-untouchable Buddhist observers in other parts of the country were inclined to attribute the greater success of the conversion movement in Maharashtra to the fact that there members of the Scheduled Castes could declare themselves Buddhists without having to forgo their state as well as their central government concessions, thus enjoying, if only to a limited extent, the best of both worlds. Such observers were, however, mistaken. While the concessions undoubtedly helped, the real reason for the greater success of the conversion movement in Maharashtra was to be found in the courage and determination of the former Mahars, in their readiness to make sacrifices, and, above all, in their unswerving loyalty to the memory of their great leader and emancipator.

But though ex-untouchable Buddhists in the state of Bombay/ Maharashtra had less inducement not to declare themselves Buddhists than did their opposite numbers elsewhere in India, this did not mean that they had no such inducement at all. The social and educational concessions given by the central government were often of greater monetary value than those given by the state government, and students from very poor families were sometimes tempted to apply for the former rather than for the latter even after taking the *Dhammadiksha* and becoming (unofficial) Buddhists. Though cases of this sort were not common, there were enough of them to give rise to serious differences of opinion not only among the students themselves but also among their elders and, indeed, within large sections of the Mahar-cum-Buddhist community. Some people thought that all true followers of 'Baba Saheb' should take *Dhammadiksha* at the first opportunity and declare themselves Buddhists regardless of consequences and that this applied to students as much as to anybody else. Others thought that it was – or that it was not – dishonest and, in effect, even a breach of the fourth precept (the precept to abstain from false speech), to apply for central government concessions after taking *Dhammadiksha*, while yet others thought that even if it was a breach of the fourth precept such a breach was – or was not – justified in the circumstances. Others, again, simply did not know what to think. Thus the subject of central government concessions was the source of a good deal of confusion, and since this confusion was never really cleared up it gave rise to a feeling of uncertainty which, in its turn, tended to have an undermining effect on the conversion movement.

The vexed subject of central government concessions was not, however, the only source of confusion among Ambedkar's followers, or even the most serious. For many years the most serious source of confusion was, perhaps, the fact that having renounced Hinduism the newly converted Buddhists – most of whom were both poor and illiterate – had little or no means of finding out what Buddhism really meant or how they were supposed to practise it and, for this reason, often continued to keep up un-Buddhistic customs and observances which they had in theory repudiated. In this they were hardly to blame. What usually happened was that they turned up at a mass conversion ceremony, were received into the Buddhist fold by a visiting politician or Maha Bodhi Society *bhikkhu*, donated some money, and then went back to their ghettoes in city, town, or village to work (if they could get work), to support their families and, in some cases, to suffer harassment at the hands of their caste Hindu neighbours. The politician they probably did not see again until the time of the next election, while the Maha Bodhi Society *bhikkhu* they probably did not see again at all. In other words there was no follow up and in virtually all cases those who had taken the *Dhammadiksha* had no one to teach them anything about Buddhism. The politicians who conducted the conversion ceremonies were not in a position to teach them because with very few exceptions they knew little or nothing about the Dharma themselves and because they were, in any case, too busy campaigning for votes, collecting funds, and (after a few years) fighting among themselves to have much time for anything else. (Some of them indeed added to the existing confusion by denying that they were Buddhists in order to be able to contest seats reserved for members of the Scheduled Castes who were, of course, by definition Hindu.) As for the Maha Bodhi Society *bhikkhus*, of whom there were less than a dozen stationed in Bombay, Delhi, Sanchi, Lucknow, and Sarnath, though these had a scholarly knowledge of the Dharma they were too busy running the Society's centres and looking after foreign Buddhist pilgrims to be able to do much more than conduct conversion ceremonies and deliver the occasional lecture.

Ambedkar had, of course, hoped that help in teaching his followers would be forthcoming from the rest of the Buddhist world and a handful of *bhikkhus* from South-east Asia did, in fact, find their way to the tiny makeshift temples that soon were springing up all over central and western India, wherever there were more than a few hundred newly converted Buddhists. But as Ambedkar had also feared, the *bhikkhus* proved to be not very adaptable and for one reason or another did not stay very long or achieve very much. Besides having trouble with the local language (or languages), they found it difficult to adjust to a standard of living so much lower than that to which they were accustomed and difficult to relate to Buddhists who, devoted as they obviously were, failed to treat them with the extreme formal deference with which they were invariably treated in their own country. They also found it difficult to understand the social, economic, and religious background of the newly converted Buddhists and still more difficult to appreciate the depth of their loyalty to Ambedkar and the extent to which the great leader's memory dominated their thinking. Above all, they found it difficult to teach the Dharma – difficult, that is, to teach it in such a way that their hearers could grasp its basic principles and apply them to their own lives. This was due partly to the fact that newly converted Buddhists did not always share their mentors' assumptions and partly to the fact that the *bhikkhus* themselves were more familiar with the letter of the Dharma than with its spirit and could present it only in the stereotype form in which it had been handed down to them. Thus the newly converted Buddhists did not learn very much and only too often were left feeling that they had, in biblical phrase, asked for bread and been given a stone. When the *bhikkhus* realized that their efforts on behalf of the Dharma were not meeting with the success they had expected they attributed it to their hearers' lack of faith and told them that, if they really wanted to understand Buddhism, they would have to go to Ceylon or Thailand (as the case might be), become monks, and spend several years studying Pāli.

Not unnaturally, the vast majority of the newly converted Buddhists had no wish to go to Ceylon or Thailand, or to become monks, or even to spend several years studying Pāli. They did, however, very much want to know more about Buddhism and if anyone took the trouble to explain it to them in a way that they could understand their joy, enthusiasm, and gratitude knew no bounds. Certainly this was my own experience when, as a result of the link that I had forged with them in Nagpur during the anxious days immediately following Ambedkar's death, I undertook a series of four preaching tours that lasted, with very little intermission, from February 1959 to May 1961. In the course of these tours I visited cities, towns, and villages in more than half the states of India, opened temples and libraries, installed images of the Buddha, performed name-giving ceremonies and after-death ceremonies, blessed marriages, conferred with leading members of the Indian Buddhist Society, held a special training course, delivered about 400 lectures and personally initiated upwards of 100,000 people into Buddhism. With each succeeding tour, however, my activities came to be increasingly concentrated in and around Nagpur, Bombay, Poona, Jabalpur, and Ahmedabad, but especially in and around Poona, where I eventually established a sort of seasonal headquarters. The reason for this was that in Poona I had the cooperation of a group of idealistic young men, mostly college students, who for more than a year before my arrival had been publicly reading and explaining *The Buddha and His Dhamma* every Sunday morning for the benefit of their less literate fellow Buddhists. Moreover, Poona was not only the centre of Maharashtrian culture but the citadel of Brahmanical orthodoxy, so that if it was possible to establish Buddhism in Poona it was possible to establish it anywhere in Maharashtra.

In 1962, not long after I had returned to Kalimpong from the fourth and longest of my preaching tours, I was invited by the English Sangha Trust to take charge of their vihara in north-west London. By this time the fighting between the politicians had led to a series of splits in the Republican Party and these had resulted in serious divisions among the newly converted Buddhists, even so far as religious activities were concerned. Partly for this reason, and partly because I had now spent twenty years in the East, I eventually accepted the Trust's invitation and accordingly left India for the United Kingdom in August 1964. Though I had originally agreed to take charge of the Hampstead Buddhist Vihara for six months, I ended up staying there for more than two years. During this period I came to the conclusion that conditions in Britain were favourable to the spread of the Dharma and therefore decided to transfer my permanent headquarters from Kalimpong to London. Before actually doing so, however, I returned to India for a three-month preaching tour that culminated in Nagpur where, on the tenth anniversary of Ambedkar's death, I addressed a gathering of 100,000 people. In the course of the tour I explained to my friends and disciples what I was doing and bade them farewell. In future, I told them, I would be dividing my time between England, the country of my birth, and India, the country of my adoption, and hoped to spend six months in each of them alternately.

This hope was not to be fulfilled. Shortly after my final departure from India it had been borne in upon me that if full advantage was to be taken of the fact that conditions in Britain were favourable to the spread of Buddhism there would have to be a new Buddhist movement there, and since the creation of this new Buddhist movement took longer than I had expected it was twelve years before I saw India again. In the meantime, however, I kept in touch with my old friends and disciples among the 'newly converted' Buddhists in Poona and elsewhere and in 1977 one of my senior English disciples paid them a fraternal visit which eventually led to the creation of a new Buddhist movement in India too. As a result of this development, between February 1979 and December 1983 I paid four visits to India and on each occasion delivered lectures and performed ceremonies in the same way as before and, in some cases, for the benefit of the very same people.

The longest and perhaps most important of these visits took place in the winter of 1981–2, when I went on a preaching tour that took me to Bombay, Delhi, Ahmedabad, and Ajmer, as well as to Poona and about fifty other towns and villages of Marathwada, as the six districts that constitute the heart of Maharashtra were collectively termed. In the course of this visit, in particular, I was able to see for myself what sort of changes had taken place among Ambedkar's followers and whether the conversion movement had made any progress. There was little doubt that as a community they were marginally more prosperous than before (few of the people attending my lectures were now dressed in rags), though perhaps it would be more correct to say that they were marginally less poverty-stricken. Quite a few of the more well off among them owned motor scooters, while one or two who had risen to gazetted officer rank in central government service had small cars and, of course, chauffeurs. It was evident, however, that whatever meagre wealth had accrued to Ambedkar's followers was very unevenly distributed, and that the vast majority of them lived well below even the Indian poverty line. It was also evident that there had been very little change in the attitude of the caste Hindus towards them. Reports of atrocities committed on 'Harijans' continued to appear with nauseating regularity in the national press, yet though the offenders were sometimes caught and punished the conscience of Caste Hindu India on the whole remained untouched.

So far as the conversion movement itself was concerned, not much had really happened. As before, it was confined mainly to Maharashtra and to the ex-Mahars, and as before the principal reason for the lack of progress was the fact that those who had taken *Dhammadiksha* had no one to teach them anything about Buddhism. In some areas they had not had an opportunity of hearing a real lecture on Buddhism since my own preaching tours of a generation ago, while in others they had never had such an opportunity, and in a community where so many were illiterate and, therefore, entirely dependent for their knowledge of Buddhism on the spoken word, this was a serious deprivation. Yet even though they had not had anyone to teach them, the vast majority of those who had embraced Buddhism in response to Ambedkar's call had lost neither their faith in their great leader's vision nor their desire to learn more about the religion to which he had directed them. The evidences of that faith and that desire were to be found all over Maharashtra, and even beyond. Wherever I went, in the course of that preaching tour in the winter of 1981–2, I saw not only scores of newly constructed Buddhist temples but hundreds of life-size – and more than life-size – busts and statues of Ambedkar. Cast in bronze, or merely moulded in plaster, the familiar figure was to be seen in every town and village, in death as in life dominating the lives of his people and reminding the whole nation of the principles for which he had stood.

Wherever I went I moreover saw, as I had seen time and time again all those years ago, how overwhelmingly grateful Ambedkar's followers were for whatever Buddhist teaching they received. This time, however, they would not have to wait for years before they heard another lecture on Buddhism. This time they were in contact with a new Buddhist movement, a movement that was the direct continuation of Ambedkar's own work for the Dharma, so that even after I had gone there would be plenty of opportunities for them to hear lectures, to learn how to meditate, and to go on retreat. There would, in short, be plenty of opportunities for them to practise Buddhism, and it was in the individual and collective practice of Buddhism that – Ambedkar believed – they would find the inspiration which would enable them, after centuries of oppression, to transform every aspect of their lives.

Lecture Tour in India
December 1981 – March 1982

NOTES FROM THE EDITORS

When Sangharakshita embarked on his tour of India in the winter of 1981–2, it was in a sense a return to a pattern established in the 1950s. In the years between Dr Ambedkar's conversion to Buddhism in 1956 and his departure for England in 1964, Sangharakshita regularly visited the new Buddhist communities, speaking as one Buddhist to another – sometimes to thousands of others – about what commitment to the Dharma life could mean. The last and longest of these tours was from October 1961 to May 1962, when Sangharakshita visited more than half the states of India, gave nearly 200 talks, and received 25,000 men and women into the Buddhist community. But when he returned to India in 1981, the situation was significantly different. Whereas he had made the tours of the 1950s and early 1960s alone, he was now accompanied by a number of Western disciples. As he toured Maharashtra, he frequently spoke about the new Buddhist movement he had founded in England, the way it was developing, and its relationship with the Indian Buddhist movement initiated by Dr Ambedkar, of whose needs he had continued to be very much aware. Now, especially through the work of Dharmachari Lokamitra, a link had been forged between the two, and the beginnings of an Indian wing of the FWBO was emerging.

It was Lokamitra who organized the 1981–2 lecture tour (as he had a shorter, previous tour in 1979). His preparations included visiting every venue beforehand to make sure everything was in place for Sangharakshita's visit. Some forty or forty-one 'programmes' were arranged, although on a few occasions Sangharakshita, suffering from a sore throat, was unable to speak and Lokamitra was required to ascend the stage and speak on his behalf. Exactly how many times this happened we no longer know, but the transcripts of thirty-three talks and three question-and-answer sessions given by Sangharakshita on that tour have survived. Many of the transcripts were edited by Sangharakshita himself in preparation for translation into Marathi and publication in *Buddhayan*, the quarterly journal of TBMSG, though in the end not all of them made it into that publication. Seven were published in English in the *Dhammamegha* series of pamphlets brought out by Triratna Grantha Mala, the publishing wing of TBMSG.[175] Most are appearing in English for the first time.

In preparing the talks for this volume we have edited them lightly, at the same time attempting to retain something of the atmosphere and feeling of the original occasion, including Sangharakshita's more informal remarks at the beginning of each lecture as he established a rapport with his audience. Of course, as Subhuti writes in his Foreword, these written texts cannot capture

> the extraordinary sights and sounds of the occasions on which
> they were given – wide-eyed children, gazing up at the orange-clad
> speaker, lines of women in gorgeous saris, flower garlands by the
> score, and crackling loudspeakers ringing on the evening air. Above
> all they cannot convey the mood, the intense joy and faith they
> awakened in their audiences: the shining faces, the soaring spirits.

The reader's imagination will have to supply this, aided, perhaps, by Nagabodhi's book *Jai Bhim!*[176] which is partly a record of this tour.

Order members

In these talks, members of what is now the Triratna Buddhist Order are variously referred to as *upāsakas*, *dasa sīla upāsakas*, and Dhammacharis. (You will find explanations of these terms in the glossary.) When the Order was founded, and up until 1982, Order members both East and West were known as *upāsakas* (m.) and *upāsikās* (f.), a traditional term for a lay Buddhist (as opposed to *bhikkhu* and *bhikkhunī*, sometimes translated as 'monk' and 'nun'). But this traditional distinction based on lifestyle was one that Sangharakshita was questioning more and more – as indeed had Dr Ambedkar – as he explains, for example, in talks 9 and 23. Thus it was that at the end of this India tour, on 9 and 10 March 1982, a meeting of the Trailokya Bauddha Mahasangha was held in Bombay when it was decided that in India the title 'Dhammachari' should replace 'Upāsaka'. This was soon adopted also in the West. From then on, Order members – whether they followed a monastic, semi-monastic, or non-monastic lifestyle – were simply Dhammacharis (m.) and Dhammacharinis (f.), all being committed to the Three Jewels and all following the same ten precepts, in other words, all 'faring in the Dhamma' – the meaning of the term Dhammachari/Dhammacharini.

Dhammamitra

This term is explained in the Glossary. Some readers may wonder at the combination of a Pāli word (*dhamma*) with a Sanskrit one (*mitra*) but for Buddhists in India, using the Pāli *dhamma* rather than the Sanskrit *dharma* avoids confusion with the Hindu dharma (see 'caste *dharma*' in the Glossary). *Mitra* is in common usage in Hindi to mean friend – so one might even regard *Dhammamitra* as a new word that has emerged in contemporary Indian Buddhist culture.

FWBO/TBMSG/Triratna Buddhist Community

The movement Sangharakshita founded in 1967 is variously referred to in these pages as the FWBO, TBMSG, and Triratna Buddhist Community. To explain this requires going into a little history. Sangharakshita founded a new Buddhist movement in England in 1967 and a new Buddhist Order the following year. They were known respectively as the Friends of the Western Buddhist Order and the Western Buddhist Order. These names translated reasonably well into other languages as the movement spread to other Western or Westernized countries across the globe. However, when Lokamitra arrived in India in 1978 and began working with local Buddhists, an Indian wing of the Order and movement began to form. Clearly the movement there could not be called Western, and another name was adopted: the Trailokya Bauddha Mahasangha Sahayak Gana (TBMSG), which translates as 'Association of Helpers of the Buddhist Community of the Three Worlds'. (The Order was known as the Trailokya Bauddha Mahasangha. The 'three worlds' are those of traditional Buddhist cosmology, *kāmaloka, rūpaloka,* and *arūpaloka,* and also the first, second, and third worlds of modern geopolitics.) Naturally there was always a slight sense that something was missing – for it was a united international Order and movement but two quite different names were in use. In 2010, therefore, in response to a request from some senior Indian Order members, and with full participation of the movement's International Chairs' Assembly, a new name suggested by Sangharakshita was adopted: the Triratna Buddhist Order and Community, the Triratna being, of course, the Three Jewels of Buddhism: Buddha, Dharma, and Sangha.

ENDNOTES

We have included quite a few endnotes, some to explain context and others so that Sangharakshita's flow of stories and references can be traced to their sources in the Buddhist canon. The aim is not at all to make this a scholarly work, which clearly it is not, but rather to encourage the reader to explore further. Sangharakshita himself has always emphasized the great value of reading the traditional texts, and we hope our notes will help.

Kalyanaprabha and Vidyadevi
April 2016

Locations for Sangharakshita's India Lecture Tour 1981–2

I

AMBEDKAR HOUSING SOCIETY
WELCOMING PROGRAMME

Poona,[177] *19 December 1981*

From the introduction by Upāsaka Sudarshan,[178] you may have noticed that I am no longer a very young man. Although I'm not exactly old, I'm certainly getting on a bit. As you get older, you begin to experience things a little differently and, in particular, time seems to pass very quickly. When I arrived here a few days ago I was thinking that the last time I came to Poona was two years ago, but then I remembered that in fact it is fully three years since my last visit,[179] and in that time a lot has happened as far as the Buddhist movement here is concerned. As soon as I arrived at the railway station and saw the faces of the friends who had come to welcome me, I felt that a change had taken place. I realized that during those three years the Buddhist movement had grown. Just by looking at people's faces, I could see that there is new life, a new heart and a new spirit in the Buddhist movement here in Poona. So I would like to begin by congratulating you all on that – the anagārikas, the *upāsakas*, the *Dhammamitras*, the *Dhammasahayaks*: I congratulate every one of you.

So much has happened here during the past three years. In England every few weeks I receive reports and minutes of meetings from Anagārika Lokamitra[180] and other friends. These reports told me that many lectures on the Dhamma were being given, not only here in Poona, but in many parts of Maharashtra, and that study groups and retreats were being held. I heard that a very successful retreat had been held at Aurangabad, at Milind College, and that Buddha Jayanti was celebrated on a grand scale, as well as the anniversary of Dr Ambedkar's birth, and the anniversary of his death. Only two weeks ago, you celebrated the twenty-fifth anniversary of Dr Ambedkar's passing away.[181] I was very sorry that I could not be here on that occasion. In fact at that time I was not in England either, but in a country in southern Europe called Italy, where we had a three-month training course for new *upāsakas*. But though I was not in India, I certainly thought about all of you here on that occasion.

Another activity here in Poona that I was very glad to hear about is the programme of publications. As you know, many booklets are being brought out by Trailokya Bauddha Mahasangha and Triratna Grantha Mala in Marathi and in English. In particular I am very glad to receive *Buddhayan*, which comes out every three months. I think that this publication is one of the best things that has happened during the whole twenty-five years since the original mass conversion ceremony in Nagpur. Many years ago, when I was going from one small village to another in Maharashtra, everywhere I went I found that people wanted to hear the Dhamma. In fact, everybody *needed* the Dhamma. In this connection there is a famous song by one of the great Tibetan Buddhist teachers, Milarepa. Perhaps you haven't heard of him, but among the Tibetans his name is as famous as the name of Dr Ambedkar is among you. Milarepa was a great Buddhist yogi and a great teacher of the Dhamma, but he didn't give lectures. Instead, he sang songs. If anyone came to him and asked about the Dhamma, Milarepa would sing a song in reply, a beautiful poem with beautiful music, produced on the spot. It is one of these songs of his that I want to tell you about now. He sang, 'Everybody needs the Dhamma. Men need the Dhamma, women need the Dhamma, children need the Dhamma, everybody needs the Dhamma.'[182] This was the theme of his song and he developed this idea in a very beautiful way. In the same way, here in India today, everybody needs the Dhamma. Here in Maharashtra, especially among the followers of Dr Ambedkar, everybody needs – and wants – to hear the Dhamma. I was very happy therefore when the magazine *Buddhayan* was started. Whenever I receive the latest copy through the post, I feel very happy because I know that now, all over Maharashtra, Marathi people can read about the Dhamma in their own language. At first, 2,000 copies were printed, then 3,000, then 4,000. Now it is 5,000, and maybe next year it will be 10,000 or 20,000. *Buddhayan* is growing! Seeing this, I feel that the Dhamma is flourishing here in Poona.

The Dhamma is growing in other ways as well. As I was coming along in the taxi with Lokamitra, he gave me a fresh piece of news. He told me that we have got Dhamma classes for small children, and that our lady mitras are taking these classes. Many years ago when I was coming to Poona, the ladies used to arrange all my programmes, and I'm very happy that they are still active. I hope that they will do more and more and that we will have hundreds of these classes for boys and girls all over Poona.

The Dhamma is flourishing not just here in Poona or in Maharashtra, but also in the West. New Buddhist centres are springing up in many places. During the last year we've started up activities in America, in Australia, and in Sweden. If you haven't heard the names of these countries and if you are a student, next time you go to school, look in the atlas, find out where these countries are, put your finger on the spot and say to yourself, 'This is where we have our activities.' Our movement is spreading throughout the world. It's not just confined to Maharashtra, nor to India, nor to the East. It's spreading in all directions.

This is very much in accordance with the wishes of the late Dr Babasaheb Ambedkar. As long ago as 1950, he wrote a very important article called 'Buddha and the Future of His Religion', which was published in the *Maha Bodhi* journal in Calcutta.[183] In the course of this short article Dr Ambedkar said a number of very important things. One of the important things he said was that Buddhism could be revived in India. So, even in 1950, six years before the conversion ceremony, Dr Ambedkar had a strong faith that Buddhism could be revived in India. Maybe nobody else in India had this faith. It's probably difficult for some of you to imagine what things were like in India in 1950. When I came to this country in 1944, before many of you were born, perhaps even before your fathers were born, you could travel from Delhi all the way to Calcutta and you would not see a single Buddhist on the way. There were almost no Buddhists in India – just a few *bhikkhus* from Sri Lanka, and a few Tibetan Buddhists in Ladakh. Who could have thought in 1950 that Buddhism could be revived in India? Only Dr Ambedkar had this imagination, this faith.

Another thing he said in his article was – and here I'm quoting his exact words – 'The Hindu masses, when they are enlightened, are sure to turn to Buddhism.'[184] And sure enough, the 'Hindu masses', the ex-Hindu masses, the ex-untouchable masses, have started turning to Buddhism exactly as he predicted. Again, he had that faith, even as long ago as 1950. He also said in his article that society must have the sanction of morality. Without morality, he said, there is no society. (I'm going to be saying something about this in my talk tomorrow night.) So you see, in this article, written in 1950, Dr Ambedkar said many important things.

Tonight I'm concerned with just one other thing that he said in that article. Dr Ambedkar had the idea of spreading Buddhism, but he was a very practical man. This was one of his great characteristics. He was a great scholar, a great thinker, but at the same time he was very practical. This combination is very rare. There are lots of people who are very good at theory, but when it comes to doing something practical, they're useless. In the same way, there are many people with energy and the capacity to do things, but they don't think, they don't have any real intelligence. Dr Ambedkar had both these things, to a very high degree.

Because he was a practical man, in 'The Buddha and the Future of His Religion' he raises a very practical question. How can this ideal of spreading Buddhism be realized? It's very easy to say, 'Let's spread Buddhism', but it is not at all easy to know how to do it. In answering this question he said that three steps appear to be necessary: first, to produce a Buddhist Bible; second, to make changes in the organization, the aims and objects, of the *bhikkhu saṅgha*; and third, to set up a world Buddhist mission. From this we can see how broad Dr Ambedkar's vision was. He didn't think just in terms of Maharashtra or even India. He wanted Buddhism to spread throughout the world. He wanted a world Buddhist mission, and that is what we now have. Our Buddhist activities are being carried on in many parts of the world, in the UK, America, Sweden, Holland, Finland, Australia, as well as in many other parts of India. In this way, Dr Ambedkar's plan is being carried out.

We mustn't forget that Dr Ambedkar was a very great man. Great men are like mountains. If you are very close to the mountain, you can't see how high it is. You can only see its height from a great distance. In the same way, a great man like Dr Ambedkar can be appreciated only from a distance. Now, from a distance of twenty-five years, we can begin to appreciate the real greatness of Dr Ambedkar, his tremendous vision, courage, and determination. Just that one person changed the lives of millions upon millions of people. This is something that happens very rarely in the history of the world. Dr Ambedkar was a universal man. He was born in India, but he was not confined to India. As you know, he received his higher education in the West. He mastered subjects like economics, political science, sociology, anthropology, law, he studied the history and the political and social institutions of the West, and he took whatever was good from the West. We can even say that Dr Ambedkar was the product of the best of the West and the best of the East. From the West he took the ideals of liberty, equality, and fraternity. From the East he took Buddhism. Dr Ambedkar was a new kind of man. He really was the modern *manu*, not just for India but for the whole world. This great man died twenty-five years ago, but his work is going on. Buddhism is spreading in many different parts of the world.

As I said, three years have passed since my last visit. Some of you might have been wondering what I've been doing during that time. Well, I've been doing what I can to spread Buddhism in the West. I've been giving lectures, taking study courses and retreats. Recently, I took a three-month Dhamma study course held in Tuscany in southern Italy and attended by twenty-six people. For three whole months we stayed in a big old building on the top of a hill, from which we had a beautiful view over the surrounding countryside and even the distant sea, and in all that time we simply studied and practised the Dhamma. That's all we did. Most people, most of the time, felt that they were in heaven. They didn't have to bother about earning money, or their family, or going to school or college. They could spend the whole day studying the Dhamma, meditating, or talking to one another.

But why did we spend three months studying and practising the Dhamma in this way? This goes back to one of the things that Dr Ambedkar mentioned in his article. He said that we need to reorganize the *bhikkhu saṅgha*. He also said that the *bhikkhu saṅgha* of today, in the Buddhist countries of Asia, can't do very much. We need a new kind of Buddhist teacher, a new kind of Buddhist worker. At the end of the course in Italy, twenty people received the *dasa sīla upāsaka* ordination. For the time being we're using this word '*upāsaka*', but we might have to change it, because we find that most of our *upāsakas* are better trained and more experienced than most of the *bhikkhus* that you meet. Some of our *upāsakas*, when they come to India, or when they go to Buddhist countries, have some quite strange experiences.

Sometimes they meet a *bhikkhu* from Sri Lanka or from Burma or from Tibet, and they ask him, 'Do you meditate?' and the *bhikkhu* says, 'No, I never meditate.' So they ask, 'Do you study the Buddhist scriptures? Can you give a lecture?' And the *bhikkhu* says, 'Oh no, that is much too difficult.' So our *upāsaka* says, 'Well, what *do* you do?' And the *bhikkhu* says, 'Well, I'm just a *bhikkhu*. People give me food, I eat it, and then they get a lot of *upāsikās puṇya*.' Our *upāsakas* are very, very surprised. Then sometimes a *bhikkhu* asks questions of the *upāsaka*. He asks, 'Do you meditate?' The *upāsaka* says, 'Yes, every day.' And then the *bhikkhu* asks, 'Do you study Buddhism?' And the *upāsaka* replies, 'Oh yes, we study Pāli texts, we study Sanskrit Mahāyāna *sūtras*, we study Tibetan Buddhism, we study Zen.' Now the *bhikkhu* is very, very surprised, and sometimes says to the *upāsaka*, 'Do you give lectures on the Dhamma?' The *upāsaka* says, 'Yes, I give lectures frequently.' And then the *bhikkhu* is more surprised than ever. He says, 'You are just an *upāsaka*, and you do all this?' So our *dasa sīla upāsaka* is a bit different from an ordinary *upāsaka*. One day it may be necessary to change the name.[185] On our three-month course in Italy, we were trying to do one of the things that Dr Ambedkar suggested – that is, to produce a new kind of Buddhist worker, a new kind of Buddhist teacher.

Another thing that I have been doing is writing. I like writing very much, even writing letters. Sometimes I don't get much time to write, but lately I have managed to do quite a lot. Upāsaka Sudarshan said something about this in the course of his introduction. He told you that I am writing a second volume of my memoirs.[186] This is quite correct. I've just been writing about things that happened in the year 1950, and the beginning of 1951 – thirty-one years ago. Some things that happened in those days are still very clear in my mind. I'll just give a couple of examples.

In 1951 the Government of India held a census. These are held every ten years, but this was the first census enumeration after India became Independent. At that time I was living in Kalimpong, which is up near Sikkim, near Tibet. The census enumerator, who was a Bengali Brahmin – some Mukherjee or Chatterjee – came to see me with the form already filled in. He said, 'Aha, yes, you are a Hindu, and your caste is Buddhist.' I said,'No, no, I am not a Hindu, I am a Buddhist, and I don't have any caste.' So he said, 'No, no, that is all wrong. You are Buddhist and that means that you must be Hindu, because Buddhism is part of Hinduism.'

I said, 'No, no. Buddhism is a separate religion. Buddhism is my religion.' But he protested, 'No, Buddhism is your caste.' He seemed to think that I was very stupid. So I said, 'First of all, I am English. In England we don't have any caste. And secondly, I am a Buddhist. In Buddhism there is no caste.' But he said, 'No, that is all wrong. Are you teaching me how to enumerate you? You are definitely Hindu by religion and Buddhist by caste.' So this was a very big lesson for me, and it taught me a lot about the attitudes of these Bannerjees and Chatterjees and Mukherjees.[187]

Another experience I had was when I was staying in a vihara belonging to some Nepali *bhikkhus*.[188] At that time there were no Buddhist activities going on, so I started some evening classes for students. Every evening I had thirty, forty, or even fifty students coming. Some of the boys were Buddhist, some of them were Hindu, some came from Nepal, some came from Bihar, some from Bengal. It was very mixed. But the Nepali *bhikkhus* were very displeased. They said, 'Sangharakshita is spoiling our vihara. He is bringing these low-caste Hindu boys from the bazaar.' Some of my students were Nepali Scheduled Caste boys, from a caste called Kami, some of them were tailors, and they were looked down on by the other Nepalese. The strange thing was that I noticed that these Kami boys were the most intelligent of all the students who came to me, and they all did well in their examinations. But these Nepali *bhikkhus* didn't like them coming to the vihara because of their low caste. That made me realize that this caste system is a very dangerous thing, a poisonous thing, if even the *bhikkhu saṅgha* in Nepal had been affected by it. So once again I learned a lesson. I learned to be very, very careful about the caste system. Afterwards, when I was working in India, people used to say, 'Sangharakshita is very narrow-minded. He is always criticizing the caste system.' People used to say to me, 'The caste system is very good. Maybe a little bit not so good here, a little bit not so good there, but on the whole it is a very good system.' But I knew better. I never forgot the lessons that I learned.

So these are some of the experiences that I have been writing about in my memoirs, and as I wrote, I thought about India and about my Buddhist friends here, and I'm very glad to be back in the midst of you all. I'm very grateful to you for the wonderful reception you've given me this evening, and for the welcome you gave me two days ago on the station platform when I arrived. My friends in England of course knew that I was coming to India, so they were asking me all sorts of questions, and one of them asked, 'Do you feel excited because you are going to India?' So I said, 'No, I don't feel excited at all.' Why should I feel excited? India is just like my own home. I am as much at home here as I am in England. I've spent half my adult life in India. Sometimes my friends in England say that they think I don't really belong in England any more because I've been so long in India that I've become more like an Indian. So yes, I am very glad to see my old friends here and very glad to see so many new friends. And I'm very glad to see with my own eyes how the Buddhist activities in Poona have grown. On this occasion I shall be spending quite a few weeks in India, travelling around and visiting a number of places, mainly in the western half of Maharashtra. I'll be going to Bombay, Mahad, Ahmednagar, Manmad, Aurangabad, Osmanabad, Sholapur, and many other places. Lokamitra has got a long list of places for me to visit, including Nagpur.

I can never forget the people of Nagpur, because they and I went through a very great experience together. I was in Nagpur on 6 December 1956, the very day that the news was received of the sad death of Dr Ambedkar. I remember that day very well. I arrived at Nagpur station in the middle of the morning. It was seven weeks after the great conversion. When the train stopped I looked out of the window, and there on the platform to receive me were 2,000 people. There was a big police *bandobast* to keep all the crowds under control. I was taken in a procession to the house of a friend, where I had something to eat and a little rest. Everybody was very happy and very much looking forward to my lecture in the evening. But at three o'clock in the afternoon someone came to the house. Tears were trickling from his eyes, and at first he couldn't speak. He said, 'We've just received some terrible news from Bombay.' This was the news that Dr Ambedkar had died. It was just as though a great thunderbolt had struck the people of Nagpur. People were crying in the streets. Thousands of people got on the trains to go to Bombay, not even buying tickets. But still thousands were left in Nagpur. After a short while one of the organizers came to where I was staying. He said, 'There are thousands of people coming, they want you to speak to them.' So I said, 'Well, if there are thousands of people, it's very difficult to speak without microphones, so please arrange something for this evening.' So a meeting was arranged for seven o'clock that night in Kasturchand Park. They had a loudspeaker, but they couldn't arrange a stage, so I had to stand on a rickshaw and give my speech. I could see people coming from all parts of Nagpur, and they were completely silent, even though there were so many of them. There wasn't a sound. People were coming from all directions in processions, each person carrying a lighted candle. There must have been more than one *lakh* – more than 100,000 people.

The condolence meeting began. I said, 'Shok Sabh',[189] but the people who got up to speak found that they just couldn't say a word. When they tried to speak they burst into tears and had to sit down. Everybody in the meeting was crying. They felt as if they had lost their mother, their father, everything. Of course, it was only seven weeks after the conversion. They were wondering, 'What are we to do? We have given up Hinduism, but we don't yet know about Buddhism. Now that Dr Ambedkar is dead, what is going to happen to the Buddhist movement?' People were afraid that the whole movement of conversion would collapse. Eventually I gave my talk. I said simply, 'Don't think that Dr Ambedkar is dead. Dr Ambedkar can never die. Dr Ambedkar lives on in you. In the same way, the movement started by Dr Ambedkar will never die; it will not come to an end. It will be carried on by all of you.' These words gave them some consolation. I stayed in Nagpur for four days, and in the course of four days I gave thirty-five lectures all over the city. Everywhere I went I said the same thing: Dr Ambedkar is not dead. The Buddhist work he started will continue.

That was twenty-five years ago. And now we know that truly Dr Ambedkar is not dead. His work has continued. There were many enemies of that work who made all sorts of pessimistic predictions, but despite what they said, the work started by Dr Ambedkar has triumphed. It is still very much alive today, and it will grow more and more. And this is, of course, why I have come again to India. I've come to help the work of Dr Ambedkar in whatever way I can. I'm very glad to see you all again, and I thank you very much for your very kind reception.

2

THE BUDDHA'S RELIGION
IS MORALITY

Ahilya Ashram, Poona,[190] *20 December 1981*

This evening I want to begin by talking about man – that is to say, about human beings. In Buddhism man occupies a very important place. It is man, in fact, who occupies the centre of the picture, not God, because in Buddhism there is no God, but only man, in various stages of development. Buddhism therefore directs all its attention to man.

According to modern evolutionary science, human beings have existed for only about 500,000 years, and of that period he has lived as a social being only for about 10,000 or 12,000 years, which is about as far back as recorded history goes. About the period before that we have only myths and legends – we don't know very much about those earlier, prehistoric times. We are, however, gradually learning more and more about them. Sometimes archaeologists dig up the ruins of ancient buried cities, and in that way we learn how people in those far-off days lived. But though we don't know much about those prehistoric times, there is one thing that we do know. We know that changes were taking place, both in man himself and in the society to which he belonged. And here there is an interesting fact to be observed. The further back we go in history, the slower is the rate at which the change takes place. The closer we come to the present, on the other hand, the faster the rate of change. During the last 500 years, especially, the rate of social change has been tremendous – particularly during the last thirty or forty years, and in the West more than the East.

But what is the reason for this? Why do changes in society take place? They take place for the very definite reason that the people belonging to that society become dissatisfied with it, and start wanting a new kind of society. Twenty-five years ago a great social change took place here in India, one of the greatest social changes that the world has ever seen. I am referring of course to the mass conversion to Buddhism (*Dhammanta*) which took place in Nagpur on 14 October 1956. Why did this great social change take place? It took place because of many, many people's deep dissatisfaction with the old Hindu society. For the caste Hindus that old society may have been very pleasant, but for millions of people who were not caste Hindus (*savarṇa*) it was simply hell. It was a hell of injustice, misery, and oppression, a hell of poverty and ignorance.

This morning I happened to be reading a speech given by Dr Ambedkar in Bombay in 1936. In the course of this speech, in which he gives his reasons for giving up Hinduism and the old Hindu society, he relates three incidents from his own life.[191] These incidents are very interesting and illuminating. The first two belong to the period when he was still very young, just a boy of five or six years old. At that time his father retired from the army on a pension after many years of service, and on his retirement the whole family went to live in Satara.[192] Up to that time Dr Ambedkar's family had been living in military quarters, and they had not had much contact with the outside world. When the family moved to Satara Dr Ambedkar, who was then just a small boy, found that no barber was prepared to cut his hair. His hair had to be cut by his elder sister. At first, not being able to understand the reason for this, he was very surprised. Eventually he realized that the barber would not cut his hair because he was an Untouchable. This was his experience when he was only five or six years of age.

The second incident involved his father, who on one occasion happened to be staying in Goregaon,[193] and wrote to his family to come and visit him there. The family went by train. Young Ambedkar had never been on a train before, so he was feeling very happy. All the members of the family were wearing new clothes and looked very respectable. On their arrival at the station, however, they found that their father was not there to meet them. Apparently he had not received the letter they had sent saying that they were coming by that train. As it was a long way from the station to Goregaon, they tried to hire a bullock cart, but this proved impossible, as none of the owners of the bullock carts were willing to drive Untouchables. Only very late in the evening did they manage to get hold of one, and even then the driver would not drive it for them. The young Ambedkar, even though he was only five or six years old, had to drive the bullock cart himself. It was a long way to Goregaon, and no one would give them water to drink because they were Untouchables. They had to drink water from a stream, and Dr Ambedkar said that the water was full of mud mixed with cow dung.

The third incident occurred many years later, after Dr Ambedkar's return from England. He had continued his education in England on a scholarship from the Baroda State,[194] and had done very well there. On his return from England he therefore went into the service of the Baroda State, and went up to Baroda city to take up his appointment. But on his arrival in the city he was unable to get a room anywhere. No Hindu or Muslim would give him a room, because he was an Untouchable. Though he was wearing a Western-style suit, though he was highly educated and spoke beautiful English, it didn't make any difference. He was an Untouchable, and so he couldn't get a room.

In this difficult situation, he decided to take a Parsi name and went to live in the Parsi *dharmasala*. On the second day of his stay there, however, people found out who he really was. As you know, in India people find out your caste very quickly. It's the first thing they want to know about you. They don't care if you are good or bad, learned or ignorant. The question is: What is your caste? I myself know this very well. It has been my own experience. On so many occasions, especially in South India, I've been walking peacefully along the road and a perfect stranger has come up to me and said 'What is your caste?' I used to reply that I didn't have any caste, but when I said that, the man would look at me as though I was mad. It was therefore not surprising that on the second day of his stay in the Parsi *dharmasala* people found out who Dr Ambedkar really was. Twenty or thirty Parsis came to the *dharmasala* with sticks and threatened to kill him. Parsis are not Hindus, but they have lived in India for centuries and have come under the influence of the caste system. So they drove Dr Ambedkar out of the *dharmasala*. He had to give up his appointment and return to Bombay.

These incidents made a tremendous impression on Dr Ambedkar. They wounded him to the heart. He thought that it was a terrible thing that human beings could treat other human beings in such a manner. Thus he became more and more dissatisfied with the old Hindu society, and eventually decided to give up Hinduism and adopt Buddhism. So on 14 October 1956 the great mass conversion took place in Nagpur. But why did Dr Ambedkar adopt Buddhism? Why did he not just give up Hinduism without adopting some other religion? After all, many people in the world today live without religion, especially in the communist countries. In these countries they are, in fact, very much against religion. So why did Dr Ambedkar adopt another religion? Why did he not just give up Hinduism and leave it at that? There are three reasons.

First of all, Dr Ambedkar himself was a deeply religious man. He had very strong feelings of faith and devotion, especially towards Bhagavan Buddha. When he was only a schoolboy someone gave him a copy of *The Light of Asia*, which tells the life of the Buddha in beautiful poetry,[195] and this book had a strong influence on him.

Secondly, Dr Ambedkar was convinced that man could not, in fact, live without religion. He believed that man is essentially a religious being, and cannot be happy or truly successful without religion. Here he did not agree with Marxist communism. Dr Ambedkar believed that if one gives up one religion, one has to adopt another.

Thirdly, according to Dr Ambedkar, religion in the sense of morality is the governing principle of every society. In his article on 'Buddha and the Future of his Religion', written in 1950, he wrote, 'Society must have either the sanction of law or the sanction of morality to hold it together. Without either, society must go to pieces.'[196]

In other words, in his view it is the law that keeps the anti-social minority within bounds, while the majority are governed by morality. Here an interesting question arises. This is not a question that Dr Ambedkar himself raises, but it occurs to me to ask what happens when there is a widespread breakdown of morality in a society? What happens when a lot of people in a society lose faith in religion? This is beginning to happen in the West. Millions of people have lost faith in Christianity, and it was of course the Christian religion that for hundreds of years held society together in the West. Now it is no longer able to hold society together, and there are signs, here and there, that society is beginning to fall to pieces.

These, then, are the three reasons why when Dr Ambedkar decided to give up Hinduism, he also decided to adopt another religion. Now here there is a point to be emphasized. Dr Ambedkar did not want simply to escape from the old Hindu society. He wanted to create a new society. Because he wanted to create a new society, and because in his view a new religion was necessary in order to do this, he had to adopt another religion. But which religion? Eventually, as you know, he chose Buddhism because of the importance that Buddhism gives to morality. In this connection I shall quote again from his article 'Buddha and the Future of his Religion':

> Hinduism is a religion which is not founded on morality. Whatever morality Hinduism has, it is not an integral part of it. It is not embedded in religion. It (i.e. morality) is a separate force which is sustained by social necessities and not by injunction of Hindu religion. The religion of the Buddha is morality. It is imbedded in religion. Buddhist religion is nothing if not morality. It is true that in Buddhism there is no God. In place of God there is morality. What God is to other religions, morality is to Buddhism. [197]

Dr Ambedkar wanted to bring into existence a new society, and this new society had to be founded on morality. This is why Dr Ambedkar chose Buddhism.

We usually think of Buddhist morality in terms of the five or the ten *sīlas*. These are indeed very important, and we cannot emphasize them too much. But it is possible to go into this matter of Buddhist morality from a somewhat different point of view, and Dr Ambedkar does this in this same article on 'Buddha and the Future of his Religion'. You might be thinking that I'm quoting a lot from Dr Ambedkar's writings, but the reason for that is that it is necessary to know what Dr Ambedkar really said. People say, 'Dr Ambedkar said this' or 'Dr Ambedkar said that', just as they say, 'The Buddha said this' or 'The Buddha said that'. Some people even say that the Buddha said there is a God! When people say such things you have to ask, 'Where did the Buddha say that? Show me the *sūtra*.' In the same way, when people say, 'Dr Ambedkar said this' or 'Dr Ambedkar said that' you must ask where Dr Ambedkar said it, and when, because it's important to know what Dr Ambedkar really did say. Unless you know what he really said, you cannot follow his path. So let us look at this article again and see what Dr Ambedkar has to say on the subject of Buddhist morality. He says:

Religion as a code of social morality ... must recognize the fundamental tenets of Liberty, Equality, and Fraternity. Unless a religion recognizes these three fundamental principles of social life, religion will be doomed.[198]

Let us, therefore, look at these fundamental principles in terms of Buddhism. First of all, the principle of liberty. I don't know whether it is the same in Marathi, but in English we distinguish between liberty and freedom. 'Liberty' is more external, and 'freedom' more internal, pertaining more to the mind and the heart than to the body. We enjoy liberty when the society to which we belong is organized on proper principles. We enjoy freedom when the mind reaches a higher state of consciousness, when the mind becomes free from greed, hatred, and delusion. We enjoy freedom when *maitrī, karuṇā,* and *prajñā* are fully developed. Buddhism attaches the greatest importance to freedom. Freedom is in fact the ultimate goal of the whole Buddhist path. In Pāli, the language of the Theravāda Buddhist scriptures, the word for freedom is *vimutti,* and in the Pāli scriptures the Buddha has quite a number of things to say about *vimutti.* On one occasion he said,

My Dhamma is just like the great ocean. Just as the great ocean has one taste, the taste of salt (*loṇa-rasa*), so my Dhamma has one taste, the taste of freedom (*vimutti-rasa*).[199]

Whether you take water from the Indian Ocean or the Atlantic Ocean, it will taste of salt. In the same way, whatever aspect of the Buddha's teaching you take up, it has just one taste, the taste of freedom – that is, it is concerned only with freedom, leads only to freedom.

Even though we can distinguish between liberty and freedom, they are still very closely connected. Almost without exception, people have to experience liberty before they experience freedom. It is very difficult to develop the mind, to raise the level of consciousness, if one does not enjoy liberty. Political liberty, social liberty, economic liberty, intellectual liberty, and of course religious liberty, are therefore all important, and Buddhism has always recognized the importance of all these different kinds of liberty. This is one of the reasons why it is so tolerant. It has always recognized the liberty of the individual to follow the religion of his own choice. Some religions do not recognize this liberty. Only 150 years ago the Pope, the head of the Roman Catholic Church, declared officially that it is wrong to believe that a man should follow the religion of his own choice.[200] All through its history the Roman Catholic Church has persecuted the followers of other religions, even the followers of other forms of Christianity, whenever it has had the political power to do so. In Europe thousands of people have been killed in wars of religion. In the past – now several hundreds of years ago – thousands of people were burnt alive for believing differently from the established Church. So Christianity, especially the Roman Catholic Church, has not recognized the liberty of the individual to follow the religion of his own choice. It is the same with Islam. Only a few weeks ago I was reading about what is happening in Iran. In Iran there are a few thousand followers of the Bahá'í religion, and according to the newspapers, many of them have been murdered by the orthodox Muslims. In Buddhism we don't find anything like that. Buddhism has existed for 2,500 years but there has never been a religious war in the name of Buddhism. Buddhism has spread only by peaceful means, and one of the reasons for this is that Buddhism believes in liberty.

Secondly, there is the principle of equality. There are some misunderstandings about this principle. Equality does not mean that everybody is exactly the same. Equality means that everybody has the same right to develop as a human being. Hinduism does not recognize this right. Therefore Dr Ambedkar says that Hinduism is not founded on morality. He says that the official gospel of Hinduism is inequality. Hinduism says that if you are born as a Brahmin, you have the right to study the Vedas. If you are born as a Kshatriya, you have the right to fight. If you are born as a Vaishya, you have the right to do business and make money. It does not matter if as a businessman you cheat a little, because that is all part of your *dharma*. If you are born a Shudra, you have the right to serve everybody else, i.e. all the members of the three higher castes. And what about the Untouchable? Well, he is not even a Shudra. The Untouchables have no rights at all. They don't even have the right to exist. In fact, of course, the Hindu caste system is much more complicated than that. There are many, many more castes, not just the original four. It is said that there are 2,000 different castes in modern Hinduism. There is even a caste of thieves, and if you are born into that caste, you have the right to steal. In fact, it is your *dharma* to steal. If you don't steal you are committing a sin. So Hinduism does not really believe in morality. It believes in caste *dharma*. It believes that it is sinful to give up your own caste *dharma* and follow the *dharma* of some other caste. For this reason someone who is a Shudra by birth is not allowed to study the Vedas, however intelligent he may be.

An orthodox Hindu writer called Kumārila Bhaṭṭa, who lived more than 1000 years ago, even criticized the Buddha on this score. In his book the *Ślokavārttika* he wrote that although the Buddha was born into a Kshatriya family he dared to act as a teacher. Teaching, however, is the duty of the Brahmin, not the duty of the Kshatriya. The Buddha, therefore, was in Kumārila Bhaṭṭa's view a very wicked person because he gave up his own Kshatriya *dharma* and tried to take up the *dharma* of a Brahmin. For this reason, Kumārila Bhaṭṭa says, the teaching of the Buddha should not be accepted, just as milk should not be accepted when it comes in the skin of a dog. There is nothing wrong with the teaching, but it comes from the wrong source, so it should not be accepted. This is the orthodox Hindu view.[201]

Buddhism takes quite a different view. It believes in equality, not in caste *dharma*. It doesn't see people as Brahmin, Kshatriya, Vaishya etc. It sees people just as human beings, and because it sees them just as human beings, it wants them all to grow. It sees them all as developing. This is the vision that the Buddha had shortly after his Enlightenment. He saw all the people of the world like a great bed of lotuses, all growing, and all in different stages of development.[202] When, some time later, he sent out his first sixty disciples to teach his *saddhamma*, he sent them out to teach it for the happiness and welfare of all.[203] He did not send them out to teach it to this caste or to that caste only. He sent out his disciples to teach all human beings, whether old or young, rich or poor, male or female. Thus we find that Buddhism believes in equality in the sense of equality of opportunity – opportunity to grow and develop as a human being.

Thirdly, there's the principle of fraternity. The English word comes from the Latin word for 'brother'. Fraternity is the sort of feeling that you have towards your own brother – in fact, it is an even stronger feeling than that. It's natural to have this sort of feeling towards your own brother. You have the same parents, you've been brought up together, you've played together, so naturally you have a good, warm, friendly feeling towards one another. The feeling of fraternity is like that, only much deeper, much broader, because it is not limited to your blood relatives. According to Buddhism all men and women are brothers and sisters, because we are all human beings. Human beings do not belong to different biological species in the way that other kinds of animals do. The proof of this is that animals belonging to different species cannot interbreed and produce offspring. The lion and the monkey, for instance, cannot interbreed to produce an animal which is half lion and half monkey. It is the same with the elephant and the horse, the cat and the dog, and so on. But human beings, men and women, can all interbreed, whatever caste or country they are from. Even the Brahmin and the Chandala²⁰⁴ can produce offspring – the Hindu *śāstras* recognize that, because they have kept a separate caste for the offspring of such unions. All men and women are brothers and sisters because we all belong to one and the same human race, so it is natural that we should all love one another. Buddhism was the first religion in the world to recognize this principle of fraternity.

In Buddhism, fraternity is called *mettā* or *maitrī*. (*Mettā* is the Pāli word and *maitrī* is the Sanskrit word.) *Mettā* or *maitrī* is the feeling of unselfish love, the heartfelt desire for the happiness and well-being of other people. Buddhism teaches that this feeling should be directed towards all human beings, not just to the members of one's own family or caste. Indeed, it should be directed towards all living beings whatsoever. What we may call the motto of Buddhism is *sabbe sattā sukhi hontu*, which means 'May all living beings be happy'. What a wonderful ideal this is! And in Buddhism it is not just an ideal. Buddhism teaches us how to develop this feeling of *mettā* through the practice of what is called *mettā bhāvanā*, about which I shall be saying something in the second talk in this series.

These, then, are the three fundamental principles of social life: liberty, equality, and fraternity. Buddhism recognizes all three principles because it gives importance to morality. Buddhism can therefore be the foundation of the new society. As Dr Ambedkar said, morality is the governing principle of every society, and it was for this reason that he chose Buddhism. He didn't simply give up the old religion. He chose a new religion, a religion that was capable of giving a solid foundation to the new society – a foundation of *śīla*, liberty, equality, and fraternity.

So far I have spoken about *śīla* as the foundation of the new society, but there is much more that could be said about it. I will now make just a few comments about *śīla* in relation to the individual Buddhist. First of all, *śīla* is something that you have to practise yourself. No one else can practise it for you. You yourself have to observe the principles of liberty, equality, and fraternity in your dealings with other people. You yourself have to practise the five, or the eight, or the ten precepts. It is good to recite them, but that is not enough. You must practise them too.

Secondly, you have to practise *śīla* regularly. Ideally you have to practise it all the time. It is not enough to practise it just once or twice a month, or just on Buddha Jayanti day. You have to practise it all the time. In Buddhist literature *śīla* is defined as habitual skilful action of body, speech, and mind. But what do we mean by skilful? Skilful means dissociated from mental states of greed, hatred, and delusion and associated with mental states of generosity, love or *maitrī*, and wisdom or *prajñā*. *Śīla* is thus the habitual performance of such skilful actions of body, speech, and mind. Here the emphasis is on 'habitual'. *Śīla* is not something you do from time to time, but something you do all the time. The individual Buddhist should be the living embodiment of *śīla*, the living embodiment of skilful mental states.

Thirdly, *śīla* makes you a true human being. Without it you are not really human. *Śīla* helps you to grow, helps you to develop. That is why it is the first stage of the threefold path taught by the Buddha, the other two stages being *samādhi* and *prajñā*. *Śīla* comes first, which is why after reciting the Three Refuges in the Buddha, the Dhamma, and the Sangha, we take the five or the eight or the ten precepts. We go for Refuge, we commit ourselves to the spiritual ideal, and when we take the precepts we actually start moving in the direction of that ideal. Therefore it is important for us to practise these precepts.

My last few comments have been about *śīla* in relation to the individual Buddhist, and before that, I spoke about *śīla* as the foundation of the new society. These two things are connected. *Śīla* is indeed the foundation of the new society, but it is not something that exists by itself. It exists only when people actually practise it. So when we say that *śīla* is the foundation of the new society, what we really mean is that people who are practising *śīla* are the foundation of the new society. If there are no people practising *śīla*, then there will be no new society. If there are no Buddhists there will be no Buddhism. Buddhism does not exist in books. Buddhism exists in the lives of people. So we must practise *śīla*. We must observe the principles of liberty, equality, and fraternity. We must practise the five or the eight or the ten precepts all the time.

If we do that, then Dr Ambedkar's purpose in giving up Hinduism and choosing Buddhism will be fulfilled. And not only that. We will lead happy, useful, and progressive lives, and in this way the foundations of the new society will be truly laid.

3

BEING A BUDDHIST MEANS CHANGING YOUR LIFE

Pimpri, 21 December 1981

Brothers and Sisters: First of all, let me say how glad I am to be here in Pimpri once again.[205] My last visit took place three years ago, and since then I've been in the West – in England, where our Buddhist activities are fast expanding. In that part of the world, more and more people are giving serious attention to the teaching of the Buddha, and becoming involved with our activities. In the course of the last year, we have started new Buddhist centres in no less than three new countries – the USA, Australia, and Sweden – and already these centres are flourishing.

Since I was last here, I myself have been very busy, giving lectures, writing books, and conducting retreats and Dhamma study courses. Our last important Dhamma study course was in Italy, where I went with a group of people to Italy, and there we stayed in a very beautiful building situated all on its own on the top of a hill. We stayed there for three months. We didn't go out into the town at all. We spent the whole time studying the Dhamma, meditating, and discussing among ourselves. People learned how to give lectures on the Dhamma in what we called the speakers' class. People learned how to chant the Pāli puja, how to lead Dhamma study classes and meditation classes, how to organize new centres, how to live in a Buddhist community, and how to get on with other people. That's very important. You may know the Dhamma very well, you may be able to meditate very well, but if you don't know how to get on with other people, you can't do very much. So for three months these people were doing just these things, and at the end of the course, some twenty of them took the *dasa sīla upāsaka* ordination. They became members of the TBM and they were given kesas like the ones you can see being worn here.[206]

So, you may be wondering, why did we take all this trouble? Why did we give people this experience, this training? Of course it was to enable them to work more efficiently for the Dhamma, but it wasn't just that. You may remember something that Dr Ambedkar wrote in 1950, in an article he contributed to the *Maha Bodhi* journal called 'Buddha and the Future of his Religion'. In that article he said, in effect, that the *bhikkhu saṅgha* must be reorganized, because the present *bhikkhu saṅgha* is useless.[207] This reorganization is what we're trying to do. We're trying to create a new body of full-time workers for the Dhamma – not only in England, but here in India also, and in many other places. This is one of the things that Dr Ambedkar saw very clearly needed to be done, and we are trying to do it. And in fact now there are altogether 160 *dasa sīla upāsakas*,[208] most of whom are working full time for the Dhamma, giving all their time and energy to Dhamma work, in eight countries of the world.

Anyway, I don't want to say anything more about that this evening. I just wanted to give you an idea of what I've been doing. You might have been thinking that I'd been sitting in my vihara in England idling my time away. Dr Ambedkar was very critical about *bhikkhus* who sit and don't do anything, so we have to be very careful!

While I was in Italy, here in India something very important was happening. You were celebrating the twenty-fifth anniversary of Dr Ambedkar's original mass conversion ceremony in Nagpur,[209] and then, just seven weeks later, you observed the twenty-fifth anniversary of the passing away of Dr Ambedkar. Twenty-five years is quite a long time. In the course of that time a whole new generation can spring up. Twenty-five years ago, I knew young men here in Poona who are now grandfathers. And many of you here this evening weren't even born then and never saw Dr Ambedkar. You've only heard about him and read about him. I myself was fortunate enough to have the opportunity of meeting Dr Ambedkar three times, and each time we had a very important discussion. The first time I met him was in Bombay, at his house, Rajagriha; the second time was also in Bombay, in his room at Siddharth College; and the third time was at his home in Delhi, just a few weeks before his death. Although I met him just those three times, in fact I'd been in contact with him by letter since 1950, though I'm not going to talk about that this evening.[210]

As I've said, twenty-five years is a very long time. It's long enough for many changes to have taken place, not only in one's appearance, but in one's way of life. It's long enough for there to be changes in one's practice of the Dhamma. We should all be much better Buddhists now than we were twenty-five years ago. But are we? Are those of us who took *dīkṣā* twenty-five years ago better Buddhists now than we were then? And if not, why not? This is a very important question. Let's consider it with the help of an incident from the life of the Buddha himself. Many of the incidents in his life have great significance for us – though we may have to think about them quite a lot before we can understand what that significance is.

You know that the Buddha was born a prince, or at least he was born into a very rich, aristocratic family. He had everything that he could possibly want – everything that was available at that time. Of course he didn't have a motor car or a television set, but he had quite a lot of things: three beautiful mansions, one for each of the seasons of the year, a beautiful horse, jewels, beautiful clothes, a beautiful wife, a kind father, high social position. He had very good prospects. But he gave it all up. He just left it. He walked out. He became what was called a *parivrājaka*. Tonight I won't go into why he became a *parivrājaka*; I want to take us to the moment when he left his palace. According to some accounts he rode out, and after a certain distance he dismounted. There was a beggar standing there, and the Buddha, the young prince, asked him to exchange clothes with him. The Buddha took off his beautiful jewels, his wonderful turban, and his sword (he was a Kshatriya, so he wore a sword). He gave all these things to the beggar, and he put on the beggar's rags. So there was a complete change. The beggar now looked like a prince, and the prince now looked like a beggar.[211] But becoming a *parivrājaka* isn't just about appearance. Becoming a *parivrājaka* means leaving home, leaving the house, but it means much more than that. It means leaving the old way of life: the old mental attitudes, the old psychological conditioning, the old reactive mind. In other words, becoming a *parivrājaka* means *changing*. When you become a *parivrājaka*, the change is not just external, but also internal. Becoming a *parivrājaka* represents a change of heart, a change of mind, even a transformation of mind. This is the important point.

Twenty-five years ago, millions of people became *parivrājakas*. They left home, in the sense that they left the old broken-down Hindu society in which they'd been living, and became Buddhists. At least, they recited *tisaraṇa* and *pañcasīla*. But since then, has there been a real change? Is the *pañcasīla* better observed now than it was twenty-five years ago? Is there less fighting and quarreling among Buddhists? Are you more honest in money matters? Are husbands more faithful to their wives? Are wives more faithful to their husbands? Has prostitution disappeared among Buddhists? Do you always speak the truth? Do you always speak kindly to one another? Do you speak about the Dhamma? Do you speak in such a way as to bring about unity among Buddhists? Have you given up drinking? Have you given up smoking? In other words, are you really observing the five precepts? After all, after twenty-five years, you should at least have made a good start. Have you given up worshipping the old Hindu gods? Have you given up the dowry system? Have you given up your fear of caste Hindu people? If you haven't done these things, then no real change has taken place.

For the last three years I've been in the West, thousands of miles away, but although I've been so far away, I've heard quite a lot about Buddhists in India, and I've heard some quite strange things. I've heard that there are Buddhists running liquor shops, Buddhists who have gone back to Hinduism, Buddhists who have lost their faith in Dr Ambedkar. I hope that these things are not true. Becoming a Buddhist means changing. It means change for the individual and change for the society. It means doing everything in a different way, a new way, a better way. It means being guided by the principles of liberty, equality, and fraternity. In the outside world, by which I mean the world outside Buddhism, things are usually done by force or by fear. But being a Buddhist is not like that. Being a Buddhist means doing everything by *maitrī*. *Maitrī* is not weak, *maitrī* is very strong. You can do everything by *maitrī* – if you want to.

So it's not enough just to say you're a Buddhist. It's not enough simply to recite *tisaraṇa* and *pañcasīla*. You must change. Your heart must change. Your life must change. Your surroundings must change. You must be a real Buddhist, not a false one. The Buddha once explained what a false Buddhist is like. He said that a false Buddhist is like a donkey who follows a herd of cows along the road, trying to join them, saying in his donkey voice, 'I'm a cow too! I'm a cow too!' But he's not a cow! His hooves are different, he hasn't got any horns, and his voice is *very* different. He just goes 'hee-haw' and everybody knows that he's a donkey![212] The false Buddhist is just like that. He doesn't practise *pañcasīla*; he doesn't really want to change.

We don't want to be donkeys. We want to be real Buddhists. It's not enough just to *look* like a Buddhist. You have to *be* a Buddhist. Simply reciting the *tisaraṇa* and *pañcasīla* without trying to practise it is no good. Of course, reciting can be good. Recite all day if you like – if you spend your time that way, at least you can't be getting up to much mischief. But whether you recite the Refuges and Precepts or not, the important thing is that you *practise* them.

This brings us to another very important point, a rather more difficult one. One of the Buddha's teachings is the teaching of the ten *saṃyojanas*.[213] *Saṃyojana* means 'fetter' or 'bond', and these ten *saṃyojanas* tie us down to the *saṃsāra*, they prevent us from going forward and realizing Nirvāṇa. They prevent us from being like the Buddha. Of these ten *saṃyojanas*, the first three are particularly important: *satkāya-dṛṣṭi*, *vicikitsā*, and *śīlavrata-parāmarśa*. I'm just going to say a few words about *śīlavrata-parāmarśa*, as this is particularly relevant here.

The word, in its Sanskrit version, consists of three parts: *śīla*, *vrata*, and *parāmarśa*. In Sanskrit, *śīla* doesn't mean quite the same thing as Buddhist *śīla*. It means 'moral rules', rules simply as rules, as it were apart from the meaning of the rules. *Vrata* means any traditional religious observance. For instance, in the Buddha's day, the Brahmins kept the sacred fire. This was called a *vrata*. Sometimes people fast on the *ekādaśī* day,[214] and this is also a *vrata*. The third part of the word is *parāmarśa*, which means 'relying upon', in a rather weak and dependent sort of way. *Śīlavrata-parāmarśa* thus means following moral rules and religious observances for their own sake, blindly. It means following them not in order to develop as a human being, but mechanically, just as perhaps you used to go to the temple when you were a Hindu. You would ring the bell – ding, ding, ding – throw some rice, and that would be that. You didn't think about what you were doing, or what it meant. You just did it, because it was the custom. This is what is meant by *śīlavrata-parāmarśa*.

But Buddhism cannot be practised mechanically. Buddhism has to be practised with thought and awareness, wholeheartedly. When we practise Buddhism, we must have a strong feeling for what we're doing, and understand what we're doing. We must do it thoroughly, we must put all our energy into it. If we don't practise it in this way, then we're not really Buddhists. But if you do practise Buddhism in this way, then changes will take place – changes in you as an individual human being, and changes in the society to which you belong. In that way you will really leave home. You will become a real *parivrājaka*. You will go from the old society to the new society.

You'll also be accepted into the Sangha. Indeed, you will not just *join* the new society; you will help *create* the new society, a society based on liberty, equality, and fraternity. The Sangha doesn't just mean the *bhikkhu saṅgha*. It means the Mahāsaṅgha, which consists of all those who are true Buddhists, all those who go for Refuge and practise the precepts.

I said that twenty-five years is long enough for many changes to have taken place, and some changes certainly have taken place in the Buddhist movement, but not enough. In fact, we can say quite frankly that until recently the Buddhist movement in Maharashtra was quite unsatisfactory. But why haven't more changes taken place in twenty-five years? Why has the Buddhist movement not flourished as it should have done? Why have people not lived up to the ideals of Dr Ambedkar? Something must have got in the way, but what?

Well, we could say that many things have got in the way, but in this connection I want to refer to another incident in the life of the Buddha. One day the Buddha was visiting the viharas where the *bhikkhus* were staying. In those days viharas were not big buildings, they were just little huts, and in one of the little huts, the Buddha found a very sick *bhikkhu*. He was suffering from dysentery, and he was lying there on the ground in his own excrement. No one was taking care of him. So the Buddha called his companion Ānanda, who was always nearby, and said, 'Bring some water'. Ānanda brought some water in his begging-bowl, and the Buddha washed the *bhikkhu* with his own hands. Then, with Ānanda's help, he lifted the *bhikkhu* up and laid him on a clean bed. After that, the Buddha called all the *bhikkhus* in the area together and asked them, 'Why are you not looking after this *bhikkhu*?' And they said, 'Well, he's useless to us.' This was a shameful reply, and the Buddha seems to have been quite displeased. He said, '*Bhikkhus*, you have no mother and no father to look after you. If you don't care for one another, who will do it?' Then he said something very, very important. He said, 'He who would serve me, let him serve the sick.'[215]

This is a very important incident, and involves a very important principle. The Buddha here is not concerned merely with the treatment of the sick, and he's not speaking just to *bhikkhus* in the literal sense. The significance of this episode is universal. Here the Buddha is concerned with difficulties of all kinds, and he's speaking to all Buddhists. What he is really saying is that Buddhists should help one another. If Buddhists do not take care of one another, who will? Hindus won't do it, we know that very well. Christians won't do it. Muslims won't do it. So if you want to serve the Buddha, you must serve your fellow Buddhists. This is very important. What is the use of offering flowers to the Buddha, or garlanding the picture of Dr Ambedkar, and then fighting and quarreling with other Buddhists, other followers of Dr Ambedkar? What is the use of criticizing the good work that they are doing? Buddhists should all be like one big family, one big, happy, spiritual family. It doesn't matter whether you're Mahars or Chamars,[216] Maharashtrian or Gujarati, Indian or English. What is important is that you're Buddhists. The Buddha himself said something like this. In his day too, all kinds of people joined the *bhikkhu sangha*. Brahmins joined it – the Buddha's great disciples Sāriputta and Moggallāna were Brahmins. Kshatriyas joined it, and so did Vaishyas and Shudras. But, the Buddha said, when they joined the *bhikkhu sangha*, they all gave up their separate castes and lineages. They became just *sākyaputtas*, sons and daughters of the Buddha. It's just like the rivers. They are called by different names – Ganga, Yamuna – but when they reach the great ocean, they lose their separate identities, their different names. They're all called simply the great ocean.

This applies not only to the *bhikkhu sangha*, but also to the Mahāsangha. The most important thing about all of us is the fact that we are Buddhists, that we've gone for Refuge. Together we form one great spiritual family. The Buddha is like our father, the Dhamma is like our mother, and we ourselves are the Sangha. Dr Ambedkar and the members of our Order are like our elder brothers. We don't always remember that Buddhists all belong to one great spiritual family. We allow ourselves to become divided, so energy goes into fights and quarrels, and unhelpful criticism. Perhaps we can't do anything for the Dhamma ourselves, so we criticize what others are doing. The result is that the Buddhist movement is weakened, and very little progress is made, even after as long a time as twenty-five years.

So, what should we do? We have to make a strong resolution that we will change the society in which we live. We should resolve to put all our energy into the Buddhist movement. We should remain united, and work with one another. We should help one another. We should remember the two incidents I mentioned from the life of the Buddha. We should remember how the Buddha changed his clothes – and more than his clothes – and how he helped the sick *bhikkhu*. If we can do all these things, then, and only then, our conversion to Buddhism will be meaningful. And only then will Dr Ambedkar's aspirations be fulfilled.

4

THE SEED OF THE DHAMMA
REVOLUTION: SAMĀDHI

Poona, 23 December 1981

Brothers and Sisters: What we know as Buddhism, that is to say the Buddha Dhamma, has now been in existence in the world for 2,500 years, and in the course of that time many different schools and sects of Buddhism have sprung up. Many of them sprang up in India itself, but others emerged in Sri Lanka, Burma, and Thailand. In China, especially, very many schools sprang up, and the same is true of Tibet and Japan. Thus there are scores, perhaps even hundreds, of different schools of Buddhism existing in the world, and very often these schools give different interpretations of the Dhamma, or at least look at it from different points of view. Not only that. In all those countries Buddhism, or the Dhamma, exists in a particular cultural context. Thus it is sometimes difficult to know what Buddhism, or the Dhamma, really is. Sinhalese Buddhists say that it is one thing, Tibetan Buddhists say that it is another, while Japanese Buddhists say that it is yet another.

There is, therefore, a difficulty, even a problem. Now this is not altogether a new problem. In a way, the same problem existed even in the Buddha's time. The Buddha taught his disciples, they learned his teaching, and they then went in different directions, to many different parts of India. Consequently they sometimes got out of touch with the Buddha, and with one another. Some disciples said that the Buddha's teaching was this, others that it was that. Some *bhikkhus* were teaching one thing, other *bhikkhus* another. In this way people sometimes got a bit confused. We might well feel the same way ourselves, given all the different teachings of different kinds that we hear. Fortunately, the Buddha himself gave clear guidelines as to how we can identify his true teachings. His advice is very useful for all of us, but it was originally given to one person: Mahāpajāpatī Gotami, his maternal aunt and foster mother. When the Buddha's mother died Mahāpajāpatī Gotami looked after him and brought him up. She loved him very much, and didn't like to be separated from him. After the Buddha's Enlightenment, therefore, she too went forth from home into the homeless life, as a *parivrājaka*. Eventually, she became a *bhikkhunī* and wandered from place to place. And on one occasion she went to the Buddha and asked him for a simple teaching that she could practise in solitude. The teaching he gave her established a clear principle according to which we can all work out which teachings are in accordance with the Buddha's understanding. He said:

> Gotami, of whatsoever teachings you can assure yourself thus: 'These teachings lead to passions, not to dispassion; to bondage, not to freedom; to discontent, not to content; to laziness, not to energy; to delight in evil, not delight in good': of such teachings you can be sure, Gotami, this is not the Dhamma. This is not the Vinaya. This is not the Buddha's Message. Conversely, of whatsoever teachings you can assure yourself thus: 'These teachings lead to dispassion; to freedom; to content; to energy; to delight in good': of such teachings you can be sure, this is the Dhamma. This is the Vinaya. This is the Buddha's Message.[217]

Here the Buddha's criterion is not theoretical but practical. The Dhamma is whatever leads to the development of the individual as a human being. We can even put it the other way round. Whatever leads to the development of the individual as a human being is the Dhamma. The great emperor Aśoka declared, 'Whatever the Buddha said is well said.'[218] But one of the Mahāyāna *sūtras* goes even further than this, and says, 'Whatever is well said is the word of the Buddha.'[219] This is a very broad principle. It means that whatever helps us to grow is Buddhism. If it doesn't help us to grow, it isn't Buddhism, and we can therefore put it to one side – even if it is found in the Buddhist scriptures. Similarly, if some teaching really does help us, then it's Buddhism, and we can use it, even if it is found in a non-Buddhist book – even if it is found in a work of literature or poetry.

Dr Ambedkar himself followed this principle. He was a widely read man – in the course of his life he read thousands of books – and in his writings and speeches he quotes from many different writers, including a number of well-known Western authors. For instance, he quotes Goethe, who was the greatest of the German poets, as well as being a great thinker, and Matthew Arnold, an English poet and literary and social critic of the nineteenth century. He also quotes Bertrand Russell, a great English mathematician and philosopher of the early twentieth century. Dr Ambedkar quotes these authors because they say good things, things he can use, things that helps human development – things that are, therefore, really part of the Dhamma.

To give a concrete example, after Dr Ambedkar conducted the great mass conversion ceremony at Nagpur on 14 October 1956, he delivered a long and important speech in which he gave the reasons for his conversion to Buddhism, and in the course of that speech he quoted a saying by one of the saints of Maharashtra, a saint who was, of course, a Hindu. This shows how broad-minded Dr Ambedkar was. The name of that saint was Ram Das. He is not known outside India. I hadn't heard of him before, and in any case in India there are hundreds of people called Ram Das, but it seems that this particular Ram Das is very well known in Maharashtra. I'll give you his exact words, just as Dr Ambedkar quoted them: 'If a man lacks enthusiasm, either his mind or body is in a diseased condition.' This is a very good saying. No wonder Dr Ambedkar quoted it. But he doesn't only quote it. He goes on to enlarge upon it, saying:

If there is no enthusiasm, life becomes a drudgery – a mere burden to be dragged. Nothing can be achieved if there is no enthusiasm.[220]

These words are very valuable. Indeed they are, as the English expression has it, 'golden words'. But Dr Ambedkar doesn't stop there. He pursues the matter even further. He asks, 'Why does one lose enthusiasm?' And he goes on to give the answer. He says:

[The] main reason for this lack of enthusiasm on the part of a man is that an individual loses hope to get an opportunity to elevate [him]self. Hopelessness leads to lack of enthusiasm. The mind is such cases becomes diseased.[221]

These words are very significant. They show how important enthusiasm is. Without enthusiasm there is no progress, and without progress there is no human development. Without enthusiasm there is no Buddhist movement, no Dhamma Revolution. So how are we to develop enthusiasm? And how are we to maintain it once it has been developed?

If we want a traditional Buddhist word for enthusiasm, perhaps the nearest we can get in Pāli is *pīti*, the Sanskrit equivalent of which is *prīti*, and according to the Buddhist tradition this is experienced in a state of *dhyāna* or *samādhi*. The Buddhist teaching about *dhyāna* or *samādhi* is rather different from the corresponding Hindu teaching. According to Buddhism there are four levels, or four degrees, of *dhyāna* – four degrees, that is to say, of what is called *rūpa-dhyāna*. Tonight I'm going to deal only with the first two. According to the Buddhist teaching, in the first *rūpa-dhyāna* there are altogether five mental factors present. These are *vitakka, vicāra, sukha, pīti*, and *cittassa-ekaggata*.[222] *Vitakka* is when the mind takes hold of something; and when it not only takes hold of something but examines it from every side, that is *vicāra*. Buddhaghosa, the great Theravāda commentator, gives a comparison: If you have a pot which you want to clean, *vitakka* is like taking firm hold of the pot with your left hand, while *vicāra* is like simultaneously scouring the outside of the pot all the way round with your right hand.[223] In English idiom, thinking *of* something is *vitakka*, thinking *about* something is *vicāra*. *Sukha* is much easier to understand. *Sukha* is happiness, bliss, to a very high degree. *Pīti* is what we've just been talking about – interest, enthusiasm, joy, delight, rapture. There are so many different words to describe this mental factor. Lastly, there is *cittassa-ekaggata*, or complete one-pointedness of mind, in which all the mental faculties are working together harmoniously. In the first *rūpa-dhyāna* there are these five mental faculties present.

When we come to the second *rūpa-dhyāna*, a change takes place. In the second *rūpa-dhyāna* there are only three mental factors, *sukha, pīti*, and *cittassa-ekaggata*, all three of them more highly developed than before; there is no *vitakka*, and no *vicāra*. What has happened is that upon your entering into the second *rūpa-dhyāna* all discursive mental activity has died away, and there is no thinking in the ordinary sense, although at the same time the mind is extremely clear, bright, and aware, and one feels intensely happy and full of energy. This is the state of enthusiasm and inspiration. And this state is the seed of the Dhamma Revolution.

The Buddha gives a beautiful simile for each of the four *rūpa-dhyānas*, so that we can understand the nature of the *rūpa-dhyānas* better, before we actually experience them for ourselves. Each simile conjures up a picture.[224] Tonight I'm going to describe only the simile for the second *rūpa-dhyāna*, the state of inspiration and enthusiasm. The Buddha says that this state is just like a beautiful big lake whose water comes not from streams flowing into the lake, or from the clouds, but from a subterranean spring. From the very bottom of the lake fresh water is continually bubbling up, and this fresh water fills the whole lake. The Buddha says that the second *rūpa-dhyāna* state is like that. There is something bubbling up deep within one's heart, just like a spring of water. We can now see how enthusiasm is to be developed, as well as how it is to be maintained. Enthusiasm is to be developed by practising, what we call in English, 'meditation'.

Twenty-five years have now passed since Dr Ambedkar's great mass conversion ceremony in Nagpur but, unfortunately, in the course of those twenty-five years not very much has been achieved. In some parts of Maharashtra people have lost enthusiasm for Dhamma work – have even lost hope. Some people, I hear, have even lost their faith in Dr Ambedkar. Consequently there has been no real Dhamma Revolution. Why is this? It's all due to lack of enthusiasm. And what is the reason for this lack of enthusiasm? There are several reasons, but one reason is that people do not practise meditation. The politicians certainly don't meditate, and even *bhikkhus* don't practise meditation, so they don't have any enthusiasm themselves, and can't inspire others. No Dhamma Revolution has therefore taken place, and not much has been achieved in twenty-five years. But in the Trailokya Bauddha Mahasangha we are trying to change this. Great importance is attached to meditation, and it is regularly taught. All the *dasa sīla upāsakas* and *upāsikās* practise meditation. Even Dhammamitras practise meditation.

Now you probably know that I returned to England from India in 1964. In England I studied the situation, especially the Buddhist situation, for two years, and I then started a new Buddhist movement. But I didn't start it by holding a big public meeting. I didn't start it by inviting government ministers along – in England people don't do things in that way, anyhow. I didn't start by collecting a lot of money. In fact, I didn't have any money at all. I didn't start it by putting out a lot of publicity. So how did I start it? I just began a meditation class, in a basement underneath a shop in the very heart of London. This class was held once a week, then twice a week. At first only ten or twelve people came, but having started in this way, our new Buddhist movement has grown fast. In the fourteen or fifteen years since it began, the Friends of the Western Buddhist Order, or Trailokya Bauddha Mahasangha Sahayak Gana, as it is known in India, has become the biggest Buddhist movement in Europe. It conducts very many different activities. It has centres for teaching the Dhamma, viharas where full-time workers live, cooperative businesses to make money for the Movement, and presses producing books and magazines. So how was it possible to do all this? How was it possible for the Movement in the West to be so successful? It was all because of enthusiasm. And where did that enthusiasm come from? It came from those meditation classes.

This is not in the least surprising. Where did Buddhism itself come from? You might say that it came from Gautama the Buddha, but where did the Buddha get the Dhamma from? Did he get it when he was living as a prince in the palace at home? Did he get it when he was living in the jungle and practising self-mortification? No. He got it sitting under the bodhi tree at Bodh Gaya. And what was he doing under that bodhi tree at Bodh Gaya? He was meditating. He discovered Buddhism in meditation. He discovered the Truth in meditation. That's where he got his inspiration – in fact the highest inspiration. He got the inspiration of Supreme Perfect Enlightenment – of *anuttara samyak sambodhi* – in meditation. First came meditation, and then came the teaching of the Dhamma.

So that's what we must do. We must first get inspiration and enthusiasm, and then teach the Dhamma, work for the Dhamma. Now, don't misunderstand me. I'm not saying you must go to the Himalayas and meditate for years and years before you can teach the Dhamma. What I do say is that meditation and Dhamma work go hand in hand. In this way you will keep your enthusiasm alive, and the Dhamma Revolution will take place. Meditation is therefore the seed of the Dhamma Revolution. We can even say that without meditation, there can be no Dhamma Revolution. The Dhamma Revolution cannot be brought about by politicians who don't meditate, however clever they may be. The Dhamma Revolution cannot be brought about by *bhikkhus* who don't meditate, however learned they may be. The Dhamma Revolution can be brought about only by those who meditate. It can be brought about only by those who are full of enthusiasm, full of energy. It can be brought about only by those who are full of *sukha* and *pīti*. It can be brought about only by those who experience *cittassa-ekaggata*. This is why, in our movement, there is such an emphasis on the importance of meditation. This is why we have meditation classes. This is why we have retreats. This is why the Trailokya Bauddha Mahasangha is able to do something for people, both in England and in other countries.

But how is one to practise meditation? I can't say very much about this. If you really want to learn how to meditate you'll have to go along to one of our classes or a *Dhamma-shibir*. One can't learn meditation from books. One can't even learn it from a lecture. Nevertheless I'll just say a few words on the subject. In the Trailokya Bauddha Mahasangha there are two methods of meditation with which we start people off. The first is called *ānāpānasati*, and the second *mettā bhāvanā*.

Ānāpāna means the in-and-out-going breath, while *sati* means 'mindfulness' or 'just watching', so *ānāpānasati* means the mindfulness, or just watching, of the in-and-out-going breath. It's very important to understand that we don't try to control the breath. We just watch it. We don't try to control it because this is a quite different kind of practice from the Hindu *prāṇāyāma*, where the breath is controlled. So how do we watch the breath? There are four stages. In the first stage we simply watch the breath coming in and going out, and at the same time we count. We breathe in and breathe out, then count one; breathe in and breathe out, then count two. In this way we count up to ten. After we've counted up to ten we go back to the beginning and start counting from one again. We breathe in and breathe out, then count one; breathe in and breathe out, then count two, and so on. We do this for five or ten minutes. Then we find that the mind becomes a little bit steady. When this happens we change to the second stage of practice. In the second stage we carry on counting, but we count in a different way. We count one, then breathe in and breathe out, count two, then breathe in and breathe out. In this second stage we're counting at the *beginning* of each in-and-out-breath, instead of at the end as in the first stage. Here also we count from one to ten, over and over again. The mind becomes a bit steadier, a bit calmer, a bit clearer. We therefore go on to the third stage. Here we don't count at all. The counting in the previous two stages was only to help concentrate the mind. In this third stage counting isn't necessary. We just follow the track of the breath.

We feel the breath coming in at the nostrils, feel it filling the lungs, feel it going up and out again. In this stage we can have quite a deep experience of concentration. Then we go on to the fourth stage. In this stage we don't concentrate on the in-and-out-breath. We concentrate our attention at the tip of the nose. There is a point just where the breath strikes the nostril, producing a sensation, a feeling. We concentrate on that sensation, on that feeling. The more we concentrate on that sensation the smaller it becomes, and the smaller it becomes the better becomes our concentration. In this way the sensation becomes smaller and smaller and, at the same time, the concentration becomes better and better. Gradually we have the experience of *dhyāna* and *samādhi*. If we want to do this practice properly we shall have to do it every day, for at least twenty or thirty minutes. We shall then find that we are gradually getting a good experience of *samādhi*. This is the *ānāpānasati* or mindfulness of in-and-out-breathing.

The other meditation practice we teach is the *mettā bhāvanā*. *Mettā* means friendliness. It is the wish for the happiness and well-being of other people. And *bhāvanā* means development; it means making bigger and bigger. *Mettā bhāvanā* therefore means making the feeling of *mettā* or friendliness bigger and bigger, stronger and stronger. So how do we practise the *mettā bhāvanā*? Here there are five stages. First we develop *mettā* towards ourselves. There is an English proverb: 'Charity begins at home.' It's not wrong to love yourself. What is wrong is to love *only* yourself. So in this stage you develop *mettā* towards yourself. You think, 'May I be well. May I be happy. May I be free from disease. May I be free from worry. May I progress. May I practise *śīla*. May I be a good Buddhist.' In that way you practise *mettā* towards yourself. Then comes the second stage. Here you think of a near and dear friend. If you are a man, you think of another man. If you are a woman, you think of another woman. In the same way you think, 'May that friend be well. May he be happy. May he be free from disease.' You do this just as you did it for yourself. In the end you'll feel the same positive feeling towards your friend as you feel towards yourself. Then you come on to the third stage. Here you think of someone who is not a friend but who, at the same time, is not an enemy. In English we call him or her the 'neutral person'. In the same way that you developed *mettā* towards yourself and towards your near and dear friend you now develop it towards that neutral person. Then you go on to the fourth stage. The fourth stage is a bit difficult, because here you have to develop *mettā* towards an enemy, that is to say, towards someone you don't like or who doesn't like you, or who has even tried to harm you. Some of our friends in England have found this stage of the practice particularly useful. If ever they have a misunderstanding with somebody, or a quarrel, when they do the *mettā bhāvanā* practice they put that person in the fourth stage. This is what we *should* do. After all, meditation is a practical thing. It's meant to help us. If you practise the *mettā bhāvanā* it will help you to get on well with everybody.

So these are the first four stages of the *mettā bhāvanā*. Then we come to the fifth and last stage, which is more complex. You have to start by thinking of the previous four people, that is to say, yourself, the near and dear friend, the neutral person, and the enemy. You have to see them as though they were standing in a row in front of you, and you have to develop the same feeling of *mettā* towards all of them and yourself equally, thinking, 'May we all be happy.' Then you have to think of all the people in your house: father, mother, brothers, sisters, aunts, uncles, cousins, children. Then you think of all the people in the locality, all the people in the city, in the district, in the state, in the country, in the continent, in the whole world. There are very many ways of practising this fifth stage. For instance, you can think of all the different centres and branches of Trailokya Bauddha Mahasangha all over the world. Or you can think of the people of all the different nationalities, all the different races, all the different religions. Of course here in India you can think of the people of all the different castes. That would be very useful. If everybody in India practised *mettā bhāvanā*, there wouldn't be any caste system left. Therefore we should try to propagate the *mettā bhāvanā* not only among Buddhists but also among our Hindu friends. If they also practise it, maybe they'll treat us a little more kindly.

So these are the two methods of meditation that we teach to beginners. Both these methods are very useful in helping us to develop inspiration and enthusiasm, but of course they are not the only methods of meditation in Buddhism. There are other methods, some of them very much more advanced, but I'm not going to say anything about them today. Instead, I want to say something on just one particular point. Earlier I used the words *dhyāna* and *samādhi*, and I used them as though they were more or less the same thing, but actually there's some difference between them, according to Buddhism. This difference is quite subtle, and not easy to understand, so please listen carefully. *Jhāna* (Pāli) or *dhyāna* (Sanskrit) is more like a state that you experience from time to time. *Samādhi* is more like that same *dhyāna* state when it has become a permanent part of your life. *Dhyāna* therefore comes first; *samādhi* comes later. Here there is a parallel with the practice of *śīla*. *Śīla* doesn't consist simply in the occasional practice of the five, or the eight, or the ten precepts. *Śīla* consists in the regular practice of those precepts. In the same way, *samādhi* is the regular and constant experience of the *dhyāna* state. In other words, *samādhi* is the experience of an uninterrupted flow of positive mental states.

From all this we can see how important *samādhi* is. *Samādhi* is the source of inspiration and enthusiasm, the seed of the Dhamma Revolution. If we want to change ourselves, we should meditate. If we want to change society, we should meditate. If we want to help others, we should meditate. Studying the Dhamma is not enough. Talking about the Dhamma is not enough. Wearing yellow robes is not enough. Running organizations is not enough. We must also meditate, must also experience *dhyāna* and *samādhi*. We must be like the Buddha. We must first of all sit under the bodhi tree. Of course the bodhi tree may be in our own room. The bodhi tree is wherever we meditate. You can say the true Buddhist carries his bodhi tree around with him. After sitting under the bodhi tree, then we can go out into the world full of inspiration, enthusiasm, and energy. Then we shall really be able to act in accordance with the Buddha's instruction to work for the good of the many, the happiness of the many. Then we shall really be able to carry on the work of Dr Ambedkar.

5
THE FIVE SPIRITUAL FACULTIES

Panchgani, 24 December 1981

Brothers and Sisters: First of all I want to say how glad I am to be in the midst of my Buddhist brothers and sisters here in Panchgani, which is such a beautiful place, and I am very glad to see so many of you here. This is not my first visit to Panchgani.[225] As some of you may know, I came here exactly twenty years ago. Quite a few of you weren't even born then, and some of you were so young that you can't remember me. But yes, I did visit this place twenty years ago. I remember that visit very well. I came here with some friends from Poona, I stayed for a couple of days, and we had a meeting. I am very glad to be here again. I am always glad to meet other Buddhists, but I am especially glad to meet those Buddhists who are followers of Dr Ambedkar.

Perhaps you don't know it, but my personal contact with Dr Ambedkar goes back to 1950. At that time, I was living in a place called Kalimpong. Like Panchgani, Kalimpong is a hill station, but it is bigger than Panchgani, and situated at a higher altitude. It is in West Bengal, in the foothills of the eastern Himalayas. At that time I had just started up Buddhist activities in Kalimpong – Dhamma classes, evening classes in English and other subjects, as well as a monthly magazine. I was then only twenty-six. (When you are young you have the energy to do such things. As you get older it becomes more difficult.) I already knew about Dr Ambedkar. In fact, I knew his name very well, having heard it in connection with the Hindu Code Bill. After carrying on my Buddhist activities for a few months I therefore thought that I should write to Dr Ambedkar, so I wrote, and told him what I was doing – this was in 1950 – and a few days later I received a reply. In his letter Dr Ambedkar expressed his great happiness that I was carrying on Buddhist activities in Kalimpong. '[*Bhikkhus*] must be more active than they have been,' he wrote, 'They must come out of their shell and be in the first rank of the fighting forces.' This exchange of letters was my first contact with Dr Ambedkar.[226]

Two or three years later I had the opportunity of meeting Dr Ambedkar personally. At that time I was visiting Bombay, and since Dr Ambedkar was also in Bombay just then I thought that I must certainly try to meet him. I therefore went along to Rajgriha, Dr Ambedkar's house at Dadar. On my arrival I found dozens of people waiting to see him, and he invited me into his office and asked me to wait while he dealt with them. While I sat there I saw delegates from many different organizations coming into his office to meet him. They had with them big garlands of flowers which they tried to put round his neck. But Dr Ambedkar would not allow this. He kept telling them, 'Take them away. I don't want them. It is a useless custom. You should spend the money on other things.' But I noticed that the more Dr Ambedkar scolded them, the happier they became. By the end of their visit they were smiling very broadly indeed. From this I could understand that Dr Ambedkar's followers were very devoted to him.

When all these visitors had gone Dr Ambedkar and I had a talk. At that time I had some connection with the Maha Bodhi Society in Calcutta. The Maha Bodhi Society was started by Anagārika Dharmapala in 1891. Dharmapala came from Sri Lanka. His principal aim was to restore the Maha Bodhi temple at Bodh Gaya to Buddhist hands, and it was in this connection that he started the Maha Bodhi Society. The Society also published a magazine, and carried on Dhamma activities.[227]

At the time that I met Dr Ambedkar, in the early 1950s, the president of the Maha Bodhi Society, strange to relate, was a Bengali Brahmin called Dr Shyama Prasad Mukherjee, who was also the president of the Hindu Maha Sabha. The Maha Bodhi Society, though a Buddhist organization, was being run by orthodox Hindus, so the Society couldn't do much for the cause of Buddhism. Dr Ambedkar knew all this, and he also knew of my connection with the Maha Bodhi Society. In fact he thought that I was a member of the Society. It was therefore about the Maha Bodhi Society that he first asked me. He said, 'How can this society of yours really work for Buddhism when its president is a Brahmin?' I said that I fully agreed with him, but that I was not a member of the Society, and was not responsible for the situation. However, I knew that some of the Buddhist workers in the Maha Bodhi Society were not happy with the present state of affairs, and wanted to change things. As it transpired, a few years later Dr Shyama Prasad Mukherjee died, and after a brief struggle the Maharajkumar of Sikkim was elected in his place.[228] This was the first time for very many years that the president of the Maha Bodhi Society had been a Buddhist. In the meantime, it was only natural that Dr Ambedkar should be concerned about the Society. Anyway, after I had made my own position clear we had a very friendly talk.

Two or three years later, at the end of 1955 or the beginning of 1956, I met Dr Ambedkar for the second time. Once again we met in Bombay, though this time it was at Siddharth College, where he had an upstairs office. He was sitting behind his desk, and I was sorry to see him looking quite ill. As I entered the room he said, in an extremely courteous manner, 'Please excuse me for not rising to receive you. I am so ill that I am having difficulty in standing up.' This time we had a very serious conversation. As you know, at that time Dr Ambedkar was very seriously thinking of giving up Hinduism and adopting Buddhism. He told me, 'I've made up my mind. I am going to become a Buddhist.' He then asked me how one became a Buddhist, and whether there was a ceremony for that purpose. I replied, 'Yes, there is a ceremony. You have to take the *tisaraṇa* and the *pañcasīla* from a *bhikkhu*.' Dr Ambedkar then asked, 'Can I take them from any *bhikkhu*?' I replied that he could, whereupon he asked, 'Could I take them from you?' I said, 'Yes, but it would be better if you took them from the oldest and most senior *bhikkhu* in India.' Dr Ambedkar then enquired who that was, and I told him it was U Chandramani Maha Sthavira of Kusinagar. Chandramaniji being my own teacher, I was very glad to mention his name. Dr Ambedkar was very pleased with my suggestions, and asked me to write everything I had told him in a letter and send it to him, so that he could know exactly what should be done. This I did, and everything happened as I had suggested. On 14 October 1956 Dr Ambedkar and *lakhs* of his followers took *Dhammadiksha* from Chandramaniji at Nagpur.

My last meeting with Dr Ambedkar took place at his residence in Delhi, just a few days before he died. I was in Delhi with fifty-six other 'eminent Buddhists from the border areas', with whom I had been touring the Buddhist holy places.[229] Knowing that the great conversion ceremony had taken place, I suggested to our group that we should all go and call on Dr Ambedkar and congratulate him on what he had done. We therefore went along to his residence. There were so many of us that there was not room for us all in the house, so Dr Ambedkar had chairs brought out into the compound. It was two or three o'clock in the afternoon, and quite hot. Dr Ambedkar was wearing a topi. We sat there talking for about two hours, but I noticed that Dr Ambedkar was very ill. Two or three times I said, 'I think we are giving you a lot of trouble. Please allow us to go.' But each time Dr Ambedkar said, 'No, no. We must have some more talk.' I could see that he was deeply concerned about the future of the movement of conversion to Buddhism that he had started. Anyway, after more than two hours of discussion we all left.

Dr Ambedkar stayed on in Delhi, of course, while I left for Bombay. From Bombay I went to Nagpur. On my arrival in Nagpur on the morning of 6 December I was given a tremendous welcome at the railway station. About 2,000 people were there to receive me. They knew that I was coming, and had made arrangements for me to give a lecture. Having been escorted to the home of the friend with whom I was to stay, I had something to eat and took a little rest. At about 3 o'clock in the afternoon I heard the sound of a disturbance outside. Someone burst into the house with the terrible news that Dr Ambedkar had died. The Nagpur people were very, very upset. I shall never forget how sad people were. Some of them were crying in the street. They felt as though they had lost their own mother, their own father. At 7 o'clock that night a meeting was held as arranged, but of course it had become a condolence meeting. I was the only speaker. Nobody else was able to speak. As soon as they stood up in front of the microphone they started crying, and had to sit down. I therefore had to do all the talking. I told people, 'Dr Ambedkar is not dead. He lives on for ever in the hearts of his followers. His work will not come to an end. It will be carried on by each one of you from where he left off.' During the next four days I addressed some thirty-five meetings in the Nagpur area. In this way I came into very close contact with the Nagpur people.[230] At the end of those four days I returned to Kalimpong. After that I used to come down from Kalimpong to Bombay, Poona, and Nagpur every winter.

In particular I used to visit Poona, and it was while I was on one of my visits that I came up to Panchgani.

Things went on like this until 1964, when I went back to England for the first time in twenty years. I stayed in England for two years, and having studied the situation there, especially the Buddhist situation, at the end of that time I decided to start a new Buddhist movement. This was in 1967. Now you may be wondering why I started that new Buddhist movement in England. At that time there were several Buddhist societies in different parts of the country, so why start a new one? First of all, the existing Buddhist societies were very small. Secondly, and more importantly, they were not one-hundred-percent Buddhist. Most of the people who belonged to these little societies were half-Buddhist and half-Christian. Though some of them said that they were Buddhist, they still believed in God and Jesus Christ. I thought to myself, this is not good. We don't want to mix Buddhism with Christianity, or Islam, or Hinduism, or any other religion. We must be one-hundred-percent Buddhist. So my experience in England was a bit like my experience in India with the Maha Bodhi Society. In England the Buddhists were half-Buddhist and half-Christian. In India, in the Maha Bodhi Society, they were half-Buddhist and half-Hindu. But if you are only half a Buddhist, how can you carry on Buddhist activities? You can do that only if you believe fully in Buddhism.

I had several quite unpleasant experiences in connection with the Maha Bodhi Society. Some years ago the Society asked me to write a short biography of its founder, Anagārika Dharmapala. This I agreed to do, and they were quite pleased. When I had written the biography it was typed, the typed copy was sent to the printer, and eventually the proofs came from the printer for correction and were lying on the desk of the general secretary. While they were lying there, a member of the governing body of the Society, an orthodox Hindu, happened to come into the office. He looked at the proofs and saw that I had made a small criticism of Swami Vivekananda, the founder of the Ramakrishna Mission, and a well-known figure in modern Hinduism. When he saw what I had done, this man said to the general secretary, 'We can't allow this sort of thing. The criticism must be cut out.' So the general secretary cut it out. I then realized that even though they were supposed to be propagating Buddhism, such people were not prepared to tolerate any criticism of Hinduism.[231]

It was the same in England, I found. In India a Buddhist is not allowed to criticize Hinduism, and in England at that time a Buddhist was not allowed to criticize Christianity. This was one of the reasons why I thought we needed a new kind of Buddhist movement. A Buddhist movement can only be run by those who are one-hundred-percent Buddhist. Otherwise one will not be allowed to say what one really thinks. A Buddhist organization should therefore consist of Buddhists, and should be run by Buddhists.

This raises a very important question: 'What is a Buddhist?' The answer is very simple, but also very profound. It is very easy to understand, but very difficult to put into practice. Anyway, I will try to give you an explanation. First of all, a Buddhist is one who goes for Refuge to the Buddha, the Dhamma, and the Sangha. But what does this mean? What do we mean by going for Refuge to the Buddha? Who is the Buddha? *What* is the Buddha? It is very important that we should understand this. In India there are many misunderstandings about the Buddha. First of all, we have to understand what the Buddha is not. The Buddha is not God, or an incarnation of God, or a messenger sent by God. The Buddha cannot save you. The Buddha shows you the way by means of which you can save yourself. But if the Buddha is not God, who or what is he? The Buddha is a human being, but he is not an ordinary human being. He is a very special kind of human being, a human being who has gained what we call 'Enlightenment', a human being who has become free from all passions, whose mind is completely pure, and full of wisdom, love, and compassion. All these qualities he possesses to the highest possible degree. This is what we mean by a Buddha. Going for Refuge to the Buddha means taking the Buddha as our ideal. The Buddha was a human being. We are also human beings. What the Buddha achieved, we too can achieve. If we accept this and act upon it, then we go for Refuge to the Buddha. This is the first Refuge.

Secondly, we go for Refuge to the Dhamma. So what is the Dhamma (Pāli) or Dharma (Sanskrit)? Here we have to be very careful. In India the word '*dharma*' means your caste *dharma*, your duty as a member of the particular Hindu caste into which you were born. But in Buddhism Dhamma means something completely different. In Buddhism, Dhamma is a *path*. It is the path leading to Enlightenment, the path of human development. Dhamma is whatever helps us to grow, whatever helps us to be wise and compassionate, whatever helps us to lead the pure life.

There are many ways of explaining the Dhamma in detail. This afternoon I am going to give an explanation which occurs frequently in the Buddhist scriptures and which describes the Dhamma in terms of the practice of what are called the five *indriyas*.[232] Usually the word *indriya* stands for the five organs of physical sense, that is to say, the eye, the ear, the nose, and so on. The function of these physical sense organs is to help us to live and move about in the world. Without them we are unable to do very much. If only one or two of them are lacking, we can just about manage, but if they are all missing we can do very little. Likewise, the five *Dhamma-indriyas* help us to live and move about and make progress in the world of the Dhamma. The five *indriyas* are therefore of great importance. If we develop them, we shall be leading lives based on the Dhamma.

The first four *Dhamma-indriyas* are divided into two groups, each group consisting of two *indriyas* that complement each other and form a pair. The first pair consists of faith and wisdom. Here faith does not mean blind faith, which has no place in Buddhism. It means the positive feeling, the love, that you feel for the Buddha, the Dhamma, and the Sangha. This is what we mean by faith in Buddhism. As for wisdom, it can be explained in a number of different ways. Usually it is explained as consisting in an understanding of the Four Noble Truths: (1) the truth of *duḥkha* or suffering; (2) the truth of craving, which is the cause of *duḥkha*; (3) the truth of the cessation of craving, which leads to the cessation of suffering, which of course is synonymous with the attainment of Nirvāṇa or Buddhahood; and (4) the truth of the Noble Eightfold Path leading to the cessation of craving and, therefore, to the cessation of suffering. If you want to understand wisdom in greater detail you will have to consult the literature on the subject. So the first pair of *Dhamma-indriyas* are faith and wisdom. Here there is a very important point to be made. According to Buddhism these two *indriyas* must be held in balance. If you have too much faith and not enough wisdom, then your faith will become blind faith. On the other hand, if you have too much wisdom and too little faith, then your wisdom will become dry, academic, and merely theoretical. Therefore the two have to be held in balance.

The second pair of *indriyas* consists of *viriya* and *samādhi*. *Viriya* means energy – energy of a specific kind. Śāntideva, the great Buddhist teacher of the eighth or ninth century, defines *viriya* as 'energy in pursuit of the good', or 'enthusiasm for the good'.[233] A Buddhist should be active, not lazy. He should take part in Buddhist activities. Only then can the Buddhist movement be successful. Together with *viriya*, there is *samādhi*, usually translated into English as 'meditation'. Basically it means purifying the mind, and raising it to higher levels of consciousness. Here also it is important to notice that Buddhism insists that these two *indriyas*, *viriya* and *samādhi*, must be held in perfect balance. Some people are extremely active, but their activity is not really effective; they are just restless. They are constantly moving from one place to another, but they don't really do anything. This is because their *viriya* is not balanced by *samādhi*. There are other people who just sit quietly all the time. Some people even go off to the Himalayas and spend their whole life in a cave. This too is one-sided. There may be *samādhi*, but there is no *viriya*, so their *samādhi* remains useless to other people. The Buddha therefore said that *viriya* and *samādhi*, too, must be balanced. You must be active, but at the same time your mind must be calm and quiet. These, then, are the first four *Dhamma-indriyas*: faith and wisdom, and energy and meditation.

The fifth and last *Dhamma-indriya* is *sati*. *Sati* means mindfulness or awareness. It means knowing exactly what you are doing at any given moment. Even if you simply raise your hand, you must know that that is what you are doing. If you talk you must know that you are talking. If you are reading you must know that you are reading. A lot of people don't know what they are doing, or what they are thinking. If suddenly you ask them, 'What are you thinking?' they can't tell you. This is because most of the time most people are in a dull, sleepy sort of state. Therefore the Buddha said, 'Wake up. Be aware. Be mindful. Know what you are doing, know what you are thinking, know what you are feeling. Always remember the Dhamma.' You will notice here that *sati* stands on its own. It is not one of a pair of *indriyas*. This is because *sati*, by its very nature, cannot go to extremes. You cannot have too much mindfulness, too much awareness, so *sati* does not need to be balanced by another *indriya*. These, then are the five *Dhamma-indriyas*. If you cultivate these five you will make good progress on the path of the Dhamma, and in the end you will gain Enlightenment.

Thirdly and lastly comes the Sangha Refuge. Some people think that the Sangha means just the *bhikkhu sangha*, but this is a big mistake. The Sangha means all those who go for Refuge to the Buddha, Dhamma, and Sangha. In practical terms the Sangha Refuge means that we help one another. We help one another because we are all Buddhists. We are all brothers and sisters. The Buddha himself is like our father, and the Dhamma is like our mother. We ourselves are the Sangha. Those who know more about the Dhamma than we do are our elder brothers and sisters. We can learn from them. And if we ourselves know something about the Dhamma, it is our duty to teach it to those who do not know anything about it. This is what is meant by the Sangha Refuge. Anyone who goes for Refuge to the Buddha, the Dhamma, and the Sangha as I have described them is a Buddhist. Whether they are a *bhikkhu* or an *upāsaka* doesn't matter. Whether they are male or female, young or old, so called 'educated' or so called 'uneducated', doesn't matter either. Some people think that you can only go for Refuge if you've got a degree, but that is nonsense. The Buddha himself didn't have a degree, neither did Sāriputta, or Moggallāna, or Ānanda. If they were living in India today people would describe them as illiterate, because they couldn't read or write. But if you can't read or write it doesn't matter very much. You can still go for Refuge. You can still be a Buddhist. I'm not saying that if you don't know how to read or write, you shouldn't learn. To learn is good. But being literate and being a Buddhist are two different things. I hope the matter is clear. A Buddhist is one who goes for Refuge to the Buddha, the Dhamma, and the Sangha.

But there is something more that the Buddhist must do. After going for Refuge you take the *pañcasīla*. Now *pañcasīla* is not something to be simply recited. It is something to be practised. So let us go through the *pañcasīla*, just very quickly. First of all you say, *pāṇātipātā veramaṇī sikkhāpadaṃ samādiyāmi*, which means, 'I accept the training which consists in not doing harm to any living being.' This is the first precept: not to harm any living being. It doesn't mean just 'not killing'. It means 'not harming'. It means not harming other living beings, not injuring them either physically or mentally. Moreover, it means not only not harming human beings, but not harming animals. There is also a positive side to the first precept, the principle of *mettā*. *Mettā* means friendliness, love. It is not enough not to harm others. We must feel love towards them.

When you take the second precept, *adinnādānā veramaṇī sikkhāpadaṃ samādiyāmi*, you undertake to abstain from taking that which is not given. This doesn't mean just not stealing. It also means not cheating, for instance not giving a false weight. It means not taking anything that is not given to you. The positive counterpart of this precept is *dāna* or giving. This means giving to those who are in need, whether they are in need of food, clothing, money, medical treatment, or education. It means giving to the Buddhist movement. In short, it means giving in whatever way one can.

The third precept consists in abstaining from *kāmesu micchācārā*, sexual misconduct. If we are married, this means remaining faithful to our marriage partner. It means not committing adultery. The positive counterpart of this precept is contentment. It means being content with your wife or husband, even as you get older, and trying to develop a good, friendly relationship.

The fourth precept consists in abstaining from *musāvādā*, or false speech. It means not telling lies. The positive counterpart of this precept is, of course, always to speak the truth.

Fifthly and lastly, one abstains from *surāmeraya majja pamādaṭṭhānā*, or indulgence in intoxicating drinks and drugs. Besides abstaining from taking these things oneself, one does not sell them to other people. One does not keep a liquor shop, or produce liquor of any kind. The positive counterpart of this precept is identical with the fifth *Dhamma-indriya*, which is *sati*, mindfulness or awareness. When a man gets drunk he loses his mindfulness. He may then do anything. He may beat his wife, throw his food about, or fall down in the road. He may start fighting with another man, and may even stab him. How can one practise the Dhamma if one behaves like that? This is why we have the fifth precept.

One who goes for Refuge to the Buddha, Dhamma, and Sangha, and observes the five precepts, is a real, true, one-hundred-percent Buddhist. Now all of you here today have taken these Three Refuges and Five Precepts. Some of you took them twenty-five years ago, perhaps from Dr Ambedkar himself. You also took the twenty-two vows or oaths. Here an interesting and important question arises. Why did Dr Ambedkar give these twenty-two vows or oaths? They are concerned with such things as not worshipping Hindu gods and not performing Hindu ceremonies such as *shraddh* and *pindadan*.[234] So why did Dr Ambedkar give you these vows? Why did he think that the *tisaraṇa* and *pañcasīla* were not enough? He gave you these vows because he saw the danger of mixing Buddhism with Hinduism, and he wanted to guard against that. So first he gave his followers the *tisaraṇa*, then he gave them the *pañcasīla*, and finally he gave them the twenty-two vows.

But what is the position now, twenty-five years later? Unfortunately some people, even among Dr Ambedkar's followers, are still mixing a little bit of Hinduism with their Buddhism. Some are still worshipping the old Hindu gods. Only a few days ago I heard that some people are still in the habit of sacrificing goats. This is absolutely against Buddhism. If you want to be a Buddhist you cannot sacrifice goats. By doing such a thing you are breaking the first precept. In fact you are breaking your Refuge in the Buddha, because you don't sacrifice the goats to the Buddha (at least I hope you don't), but to some Hindu god. When you sacrifice the goat you are worshipping that god, and that breaks your Refuge in the Buddha. I have also heard that there are some people who are still practising 'talwa pūjā'.[235] I don't know whether this kind of puja is customary in Poona or Panchgani, or even in Maharashtra, but I do know that there are some people who call themselves Buddhists and who are still performing this talwa pūjā. If you perform talwa pūjā you are worshipping violence. This un-Buddhistic practice must therefore also be given up.

Then there is the question of the dowry system. I don't know what the present position is, but I very much hope that all Buddhists have now given up this system. The dowry system was one of the causes of the poor economic condition of the Buddhists before conversion. It very often happened that if the father of the bride did not have money for the dowry he borrowed it from the moneylender, usually at a very high rate of interest. This debt remained as a great load on his back. It was always there. Even though he was paying out money all the time in the form of interest, the debt just got bigger and bigger. He couldn't understand it. So if you haven't already given up the dowry system, give it up at once. People also used to spend far too much money on marriage ceremonies. They used to borrow for that purpose too. In this way also they got into debt. This was one of the points I used to make twenty years ago, when I was going round the villages of Maharashtra. I used to say, 'Don't spend much money on marriage ceremonies. This is not the Buddhist custom. Perform the marriage ceremony properly. Do it beautifully, do it in a dignified way, but don't spend a lot of money. Above all, don't borrow money. Also, when you give the marriage feast, don't serve liquor.'

These are just a few examples. You have to give up the old, bad customs. Now you are Buddhists. You are sons and daughters of the

Buddha. So you should act like that, behave like that; then you will be strong. You must really go for Refuge, really practise the *pañcasīla*, really observe the twenty-two vows or oaths. You must do as much as you can to spread the Dhamma. Those of you who can read should read Buddhist literature and explain it to those who cannot read. There is now quite a lot of Buddhist literature in your own Marathi language – *Buddhayan*, for instance. *Buddhayan* was started in Poona three years ago by Lokamitra and his helpers. It comes out every three months, and contains articles about both the theory and practice of Buddhism. So you have *Buddhayan* to study. Lokamitra has also brought out, under the auspices of the Trailokya Bauddha Mahasangha Sahayak Gana, Poona, a number of Marathi booklets. This is a very noble work, and I am very happy to see it being carried on. People must know about Buddhism. They must understand Buddhism. There is no place for blind faith. You must all develop and grow as human beings. You must create a new society in place of the bad old society. If you can do all these things you will be a real Buddhist. You will be a true follower of Dr Ambedkar. You will fulfil the ideas which Dr Ambedkar set up before you.

6

TURNING POINTS IN THE LIVES OF
THE BUDDHA AND DR AMBEDKAR

Mahad,[236] *25 December 1981*

Mr Chairman, Brothers and Sisters: Ever since I was a boy, I have been very fond of reading, and especially I enjoy reading the biographies of great men. And when reading the lives of various great men from various countries, I have noticed that they have something in common. In the lives of all these great men there were certain turning points – points at which their whole lives seemed to take an entirely new direction. Not only that, there were also points at which their lives seemed to reach new heights of achievement. Now the Buddha, as you all know, was a great man, perhaps the greatest man the world has ever seen. In his life we certainly see there were great turning points, points at which his life took an entirely new direction.

The first of these turning points was when he left all the comforts of home, when he left his high social position as a prince, his wealth, his beautiful clothes, his jewels, his wife, and his son, and went out into the jungle as a homeless wanderer, a *parivrājaka*. Then there was a second great turning point. After going into the jungle the Buddha practised self-mortification. At that time in India many people believed that one could realize the truth by self-torture, and the Buddha followed that path for some years. He cut down his food – cut it down almost to nothing. He became just skin and bones. Afterwards when he was describing his experiences to his disciples he said he was so thin that if he touched the skin of his belly in front he could feel his backbone.[237] He continued like this for some years, but in the end he realized this was not the way to realize the Truth, so he gave up self-mortification. This was the second great turning point in his life. And the third great turning point was of course when he sat under the bodhi tree at Bodh Gaya and became Enlightened. At that point he became the highest of all beings. He became full of wisdom (*prajñā*) and compassion (*karuṇā*).

Now you might think, what could there be after Enlightenment? Surely there can't be any great turning point after that. But it is not correct to think that once you've gained Enlightenment all you do then is just sit down and enjoy it. No, there were two more great turning points in the Buddha's life. The fourth great turning point was when the Buddha decided to teach the Truth he had realized. It wasn't enough that he had realized the Truth himself. He realized that he must now go out into the world and teach the path to the Truth he had discovered to all living beings.

And there was one more turning point: the fifth. This was when the Buddha formed the *saṅgha*. He brought together his first sixty disciples and said, 'Go forth. Teach my Dhamma, which is beautiful in the beginning, beautiful in the middle, beautiful in the end, which is perfectly pure. Teach this pure Dhamma for the benefit, for the welfare of all living beings.'[238] In this way the Buddha formed his *saṅgha* and sent them out to teach the Dhamma, to help all living beings.

We find much the same sort of thing in the life of Dr Ambedkar. Dr Ambedkar was also a great man, perhaps the greatest man that modern India has produced, and in his life also we find that there are certain great turning points. This afternoon I'm going to mention just three of them, perhaps the three most important turning points in his life. First of all, one great turning point, as you know very well, was the Mahad Chowdar Tank *satyāgraha* and the burning of the *Manusmṛti*. This took place in 1927. At that time I was two years old and had no idea what was going on in Mahad, but now I know very well. It's the fifty-fourth anniversary of that great event here in Mahad that we are celebrating on this occasion. I'm not going to go into a lot of detail about what happened. You've heard the story many times before, and of course it happened here, on your doorstep, as we say in English, but sometimes people do forget – after all, it is quite a long time ago, and a whole new generation has sprung up since then. Those who were young men in 1927, full of fire and energy, are old men now. So let me refresh your memories.

It all started at the beginning of 1927 when there was a great conference here under the leadership of Dr Ambedkar. Ten thousand people are said to have gathered under his leadership, and they all went to the Chowdar Tank and took the water. On my way here, I saw that tank and looked at the water in it. I wouldn't like to take water from it – it was all green – but of course people didn't take water from that tank at that time because it was nice water. That wasn't the point. They took water from the tank to establish their right to take it. They were taking it not just to establish the right of the Mahars, but to establish the right of all human beings to equal treatment.

The orthodox Hindus were very upset, of course, and they hastenend to 'purify' the water with the five products of the cow. In India, of course, the cow is a very holy animal. In England it's not like that. If you call someone a cow, especially a lady, it's a great insult. Anyway, our orthodox Hindu friends purified the water with the five products of the cow, including the cow's urine and dung. It is astonishing that people should think that an animal is pure, and that a human being is impure, but this is what they thought. They thought that if you touch the dung of the cow you become pure, but if you touch the skin of a human being you become impure. This is madness. Those caste Hindus must have been quite mad.

That was not the end of the matter. As you know, there was a great struggle. Dr Ambedkar called for *satyāgrahis*[239] and 4,000 of them came forward and were enrolled. But it wasn't so easy. These *satyāgrahis* wanted to take water from the tank again, but there was an obstacle. The local caste Hindus said that the tank was private property, and they got an injunction from the court to stop the *satyāgrahis* taking water from the tank a second time. At this point the situation became very difficult, and very dangerous. The followers of Dr Ambedkar were ready to take water from the tank, but there was the injunction of the court preventing them. There were the police, the magistrates were there, and the collector came. There was the danger of an outbreak of violence. Dr Ambedkar handled the situation very skilfully and violence was avoided. They didn't take the water, but instead they marched peacefully all the way round the tank, just to establish their right as human beings, and then in the evening they ceremonially burned the *Manusmṛti*.

These were very great events. Under the leadership of Dr Ambedkar the Untouchables asserted that they were human beings, and they showed their determination not to submit to slavery by burning a symbol of slavery. Afterwards, Dr Ambedkar explained that they did not burn the *Manusmṛti* out of hatred. He also said that not all parts of the *Manusmṛti* are bad. The *Manusmṛti* also contains some good principles. After all, it is a very big book. It would be difficult for such a big book to be all bad. (You see what a broad-minded person Dr Ambedkar was.) But for the Untouchables the *Manusmṛti* was a symbol of injustice. They had been crushed under it for centuries, and because of its teachings they had been ground down in misery and poverty. That's why Dr Ambedkar and his followers, on that day which we are celebrating now, burned the *Manusmṛti*. With it they burned the injustice, oppression, and slavery of the bad old orthodox Hindu society. This was the first great turning point in Dr Ambedkar's life. It was a turning point also in the lives of his followers, and in the history of modern India.

The second great turning point in Dr Ambedkar's life was the Yeola conference of 1935. No doubt you are familiar with the events that led up to that conference. For years and years Dr Ambedkar had been trying to change the hearts of the caste Hindus. He had begged and pleaded with them, asking them to treat the Untouchables as human beings, but they didn't listen. At the most he got a few sweet words, but the hearts of the caste Hindus remained as hard as ever. Dr Ambedkar became almost desperate, and he decided that drastic measures were necessary. At the Yeola conference he made a long speech in which he described the plight of the Depressed Classes in all spheres of life. He described their sufferings under Hinduism, and how the caste Hindus refused to change their ways. He said, 'It's time you considered your position. It's time that we cut off our connection with Hinduism. It's time to look for another religion.' Then he made his famous declaration. 'I may have been born a Hindu, but I solemnly assure you, I do not intend to die a Hindu.'[240]

This great declaration echoed all around India, and created a tremendous impression throughout the country. The caste Hindus were deeply upset and shocked, but still they wouldn't change their ways. They didn't want the Untouchables to leave the Hindu religion, and kept on telling them what a wonderful religion Hinduism was. But all the time they continued to treat them like animals, in fact worse than animals. So this was the second great turning point in Dr Ambedkar's life as well as in the lives of his followers.

Now we come to the third great turning point, and I'm sure you know what that is. This was the Nagpur mass conversion ceremony of 1956, when Dr Ambedkar and many of his followers took Refuge in the Buddha, Dhamma, and Sangha, recited the five precepts, and took the twenty-two vows. That was a great and glorious day, the greatest turning point in Dr Ambedkar's whole life and those of his followers. Indeed, it was a turning point in the history of India, and in the history of Buddhism itself.

Unfortunately, seven weeks after that mass conversion ceremony Dr Ambedkar passed away, and when that happened his followers were plunged into grief. On the day he died I myself was in Nagpur, so I know very well how his followers received the news of his death. They felt as though they had lost their own mother, their own father. I did what I could on that occasion to help. I gave many lectures in Nagpur, and I told people mainly two things. First of all, they should not think that Dr Ambedkar was dead, for his memory would live on for ever in the hearts of his followers. Secondly, his work would continue, and they themselves had to carry it on.

That was twenty-five years ago, and since then a whole new generation has sprung up. Many of you have never seen Dr Ambedkar in the flesh. It's now fifty-four years since the Chowdar Tank *satyāgraha* and the burning of the *Manusmṛti*. It's forty-six years since the Yeola conference and Dr Ambedkar's great declaration. It's twenty-five years since the mass conversion at Nagpur. So at this point a very important question arises. In the course of the last twenty-five years, since everybody became Buddhist, how much progress has there been in the Buddhist movement? After all, in twenty-five years it's possible to do quite a lot. Unfortunately, we have to admit that in the course of the last twenty-five years it's not been possible to do in Maharashtra as much for this Dhamma movement as Dr Ambedkar wanted.

What is the reason for this? Let's look into this matter briefly. In 1950 Dr Ambedkar wrote in English a very important article called 'Buddha and the Future of his Religion' which appeared in the *Maha Bodhi* journal of Calcutta. In this article Dr Ambedkar makes some very important points. This afternoon I'm going to be concerned with just one of them. In writing about the ideal of spreading Buddhism, Dr Ambedkar asks how this ideal could be realized, and he says that three steps appear to be necessary. First, to produce a Buddhist Bible.

Secondly, to make changes in the organization, aims, and objectives of the *bhikkhu sangha*. Thirdly, to set up a world Buddhist mission.[241] So these are the three steps that have to be taken according to Dr Ambedkar before the ideal of spreading Buddhism can be realized. Let us see how many of these steps have already been taken, and that will perhaps help us understand why more progress has not been made. First of all, the production of a Buddhist Bible. Well, a Buddhist Bible was produced by Dr Ambedkar himself. His great work *The Buddha and His Dhamma* was published by the People's Education Society one year after his death. The PES is one of the most important Buddhist organizations in India, as you know. Over the years it has done very solid work, bringing the right sort of education to the people. But not only that. It was the PES that took up the publication of the writings of Dr Ambedkar. Besides bringing out *The Buddha and His Dhamma*, they also brought out under the auspices of the Government of Maharashtra the first volume of Dr Ambedkar's writings and speeches. (I understand the second volume is on the way.) So the PES is to be congratulated, not only for its educational work, but for bringing the writings of Dr Ambedkar into circulation. So the first step towards spreading Buddhism has been taken.

What about the other two steps, that is to say, reorganizing the *bhikkhu sangha* and setting up a world Buddhist mission? Unfortunately not much has happened, at least in Maharashtra. In fact, we can say that nothing has happened. The *bhikkhus* go on in the old way. I don't want to criticize them: some of them are very good people, especially the younger ones, but they're trapped in an out-of-date system, and for this reason they cannot do as much as they would like. So changes still need to be made. We need a new kind of *sangha*, a new kind of Buddhist worker, just as Dr Ambedkar said. As for a world Buddhist mission, people haven't even thought about that yet here.

But although not much has happened in Maharashtra, a lot has happened elsewhere. As some of you know, I myself spent some twenty years in India, and from 1956 to 1964 I was closely connected with the movement of mass conversion started by Dr Ambedkar. Then in 1964 I went back to England and there in 1967 I started a new Buddhist movement which is now active in eight different countries including India. In English we call this Buddhist movement the Friends of the Western Buddhist Order and in India we call it Trailokya Bauddha

Mahasangha Sahayak Gana. It is the biggest Buddhist movement in Europe.

So why have we been able to be so successful in such a short time? There are several reasons. Today I'll mention only two. First of all, we have reorganized the *bhikkhu sangha*. In fact we've created a new *sangha*. It's a *sangha* fully dedicated to the Three Jewels; a *sangha* of people who practise the ten *kusala dhammas*, meditate, and work for the good of society. This *sangha* is not just in England. Our movement is spreading to other countries. In India we have created our Trailokya Bauddha Mahasangha. So you could say we are in the process of creating a world Buddhist mission.

Dr Ambedkar was a very far-sighted man. He didn't confine his attentions to Maharashtra, or to India. He thought in terms of the whole world. After all, Buddhists are all members of one great spiritual family. Buddhists are all brothers and sisters regardless of the country they belong to. In that spirit I'm very glad to be able to be present with you today and address you on this occasion. I had of course heard of Mahad before, but I hadn't been here. I'm very glad to see the beautiful pillar that has been constructed, and the bust of Dr Ambedkar, and I heartily congratulate all those who had anything to do with the construction of these two monuments. I'm very glad to have seen all of you. Before I finish I would like you to consider very seriously why more progress has not been made in the Buddhist movement in Maharashtra over the last twenty-five years. I'd like to suggest you give very serious consideration to the reorganization of the *bhikkhu sangha*, and I suggest that you have more contact with your Buddhist brothers and sisters from other countries. In this way progress will be made. Fifty-six years ago Dr Ambedkar burnt the *Manusmṛti*, but there are a lot of other things left to burn. We must burn up our separatism. We must burn up out-of-date customs. We must burn up the old society. We must create a new society, a society based on the Dhamma, on *śīla*, on liberty, equality, and fraternity. If we can do this, this will be yet another great turning point. And in this way the mission which Dr Ambedkar started on this very spot fifty-six years ago will at last be fulfilled.

7

SEEING THE TRUE NATURE
OF EXISTENCE: PRAJÑĀ

Ahilya Ashram, Poona, 27 December 1981

Brothers and Sisters: Gautama the Buddha gained Supreme Perfect Enlightenment at the age of thirty-five, and attained *mahāparinirvāṇa* at the advanced age of eighty, so he spent some forty-five years of his life teaching the Dhamma. In the course of this time he taught the Dhamma to many different kinds of people. He taught the Dhamma to people of high social position, to people of low social position, and to people of no social position at all. He taught it to the rich and the poor, to the powerful and the weak, to those who were highly intelligent and those who were not so intelligent. Since the Buddha taught the Dhamma to so many different kinds of people, he developed a number of different methods of teaching the Dhamma. Sometimes he was inspired, and beautiful verses of Pāli poetry flowed from his lips. We find verses of this sort in, for instance, the *Dhammapada*. We sometimes find the Buddha giving very long, detailed, and systematic expositions of his teaching. Sometimes we find him expressing himself in short, pithy sayings. Occasionally we find him not saying anything at all. Someone asked a question and the Buddha remained absolutely silent. It wasn't that he was not answering the question. The silence *was* the answer. It was a profound, meaningful silence. It wasn't the silence of ignorance, but the silence of wisdom. We also find the Buddha teaching the Dhamma by telling stories. These stories were very popular, and they're still very popular in the Buddhist world. Stories are easy to understand. They're very enjoyable, sometimes they're quite amusing, and people usually remember them. It has been my own experience, both in India and in England, that sometimes people come up to me and say, 'Bhante, I heard you give a lecture twenty or twenty-five years ago. I don't remember very much about it, but one thing I do remember. I remember a story that you told.' Stories stick in people's minds. This is why the Buddha very often taught the Dhamma through the medium of stories, and many of his stories are found in the Pāli scriptures. Some of them are very short, but though short they have a profound meaning.

In English a short story of this sort, with a profound spiritual meaning, is called a parable, and this evening I'm going to tell one of the most famous of the Buddha's parables, the parable of the blind men and the elephant. The Buddha relates how once upon a time there was a certain king who was feeling rather bored. Wanting to be amused, he called together all the blind men in the city and caused an elephant to be presented to them. When the blind men had all stretched out their hands and felt the elephant, the king asked them what they thought an elephant was like. The one who had felt the elephant's head said that an elephant was like a pot, the one who had felt its ear said it was like a winnowing basket, the one who had felt its tusk said it was like a ploughshare, and so on. All the blind men described the elephant differently, in accordance with the part of it they had laid their hands on. In the end they started shouting and arguing about what an elephant was like, and even came to blows about it. The king was very much amused by the scene, and laughed heartily.[242]

So what is the meaning of the parable? What did the Buddha mean by telling this story? Here the first question that arises is: What does the elephant represent? Well, we can give a very short and simple answer to that question. The elephant is Life. Or, to put it more philosophically, the elephant represents the nature of existence. Who, then, are the blind men? The blind men are the founders of the different philosophical systems, and the fact that they are all blind means that they have no *prajñā*. Because they have no *prajñā*, they cannot 'see'. They cannot appreciate the true nature of existence, just as the blind men cannot see the elephant. The accounts that the founders of the different philosophical systems give of the true nature of existence are, therefore, incorrect. They are just like the blind men's descriptions of the elephant. Maybe their descriptions are not absolutely wrong. After all, one part of an elephant is a bit like a pot, and another part is a bit like a winnowing basket, and so on. But the 'views' given by the founders of the different philosophical systems are very one-sided and misleading, just like the 'views' the blind men have of the elephant. However, although the blind men cannot see the elephant, the king can see it. He can see the whole elephant. He can see exactly what it is like. Who, then, does the king represent? The king is the Buddha. The Buddha is able to see the true nature of existence because he has *prajñā*, just as the king is able to see the whole elephant because he has two good eyes. From this parable, we can understand how important *prajñā* is in Buddhism. Without *prajñā* we cannot see the true nature of existence.

But what exactly do we mean by *prajñā*? Let us go into this a little. Before we do this, however, I want to say something about the blind men's different descriptions of the elephant. As I mentioned, these blind men represent the founders of the different philosophical systems, and their one-sided descriptions are the philosophical systems themselves. Let me give you a few examples of these philosophical systems. I'll mention just three of them – these are perhaps the most important, and all three have a number of different forms. The first of these is what we call in English 'theism'. Theism means belief in a personal God, or what the Hindus sometimes call *Saguna Brahman*. According to theism God has created the whole world, the whole universe, and everything that is in it. But God himself was not created by anybody. According to theism, God is eternal, God is almighty. He knows everything, he sees everything. God has not only created the universe. According to theism, he also governs it and rules it by his will. It is because of the will of God that fire burns. It is because of the will of God that the wind blows. Nothing can happen except by the will of God. This is what theism says. Theism not only says that God has created the external universe, but also that God has created man from the dust and controls whatever he does. According to theism, whatever happens to man happens by the will of God. Compared with God, man is weak, helpless, powerless. He cannot do anything, or change anything. He can only submit to God, and pray to God to help him. This, in brief, is theism.

Secondly, we come to pantheism. Pantheism means the belief in an impersonal God who is identical with the universe. This is what the Hindus sometimes call *Nirguna Brahman*. According to pantheism, everything is God, everything is *Nirguna Brahman*. The tree is God. The stone is God. This microphone is God. Everything is God. According to pantheism, in the beginning everything comes out of God, and in the end everything goes back to God. One of the Upanishads (these are technically a part of the Vedas) gives a comparison for this. Just as the spider spins the thread from its body and then draws it back, so God produces the whole universe from his own substance and then merges it into himself again.[243] According to some forms of pantheism, however, the universe does not really come out of God. It only appears to come out. This form of pantheism is called Māyāvāda, and it's very popular with some Indian intellectuals. This is pantheism in brief.

Thirdly, there is materialism. Materialism is the belief that nothing exists except matter. According to materialism, there is no such thing as mind, no such thing as consciousness, apart from matter. In other words, there is no such thing as mind separate from, and independent of, matter. Mind is just a by-product of matter, just as butter is a by-product of milk. This, in brief, is materialism.

All these three philosophical systems are what Buddhism calls *micchā-diṭṭhis*, that is to say, they are wrong, mistaken, views. They are one-sided accounts of the true nature of existence. They are accounts of the nature of existence given by men without *prajñā*, men who are spiritually blind and have no personal experience of the true nature of existence. It is time, therefore, that we try to understand what *prajñā* is. Without *prajñā* there is no Buddha, and therefore no Buddhism.

The word *prajñā* in Sanskrit (or *paññā* in Pāli) has several different meanings. According to Buddhism, there are three different levels, or grades, of *prajñā*, each higher than the one preceding.[244] The first is called *śruta-mayī prajñā* (Sanskrit) or *suta-mayā paññā* (Pāli). This literally means the *prajñā* that comes from hearing, but we could think of it as the *prajñā* that comes from learning. We must remember that in the Buddha's own day there were no such things as books. Knowledge had to be imparted orally, and learned by heart. A learned man was *bahu-śruta*, one who had 'heard much'. The Buddha's disciple Ānanda was called *bahu-śruta* because he had heard much, or learned much, from the Buddha. Nowadays we usually learn from books; reading has taken the place of 'hearing'. *Śruta-mayī prajñā* therefore really means, in effect, book knowledge. This is the lowest form of *prajñā*. (Nowadays in India this form of *prajñā* is sometimes called *apara-vidyā*, or just *vidyā*.) Although *śruta-mayī prajñā* is the lowest form of *prajñā* it is still very necessary. It is the basis, in fact, of the other forms of *prajñā*. It is their raw material.

Secondly, we come to *cintā-mayī prajñā* (Sanskrit) or *cintā-mayā paññā* (Pāli). *Cintā* means simply 'thought', that is to say, rational thought or rational thinking. It also means 'independent thought'. In the case of *cintā-mayī prajñā*, we think about what we have read, what we've learned. We turn it over and over in our mind and try to understand it for ourselves. It's not enough merely to repeat the words we have learned. This is, of course, what students very often do. Before examinations students study very hard, and many of them try to learn the textbook by heart. When they come into the examination hall and read the question paper, they answer the questions by writing out bits and pieces of the textbooks that they've committed to memory. They don't try to understand the subject, and a few weeks after the examination they have very often forgotten everything. This sort of education is of no use. Study is indeed very important, but we should think about what we study. Not only that. We should try to come to our own conclusions, form our own judgements. In other words, we should think for ourselves. We shouldn't just accept whatever we read or hear.

Dr Ambedkar was a very good example of this. He studied very widely, and read many books on politics, economics, anthropology, history, sociology, religion, and many other subjects. But he didn't just read. He thought about what he read and came to his own conclusions – this is one of the reasons why he was such a great man. He came to his own conclusions about who the Shudras were, about the origins of untouchability, and about Buddhism. So *cintā-mayī prajñā* is very, very important, and without it we should not even think of speaking about the Dhamma. It's very easy to read books on Buddhism and to blurt out – to vomit out – whatever we've read, without any proper understanding. But speaking and writing on Buddhism in this way is of no use to anybody. Just recently there was an example of this sort of thing in London. The Sri Lankan embassy in London organized a big exhibition devoted to the history and culture of Sri Lanka, and as part of the exhibition they arranged some lectures on Buddhism. But they invited three dry-as-dust academic writers to speak. One was a *bhikkhu* from Sri Lanka, and the other two were academics from English universities. All three were extremely learned men, and they had read a lot of books, but they hadn't thought seriously about what they had read. They simply blurted out the contents of the books, together with a lot of Pāli quotations. So the lectures didn't really help anybody. In fact, very few people attended. This sort of thing often happens, even in India. People are invited to give lectures on Buddhism who have simply read a lot of books about Buddhism. They haven't *thought* about Buddhism, or tried to practise it. As I say, without *cintā-mayī prajñā* you shouldn't even think of speaking about the Dhamma.

Thirdly and lastly, we come to *bhāvanā-mayī prajñā* (Sanskrit) or *bhāvanā-mayā paññā* (Pāli). The word *bhāvanā* means 'development'. In this context this means the development of the mind, the development of consciousness. In particular it means the development of mind, or the development of consciousness, through the experience of *dhyāna* and *samādhi*, that is to say, through the experience of meditation. Through *dhyāna* and *samādhi* the mind becomes pure, one-pointed, and steady, and in this way we become able to see the true nature of existence. *Bhāvanā-mayi prajñā* is therefore the real *prajñā*. When we say just *prajñā* we mean, or we should mean, *bhāvanā-mayī prajñā*. It's *bhāvanā-mayī prajñā* that makes the Buddha a Buddha. The development of *prajñā* in the highest sense, that of *bhāvanā-mayī prajñā*, is therefore necessary. *Dhyāna* and *samādhi* are necessary.

But what is necessary in order to develop *dhyāna* and *samādhi*? The answer is that *śīla* is necessary. There is no *dhyāna* and no *samādhi*, certainly no *prajñā* to any great extent, without *śīla*. Therefore we can say that there is no *bhāvanā-mayī prajñā* without *śīla*. In his book *The Buddha and His Dhamma* Dr Ambedkar says, '*Prajñā*, without *śīla*, is dangerous.'[245] That is to say, *śruta-mayī prajñā* and *cintā-mayī prajñā* are dangerous when they are by themselves. They are dangerous without *śīla*, dangerous without *bhāvanā*. Mere *prajñā*, Dr Ambedkar says, is like a sword in the hand of a man. A man who is merely learned, who is just well read, can do a lot of harm. The man who merely thinks can do a lot of harm. *Śīla* and *bhāvanā* are also necessary. But Dr Ambedkar goes even further than this. He says that even *prajñā* is not enough. Even *bhāvanā-mayī prajñā* is not enough. What else, then, is necessary? What else *could* be necessary? *Karuṇā* is also necessary. *Karuṇā* is one of the twin pillars of Buddhism. The Mahāyāna says that the Dhamma is like a great bird. One of its wings is *prajñā*, and the other wing is *karuṇā*, and with these two wings the bird of the Dhamma is able to fly.

I said a little while ago that with *bhāvanā-mayī prajñā* we are able to see the true nature of existence. But when we see the true nature of existence, what exactly do we see? What does the Buddha see? He sees three things. He sees *duḥkha*, he sees *anitya*, and he sees *anātman*. He sees that conditioned existence is painful and unsatisfactory, that it is impermanent, and that it is devoid of any unchanging self or *ātman*. In Buddhist literature these three are known as the three *lakṣaṇas* or 'characteristics' of conditioned existence.[246] Out of these three the second, *anitya*, is in a way the most important. The other two, we may say, are derived from it. Things are painful and unsatisfactory because they are impermanent, because they change. Even if we have a pleasant experience we can't hold on to it – we can't make it last for ever. We can't hold on to our youth. It fades, just like the flower. We can't hold on to our health. One day we're well, the next day we're sick. We can't hold on to life itself. We want to hold on to all these things, but we can't, and because we can't, we suffer. In the same way, things are *anātman* because they change. Or, to put it the other way, because they change, they're *anātman*. They don't remain identical for any two consecutive instants. Therefore, there is no permanent, unchanging self or *ātman*. In this way, we see that impermanence, *anitya*, is the most important of these three *lakṣaṇas* or characteristics.

Let us therefore look at *anitya* a little more closely. Everything in the universe changes. Man also changes. The body changes, the mind changes. However, the mind does not merely change. The mind can also develop. The mind can rise to higher and ever higher levels of purity, concentration, and *prajñā*. Change may be from a lower to a higher state, or from a higher state to a lower one, or to a state which is merely different, neither higher nor lower than the previous one. Development, however, is always from a lower state to a higher state. You can have change without development, but you cannot have development without change. *Prajñā*, in the sense of *bhāvanā-mayī prajñā*, not only sees that everything in the universe changes, not only sees that man changes, it also sees that man can *develop*. *Prajñā*, in the highest sense, sees not only that the true nature of existence is change, but also that the true nature of human existence is development from a lower to a higher state. *Bhāvanā-mayī prajñā* sees that to be human, truly human, is to grow, is to develop.

This is the significance of the Buddha's vision after his Enlightenment. He saw the whole of humanity as being like a great bed of lotus flowers, all in different stages of development. Some were sunk deep in the mud, and some had risen to the surface of the water, but they were all growing.

This is how the Buddha saw humanity.[247] This is how Buddhism sees humanity – as full of potential to grow and develop.

But it's not enough just to see. One must also help people to grow. *Prajñā* must be accompanied by *karuṇā*. True *prajñā*, in fact, is always accompanied by *karuṇā*. We see this demonstrated many times in the life of the Buddha. I'll give just one example. This is not a parable but a story of another kind. There was a young woman called Kisā Gotamī. 'Kisā' means 'thin', so, her clan name being Gotamī, she was called Kisā Gotamī, because she was thin. She had not been long married, and was the mother of a small son. One day the boy was bitten by a snake, and unfortunately he died. Kisā Gotamī nearly went mad with grief. She refused to give up the body of her son. Instead, she carried it from door to door asking people for medicine to bring her son back to life. Eventually someone told her that she had better go to the Buddha. *He* would surely be able to give her the medicine she needed. So Kisā Gotamī came to the Buddha, laid the body of her son at his feet, and said, 'Please give me the medicine. Please bring my son back to life.' What did the Buddha say? What *could* the Buddha say? For a while he was silent, then he said, 'All right, I will give you the medicine. But first, you will have to bring me something. You will have to bring me some mustard seed from a house where no one has ever died.'

Thinking that this task would be easy, off Kisā Gotamī went to the nearest house. There she asked for some mustard seed. People were ready to give her as much as she wanted, but when she asked, 'Has anyone ever died in this house?' they replied, 'What is this that you are saying? The dead are many, the living are few.' She therefore had to go to another house, and there she had the same experience. She went to another house and the same thing happened. In this way she eventually came to understand that death comes to every house, to every man, to every woman. Everybody must die one day. Death wasn't something that had happened just to her son. Death happens to everybody. So she left the dead body of her son at the cremation ground, came back to the Buddha, knelt in front of him, put her hands together, and said, 'Lord, please give me a Refuge.' So the Buddha gave her a Refuge. Indeed, he gave her Three Refuges: the Buddha, the Dhamma, and the Sangha. She left home and became a *parivrājakā*, practised meditation, developed *prajñā*, and saw the true nature of existence.[248] Here we have another example of the Buddha's method of teaching. He not only exhibited great *prajñā* in dealing with Kisā Gotamī, not only saw the cause of her suffering; he also demonstrated *karuṇā* in helping her to overcome her suffering and attachment, her narrow outlook. In other words, he helped her to develop, helped her on the path to Enlightenment.

We can now see, perhaps, what *prajñā* really is. True *prajñā* is always accompanied by *śīla* and *bhāvanā*, and it always manifests as *karuṇā*. True *prajñā* sees the true nature of existence, and especially it sees that the true nature of human existence is to develop. The true Buddhist therefore practises *śīla* and *bhāvanā*, and develops *prajñā* and *karuṇā*. He tries to develop himself, and to help others to develop. He tries to follow in the footsteps of the Buddha, and in the footsteps of Dr Ambedkar. In short he tries to be a source of happiness, welfare, and progress, not only for himself, not only for his own family and friends, his own immediate society, but for all living beings.

8
HAS THE DHAMMA REVOLUTION FAILED?

Currey Road, Bombay,[249] *30 December 1981*

Brothers and Sisters in the Dhamma: When we are at school or college, among all the subjects that we can study, one of the most interesting is, in my opinion, world history. If we study world history we see great cultural and religious movements rising from time to time and exercising an enormous influence on the lives of millions of people for hundreds of years. And one of the biggest and most important of these world movements is Buddhism. Buddhism began more than 2,500 years ago and it started, as you know, here in India. It started with Gautama the Buddha seated in meditation under the bodhi tree at Bodh Gaya. Sitting there, he discovered for himself the highest Truth. He saw the true nature of existence, the cause of sorrow and the way leading to Enlightenment for every man and woman.

Having discovered the Truth, the Buddha did not keep it to himself but communicated it to other human beings because he wanted to help others to grow and develop. So he taught the Truth he had discovered – the Dhamma – to his disciples, and more and more people came to him for teaching and then saw the Truth for themselves. In this way, a short time after the Enlightenment, the Buddha had gathered together a band of about sixty disciples, whom he sent out to proclaim the Dhamma, saying, 'The Dhamma is lovely in the beginning, lovely in the middle and lovely at the end. It is perfectly pure. Go and proclaim it for the benefit and the happiness of all living beings!'[250] So the disciples went forth and proclaimed the Dhamma, and the Dhamma spread. By the time of the Buddha's *parinirvāṇa*, the Dhamma had spread over the greater part of northern India, and wherever it went, people gave up their old customs, practices, and beliefs. They gave up animal sacrifice, which was very popular at that time and was thought to be religion by some people. They gave up the caste system. They started thinking more in terms of liberty, equality, and fraternity. Not only that; everywhere the Dhamma went, people started practising *śīla*, *dhyāna* and *samādhi*, *prajñā* and *karuṇā*. In this way, in the course of a few hundred years, India became just like heaven on earth. We cannot even imagine what India was like then. In this way the Dhamma continued to spread more and more.

Among other places it spread to Maharashtra; we know this because of all the cave viharas and cave temples that still remain here. In fact, Maharashtra must have been one of the most important centres of Buddhism in the whole of India. Buddhism also spread to Kashmir, Sri Lanka, Central Asia, China, Japan, and Tibet. In the course of a thousand years Buddhism spread all over Asia and wherever it went it brought peace, a higher culture and a true system of education. Wherever Buddhism went people were able to lead better and happier lives. In the course of 1000 years one third of the population of the entire world was Buddhist. This was a great victory for Buddhism, a victory that was gained entirely by peaceful means. Other religions have spread very widely in the world but unfortunately these other religions have not always spread by peaceful means. Sometimes they were spread by the sword, sometimes with the help of money. But in the case of Buddhism, it was not like that. Buddhism spread so widely over such a vast area only by peaceful means. Unfortunately, however, while Buddhism was spreading in the rest of Asia it was already declining in India, and eventually it disappeared from India.

There were various reasons for this and I'm going to mention the important ones. Firstly, there was the hostility of the Brahmins. The Brahmins as a caste had never liked Buddhism and had always been against it because it deprived them of their superior position in society. Buddhism said that your position in society should not depend upon your birth but upon your worth and the Brahmins did not like this so they were always against Buddhism. The second cause of the decline and disappearance of Buddhism was the Muslim invasion. The Muslims came down from the north-west of India and spread right across the Ganges valley, and wherever they went they destroyed Buddhist viharas and temples and images. The third reason for the decline of Buddhism was the fact that, in the course of hundreds of years, the *bhikkhu saṅgha* had become centralized, with more and more *bhikkhus* living in bigger and bigger viharas. Formerly they were spread out, with two or three here, four or five there, and fifteen or twenty somewhere else. But after hundreds of years the *bhikkhus* built bigger and bigger viharas and hundreds, even thousands, of *bhikkhus* were living in them. In this way, unfortunately, they lost contact with ordinary people. They just lived in the big viharas and were supported by the kings. Moreover they became more and more academic and intellectual. In this way Buddhism also became weaker. The fourth reason for the decline of Buddhism was the development of a new kind of Hinduism which borrowed many things from Buddhism. In this way it became more and more difficult to tell the difference between Hinduism on the one hand and Buddhism on the other.

So for these four main reasons, Buddhism declined in India until eventually it disappeared. For a period of about 600 years Buddhism was hardly known in India. Even the name of the Buddha was forgotten, which is really astonishing. Buddhism is the great glory of India but it was completely forgotten for such a long time. And the reason it was forgotten was again the hostility of the Brahmins. They destroyed the Buddhist books – or at least they allowed them to perish – and the result was that not a single Buddhist *sūtra* survived in India. They only survived in Sri Lanka, central Asia, China, Japan, and Tibet. However, the Brahmins could not completely destroy the remains of the Buddhist viharas and many of these survived. Sometimes they survived underground and then, in the nineteenth century, these ancient viharas started to be rediscovered and were excavated by British archaeologists. This happened at Bodh Gaya, Sarnath, Kusinara, Lumbini, and many other places. And at that time, about one hundred years ago, people started to realize that India had once been Buddhist.

Not only that. A Buddhist came from Sri Lanka and started propagating Buddhism in India. His name was Anagārika Dharmapala and he started an organization called the Maha Bodhi Society in Calcutta in 1891, the year in which Dr Ambedkar was born. Dharmapala spread the knowledge of Buddhism among educated Bengali Hindus but hardly any of them actually became Buddhists. They remained Hindus. This brings us down very nearly to the present day. I myself came to India in 1944 and at that time there were very few Buddhists in India. You could travel all the way from Delhi to Calcutta and not meet a single Buddhist. Today the situation is very different. If you travel from Delhi to Calcutta you will meet thousands of Buddhists on the way. Even if you travel from Dadar station to this place you will meet thousands of Buddhists on the way.[251]

This great change was brought about by Dr Babasaheb Ambedkar on 14 October 1956 when he, along with *lakhs* of his followers, embraced Buddhism. This was an epoch-making event because after hundreds of years Buddhism had come back to India. Nothing like it had happened in the history of the world before. Unfortunately, only seven weeks after the mass conversion, Dr Ambedkar died and his followers were plunged into grief. Nonetheless the movement of mass conversion continued, and I myself took an active part in that movement. At that time I was living up in the hills in Kalimpong in West Bengal and I came down to Maharashtra every winter. I used to go from town to town, and village to village, sometimes travelling by bullock cart, and in this way I gave many lectures, especially in Bombay and Poona.

In 1964 I went back to England for the first time in twenty years. I remained there for two years working for Buddhism and in 1967 I decided to start a new Buddhist movement in England and in the West. For the next twelve years I was very busy establishing this Buddhist movement and during this period the only contact I had with my Indian Buddhist friends was by letter. You may be wondering why I started a new Buddhist movement in the West, so this evening I want to tell you something about that, and compare our new Buddhist movement in England and the Buddhist movement here in India. I shall also say something about whether the Buddhist conversion movement in India has failed, which has been advertised as the title of this talk – though without my knowledge, I must point out. Before dealing with these matters, however, I want to make a more general point. I have said that Buddhism spread all over Asia. This is very true, but we have to accept that Buddhism is no longer as active in Asia as it was before. In some parts of Asia Buddhism has entirely disappeared. Java and Sumatra, nowadays called Indonesia, are no longer Buddhist but Muslim. China, Tibet, and Vietnam are no longer Buddhist – at least not in the old sense – but communist. In this way, in the course of the last thirty years, Buddhism has suffered serious losses. There are two places, however, in which Buddhism has grown in recent years. The first of these places is India, especially Maharashtra, and the second is the West, especially England. So India and England have this in common: they both have a growing, active, flourishing Buddhist movement.

Let me get back to England, and tell you why I started the new Buddhist movement there in 1967. At that time, there were already a few Buddhist groups in England. By Indian standards these groups were very small indeed and some only consisted of ten or twelve people. This doesn't matter too much, provided that those people are one-hundred-percent Buddhist. But at that time in England those who thought of themselves as Buddhist were really half-Buddhist and half-Christian. They believed in the Buddha but they also believed in God and this was of course a big mistake. And at that time the Buddhist groups and organizations and societies were run by these half-Buddhists, so the Buddhist movement in England could not make very much progress. I therefore decided to start a new Buddhist movement in which membership was only open to one-hundred-percent Buddhists. This new movement is called, in English, the Friends of the Western Buddhist Order and in Marathi, Hindi, and Gujarati we call it Trailokya Bauddha Mahasangha Sahayak Gana. In this organization membership is only open to real Buddhists. The activities are only conducted by Buddhists, the Dhamma is only taught by Buddhists, and control is only in the hands of Buddhists. Consequently our new Buddhist movement has made tremendous progress and now we are active not only in England but also in a number of other countries.

Here we can make a comparison with India. A little while ago, I mentioned the work of the Maha Bodhi Society of Calcutta, and I said that Anagārika Dharmapala spread the knowledge of Buddhism amongst educated Bengali Hindus who were interested in Buddhism but who did not become Buddhists. At the most they became half-Buddhists or even quarter-Buddhists. They believed in the Buddha but they continued to believe in their old Hindu gods and goddesses. Not only that. Some of them joined the different Buddhist societies and in this way they controlled them. After Anagārika Dharmapala's death these people controlled the Maha Bodhi Society, which is why it could not do very much for Buddhism. The situation changed only after the great mass conversions. On that occasion Dr Ambedkar gave his followers *tisaraṇa* and *pañcasīla* and following this he gave them twenty-two vows in order that his followers would be one-hundred-percent Buddhist. He didn't want them to be half-Buddhist and mix Buddhism and Hinduism, and therefore he gave the twenty-two vows. At the time some people criticized him for this but actually it was a very wise and far-sighted move on his part.

So there are some parallels between the Buddhist situation in England and that in India. In both places there has been a danger of mixing Buddhism with other religions. In India this danger was counteracted by Dr Ambedkar and in England it was counteracted by our own new Buddhist movement. Now I know that here in India people think it may be easy to spread the Dhamma in England, but this is not the case. It is just as difficult to spread Buddhism in England as it is to spread it here in India. In England the difficulty is due very largely to Christianity, since most people in England are brought up as Christians. Christianity teaches them that man is sinful and weak and that he can't do anything for himself or save himself, but has to ask God or Christ to save him. Even after people become Buddhists, sometimes this way of thinking continues, at least unconsciously, and because of it, people in England often suffer from a feeling of inferiority. So, once again, there is a parallel with the situation here in India. Here people were Hindu before becoming Buddhists and they find it difficult to get rid of their Hindu mentality. Not only that. Before becoming Buddhists, many of them were Hindus of a very low caste, even Untouchables, and they were accustomed to the higher caste Hindus regarding them in a certain way. Even after conversion it was very difficult for some people to shake this off and feel that they were just human beings, neither superior to anybody nor inferior to anybody. In England it is the Christian God who makes people feel inferior whereas in India it is not so much God but the higher caste people who make other people feel inferior. So we have to get rid of both God and the caste system and then we can become real hundred-percent Buddhists. We can become real human beings.

There was another reason why I started this new Buddhist movement in England. In England we have what we call the class system which is not quite the same thing as the caste system but it is still quite bad. We have an upper class, a middle class, and what is usually called the working class, and these have many, many subdivisions. In England people can usually tell which class you come from. Before 1967 most Buddhists and half-Buddhists in England belonged to the upper middle class and for this reason they were not especially interested in the social aspect of Buddhism. To them Buddhism was just a philosophy or even just a hobby. But now the FWBO/TBMSG has changed all that in England. Our members come from all classes. Some are rich, some poor. Moreover, in England, the FWBO/TBMSG wants to change society, and even to create a new society. It doesn't see Buddhism just as a philosophy but also as something that can change society. For this reason we've set up a number of businesses which are all organized on cooperative principles. Our members work together in these businesses in the spirit of Buddhism. There is no distinction between bosses and workers, or between capital and labour. Everybody has a share of the responsibility and, working in this way, the co-op members support themselves and their families. These cooperative businesses make a profit which doesn't go to any individual but it goes towards the running of Buddhist activities. Our biggest centre of activities in England is in London and there activities go on every day – lectures, classes, study groups and so on. Of course it costs a lot of money to run all these activities, and most of this money comes from our co-op businesses. Only a small part comes from donations. Here too is a parallel with the situation in India. In India too, people don't regard Buddhism just as a philosophy. Dr Ambedkar did not regard Buddhism as a philosophy. He saw it as a means of social, economic, educational, cultural, and spiritual uplift for millions of people, and as a means of the all-round development of the individual human being.

From this we can see that there's quite a similarity between the Buddhist movement in England and the Buddhist movement in India, especially in Maharashtra. Many of our members and friends in England are very interested in the Buddhist movement here in Maharashtra, and in the life and work of Dr Ambedkar, which is why some of them, like Lokamitra, have come out here to India. The FWBO or TBMSG is in fact the only Buddhist movement in the West which gives information to the people there about Dr Ambedkar and his movement, mainly through activities and reports in its quarterly magazine, which is published in London and circulates throughout the world. Some of you may know that the editor of this magazine, Nagabodhi, is here this evening.[252]

English Buddhists now have a strong feeling towards Indian Buddhists and would like to have more contact with them. They would like to help in whatever way they can because, after all, Buddhists everywhere are brothers and sisters and therefore we should do whatever we can for one another.

I have now said something about our new Buddhist movement in England and the West, but what about the Buddhist movement here in India which was started by Dr Ambedkar? Twenty-five years have passed since the original mass conversion in Nagpur, which is long enough for a whole new generation to spring up and for many changes to have taken place. Unfortunately, not as many changes have taken place as people hoped. People haven't changed very much and therefore some people think that the movement of conversion to the Dhamma has failed and that Dr Ambedkar has failed. Now I must say very strongly that I do not agree with this. In my view Buddhism cannot fail; the Dhamma cannot fail; Dr Ambedkar cannot fail.

But *we* may fail. It is important that we accept personal responsibility for the situation. It is *we* who have become Buddhists and can therefore work for Buddhism. *We* must practise the *tisaraṇa* and *pañcasīla*, since nobody else can do it for us. In India people are very much accustomed to looking to some great man to deliver them. But as Buddhists we cannot do that. As Buddhists we have to deliver ourselves. If we want the Buddhist movement in India to be more successful we must simply work harder. Not only must we work harder, but we must work along the right lines, systematically and in cooperation with one another. We must study the Dhamma, so that we know what the Buddha taught. Also, we must learn what Dr Ambedkar taught. We must attend Dhamma lectures, that is, real Dhamma lectures given by real Buddhists who understand and practise Buddhism and who can make it understandable to others. Whenever we get the opportunity we must go on *Dhamma-shibir*. We must attend Dhamma study groups, and we must practise meditation.

In our new English Buddhist movement great importance is attached to meditation because it's a source of energy and inspiration. If we meditate we can work better for the Dhamma and we ourselves will grow and develop. We will be able to understand life better and understand ourselves and other people better. We will be able to understand the Dhamma better. We will be one-hundred-percent Buddhists and so we will be able to give up all our old, bad Hindu customs. We shall be able to create a new society and to really bring back Buddhism to India. In this way we shall give meaning and value to our lives and also fulfil the ideals of Dr Ambedkar. We shall help spread Buddhism throughout the world.

9

GOING FOR REFUGE

Theosophy Hall, Bombay,[253] *31 December 1981*

Mme Wadia[254] and Friends: I cannot begin my talk this evening without saying how glad I am to be back in Bombay. I almost said glad to be back *even* in Bombay. With its problems of pollution and overpopulation one has to admit that this is in some respects not the most attractive of cities, but it has its compensations, and for me the place has a special appeal. My associations with the city go back to 1944, when I had my first glimpse of the docks from the deck of a British troopship. Thereafter, I often had occasion to visit Bombay, and with every visit became better acquainted with it. Though living in the foothills of the eastern Himalayas, amidst beautiful and inspiring scenery, I came to look forward to my annual winter visits to Bombay, even though I was a little saddened each time to see how the once lovely city had deteriorated. The people, however, never deteriorated. Each time I came down I received a warmer welcome than ever from my friends. Not the least of my associations in Bombay was with Theosophy Hall, where I spoke on a number of occasions. In fact, I think I have hardly ever visited Bombay, even for a short period, without speaking here at least once or twice. Last time I spoke here was, I believe, in the winter of 1966, when I addressed you on the subject of Tibetan Buddhist meditation.

Tonight my subject is Going for Refuge (Pāli *saraṇa-gamana*, Sanskrit *śaraṇa-gamana*). I am happy to have been invited to speak on this topic, since it is one which for many years has been very close to my heart. However, I am going to approach it indirectly, via my experience of living and working for Buddhism in England. As some of you know, for twelve or thirteen years my face has not been seen in Bombay, or indeed in India. During that period I have been busy with the creation and consolidation of an entirely new Buddhist movement in the West, beginning with England, and it is via my experience of that new Buddhist movement that I am going to approach the subject of going for Refuge tonight.

At the various urban centres of this new Buddhist movement (known in England as the Friends of the Western Buddhist Order and in India as the Trailokya Bauddha Mahasangha Sahayak Gana), we conduct a wide range of activities including lectures on Buddhism, literature and the fine arts, meditation classes, hatha yoga classes, and courses in communication. From time to time day retreats are held which involve spending the whole day engaged in meditation, study, discussion, and communication.

People come to hear about our activities in various ways. Some come into contact with them through our publicity, but more often they hear about them simply by word of mouth. One friend tells another that there is a place where you can meditate, or where you can learn about Buddhism, or practise hatha yoga. By one means or another people make contact with their local FWBO centre, and thus with our new Buddhist movement. At first they may be interested simply in meditation, or Buddhist philosophy, or yoga, and come to see us just for that. But however it happens, they start coming. Nowadays in England, as in most Western countries, there are thousands of people who are engaged in sampling all kinds of spiritual groups. They go along to one group for a while, then to another, and so on. In this way they sample quite a number of groups. Some of the people who come to see us are of this type. They come to us for a time, then leave to continue their search elsewhere. Some of them, however, like our approach and feel at home with us, so they stay and get more deeply involved in our activities. One day it dawns on them that they would like to identify themselves with us and, in a word, 'belong'. When they reach that point they can become what we call a Mitra, which is simply the Sanskrit word for friend.

Here I should perhaps explain that in our new Buddhist movement, the FWBO or TBMSG, we have no membership in the ordinary sense. You cannot join simply by filling in a form and paying a subscription. We have a different system, and it is this system, in fact, that I am in the process of describing. When you reach the point of wanting to belong to the FWBO and become a Mitra, you make your wishes known and, if your desire is genuine and you have a real interest in the work of the FWBO, a simple public ceremony is held at which you offer a flower, a lighted candle, and a stick of incense before an image of the Buddha. In this way you become a Mitra. Until then you have been a Friend, with a capital 'F'. Anybody who comes along and participates in any of our activities, to however small an extent, is regarded as a Friend. You don't have to join in any formal sense. You are free to derive whatever benefit you can from our activities without incurring any obligation or responsibility. We are quite happy for you to do this. If you want to become more deeply involved, however, then you become a Mitra in the manner I have described.

In becoming a Mitra you show that your search for a spiritual group has now ended, and that henceforth your time, energy, and interest will be devoted exclusively to the FWBO. Four things are expected of a Mitra: (1) to attend the local FWBO centre regularly and participate in its activities; (2) to keep up a daily meditation practice; (3) to maintain contact with the *dasa sīla upāsakas* who conduct all centre activities and to do one's best to develop *kalyāṇa mitratā* or 'spiritual fellowship' with them; and (4) to help the centre, and the Movement generally, in any practical way one can.

As a Mitra you will probably find yourself becoming increasingly involved with the Movement, and increasingly attracted by the beauty of the Buddhist spiritual ideal, the ideal of human Enlightenment. You may find that your experience of meditation is becoming deeper, that your communication with other people is expanding, and that psychological conditionings are being removed. Eventually, you may find that the centre of gravity of your whole existence has been subtly shifted, and that you now want to give up your old interests and activities and commit yourself wholly to Buddhism, to the Dharma, to the spiritual life. When that point is reached you start thinking in terms of joining the Order or, to put it more traditionally, in terms of going for Refuge to the Buddha, the Dharma, and the Sangha. If the existing Order members are convinced that your aspiration is genuine, and that you really are able to Go for Refuge – by no means an easy thing to do – then your application is accepted and in due course the very beautiful ordination ceremony is held. You become a *dasa sīla upāsaka*, i.e. one who goes for Refuge to the Buddha, the Dharma, and the Sangha and who, in addition, takes upon himself or herself the ten *sīlas* or moral precepts by means of which body, speech, and mind are progressively and systematically purified.

But where does this 'going for Refuge' have its origin, and why does it seem to represent the culmination of one's involvement not only with our new Buddhist movement but even with Buddhism itself? The tradition of going for Refuge is a very ancient one, and in order to understand where it had its origin and why it is of such tremendous importance, we shall have to go back a very long way to the Buddha's own lifetime and to certain incidents in his career.

After his Enlightenment the Buddha spent a great deal of his time wandering from place to place making known the Truth he had discovered, and the way leading to its realization. Much of what he said is preserved in the Pāli scriptures, but although in some cases we have what may well be the Buddha's actual words, we probably do not appreciate how powerful was the effect of those words on the listener when spoken by the Enlightened One himself. What we usually find happening is that, in the course of his wanderings, the Buddha meets someone, whether a wealthy Brahmin, a beggar, a fellow wanderer, or a young prince, and the two of them get into conversation. As the conversation deepens, the Buddha begins to speak from the depths of his spiritual experience. In other words, the Buddha expounds the Dharma: the Dharma *emerges*. Sometimes, when reading the Buddhist scriptures, we get the impression that the Dharma is a matter of lists, the five of this and the six of that and so on, and that it is an excessively schematized and tabulated thing. But it certainly wasn't like that at the beginning. It was all fresh, original, and creative. The Buddha would speak from the depths of his spiritual experience. He would expound the Truth and show the way leading to Enlightenment, and the person to whom he was speaking would be absolutely astounded, absolutely overwhelmed. In some cases he might not be able to speak, or to do more than stammer a few incoherent words. Something had been revealed to him. Something had burst upon him that was above and beyond his ordinary understanding. For an instant, at least, he had glimpsed the Truth, and the experience had staggered him. Time and time again, on occasions of this sort, the scriptures tell us that the person concerned exclaimed,

Excellent, lord, excellent! As if one should set up again that which had been overthrown, or reveal that which had been hidden, or should disclose the road to one that was astray, or should carry a lamp into darkness, saying, 'They that have eyes will see!' Even so has the Truth been manifested by the Exalted One in many ways.[255]

In this manner he would express himself. Then, out of the depth of his gratitude, such a person would fervently exclaim, '*Buddhaṃ saraṇaṃ gacchāmi! Dhammaṃ saraṇaṃ gacchāmi! Saṅghaṃ saraṇaṃ gacchāmi!* To the Buddha for Refuge I go! To the Dharma for Refuge I go! To the Sangha for Refuge I go!'

So this is where the Going for Refuge had its origin, and it gives us an idea of its tremendous spiritual significance. The Going for Refuge represents your positive emotional response – in fact your total response – to the spiritual ideal when that ideal is revealed to your spiritual vision. Such is its appeal that you cannot but give yourself to it. As Tennyson says, 'We needs must love the highest when we see it.'[256] Going for Refuge is a bit like that. You've seen the highest – the highest has been shown to you – so you needs must love it, needs must give yourself to it, needs must *commit* yourself to it. That commitment of yourself to the highest is the Going for Refuge.

The object of Refuge is threefold: one goes for Refuge to the Buddha, the Dharma, and the Sangha – the Triple Gem or Three Jewels. But what does going for Refuge to each of these three things specifically mean? The Buddha is an Enlightened human being. He is not God, nor an avatāra, a messenger of God. He is a human being who, by his own efforts, has reached the summit of human perfection. He has gained the ineffable state which we designate Enlightenment, Nirvāṇa, or Buddhahood. He is, indeed, not only a Buddha but a *samyak-sambuddha*, a fully and perfectly Enlightened One. When we go for Refuge to the Buddha, we go for Refuge to him in this sense. We don't just admire him from a distance. We admire him indeed, and certainly he is very distant at present, but great as the gap between the Buddha and ourselves may be, that gap can be closed. We can close it by following the Path, and by practising the Dharma. We too can become as the Buddha. We too can become Enlightened. That is the great message of Buddhism. Each and every human being who makes the effort, who follows the Noble Eightfold Path to Enlightenment, can become what the Buddha became. When we go for Refuge to the Buddha, we go for Refuge to him as the living embodiment of a spiritual ideal which is a spiritual ideal for us, a spiritual ideal that we can realize. When we go for Refuge to the Buddha it is as though we say, 'That is what I want to be. That is what I want to attain. I want to be Enlightened. I want to develop the fullness of Wisdom, the fullness of Compassion.' Going for Refuge to the Buddha means taking Buddhahood as our personal spiritual ideal or as something we ourselves can achieve.

The Dharma is the path or way. It is the path of what I have sometimes called the higher evolution, a stage of purely spiritual development above and beyond ordinary biological evolution. As a path, the Dharma can be described in terms of a number of different formulations. We speak of the threefold path of morality (*śīla*), meditation (*samādhi*), and Wisdom (*prajñā*), as well as the path of the six perfections (*pāramitās*) of giving (*dāna*), morality (*śīla*), patience and forbearance (*kṣānti*), vigour (*vīrya*), higher consciousness (*samādhi*), and Wisdom (*prajñā*) – the path of the bodhisattva. Thus there are many different formulations. But although the formulations are many, the basic principle of the path is one and the same. The path is essentially the path of the higher evolution. It is whatever helps us to develop. The Dharma is not to be identified with this or that particular teaching. According to the Buddha's own declaration the Dharma is whatever contributes to the spiritual development of the individual. When his maternal aunt and foster mother, Mahāpajāpatī the Gotamid, asked him for a criterion by means of which she should distinguish between what was his *Dharma-Vinaya* and what was not, he replied,

> Of whatsoever teachings, Gotamid, thou canst assure thyself thus: 'These doctrines conduce to passions, not to dispassion; to bondage, not to detachment; to increase of (worldly) gains, not to decrease of them; to covetousness, not to frugality; to discontent, and not content; to company, not to solitude; to sluggishness, not energy; to delight in evil, not delight in good': of such teachings thou mayest with certainty affirm, Gotamid, 'This is not the Norm [i.e. the Dharma]. This is not the Discipline [i.e. the Vinaya]. This is not the Master's Message.' But of whatsoever teachings thou canst assure thyself (that they are the opposite of these things that I have told you), – of such teachings thou mayest with certainty affirm: 'This is the Dharma. This is the Vinaya. This is the Master's Message.'[257]

When we go for Refuge to the Dharma we therefore commit ourselves to the path of the higher evolution. We commit ourselves to whatever helps us develop spiritually, to whatever helps us grow towards Buddhahood.

Sangha means 'spiritual community'. Primarily this is the community of all those who are spiritually more advanced than we are: the great Bodhisattvas, the Arahants, the Stream Entrants and so on. Together they form the Āryasaṅgha or the spiritual community in the highest sense. Secondarily, the Sangha is the community of all Buddhists, all those who go for Refuge to the Buddha, the Dharma, and the Sangha. In the case of the Āryasaṅgha, going for Refuge to the Sangha means opening ourselves to the spiritual influence of the sublime beings of whom it consists. It means learning from them, being inspired by them, reverencing them. In the case of the *sangha* in the more ordinary sense, that of the community of all Buddhists, it means enjoying spiritual fellowship with one another and helping one another on the path. Sometimes you may not need a highly advanced bodhisattva to help you. All you need is an ordinary human being who is a little more developed spiritually than you are, or even just a little more sensible. Only too often people are on the lookout for a great, highly developed, preferably god-incarnate guru, but that is not what they really need, even if such a person was available. What they need is a helping hand *where they are now*, on the particular stage of the path which at present they occupy, and this can generally be given by an ordinary fellow Buddhist.

This, then, is what it means to go for Refuge to the Buddha, the Dharma, and the Sangha specifically, and it is this threefold going for Refuge that makes one a Buddhist. Going for Refuge is therefore of crucial importance in the Buddhist life. But having said that, one must sound a note of regret. Unfortunately, the Going for Refuge, despite its crucial importance, is often undervalued in the Buddhist countries of Asia. I shall have something to say about this in a minute. In our new Buddhist movement it is certainly not undervalued. Some people might think that we overvalue it, but I would say that is not possible. You *cannot* overvalue the Going for Refuge, because the Going for Refuge is the basis of everything else. When in the FWBO or TBMSG we emphasize the importance of the Going for Refuge we are trying to get back to the way things were in the Buddha's own time. We are trying to restore the original significance and value of the Going for Refuge.

Returning once more to the Buddha's own time we find something else of great interest happening. Not only may someone be so impressed and thrilled by the Buddha's exposition of the truth that he goes for Refuge but, even as he listens, insight into that truth may arise in his mind. In the language of the Buddhist scriptures, there arises for that person the pure and stainless Eye of Truth (*dharma-cakṣus*) – a profound spiritual experience. This 'Eye of Truth' is one of the five 'eyes' known to the Buddhist tradition. Firstly, there is the eye of flesh (*māṃsa-cakṣus*). This is the eye with which we see the ordinary world, the organ of physical sight, by means of which material objects are perceived. Secondly, there is the divine eye (*divya-cakṣus*). If you were able to 'see' what was happening on the other side of Bombay, or what was happening in Poona, or even in England, it would be this eye that you were using. This is known in English as the faculty of clairvoyance, and it is one of the supernormal powers that may arise spontaneously in the course of meditation practice. Thirdly, there is the Eye of Truth (*dharma-cakṣus*), the eye with which we are concerned at the moment. This is the inner spiritual eye, or inner spiritual vision, with which you 'see' the truth of things. I will say more about this in a minute. Fourthly, there is the Eye of Wisdom (*prajñā-cakṣus*). This eye, which sees even further than the Eye of Truth, arises only when one becomes an Arahant. Fifthly and lastly, there is the Universal Eye (*samanta-cakṣus*), also known as the Buddha Eye. When *this* eye arises, one is fully Enlightened and one's spiritual vision is total and absolute.

So let us consider this Eye of Truth, this Dharma Eye or Dharma Vision. There is a formula in the Buddhist scriptures which gives succinct expression to the Truth meant here. This formula simply states that whatever arises – whatever comes into existence – must pass away. That sounds so simple and so straightforward that you might think you knew it already, but do you really? What the Eye of Truth represents is not a theoretical knowledge of the fact of universal impermanence or transitoriness but a deep spiritual insight into it, a real understanding. Now the fact that all things are impermanent – that you have to give up everything, lose everything, in the end – may seem to some people very terrible. Yet this is not really so, because impermanence implies not only change but also development and transformation. If things were *not* impermanent and did *not* change – if you were the same today as you were yesterday, and the same yesterday as you were the day before – *that* would be terrible indeed, for then you would not grow and develop. The law of impermanence guarantees the possibility of development. This is what one sees when one's Dharma Eye opens. One not only sees the fact of impermanence, the fact that everything changes; one also sees the possibility of human growth and development. One sees the possibility of the transformation of ordinary humanity into Enlightened humanity or Buddhahood.

When that kind of insight is developed, something tremendous happens. In the language of Buddhism, you 'enter the stream' – the stream that leads directly to Nirvāṇa. Your whole being now flows irreversibly in the direction of Enlightenment or Buddhahood. This is what we call the 'real' Going for Refuge or, if you like, the 'Transcendental' Going for Refuge. By entering the stream, by going for Refuge in this higher, transcendental way, you at once break three of the ten fetters binding you to mundane existence. It is, indeed, by breaking these three fetters that you 'enter the stream', thus becoming what is known as a 'Stream Entrant' (srotāpanna). Since they occupy an important place in Buddhist teaching, let me say a few words about each of the three fetters in turn.

The first fetter is that of 'self-view' (satkāya-dṛṣṭi). When you are the victim of self-view your attitude is that what you experience as the self or the ego is something fixed, irreducible, and ultimate. You think there is a core of selfhood in you which is never going to change, and which is the real 'you'. Such an attitude blocks change and inhibits growth because you think that you are you, and that as you are now so you will be for ever. It is very difficult to break this fetter, very difficult to imagine oneself as different from what one is now. But it can be done. If you are genuinely committed to the spiritual path the time will come when you will be able to look back and see that great changes have taken place. You will see that you have grown, even that you have been transformed. But so long as the fetter of self-view remains unbroken there is no real spiritual development and no Stream Entry.

The second fetter is that of 'doubt' (vicikitsā). This is not doubt in the intellectual sense so much as indecision. In fact, it is deliberate, culpable indecision. You actually refuse to make up your mind and commit yourself. Rather than give yourself wholeheartedly to something you prefer to keep all your options open, so you make excuses, you wobble, you shilly-shally, you delay, you hesitate, you temporize, you rationalize. It is doubt that prevents you from throwing yourself into the spiritual life – from plunging in at the deep end, as we say. Consequently you get nowhere with the spiritual life; you fail to make real spiritual progress.

The third fetter is that of 'dependence on moral rules and religious observances' (*śīlavrata-parāmarśa*). It could be paraphrased as the belief that going through the motions will do. You go through the motions when your heart is not really in what you are doing. You think that if you keep up appearances externally, i.e. if you observe the moral rules because that is what society requires, and maintain the religious observances because that is what your co-religionists require, then everything will be alright. In other words, there is a split between the external observances and your inward state of being. Although the things you are doing may be good in themselves your heart is not in them and your performance of them is therefore empty, mechanical, rigid, and artificial. Hence these observances don't really help you to develop; they don't get you anywhere spiritually.

Such are the three fetters. When you enter the stream, they are broken; when they are broken, you enter the stream. When your Dharma Eye is opened you see the truth of impermanence, including the truth of the possibility of total transformation, and it is that insight, or higher spiritual vision, that causes the three fetters to break. Thus we have two things happening together. We have the Transcendental or Real Going for Refuge to the Buddha, the Dharma, and the Sangha and, at the same time, we have the opening of the Dharma Eye, or higher spiritual vision, leading to the breaking of the three fetters and to entering the stream. Indeed, we have these two things, (i.e. Transcendental Going for Refuge and Stream Entry), not just happening together but as different aspects of one and the same spiritual experience or spiritual process.

Still remaining in the Buddha's own time, we can go a little further. Suppose someone hears the Buddha expound the Dharma. Suppose he is impressed and thrilled and goes for Refuge. Suppose he gains Stream Entry. There is still something else that may happen at this point, something else that he may do. He may leave home and become a *bhikkhu*. Not that this was invariably the case. Sometimes people went for Refuge and, at the same time, their Dharma Eye opened, but they did not leave home. But very often they did. In such cases we have not two but three things happening together: Going for Refuge, Stream Entry, and what subsequently became known as 'ordination', i.e. 'Going

Forth' into homelessness and becoming a *bhikkhu* or monk. This was the situation during the Buddha's lifetime.

After the Buddha's death, or what we call his *parinirvāṇa*, many changes took place. Perhaps inevitably, a certain spiritual deterioration set in. Stream Entry became rarer and rarer and as centuries went by, the emphasis came increasingly to be placed on becoming a monk in the more formal sense and the Going for Refuge gradually lost its significance as the central act of the Buddhist life. This happened especially in the Theravāda countries of South-east Asia. Today, if you visit these countries, or talk to a Theravādin Buddhist, they will not say very much to you about the importance of going for Refuge. They will be much more likely to speak in terms of becoming a monk in the more formal sense, shaving one's head and donning the yellow robe. For the Theravādins there are two kinds of people: the monks and the lay people. On this side there are the monks, who are the 'real' Buddhists, and on that side the lay people, who are the not so 'real' Buddhists. One could even speak of them as the first class Buddhists and the second class Buddhists – sometimes the difference seems to be almost as great as that.

Looking at things from a different point of view, however, and seeing them more as they were in the Buddha's day, one might say that though there certainly is a difference, it is of a different kind. The real difference is not between monks and lay people but between those who go for Refuge and those who do not. Whether you are a monk who goes for Refuge or a layman who goes for Refuge, a man who goes for Refuge or a woman who goes for Refuge, that is of secondary importance. That you live in a certain kind of way, or follow a certain discipline, is of secondary importance. What is of overriding importance is your spiritual commitment, your going for Refuge. That is why in the FWBO we have a sort of saying, or slogan: 'Going for Refuge – or commitment – is primary; lifestyle is secondary.'

Although in the Theravāda countries the distinction between monk and layman was unnecessarily insisted upon, and the significance of the Going for Refuge lost sight of, this did not happen in the Mahāyāna countries to nearly so great an extent. As their designation suggests, the Mahāyāna countries followed the Mahāyāna, the Great Way. They followed the bodhisattva ideal which stresses the ideal of attaining Enlightenment not just for one's own sake but for the sake of all.

Ultimately, of course, the distinction between the two ideals falls to the ground. You cannot really gain Enlightenment for the benefit of others unless you are a person of considerable spiritual development yourself, and you cannot develop spiritually yourself unless you are to some extent mindful of the needs of other people. In the long run spiritual individualism and spiritual altruism coincide. But as a necessary corrective to the earlier, more individualistic approach of the Theravāda, and of the Hīnayāna generally, the Mahāyāna stressed the bodhisattva ideal. The attitude of the bodhisattva is: 'I don't want Enlightenment only for myself. If it's to be only for myself, in a sense I'm not interested. I want Enlightenment for all. I am therefore working for Enlightenment for all – including myself.' The bodhisattva doesn't leave himself out; he includes himself, but only as one among many. His mission is to work for the spiritual progress, the ultimate Enlightenment, of all living beings.

After the Mahāyāna developed the bodhisattva ideal, all lesser distinctions lost their significance. Mahāyāna Buddhists insisted that everybody should aim for bodhisattvahood, everybody should follow the bodhisattva ideal. Be they a monk or a lay person, literate or illiterate, rich or poor, spiritually developed or spiritually not so developed, all should aspire to Enlightenment for the sake of all living beings. On account of the presence of the bodhisattva ideal, therefore, we find that in the Mahāyāna there is less of a difference between monk and layman, or at least that the difference is less insisted upon.

But what is a bodhisattva, and what does it mean to aim at Enlightenment for the sake of all? According to Mahāyāna tradition a bodhisattva, in the real sense, is one in whom the *bodhicitta* or 'Will to Enlightenment' (as I translate the term) has actually arisen as a vital spiritual experience. The *bodhicitta* is not a mere pious aspiration. It is not a concept, nor an abstract ideal. When, within the depths of your being, there arises an immensely powerful impulse towards Enlightenment for the benefit of all, and when the impulse dominates your whole life, and becomes the master-current of your existence, *that* is the *bodhicitta*.

Here an interesting question arises. What is the nature of the relation between, on the one hand, the arising of the *bodhicitta*, and on the other hand the Going for Refuge, the opening of the Dharma Eye, Stream Entry, and even Going Forth into homelessness and becoming a monk? The arising of the *bodhicitta*, represents, we may say, the altruistic dimension of these four other experiences. Or rather, all five of them, including the *bodhicitta* itself, represent the five different aspects of a single basic, crucial, and unique spiritual experience. The Going for Refuge draws attention to the emotional and volitional aspect of this experience, the opening of the Dharma Eye to the unconditioned depth of its cognitive content, Stream Entry to the permanent and far-reaching nature of its effects, while Going Forth into homelessness draws attention to the extent of the reorganization which, regardless of whether or not one becomes a monk in the formal sense, the experience inevitably brings about in the pattern of one's daily life. As for the *bodhicitta*, it represents, as I have said, the altruistic or other-regarding aspect of the experience.

Perhaps we now have a broader conception of the Going for Refuge. Much more is implied by it than people usually think, and this is why it is so greatly emphasized in our movement. Incidentally, the use of the word 'refuge' sometimes creates confusion, because it is associated in people's minds with 'refugee'. Expressions like 'taking Refuge' or 'going for Refuge' have distinct connotations of running away from difficulties, taking the easy way out, and so on. From what I have already said it should be clear that going for Refuge in the Buddhist sense has nothing to do with running away. However, in order to avoid the possibility of misunderstanding on the part of people who are unfamiliar with the expression, we often speak not of going for Refuge but of commitment. So we often speak not of going for Refuge to the Buddha, Dharma, and Sangha, but of committing oneself to the Buddha, the Dharma, and the Sangha.

Nor is that all. In the course of years we have come to distinguish four levels of going for Refuge, four levels of commitment. First of all there is *provisional* going for Refuge, sometimes called ethnic going for Refuge. This consists in simply reciting the Refuge-going formula in Pāli, or some other language, just because it is part of your national culture. In Buddhist countries like Sri Lanka, Thailand, and Burma, and even here in India, one often finds people reciting the Refuge-going formula, *Buddhaṃ saraṇaṃ gacchāmi* etc., without understanding its meaning. It is just part of their culture, and has no real spiritual significance for them. That one should recite the Refuge-going formula, even without understanding, is by no means a bad thing but it is certainly not sufficient. In much the same way, one sometimes finds people in the Buddhist countries of Asia, and again, even in India, describing themselves as 'born Buddhists'. But how can you be a born Buddhist? Do you issue from your mother's womb reciting *Buddhaṃ saraṇaṃ gacchāmi*? A 'born Buddhist' is a contradiction in terms. You can become a Buddhist only consciously and deliberately, as a result of personal choice. You cannot possibly be *born* a Buddhist. The Buddha himself criticized the Brahmins of his day for thinking that one could be born a Brahmin. You were a Brahmin, he insisted, only to the extent that you acted like one. If truth and righteousness were in you, then you could be called a Brahmin, not otherwise. Similarly, you cannot be a Buddhist by birth. People in Buddhist countries who say they are Buddhists by birth are no better than the ancient Brahmins who said that they were Brahmins by birth. What it really means is that Buddhism, so called, has simply become Brahmanism. This is a very important point. The going for Refuge must be a real going for Refuge. If you are a Buddhist it must be on account of your own, individual, independent volition – your own understanding. Thus you cannot be born a Buddhist. If you think you can, you are still on the level of provisional going for Refuge, the significance of which is cultural rather than genuinely spiritual. Secondly, there is *effective* going for Refuge. This is a wholehearted, conscious commitment to the Buddha, Dharma, and Sangha. Though such commitment is sincere and genuine, it is not powerful enough to break the three fetters and does not amount to Stream Entry. From effective going for Refuge you can fall away. Thirdly, there is *real* going for Refuge. This coincides with Stream Entry, which occurs with the breaking of the three fetters. From this going for Refuge you cannot fall away. Fourthly and lastly, there is Absolute going for Refuge. On this level there is, in a sense, no going for Refuge. Though you indeed go for Refuge to the Buddha, now that Enlightenment has been attained you are yourself the Buddha. Here, the goal of your quest having been reached, the subject of going for Refuge and the object of going for Refuge are one and the same. Buddha goes for Refuge to Buddha.

Such are the four levels of going for Refuge, or four levels of commitment, and it is very helpful to think of going for Refuge in this way. A little more might be said, however, in connection with the highest level, that of Absolute going for Refuge. In the Mahāyāna it is sometimes stated that ultimately there is only one Refuge, and that is the Buddha. In a sense there is a Dharma Refuge, and a Sangha Refuge, but again in a sense there is not. After all, the Dharma comes from the Buddha. It is the product, the creation of the Buddha's Enlightenment experience – the means by which that experience is communicated to other human beings in such a way as to help them. Similarly, the Sangha is the spiritual community of those who practise the Dharma. Just as the Dharma is dependent on the Buddha, the Sangha is dependent on the Dharma, so that the Sangha is also dependent on the Buddha. Thus there is only the Buddha: only the Buddha Refuge. Though we speak of Three Refuges, ultimately the Three Refuges are one Refuge. For the time being, however, it is no doubt helpful for us to think in terms of the Three Refuges, or the Threefold Refuge.

So far I have spoken about the Going for Refuge more or less within the context of our new Buddhist movement in England. I want to conclude with a few words about the Buddhist movement in India, especially in Maharashtra. As some of you know, in the course of the last few decades there has been a great expansion of the Buddhist movement in India, particularly here in Maharashtra, an expansion associated with the name of the late Dr Ambedkar. You may also know that at the time of the historic mass conversion of his followers to Buddhism on 14 October 1956, at Nagpur, Dr Ambedkar emphasized the Going for Refuge very strongly indeed. All that he asked his followers to do, in fact, was to go for Refuge. They should go for Refuge to the Buddha, Dharma, and Sangha as a means of all-round development of themselves and the society to which they belonged. It is significant that Dr Ambedkar did not emphasize becoming a *bhikkhu*. He did not ask his followers to become monks. He simply asked them to go for Refuge, and this fact is worth considering. Nor is that all. On more than one occasion Dr Ambedkar went so far as to criticize the *bhikkhus* of today. He even went so far as to say that the present day *bhikkhu saṅgha* was useless, i.e. useless for spreading the Dharma.[258] A new kind of *saṅgha* was needed, he declared, a new kind of Buddhist worker.

This new kind of *saṅgha*, this new kind of Buddhist worker, is what our new Buddhist movement has succeeded in creating in England in the course of the last twelve or thirteen years. At the heart of that movement is the Order. This Order is a spiritual community of people who have gone for Refuge, that is to say, who have *effectively* gone for Refuge. Few of them, perhaps, indeed if any, have got so far as the real going for Refuge, but at least they have got so far as the effective going for Refuge. At least they have transcended the provisional going for Refuge. What we have succeeded in creating in the course of the last so many years is this Order, this *sangha* or spiritual community, of people who go for Refuge, who make the act of going for Refuge central in their lives, and who place the emphasis *there*. Some of them live at home with their wives or husbands and families. Some live in communities. There are communities for men and communities for women. A few of them are *anagārikas* who take a vow of celibacy. As I mentioned earlier on, all members of the Order observe the ten precepts. These are: abstention from injury to living beings; from taking what is not given; from sexual misconduct (in the case of the *anagārikas*, from non-celibacy); from false speech; from frivolous, idle, and useless speech; from speech which divides and disunites people; from craving, from hatred, and from wrong views. According to Buddhist tradition, *bhikkhus* or monks observe 227 (or 250) precepts, but in the course of ages quite a few of these have been lost on the way, so to speak, and are nowadays honoured more in the breach than in the observance. We therefore decided to have a short list of precepts that people would take and actually observe.

Thus we have the Order, this *sangha* or spiritual community of people who have gone for Refuge to the Buddha, Dharma, and Sangha: people who actually practise the Dharma; who observe the ten precepts. Some of them have been members of the Order for eight or ten or twelve years or more, and are gathering experience all the time – from taking meditation classes, giving lectures, and running our cooperative businesses. It is, in fact, this dedicated, committed core of people at the heart of the Movement that is responsible for running everything. From this we can see more clearly, I hope, the vital importance, both for ourselves individually and the society to which we belong, of the Going for Refuge. It is my hope that, just as we have been able to create in England – in fact in the West – a *sangha* or spiritual community of those who have gone for Refuge – so we shall be able to create a similar *sangha* or spiritual community here in India, and create it on an even larger scale. If we are to do this, however, it can be only on the basis of the Buddha, the Dharma, and the Sangha. It can be only on the basis of the Going for Refuge.

IO

LOSING AND FINDING THE
JEWEL OF THE DHAMMA

Worli, Bombay, 2 January 1982

Brothers and Sisters in the Dhamma: I am very glad to be back in
Bombay, and especially glad to be back here in Worli.[259] I am glad to be
back not in order to see the Gateway of India or the Taj Mahal Hotel
but because I can meet all of you. I am glad to meet you particularly
because you are Buddhists and also followers of Dr Ambedkar. It is
very good that Buddhists of different nationalities should meet together
from time to time because, after all, Buddhists are brothers and sisters.
We have the same father, the Buddha himself, and we have the same
mother, the Dhamma. So we are all brothers and sisters. In fact we are
even closer than that. We are friends – friends in the Dhamma. So for
this reason I'm very glad to be here tonight speaking to you, among all
these beautiful decorations. Unfortunately I can't speak loudly because
your Bombay air has affected my throat and I may not be able to speak
for as long as I'd hoped.

This is certainly not the first time I've spoken in Worli. I first spoke
here in 1955–6 when I gave a lecture at the invitation of Dr Ambedkar.
I had met him a few days before, at Ananda Bhavan at Siddharth
College.[260] We had a good talk in the course of which we spoke about
the forthcoming conversions to Buddhism. At the conclusion of our
conversation, Dr Ambedkar asked if I would like to give a talk about
the meaning of conversion to some of his people. I accepted happily
and so the meeting was arranged here. Some of the older ones among
you may have been present. I remember that the meeting was held late

at night – about 11 o'clock – and it was a cold, windy night. I was wearing my thin *bhikkhu's* robe and even though I was much younger then, I felt the cold. On that occasion I spoke to about 2,000 people. I explained the meaning of conversion to the Dhamma. Firstly, I said, it meant going for Refuge to the Buddha, the Dhamma, and the Sangha. Also, it meant observing faithfully the *pañcasīla*, the five precepts. The people present listened very carefully. They realized how important it was. Unfortunately Dr Ambedkar could not attend because he was unwell. However, he was very pleased when he heard about the meeting.

That occasion, twenty-five or twenty-six years ago, was my first contact with the people of Worli. For a few years following that, I spoke here again a number of times. Sometimes we met in the chawls, in the corridors, quite late at night so people could come after work, but nevertheless they were good meetings. I also spoke more than once in the Japanese Buddhist temple. One of the lectures I gave there was called 'The Parables of the *White Lotus Sūtra*', that is, the *Saddharma Puṇḍarīka Sūtra*. I chose to speak on that subject on that occasion because the Japanese temple is run by monks who follow a particular kind of Japanese Buddhism called Nichiren Buddhism and the followers of this particular school think very highly of this particular *sūtra*. Indeed, they think so highly of it that they recite salutations to the *White Lotus Sūtra*. In Japanese the phrase they recite is *namu myōhō renge kyō*. At the Japanese Buddhist temple the monks used to recite this for one and a half hours every evening to the beat of a drum. Many Indian Buddhists also went to the temple so they also recited *namu myōhō renge kyō*, but they didn't know what it meant. This is why I decided to give a lecture on the *White Lotus Sūtra*, in which I explained the meaning of the title of the *sūtra* and then spoke about the meanings of the parables within it.

Tonight I am also going to speak about an important parable from the *White Lotus Sūtra*. This parable is important for all followers of Dr Ambedkar, particularly now, twenty-five years after the original mass conversion. It begins simply with two men who were friends. One man was rich and the other poor, and one day the rich man invited his poor friend to a meal at his house. It was a very good meal with many courses and lasted for one or two hours. The rich man fed his friend so well that in the end he couldn't eat any more, and started to feel very sleepy. Soon he fell asleep, and while he was sleeping his friend took a beautiful, precious jewel and tied it in a corner of his cloak, thinking, 'When my friend wakes up he'll be able to use this jewel and live happily.' After two or three hours the poor man woke up, gave a big yawn and went home, taking the jewel with him in his cloak, but he didn't know it was there. In fact, he never found it, so he remained very poor. He led a very miserable life and he never knew that the jewel was hidden in his cloak. This continued for many years and then one day he happened to meet his rich friend, who asked him, 'How is it that you are living so miserably?' The poor man replied, 'Well, I don't have any money. I don't have a job.' Then his friend said, 'You foolish person! While you were sleeping I tied a jewel in the corner of your cloak. Bring that cloak and take the jewel out!' So the poor man found the jewel and afterwards lived happily.[261]

So what is the meaning of this story from the *White Lotus Sūtra*? All stories in Buddhism have a meaning. It's alright to enjoy the story just as a story but we must also understand its meaning. So what is the meaning of that precious beautiful jewel? Who is the poor friend? Who is the rich friend? A number of different interpretations are possible. For instance, the jewel can represent the potential of each human being for gaining Enlightenment. People don't realize they have this potential. They don't realize their own strength and what they can do. Instead they think that they are weak and poor. So this is one meaning of the jewel.

However, tonight I am concerned with another meaning. We can also say that the jewel represents Buddhism, represents the Dhamma itself. The poor friend represents the people of India in the Buddha's time and the kind rich friend is the Buddha. In the story the rich friend fed the poor friend, and in the same way, 2,500 years ago Gautama the Buddha gave the food, the *amṛta*, of the teaching to the people of his time. The Buddha gave the people so much teaching in the forty-five years during which he taught that they found it too much and they fell asleep. Now I myself have experienced this with people. Sometimes I am giving a lecture and I look around the audience and here and there I see that someone has fallen asleep. I don't see anyone sleeping tonight, but sometimes the Dhamma is too much for people, and this is what happened in the Buddha's time too. But although people fell asleep, the Buddha continued to teach, regardless of whether or not anyone was listening. His duty was to teach, so he went on teaching and gave teachings that would be useful later on. In terms of the story, the Buddha tied a priceless jewel in the corner of the cloak of the people of his day.

In the story, the poor friend wakes up after a while, and he goes away and leads a miserable life, forgetting all about the jewel. Similarly, the people of India forgot about the Buddha, and they lived without the Dhamma for many years. The very name of the Buddha was forgotten in India, and the people suffered because they did not know about the Buddha. In particular, the so-called low-caste people suffered. This went on for 600 or 700 years. Then someone pointed out that the jewel was still there in the corner of the cloak. Someone said, there is no need for the people to live miserably. They can live happily, they can grow and develop. So who was it who pointed out the jewel that had been lost and forgotten for so many hundreds of years and reminded the Indian people of their priceless possession? It wasn't Gautama the Buddha, who had died 2,500 years before. It was, of course, Dr Ambedkar, who, on 14 October 1956 in Nagpur, together with *lakhs* of his followers, took the *Dhammadiksha*. On that occasion he held up the jewel of the Dhamma for everyone to see and he said, 'This is our precious possession, which we have forgotten. It will make us rich, culturally, spiritually, and in every way.' In this way Dr Ambedkar pointed out the jewel that had been hidden for so many hundreds of years. Unfortunately, we know that only seven weeks after that great conversion Dr Ambedkar died. I was in Nagpur at that time and remember the occasion very well. I remember how the followers of Dr Ambedkar felt as though their own father and mother had died. But though they had lost Dr Ambedkar, they still had one consolation. They still had Buddhism, which Dr Ambedkar had given them. They still had the jewel of the Dhamma.

All that happened twenty-five years ago and some of you have been Buddhists for twenty-five years, which is a very long time. So a question arises: What have you done with that jewel of the Dhamma? What use have you made of that jewel? Some of you may not find that question easy to understand so let's go back to the parable from the *White Lotus Sūtra*. You remember that at the end of the story, the rich man points out to his poor friend that the jewel is there in the corner of the cloak where it had been hidden all the time, and he tells the poor friend that now he has got the jewel in his hand he can live happily. Once the poor man has the jewel, he goes and sells it so that he has money for food, clothing, shelter, and medicine. The poor man sells the jewel even though it is very beautiful, valuable, and precious because he cannot eat it. The jewel is only useful when it is turned into something that he can eat.

There is an old story that illustrates this point, about a merchant who went on a long journey.[262] He was on a business trip but he lost his way in the desert. He was alone without a horse so he had to walk with no food and no water. The man was in a terrible state, almost dying of hunger; and around him there was only desert – no trees, no bush, no animals – just sand in all directions. Eventually he lay down in the sand and he thought, 'If I don't get any food soon, I shall die.' While he lay there thinking this, he saw something in the distance lying on the ground. Judging from its size and shape he guessed it must have fallen off the back of a merchant's horse or camel. So he went quickly towards it, thinking it must be a sack of rice and hoping that now he would have something to eat. With his last strength he caught hold of the sack and pulled it open only to find not rice but pearls. He was very disappointed and he died, because you cannot eat jewels, you can only eat food. You cannot even eat the jewel of the Dhamma; you have to sell it for something that you *can* eat. This selling or exchanging of the jewel of the Dhamma means translating the ideal of the Dhamma into practice. Buddhism, that is the Buddha's teaching, is like a jewel. It is very beautiful with many lovely colours and very valuable, indeed priceless, but it only becomes useful to us when we practise it.

As I mentioned earlier, it is now twenty-five years since the original *Dhammadiksha* but in some ways not much has happened since then. There has not been much progress in the Buddhist movement. The reason for this is that we have not made full use of the jewel of the Dhamma. We have got the jewel but we have not yet exchanged it for anything. We keep the jewel in our house and we are pleased to have it there, but we go on living in the same poor old way. So how can we make use of the Dhamma? How can we exchange the jewel and translate theory into practice? We can do this in two ways. I shall explain it very simply so that everybody can understand, including the small children. We have to get rid of certain things and we have to develop certain things, and by doing these two things we shall translate theory into practice.

There are three things we have to give up. To begin with, we have to get rid of the old Hindu customs and attitudes and we have to stop worshipping the old Hindu gods. A few years ago I heard that in some of the villages in Maharashtra the people were going back to the worship of the old gods, and this made me very sad. Dr Ambedkar realized this might happen so at the time of the *Dhammadiksha* he not only gave his followers the Three Refuges and the Five Precepts, but also gave them twenty-two vows so that they would not mix Buddhism with Hinduism. He wanted his followers to be one-hundred-percent Buddhists. We have to give up Hindu customs like sacrificing goats; we can't do this sort of thing and say that we are Buddhist, because this practice is not in accordance with Buddhism. In the same way, at the time of marriage we should not ask for a dowry, because the dowry system is not in accordance with Buddhism. Not only that, we should not celebrate the marriage of Buddhists in the old Hindu way but in the Buddhist way. We should celebrate in a decent, dignified way without spending too much money. In the old days people used to spend a lot of money on food and drink at weddings, but they often did not have the money so they had to borrow it and go into debt, and for the rest of their life they carried a load of debt on their back. These are the kinds of bad old customs we have to give up now that we are Buddhists. As Buddhists we are going to do things in a new way, and as new individuals we shall make a new society.

Also we have to practise the precepts. We should not do any injury to human beings or even to animals. We should not take what is not given, should not steal or cheat. We should not commit adultery. We should not tell lies or use rough or harsh speech, and finally we should not drink or take drugs. This last precept is especially important. These are, of course, the five *sīlas* and if you do not practise the fifth one you may not be able to practise the other four. Here the precepts are expressed in their negative form – you shouldn't do this or that; I'll give the positive form in a few minutes.

Secondly, we should give up wrong views about Buddhism. There is one particular wrong view about the Buddha which is very common in India, namely that the Buddha is the *avatāra* of Vishnu. This is absolutely untrue, and if you are a Buddhist you will give up this view. In Buddhism there is no Vishnu or any other god, so there cannot be the *avatāra* of any god. The Buddha was not the messenger of any god, nor the son of any god; he was a human being, an extraordinary human being who gained Enlightenment by his own efforts. If we make that effort we too can become Buddhas. So the Buddha is not an *avatāra*, and to see him as such is a wrong view which we must give up.

We must also give up the wrong view that the Dhamma is the same as *dharma*. *Dharma* means your duty as a member of a particular caste, the duty that means that if you are born a Kshatriya you must fight; if you are born into a Bania family[263] you must make money; if you are born into the thieves' caste then you must steal, and so on. The *Bhagavad Gītā* says that you mustn't give up your own *dharma* and take the *dharma* of another person. So this is the meaning of *dharma* and it depends on caste and birth.

However, the meaning of the Buddha's Dhamma is quite different. The Dhamma is that which helps in the growth and development of the individual and contributes to their happiness. It is the same for all and it does not depend on caste. The Dhamma depends on your personal qualities as a human being. This then is another wrong view that we must give up: that the *dharma* is the same as Dhamma.

The third thing we must give up is the mechanical practice of Buddhism. Earlier I spoke of reciting *namu myōhō renge kyō*. It is good to recite this, and to recite the *tisaraṇa* and the *pañcasīla*, but it is not good to recite something without understanding what you are doing. If you want to be a real Buddhist, you must understand the practice you are doing. In the Buddhist countries of Asia there is still quite a lot of mechanical practice of Buddhism, and Dr Ambedkar himself gave an example of this. In 1950 he visited several countries in South-east Asia to see how Buddhism was practised there. In particular he wanted to see how a *bhikkhu* gave a lecture, so his Buddhist friends arranged this for him. They took him to a very small room, not much bigger than a table, and after a while a *bhikkhu* in a yellow robe came in, sat down and some of the people came forward and washed his feet. This took some time and then the *bhikkhu* held a fan in front of his face and spoke for two minutes, after which he went away. Dr Ambedkar was very disappointed. He had wanted to hear a good lecture on Buddhism, but instead of giving a proper explanation someone had just spoken mechanically for a couple of minutes. We don't want this sort of mechanical practice of the Dhamma, we don't want a religious routine. Instead we want to put our hearts into the practice of the Dhamma. These then are the three things that we have to get rid of – the old Hindu customs, wrong views about Buddhism, and the mechanical practice of the Dhamma.

Now turning to the things we have to develop, I shall mention briefly six things. There are many more, but these six are particularly important.

Firstly, we have to develop our going for Refuge to the Buddha, the Dhamma, and the Sangha. It is not enough just to recite the *tisaraṇa*; we have to feel it in our heart, we have to have devotion and a proper understanding. We have to understand who the Buddha was, what the Dhamma is, and what the Sangha is.

Secondly, we have to develop the five positive precepts. (I have already explained the negative precepts.) We have to develop *mettā* – love – for all living beings. This is not just love for the people in our own home or locality, nor even just human beings, but animals too. And then we have to develop *dāna*. *Dāna* means giving – giving especially for the sake of the Buddhist movement, to help it grow strong. The third precept is *santuṭṭhi* or contentment. This means not being discontented but working to improve your own condition while at the same time not wasting mental energy on being discontented. The fourth precept is *satya* or truth – speaking the truth, thinking the truth, and acting the truth. Finally there is *sati* or recollection or mindfulness, which means always keeping a clear mind and knowing what you are doing, not doing things in a muddle.

Thirdly, we have to develop right means of livelihood. It is a very important principle in Buddhism that we should not earn our living in any way that goes against the Buddha's teaching. Sometimes it's quite difficult to practise right livelihood. That is the case here in India, and it's also the case in England. In some ways it is more difficult in England than it is here, and so in England some of our Buddhist friends have set up their own cooperative businesses, in which the principles of right livelihood are strictly applied. People can work happily together in these businesses in the spirit of Buddhism and they have achieved a good reputation even among non-Buddhists. The profits that accrue from these businesses go to support the Buddhist movement. So perhaps it will be possible to organize something of this sort in India too.

Fourthly, we have to meditate. Meditation is not just for the *bhikkhus* but for all Buddhists who go for Refuge since it purifies the mind and gives energy and inspiration. You may be wondering how you can learn to meditate, but it is not difficult; you can learn in a class or on retreat.

Fifthly, we should study the Dhamma. We should study the writings of Dr Ambedkar, particularly his book, *The Buddha and His Dhamma*, which is available in English, Hindi, and Marathi. It is important that we understand the Dhamma and if we don't study it we won't understand it. To support our Dhamma study, we can also read the publications put out by the TBMSG like the monthly magazine, *Buddhayan*. Study the Dhamma as much as you can; hold study classes; read the Dhamma literature.

Sixthly and lastly, we need to develop the ability to work together. There is no strength without unity. As I said at the beginning, all Buddhists are brothers and sisters, so we have to work together, help one another, practise the Dhamma together and spread the Dhamma together. As some Buddhists become a little richer and get better jobs, it is very important that they do not separate themselves from Buddhists who have not got such good jobs or who are poorer. Buddhists should all remain in contact with one another. We have given up the caste system and we don't want to introduce any other sort of division between us. We have to give up all divisions. Buddhists should remain united.

So these are the six things we should develop. We should develop going for Refuge, the five positive precepts, right livelihood, meditation, the study of the Dhamma, and the habit of working together. If we can get rid of the three things I mentioned earlier and cultivate these six things then our success is assured and theory will be translated into practice. We shall not just keep the jewel of the Dhamma uselessly in the home but will be able to make full use of it, and base our lives upon it. If we can do that, we shall be real one-hundred-percent Buddhists and real followers of Dr Ambedkar.

I don't want to say any more – my throat is nearly finished – but I'm very glad to have had the opportunity of speaking to you this evening. I am glad to have met you and to see the beautiful decorations and I am happy to feel that you are all friends of mine, just as I am a friend of all of you. I hope we shall meet again and have closer and ever closer contact with one another. I feel very inspired to be here this evening. I spend most of my time in England where the Movement is going very well. However, there is one big difference between England and India. In England we don't have such big meetings as this. Only a few hundred people attend a meeting at a time and if 500 people come to a Buddhist meeting in England, we think we are doing very well, but here in India we don't just have hundreds but tens of thousands, all going for Refuge to the Buddha, the Dhamma, and the Sangha. So I am very happy to be in the midst of not just a few Buddhists but thousands of Buddhists. I am very happy to hear thousands of Buddhists chant *buddham saraṇaṃ gacchāmi*, and I hope before too long we shall have thousands and tens of thousands of one-hundred-percent Buddhists. This is what the Buddha wanted, and likewise this is what Dr Ambedkar wanted twenty-five years ago. Dr Ambedkar told you frankly that Buddhism is very difficult to practise and he understood this well. But if you practise Buddhism, even though it is difficult, it will do you real good and Dr Ambedkar realized this. Both Dr Ambedkar and I want one-hundred-percent Buddhists and I hope all of you also want to be one-hundred-percent Buddhists. I wish you all success in your work for the Dhamma.

11

HOW TO DISTINGUISH BETWEEN THE TRUE AND THE FALSE BUDDHIST

Ulhasnagar, 3 January 1982

Venerable Bhikṣu, Brothers, and Sisters in the Dhamma: First of all I want to say how glad I am to be here among you all tonight.[264] This is my first visit to Ulhasnagar, but even before coming here I heard about this place from Lokamitra, who told me, 'We have got some very good Buddhists in Ulhasnagar.' I was very happy to hear this, and I am very happy to be speaking to you this evening. Unfortunately, I may not be able to speak for as long as I had intended. For the last few days I have been staying in Bombay and the air has affected my throat. Lokamitra tells me that next time he brings me to this area he will arrange for me to stay in Ulhasnagar, not in Bombay. Here, he says, the air is better. I can certainly feel the fresh air of Ulhasnagar and also see the beautiful view on all sides.[265]

I want to start by speaking about the Buddha. As you know, Gautama the Buddha lived some 2,500 years ago. He left home, left his parents and his beautiful wife, at the age of twenty-nine, gained Supreme Enlightenment six years later at the age of thirty-five, and died, or entered *parinirvāṇa*, as we say, at the age of eighty. This means that he spent forty-five years going from place to place teaching the Dhamma. In those days there were no trains or buses, so he went everywhere on foot, and wherever he went he met different kinds of people. He met people of high caste and people of low caste, and to all of them he taught the Dhamma. He taught the Dhamma in many different ways. Sometimes he gave a long lecture; sometimes he spoke just a few words. Sometimes he recited some verses of poetry, and sometimes he told a story. But whatever form they took, he gave all his teachings through the spoken word. In his day there were no books. Then, people only used writing for business arrangements, keeping accounts, and that sort of thing, and they didn't think it was right to use writing for religious purposes. So the Buddha and his disciples taught by word of mouth, and what we now call the Buddhist scriptures were not written down in book form until several hundred years after the Buddha's death. The scriptures were known as the *Tripiṭaka*, which means the 'three collections' of the teachings of the Buddha. It is very important that we should understand that the Buddhist scriptures did not come down from heaven. They were not given by God. They are simply the written form of the teachings given on this earth by an Enlightened human being or Buddha.

The *Tripiṭaka* is very large – in the Royal Thai edition it comprises forty-five volumes[266] – and it is divided into many different sections, one of the best known of which is the *Dhammapada*, which is quite short, consisting of 423 *gātha*s or verses arranged in twenty-six chapters. Each chapter deals with one subject; for instance, there is a chapter on the mind, a chapter on the wise man, a chapter on the fool, a chapter on the world, a chapter on the Buddha, a chapter on the path, and so on. Tonight I want to talk about the first chapter, which in Pāli is called *yamakavagga*, which means the chapter of the pairs. The verses are all arranged in pairs, each of which deals with two things, one good and one bad. Thus the first pair of verses deals with the pure mind and the impure mind. If we do something with an impure mind, the Buddha says, then we will experience suffering; if we do something with a pure mind, we will experience happiness. Another pair of verses deals with enmity. Here the Buddha says enmity never comes to an end through hatred; enmity comes to an end only through love. Yet another pair of verses deals with those who wear the yellow robe, that is to say the *bhikkhus* and *anagārikas*. The Buddha says that if one is not free from impurities then one does not deserve to wear the yellow robe; similarly, if one is free from impurities then one deserves to wear the yellow robe. Thus each pair of verses deals with two things, one good and one bad.

But why are the verses on the *yamakavagga* arranged in this way? What is the principle here? The principle is that it is very important to make clear distinctions. It is very important, for instance, to make the distinction between good and bad, or between what we call in Buddhism *kuśala* and *akuśala*, as the Buddha does in the *Dhammapada* when he speaks of the pure mind and the impure mind, and of the good *bhikkhu* and the bad *bhikkhu*. It is important to make the distinction between the path that leads to Enlightenment and the path that does not lead to Enlightenment, between what is Buddhism and what is not Buddhism, between what Dr Ambedkar taught and what he did not teach. But why is it so important to make clear distinctions? It is important because if we don't make clear distinctions we won't know what to do. We won't know which path to follow, and because we don't know which path to follow, we won't make any progress. This is why the *yamakavagga* is the first chapter of the *Dhammapada*. It is as though the Buddha is telling us that first of all we must think clearly, and distinguish clearly between right and wrong, between the false path and the true path, between what is Buddhism and what is not Buddhism.

To give an example of being confused and not making clear distinctions, let us suppose that you are a shopkeeper, and let us suppose that in the course of your business you use false weights and measures and also adulterate the foodstuffs that you sell. If you do these things, in plain language, you are cheating; you are stealing. But you don't like to think that you are stealing, so you say to yourself, 'I am taking only a very small amount from each customer, so it doesn't really matter. By taking that very small amount from each customer I can make some extra profit, and with that extra profit I can do something good. Maybe I can build a temple.' In this way people confuse themselves. They lose sight of the distinction between what is right and what is wrong, what is *śīla* and what is not *śīla*. They may build many temples and *dharmasalas*, and they may have the reputation of being good, pious people, but in reality they are just thieves.

The Buddha emphasized the importance of distinguishing clearly between the right path and the wrong path because only if you distinguish between them can you follow the right path. It is extremely important for us to remember this. So we have to ask ourselves some questions. We have to ask ourselves whether we are really following the path shown by the Buddha, the path shown by Dr Ambedkar? Do we know what is Buddhism and what is not Buddhism? Do we know who is the true Buddhist and who is the false Buddhist? Tonight, therefore, I am going to go into the matter a little. I am going to say something about the true Buddhist and something about the false

Buddhist, so that you can distinguish between them and know to which category you belong.

First of all, what is the false Buddhist like? The Buddha said that the false Buddhist is like a donkey. Actually, he says that the false *bhikkhu* is like a donkey, but the comparison is applicable to all Buddhists. The Buddha says that the false Buddhist is like a donkey who is following after a herd of cows and as he follows them he brays, 'I'm a cow too! I'm a cow too!' But everybody can see that he is not a cow. His head is different, his hooves are different, and his voice is very different indeed. Everything, in fact, is different.[267]

I am quite happy with this comparison of the false Buddhist to a donkey, but what about the good Buddhist? Can we really compare the good Buddhist to a cow? I know that in India people honour the cow very highly. There is even a special cow puja, when they put garlands round the cow's neck. But in England and in the West generally, people do not respect the cow like that; in fact, in the West, to call someone a cow is a great insult. So I am going to change the Buddha's comparison. I am going to say that although the false Buddhist is like a donkey, the true Buddhist is like a *horse*.

Let us go into this in a little more detail. First of all, how is the false Buddhist like a donkey? The false Buddhist is like a donkey in five ways.

1. *The donkey has a very big head.* What does this mean? It means that the false Buddhist thinks a lot of himself. He is what we call in England 'swollen-headed'. Sometimes we say, 'His hat is not big enough for him.' Not only that. The donkey's head is very big in proportion to his body. This means that the false Buddhist may know a lot about Buddhism, he may have read a lot of books about it, but he doesn't actually practise it.

2. *The donkey has very big ears.* This means that the false Buddhist listens to all sorts of idle, useless gossip, all sorts of criticisms of other people. Moreover, the donkey's ears are very big in relation to his head, just as the head is very big in relation to his body. This means that the false Buddhist hears more than he understands. Many scholars are like that. They may have read a lot of books, but they don't really understand Buddhism at all.

3. *The donkey has a very loud voice.* Though he is a small animal, his voice is very loud. You can hear it miles away. This means that the false Buddhist talks a lot. For example, he talks a lot about organizing

Dhamma programmes in his village or locality, but he doesn't do very much. Perhaps he doesn't do anything at all. Moreover, the donkey's voice is not only very loud but harsh and unpleasant. Nobody likes to listen to the voice of a donkey. It is not like listening to the voice of a nightingale. This means that the false Buddhist talks in a very unpleasant sort of way. He talks about all sorts of foolish things. He does not talk about the Dhamma.

4. *The donkey has a tail like a rat.* It is long and thin, like a piece of old rope. This means that the false Buddhist has very few good qualities, just as there are very few hairs on the tail of a donkey.

5. *The donkey is a very obstinate animal.* He likes to go his own way. Sometimes he doesn't want to go at all! He just stands still. He digs his hooves into the ground and refuses to move. You may beat him, but it doesn't make any difference. He just stands there. He doesn't care at all. He has no shame, no conscience. He won't listen to anybody. The false Buddhist is just like that. He won't go on the right path. He likes to go on the wrong path, or he may even just stand still. He takes no notice of what you say. Whatever you say to him about *pañcasīla*, or about meditation, or about working for the Dhamma, it doesn't make any difference. The false Buddhist doesn't care. He doesn't even listen to you. He just stands there.

The false Buddhist is like a donkey in these five ways. But what about the true Buddhist? The true Buddhist, as I said, is like a horse. He is like a horse in five ways.

1. *The horse has a small head.* In the same way, the true Buddhist doesn't think a lot of himself. He is not proud, not arrogant. The horse's head is also small in relation to his body. This means that whatever the true Buddhist knows and understands he puts into practice. Theory and practice are well balanced, just as the horse's head is proportionate to the rest of his body.

2. *The horse has very small ears.* This means that the true Buddhist doesn't listen to idle, useless gossip. He listens only to the Dhamma. Not only that. His ears are small in relation to his head. This means that he thinks about what he hears and does his best to understand it.

3. *The horse has a soft voice.* At least, it is soft in comparison with the sound of the donkey's voice. This means that the true Buddhist doesn't talk very much. Moreover, if he promises to do something he does it – he may even do more than he promises – so you can rely on

his words. The horse's voice is not only soft but pleasant. People like to hear the voice of the true Buddhist. The true Buddhist speaks truthfully, speaks kindly, speaks about the Dhamma, and speaks in such a way as to bring people together.

4. *The horse has a beautiful tail*, which consists of thousands of very long hairs. This means that the true Buddhist has many good qualities. The true Buddhist is kind, gentle, energetic, truthful, mindful, intelligent, and so on.

5. *The horse is not obstinate.* The horse responds very well to training. He learns quickly. Similarly, the true Buddhist listens carefully. He takes notice of what is said to him. If you talk to him about *śīla*, he will try to practise it. If you talk to him about meditation, he will try to practise that too. The true Buddhist feels ashamed if he cannot do very well in his practice of the Dhamma. He is always trying to do better.

The true Buddhist is like a horse in these five ways. But we can go even further than that. The true Buddhist is not just like a horse, but like a very special type of horse. I am now going to describe this special type of horse, or rather I am going to describe a picture of him that I have seen. This picture is at our London Buddhist Centre, and it is painted on a wall. It is a very big picture, maybe twenty feet in height and twenty-five feet long, and it depicts a big, beautiful horse. This horse is white in colour. He is flying through the air, and the harness with which he is equipped is magnificently decorated. Flames issue from his nostrils and his hooves. As he flies through the air he carries on his back a big red lotus-throne. On the red lotus-throne there is a white mat, and on the white mat there are three bright jewels. One jewel is yellow, one jewel is blue, and one jewel is red, and all three are surrounded by golden light.

This white horse is what we call the Windhorse. He is the horse of *vīrya* or energy, the horse of inspiration. His pure white colour represents the purity of *śīla*. And he flies through the air. This means that he travels far and wide. His magnificently decorated harness signifies his many good qualities. The fact that he carries the red lotus throne on his back means that he carries thoughts of *mettā*, or maitrī, and *karuṇā*. As for the white mat on the red lotus throne, this stands for *prajñā*. Of the three jewels on the white mat, the yellow jewel is the Buddha, the blue jewel is the Dhamma, and the red jewel the Sangha, and the golden light by which they are surrounded represents the influence of the Three Jewels radiating in all directions.

This, then, is the Windhorse. The true Buddhist must be like not just an ordinary horse, but a Windhorse. He must be full of energy, must be pure, must practise *śīla*, *maitrī*, and *karuṇā*, must develop *prajñā* and, most important of all, he must carry the Three Jewels – that is, he must carry the message of Buddhism in all directions. If you can do all this, then you will indeed be a true Buddhist.

12

MY LIFE AND MISSION AND THE
TEACHING OF DR AMBEDKAR

Daund, 12 January 1982

Brothers and Sisters in the Dhamma: The first thing I want to say is that I am very happy to be here in Daund this evening with you all.[268] In order to be here I've come a very long way. I've come from London to Bombay, from Bombay to Poona, and finally from Poona to Daund. Getting from Poona to Daund took nearly as long as getting from London to Bombay because the train was late. So if you have been waiting here a long time I'm very sorry but it wasn't my fault. It was the fault of the railways. Anyway, I really am glad that I could get here in the end, because I'm always glad to meet other Buddhists. I'm always glad to meet followers of Dr Ambedkar. I feel that we're all brothers and sisters. We belong to the same spiritual family. We have the Buddha for our father, we have the Dhamma for our mother. Of course I've been in Maharashtra before, but so far as I remember this is my first visit to Daund. Certainly it is the first time I've been able to speak to Buddhist people here. This evening I may not be able to speak as much as I would like to because I'm suffering from a sore throat, but I want to say at least a few things about the Dhamma. But before that I'm going to say just a few words about myself.

As some of you may know, I was born in London in 1925, and of course I wasn't born into a Buddhist family. I can't even say I was born into a Christian family, because my family, like so many other English families, was sort of 'half-Christian'. At that time there was no Buddhism in England. Only a handful of people were even interested in Buddhism. At school I heard nothing about it and I never even heard the name of the Buddha. But when I was about eight years old I became quite ill and was confined to bed. All I could do was read, and in the course of a few years – even once I was better and could go back to school – I read quite a lot of literature and poetry. One day when I was about fifteen years old I thought to myself, 'Why should I read only the poetry of the West? I must also read something of the poetry of the East.' I therefore started reading translations of Persian, Chinese, and Indian poetry. As you probably know, many Indian poetical works are at the same time works of religion and philosophy, so when I started reading these poetry books, at the same time I started reading books on Hinduism and Buddhism.[269] In this way I came into contact with Buddhist literature, which made a very great impression on me. I was particularly impressed by two Buddhist *sūtras*, the *Diamond Sūtra* (*Vajracchedika-prajñāpāramitā Sūtra*) and the *Sūtra of Wei-Lang* (Huineng). When I read those two *sūtras* – I was then sixteen – I thought to myself, 'This is the Truth. This is what I believe.' There was no doubt in my mind about this at all. I therefore thought to myself, 'I am a Buddhist'.[270] But I wasn't in contact with any other Buddhists. No one else with whom I was acquainted knew anything about Buddhism. For the next two years I was completely on my own. I just continued reading books about Buddhism. But when I was eighteen I discovered that there was a small Buddhist society in London, and I started attending its meetings. The president of the society was Mr Christmas Humphreys, the well-known English lawyer and judge. Meetings were held once a week and were attended by not more than twelve or fourteen people. That was all the Buddhism there was in England at that time.[271] It was wartime, and I remember that once, during a meeting, when we were all meditating, a bomb fell nearby. But everyone just went on meditating.

Around that time I started thinking that if I want to learn more about Buddhism I would have to go to India. But how was I to get there? Since it was wartime, travelling abroad was difficult. In the end the problem was solved in a strange way. I was conscripted into the army, and the army sent me to India. When this happened I was very pleased, and thought that it must be due to my past good karma. I didn't want to be a soldier, but I certainly wanted to go to India.[272] I arrived in Bombay in 1944, and went straight to Delhi. I was then nineteen. While in Delhi I was constantly on the lookout for some vestige of Buddhism. At that time there was a small Buddhist vihara in Delhi, which naturally I was interested in seeing, but to my disappointment it was closed. Outside the vihara there was a patch of grass on which a *bhikkhu's* yellow robe was spread out to dry, but of the *bhikkhu* himself there was no sign. That was as much as I could find of Buddhism in India at that time.

Being still in the army I applied for a transfer to Sri Lanka. Since Sri Lanka was a Buddhist country I hoped to be able to make contact with Buddhism there, but there too my efforts did not meet with much success. Buddhism in Sri Lanka seemed dead, or at least asleep. I went to Kandy, where I visited a fine temple containing what was supposed to be a tooth of the Buddha, and I also met one or two *bhikkhus*, but they didn't know much about Buddhism and again I was disappointed. After spending a year in Sri Lanka I went to Calcutta, and from there to Singapore. All this time I was still in the army. In Singapore I happened to meet some Chinese Buddhists. This was a much more beneficial experience, and I had some good contact with them. It was at this time, when I was about twenty-one, that I started giving lectures on Buddhism. I gave many lectures in Singapore, in fact, and made many Buddhist friends.

By that time the war was over. I had been in the army for four years, and thinking that was long enough, I left the army and went to Calcutta, where I stayed for a while at the Maha Bodhi Society. Not getting much inspiration there, I left for Ahmedabad, where I attended a series of meetings organized by the All-India Dharma Parishad. At these meetings there were representatives of all the different religions of the world. I was the Buddhist representative, and in that capacity spoke on Buddhism. From Ahmedabad I journeyed to Kasauli, a hill station in West Punjab, and I was there on Independence Day, 15 August 1947. Three days later, deciding that I too would become independent, I became an *anagārika*. I dyed my clothes yellow, cut off my hair and beard, and 'went forth', walking from Kasauli down to the plains. From there I travelled to South India, where I lived as an *anagārika* for two years. Sometimes I stayed in ashrams, sometimes in caves. Once, when I was staying in a ruined temple, I heard leopards snarling on the roof, but they did me no harm. Wherever I stayed I passed my time meditating and studying Buddhism.

During this period I had contact with no other Buddhist. I was surrounded by Hindus. Whenever they saw me they would ask only one thing: 'What is your caste?' Sometimes I would be walking quietly along the road, giving no trouble to anybody, when a perfect stranger would come up to me and, after looking me up and down, would ask, 'What is your caste?' I would say, 'I don't have any caste. First of all, I'm from England, and in England we don't have any caste. Secondly, I'm a Buddhist, and in Buddhism there is no caste system.' When I said this, these people used to become very suspicious. They used to think that I belonged to some very low caste and was ashamed to admit it. It was impossible for them to understand that I didn't have any caste. They thought every man, woman, and child must have a caste. Sometimes they would argue with me, saying, 'You must have a caste. Everybody has a caste.' I used to insist that I really didn't have a caste, but they wouldn't believe it.

The reason why I stayed in South India, just one solitary Buddhist, was because I wanted to see how strong as a Buddhist I was. At the end of the two years I thought, 'Yes, I am quite strong as a Buddhist. Even though I am surrounded by Hindus it does not affect me at all.' I therefore decided to become a *sāmaṇera*, and for this purpose I travelled to Sarnath. There I met the Maha Bodhi Society *bhikkhus* and asked them to make me a *sāmaṇera*, but these *bhikkhus*, who were from Sri Lanka, were quite suspicious of me, mainly because I had no money. Thinking that it was one of the monastic rules, for two years I had not touched money, but the Sri Lanka *bhikkhus* thought this very strange. In their opinion a modern monk ought to have money, so because I had none they were unwilling to make me a *sāmaṇera*.

From Sarnath I walked up to Kusinara, which of course is the place where the Lord Buddha attained *parinirvāṇa*. Here I was more fortunate. I met U Chandramani Maha Thera, of whom I am sure you have heard, because it was he who gave the Three Refuges and the Five Precepts to Dr Ambedkar in Nagpur in 1956. A week after my arrival I took the *sāmaṇera* ordination from U Chandramani. Although I didn't know it at the time, this gave me a sort of connection with Dr Ambedkar, because U Chandramani was now my guru and he was afterwards to become the guru of Dr Ambedkar.

Having become a *sāmaṇera*, I went on foot up into Nepal, finding my way there through the jungle. I visited Lumbini, the birthplace of the Buddha, as well as Butaol and Tansen, where I gave lectures on Buddhism to the local Buddhists. From Nepal I came down to

Benares and stayed at the Benares Hindu University studying Pāli and Abhidhamma with the famous Indian *bhikkhu*, the venerable Jagdish Kashyap. When I had been with him for nearly a year, Kashyapji took me up to Kalimpong, a small town in the eastern Himalayas, in the Darjeeling District of West Bengal, not far from Tibet. Here he left me, saying, 'Stay here and work for the good of Buddhism.'

In this way I was left on my own in Kalimpong, while Kashyapji returned to Benares. I was then twenty five years old. Since I had been told to work for the good of Buddhism I started a Buddhist organization, and later on a Buddhist magazine. At the same time I made my first contact with Dr Ambedkar. An article he wrote for the May 1950 issue of the *Maha Bodhi* journal entitled 'Buddha and the Future of His Religion' impressed me very much, so I wrote to Dr Ambedkar telling him what I was doing in Kalimpong, and adding that I liked his article. He replied saying that he was glad to hear what I was doing and that *bhikkhus* must be more active than ever.

A few years later I came to Bombay and met Dr Ambedkar. I'm not going to give a detailed account, but I met him altogether three times, twice in Bombay and once in Delhi, and we had important discussions on Buddhism, conversion, and other matters. On the very day that Dr Ambedkar died I was in Nagpur and for four or five days I had very close contact with his followers in the area. Thereafter I used to come down from Kalimpong to Maharashtra every winter, and go from place to place giving lectures. This went on for several years.

In 1964 I returned to England for my first visit in twenty years. Originally I was going to spend four months there, but the four months gradually became two years, and in the course of that time I came to realize that England was a very good place for a Buddhist movement. I therefore decided to stay on there for a while, and in 1967, having paid a short visit to India, I started a new Buddhist movement in England. There was already a small Buddhist movement there, but it was not one-hundred-percent Buddhist; the people belonging to it were mostly half-Christian and half-Buddhist, just as in India there are people who are half-Hindu and half-Buddhist. I was not satisfied with this state of affairs. I wanted to have a movement that was one-hundred-percent Buddhist. The new Buddhist movement I started is called, in English, the Friends of the Western Buddhist Order. In Hindi and Marathi it's called Trailokya Bauddha Mahasangha Sahayak Gana. Despite the difference of nomenclature, these are one and the same organization.[273] So how did I start this new Buddhist movement? I'll tell you a little about this, as it may be of interest to you. First of all, I established a small centre, consisting of just one room, and started holding meditation classes there. At first these classes were held just once a week and were attended by eight or ten people. After a while, however, as more and more people started attending them, the classes were held twice a week, and I started giving lectures, which meant that still more people came to us. All this took place in London, since I thought that if we were to have a Buddhist movement in England it must start from London. Within a year there were quite a lot of people coming to us and taking part in our activities.

Some of these people started thinking that just coming along to classes once or twice a week wasn't enough. We therefore started holding *Dhamma-shibirs*. We used to go away, out of London, into the country, rent a big house for one or two weeks and stay there all together. Sometimes there were forty, fifty, or even sixty people. The whole of our time would be devoted to the Dhamma. We used to meditate together, listen to lectures together, discuss the Dhamma together, and do communication exercises together. In this way, we spent one, two, or even three weeks. Day and night it was nothing but the Dhamma. People used to enjoy this so much that they forgot all about their work, all about their home, all about their worldly troubles. They became so happy. They felt as though they were living in heaven – in the real *dhammaloka*, the world of the Dhamma. They felt able to be real Buddhists. They felt that their lives were being completely changed. In this way the *Dhamma-shibirs* had a very powerful effect. Here in Maharashtra, I think, you've already started having these *Dhamma-shibirs*, and those of you who have been on them know how powerful the effect can be.

In England this meant that at the end of the *shibir* there would be a problem. The problem was that the *shibir* came to an end. Usually it ended on a Sunday evening and on the Monday morning people had to go back to work, but they didn't *want* to go back to work. They wanted to stay at the *Dhamma-shibir*. They wanted to devote all their time to the Dhamma. At the end of the *shibir* people would be standing at the gate unwilling to leave. Sometimes they would be so sad that the *shibir* had come to an end that they wept. And some of them started thinking that they would like to live as though they were on *shibir* all the time.

So, having decided that they wanted to live together, when they got back to London they rented or bought a big house and made it into a sort of vihara. First a vihara was made for the men, then a vihara was made for the women; so in this way the people who had been on *shibir* were able to live together, meditate together, and practise the Dhamma together.

But then another problem arose – an economic problem. How were they to support themselves? Since they didn't want to go outside the Movement and work in the world they decided to start their own businesses, where they could work together. They wanted to run these businesses in accordance with the Buddhist principle of right livelihood, so they organized them along cooperative lines. In this way, in the course of a few years, we established Buddhist centres, Buddhist communities or viharas, and also Buddhist cooperative businesses. We established them in London and many other parts of England, as well as in other Western countries. In this way quite a big new Buddhist movement developed, a movement which is now certainly the biggest Buddhist movement in Europe.

You may be wondering what it is that makes people in England become Buddhist. Here in India it is only natural that you should become Buddhist. You might even say that it is right and proper for you to do so. After all, the Buddha lived and taught in India, and Buddhism flourished in India for 1,500 years. But England has no connection with Buddhism. The Buddha never went there. It's only very recently that people in England have even heard about Buddhism. Why is it, then, that so many hundreds and even thousands of people in England, and in the West generally, are now becoming Buddhist? Tonight I shall give you just a few of the reasons.

One of the main reasons is that many people in the West can no longer believe in God. They want to believe in some religion, but they don't want to believe in God. In Christianity, the idea of God is very important, so people who can't believe in God can't believe in Christianity. What they want is a religion which is definitely a religion but which, at the same time, involves no belief in God. Such people find that Buddhism is a religion of this kind. Though Buddhism is a religion, in fact the greatest of religions, in Buddhism there is no belief in God, no belief in an omniscient and omnipotent creator of the universe. It is therefore possible for someone who doesn't believe in God to accept Buddhism. This is one of the main reasons why so many people in England become

Buddhist, but there are other reasons too. Nowadays people in England have lost faith not only in Christianity but in politics. In England there are a number of different political parties, and all these parties and groups conduct a very active propaganda on behalf of their respective ideologies. But a lot of people believe that the problems of the world are not going to be solved by politics. They see that people in capitalist countries are not happy, and neither are people who live in socialist countries, or communist countries. Many people have therefore started feeling that politics cannot solve the problems of humanity. They feel that there has to be some other solution – a religious solution, a spiritual solution. This is the conclusion that Dr Ambedkar came to. He said that Dhamma is morality, and that morality is necessary to hold society together. A lot of people in England feel this too, and this is why some of them take to Buddhism.

There is another reason. England is a very prosperous country. Nobody starves, and if you don't have a job the government will give you money for yourself and your dependants, every week and, if necessary, year after year. People therefore don't have to worry about material things. They have a nice house, nice clothes, a motor car, a motorbike, a refrigerator, a television set, and all the rest of it. But at least some people have realized that these things are not making them happy. It is not that these things are bad. On the contrary, they are quite good, quite useful, they make life a little easier. But you don't become happy, you don't become a complete human being, just by having these things. You need more than material prosperity. This is the way a lot of people in England feel. They have material prosperity, but they feel that this is not enough. They want something more. They want to develop their minds and their hearts, to develop a higher vision. People who start feeling in this sort of way may become Buddhist.

I'll mention just one or two more reasons why people become Buddhist in England. As some of you may know, England is a very well-organized country. Some people, indeed, think it is too well organized. We have many civil servants, many laws, many rules. For this reason it is sometimes difficult for people to feel that they are really free. The government and big organizations are doing everything for you, and very often things happen over which you have no control, so people start feeling that the individual is weak and powerless. Of course, every individual has a vote, but then people wonder what use a single vote is.

You may vote this way, or you may vote that way, but does it really make any difference to anything? Thus they start feeling that the individual has no power, no importance in society. They feel that it is the group that is important, and this gives them a feeling of helplessness. They feel that they have no control over their own lives. This is one of the reasons they are attracted to Buddhism, because Buddhism places the individual in the centre of the picture. Buddhism stresses that the individual must develop, must grow, and that society exists for the sake of the individual, not the individual for the sake of society. Many people are attracted to Buddhism because of this emphasis on the importance of the individual. In particular Buddhism emphasizes that the individual can change. The individual can change from an unenlightened individual to an Enlightened individual, a Buddha. This is what Buddhism is all about: to transform the ordinary, unenlightened human being into a Buddha, an Enlightened human being. Buddhism in fact says that every individual can become a Buddha. This teaching, too, very much attracts many people in England.

Not only that. Buddhism not only says that the individual can change, but also that society can change. Buddhism says that society must change from a society that does not help the individual into one that does. This teaching also appeals to many people. Many of our friends in England feel that politics cannot change society, but that Buddhism can. This is what Dr Ambedkar also felt. This is why he himself took the *Dhammadiksha*, and why he encouraged his followers to do likewise. The purpose of taking the *Dhammadiksha* is not only to change the individual, but also to change the whole society. Its purpose is to make a new society, a better society, a society governed by the principles of liberty, equality, and fraternity.

I have now given you some idea about our Buddhist movement in England, as well as some idea of why people in England become interested in Buddhism. Though I have been busy with Buddhist work in England and other Western countries for the last twelve or thirteen years, I have not been so busy that I forgot my friends in India. At first I thought of dividing my time between the two countries, spending first six months in England and then six months in India, but this proved to be impossible. There was so much work to be done in England, and so much was happening both in England and in other Western countries, that for many years I have not been able to visit India at all. But I was thinking about India all the time, and exchanging letters with some of my friends here. Then about four years ago Anagārika Lokamitra came to India. He came to Poona to study hatha yoga. When I heard that he would be going to Poona I asked him to meet our Buddhist friends there, and this is what he did. In fact he got to know these friends, and took a great liking to them. He started thinking, 'These Indian Buddhists are very good people. They really love the Dhamma. They are very devoted to Dr Ambedkar.' On his return to England he told me what he had been thinking, adding, 'I think I'd like to go back to Poona. I think I'd like to work with our Indian Buddhist friends.' When I heard him say this I was very pleased indeed. I thought, 'Even though I myself am unable to go back to India, Lokamitra will go instead.' Four years ago, therefore, he came back here to stay, and started our Trailokya Bauddha Mahasangha Sahayak Gana.

Three years ago I myself was at last able to pay a visit to India, and saw what Lokamitra and our other friends were doing here. On that occasion twelve of these friends took the Three Refuges and Ten Precepts from me, thus becoming *dasa sīla upāsaka* and *upāsikā* members of the Trailokya Bauddha Mahasangha. Thus in the same way that our activities were being carried on in England and in the West generally, so they were beginning to be carried on here in Maharashtra. That was three years ago. Now I have come on another visit, this time for three months. I have already spent some time in Poona and Bombay, and have been to Panchgani and Mahad. Just now I'm on a tour of this part of Maharashtra, and this is the first lecture of this part of the tour. I'm very happy to be here, and to start my present tour in this place.

When I was here in Maharashtra three years ago, I saw that many changes had taken place since my earlier visits. And now, only three years later, I can see that even more changes have taken place since I was last here. I can see that the economic condition of the Buddhists is much better than it was, and I am very happy that this is so. Buddhism doesn't say that it is wrong to have money. What is wrong is to be a slave to money. Have money, yes, but use it properly, to secure a decent standard of living, and to spread the Dhamma. If you can do this there is nothing wrong with having money, even being rich. I also see that people are more educated than before. In Mahad and Bombay I've seen the great work of the People's Education Society. In the course of my present tour I am also going to Aurangabad where I shall be giving some lectures at Milind College. In short, I am very pleased that educational work is continuing among the Buddhists.

But I must say that the work of the Dhamma has not kept pace with the economic development and the educational development. We still need a lot more Dhamma activity. We need a much better understanding of the Dhamma. We need to know what the Dhamma is. I'm therefore going to conclude with a few remarks on the fundamental nature of the Dhamma, and I'm going to take my headings from Dr Ambedkar's book *The Buddha and his Dhamma*. In that book Dr Ambedkar lists six things which, he says, constitute the Dhamma.[274]

1. First of all he says, *to maintain purity of life is Dhamma*. According to Buddhism the individual human being consists of three parts, the physical body, speech, and the mind or heart, and all three must be purified. You purify the body by not injuring any living being, by not taking what is not given, and by not committing adultery. You purify speech by always speaking the truth, by speaking kindly and affectionately, by speaking about what is useful, and by speaking about the Dhamma. Finally, and this is a much more difficult thing to do, you purify the mind by getting rid of greed and craving, by getting rid of hatred, and by giving up all *micchā-diṭṭhis* or wrong views. Once you have removed these three things, the mind becomes pure. If the body is pure, the speech is pure, and the mind is pure, then you are pure. If you are pure, your life is pure, and if you maintain purity of life, that is the Dhamma. (The ten 'purifications' described in this section correspond to the ten *kusala dhammas* taken by all Order members of the Trailokya Bauddha Mahasangha.)

2. Secondly, Dr Ambedkar says, *to reach perfection in life is Dhamma*. 'Perfection in life' means that it is not a matter of reaching perfection after death, when you go to heaven. Perfection is to be reached here and now, in this life. You reach it by practising *dāna* or giving, *śīla* or morality, *kṣānti* or patience, *vīrya* or energy, *samādhi* or meditation, and *prajñā* or wisdom. If you practise these six *pāramitās* or perfections, then you reach perfection in this life, and to reach perfection in this life is Dhamma.

3. Thirdly, Dr Ambedkar says, *to live in Nibbāna is Dhamma*. Nibbāna is not something you attain after you die; it is something you attain here in this life itself. If you don't attain it in this life, it isn't Nibbāna. Some religions say that you must wait for your reward until

after death. Buddhism says that if you practise the Dhamma now you will get the result now. If you practise the Dhamma in this life you will get the result in this life. Therefore to live in Nibbāna in this life is Dhamma.

4. Fourthly, Dr Ambedkar says, *to give up craving is Dhamma*. In English we distinguish between desire and craving. If you feel very hungry, you start desiring food. It's natural. You desire food, you eat, and the desire is satisfied. There is nothing wrong with that. But if after filling your stomach you still want more, that is craving. This reminds me of a story. You've been listening to a rather serious lecture all this time, so let me tell you a little story just to make things a bit lighter. This story is about a Brahmin. I don't know why it is, but in India Brahmins have a reputation for being very greedy. So there is a story that a certain Brahmin went to a big feast and ate so much that he could hardly walk. He therefore left the feast and went to the house of one of his friends. 'Oh, I'm so full,' he groaned, 'I feel quite ill.' His friend said, 'What you should do is put two fingers down your throat, vomit up part of the food and get some relief.' But the Brahmin said, 'Oh no, I can't do that. If there had been room to put two fingers I would have taken another banana.' This is an example of greed. Desire is not wrong, but craving or greed is wrong. Therefore Dr Ambedkar says, 'To give up craving is Dhamma'.

5. Fifthly, we come to something a bit more philosophical. Dr Ambedkar says, *to believe that all compound things are impermanent is Dhamma*. This is very important. Science teaches us that everything changes. Whether you look through a microscope or a telescope you will see that things are changing. However small something is, it is changing. However big it is, it is changing. The earth is changing all the time. The sun is changing. The stars are changing. The whole universe is changing. Everything is changing. Everything is impermanent. It is the same with us. We are changing all the time. Our body is changing. Our mind is changing. This is a good thing, because if you can change, you can change for the better. When Buddhism says that everything is impermanent, that everything changes, it also says that everything can become better. A human being can change and become better, and so can society. This principle of impermanence, of transitoriness, is very important. I haven't time this evening to say anything more about it, but from the little I have said we can understand what Dr Ambedkar means

when he says, 'To believe that all compound things are impermanent is Dhamma.'

6. Sixthly and lastly, Dr Ambedkar says, *to believe that karma is the instrument of moral order is Dhamma*. This means that as you act, so will be the result. Perform skilful actions and you will experience happiness. Perform unskilful actions and you will experience suffering. This is a natural thing. No god is required to operate this law; it operates itself. It's a natural law, and this law is the law of karma, because of which we can be sure that any effort we make to follow the Dhamma will bear fruit. Therefore Dr Ambedkar says, 'To believe that karma is the instrument of moral order is Dhamma.'

So these six things, according to Dr Ambedkar, constitute Dhamma. This Dhamma can be practised by anybody, by any man or woman, even by any child. It can be practised by someone in India and it can be practised by someone in England, or America, or China. If there are people on the moon, they can practise it too. The Dhamma is universal. It's not only something that only the Brahmin can practise, or only the Kshatriya. It's for every human being. And because every human being can practise the Dhamma, every human being is the brother or sister of every other human being. The more we practise the Dhamma, the more we come together. It doesn't matter whether we are born in India or England. If we practise the Dhamma, we are brothers and sisters. Whether I'm talking about the Dhamma here in Daund or in London, it's the same Dhamma. It doesn't make any difference. In England they all sit on chairs and listen, whereas here you all sit on the floor. Here in India people like to have lots of these coloured lights. In England they don't care for such things. But everybody cares for the Dhamma. That is the same everywhere. Wherever the Dhamma is, there is your home. Wherever Buddhists are, there is your family.

This evening I've told you something about Buddhism in England, and I hope you've found it of some interest. Our Buddhist friends in England are very interested in the Buddhist movement here in India. They are very interested in what the followers of Dr Ambedkar are doing. They can see that here in India, here in Maharashtra, a great social revolution is going on. The whole society is being changed. People's lives are being changed. This is of interest to Buddhists everywhere. We have in England a Buddhist magazine that comes out every three months.[275] It's quite big, and contains many illustrations. Every now and then there are articles and pictures about our Buddhist movement here in Maharashtra. Our English Buddhist friends are very interested to read these articles, and see these pictures. Through this magazine of ours news about the Buddhist movement here in India, news about Dr Ambedkar and his work, goes all over the world. This Buddhist magazine is edited by one of our Buddhist friends. His name is Nagabodhi. Like me he was born in England, and like me he is here this evening. You may have noticed him taking pictures. What is he going to do with those pictures? He's going to print them in his magazine. Thus not only people in England but Buddhists in many parts of the world will know about this meeting here this evening. This is a very good thing. Buddhists in one part of the world should know what Buddhists in other parts of the world are doing. In this way we shall be able to develop a spirit of brotherhood and sisterhood, and if more and more people develop such a spirit then certainly the world will be a very much better place.

13

THE SEVEN BODHYAṄGAS

Manmad,[276] *16 January 1982*

Brothers and Sisters in the Dhamma: One month ago I was in England, and the weather was very different from what it is in Maharashtra today. It was very cold, and there was snow on the ground, such as you have probably seen only in pictures of the Himalayas. Looking out of my window in the morning, I would see the whole countryside covered with this white snow. From that cold England I came to this hot Maharashtra. Though my mind was very happy, my body wasn't so happy, and I started getting a sore throat. For that reason I cannot speak as much tonight as I would like, and cannot speak very loudly. Since I can't speak very loudly, and don't want to strain my throat, please listen quietly. In any case it is the Buddhist tradition that when anyone is speaking about the Dhamma we listen very quietly and attentively, because the Dhamma is very precious, very important, and very useful to us, so we don't want to miss any of it. It is just like water in the desert: every drop is precious. For you, every drop of the Dhamma is precious, like *amṛta*. You are very fortunate to have this opportunity of hearing the Dhamma, of receiving this *amṛta*, so please take full advantage of the opportunity. Life is short. We don't know when we are going to die; we don't know when we are going to get another opportunity of hearing the Dhamma. So when we do get an opportunity, we should listen carefully.

During the month that I have been in India I have been quite busy. I have been going from place to place, and we have had many programmes, in Poona, where I gave many lectures, then in Bombay, in Panchgani, and in Mahad. I was especially pleased to go to Mahad because, as you know, Mahad occupies a very important place in the life of Dr Ambedkar. It was there that he burned the *Manusmṛti*,[277] thus starting his great movement of Dhamma Revolution. In Mahad the programme was organized by the People's Education Society.[278] Members of the Governing Body of the Society came from Bombay for the occasion, and the meeting was held in front of the memorial column erected in honour of Dr Ambedkar. After Mahad, we had more programmes in Poona, and nearly a week ago we started on this present tour, in the course of which we have visited Daund, Ahmednagar, Sangamner, and Koperagaon, in all of which places we had highly successful meetings. Yesterday we left Koperagaon and came to Yeola, a place which also had a very important place in the life of Dr Ambedkar. It was there that he made his great declaration, 'Though I may have been born a Hindu, I do not intend to die one.'[279] This morning the Buddhist people of Yeola gave us a wonderful reception, and afterwards they took us to see the ground where Dr Ambedkar made his great declaration. We were very happy to see it.

From Yeola we came here. On our arrival we were again given a wonderful reception. Ladies were waiting outside the hotel with garlands. After a little time at the hotel we were taken to somebody's house for lunch. Here the arrangements for lunch were very beautiful, and in truly Buddhist style. For me this last week has been a very wonderful experience. Every time we arrived at a new place, there would be fresh interest, fresh enthusiasm. Meetings were getting better all the time, with people showing more and more interest, more and more enthusiasm for the Dhamma. Tonight we have this meeting, which I think is the biggest and best of the whole week. When I arrived for the meeting, I was glad to see the ladies lined up in two rows in their white saris. It was a very beautiful sight, in the real Buddhist style. They are real *upāsikās*. I was also glad to see them holding lighted candles in their hands and carrying flowers. Then I saw how beautifully the whole place had been decorated. I saw the beautiful bust of Dr Ambedkar. Since I am getting a bit old, I couldn't climb up and garland it myself, but Anagārika Lokamitra, who is young and strong, climbed up and did the garlanding for me. Then I saw all these beautiful coloured lights. This means something. It is the multi-coloured radiance of the Dhamma. I can also see the five-coloured Buddhist flag. This also has a great meaning, but I have no time to go into it tonight. Finally, when I look out at the audience, I see all of *you*. I see thousands and thousands of Buddhists. This is a truly wonderful sight. As Anagārika Lokamitra told you, in England we never see so many Buddhists all together. Sometimes we may see four or five hundred, sometimes seven hundred, but we never see four or five thousand like this. I am very happy to see you all. I am very glad that there are so many good, devoted, sincere Buddhists in Manmad.

I am also glad to see so many friends of mine here on the platform. Some are old friends, some are new friends, some are in yellow robes, and some are in white robes, but they are all working for the Dhamma. I am very happy to see this. I am very happy that over the last week we have had the help and cooperation of so many Buddhist organizations. The People's Education Society has helped us very much, as has the Bharatiya Bauddha Mahasabha.[280] Thirty or forty different organizations, in fact, have helped us. Everybody has been giving us a welcome. This too makes me feel very happy. Someone was telling me that all the different localities of Manmad are represented in this meeting. Not only that. I heard that all seventeen *talukas* of this District are represented. This shows very good organization. A lot of people must have worked very hard.

Thus I feel that this whole week, and especially today, I've had a wonderful experience. It is as though the meetings and receptions have been getting bigger and better the whole week. But really this is not surprising. It is the effect of the Dhamma. If you practise the Dhamma, everything gets better, and it also becomes bigger. People become happier and happier, wiser and wiser, kinder and kinder. This is all the effect of the Dhamma. It is as though this progressive effect of the Dhamma has been illustrated, indeed exemplified, by the events of this last week.

There are many teachings of the Buddha that show the expansive nature of the Dhamma. Tonight I am going to speak about one of these formulations, a teaching called the seven *bodhyaṅgas*.[281] Once again I must ask you to listen very attentively. If we don't listen attentively, we won't hear, we won't understand. When you go to the cinema you listen and watch very attentively, and you must pay at least as much attention as this when you listen to the Dhamma. The Dhamma is much more valuable than anything you can see at the cinema. Even the best cinema can't compete with the Dhamma. *We* are the best cinema! *This* is the best cinema show! So please listen attentively.

The word *bodhyaṅga* (*bojjhaṅga* in Pāli) is made up of two parts, *bodhi* and *aṅga*. *Bodhi* means the higher knowledge, the higher wisdom and compassion. The Buddha is called 'Buddha' because he is a human being who has attained, or who has realized, this *bodhi*. *Aṅga* means simply limb, as in Hindi or Marathi. The seven *bodhyaṅgas* are the seven limbs or parts of *bodhi*. *Aṅga* can also mean the limb or branch of a tree. When a tree grows, first a little shoot comes out of the ground. This shoot grows bigger and stronger. Then it puts out a branch, then another branch, then another. These can also be called *aṅgas*. The seven *aṅgas* of *bodhi* are the seven limbs, or seven branches, that we develop as we attain to *bodhi*. They are the seven stages of progress. I am going to say a few words about each of the seven, giving an illustration for each one.

Smṛti (Pāli: *sati*). This is what we call in English 'recollection' or 'awareness'. It is knowing what is happening, knowing what is going on. Four levels of practice are usually distinguished. At one level, we are aware of what we are doing, i.e. aware of bodily movement, and aware of what we are saying. Very often people don't really know what they are saying; their mind is somewhere else. At another level, we have to know what we are feeling. We have to know whether we are happy or sad, greedy or angry, and whether there is *mettā* and *karuṇā* in our minds. Thirdly, we also have to be aware of what we are thinking. Sometimes people don't know this. At this very moment, even, you may not know what you are thinking. Though in a sense you are listening to what I am saying, maybe your mind is busy thinking about something else. Maybe you are wondering what time it is, and whether you ought to be going, but you aren't really conscious of this. We have to know what we are thinking from moment to moment, otherwise the mind will be simply scattered and confused. And fourthly, we have to be aware of the Dhamma. We must never forget the Dhamma. Whatever we do, the Dhamma must be in our minds. We must always be in touch with the Dhamma. This kind of mindfulness is very important. We may find the second, third, and fourth aspects of the practice of recollection or awareness a little difficult, but at least we should practise the first aspect, awareness of what we are doing and saying.

Let me tell you a little story to illustrate this. Twenty years ago I was travelling around Maharashtra giving lectures, and some of the people who attended those lectures are still in contact with me. Sometimes they remember things I said twenty years ago, but most of all they remember the stories. They may forget the philosophy, but the stories they remember. So I am going to tell you a little story now – a story to illustrate the importance of being mindful of everything that you do. I hope you will remember it.

The story is about a young Japanese Buddhist who wanted to practise meditation, so he thought he should find a guru who could teach him to meditate. After searching for some months, and travelling many hundreds of miles, he came to a vihara where there lived a great guru. The young man asked if he could see the guru, and having been told that he could, he entered the guru's room. Now at the time of his arrival at the vihara it was raining, and he was carrying an umbrella. Before entering the guru's room he folded up the umbrella and put it to one side; then he entered. The guru asked him what he wanted. He said: 'I want to practise meditation. Please teach me.' The guru said: 'All right. Let me ask you one or two questions.' The young man was quite pleased to hear this, thinking that he would be questioned about the theory of meditation, but the guru asked: 'When you arrived just now, was it raining?' The young man replied: 'Yes, it was raining quite heavily.' Then the guru asked: 'Did you come carrying an umbrella?' The young man thought this was an odd question, and that it was strange that the guru was not asking him anything about meditation. But anyway, he said, 'Yes, I was carrying an umbrella.' The guru then asked another question. He said, 'When you entered my room, on which side of the door did you leave the umbrella?' But try as he might, the young man could not remember. Then the guru said, 'You are not yet ready to practise meditation. First you must practise mindfulness.' So the young man was sent away. He had to practise mindfulness first.[282]

We too have to practise mindfulness. Whatever we do, we should do it carefully, with proper thought. We may be studying, or cooking, or sweeping the floor, or mending a transistor set, or driving a car, or talking with our friends, or even giving a lecture – but whatever it is, we must do it with a clear mind. We must do it with *smṛti*, with recollection and awareness. This is the first *bodhyaṅga*, and I have spoken a lot about it not only because it is the first but because it is very important. I shall deal with the other *bodhyaṅgas* rather more quickly.

Dharma-vicaya (Pāli: *dhamma-vicaya*). Usually the term 'Dharma' or 'Dhamma' means the Buddha's teaching, but here it has the special meaning of 'mental state'. As you know, there are all kinds of mental states. Sometimes we are happy, sometimes sad. Sometimes greed is present in the mind, sometimes it is not present. In Buddhism, especially in the *Abhidharma*, these mental states are analysed in very great detail. In fact, the mind is analyzed into hundreds of different states. As for the word *vicaya*, it means distinguishing or sorting out. *Dharma-vicaya* therefore means distinguishing or sorting out our mental states, especially into those that are termed *kuśala* and those that are termed *akuśala*. It isn't enough just to let mental states happen. We have to keep watch over the mind; we have to sort out the *kuśala* states from the *akuśala* states. Unless we can do that, we can't get rid of the *akuśala* states, and we can't develop the *kuśala* states.

At this point, let me give you an illustration which will be of special interest to the ladies. Ladies have a lot of work to do in the house, and one of their biggest jobs is cooking. Every day they have to cook two or three times. In India it is usually rice that is cooked, sometimes *roti*. But before you can put the rice in the pot and cook it, as you know very well, you have to clean it. You spread it out on a kind of wicker tray and you go over it very carefully. On one side you put the rice, and on the other side you put all the bits of stone and dirt, and at the end of half an hour, you have a big heap of nice clean rice, and a little pile of dirt and stones. This is what we call *vicaya*. You are already doing a *vicaya* with the rice, and that is what you must also do with your mind, with your mental states. You must put all the *kuśala* states on this side, as it were, and all the *akuśala* states on that side. You must distinguish between them. You must say to yourself: 'This is good, that is bad; this I must cultivate and develop, that I must get rid of.' This is what we must do every day. Just as we clean the rice, we must clean our minds. The ladies should find it quite easy to do this, because they get a good reminder every day. When you are cleaning the rice, you should think: 'This is the way I must clean my mind. I must make my mind pure by getting rid of all the dirt, all the grit, all the unskilful mental states. Then my mind will be quite pure. Then I can practise the Dhamma.' As I said before, I am glad to see the ladies in their white saris. They look like real *upāsikās*. But the mind also must be pure and white. Then you will be real, one-hundred-percent Buddhists.

Vīrya (Pāli: *viriya*) means energy. A Buddhist must have energy. If you don't have energy, you can't do anything, either ordinary work or Dhamma work. Therefore you must build up your energy and your strength. You must build up your physical energy, your mental energy, your emotional energy, and your spiritual energy. A Buddhist must be the embodiment of energy. A Buddhist should never be dull or slothful, but should be always working for good things. The great Buddhist poet Śāntideva defines *vīrya* as 'energy in pursuit of the good'.[283] You may have a lot of energy, but if you use it for a bad purpose, then that is not *vīrya*.

Śāntideva gives a very beautiful illustration of what a person with *vīrya* is like. He is like an elephant – not a tame elephant but a wild elephant. The wild elephant is a very playful beast, and one of the things he likes doing in hot weather is plunging into a pool – especially into a lotus pool. After plunging into one pool and spending a few minutes there, he comes out and plunges into another pool. Thus he goes on plunging into one pool after another, and in this way he enjoys himself. Śāntideva says that the bodhisattva's *vīrya* is like that. As soon as one work is finished, he plunges into another, just as the elephant plunges into another lotus pool.[284] If we are full of energy, that is what we will be like. We will enjoy our work, particularly our Dhamma work, and as soon as one work is finished, we will plunge into another. As soon as one meeting is finished, we start planning another. As soon as we have given one lecture, we are ready to give another. As soon as we have finished selling Dhamma literature in one town, we are ready to move on to the next. In this way we enjoy ourselves more and more, and our energy increases all the time.

Prīti (Pāli: *pīti*). *Prīti* is enthusiasm. If you have developed energy, you will develop enthusiasm and joy. You will not only have energy, but that energy will radiate in all directions. You will be full of life. You will be bubbling over, as it were. You will feel really wonderful. Let me give you an illustration, this time from Buddhaghosa, the great Pāli commentator. *Prīti*, Buddhaghosa says, is like a great silken bag filled with air, or what we nowadays call a balloon.[285] When you are full of *prīti*, you feel just like a balloon. You feel very light, as though you were floating through the air. You feel very happy. And you get this sort of feeling especially when you meditate. This evening I have no time to say anything about meditation. If you want to learn to meditate, you should come on one of our *Dhamma-shibirs*, or attend one of our meditation classes.

Praśrabdhi (Pāli: *passaddhi*). This means 'calming down'. The excitement, as it were, of the *prīti* has died away, and you are left with a feeling of pure happiness. This feeling is very calm, and very steady. It is like what happens when the bee is collecting nectar from the flowers. First it locates the flower, then it alights on the flower with a loud buzzing sound and crawls inside the petals. So long as the bee has not found the nectar, the buzzing sound continues, but as soon as it finds it, the sound stops. *Praśrabdhi* is like that.

Samādhi (Pāli: *samādhi*) This usually means one-pointedness of mind. It means bringing the energies of the mind together, thinking of one thing only, concentrating on one thing only, ignoring everything else. Here I am going to give you not one illustration, but two. One illustration is from the life of the Buddha, and the other is from the life of Dr Ambedkar.

As you know, the Buddha always walked from one place to another, even when he was a very old man. Sometimes he felt quite tired, and quite thirsty. On one such occasion he sat down at the side of the road and asked Ānanda to fetch some water from a nearby river. While Ānanda was away, the Buddha passed the time in meditation. After a while Ānanda returned and told the Buddha that he was unable to get any water because 500 bullock carts had just crossed the river and made it very dirty. They had in fact been passing along the road by the side of which the Buddha was sitting. But the Buddha said: 'I heard nothing at all.' Ānanda was very surprised. Five hundred bullock carts had passed by right in front of the Buddha, but the Buddha had not heard them.[286] This is an example of what we mean by *samādhi* or one-pointedness.

There is a similar example from the life of Dr Ambedkar. At the beginning of 1956, Dr Ambedkar was working on his book *The Buddha and His Dhamma*. He was quite ill at that time, but he wanted to finish the book and was working hard on it. One Saturday evening, when he was writing at his desk, he told his secretary to go home and come again the following morning. When the secretary returned seven or eight hours later, he was astonished to find Dr Ambedkar sitting in the same chair, at the same desk, still writing. Since Dr Ambedkar had not heard him come in, the secretary made a slight noise. Dr Ambedkar said: 'Haven't you gone home yet?' The secretary replied: 'I've been home. I've slept. It's now Sunday morning.' Dr Ambedkar said: 'Is it Sunday morning? I've been writing all this time!' This too is an example of *samādhi* or one-pointedness of mind.

Dr Ambedkar was quite indifferent to external circumstances. He was able to focus his mind entirely on one thing. We find this very difficult.

Dr Ambedkar was able to write all night, but you might find it difficult even to listen to a lecture all night, or even for one hour. So we have to develop one-pointedness of mind; we have to develop *samādhi*. Not that we have to go and live in a cave in order to do this. We have to learn to do it in all the affairs of life. Whatever we do, we must give our whole mind to it. When we go for Refuge, we must go for Refuge with our whole mind. The same should be the case when we observe the *pañcasīla*, or listen to a lecture. Even if people are coming and going, don't take any notice. Even if trains are making a noise, don't take any notice.[287] Take no notice of anything else. Just listen to the Dhamma. Apply this principle to whatever you are doing.

If you are a student, study with your whole mind. When Dr Ambedkar was in London, he studied eighteen hours a day. He never wasted his time. He never went to see films. He just concentrated on his studies. This is one of the things that made him a great man. But he wasn't born a great man. He made himself a great man by his own efforts, his own struggles, and especially by his own *samādhi* or one-pointedness.

Upekṣā (Pāli: *upekkhā*). Here I am not going to give you any explanation. I am just going to give you an illustration. If you have *upekṣā*, you will be like a mountain. A mountain is made of solid rock. It is very big, and nothing can shake it. Even if all the winds blow, the mountain is not in the least affected. This is what we must be like. Whatever wind may blow, we mustn't mind. Whether we experience happiness or sorrow, praise or blame, loss or gain, fame or infamy, we mustn't let it affect us. We must be just like the mountain. This also we see in Dr Ambedkar's life. He was just like a great mountain. In fact, he was like the great Himalaya itself. He was loftier than all other men, and more unshakeable. He had to bear enormous difficulties. Many people criticized him. Many people were against him. He suffered a great deal. His wife died; his children died. All this he had to bear. He had to endure ill-treatment at the hands of other people. But he was unmoved, unshaken. He remained just like the mountain. He was an example of *upekṣā*.

I have now described, very briefly, the seven *bodhyaṅgas*. You may have found them a little difficult to understand, but at least you will remember the stories. We shouldn't always be talking about the *tisaraṇa* and the *pañcasīla*, even though these are very good things. We should try to learn about something new. In fact, you should be trying to learn something new about the Dhamma all the time. This is why I have talked this evening about the seven *bodhyaṅgas*.

The seven *bodhyaṅgas* represent the Dhamma. When we say *Dhammaṃ saraṇaṃ gacchāmi* we mean that we are going for Refuge to the teachings of the Buddha, and the seven *bodhyaṅgas* is one of these teachings. Unless we understand and practise such teachings, how can we really go for Refuge to the Dhamma? So we should try to understand these things, and try to practise them. Then we shall be real Buddhists.

As I said at the beginning, the Dhamma is very precious, and very valuable. It is just like a jewel. The jewel is the most precious of all material things. If we get a diamond, or a pearl, or a ruby, which may be worth *lakhs* of rupees, we shall be very rich and very happy. But we have got the biggest of all jewels, the jewel of the Dhamma. We are very rich, now that this jewel has been given to us. We haven't earned it; we didn't make any sacrifice to get it. It was just given to us. It was given twenty-five years ago, when Dr Ambedkar took the *Dhammadiksha* himself and gave this *Dhammadiksha* to his people. It is Dr Ambedkar who has given you this jewel of the Dhamma. So you must look after it properly, and make good use of it. You must make your life rich with it.

Not only is the Dhamma like a jewel. The Buddha said the Dhamma is like a raft.[288] The function of the raft is to enable us to cross the river. We don't worship the raft, or just repeat the word 'raft' over and over again. We get onto the raft, and then, paddling with hands and feet, we cross the river and land safely on the other shore. In this way we use the Dhamma. We use the Dhamma to improve our lives. We use the Dhamma to help us grow. We use the Dhamma to create a new life for ourselves. We use the Dhamma to create a new society.

I am very happy to have had the opportunity to speak to you all this evening, and to say something about the seven *bodhyaṅgas*. If you have found the lecture difficult to follow, never mind. It is being tape-recorded, and the Marathi version will appear in a future issue of *Buddhayan*.[289] I am very happy to be here in Manmad, and to have seen you all. I am very happy with the beautiful arrangements for the meeting, and with the reception you have given me. People in many other parts of the Buddhist world will come to know about what is happening here. As you know, Upāsaka Nagabodhi is present tonight. During the last month, especially during this last week, he has been taking photographs of our meetings and writing about them. Both the articles he writes, and the photographs he takes, will be appearing in our English Buddhist magazine, published in London.[290] Buddhists all over the world will therefore know about our meeting here tonight. The Buddhist world is very large and includes Buddhists from many different countries, but though it is a big world, it is one world. Buddhists are all united. Whether they come from England or India, New Zealand or America, Malaysia or Japan, they are all brothers and sisters. They have the same father: the Buddha; the same mother: the Dhamma. They form one great spiritual family. It is therefore a very good thing that Buddhists from different parts of the world can meet together from time to time. If we do this, we strengthen the Buddhist movement. By organizing this meeting this evening, you have strengthened the Buddhist movement not only in Manmad, but in many parts of the world.

This is the first time that I have been to Manmad. Twenty years ago I managed to get as far as Bhusawal, and one of my friends wanted to bring me to Manmad, but for some reason this was not possible. I felt quite disappointed, because even at that time I had heard of the Buddhists of Manmad. Anyway, tonight I have been able to come here, even though I am twenty years late, and I am very glad it has been possible for me to do so. Thank you for the reception you have all given me, and thank you for listening to my Dhamma talk. I hope you may remember some of the things I have said. May you live happily. May you become more prosperous. May you obtain a better education, a better culture, and better jobs. Above all, may you become better Buddhists day by day. May you become one-hundred-percent Buddhists. May you become true followers of the Buddha, and true followers of Dr Ambedkar. If you can do this, you will be able to turn Manmad into a heaven on earth. I hope we shall meet again one day. Meanwhile, may you all be happy.

14

WORKING TOGETHER FOR
THE DHAMMA

Milind College, Aurangabad, 20 January 1982

Brothers and Sisters in the Dhamma: This is my first public lecture in Aurangabad, and indeed my first visit to the city.[291] I've been to many parts of Maharashtra before, some twenty years ago, but this is the first time I've had the opportunity to visit Aurangabad, and I'm very glad to be here this evening. I'm very glad to see so many people at this meeting, and I'm very grateful to you for the fine reception you have given me. I'm especially grateful to the ladies for the devotion they have shown. It was very nice to see them lined up at the entrance, in two rows, all wearing their white *upāsikā* saris. I'm also grateful to the organizers of this meeting. I understand from Anagārika Lokamitra that this meeting has been organized by the Trailokya Bauddha Mahasangha *Dhammamitras* and *Dhammasahayaks* of Aurangabad, and I am very pleased indeed to know this. Usually it is the *anagārikas* and *dasa sīla upāsakas* who take the initiative in organizing programmes and activities of this kind, but here it is the *Dhammamitras* and *Dhammasahayaks* who have done so. This is a very good sign indeed for the future. It is a sign that our movement will surely flourish here in Aurangabad.

In fact, it is only right that our Buddhist movement should flourish here. Aurangabad, as you well know, is associated with the illustrious name of Dr 'Babasaheb' Ambedkar. Not only that; there is an important educational movement flourishing here in Aurangabad. I refer of course to the People's Education Society. I think everybody in Maharashtra has heard of the People's Education Society, and I think that in the future quite a lot of people in the West will know its name too. Moreover, in Aurangabad you have Milind College, established, of course, by Dr Ambedkar, and giving the right sort of education to so many thousands of students. In view of these facts it is only natural that there should be in Aurangabad a flourishing Buddhist movement. I am quite sure, in fact, that in the future Aurangabad could be one of the greatest Buddhist centres in the whole of India. If enough people take the initiative, this will surely happen.

Taking initiative is extremely important. We should not sit back and wait for other people to do things. We should do those things ourselves. Taking initiative in this way implies a deep sense of responsibility and a comprehensive understanding of the situation. When we see that something needs to be done, we don't wait to see what somebody else is doing about it. We just go ahead and do it, and this also implies self-confidence. We know that we have the capacity to take the initiative, so we go ahead and do what needs to be done. But here there is a misunderstanding to be avoided. Taking the initiative does not mean becoming a leader and just telling other people what to do. It means doing the thing oneself. It means encouraging people by our example. If we ourselves do things, there is a chance that other people may do them. If we work for the Dhamma, then others may work for the Dhamma too. It's no use just complaining that nobody is doing anything. If other people are inspired by our example then we can all work for the Dhamma together. There is no question of just one person leading all the others. Certainly there is no question of one person dominating others, or bossing others around, or telling them what to do. Unfortunately, a lot of people are just looking for a leader, but this is a weakness, and it is not in accordance with true Buddhist thinking. Rather than looking for a leader, we should think in terms of taking the initiative ourselves, within the limits of our own understanding and capacity.

What usually happens is that we have one very active leader and a lot of very passive followers. That is to say, we have one shepherd and a lot of sheep – or, since this is India, perhaps I had better say we have one cowherd and a lot of cows. The leader is usually very ambitious. He wants to have power over other people. He may also want money and fame. So he encourages people just to believe in him, even to have blind faith in him. He doesn't allow criticism. The followers, on the other hand, are usually very weak and lacking in self-confidence, so they want to believe in a great leader. They want him to do everything for them. They want him to take responsibility. They even want him to save them. As we know very well, in the political field we have many such leaders in most countries of the world, maybe in all. But we don't have them only in the political field. We also have them in the religious field, in which such leaders are usually called 'great gurus'.

Now, 'guru' is not in itself a bad word. In itself it's quite a good word. It's usually explained as 'one who gives light'. But in modern times the meaning of the word has become very much debased. The 'great gurus' talk a lot about themselves. In a place like Bombay you can hear them nearly every day. They give themselves big titles. In English they give themselves such titles as 'His Holiness', or 'His Divine Grace', which – you can take it from me – are very high-sounding titles indeed. Not only that. They make very big claims for themselves. They say that they have come from God, or that they are *avatāras* of God. They say that they are Enlightened. They even say that they were Enlightened from birth, and that they didn't have to learn anything, so that whatever they say – whatever they happen to blurt out – is the truth. Moreover, they say that everybody should believe in them. If you believe in them you will be saved. There are a lot of these 'great gurus' in India. Some of them have even come to the West.

But this is not at all in accordance with the Buddhist ideal. In Buddhism we are not divided into leaders and followers. In Buddhism we *all* take the initiative, we *all* exercise responsibility, and at the same time, we *all* work together. And because we all take the initiative, all exercise responsibility and all work together, we form what is called a 'team'. This team is the *saṅgha* in the true sense: the living, working, active *saṅgha*.

To make things a little easier, especially for the children present, I'm going to make a comparison. This team of which I have spoken, this *saṅgha* in the true sense, can be compared to a football team. As I expect you know, a football team consists of eleven men, all of whom are experienced footballers. When they play a match, members of the team all occupy different positions on the field, all fulfil different functions. There's the centre forward, the half back, the goalkeeper, and so on. Thus you have all these people in the team playing their different parts, fulfilling their different functions. But they all work together for victory. Of course, there is a captain, but he is simply the most experienced member of the team. While the game is going on the captain doesn't run here and there on the pitch telling the members of his team what to do. If he did that it would spoil the game. What happens is that in the course of the game, everybody takes his own initiative. At the same time, nobody tries to be the leader. If you have got the ball, you don't necessarily try to score the goal yourself. You may see that some other member of the team is in a better position to score than you are, so you pass the ball to him and let him score the goal. You don't just want to play a prominent part yourself. The important thing is that your team wins the game. It doesn't matter who scores. The game is won with the support of the whole team, by virtue of teamwork.

The same is the case with Dhamma activities. For example, here I am in Aurangabad this evening, standing in front of the microphone giving a lecture. At this moment I am the most prominent member of the team. You could say I'm scoring the goal. But I'm not the leader. I'm not doing everything myself. I'm not taking all the responsibility. I'm working with the support of other people, and without that support I wouldn't be able to give this lecture. In order to make it possible a lot of other people have done a lot of work. Not only have people organized this programme. Some of them brought me here by car. Someone has been putting me up in his house for the last few days. Someone has been feeding me. Someone has been giving me medicine. Someone has been supplying me with writing paper for my notes. In this way everybody has been helping. We are all working together as a team. Everybody is important. Everybody is necessary. If it wasn't for all the people who've been helping I couldn't be standing here talking to you at this moment. So in Buddhism we don't have leaders and followers; we just have teams and teamwork. This has been the principle of Buddhism from the beginning, and this is the principle that we try to follow in the Trailokya Bauddha Mahasangha Sahayak Gana.

The Buddha lived for quite a long time. He taught the Dhamma he had discovered for forty-five years. Towards the end of his life, when he was a very old man, his disciple Devadatta, who was rather ambitious, said to him, 'You have become very old. It is not so easy for you to work as before. You should take things easy, rest and enjoy the fruits of your labours. I will take charge of the *bhikkhu sangha*.' But the Buddha refused Devadatta's offer in the strongest terms, saying, 'Even to Sāriputta and Moggallāna I would not entrust the *bhikkhu sangha*.

I would certainly never entrust it to a despicable person like you.'[292] When Devadatta heard these words he became extremely angry. In fact he became the enemy of the Buddha and even tried to kill him. This shows what a terrible thing personal ambition and the desire for leadership is. Because of it people are not only ready to kill the Buddha, they are ready to kill their own brother, or even their own father or mother. History is full of examples of this sort. The desire for leadership is such a dangerous thing.

There is another incident from the life of the Buddha that sheds light on this subject. As you know, Ānanda Thera was very close to the Buddha. Wherever the Buddha went, Ānanda went. Ānanda looked after the Buddha, cared for the Buddha, and from time to time he asked the Buddha questions. Shortly before the Buddha's *parinirvāna*, Ānanda asked him quite a number of questions, one of which related, in effect, to the leadership of the *bhikkhu saṅgha* after the *parinirvāna*. In reply the Buddha made two interesting and important statements. First of all he said, 'I do not consider that I lead the *bhikkhu saṅgha*, or that the *bhikkhu saṅgha* is dependent upon me.'[293] This statement is of tremendous significance. It shows that the Buddha is not a sort of spiritual dictator. The Buddha is not like the Pope or the Aga Khan. Just before making this statement the Buddha had made it clear that if anyone thought that he should lead the *bhikkhu saṅgha*, or that the *bhikkhu saṅgha* was dependent upon him, then he should come forward. The Buddha's second statement is no less significant. What he tells Ānanda, in effect, is that after his *parinirvāna* the Dhamma will be their leader. His actual words are, 'Hold fast to the Dhamma as a lamp. Hold fast as a Refuge to the Dhamma.'[294] In other words, no individual will be the leader. It is as though the Buddha was saying that personalities are not important. It is the practice of the Dhamma that is important. If we all practise the Dhamma we will all be following the same path, and if we are all following the same path then we can all work together.

This represents the spirit of Buddhism. As I said, in Buddhism we don't have very big gurus and very small devotees. We don't have power and arrogance on the one hand, and weakness and submission on the other. No, we have teams and teamwork. We have initiative and cooperation. We have shared responsibility. This has been the principle of Buddhism from the beginning, and this is the principle we try to follow in the Trailokya Bauddha Mahasangha Sahayak Gana.

How do we follow this principle? The Trailokya Bauddha Mahasangha Sahayak Gana was started in England in 1967. It's known as the Friends of the Western Buddhist Order and it now has regular activities in eight different countries of the world, including India. Though we've been functioning for less than fifteen years, already we have achieved, I may say, a considerable success, and sometimes people, especially other Buddhist organizations, wonder how we have managed to be so successful. Tonight I'm going to mention just two reasons for our success, and these two reasons are closely interconnected. The first reason is that the Trailokya Bauddha Mahasangha Sahayak Gana is a one-hundred-percent Buddhist movement. The second reason is that the TBMSG is based on the principle of teams and teamwork, which it applies in a highly practical manner.

First of all, the TBMSG is a one-hundred-percent Buddhist movement in the sense that it consists only of people who actually practise the Dhamma. You can be a member of the Trailokya Bauddha Mahasangha Sahayak Gana only to the extent that you practise the Dhamma. The more you practise the Dhamma, the more you are a member of the TBMSG. You cannot join the TBMSG simply by filling in a form and paying a membership subscription. Now this is not the case with some other Buddhist organizations. You can join some so-called Buddhist organizations simply by paying a subscription, even though you may not be a Buddhist, even if you are against Buddhism. Not only can you become an ordinary member, you can even become secretary, even become president. No wonder such organizations cannot do very much for Buddhism!

Again, I'm going to make a comparison with a football team. Suppose there is a very big, fat man. Such a man can't run. It's even difficult for him to walk. So can he play football? Of course not. But suppose that for some reason or other he wants to join the local football team, and he happens to be rich as well as fat. He therefore gives the team some money, maybe ten rupees, or a hundred rupees, or one thousand, or ten thousand, or even a *lakh*. The football team may let him join, because he has given so much money, and may even let him play in the team. But what use will he be? He will be no use at all. Some Buddhist organizations are just like that. They admit people to membership simply on payment of a subscription. So what can such organizations do for Buddhism? We have such so-called Buddhist organizations in both India and England.

Then there are other Buddhist organizations that admit people to membership simply because they *say* they are Buddhists. This also is not very useful. This is like a football team that allows people to join it simply because they say they can play football very well. It doesn't give them any test, or any training. Such a team won't win many matches. Similarly, such a Buddhist organization won't be able to do very much for its members. Therefore the TBMSG admits to membership only those who are actually practising the Dhamma wholeheartedly. The TBMSG is therefore a one-hundred-percent Buddhist movement. It consists only of practising Buddhists. We don't have any people who are half-Christian and half-Buddhist, or half-Hindu and half-Buddhist. We have only people who are one-hundred-percent practising Buddhists.

Now some people practise the Dhamma more than others and some less, so in the TBMSG we have different kinds of membership. We have, in fact, three levels of membership: *Dhammasahayaks*, *Dhammamitras*, and *dasa sīla upāsakas*, sometimes called Dhammacharis. *Anagārikas* are included in the third level of membership.

A *Dhammasahayak* is someone who has occasional contact with the TBMSG. He may also have contact with other Buddhist organizations. Sometimes he comes along to programmes, sometimes he does not. He may attend *shibirs* and lectures, and so on, from time to time. He may buy and read our publications occasionally. He may even be very helpful at times. But he doesn't have regular contact.

Secondly, there is the *Dhammamitra*. A *Dhammamitra* is someone who has regular contact with the TBMSG. He does not take part in the activities of other Buddhist organizations. He observes the *pañcasīla*. More specifically, the *Dhammamitra* is expected to do four things. First of all, he is expected to attend the local TBMSG centre regularly and attend the meditation classes, Dhamma study groups, lectures, and so on. Secondly, he is expected to meditate regularly by himself and practise the *ānāpānasati* and *mettā bhāvanā*; and he may also do the stupa visualization and Śākyamuni visualization practices. What is important is that he should practise some form of meditation at least once every day, preferably twice. This may not be very easy, especially for those who are living at home with their families and have jobs, but they must try. Thirdly, the *Dhammamitra* is expected to keep in close and regular contact with the Dhammacharis, including the *anagārikas*. In fact they should try to make their contact with them deeper and deeper.

This is what we call *kalyāṇa mitratā*. *Kalyāṇa mitratā* is considered extremely important in Buddhism. There is an incident in the scriptures that illustrates this point. This incident also concerns the Buddha and Ānanda. Ānanda once said to the Buddha, 'Lord, I think that *kalyāṇa mitratā* is half the spiritual life.' But the Buddha said, 'Do not say such a thing, Ānanda. *Kalyāṇa mitratā* is not half the spiritual life, but the whole of it.'[295] This shows how important *kalyāṇa mitratā* was considered by the Buddha. It shows how important it is considered in Buddhism. But why is it so important? It's important because we learn best from personal contact. In the case of learning the Dhamma, we learn best from people who are spiritually more developed than ourselves. We don't just get knowledge from them. We get encouragement, practical help in our Dhamma life, inspiration, and enthusiasm, just like one candle being lit by another. This does not mean that those who are spiritually more developed than we are do things for us. They show us how to do them, and then they encourage us to do them ourselves. This is what we call *kalyāṇa mitratā*. Fourthly, the *Dhammamitra* is expected to help the TBMSG, and especially the local TBMSG centre, in practical ways. There are lots of ways in which we can help. I'll mention just a few of them. We can organize programmes, just as some of you have done today. We can help keep the centre clean and beautiful, especially the shrine-room. We can help sell *Buddhayan*, as well as other TBMSG publications. We can lend our motor car, if we have one. We can tell our friends about the TBMSG and its activities. These are just some of the ways in which *Dhammamitras* are expected to help.

From this you can see that it's not an easy thing to become a *Dhammamitra* in the TBMSG. It's quite difficult. We expect quite a high standard of our *Dhammamitras*. If you go to Thailand or Sri Lanka, they will make you a *bhikkhu* almost immediately. You arrive one day, and they make you a *bhikkhu* the next. But it's not so easy to become one of our *Dhammamitras*. You may have to wait a year or two and prepare yourself. As Dr Ambedkar said, to practise the Dhamma is very difficult. For this reason, becoming a *Dhammamitra* is difficult.

Thirdly and lastly, we come to the *dasa sīla upāsaka* or Dhammachari. The *upāsaka* is one who really and truly goes for Refuge, not just with his lips but with his whole heart. He also observes the ten *sīlas*, or ten *kusala dhammas*. He abstains from injury to living beings, abstains from taking what is not given, abstains from sexual misconduct. In the case of the *anagārika* he abstains from non-celibacy or *abrahmacariya* or, in others words, practises *brahmacariya*. These three *sīlas*, these three *kusala dhammas*, purify the body. Further, the *dasa sīla upāsaka* abstains from false speech, abstains from harsh speech, abstains from all idle talk and gossip (one of the most difficult precepts), and abstains from slander and backbiting. These four *sīlas*, these four *kusala dhammas*, purify one's speech. Finally, the *dasa sīla upāsaka* abstains from greed and craving, abstains from hatred, ill will, and enmity, and abstains from wrong or false views – views, teachings, and beliefs that are contrary to the Dhamma, for example the wrong view that the Buddha was the *avatāra* of Vishnu. These three *sīlas*, these three *kusala dhammas*, purify the mind. In this way the whole being is purified.

The ten *upāsaka sīlas*, or ten *kusala dhammas*, also have a more positive aspect. This more positive aspect consists, first of all, in practising love, generosity, and contentment. Further, it consists in speaking the truth, speaking kindly and affectionately, speaking what is useful – that is to say, speaking about the Dhamma, about those things that will help human beings to develop and become better human beings – and speaking in such a way as to promote concord, unity, and harmony within the Buddhist community. Finally, it consists in developing generosity, love and compassion, and wisdom. So you can see that a great deal is expected of our *dasa sīla upāsakas* – even more than is expected of the *Dhammamitras*.

Dasa sīla upāsakas and *upāsikās* make up the Trailokya Bauddha Mahasangha, and *Dhammasahayaks*, *Dhammamitras*, and *dasa sīla upāsaka* and *upāsikās* together make up the Trailokya Bauddha Mahasangha Sahayak Gana. Our local centres are run by five or more *upāsakas* together with the assistance of the *Dhammamitras* and *Dhammasahayaks*. More than this it probably isn't necessary for me to say. I hope that I've been able to give you some idea about the TBMSG.

I'll close with another comparison with the football team. I hope you're not tired of the football team. This comparison may help to fix what I have said more firmly in your minds. We can say that the *Dhammasahayaks* are like the spectators at the football match. Sometimes they come to see the match, sometimes they don't. They don't actually play football. They may sometimes just kick the ball around at home, or on some waste ground, but that is all. Then there are the *Dhammamitras*. They are like those who are actually learning to play the game of football. Because they are learning they practise every day, and they learn as much as they can from the seasoned, experienced football players. Some of them may even be in the reserve team. As for the *dasa sīla upāsakas*, they are the seasoned, experienced players who make up the football team. They work together. They play together. In a word, they cooperate. They even have team colours – the yellow, blue, and red of the Three Jewels embroidered on the *kesa*.

In this way we come back to the team. We come back to the great principle of cooperation. We come back to the fact that we must take the initiative ourselves. We must work together with others who are also taking the initiative. We must work for the Dhamma. Then we will be real *Dhammasahayaks*, real *Dhammamitras*, real *dasa sīla upāsakas*.

In conclusion I'd just like to congratulate the *Dhammamitras* and *Dhammasahayaks* who have been responsible for organizing this programme tonight. I hope it will not be very long before those *Dhammamitras* and *Dhammasahayaks* 'join the team'. I hope they will score many goals. In fact, I hope that one day you will all score many goals.

15
THE SANANTANA-DHAMMA

Milind College, Aurangabad, 21 January 1982

Principal Chitnis,[296] Brothers and Sisters in the Dhamma: During the last three years I have spent most of my time in England, but although I've been away from India I've been hearing quite a lot about Aurangabad, and about Milind College in particular, as well as about the work of the People's Education Society here. I have been hearing about them from Anagārika Lokamitra, who has been telling me in his letters that he thinks Aurangabad is a very good place for our Buddhist activities. In fact he seems to think that it is just about the best place for our Buddhist activities in the whole of India. I have therefore come to see things for myself, and I am very glad to be here and to see you all. I am very grateful to the People's Education Society's Buddhist centre for arranging this function this morning. Wherever I have gone in the course of my present tour, whether to Bombay, to Mahad, or now to Aurangabad, the People's Education Society has treated me and my friends with very great hospitality and friendliness.

Aurangabad is an important place, having many important historical associations, especially with the great Mughal emperor Aurangzeb, and many important historical monuments. In modern times, however, the city has become famous for its association with the illustrious memory of Dr Babasaheb Ambedkar. I am told by some of my friends here that Dr Ambedkar loved Aurangabad very much and spent quite a lot of time here. Here, as long ago as 1950, he established this great institution and named it Milind College, from this we can see the direction in which his mind and heart were moving even in 1950. After all, he could have called it Mahatma Gandhi College, or Jawarhalal Nehru College, or even Shivaji College – that would have been very popular. But he called it Milind College, and Milinda or Menander was the Bactrian Greek king who was converted to Buddhism by Nagasena Thera.

To people from other countries Aurangabad is famous mainly on account of the Ajanta caves and their wall paintings. Many visitors come from all over the world to see the Ajanta caves, which are one of the great wonders of the whole Buddhist world. As I am sure you know, there are altogether more than thirty rock-cut caves, some of which are what we call *caityas*, used for purposes of *vandanā* or worship, while others were viharas, that is to say, they were used for residential purposes by the Buddhist *bhikkhus*. The walls of the caves at Ajanta are covered with dozens upon dozens of beautiful paintings which constitute a landmark in the history of ancient Indian art. I myself saw them more than twenty years ago, and I have a very vivid recollection of their beauty. I especially remember that world-famous picture of the Bodhisattva Padmapāṇi. He is represented as a young prince wearing a beautiful jewelled headdress and holding a blue lotus flower in his hand – which is why he is called Padmapāṇi. He is looking down with a beautiful expression of compassion on his face, looking down on the sufferings of humanity and wanting to help. He is the embodiment of *karuṇā*. This figure thus represents a very important aspect of the Buddhist ideal. In Buddhism *prajñā* is important, but *karuṇā* is no less important.

There are many of these rock-cut caves in Maharashtra, not just at Ajanta and Ellora, and most of them are Buddhist caves, which shows that Buddhism must have been very widespread in this area, and very influential, not just for a short time but for hundreds of years. In this connection, I want to point out something important. Although it is important that we should know about, and appreciate, Ajanta and the other Buddhist caves, there is a danger in this. We may start thinking that Buddhism is just something very old, belonging just to the remote past. We may start thinking that Buddhism is just part of the ancient history of Bharat and therefore that it has nothing to do with today. We may even think that it is out of date. To think in this way would be a great mistake. Buddhism belongs not only to the past but also to the present, and to the future. In fact we may say that Buddhism belongs more to the present than to the past, and more to the future than to the present. That is why Dr Ambedkar embraced Buddhism, and why he encouraged his followers to do likewise. He did not mean that his followers should all become students of ancient Indian history and go and live in some dusty old museum. That was not his intention.

The Dhamma is the *akāliko-dhamma*. The principles taught by the Buddha are timeless, not limited by time. In the same way they are not limited by space. The Dhamma can be practised in both the East and the West, the North and the South. At present many people in the West are becoming Buddhists. They don't see Buddhism as something old. It has nothing to do with their ancient culture. They see it as something very new. In the same way they don't see the Buddha as an old man. After all, when he gained Enlightenment he was only thirty-five – in the prime of life. In India people sometimes say that when you are thirty-five you are old, but that is not true. When you are thirty-five you are in the prime of life, and that is when the Buddha gained Enlightenment.

The Dhamma is not only called *akāliko-dhamma*; it is also called *sanantano-dhamma*. There is a famous verse in the *Dhammapada* which goes like this:

na hi verena verāni sammantīdha kudācanaṃ
averena ca sammanti esa dhammo sanantano.

In this verse the Buddha says that here in this world hatred, or enmity, never ceases by hatred or enmity.[297] Hatred or enmity, he says, ceases only by non-hatred or non-enmity, or in other words by love. Then he adds that this teaching, or this principle, is the *sanantana-dhamma*. Here we must be very careful to distinguish *sanantana-dhamma* from *sanātana-dharma*. There is only a difference of one letter between them, just a difference of M or R, but whether you put the one or the other makes a very big difference indeed. *Sanātana-dharma* is *varṇāśrama-dharma*, in other words the caste system. So far as some people are concerned this still means treating others as lower, even treating them as untouchable.

I remember a little story in this connection. As you may know, I once spent two years in South India, wandering about from place to place, sometimes on foot. In the course of these wanderings I had many interesting experiences, and heard many interesting stories. One of these stories illustrates the meaning of *sanātana-dharma*. Some of my friends in South India told me that there was an old high-caste Hindu woman who became converted to Christianity. After a few months Christmas came along. As I expect you know, Christmas is the birthday of Jesus Christ, and Christians like to celebrate it on a grand scale. The church with which this old lady had become connected celebrated it, and as part of the celebrations there was a big feast to which all the Christian people, most of them converts, were invited. The old woman was invited, but when she saw the other Christians all sitting ready for the feast she said, 'I'm not going to eat with those people – they are low-caste people. I'm high caste.' When she said this the priest became quite annoyed. He said, 'You are a Christian now. You have got to sit and eat with these people. It is Christmas time.' But the old woman said, 'Father, I may have become a Christian, but does that mean I have to give up my *dharma*?' So for her '*dharma*' meant simply not eating and drinking with people of another caste.

So we all know what *sanātana-dharma* is. But what is *sanantana-dhamma*? *Sanantana-dhamma* can be defined as those moral and spiritual principles that are true irrespective of time and space. By moral and spiritual principles we mean those principles that conduce to the development of the individual human being as a human being. In other words they are those principles that are conducive to Enlightenment. One of those moral and spiritual principles is enunciated in the *Dhammapada* verse I quoted a few minutes ago. 'Enmity and hatred never ceases by enmity or hatred.' This is a principle which is eternally true. It was true in the past, it is true in the present, and it will be true in the future. It is true in the East, true in the West; true in India, true in England. Therefore it is a *sanantana-dhamma*.

Now *sanātana-dharma* is not like that. *Sanātana-dharma* cannot be really fully practised outside India, outside the *puṇyabhūmi*.[298] Only a hundred years ago a Hindu was not permitted to cross the *kālapāni*.[299] If he did so he was outcasted. In this connection I remember that in 1947 I met a very old Bengali gentleman, a famous Sanskrit scholar, called Pandit Jagadish Chandra Chatterjee. He told me that he had gone to England in about 1890, and spent two or three years there translating the Upanishads into English. When he returned to India, however, he was outcasted. Even his wife would not speak to him. He was not allowed to stay in the house. Instead he was put in the cowshed, and kept there for two or three months. He had to swallow cow dung and cow urine, as well as having them poured over him by Brahmin pandits, and in this way he was made 'pure'. Only then was he allowed to enter the house. Therefore I say that it is difficult to practise Hinduism, certainly orthodox Hinduism, outside India. After all, in foreign countries you can't get *gaṅgāpāṇi*,[300] you can't get cow dung, at least not the real Indian cow dung. There are some Hindu religious movements in the West, but they don't represent the real *sanātana-dharma*. They are mostly Vedanta teachings mixed with a bit of modern science or a bit of Christianity. But when we speak of Buddhism we mean *akāliko-dhamma*, *sanantana-dhamma*. We mean certain moral and spiritual principles. We mean *śīla, maitrī, karuṇā*, and *prajñā*. We don't just mean something old. We mean something new – in fact something eternally new. We mean something which is of universal validity, universal applicability.

There are other things besides the Buddhist rock-cut caves which may give us the wrong impression that Buddhism is just something old. One of these things is the *bhikkhu's* robes. Lay people like you usually wear modern dress. You are not wearing *dhoti* or *lunghi* but trousers and shirts, because you like new things. Ladies of course still wear a sari, but young men like modern dress. But the *bhikkhus* wear *ticīvara*, the same dress they wore 2,500 years ago.[301] I'm not saying that this is wrong. After all I'm wearing *ticīvara* myself. But it may give people the wrong impression that Buddhism is just something very old, something belonging to the remote past.

There is also the question of the Pāli language. Actually, Pāli is not really the name of a language at all. The word 'Pāli' means a line of writing. In the course of time, however, it has come to be used as the name of a language and I shall use the term in that sense. Pāli is the name of the language of the Theravāda Buddhist scriptures. It is a very beautiful and expressive language, but at the same time it is a dead language. Like Sanskrit, Pāli is not spoken by people today, though Buddhists often use it for chanting. Sometimes Pāli alone is used for chanting, and this too may give the wrong impression that Buddhism is just something old, even dead.

What then must we do? We have to adapt Buddhism to the needs of modern life. By adaptation I do not mean changing the fundamental moral and spiritual principles. They cannot be changed; they are *akāliko* and *sanāntana*. By adaptation I mean presenting and explaining these moral and spiritual principles in a new kind of way. Buddhism has now been in the world for more than 2,500 years. During that time it has undergone many developments. It has gone to many countries – to Sri Lanka, Burma, and Thailand, to China, Japan, and Tibet and so on – and in all these countries it has come, in the course of hundreds of years, to be very much mixed up with the local culture. What we have to do, therefore, is separate the Dhamma in the sense of the universal moral and spiritual principles from the various later, purely local, cultural accretions. We have to emphasize the moral and spiritual principles and apply these principles directly to our own lives. We can do this because we are new Buddhists. We don't want Thai or Japanese manners and customs. We just want the Dhamma, the *akāliko, sanantana* Dhamma. We want to be able to learn it in our own language. We want to be able to practise it in our own way, in accordance with our psychological and spiritual needs, and our own modern cultural background. This applies to Buddhists in England as well as to Buddhists in India. We want to practise the Dhamma here and now in the twentieth century. We don't want to practise it in the fifth century BCE or the tenth century CE.

But before we can practise the Dhamma we must learn it, and in order to learn it we must have a proper teacher. In other words, we must have a *kalyāṇa mitra*. But where are we going to get these Dhamma teachers or *kalyāṇa mitras* from? In order to help us answer this question I want to refer to an important article written by Dr Babasaheb Ambedkar entitled 'Buddha and the Future of His Religion' which appeared in the Calcutta *Maha Bodhi* journal in May 1950. I read this article soon after it came out and liked it very much, so I wrote to Dr Ambedkar and told him about the Buddhist work that I was doing, and he wrote back a very kind and encouraging letter. That was in 1950, and that was my first contact with Dr Ambedkar.

In this article Dr Ambedkar raises a number of important points. For instance, he says that it is very important to spread Buddhism, not only in India but throughout the world. He then asks how this ideal of spreading Buddhism could be realized, and he says that three steps are necessary: first, the production of a Buddhist Bible; second, the making of changes in the organization, aims, and objects of the *bhikkhu saṅgha*; and third, the setting up of a world Buddhist mission. This morning I am concerned just with the second of these three points, that is, making changes in the *bhikkhu saṅgha*. Dr Ambedkar was quite dissatisfied with the present-day *bhikkhu sangha*, which he said was of no use in the spreading of Buddhism. He was quite right. You may have heard the name of Anagārika Dharmapala, the founder of the Maha Bodhi Society. He did a lot for the revival of Buddhism in India and Sri Lanka, but he spent most of his life as an *anagārika*, thinking that if he became a *bhikkhu* it would not be possible for him to work for the Dhamma. *Bhikkhus* have to observe so many different rules, and the observing of these rules gets in the way of practising the Dhamma. This is really a ridiculous situation. The Buddha sent out his disciples into the world simply to teach the Dhamma. He didn't send them out into the world to observe very minor rules. So Dharmapala became a *bhikkhu* only at the very end of his life, when he was confined to a wheelchair and could no longer work for the Dhamma. You could say he retired and became a *bhikkhu*. Dr Ambedkar was very aware of all this, and what he said, in effect, was that we need a new kind of *bhikkhu*, a new kind of *sangha*. Unless we have this new kind of *sangha* Buddhism will not spread.

In this connection Dr Ambedkar made a few practical suggestions. He said that we want fewer *bhikkhus*. At present there are too many; he said that we want quality, not quantity. We want highly educated *bhikkhus*, but this does not necessarily mean *bhikkhus* with university degrees. Nowadays we have quite a lot of such *bhikkhus*, and most of them are quite useless for Dhamma work. By an educated *bhikkhu* we mean one with a good general education and a sound understanding of the Dhamma. In this connection Dr Ambedkar made a very interesting suggestion. He said 'The Bhikshu Sangha must borrow some of the features of the Christian priesthood, particularly the Jesuits.'[302] To understand what he meant by this, we need to know who the Jesuits were. I want to go into this just a little before closing. The Jesuits are an order of Roman Catholic Christian monks which was founded in the sixteenth century, by a Spanish Roman Catholic called Ignatius Loyola. This was the time of Martin Luther and what is called the Protestant Reformation. As a result of this Reformation the Roman Catholic Church was greatly weakened, and lost nearly half its followers. Ignatius Loyola wanted to strengthen the Roman Catholic Church, and for this purpose he founded his Jesuit Order and succeeded in saving the Roman Catholic Church.

When Dr Ambedkar said that the *bhikṣu sangha* could borrow from the Jesuits he did not mean that Buddhist *bhikkhus* should become just like the Jesuits. That is impossible. They were Christians; we are Buddhists. But there are some things that we can learn from them, and Dr Ambedkar recognized this. The Jesuits were highly educated, very dedicated, prepared to give their lives for their religion. Hard-working and adventurous, they carried Roman Catholicism all over the world, even to India. They were very strong in Goa, for instance, as you may know. Another point about the Jesuits is what they wore. The older orders of Christian monks wore a special kind of robe. Some wore white robes, some brown ones, some black ones, and some wore robes that were half white and half black. Some wore a special kind of hat, or special shoes. This special costume differentiated them from ordinary lay people. But the Jesuits did not follow this custom. They wore ordinary clothes so that they looked like other people, which meant that they could mix with people easily. It is not surprising that being possessed of all these qualities and characteristics, the Jesuits were able to save the Roman Catholic Church.

Here we can make a comparison. In the sixteenth century the Roman Catholic Church was seriously threatened by Protestantism. Half of Germany became Protestant, and so did England, Switzerland, Holland, Sweden, and a number of other countries. In this way the Roman Catholic Church became very much weakened. Similarly, in the twentieth century, Buddhism is seriously threatened by all sorts of forces. It is threatened by materialism and by communism. In several Asian countries it has been practically wiped out. Here in India Buddhism is of course threatened by Brahmanism. We therefore need a very strong *saṅgha*, otherwise Buddhism may disappear altogether from the world. The present-day *bhikkhu saṅgha* is too weak to cope with the situation. It is too easy-going, too lazy. We want a new kind of *saṅgha*. We want a team of educated, dedicated, active people all working together for the Dhamma. Only if we have such a new kind of *saṅgha* can Buddhism survive and flourish in the modern world, not only in India but in other parts of the world as well.

For the last seventeen years I have been in England, spreading the Dhamma there, as well as in other Western countries. I have also been trying to create a new Buddhist *saṅgha* – the kind that Dr Ambedkar had in mind. This is an Order of what we call *dasa sīla upāsakas*, including *anagārikas*. It now consists of 163 members belonging to twelve different nationalities, nearly all of whom are working full-time for the Dhamma. Between them they are running Buddhist centres in eight countries including India. They are giving lectures, producing books and magazines, running cooperative businesses, leading retreats, and so on. This new Buddhist Order is known as the Trailokya Bauddha Mahasangha. It is working for Buddhism and teaching the *akāliko-dhamma*, the *sanantana-dhamma*, in a new way. It is presenting the Dhamma in the way in which people can understand and practise it. Because the Dhamma is not just something old. It is eternally new. It doesn't just belong to the past. It belongs also to the present and the future. In fact, as I said at the beginning, it belongs more to the present than to the past, and more to the future than to the present. We know that Buddhism has had a very glorious past, but I am sure it could have an even more glorious future. We could have a hundred Ajantas.

Most of you are young men. You like new things. You even like new styles of dress. Buddhism should therefore appeal to you very strongly. The *akāliko, sanantana-dhamma* should appeal to you very strongly. The idea of a new kind of Buddhist teacher – a *kalyāṇa mitra* – and a new kind of Buddhist order should appeal to you very strongly. I therefore hope that all of you, or at least a large number of you, will eventually come forward and do your part. Meanwhile, in conclusion, I would like to thank the People's Education Society very heartily for arranging this function this morning. Where you have the Dhamma, there you will have education, and where you have the right kind of education, there you will have the Dhamma. I am really glad to have had this opportunity of meeting you all – office-bearers of the People's Education Society, members of the different faculties and, of course, all of you, the students. You are the most important, because the college exists for your sake, not you for the sake of the college. I hope we shall all meet again.

16

REASON AND EMOTION IN THE SPIRITUAL
LIFE: DR AMBEDKAR'S GREAT EXAMPLE

Vaijapur,[303] *22 January 1982*

Brothers and Sisters in the Dhamma: Great men are like mountains.
When you get close up to a mountain, especially when you are right
underneath it, you can't see how big it is. You can see its true size only
when you are some distance away. Great men are like that. When you
are close to them, especially when you are actually living with them,
you can't see how great they are. Since the great man eats, drinks, and
sleeps, at first he seems just like everybody else. In order to see how great
he is you have to get some distance away. Indeed, you may not begin
to appreciate how great a great man is until some time after his death.

Dr Ambedkar was a great man, one of the greatest men of modern
India, or perhaps even the greatest, but during his lifetime a lot of people
did not appreciate him. In fact a lot of people were against him, and
even hated him. Now that Dr Ambedkar has been dead for twenty-five
years, people are beginning to appreciate his importance. During the
last month I have been visiting different parts of Maharashtra, and
wherever I have gone I have seen statues and busts of Dr Ambedkar –
some of them put up by the government, others by the Buddhist people
themselves. This shows that more and more people are beginning to
appreciate the greatness of Dr Ambedkar and to see his significance in
the history of modern India.

There are a number of reasons why Dr Ambedkar was a great man.
This afternoon I am going to mention just one or two of them. First of
all, he had a very great brain. He was what we call an intellectual giant.

He himself once said that he was as good as 500 ordinary graduates, but perhaps even that was an underestimate. Maybe he was as good as 5,000 graduates. What one Dr Ambedkar did, even 5,000 ordinary graduates could not do. He had read many books, studied many subjects: law, political science, economics, commerce, banking, history, sociology, international relations, literature, and many others. In all these subjects he become a master. He was not an amateur, but a professional. On one occasion he declared that he was so highly educated that he was qualified to fill any position in India, even that of Viceroy. (This was, of course, before Independence.)

But though Dr Ambedkar was one of the intellectual giants of the modern world, he was not like those people who have a very well-developed head but not a very well-developed heart. On the contrary, though he had such a powerful intellect he also had very powerful emotions. He had, in fact, a great and noble heart, which felt deeply and sincerely. He loved his friends. He loved his wife and children. When his first wife died he was so upset that for a while he lived as a sadhu. When his young children died, he was so deeply upset that he wept for days and nights together.

So he had a very tender heart. And when he saw how great were the sufferings of his own people, how they were not permitted to draw water from the common well, or wear proper clothes, or eat good, nourishing food, or wear decent ornaments, he felt the injustice and inhumanity of all this very strongly. He felt that he must help these unfortunate people and rescue them from their misery. He felt great compassion for them, great *karuṇā*. Being such a highly educated man, he could easily have led a life of comfort and prosperity, but he had no wish to do that. Instead, he sacrificed his own life, his own leisure, his own money, working for the uplift of his people. In this way he lived like a real bodhisattva. This is why even today people sometimes call him 'Bodhisattva Dr Babasaheb Ambedkar'.

Thus we see that Dr Ambedkar had this very wonderful and very important combination of intellectual capacity and emotional feeling. Emotion is very important in life. Knowledge is not enough. If we have only knowledge we cannot do very much. We also need emotions; then we can put our knowledge into action. In ordinary life, without strong feelings we cannot do anything, and it is the same in our Dhamma life. First of all, we must have a feeling for the Dhamma itself. Just learning about the Dhamma intellectually, as we do by reading books, is not enough. We must have a feeling for the Dhamma – must give our hearts to the Dhamma. Only then will we start practising the Dhamma. And besides feeling for the Dhamma, we must feel for other people – not just for ourselves. We must develop emotion in this kind of way too.

In the Buddha's teaching there are three kinds of emotion which are of importance: *maitrī*, *karuṇā*, and *śraddhā*. I shall say a few words about each of these in turn.

The word *maitrī* (*mettā* in Pāli) comes from the Sanskrit word *mitra*. It means seeing everybody as a friend and treating them as such, having the same feeling of love towards all living beings that you have towards your own nearest and dearest friend. There is a celebrated Pāli saying that gives expression to this kind of attitude: *sabbe sattā sukhi hontu*, may all beings be happy. Buddhists want that everybody should be happy. Not just Buddhists, but non-Buddhists too. Not just human beings, but even animals. This is the sort of feeling that we should have, and we call this sort of feeling *maitrī*.

Coming to *karuṇā*, there is no basic difference between *karuṇā* and *maitrī*. If we see someone who is in difficulties, or who is suffering, perhaps without food or without proper clothes, then, if there is *maitrī* in our heart, we will feel *karuṇā* towards such people. Thus *karuṇā* is the emotion that develops when *maitrī* comes into contact with human – or animal – suffering. If we have this *maitrī*, this *karuṇā*, then we will try to help those who are suffering, just as Dr Ambedkar did.

As for the difference between *śraddhā* and *maitrī*, and therefore between *śraddhā* and *karuṇā*, once again there is no fundamental difference between the two. *Śraddhā* is the feeling that develops when, with *maitrī*, we look up to another human being who is spiritually more developed than we are ourselves. When, with *maitrī* in our hearts, we look at the image or picture of the Buddha, or when we simply think of the Buddha, that *maitrī* develops into what we call *śraddhā*. *Śraddhā* is not belief in the sense of thinking that this or that statement is true. It is what we may call our healthy, positive emotional response to the spiritual ideal. And the spiritual ideal represents something that we ourselves can become.

If we feel *karuṇā* towards those who are suffering, we will try to help them. Similarly, if we feel *śraddhā* towards the Buddha we will perform the Buddha puja. The puja is the outward expression of the *śraddhā* we feel towards the Buddha, the expression of our positive feeling for the spiritual ideal. Puja is generally directed towards an image or picture of the Buddha. This is because it is very difficult for us to form an idea of what the Buddha actually looked like, and the image or picture helps us to do this.

Buddhist puja is a very simple affair. There is no ringing of bells or breaking of coconuts. It consists simply in offering flowers, lights, and incense. When we make our offerings we have to understand the meaning of what we are doing, otherwise our puja will not be Buddhistic but only a sort of superstitious practice. We offer flowers because flowers, though they are bright and beautiful, do not last very long. Today they are fresh, but tomorrow they will be dry and withered. When we offer flowers we have to reflect on this, and that we too are like flowers. Today we may be young and beautiful, perhaps wearing a nice bright sari or a fine suit, but it won't be so very long before we shall be wrapped in a white sheet and carried to the burning ground. So we should reflect on the meaning of life. We should resolve to develop ourselves mentally and spiritually, and become as perfect as possible. In other words, offering flowers to the Buddha should make us think seriously.

We offer lights, usually in the form of lighted candles, because light too is a very beautiful thing. Light shines in the midst of the darkness. Where there is light, darkness cannot exist. Light represents *prajñā*. When you have *prajñā*, ignorance disappears. *Prajñā* means Enlightenment or *bodhi*. When we offer a lighted candle to the Buddha we do so with the aspiration that we may light the light of *prajñā* in our own mind, that we may get rid of ignorance and develop mentally and spiritually – that we may become, like the Buddha, Enlightened.

We offer incense because it is very sweet. The fragrance of even a small stick of incense can be perceived hundreds of yards away, and thus incense represents the widespread influence of the good life. If you observe the *pañcasīla*, that will have a positive influence on the surroundings. It will affect people even a long way off, and bring about an improvement in the whole environment. When offering incense it should be with the aspiration that, through your practice of the *pañcasīla*, you may influence your family, your locality, and eventually the whole society, in a positive and constructive manner.

Thus Buddhist puja consists simply in the offering of these three things: flowers, lights, and incense. This puja is the outward expression of our *śraddhā*, or positive feeling towards the Buddha.

We must not think that *śraddhā* can be separated from *prajñā*. If *śraddhā* is separated from *prajñā*, it is not really *śraddhā*. This is why we have to understand the meaning of the offerings we make in the way I have explained. *Śraddhā* and *prajñā* must be balanced. If we have *prajñā* without *śraddhā* we are just intellectuals, just rationalists, and if we have *śraddhā* without *prajñā*, we shall very easily sink into a morass of superstition and blind belief. Therefore we have to have both *śraddhā* and *prajñā*. We have to develop both our intellect and our emotions.

This is what Dr Ambedkar did on a grand scale. He was a man of exceptionally powerful intellect, and also a man of exceptionally positive emotions. This is why he could do so much for India, especially for his own people. This is why he could bring back the Dhamma to India. Besides a deep understanding of the Dhamma, he had a strong feeling for the Dhamma. He had both great *prajñā* and great *śraddhā* – as well as great *karuṇā*. Thus we can see that Dr Ambedkar was a very balanced man. He was not only a great man, but an all-round-developed great man. In this way he provides us with a model, an example.

We too should try to develop our understanding of the Dhamma. All Buddhists should understand the Dhamma – not only the men, but also the women; not only the old, but also the young. Nowadays, there is no excuse for anybody not understanding the Dhamma. Twenty or thirty years ago it was not easy to learn about it, but now it is much easier. Now we have lectures on the Dhamma and literature on the Dhamma in Marathi. If you cannot read, you should get someone to read it to you. You can discuss what you read, and in this way you will come to understand the Dhamma more and more deeply. Nor is that all. You must not only understand the Dhamma but also develop a feeling for it through the performance of puja.

Sometimes we see that men are stronger in intellectual development, whereas women are stronger in emotional development. Wherever I go, it is the women who come rushing forward with their trays of lighted candles and their garlands of flowers. This is very good to see. It shows great *śraddhā*. But that *śraddhā* must be joined with *prajñā*. In the same way, it is the men who always ask questions about the Dhamma. Theirs is an intellectual interest. They want to know why Dr Ambedkar wrote this in *The Buddha and His Dhamma*, and why he wrote that. The women do not bother with such questions. To generalize, one could say that in the men *prajñā* is more developed, so they need to develop *śraddhā*. Men need more *śraddhā*, just as women need more *prajñā*.

We must have both these things. If we have them both, we will be real Buddhists, and real followers of Dr Ambedkar. Indeed, we shall be more than that. We shall be a little bit like the Buddha, a little bit like Dr Ambedkar. We won't be just followers, we shall be sons and daughters of the Buddha, sons and daughters of Dr Ambedkar. And if that is what we are like, we can transform the whole of society. So develop *prajñā*, develop *śraddhā*; develop *maitrī*, develop *karuṇā*. Develop all those positive qualities, and progress will be sure.

I am very happy to have had the opportunity of meeting you this afternoon, and very grateful for the reception you have given me. I very much appreciate the work of the Bharatiya Bauddha Mahasabha in organizing this fine gathering. May you carry on Dhamma activities vigorously, and one day may we all meet again.

17

QUESTIONS AND ANSWERS
AT MILIND COLLEGE

Aurangabad, 23 January 1982

Before trying to answer the questions that have been handed to me, I would like to make a few remarks of a general nature. In the course of my travels in different parts of the world I am often asked questions about Buddhism, both theoretical and practical, spiritual and historical. But one thing I always like to make clear is that I am not a sort of oracle. So many questions come in, but it is not that to each specific question there is one specific answer which Sangharakshita is going to give you so that you then know the answer and can write it down for future reference. It isn't as simple as that. Asking questions about the Dhamma is not like asking questions about history or geography or physics or chemistry. If you were to ask me how far it is from the earth to the sun I could give you a straightforward factual answer, and it would be similar if you were to ask me the speed of light – not that I could tell you, but I could tell you what scientists who have studied the subject have said it is. (Not that *they*, even, really know what the speed of light is in another sense, but that is another question again.) If you were to ask me the date of the Battle of Hastings, or the date of Indian Independence, I could tell you. These are all factual questions, and to factual questions there can be factual answers.

But questions about the Dhamma are very rarely of this nature. Of course if you were to ask me in which century the Buddha lived, I could discuss the question on a factual basis and perhaps come to a definite conclusion. If you were to ask me whether, in the *āryamārga*, there are seven *aṅgas* or eight, then on the basis of the Pāli and Sanskrit texts I could tell you.[304] But most questions about the Dhamma are not of this factual nature; they are questions pertaining to what we call values, and these are very much more difficult to answer. Indeed, they are not just more difficult to answer: they have to be answered in a different sort of way.

Though I shall respond to your questions as best I can, I therefore doubt very much whether it will in the very nature of things be possible for me to give straightforward, factual answers. It is in this sense that I am not an oracle. What I may be able to do is to throw some light on the questions themselves, or to uncover some of the assumptions underlying the questions – assumptions of which the questioners themselves are perhaps not aware. I may also be able to point out the general ethical and spiritual principles which have to be taken into consideration in attempting to answer these questions.

We have to be very careful that we do not develop, in relation to the Dhamma, a sort of examination mentality. It is not as simple as that. In some ways it is *more* simple. It's a question of values. In my response to the questions that have been submitted I shall be trying to throw light on the *values* of Buddhism – on its basic, underlying ethical and spiritual principles. You have to try to apply these principles to your own life situation: to your practical problems, as well as to your theoretical difficulties. I can't hand you the answers, ready-made, on a plate.

So much by way of preliminary. There are about thirty questions, and I have an hour or so in which to answer them. That means two minutes for each question. Since some of the questions have been discussed for the last 2,500 years, that isn't a very long time, but I shall do my best. I have organized the questions into five groups, though between these groups there is a certain amount of overlap. This will enable me to deal with the questions more systematically, since it is rather irritating if one keeps jumping from one topic to another in a haphazard fashion. The five categories are as follows: (1) questions of a biographical – or autobiographical – nature. These come first, because they are the easiest to answer; (2) questions about Buddhist organizations; (3) questions about the social aspect of Buddhism, e.g. about Buddhist manners and customs; (4) questions about Buddhist spiritual practices; (5) questions of a philosophical nature. A number of these questions are about God. I don't know why you are still bothering about God, but apparently some of you still are. You will notice that I have arranged the questions in such a way that we start with relatively simple questions and progress towards questions that are rather more difficult.

1. QUESTIONS OF A BIOGRAPHICAL NATURE

Q: *Bhante, you discussed conversion with Dr Ambedkar, and you helped the propagation of Dhamma [in India], but after a few years you left for England and were busy with the propagation of the Dhamma in your motherland. It seems you could not concentrate fully on India.*

S: So the question is, why did I go back to England in 1964 instead of continuing to help the Buddhist conversion movement in this country? There were basically two reasons: a reason why I felt I should be in England, and a reason why I felt I should not be in India. The reason why I felt I should be in England was that, after what was originally intended to be only a brief visit, I came to the conclusion that there was great scope for the teaching of the Dhamma in England – in fact in the West generally. This is why I decided to prolong my stay there. But was there not scope for spreading the Dhamma in India? There certainly was, and I had been trying to spread the Dhamma here for a number of years. I lived here for more than twenty years, and for the last eight of those years I was associated with the movement of mass conversion. After the passing away of Dr Ambedkar I gave hundreds of lectures in different parts of Maharashtra.

Why, then, did I not carry on in this way? Why, having gone back to England, did I decide to start up my Buddhist work there? There were two connected reasons for this. In India I had usually worked on my own, and though I had gone from place to place giving lectures there was at that time no possibility of any follow-up. For follow-up a team is required, and at that time there was no team, no *sangha*, as we now have in Poona and even here in Aurangabad, and there seemed to be no possibility of developing a team. I therefore felt that I had gone as far as I could in India for the time being, and since I did not want to be giving lectures indefinitely, without the possibility of any follow-up, I decided to stay on in England. There I did create a team. Some members of that team have come to India, and we are in the process of creating a team here. This is the first of the two connected reasons why I felt I should not stay in India. Now, of course, I am working both in England and in India, as well as in a number of other countries.

The second reason for my not carrying on in India at that time was politics. After Dr Ambedkar's death there was, as you know, a great deal of confusion among his followers. There were a number of different political leaders, and these leaders were not always in agreement. As I went from place to place giving lectures, just an individual Buddhist monk, these leaders would try to induce me to identify myself with their political party. This sometimes created a very difficult and even unpleasant situation for me, because I did not want to identify myself with any particular group. I wanted to be the friend of all Buddhists, regardless of their political affiliation, regardless of whether they belonged to this or that faction. I saw them just as Buddhists. But some of the leaders did not want me to see people in that way. They tried to pull me in the direction of their own group, their own party, and this I could not tolerate. In the end the situation became so difficult and unpleasant that I felt I had better leave India for a while, to give the politicians time to come to their senses. Later on, I hoped, it might be possible for me to continue my work in India – and this is in fact what happened. Now, for a few weeks at least, I am concentrating fully on the Dhamma work in India.

Q: *Reverend Sir, have you forgotten your native place when doing religious work? If yes, is it necessary to forget it? If no, how can you devote [yourself] to religious work? Will you be successful in it?*
S: This question of forgetting one's native place is quite important, and quite relevant from the point of view of Dhamma work. I have already mentioned that I lived in India for upwards of twenty years. At that time I had no intention of ever returning to England. The idea never occurred to me until I received an urgent invitation from Buddhists in London, and even then I did not think of going immediately. The person who persuaded me to go was Bhikkhu Khantipalo, an English Buddhist monk who stayed with me for some time in Kalimpong. He put it to me that, inasmuch as I had been born and brought up in England, it was my duty to spend some time there.[305] I therefore agreed to go for four months. Four months became six months, six months became two years, and then, as I have explained, I decided to stay for a longer period.

I have come to the definite conclusion that it is a very useful thing, from the Dhamma point of view, to spend some time, preferably several years, away from the country of one's birth. On account of our having been born in a particular place, we have all sorts of limitations. We see things in a particular way, or from a particular point of view. We grow up with a particular kind of psychological conditioning. If we want to overcome that conditioning and develop a broader outlook – if we want to see things from a loftier standpoint – it is very helpful to go and spend some time in another country. This helps us to see things just as a human being – not as an Englishman, or an Indian, or an American, or a Frenchman. As Buddhists we ought to have this wider experience and this wider outlook. Therefore, though I would not say it is *necessary*, from the point of view of the Dhamma work, to go and work in another country, it is often very helpful.

The situation in India is not quite the same as it is in England. To begin with, India is not just a country but a subcontinent. There are a number of states and union territories, each with its own language and, very often, its own culture. Therefore, in the case of people working for the Dhamma in India it is not, perhaps, so much a question of going outside India as of going to another state. If you are a Maharashtrian, go and work in Gujarat; if you are a Gujarati, go and work in Andhra Pradesh, and so on. This will give you a broader outlook, as we sometimes find happening in the case of central government officials and university professors. In the course of their careers they are transferred from one part of the country to another, and this broadens their outlook. They become less parochial, less identified with purely local attitudes and interests.

From the Dhammic point of view, we don't *have* to forget our native place, we don't have to forget our own state or our own language, but it is a very good and helpful thing if we can go outside our own place for a while and gain a broader perspective, a more universal, a more truly human outlook. The more we are able to emancipate ourselves from exclusive local loyalties and patriotisms the better shall we be able to work for the Dhamma.

In the different areas where different Buddhist 'locality loyalty' as we may call it, or 'locality patriotism', is very strong, it is sometimes to the detriment of the overall Dhamma activities. People are intensely devoted to their own locality, to the place where they live, and where their parents and grandparents lived before them. They want everything to happen there. They want every meeting to be held there. They don't like it if sometimes meetings are held in other places. That kind of locality loyalty, or locality patriotism, we must learn to transcend.

2. QUESTIONS ABOUT BUDDHIST ORGANIZATIONS

Q: *There is only one world Buddhist organization in the world. Why is there no homogeneity in the moral principles of Buddhism?*
S: I take it that the questioner is referring to the World Fellowship of Buddhists. The WFB meets every two years, and meetings are attended by Buddhists from all over the world. They discuss matters of general interest. The great weakness of this organization is that it has not yet devised any way of implementing its resolutions. Since the WFB was founded in 1950 I believe some hundreds of resolutions have been passed, but very few of them have actually been implemented in the different Buddhist countries.[306]

The questioner goes on to ask why there is no homogeneity in the moral principles in Buddhism. I am not so sure that there is no such homogeneity. I don't think that Buddhists in any Buddhist country would refuse to accept, for instance, the five *sīlas*, and very likely there are none that would refuse to accept the ten *kusala dhammas*. To that extent, I would say, there is in fact homogeneity in the moral principles of Buddhism. If you go beyond the five *sīlas* and the ten *kusala dhammas* there may not be unanimity, but so far as *they* are concerned, I am reasonably certain that there is. I would even go so far as to say that if you consciously reject the five *sīlas* or the ten *kusala dhammas*, you cannot really be considered a Buddhist. Thus there is homogeneity, there is unity, at least on that very basic level.

Q: *Dhamma and politics are two different fields, so why is a missionary, instead of working for religion, involved in politics?*
S: I take it, though I can't be completely certain, that the missionary referred to is a Christian missionary. Is this the case, or am I jumping to conclusions? Is the gentleman who handed in this question present? (*Comment from the audience to the effect that a Buddhist missionary was meant.*) A Buddhist missionary! Well, I don't personally like the word 'missionary'. The term 'missionary' arose in connection with Christianity. In Buddhism the equivalent term is *dhammadūta*. If the question is, 'Why is a Buddhist missionary or *dhammadūta*, instead of

working for religion, involved in politics?' I must confess I just do not know. I would have to meet such a person and ask him.

My personal conviction is that being a Buddhist *dhammadūta*, and working for religion, is quite incompatible with being involved in practical politics. One can certainly, as a Buddhist *dhammadūta*, have one's own personal *philosophical* views about politics. That is another matter. If, for instance, as a Buddhist *dhammadūta*, you say that in your opinion a republican type of political organization is more in accordance with the spirit of the Dhamma than a monarchical type of political organization, *that* is not being involved in politics. That is a matter of political philosophy. You can discuss the relationship between the Dhamma on the one hand and political philosophy on the other without ceasing to be a *dhammadūta* and without becoming involved in politics in a practical sense. What the *dhammadūta* must not do, I believe, is become actively involved in party politics, because this will inevitably bring you into conflict with other people of other parties: it will almost inevitably engender unskilful mental states; and to that extent your usefulness as a *dhammadūta* will be limited.

3. QUESTIONS ABOUT THE SOCIAL ASPECT OF BUDDHISM

Q: *It has been repeatedly written by Dr Babasaheb Ambedkar that morality is Dhamma and that Dhamma is morality. What is the sanction behind morality?*
S: In other words, what is the sanction behind the sanction? Or, what is the sanction behind the sanction behind the sanction? If you are not careful, you have here what is known in logic as a *regressus ad infinitum*. You just go back and back, as when you ask, 'Who made the world?' 'God made the world.' 'Well, who made God?' 'Some higher God.' 'Well, who made *him*?' 'Some higher God still.' In that way you go back and back and back. So what is the sanction behind morality? Does morality have to have a sanction? Perhaps you should consider that question. Perhaps you should ask yourself what you mean by a sanction, what you mean by morality.

Well, what is morality? What is *sīla*? Dr Ambedkar seems to use the word 'morality' in a very broad sense, in the sense in which it is used by Western moral philosophers, that is to say, as pertaining to anything that concerns the development of the individual human being. So what is the sanction behind that development? What is it that says, 'You must be moral'? It can't be God – not for Buddhism. What, then, can it be? *Who* can it be? It cannot be an abstract principle, because then you become involved in a *regressus ad infinitum*. So what is it? What is the sanction behind morality, behind *śīla*?

Perhaps so far we've been on the wrong track. Perhaps it isn't a question of *what* is the sanction at all. Perhaps it's a question of *who* is the sanction. I am only making suggestions, so please don't think I am giving answers. Who, then, is the sanction? Well, perhaps *you* are the sanction. You practise *śīla* because *you* want to practise *śīla. Why* do you practise *śīla*? You practise *śīla* because you want to develop. And why do you want to develop? You want to develop because it is your nature as a human being to want to develop. *That* is the sanction. You can't have a more ultimate sanction than that. Therefore I would say that the sanction of morality is the individual's own innate desire to develop to higher and ever higher levels of being and consciousness. Morality requires no further, no higher, sanction than that.

Q: *Does the Buddha give a social message? If so, is it beyond that of fundamental human rights?*
S: I take it that the fundamental human rights referred to are those laid down by the United Nations organization. From a Buddhist point of view there cannot be a greater or more fundamental right than the right to evolve, the right to develop as a human being; and that right cannot be given to you by any external authority or organization. You as it were give yourself that right inasmuch as you are a human being. You say, 'I will evolve, I will develop, I will lead a better life. I will attain to higher levels of being and consciousness.' Thus you give yourself that right. That you wish to go further, wish to go higher – that you wish to *develop* – is an expression of your very nature as a human being. No external sanction, no external permission, is necessary.

The Buddha gives a social message in that according to the Buddha's teaching the type of social organization under which men live should be of such a nature as to help rather than hinder them in their development as human beings. If 'fundamental human rights' fail to make that clear, then they are not truly fundamental and the Buddha's social message goes beyond them.

Q: *It is observed that various religious rituals are followed in different parts of the country. In such a situation which marriage rituals should be observed among the Buddhists? Explain.*

S: I must admit I am a little out of practice here. It is a long time since I blessed a Buddhist marriage, though some of my *dasa sīla upāsaka* friends have been involved in this way. But when I started travelling around Maharashtra in the early days of the mass conversion movement, immediately after the passing away of Dr Ambedkar, the first question I was asked was, 'How do we celebrate Buddhist marriage?' People seemed more interested in this topic than in any other, because whether you were a Hindu or whether you were a Buddhist, life went on. People were being born, people were getting married, and people were dying, so that there had to be the *namkaran-vidhi*,[307] the *lagna-vidhi*,[308] and so on. For some reason or other the newly converted Buddhists seemed to attach extraordinary importance to the *lagna-vidhi*. They wanted bigger and bigger, and grander and grander, wedding celebrations. Admittedly the celebrations were conducted in a neater and more artistic manner than when they were Hindus, but a lot of money was still being spent. Bride and bridegroom would be dressed in white, the pandal would be decorated in white, and two, three, or four hundred guests would be fed. Usually no liquor would be served, though I would sometimes hear of this being done in out-of-the-way villages where the conversion movement had not really penetrated.

I started thinking that giving so much importance to the *lagna-vidhi* or marriage ceremony was a sort of leftover from the old Hindu way of thinking. I am not saying that the *lagna-vidhi* should not be celebrated properly. It represents a very important event in the lives of the people concerned. But we must have a sense of proportion. What I started finding was that everybody wanted to have their *lagna-vidhi* on Vaiśākha Pūrṇimā Day, i.e. the Buddha Jayanti Day.

[At this point there was a contribution from the floor, enlarging on the importance of the question inasmuch as the courts do not recognize the legality of the Buddhist marriage ceremony unless the Hindu *saptapadas* or 'seven steps' are performed. Sangharakshita then enquired whether it was possible, in India, for those who are Buddhist by faith to undergo a civil marriage ceremony. No clear reply to this question being forthcoming, he pursued the topic as follows.]

Perhaps I could say a few words about Buddhist marriages in England and in New Zealand, as I know a little about both of these. In England Buddhist marriages as such, i.e. marriages celebrated solely with Buddhist rites, are not legally recognized. If two Buddhists want to get married they have to have a civil wedding at the local Registry Office. Afterwards, if they so wish, they can have a Buddhist blessing on their marriage, but that does not add anything to the legal status of the marriage. We have been informed that if we have a registered place of worship we can apply for a member of the Order to be recognized as competent to perform legal marriages. That person would be *individually* recognized, and a Buddhist marriage ceremony performed by him in a Buddhist registered place of worship would be recognized in law without the civil ceremony at the Registry Office. That is the position in England. So far no member of the Order has cared to apply for the necessary recognition. Most Western Buddhists feel that it is sufficient to have a civil marriage at a Registry Office, with perhaps a Buddhist ceremony afterwards. In New Zealand, one member of our Order has applied for, and received, permission to celebrate legal marriages in a Buddhist registered place of worship, and I believe he has actually performed one or two such marriages. [If there is such a thing as a civil marriage in India, it might be possible for Indian Buddhists to have a civil wedding followed by a Buddhist marriage ceremony *without* the *saptapadī*[309] in much the same way that Buddhists in England and New Zealand do.]

It is interesting that there have been contributions from the floor in connection with this question, but not in connection with any other question. As Principal Chitnis remarked, it is a burning topic. All the same, now that we are Buddhists, the question of the *lagna-vidhi* or marriage ceremony should not loom so large in our consciousness as perhaps it did when we were Hindus. Whether or not it has legal status, let us celebrate the Buddhist *lagna-vidhi* with simplicity and dignity, and in a manner which is appropriate to the Dhamma and to ourselves as followers of the Dhamma. As for which marriage rituals should be observed, this is mainly a question of our unifying existing practices. If the *namkaran-vidhi*, the *lagna-vidhi*, and the *antima sanskar vidhi*[310] are all celebrated in the same manner everywhere in India, particularly in Maharashtra, this will contribute to the unity of the whole Buddhist movement.[311]

Q: *Bhante, will you please make it clear how we should respect or honour the* bhikkhus *who come to our place at home. Is it that we should fold our hands, or do prostration, or are there other ways?*

S: The answer to this question is quite simple. It is found in the Buddhist texts themselves. A number of *suttas* tell us how various people came to see the Buddha, and to listen to the Dhamma. Some of these people, the *suttas* say, on coming into the Buddha's presence saluted him with folded hands and announced their names. This was the ancient Indian custom. Others, on coming into the Buddha's presence, sat down without any salutation and without announcing their names. Others, on coming into his presence, prostrated themselves before him, even embracing his feet. People behaved in all these different ways. But the Buddha never told them that they should salute him in this or that particular way. He never said anything about it. People were free to salute him in whatever way they wished.[312]

Different people have different feelings, and different ways of showing respect. In Western countries people don't show respect by the *namskara*, the salutation used in India. They greet you by shaking you by the hand. It means the same thing. Muslims, I believe, have to cover the head when they pray. Without covering the head they cannot enter the mosque. But if you were to enter a Christian church in England with your head covered (if you were a man, that is) it would be considered highly disrespectful. So in one religion, *covering* the head is a sign of respect, and in another religion *uncovering* it is a sign of respect. The external action is of no significance in itself. It is the inner feeling that counts.

Thus if the Buddha did not lay down, with regard to himself, any precise mode of salutation, how can we say that there is a way in which we should, or should not, show respect to *bhikkhus*? It is a question of your personal feeling. If you feel like saluting the *bhikkhu* with a *namskara*, salute him with a *namskara*. If you feel like prostrating, very well, prostrate. If you feel like shaking hands with him, then shake hands! It doesn't matter, it's just a question of your personal feeling. When Eastern *bhikkhus* come to England they are sometimes surprised that people don't prostrate themselves, but Western Buddhists are not in the habit of prostrating. They don't even salute with a *namskara*. They just say, 'Hello, Bhante!' This tends to upset our Thai and Sinhalese *bhikkhu* friends, and they say, 'These Western Buddhists have no *śraddhā*.' But that is not true. Western Buddhists have just as much *śraddhā* as Buddhists in the East, but they show it in a different way. We can't lay down any hard and fast rule. If you invite a *bhikkhu* to your house, receive him in accordance with your own feelings. Presumably if you didn't have a positive feeling of *śraddhā*, you wouldn't invite him. But the way you show that feeling when he enters the house, whether by a salutation with folded hands or in any other way, is entirely a matter of your personal choice. In some Theravāda Buddhist countries they insist that the *upāsaka* must do a full *panchang-pranam*[313] to every *bhikkhu* and *sāmaṇera*, but this is not really in accordance with the Buddhist texts and, I would say, not in accordance with the spirit of Buddhism. So follow your own feeling. What is important is that you should actually feel *śraddhā* and express it in the way that is natural and appropriate to you.

Q: *Oldenberg, the German scholar on Buddhism, says, 'Buddhism is not a religion for the lowly and ignorant.'*
S: Well, Oldenberg lived a long time ago. He was a distinguished Pāli and Sanskrit scholar and wrote a famous book called *Buddha: His Life, His Doctrine, His Order*. But I am afraid he has been superseded. He is out of date.[314] He may have been a good scholar, but he didn't have a deep understanding of Buddhism as a spiritual tradition. Buddhism is for everybody, whether high or low, learned or ignorant. (I take it that by ignorant is meant uneducated, or illiterate.) I remember that when I was going round the towns and villages of Maharashtra giving lectures to the newly initiated Buddhists, some of my highly educated caste Hindu friends used to ask me what I talked to them about. I used to reply that I talked about *śīla, samādhi,* and *prajñā,* about *anātmavāda,* about Nirvāṇa, and about *śūnyatā.* These Hindu friends of mine would then say, 'But do the villagers understand such things? They are very ignorant people: they are illiterate.' I would say, 'They may be ignorant in the sense of not being highly educated, but their natural intelligence is as good as that of the educated person. It is simply that they have received no formal education.' In my experience, a so-called uneducated or illiterate audience is just as capable of understanding the finer points of Buddhist philosophy as any other. People who have been to college very often have a superiority complex and think that they are the only people with any intelligence, but actually villagers without any education are often highly intelligent. They are capable of understanding anything

of Buddhist philosophy that you care to explain to them – provided, of course, that you explain it clearly and simply, in a practical way, with illustrations. So we should not make too much of the distinction between those who are 'ignorant', in the sense of having received no formal education, and those who are not so ignorant.

As for the lowly, what does one mean by 'lowly'? Is it 'socially low', i.e. low in the social scale? In that case I don't see that your social position makes any difference to your understanding of Buddhism. The fact that you are rich and live in a large and luxuriously appointed house doesn't make you any more capable of understanding Buddhism than you would have been if the conditions under which you lived were different.

There is a curious misunderstanding in Buddhist countries such as Sri Lanka and Thailand. *Bhikkhus* from these countries often maintain that in the West it is only highly educated, upper class intellectuals who are capable of understanding Buddhism, but I have certainly not found this to be the case. In our own Buddhist movement, we have people of all social classes and all types of educational background – including one or two who cannot read or write. Many people in our movement have received only an elementary education, but some of them have a better understanding of the Dhamma than some of those who went to university. Academic qualifications have very little to do with ability to understand the Dhamma. We mustn't fall victim to this educational-cum-intellectual snobbery and think that because we have been to college or university, we alone are capable of understanding Buddhism.

Q: *In ancient India during the lifetime of the Buddha and after, until the fall of Buddhism, there was only the Buddhist Order and no Buddhist society. After the conversion of Dr Babasaheb Ambedkar the Buddhist community has become distinct. Is it not desirable to have separate rites and rituals for the sustenance of the New Society?*
S: The answer is definitely yes. When Dr Ambedkar observed that in India there was for many centuries a strong Buddhist *sangha* but a weak Buddhist laity, he put his finger on a very important point. Very often the ordinary layman, even the *upāsaka*, patronized not only the *bhikkhus* and the viharas but also the Hindu temples. Thus the lay community was on the whole quite weak: it was only the *bhikkhu sangha* that was

strong. When the *bhikkhus* and the viharas or Buddhist monasteries were destroyed, Buddhism itself gradually disappeared. It is therefore very important that we now build up a strong Buddhist community. This is why in England, in our Friends of the Western Buddhist Order [called here TBMSG], we place so much emphasis on the Going for Refuge. It is the act of going for Refuge that makes you a Buddhist. Whether you are a *bhikkhu* or an *upāsaka* is of secondary importance. What is really important is the fact that you go for Refuge and practise Buddhism. All of you who practise Buddhism together, whether you are *bhikkhus*, *anagārikas*, or *upāsakas*, *you* make up the Buddhist community. It is not a question of having a *bhikkhu saṅgha* and a semi-Hindu or semi-Christian lay following. Such an arrangement is worthless. By virtue of the fact that you have all gone for Refuge you constitute a fully integrated Buddhist community, or Buddhist society, with its own distinctive rituals, as Dr Ambedkar suggested. A community of this type is absolutely necessary for the safeguarding and perpetuation of the Dhamma – certainly in India, where there are so many powerful non-Buddhist and even anti-Buddhist influences working upon us all the time.

Q: *Poverty-stricken people welcome communism. How can we convince poor people of the philosophy of Buddhism unless their primary material needs are fulfilled?*
S: It has been said that one should not preach religion to a man with an empty stomach. If you are hungry it is very difficult to listen to a religious discourse. In a society where people's primary material needs are not being met, a dynamic to change society is needed. It was Dr Ambedkar's conviction that that dynamic, so far as Indian society was concerned, could come ultimately only from religion, and especially from Buddhism. I observed this myself when I was moving around in Maharashtra all those years ago. When I asked ordinary, illiterate village people what difference conversion had made to them they invariably gave the same answer. What answer people would give now I don't know, but at that time they always gave the same answer, quite spontaneously. They said, 'Now that we are Buddhists we feel free!' If you have that sort of spirit, you can do anything, you can change anything. You can change the conditions under which you live. If someone is hungry, you have to feed him, and *then* give him the Dhamma; but from a broader point of view

it is only the Dhamma that can supply the social dynamic which is going to change the whole society.

Q: *Is it possible to eradicate Hinduism and substitute Buddhism in the present situation?*
S: In my lectures in Maharashtra twenty years ago, I used to say that it wasn't possible for anyone to be a one-hundred-percent Buddhist unless everybody was a Buddhist. In India, unfortunately, other people won't let you be a one-hundred-percent Buddhist. If you want to be a one-hundred-percent Buddhist then you have to have a one-hundred-percent Buddhist society. If you want to have full social equality, for instance, what you really have to do is convert everybody to Buddhism. This is what I used to say, and I still think it is true. In India you can't just have a minority that is Buddhist. Formerly there were millions of Buddhists in India, but even so Buddhism died out. I therefore propose it as a really serious objective that we should spread Buddhism all over India and bring everybody into the Buddhist fold. It seems a tremendous task, but during my early days in India, there were only a few thousand Buddhists. Had you told me at that time that within fifteen or twenty years there would be 3,000,000 Buddhists I wouldn't have believed you. So if I now tell you that within a hundred years time there will perhaps be 100,000,000 Buddhists, you may not be able to believe me. But there *could* be as many as that. It really is possible. Therefore I think we should take as our penultimate – not our ultimate – aim the conversion of everybody in India to Buddhism. We have made a very good start in Maharashtra, where there are now 3,000,000 Buddhists. I know very well that they are not perfect Buddhists, but at least they say they are Buddhists and they are willing to try to be Buddhists, and that's a very good start. If by Hinduism one means the *varṇāśrama-dharma*, or what is generally known as the caste system, to eradicate Hinduism in that sense must clearly be our aim. It is very difficult to live as a Buddhist when that pernicious system is being practised all around one, and when other people are constantly trying to draw you into it and treat you in accordance with its requirements, instead of treating you as a Buddhist or just as a human being. So yes, we must work for the eradication of Hinduism in the sense of the caste system. We should work peacefully and non-violently, of course, and by democratic means, but there should be no doubt what our objective really is.

4. QUESTIONS ABOUT BUDDHIST SPIRITUAL PRACTICE

Q: *Does faith play a part in our lives, and is this connected with the existence of God?*

S: Faith plays a very important part in our lives inasmuch as we often have to act without full knowledge of a situation; that is, we have to act, to some extent at least, out of faith. If we have never been to Bombay, for instance, we do not really *know* that there is such a place, but we buy a ticket and take the train to Bombay nevertheless. We have *faith* that Bombay is there. Faith in God is rather a different thing. There are many things the causes of which we do not understand, so we say they are caused by God. Faith in God means using the concept of God as a principle of explanation for all those things the reason for which we do not understand. People used to think that God sent the rain, but now they know that rain falls on account of certain meteorological conditions, so they no longer have faith in God as the sender of rain.

In Buddhism, faith (*śraddhā*) has quite a different meaning. It means our positive emotional response to the Buddha, the Dhamma, and the Sangha, i.e. to the ideal of Human Enlightenment, to the path leading to the realization of that state of Enlightenment, and to all the people who are treading that path. It means the happiness and joy with which we are filled by the very thought of these three things. Faith is one of the five spiritual faculties, i.e. one of the five human qualities which are to be cultivated if we wish to attain Enlightenment.[315] It must always be balanced by wisdom. In Buddhism there is no such thing as blind faith.

Q: *What are the methods to obtain* vimukti?

S: One could say a lot on this topic, but the simplest answer is the traditional one, i.e. that *vimukti* is obtained by the practice of *śīla*, *samādhi*, and *prajñā* – not forgetting *maitrī* and *karuṇā*, because where there is *prajñā* there will be *karuṇā*. There is no esoteric answer to this question, no special mantra that gives realization immediately. We just have to plod on, day after day, month after month, with our *śīla*, i.e. *pañcasīla* and *dasa-sīla*; we have to plod on with our *samādhi*, i.e. *ānāpānasati* and *mettā bhāvanā*, and finally plod on with our *prajñā*, i.e. *śruta-mayī prajñā*, *cintā-mayī prajñā*, and *bhāvanā-mayī prajñā*.

Plodding on in this way, gradually we will become liberated and experience *vimukti*. Gradually we will become free from the *saṃskāras*, free from ignorance, free from psychological conditioning.

5. QUESTIONS OF A PHILOSOPHICAL NATURE

Q: *Can Buddhism as taught by the Buddha be regarded as thoroughly empirical, having no reference to a supersensuous world?*
S: Buddhism is thoroughly empirical – I think that is obvious – but it is not necessarily empirical in the sense of being confined to the world of the five senses. You can be empirical with regard to higher levels of consciousness as well, inasmuch as you actually experience those levels and draw conclusions from them. So far as Buddhism is concerned, what is important is that you should not merely have faith in the existence of supersensuous worlds, or supersensuous levels of consciousness, but that you should have actual experience of them, for example through meditation, and then draw conclusions from your experience. In so doing you are still being thoroughly empirical.

Q: *If the answer to this is positive, how can rebirth be explained?*
S: The question of rebirth seems to be quite a difficult one for a number of people. In this regard one can say that if one distinguishes the material or physical level of existence from the mental or supersensuous level, then clearly when somebody dies and when the physical body disintegrates, if there is any continuity of anything it can only be on the mental or supersensuous level. Hence if one is to accept rebirth one needs to accept, also, a supersensuous level of existence on which it is possible for the kind of continuity that rebirth implies to take place. The important point to remember is that when one speaks of rebirth one is not speaking of it in the sense of the continuation of an unchanging mental entity or *ātman*. One is speaking of the continuation of a process. For this reason rebirth does not, for Buddhism, involve any *ātman*. It is a process without any subject which undergoes that process. For example, in English we say, 'It's raining.' Now where is this 'it' to be found? What is this 'it' which is said to be raining? Well, it doesn't exist. It is a mere linguistic convention – a grammatical subject without any objective reality to which it corresponds. All that exists is the process of the rain falling. There is no 'rain' which is falling separate from 'the falling of

the rain'. In the same way there is no 'being' being reborn apart from the actual process of rebirth itself. There is no subject, especially no unchanging subject, of that process. Therefore in Buddhism we have rebirth, but we do not have anyone that is reborn.

Q: *Buddhism does not believe in the existence of God or Ātman, yet in the* Tripiṭaka *such words as Brahmā and Indra are used. Please explain in what sense these words have been used in the* Tripiṭaka.
S: In Buddhism there is no God with a capital G, but in the *Tripiṭaka* we do find references to gods – in the plural – with a small 'g'. Whether the Buddha himself literally believed in the existence of these gods, or whether he was simply using the language of his times and they were just figures of speech, it is now very difficult to know. In a sense it does not matter, because it is very clear from the Pāli *Tipiṭaka* that these gods – Brahmā, Indra, and so on – have nothing at all to do with the path to Nirvāṇa. They are, so to speak, personifications of worldly or natural powers. In the case of Indra this is very clear. Indra is a Vedic deity connected with thunder and rainstorms. When you speak of Indra it is thunder, or the rainstorm, to which you are really referring. Indra is a sort of poetic personification of that particular natural phenomenon. Thus even though the names of these deities occur in the Pāli *Tipiṭaka*, the reference is ultimately to the phenomena of the natural world. They have nothing whatever to do with the path to Nirvāṇa, so recognizing them has nothing to do with Buddhism. As Buddhists we do not recognize them as gods, but we may recognize them as poetic descriptions of natural phenomena – descriptions which came naturally to people of former times.

Q: *Does God exist? If not, how would you explain the phenomenon of miraculous success in hopeless cases where only God was expected to help?*
S: There are two questions here. First of all, it is not incumbent upon the Buddhist to prove that God does *not* exist. It is incumbent upon the believer in God to prove that he *does* exist. There are, in fact, quite a number of arguments purporting to prove that God does exist, but the Buddhist is not convinced by any of them. Therefore it is up to the non-Buddhist, up to the theist, to produce better arguments and convince the Buddhist. As for the phenomenon of miraculous cures in hopeless cases where only God was expected to help, before we can assign a cause to

something we must know all the conditions under which it took place. In every country so-called miraculous cures do happen. Someone is treated by all the best doctors, but he doesn't get any better. A holy man then comes along and says, 'Bless you my son,' gives some *bhasma* or, in a Christian country, makes the sign of the cross, and the person gets better. The fact that he gets better does not constitute a proof that the holy man, or the *bhasma*, or the sign of the cross cured that person. To think that it does involves the logical fallacy of 'consequent to, therefore because of'. Before you can say that any of these factors was the cause of the so-called miraculous cure you have got to be able to show an actual causal connection and reproduce that experimentally in a laboratory, under test conditions. Sometimes people just get better, even without treatment. Sometimes it so happens that, by sheer coincidence, they get better at the very moment that the holy man comes along. So they say that it is all due to his blessing, but there is no proof of this. The fact that two events occur at the same moment does not mean that one is the cause of the other. God, as represented by the holy man etc., cannot be invoked as the author of the miracle. 'Miracles' of this sort do not therefore constitute a proof of the existence of God.

Q: *What is God?*
S: As a Buddhist, I don't have to answer this question. It is otiose, as the lawyers say.

Q: *What is Nirvāṇa?*
S: The traditional Buddhist definition is that it is the complete eradication of craving, hatred, and delusion, and the development of the spiritual qualities which are the positive counterparts of those states, i.e. unlimited generosity (*dāna*), universal love (*maitrī*), and infinite wisdom (*prajñā*). More than that we can hardly say. Nirvāṇa consists of the very best, the very greatest, and the very highest human qualities developed to a degree which, in our present unenlightened state, we find it difficult even to imagine.

Q: *Could you define* śūnyatā *in accordance with Buddhism?*
S: There are many bulky Mahāyāna *sūtras* dealing with *śūnyatā*, but after thinking about the matter for thirty or forty years I have come to the conclusion that it is really quite simple. All that the teaching of

śūnyatā means is that words, and even thoughts, are not adequate to explain the nature of reality. Even our experience as ordinary human beings transcends thought and speech. You see a beautiful sunset, but can you describe it? Do you have the words for it? You would like to be able to describe it, but you can't. Words and thoughts are both inadequate. *That* is *śūnyatā*.

18

RELIGION AND THE SECULAR STATE

Vishwa Hindu Parishad, Aurangabad, 23 January 1982

Brothers and Sisters: I am happy to be here this evening addressing members and friends of the Vishwa Hindu Parishad, the local branch of which has organized this function.[316] Until a few days ago, I had not heard of the existence of the Vishwa Hindu Parishad, but I have been given to understand that it was founded here in India some twenty years ago, that it is an international organization having activities in some thirty different countries throughout the world, and that it has three main objects. These objects are: (1) to bring together all Hindus regardless of sect, (2) to remove corruptions and abuses from the present-day Hindu society, and (3) to render service to the poor and downtrodden sections of society. These are very laudable, indeed excellent objects, with which nobody could disagree and which everybody must welcome. I believe that the Parishad has already achieved considerable success in carrying them out, and on this it is to be congratulated.

As you will have gathered from the introductory remarks, I have spent upwards of twenty years in India. From 1944 to 1964 I was, in fact, here almost continuously, my stay being interrupted only by visits to Sri Lanka, Singapore, and Nepal. During this time I came to know many Hindus, of many different sects and spiritual lineages, and had many Hindu friends. Even more importantly, I had the opportunity of meeting famous Hindu teachers and lineage gurus such as Anandamayi Ma, Swami Ramdas of Kanhangad, and Ramana Maharshi, with each of whom I spent several weeks. Moreover, on other occasions I had the opportunity of meeting the Shankaracharya of Shringeri Math and the Shankaracharya of Puri. With all these great personalities I entered into religious discussion.[317]

While I was in India I came to know not only many Hindus, which was perhaps natural, but also many people of other religions. Indeed, I became friends with people of many different religions, and was quite happy that this should be the case. For instance, I had many Sikh friends. The Sikhs, as you know, are followers of Guru Nanak and the other Sikh gurus. Sikhs are very well known. Since they wear turbans and beards, and sometimes carry *kirpans*,[318] they are easily recognizable, even in London. I also had many Parsi friends, especially in Bombay. The Parsis, of course, are followers of the great prophet Zarathustra, and therefore fire-worshippers. Then again I had Jain friends, both sannyasis and laymen. The Jains, as you know, are followers of the *tīrthankaras*, especially the last of them, Mahāvīra. Similarly I had many Christian friends, both Catholic and Protestant, who, though they might fight with each other, did not fight with me. I even had a few Jewish friends. One of these Jewish friends was a rabbi, or minister of the Jewish religion, but he got into trouble with his congregation for introducing some of Krishnamurti's ideas into his sermons. Besides these, I had friends who were Bahá'ís, or followers of the Bahá'í faith. All these friends, following so many different religions, used to organize meetings and lectures for me. Of course I also had many Buddhist friends during my twenty years in India. Even though, at the beginning of that period, the number of Buddhists in India was very small, I still had quite a few Buddhist friends in different parts of the country.

The question which therefore arises is: How was such a thing possible? How was it possible for me to have friends from all these different religions? First of all, it was possible because they all lived in one country. In India there are many different religions. Besides Hinduism and Buddhism, religions here include Jainism, Zoroastrianism, Sikhism, Islam, Christianity, and Judaism, together with their various sects and subdivisions, and their hundreds of different traditions. India is, in fact, very rich in religions, both those originating here and those introduced from abroad. On the whole, all these religions live together peacefully. Sometimes there are misunderstandings, even a little fighting, but generally speaking, they manage to live together quite peacefully. Now how is it possible for so many different religions to live peacefully together in this one country? It is possible because India is a secular state.

What, then, is a secular state? It is a state in which no religion in particular is favoured by the government above the rest, a state in which no particular religion is the official religion, no religion is discriminated against, and each individual is free to follow the religion of his own choice. Moreover, in a secular state everybody is free to propagate his own religion, subject only to considerations of law and order and public decency, and provided that in practising and propagating his own religion he does not infringe the rights of other people. This is what we mean by a secular state.

I was born and brought up in the United Kingdom, which is not a completely secular state. To begin with, the sovereign has to be a Christian, not a Roman Catholic but a Protestant, and has to belong to the Church of England. If the sovereign changes his religion he (or she) cannot remain on the throne. In England the Church of England enjoys various special privileges. We therefore cannot say that the United Kingdom is a completely secular state.

Similarly, Soviet Russia was not founded as a secular state, at least not in the sense in which I am using the term. In Soviet Russia Marxism-Leninism was established as the official religion, so to speak. Other systems of belief might be practised, but only to a limited extent. Propaganda on behalf of religion was not allowed, and religious books and magazines, whether Christian or non-Christian, could not be published. In Soviet Russia printing and publishing was, in any case, a government monopoly, and they only permitted the publication of Marxist literature, so that there was a black market in Bibles.

When I visited Nepal in 1949 and 1952 I found that it was not a secular state, but a Hindu kingdom, where the caste system was not only established but enforced by law. If you failed to observe the caste system you could be arrested by the police, and fined or even imprisoned. Sometimes people used to lose their caste by accident. For example, once when I was staying at the Buddhist monastery in Palpa Tansen there came a knock at the door very late one night. On opening it we found a Hindu gentleman standing outside, and the following conversation ensued:

'Could I stay at the monastery tonight?'

'Why do you want to stay?'

'I've had the misfortune to lose my caste, so I can't go home. My wife won't let me into the house, because if she did she would lose her caste too.'

'But how did you lose your caste?'

'It happened like this. I had been to Butaol on business, and on my way back to this place I fell ill and had to stay at an inn. There was no one to look after me except a very low-caste man, and since I ate food cooked by him I lost my caste. Please allow me to stay here tonight. In the morning I shall go to the police station, tell them what happened, and pay the fine. They will give me a certificate saying that I have got my caste back. I can then go home, and my wife will let me in.'

This is just one example of the sort of thing I witnessed many times in Nepal. The caste system was really very strong there. Indeed, even to criticize the caste system was against the law. Only a few years earlier a Nepalese Buddhist monk who had received his training in Burma had started speaking out against the caste system, saying that it was not in accordance with Buddhism, and that Buddhists should not observe caste. The result was that he was arrested by the police and taken before the hereditary Prime Minister who, after hearing what he had to say, personally flogged the *bhikkhu* with a whip, remarking, 'We can't allow that sort of talk in our Nepal.' The story was well known in Nepal, and years later I heard it from the *bhikkhu's* own mouth.[319] When I visited Nepal it was certainly not a secular state.

Thailand is not a secular state either. In Thailand Buddhism is the official religion, and the *bhikkhu saṅgha* or Order of Monks is controlled by the education department. Nonetheless, even though Buddhism is the official religion, all religions are tolerated, and religions other than Buddhism all enjoy complete freedom. One of the titles of the king of Thailand is 'Protector of All Religions'. Thus the King is not just the protector of Buddhism, but the protector of Hinduism, Christianity, and Islam as well, even though he himself is a Buddhist.

Malaysia too is not a secular state. Islam is the official religion of the country, and only very limited religious tolerance exists there. In Malaysia a Muslim is not, in fact, allowed to change his religion, so he cannot cease to be a Muslim even if he wants to. Such a state of affairs is, of course, usual in Muslim states, the traditional penalty for apostasy from Islam being death.

The United States of America is officially a secular state, but it is not totally secular. It resembles the United Kingdom a little in this respect. The Creator, i.e. God, is referred to in the Declaration of Independence, people take religious oaths prior to giving evidence in a court of law, and Christianity is taught in United States schools, whereas other religions are not.

I could go on giving examples in this way, but probably I have given enough. As I pointed out at the beginning, India is a secular state. Here one is free to follow the religion of one's choice, and the state neither favours any religion nor discriminates against any religion. That is the legal position, at least. In India it is therefore possible for the followers of many different religions to live together peacefully. Thus Indian society is what we call a pluralistic society, a society in which many different religions and cultural trends co-exist. Hinduism is the dominant trend, but this is not because it enjoys any special official recognition. It is due simply to the numerical superiority of the Hindus.

At this point I want to raise a question. We have seen that the secular state neither favours nor discriminates against any particular religion, and that in the secular state different religions co-exist in a peaceful manner, but what is it that makes this peaceful co-existence possible? It cannot be simply the *force majeure* of the state. This by itself would not be sufficient, because religious passions are very strong. What, then, are the general principles that all the different religions accept, the acceptance of which enables them to live together peacefully in the same state? This is the question into which I want to enter a little this evening.

There is quite a lot that could be said on the subject, but I am going to consider just one main principle, which I think underlies all the others. The main principle that allows different religions to co-exist in the same state is the principle that a human being is first and foremost a human being. All religions have to accept this principle if they want to live together in the same state. They may accept it explicitly or implicitly, willingly or unwillingly, but they have to accept it. They have to accept that man is first and foremost a human being and that he is, therefore, only secondly a Hindu, a Buddhist, a Muslim, a Christian, etc. If we accept that we are first and foremost human beings then we can relate to others as human beings. We can treat one another as human beings, live together as human beings. Regardless of whether we are Hindu, Muslim, or whatever, we can live together in the same state.

This idea that man is first and foremost a human being is comparatively recent. For a long time it was thought that a man was first and foremost a member of a particular tribe. Men who belonged to other tribes were not human beings, so to speak, and it was not wrong to kill them. It was wrong only to kill members of one's own tribe. This 'tribal' kind of thinking is still very strong, even in some religions.

If we accept the principle that a human being is first and foremost a human being, certain consequences follow for the different religions co-existing in the world. In particular, if a human being is first and foremost a human being, and only secondly a Hindu, Buddhist, Muslim, Christian, or whatever, it means that human beings are more important, and religion is less important. It means that religion exists for the sake of man, not man for the sake of religion. The real purpose of religion is to help human beings to develop, to help us become better human beings, to become perfect human beings, or to become what, in Buddhism, we call Enlightened.

Not all religions accept the essentially humanistic attitude, as we may call it, that a human being is first and foremost a human being, and that man is more important than religion – that religion exists for the sake of man. What, then, happens when a non-humanist religion exists within the framework of the secular state along with other religions, whether humanist or non-humanist? What happens is that it is forced to change. Let us look into this a little. Let us look at one or two of the ways in which certain religions have been forced to change.

First of all, Christianity. Though one speaks of Christianity it is not really possible to be just a Christian. You may try, but it isn't possible. You have to be either a Protestant, or a Roman Catholic, or some other variety of Christian – just as you can't really be just a Hindu but have to be a Brahmin Hindu, or a Kunbi Hindu, or a Chamar Hindu, and so on. Protestantism came into existence only towards the middle of the sixteenth century, and before that western Europe was dominated by the Roman Catholic Church. According to Roman Catholicism you were a Christian (i.e. a Roman Catholic) first and a human being afterwards – and only Christians were human beings at all. Other people were just pagans. If you killed them it was not a sin. In fact, it was a good deed. Nor was this all. Because you were first and foremost a Christian, you were not allowed to be anything *except* a Christian. You were not allowed to give up Christianity or to adopt another religion, and if you tried, you were executed, usually by being burned alive at the stake. This fate befell thousands of people, because at that time the Roman Catholic Church had political power in western Europe, and Christianity was the state religion in all the countries there.

This state of affairs lasted for many years, but now the situation has changed. In many western European countries (as in many eastern European ones), the Church no longer has political power, and Christianity is no longer the state religion. Now the Christian is free to change his religion if he wishes, and the Church cannot prevent him from doing this. In other words, Christianity has been forced to recognize that a human being is first and foremost a human being. Christianity has been made more humanistic. It has been forced to change, because now it exists within the secular state.

It is much the same in the case of Islam. A Muslim who lives in India is free to give up Islam and adopt some other faith, because India is a secular state. But a Muslim who lives in an Islamic state is not free to change his religion, and if he tries to do so, he may be executed. This is still the case, even today, in some Muslim states in the Middle East. In India, however, Islam has been forced to adopt a more humanistic attitude, because India is a secular state.

What about Hinduism? As I said earlier, one cannot be just a Hindu. You have to belong to a particular caste. Caste is determined, of course, by birth. You are a Brahmin because your parents were Brahmins, a Kunbi because your parents were Kunbis, a Chamar because your parents were Chamars. In this way Hindu society is divided into numerous castes – according to some authorities, not less than 2,000. These castes, and the various relationships between them, make up what we call the caste system. The basic feature of this system is inequality. Every caste is higher than some other caste or castes, every caste lower than some other caste or castes – except, of course, the caste at the very top and the caste at the very bottom. When it comes to deciding who is highest and who is lowest, there is no agreement, because while everybody would like to be highest nobody wants to be lowest. The caste system is therefore what Dr Ambedkar called a system of graded inequality.

Now I am not concerned this evening with the question of whether or not the caste system in this sense is really in accordance with the Hindu *dharma śāstras*. I am concerned with the caste system as it actually exists, and as it actually exists it is based on the principle of heredity and is a system of graded inequality. In what, then, does this inequality consist? Let me give you a few examples. Some people were not allowed to receive education, just because of their birth. They were not allowed to own property, not allowed to draw water from the common well. Some of them were even treated as untouchable. There is no need for me to multiply examples. Instances of inequality such as these are well known to every single one of you. In any case, the whole subject is extremely unpleasant and painful, and one does not wish to dwell on it unnecessarily.

In a secular state, certainly in a democratic secular state, everybody is equal, that is to say, everybody has exactly the same political and civic rights. All are equal in the eyes of the law. Everybody is entitled to receive education, to own property, to draw water from the common well. Nobody is branded as untouchable. Now, equality and inequality are incompatible. They cannot co-exist. The caste system cannot, therefore, survive in the secular state – not if that state is truly secular. In other words, Hinduism will be forced to change when it exists in the secular state. It will be forced to recognize that human beings are first and foremost human beings, and only secondly followers of a particular religion, or members of a particular caste. Nor is that all. In the secular state Hinduism will be forced to abandon the caste system altogether. One cannot treat people as equal and as unequal at the same time. The secular state obliges you to treat people as equal: it obliges you *not* to practise the caste system. To the extent that India is a secular state the caste system will not be practised. Conversely, to the extent that the caste system is practised, India is not a secular state. I am sure that members of the Vishwa Hindu Parishad are well aware of all this. As I mentioned at the beginning, you have three main objects. The second of these is to remove corruptions and abuses from present-day Hindu society, and the greatest of the corruptions and abuses is the system of hereditary caste, the system of graded inequality.

So how is one to get rid of this particular corruption? In my opinion there is only one way. Caste is based on the hereditary principle: you are a Brahmin on account of your having been born into a Brahmin family.

The caste system can be destroyed, therefore, only by destroying the hereditary principle. But how is this to be done? There is only one way. The hereditary principle can be destroyed only by intermarriage between the different castes – between *all* the different castes. If no Brahmin family exists, then it will not be possible for anyone to be born into a Brahmin family, and if no one is born into a Brahmin family there will be no Brahmins. Similarly with the other castes. In this way – and only in this way – will the caste system be abolished. I would request my friends of the Vishwa Hindu Parishad to give this matter of inter-caste marriage their very serious consideration.

I have spoken about Christianity in connection with the secular state, as well as about Islam and about Hinduism. But what about Buddhism? Buddhism has no difficulty at all in existing in the secular state. Indeed, Buddhism flourishes in the secular state. This is because Buddhism always puts human beings first and religion afterwards. According to Buddhism, the Dhamma is simply the means of human development. It is the means by which human beings become better, by which they become perfect or become what we call a Buddha. There is no need to have Buddhism as the state religion, as in Thailand. Buddhism does not need official support or encouragement. Under the conditions at present obtaining in the world, the less official support it has the better. Buddhism needs only the freedom that a secular state can give – a secular state like India. Indeed, we can see that the more truly secular India becomes, the more Buddhism will grow. Similarly, the more Buddhism grows, the more truly secular India will become. That is perhaps the significance of the Aśoka *cakra* – the *dhammacakka* – on the Indian national flag.

Buddhism is the religion of humanity. It is the religion of liberty, the religion of equality, the religion of fraternity. It is therefore inevitable that a free and independent India should turn more and more in the direction of Buddhism. It is inevitable that all thinking Hindus should move more and more in the direction of Buddhism, especially those who want to remove the corruptions and abuses of present-day Hindu society – especially those who are members and friends of the Vishwa Hindu Parishad, which has so kindly arranged this function tonight.

19

GETTING OUT OF THE BURNING HOUSE – TOGETHER

Aurangabad, 24 January 1982

Brothers and Sisters in the Dhamma: I am very happy to have the opportunity of addressing you this afternoon. I have now been in Aurangabad for practically a week, and in the course of that time I have met many people and addressed a number of meetings. This, however, is the last lecture I shall be giving in Aurangabad city – at least for the time being.

This afternoon I want to talk a little about Buddhist literature. More specifically, I want to talk about the Buddhist *sūtras*. The Buddha, as you know, did not actually write anything himself. He spent most of his time walking from village to village, and from town to town. In this way he met people of many different kinds, and he talked to them about the Dhamma, and answered their questions about the Dhamma, as well as about life itself.

In those days, 2500 years ago, there were no such thing as a tape-recorder, so the Buddha's teachings were preserved with the help of his disciple, Ānanda, the constant companion of his later years. Ānanda was a sort of human tape-recorder. As he had an exceptionally good memory, he was able to remember whatever the Buddha said, and what he remembered he repeated to the other disciples. After the Buddha's *parinirvāṇa* he repeated all the teachings he remembered in the presence of the entire *bhikkhu saṅgha*, and those *bhikkhus* who were present repeated what they had learned from Ānanda to their disciples, and they to their disciples. In this way the Dhamma was preserved, and eventually all these teachings were written down in book form.

In this written form the teachings were called *suttas* (Pāli) or *sūtras* (Sanskrit). The term *sutta* or *sūtra* literally means 'a thread', and as a literary term it signifies a number of teachings strung together, as it were, on a single thread, that is, connected by a common theme – just like the beads of a *jap-māla*.[320] *Sūtras* are therefore sometimes quite long. Some are in Pāli, while others are in what is known as Buddhist Hybrid Sanskrit, which is quite different from Classical or Paninian Sanskrit. Scholars used to think that Buddhist Hybrid Sanskrit was simply bad Sanskrit, that is to say irregular, ungrammatical Classical Sanskrit. But now Buddhist Hybrid Sanskrit is recognized as a distinct and separate language.

One of the most important *sūtras* to be written in Buddhist Hybrid Sanskrit is the *Saddharma Puṇḍarīka Sūtra*, or the *Sūtra of the White Lotus of the Real (or True) Dhamma*. This is quite a long *sūtra*. In fact it is as long as an average book. It is particularly popular with the Buddhists of China and Japan, and it is also quite popular with Western Buddhists. No less than three complete translations of this *sūtra* have been made into the English language. There are various reasons for the great popularity of the *Saddharma Puṇḍarīka Sūtra*, one of them being that it contains many beautiful stories. These are not ordinary stories, but stories with a profound Dhammic meaning, or what are known in English as parables.

This afternoon I want to talk about one of these parables. It is called the Parable of the Burning House, and the story is told, of course, by the Buddha. Once upon a time, the Buddha said, there was a very rich old man who lived with a large number of dependants in a big old house with very many rooms. Because it was so old the house was in very bad condition, and in danger of falling down any minute. Moreover, though there were so many rooms, there was only one door. One day a great fire broke out, and soon the whole house was ablaze. Now among the old man's dependants were many children. The *sūtra* says that the old man had thirty children, and all these children were in the house at the time the fire broke out, and they were all playing – even though the house was on fire.

The old man, their father, had to think very quickly. He knew it wasn't difficult for him to get out of the burning house himself, but he wanted to save the children too, because he loved them very dearly. The children did not realize that the house was on fire and that their lives were in danger. As the custom is with children, they were totally absorbed in their games, and had no care for anything else. The old man called out to them, 'Come out quickly! The house is on fire!' – but the children were so deeply absorbed in their games that they took no notice of their father.

The old man therefore thought of a stratagem. Knowing that his children were very fond of toys, especially carts, he again called out to them, saying, 'Come out quickly, all of you! I have beautiful riding carts for you – carts drawn by goats, by deer, and by bullocks. They are standing right outside the door. Come and get them!' This time the children all came rushing out – out through the single door, and out of the burning house. They were saved, and the old man, their father, was overjoyed. He gave all of them the same kind of carts – the best kind. He gave them big, beautifully decorated bullock carts drawn by bullocks that were as fast as the wind.[321]

What is the meaning of the story? What is the burning house? Who is the rich old man? Who are the children? What are the carts? Let us go into this a little. The burning house is easily explained. It is this world, this *saṃsāra*. It is inhabited by all kinds of living beings and it is very old – according to modern science, millions of years old. Since it is so old it is in quite a bad condition, and in danger of falling down any minute. In other words, the world is impermanent. No worldly thing lasts for very long. Besides this, the world, the *saṃsāra*, is burning with the fires of greed, hatred, and delusion. This is what the burning house represents.

As for the rich old man, he is the Buddha. Just like a father he feels *maitrī* and *karuṇā* towards all living beings. He wants to help them get out of the *saṃsāra* – wants them to overcome their difficulties and be happy. He wants them to overcome greed, hatred, and delusion. In short, he wants to show everybody the path to Enlightenment. So he calls out. This calling out is the Buddha's teaching of the Dhamma – his teaching of *śīla*, *samādhi*, and *prajñā*. But the children take no notice.

Who, then, are the children? The children represent all human beings. *We* are the children. We don't listen to the Buddha. We don't really want to get out of the burning house; we don't really want to get rid of greed, hatred, and delusion. The reason we don't want to listen to the Buddha or practise the Dhamma is that we are absorbed in our own little games. There are many different kinds of games that human beings play. Some people don't hear the Dhamma because they are busy making money, some because they are busy running after political power, some because they are busy fighting and quarrelling, and some because they are busy drinking. These are just some of the games in which people get absorbed. The result is that they don't want to listen to the Dhamma. They think such things as *śīla*, *samādhi*, and *prajñā* very dull and uninteresting.

This reminds me of something that happened in Kalimpong, a town in the Darjeeling District of West Bengal where I lived for many years. One day I was sitting in my room writing. It so happened that I was writing something about *śīla*, *samādhi*, and *prajñā*. As I sat at my desk, a very elderly, quite senior *bhikkhu* came to see me. When he saw what I was writing he was very surprised. He said, 'Sangharakshita, why are you wasting your time writing about that dull, old-fashioned stuff?' I too was very surprised. I thought, 'Even a very elderly, quite senior *bhikkhu* doesn't want to get out of the burning house!' This is the situation nowadays.

Anyway, in the *sūtra* the Buddha again calls out to the children. He doesn't relax his efforts. He speaks to the children in their own language, as it were – speaks in a way that will appeal to them. He promises them different kinds of carts to play with. These carts represent the different ways in which the Buddha teaches the Dhamma. The Buddha doesn't always teach the Dhamma in the same way; he teaches it in different ways in accordance with the different temperaments of people, and their different understandings. To some people the Buddha teaches the Dhamma in a highly philosophical form, to others in the form of stories. To some he gives a long, complex teaching, while to others he gives a short, simple one. Some he teaches in prose, others in poetry. And so on. But in whichever way the Buddha teaches, it is the same Dhamma that he proclaims. When the children come out of the burning house they all get the same kind of cart, the best kind of cart. They all get big, beautiful bullock carts.

What this signifies is that in reality there is only one Dhamma. There is only one *yāna*, not two, much less three. This is the *Saddharma Puṇḍarīka Sūtra*'s famous teaching of *ekayāna*. (In the *sūtra*, the word for cart is *yāna*.) This *ekayāna* is the *Buddhayāna*. Even though they understand and practise the Dhamma in slightly different ways, all Buddhists are on the same spiritual path. All Buddhists go for Refuge to the Buddha, the Dhamma, and the Sangha. All Buddhists practise the five precepts. Therefore all Buddhists together form one great, universal, worldwide Buddhist spiritual family. All Buddhists are brothers and sisters. It doesn't matter whether you live in India or in England, whether you come from Japan or from Sri Lanka. All should help one another. All should work together for the Dhamma.

In our Trailokya Bauddha Mahasangha Sahayak Gana, we have people belonging to twelve different nationalities. Having gone for Refuge to the Buddha, the Dhamma, and the Sangha, they are all observing the ten *kusala dhammas* and all are working together for the Dhamma in eight different countries, including India. This is what Dr Ambedkar wanted. He wanted to see a world Buddhist mission.

The interpretation of the Parable of the Burning House that I have given this afternoon is the traditional one, but now I want to give you a new, up-to-date interpretation. I don't mean that the old interpretation is out of date, but I'm going to give you a different interpretation. Let us go through the story again. What, then, is the burning house? The burning house is the old, corrupt Hindu society, which is burning with the three fires of slavery, inequality, and oppression. Even though people may not realize it, it is a terrible place in which to live. The rich old man is Dr Ambedkar. He feels *maitrī* and *karuṇā* for the people who are so unfortunate as to live under the old society. Since he doesn't want to escape just by himself, but to take everybody with him, he calls out to them. He calls out to them to go for Refuge and take the *Dhammadiksha*. This is what he did in Nagpur in 1956. Many people answered his call and left the burning house. They left the old, corrupt Hindu society. They took the *Dhammadiksha* and became Buddhists. But many did not do so. They remained in the old, corrupt Hindu society. They went on playing their old games: the game of worshipping the old Hindu gods, the game of drinking liquor; the game of giving dowry and asking for dowry; the game of marrying only within one's own sub-caste. So what did Dr Ambedkar do, and continue to do even after his passing away? He gave his followers carts in the form of the writings that have been published since his death, especially his book *The Buddha and His Dhamma*, published by the People's Education Society. If these writings of Dr Ambedkar can't get people out of the burning house, then nothing can! But in fact, more and more people have been coming out of the burning house. I hope that eventually everyone in India will come out.

In his book *The Buddha and His Dhamma* there is something for everybody. There are stories from the life of the Buddha, and there are philosophical teachings. There are teachings for monks and teachings for lay people, teachings about *prajñā* and teachings about *karuṇā*. In *The Buddha and His Dhamma* all the carts are represented. There are sections taken from the Pāli scriptures, and sections taken from the Hybrid Buddhist Sanskrit scriptures. There are Theravāda teachings and there are Mahāyāna teachings. For instance, on page 163 of the original English edition, Dr Ambedkar quotes an important passage from one of the Prajñāpāramitā *sutras*. This passage deals with the six *pāramitās*, i.e. *dāna, śīla, kṣānti, vīrya, samādhi,* and *prajñā*. The Prajñāpāramitā *sutras* are of course, Mahāyāna *sutras*, and they are written in Buddhist Hybrid Sanskrit. From this we can see how broad, indeed how universal, Dr Ambedkar's approach was. He took the Dhamma from wherever he could find it, whether it was from Pāli, or Buddhist Hybrid Sanskrit, or even Chinese sources. Dr Ambedkar's book *The Buddha and His Dhamma* doesn't just contain all the *yānas*. It contains the *ekayāna*, the *Buddhayāna*. In other words, it contains just the Dhamma.

In this connection an important point arises. When I was travelling around Maharashtra in the years immediately following the *Dhammadiksha* in Nagpur, and giving lectures on the Dhamma, there was one question which people often used to ask me. They used to say, 'Now we have taken the *Dhammadiksha*, have we become Hīnayāna Buddhists or have we become Mahāyāna Buddhists?' This is a very dangerous question, and it didn't come from the Buddhists themselves, but from our Hindu friends. After the great conversion ceremony they started asking the newly converted people if they had become Hīnayāna Buddhists or Mahāyāna Buddhists. In my opinion they did this simply to create confusion and disunity. When people questioned me about the matter I therefore always used to say, 'You are neither Hīnayāna Buddhists nor Mahāyāna Buddhists. You are just Buddhists. You are all followers of *ekayāna*, followers of *Buddhayāna*. You go for Refuge simply to the Dhamma, not to any particular interpretation of the Dhamma.'

This principle is of great importance for Indian Buddhists, and also for English Buddhists. In England we have many *bhikkhus* and lamas from different Buddhist countries. Some want us to follow only the Theravāda, others want us to follow only the Mahāyāna. Some would like us to follow Tibetan Buddhism, while others would like us to follow

Japanese Buddhism. But English Buddhists simply want to follow the Dhamma. In our own movement, the Western Buddhist Order/Trailokya Bauddha Mahasangha Sahayak Gana, we are ready to take whatever is helpful from the whole Buddhist tradition. After all, the Dhamma is whatever helps us to develop as individuals, as human beings. But we don't want to identify ourselves exclusively with any one yāna. We want to be just Buddhists, just followers of the Dhamma.

The situation in India is very similar. Here too people want to be just Buddhists, just followers of the Dhamma. If we are all just Buddhists, there will be unity and *maitrī* among us. If there are unity and *maitrī* among us we shall be able to work together, and if we can work together we shall surely succeed. We shall get out of the burning house, and take others with us. This is the message of the *Saddharma Puṇḍarīka Sūtra*. This is the message of *ekayāna* and *Buddhayāna* – the message of unity, the message of strength.

I am very happy to have had the opportunity of speaking to you on this subject this afternoon, and very grateful to the Bharatiya Bauddha Mahasabha for having arranged this very successful meeting. In the course of the last month different branches of the Bharatiya Bauddha Mahasabha have been responsible for arranging many of my meetings. I very much appreciate the spirit of unity and *maitrī* which they have shown. I am also very happy to have seen you all this afternoon, and hope that we may meet again.

20

THE FOUR ANIMALS OF AŚOKA
AND WHAT THEY REPRESENT

Jaikwadi, 25 January 1982

Brothers and Sisters in the Dhamma: First of all, I would like to say that I am very glad to be with you here this evening in Jaikwadi.[322] This part of Maharashtra is famous for its association with Buddhism, and especially for its hundreds of rock-cut Buddhist caves, of which the most famous of all is Ajanta. At Ajanta not only are there rock-cut caves but the walls of the caves are covered with hundreds of beautiful paintings. People come to see these paintings from all over the world. From the size and number of these Buddhist cave viharas and cave temples we can see that Buddhism must have flourished here in Maharashtra for hundreds of years.

This is of course true not only of Maharashtra but of practically the whole of India. Buddhism flourished here for about 1,500 years, and during that time India must have been a heaven on earth. Buddhism flourished especially during the reign of Aśoka, who lived about 200 years after the Buddha, and who was not only the greatest ruler of the Maurya dynasty but perhaps also the greatest king that India has ever seen. (This is not just my personal opinion, but the opinion of several leading Western historians.) During the first part of his career Aśoka was known as Chaṇḍāśoka, which means Aśoka the Fierce. He was given this name because he was always at war, always engaged in campaigns of military conquest, and because he was very cruel. During the second part of his career, however, he was known as Dharmāśoka or Aśoka the Righteous. He gave up war, gave up his campaigns of military conquest, and became very kind and compassionate. This great change came about because he was converted to the Dhamma. He turned from Brahmanism to Buddhism, and from the path of war to the path of peace. He turned from *himsā* to *ahimsā*, from enmity to *maitrī* and *karuṇā*. It was one of the greatest revolutions the world has ever seen.

After his conversion Aśoka did a number of remarkable things, and tonight I am going to speak about just one of them. This remarkable act was that he put up inscriptions all over India telling people about his conversion to Buddhism and exhorting them to practise the Dhamma. Some of these inscriptions were on rock, some on pillars of stone, but they were all written in the local language, or local dialect, because Aśoka wanted the ordinary people of the country to understand what he was doing and what he was thinking. Now tonight I am going to speak about the images carved on the Aśoka pillars (*stambhas*). These are twenty or thirty feet in height, and very beautiful, being very highly polished, just like glass. Even today it is difficult for craftsmen to achieve this sort of polish on stone. The capital of each pillar was surmounted by the figure of an animal or animals, and in some cases these animals supported a *dhammacakka*, an eight-spoked Dhamma wheel. Moreover, the capitals of certain pillars were decorated on their four sides with the figures of four different animals which seemed to be running round the capital. These four animals were the elephant, the bull, the horse, and the lion, and it is about the meaning of these four animals, and the nature of their connection with the Buddha and the Dhamma, that I want to speak tonight.

To begin with, the four animals are connected with four important events in the life of the Buddha: his conception, his birth, his leaving home, and his teaching of the Dhamma. Let us therefore look at each of them in turn.

1. The elephant is connected with the *conception* of the Buddha. Ten months before the Buddha's birth his mother, Mahāmāyā, had a dream. She dreamt that a beautiful white elephant, bearing a beautiful silver lotus flower in his trunk, descended into her womb. She then knew that she was going to give birth to a very great man. So she behaved very mindfully, and observed the precepts. There is a lesson here for other women. When one is pregnant one should not allow oneself to get angry, or to quarrel, or to partake of intoxicants. (As a Buddhist, one should not, of course, partake of intoxicants at any

time.) If one behaves mindfully in this way it will have a beneficial effect on the unborn child.

2. The bull is connected with the *birth* of the Buddha. This is because according to tradition the Buddha was born in the month of Vaiśākha and therefore under the zodiacal sign of *vrishabha* or the bull. Now it is important to avoid a misunderstanding here. Buddhism believes in astronomy, but it does not believe in astrology. Astronomy is a science, the science of the stars; but astrology is not a science. It is, in fact, difficult to say *what* astrology is. The Buddha was not a great man simply because he was born under a certain zodiacal sign. After all, many people were born under the sign of *vrishabha* in the same year as the Buddha, on the same day, and even at the same minute; but they did not become great like the Buddha. To say that the Buddha was born under the sign of *vrishabha* is therefore simply a way of saying at what time of year the Buddha was born, because in the Buddha's day there were no calendars in the modern scientific sense.

3. The horse is connected with the Buddha's *leaving home*. The Buddha was born into a rich and noble family, and had every comfort and luxury. He had three magnificent palaces, one for each of the three seasons of the year. He had a beautiful wife, and an infant son. He had high social position. But he gave it all up. He gave it up because he wanted to discover the cause of human suffering or, if you like, of human conflict. So one night he left his palace, and he left it riding on his favourite horse. The horse is therefore connected with the Buddha's leaving home.

4. The lion is connected with the Buddha's *teaching of the Dhamma* to his five former disciples in the Deer Park at Isipatana, near Benares. There are two reasons for this. Firstly, the lion is a very noble animal. It is, in fact, the noblest of animals, or even the king of animals. In the same way the Buddha is the noblest of men. He is the king of men, so to speak. For this reason, he is called *narasīha* in Pāli, or *narasiṃha* in Sanskrit. The Hindus have a *narasiṃha* who has the head of a lion and the body of a man. He is one of the *avatāras* of Vishnu. But this *narasiṃha* has nothing to do with the Buddha. The Buddha is a human being – an Enlightened human being. He is simply *like* a lion. He is called *narasīha* because he is among men as the lion is among animals. Secondly, the lion represents the Buddha because the lion has a very loud and terrifying roar. When the lion roars, it is said, all the other

beasts in the jungle become silent out of fear. In the same way, when the Buddha teaches the Dhamma, all the other religious teachers become silent. They are unable to speak so much as a single word.

Then, the four animals represent four characteristics, four attributes which the Buddha possessed and which all Buddhists should aim to develop:

1. The elephant represents *strength*, because the elephant is capable of bearing great burdens. It represents a sense of responsibility, as well as of patience and tolerance. A whole chapter of the *Dhammapada*, one of the most important Buddhist texts, is devoted to the elephant from this point of view. This chapter is called the *Nāgavagga*, or the Chapter of the Elephant, and in the first verse the Buddha says – or represents his true disciple as saying: 'Even as an elephant in battle withstands the arrow shot from a bow, even so shall I endure abuse.'[323] Life itself is a battlefield. All the time people are shooting at us with the arrows of harsh words, the arrows of abuse. But like the elephant we must practise patience and tolerance. It is said that when the elephant walks through the village all the dogs bark at him, but the elephant takes no notice. In the same way, we should take no notice of criticism, but just go on practising the Dhamma and working for the Dhamma. If we work for the Dhamma we are sure to be criticized, regardless of how well we work. Even the Buddha was criticized. So we should take no notice of criticism, or slander, or abuse, but just go on our way like the elephant.

2. The bull also represents *strength*, but the kind of strength represented by the bull is different from the kind of strength represented by the elephant. Whereas the elephant's strength is a passive strength, and consists in bearing, suffering, and enduring, the bull's strength is an active strength. It is a sort of fiery energy. The bull will get angry if necessary. It will put its head down and charge. It will attack, and even toss people on its horns. Thus the bull represents the active, fighting strength that is capable of breaking through opposition – the strength that is capable of putting the enemy to flight. Of course, in our case we will use this kind of strength in a completely peaceful, non-violent way, but we shouldn't be afraid to take the initiative and assert ourselves when necessary.

3. The horse represents *energy* and *speed*. In other words, the horse represents *vīrya-pāramitā*. This is a very necessary quality. Without energy we cannot practise any of the other *pāramitās*. We cannot

practise either *dāna* or *śīla*. We cannot practise *kṣānti* – which is not something weak and passive, but is the kind of strength represented by the elephant, as we have seen. And similarly, if we want to practise *samādhi* and *prajñā*, energy or *vīrya* is necessary. This quality also is mentioned in the *Dhammapada*, where the Buddha says: 'The wise man forges ahead, just as the racehorse outdistances a feeble hack.'[324] Here two kinds of horse are mentioned, the racehorse and the feeble hack. The Buddhist should be like the racehorse. He should forge ahead, leaving the non-Buddhists behind. And we forge ahead by practising the Dhamma.

4. The lion represents *fearlessness*, or courage. It isn't afraid of any other animal. The Buddhist should therefore be like the lion. He should not only be strong, and patient, and full of energy, but he should also be fearless. There is a particular kind of Buddha image which depicts the Buddha in what is called the *abhaya mudrā*, or gesture of fearlessness, which consists in raising the right arm and showing the hand palm outwards. Here the Buddha is, as it were, saying, 'Fear not!' Do not fear anybody; be free from fear. If you are completely free from fear you will be very near to Nirvāṇa.

Now I want to compare the characteristics of the four animals seen on Aśoka's great pillars with the qualities of Dr Ambedkar, who exemplified all the virtues of the true Buddhist to an extraordinary degree:

1. *Strength, patience, tolerance*: Dr Ambedkar possessed enormous strength, both intellectual and emotional, and he bore an enormous weight of responsibility. I am not referring to his responsibilities as a minister in the central government, because although those responsibilities were indeed weighty, he took on even bigger responsibilities than that. He bore the responsibility of lifting millions of Depressed People from a state of degradation to a state of human dignity. He bore the responsibility of pointing them in the direction of the Dhamma. Moreover, Dr Ambedkar was a very patient man. In his lifetime he had to bear a lot of criticism, and a lot of personal abuse. But he didn't retaliate. He just ignored it all and went his own way, just as the majestic elephant goes its own way ignoring the barking of the dogs.

2. *Active strength*: Dr Ambedkar had a great deal of active strength, a great deal of fiery energy. He was able to break through all obstacles, even the greatest, and he did this throughout his life. He broke through social obstacles, educational obstacles, economic and political obstacles, and

religious obstacles. He was born into a so-called low-caste community, yet he attained high social position. He was born into a community in which no one had even matriculated before, yet he attained to the highest academic honours. He was born into a very poor community, yet he achieved prosperity for himself and for numerous other people. He was born into a community without human rights, yet he attained to high political office. He was born into the Hindu religion, yet he took *Dhammadiksha* and became a Buddhist. In this way he broke through all obstacles, just like a bull.

3. *Energy and speed*: Dr Ambedkar not only did a lot of work, but he did it very quickly and very well. In a number of different fields he outdistanced not only other members of his own community but everybody else in India as well. He alone in India had the vision to see that India needed the Dhamma and the courage to take steps in that direction. Sometimes Dr Ambedkar was so far ahead of other people that they couldn't even see him. In this respect he was like the noble racehorse. He won every race.

4. *Fearlessness and courage*: Dr Ambedkar had fearlessness and courage to a very high degree, otherwise he could never have done the work that he did. At one time practically the whole of Caste Hindu India was against him. He himself said he was the most hated man in India.[325] His life was threatened, even, but he didn't flinch. He went on doing what he thought was right. A lesser man would have given up, but not Dr Ambedkar. He was devoid of fear. Nor was that all. He uttered his lion-roar, and when he did that everybody became silent. Nobody could stand against him. Nobody could resist his powerful logic. They might abuse him, but they were unable to find fault with his arguments.

Dr Ambedkar uttered many lion-roars in his lifetime. He uttered a lion-roar when he burned the *Manusmṛti*. He uttered a lion-roar when he declared, 'I may have been born a Hindu, but I do not intend to die one.' But his greatest and loudest lion-roar, the lion-roar that resounded throughout India and throughout the world, was when he said, '*Buddhaṃ saraṇaṃ gacchāmi, Dhammaṃ saraṇaṃ gacchāmi, Saṅghaṃ saraṇaṃ gacchāmi*', when he took the *Dhammadiksha* and advised his followers to take it too. That lion-roar was heard by millions of people, and we can still hear it even now. We can hear it in Maharashtra, we can hear it in the Aurangabad District, and we can hear it in Jaikwadi. That is why we are here today. That is what has brought us together.

So let us remember the example of Aśoka. Let us remember the example of the Buddha. Let us remember the example of Dr Ambedkar. Let us be like elephants and bulls, as well as like horses and lions. Let us have the strength that endures. Let us have patience and tolerance. Let us have the strength that breaks through obstacles. Let us have energy and speed. Let us have fearlessness and courage. We shall then be true fellow-countrymen of Aśoka, true disciples of the Buddha, and true followers of Dr Ambedkar.

21

THINGS THAT CAN HELP US
TO CHANGE

Ambad, 27 January 1982

Brothers and Sisters in the Dhamma: First of all I want to say how very glad I am to be here this evening.[326] It took me a little longer to get here than expected, because on the way from Aurangabad there were three impromptu receptions.[327] We were therefore a little late in getting here, and the meeting is a little late in starting. Even so, I am very glad to see you all. In the course of the last year I have been in no less than eight different countries. I have spent three months in Greece, five months in England, and three months in Italy. Now I am spending three months in India, mainly in Maharashtra.

In each of the countries in which I have stayed in the course of the last year or so I have been doing different things, seeing different things, and living in a different kind of way. Here in Maharashtra, I have been constantly giving lectures – usually one or more a day, and constantly meeting people – tens of thousands of people. I have been going from town to town, and from village to village, maybe not exactly like the Buddha, but at least in my own way. During the last six weeks I have been to Poona, to Panchgani, and to Mahad, which is of course famous for its connection with Dr Ambedkar, as well as spending some time in Bombay. I have also paid visits to Ulhasnagar, to Daund, to Ahmednagar, to Sangamner, to Koperagaon, to Yeola – which is also famous for its connection with Dr Ambedkar – to Manmad, and to Kannad. I then spent a week in Aurangabad, after which I visited Vaijapur and Jaikwadi. In all these places we had programmes and I met very many people. Everywhere I have gone I have been given a wonderful reception by our Buddhist friends. Now tonight I am in Ambad and I am very glad to see you all sitting and listening to me.

So I have done quite a lot of travelling during the last year, and in fact I am still travelling. I still have many more programmes to get through in Maharashtra, as well as others in Gujarat, Rajasthan, and Delhi. I am not going to Nagpur this time, but I shall certainly be going there in the course of my next visit to India. The people of Nagpur should not think I have forgotten them – that is quite impossible. But for the present, at least, I am concentrating on this part of Maharashtra.

Everything we do has an effect on the mind, especially if we do a great deal of it, and this certainly applies to travel. This is particularly the case if we travel from one country to another. We begin to see things in a new way. We even learn to do things in a new way. We start realizing that our way of doing things is not the only way, and that there is no question of our way being the right way and all the other ways being wrong. As the English proverb says, 'Travel broadens the mind.' If we travel we no longer see things just as an Indian, or an Englishman, or an American, or a Frenchman, or a Pakistani. We start seeing things just as human beings. Let me give you a simple example. Here in India, in Maharashtra, you eat your food with your right hand. But in England people don't use their hand for eating. They use a knife and fork for everything. When English people come to India they are very surprised to see Indians using their hand to eat with. They may even think it a very bad habit. But if they stay in India for some time they get used to it, and even start thinking it quite natural. Similarly, when Indians go to England they find people eating everything with a knife and fork. Indians who go to England at first find it very strange, even very awkward, to eat everything with a knife and fork, but after a while they get used to it. They realize that it is neither good nor bad, but just the custom of the country.

So in this way travel broadens the mind. We see that although people living in different parts of the world live in different ways, and have different manners and customs, and different beliefs, they are all human beings just like ourselves. If we stay at home all our lives we may not realize this – especially if we happen to live in a small village. If we live in a small village we may think that the way we do things in our village is the only way to do them, or at least the only right way, and therefore we may look down on everybody else. We could call this sort of attitude the 'frog in the well' mentality. The story goes that there was a frog who lived in a well. He thought his well was a very fine place. In fact, he thought his well was the whole world. One day he had a visitor. This visitor was an ocean frog, a frog who lived in the great ocean. The well frog asked the ocean frog,

'Where do you come from?'
'I come from the ocean,' the ocean frog replied.
'The ocean? What is that?'
'It is a very big body of water.'
'Is the ocean as big as my well?' the well frog then asked.
'Don't be so foolish,' said the ocean frog, laughing, 'the ocean is many times bigger than your well.'
'That's impossible!' shouted the well frog. 'Nothing is bigger than my well.' So saying, he drove the ocean frog away.

The man who never travels is like the frog in the well. His outlook is very narrow and rigid. To him his village is the whole world. Travel is one of the things that can help us overcome this sort of mental attitude. Travel can help us to change.

We find this in the case of Dr Ambedkar. When he was still quite a young man he spent some time in America, as well as in England and Germany. This is one of the reasons why he had such a broad outlook and could see things from such a universal point of view. In later life he went to Sri Lanka, to Burma, and to Nepal, in order to see for himself the way in which Buddhism was practised in these countries. Thus travel, we can say, is one of the things that can help us to change.

Another thing that can help us to change is education. By education I don't mean learning textbooks by heart, or acquiring qualifications. I mean genuinely increasing our knowledge and understanding of the world in which we live, as well as of the whole human race, and of ourselves. Take, for instance, the subject of history. History is not just learning dates or isolated facts. It is learning about the great historical movements that have shaped the lives of millions upon millions of people for hundreds of years, and understanding the effects of these movements and how they influence our lives even today. The sort of great historical movements that I have in mind are the spread of Buddhism throughout

Asia, the conquest of India by the Mughals, and the French Revolution. The French Revolution was fought for the sake of liberty, equality, and fraternity, and if we don't know something about the French Revolution we won't know what these terms really mean. Simply looking them up in the dictionary is not enough. Thus education too gives us a broader outlook. Travel enables us to move about in space; education enables us to move about in time. Travel opens up the physical world to our personal experience; education opens up the mental and spiritual world. Through education we learn what men and women have done in the past and in other parts of the world. We learn what they have thought and how they have felt, thus sharing their experience, as it were. In this way we become less limited, and more truly human. Thus education is one of the things that helps us to change. We find this, too, in the life of Dr Ambedkar. He was a highly educated man, one of the most highly educated Indians of his time – certainly the most highly educated Indian in politics. He had studied in the United States, in England, and in Germany. Indeed, it was for the sake of his studies that he went to these three countries. His outlook was therefore very broad. His knowledge was very wide, and his understanding very deep.

Travel and education are not the only things that can help us to change. There are other things that can help us to change even more than travel and education, things that can help us grow and develop, things that can help us become better human beings – even help us become Enlightened. This evening I want to mention just a few of them.

1. *Taking part in Dhamma activities* can help us to change. You can change just by listening to this lecture! As you listen you may hear something you have not heard before, and that may change your outlook. It may make you see and understand things in a new way. You may act upon that new understanding, and in this way you may eventually change your whole life. This can come about just by listening, carefully and thoughtfully, to this lecture! There are many examples of this kind of thing in the life of the Buddha. Take the case of Aṅgulimāla, the famous dacoit.[328] Even the king was afraid of him, because in order to collect the garland of fingers which he wore around his neck and from which he derived his name he had killed ninety-nine people.[329] But then, the story goes, when he was looking for his hundredth victim, he happened to meet the Buddha. The Buddha spoke just a few words about the Dhamma, but when Aṅgulimāla heard those words he changed

completely. He became a *bhikkhu*, and eventually gained Enlightenment – just in response to hearing those few words from the Buddha.³³⁰ So taking part in Dhamma activities can help us to change. This does not only mean listening to lectures. Helping to organize programmes, and selling *Buddhayan*, can also help us to change.

2. *Actually practising the Dhamma* can help us to change more than anything else – more than travel, more than education, more than taking part in Dhamma activities. In fact, it is the function of the Dhamma to help us to change. It has no other purpose. The Dhamma was made for man; man was not made for the Dhamma. The Dhamma helps us to grow, to become better human beings, to gain Enlightenment. The Buddha said that the Dhamma is just like a great raft.³³¹ This raft helps us to cross over the river of suffering to the other shore of peace and happiness, of *maitrī, karuṇā*, and *prajñā*. It helps us to cross over not in some future life, not after death, but here and now, in this present life. Thus actually practising the Dhamma can help us change, help us to grow.

3. *Śīla* can help us to change. We can practise the Dhamma in many different ways. For instance, we can practise the Dhamma by observing the five *sīlas*: (a) refraining from injuring living beings, and practising *maitrī* instead; (b) refraining from taking the not-given, and practising generosity; (c) refraining from committing adultery, and practising contentment; (d) refraining from false speech, and practising truthfulness; (e) refraining from taking intoxicating drinks and drugs, and instead practising mindfulness.

These are the *pañcasīlas*. Buddhists recite them every day, and you all recited them yourselves half an hour ago. But it is not enough just to recite them. You must also practise them. If you don't practise them you are not a real Buddhist. *Śīla* is the foundation of our whole practice of the Dhamma. If we practise *śīla* then we will change. This should be quite obvious. If we practise *śīla* we will become more like real human beings and less like animals. Without *śīla* a man is no better than a cow or a dog; in fact he is worse than a cow or a dog. Without *śīla* society is no better than a jungle full of wild animals. *Śīla* is not just the foundation of our practice of the Dhamma. *Śīla* is the foundation of human life itself, both individual and collective.

4. *Meditation can help us to change.* Meditation changes the mind. One of the Buddhist words for meditation is *bhāvanā*, which literally

means development. Meditation makes the mind more concentrated. It makes the mind clearer. It fills it with positive thoughts, so that it consists entirely of what we call 'skilful mental states'. In Buddhism there are many different ways of practising meditation. Tonight I am going to mention only two of them.

i. *Ānāpānasati*: Here we just watch the breath, the process of inhalation and exhalation, and as we watch, we count. We count 'one' at the end of the first inhalation and exhalation, 'two' at the end of the second, and so on up to 'ten', after which we start again from 'one'. We do this for five or ten minutes. Then we count at the beginning of each inhalation and exhalation, counting from 'one' up to 'ten' in the same way, over and over again. We do this also for five or ten minutes. Having completed these two stages we drop the counting. Instead, we mentally follow the track of the breath as it goes down into the lungs and comes out again. We do this, also, for five or ten minutes. Finally, we concentrate our attention on the sensation of touch produced by the breath at the end of the nose as it goes in and out of the nostrils. Again, we do this for five or ten minutes. In this way we practise, and we practise every day – regularly. This is what we call *ānāpānasati*. I have explained it very briefly. If you want to understand it properly, and learn how to do it, you will have to attend one of the TBMSG meditation classes, or go on one of the TBMSG *Dhamma-shibirs*.

The *ānāpānasati* practice should not be confused with the Hindu practice of *prāṇāyāma*. In *prāṇāyāma* the breath is controlled, but in the *ānāpānasati* practice we simply watch the breath without trying to control it. If we practise the *ānāpānasati* regularly the mind will become more and more deeply concentrated. *We* shall become more deeply concentrated. We shall become less scattered, less distracted. All our mental energies will start flowing together. We shall feel better, and happier, and lighter. We shall feel free.

ii. *Mettā bhāvanā*: Here we develop thoughts of friendliness towards all living beings. The word *mettā* in Pāli, or *maitrī* in Sanskrit, means 'friendliness'. It is the feeling we naturally have towards a very near and dear friend. *Bhāvanā* simply means development. So *mettā bhāvanā* means the development of the same feelings of friendliness that we have for our nearest and dearest friend towards all living beings. We practise this meditation sitting cross-legged, just as we do for the *ānāpānasati*. First we think of our own self, and develop *mettā* towards our own self. We repeat mentally such words as, 'May I be well! May I be happy! May I progress!' We do this for five or ten minutes. Then we think of a very near and dear friend, someone we go about with, or with whom we spend a lot of time, and whom we love very much. The same feelings of *mettā* or *maitrī* that we first felt towards ourselves, we now try to feel towards him or her.[332] We think, 'May he be well! May he be happy! May he progress!' We do this too for five or ten minutes. Then we think, thirdly, of what we call a neutral person, someone with whom we are acquainted but whom we neither like nor dislike. And we try to develop the same feeling of *mettā* or *maitrī* towards him too. We think, 'May he be well! May he be happy! May he progress!' We do this for five or ten minutes. Fourthly, we do exactly the same thing with regard to someone we dislike – someone who is an enemy, even. We put all thoughts of enmity aside. We think, 'May he be well! May he be happy! May he progress!' We develop the same feeling of *mettā* or *maitrī* towards that person that we had developed before towards ourselves, our near and dear friend, and the neutral person. This also we do for five or ten minutes. Lastly, we develop this same feeling of *mettā* or *maitrī* towards all living beings. First we think of all the people in our own house, then all the people in our locality ... all the people in our district ... all the people in our state ... our country ... the whole world. Thus in the end we have a very strong, powerful feeling of *mettā* or *maitrī* going towards all living beings. This fifth stage we have to practise for a somewhat longer time, maybe ten or fifteen minutes, or even twenty minutes if we can. If we do this practice regularly, every day, then we shall develop a very strong and powerful feeling of *mettā* or *maitrī*. We will get rid of all feelings of enmity and ill will. We will not get angry or impatient so easily. We will feel very happy. The world will seem like a different place. Everybody will seem like a friend. Even if someone does us an injury we will just feel *karuṇā* towards him.

These are just two of the many ways of practising Buddhist meditation. It is not difficult to see from this that meditation can help us to change. Meditation can change our mind. Meditation can raise our mind to a very high level. It can make our mind more like the mind of the Buddha.

5. *The study of the Dhamma can help us to change.* By this I don't mean just intellectual study. Dhamma study doesn't just mean the reading of books. When we do Dhamma study in the real way, we should study with a *kalyāṇa mitra*, that is to say, with someone who has

already understood the Dhamma deeply himself, and who also practises it. With the help of this kind of study of the Dhamma, we can develop real insight, real *vipassanā*. We can develop a real understanding of life, a real understanding of the world, and a real understanding of our own self. We can develop what the Buddha himself called *yathābhūta-ñāna-dassana* or knowledge and vision of things as they really are. Some people have the wrong sort of idea about Dhamma study. They think it's just like studying a school subject like history, or arithmetic, or physics. But studying the Dhamma is much more interesting than that, because when you study the Dhamma you are studying yourself. You are studying your own life – studying the process of your own development. Dhamma study can therefore certainly help us to change.

6. *Right Livelihood can help us to change*. Work is something we do every day, so it affects us very much indeed. We therefore shouldn't do the wrong kind of work. As Buddhists we should practise Right Livelihood, which is the fifth step of the Buddha's Noble Eightfold Path. Right livelihood means we should earn our living in a way that does not injure our health, that does no harm to any living being, including ourself, and that is in accordance with the five *sīlas*. Our work should ideally produce something really useful for the community, whether in the way of goods or services. So if we are engaged in any form of wrong livelihood we should give it up and follow right livelihood. This alone will bring about a tremendous change in our life.

7. *Communication can help us to change*. Communication means speaking to another person just as a human being, not as a member of a particular caste or as belonging to a particular nationality. It also means speaking to him truthfully, speaking to him kindly and affectionately, speaking to him about what is useful, i.e. about whatever helps him to develop as a human being, and speaking to him in a way that promotes harmony, concord, and friendship. If we communicate in this way, it will bring about a change in our attitude to other people. Our attitude will become truly human. And if our attitude towards human beings changes in this way, then *we* shall change.

8. *A Dhamma-shibir can help us to change*. A *Dhamma-shibir* is when you go away with anything up to a hundred other Buddhists and stay in a quiet place for a week or ten days or more. While you are there you all live together, eat together, and practise the Dhamma together. You observe the five *sīlas*, you practise meditation, and you engage in Dhamma study.

You practise right livelihood, because on a *shibir* you don't work in the ordinary sense so the question of your practising wrong livelihood doesn't even arise. You also practise communication with one another. Thus the *Dhamma-shibir* helps us to change. Perhaps the *Dhamma-shibir* helps us to change more than anything else, because there so many of the things that help us to change are found. People who go on *Dhamma-shibir* therefore change very quickly indeed. At the beginning of the *shibir* they may be only fifty-percent Buddhist, or at the most seventy-five-percent, but by the end they are one-hundred-percent Buddhist. So everybody who possibly can should go on a *Dhamma-shibir*. To go on a *Dhamma-shibir* means to change. It means to develop. It means to become a real Buddhist.

Twenty-five years ago Dr Ambedkar took the *Dhammadiksha* himself, and encouraged his followers to take it; but he didn't want them simply to recite the *tisaraṇa* and *pañcasīla* like parrots. He wanted them really to change. He wanted his followers to change individually, and he wanted society as a whole to change. He wanted people to grow and develop. He wanted them to be happy. He wanted them to progress. This is what Dr Ambedkar wanted, and this is what the Buddha wanted too. After his attainment of Enlightenment the Buddha looked out over the world and saw the whole of humanity just like a bed of lotuses in various stages of development. Some of the lotuses were still deeply immersed in the mud, some had almost reached the surface of the water, while some had just broken through into the air. A few lotuses had even risen completely above the water. The Buddha saw that human beings were also in various stages of development, just like the lotuses.[333]

In order to develop, the lotus needs sunlight, water, and air. It even needs mud. In the same way, there are various things that help human beings to develop. I have mentioned some of them this evening. We may not all be able to travel widely, or to obtain a good education, but we can all take part in Dhamma activities – just as you are doing here tonight. We can all practise the Dhamma. We can practise *sīla* and meditation. We can study the Dhamma. We can practise right livelihood and skilful communication. We can attend the *Dhamma-shibir*. All these things can help us to change, to develop as human beings. They can help us develop spiritually and bring us nearer to Nirvāṇa, to Buddhahood. I hope that here in Ambad you are all practising at least some of these things that can help us to change. If you can do that you will be true disciples of the Buddha, and true followers of Dr Ambedkar.

22

THE FIVE MUDRĀS OF THE BUDDHA

Parbhani, 28 January 1982

Brothers and Sisters in the Dhamma: For the last two to three weeks I have been touring Marathwada[334] and in the course of that time I've visited quite a number of places, given quite a few lectures, and met quite a lot of people. Today I have come to Parbhani.[335] I'm very glad to be here, and I'm very pleased that people have come to this meeting in such large numbers. Some of you, I understand, have come from distant towns and villages. This shows your great enthusiasm for the Dhamma. I'm very glad to see you all. Even though I can't actually see you all with my eyes – I can only see those sitting at the front – I can see everybody in my mind. I'm always really happy to meet other Buddhists. All Buddhists are brothers and sisters. It doesn't matter whether we come from India or England, from Japan or Sri Lanka; we all belong to the same spiritual family. We all have the same father, the Buddha. We all have the same mother, the Dhamma. And we ourselves make up the *sangha*, the Mahāsaṅgha. In an ordinary family we have elder brothers and younger brothers, elder sisters and younger sisters. It's just the same in our Buddhist spiritual family. We have *anagārikas* and *dasa sīla upāsakas* and *upāsikās*. They are like the elder brothers and sisters. We also have the *pañcasīla upāsakas* and *upāsikās*. They are like the younger brothers and sisters.

You are not only Buddhists, you are followers of Dr Babasaheb Ambedkar, and for that reason also I am very happy to see you. Dr Ambedkar, as you know, is very famous in Maharashtra and throughout India, and now he's also beginning to be well known among English Buddhists, especially among the members of the Western Buddhist Order/Trailokya Bauddha Mahasangha Sahayak Gana. This is the new Buddhist organization which I started in England in 1967. It's now the biggest and most active Buddhist organization in Europe and many of our members are very interested in Dr Ambedkar's work and in his approach to Buddhism. Some of them particularly like his emphasis on the social relevance of Buddhism. So far there are no statues of Dr Ambedkar in England as there are in Maharashtra, but I'm sure that we shall have statues of Dr Ambedkar in England one day.

This is my first visit to Parbhani. I came to Maharashtra many times between 1957 and 1967, but I've not been to this place before. It is not Anagārika Lokamitra's first visit however. He came here some months ago and gave a lecture here. I wonder if you remember what he spoke about? I wonder if you made any notes? Well, he told me that he spoke about the Three Jewels, about the Buddha, the Dhamma, and the Sangha. Buddha, of course, means Gautama the Buddha. Gautama the Buddha was not a god, but a human being, an Enlightened human being. He was a human being who had completely got rid of greed, hatred, and delusion, a human being who was completely pure, and full of *maitrī*, *karuṇā*, and *prajñā*. The Buddha was not just himself a perfect human being. He represents the ideal of moral and spiritual perfection for all other human beings. The Buddha shows us what it is possible for us to become if we make the effort. It's not only he who can become Buddha. Everyone can become Buddha. Everyone can grow and develop. And the Dhamma is the means of that growth and development. Dhamma means, of course, the Buddha-Dhamma, the path taught by the Buddha, the path of *śīla*, *samādhi*, and *prajñā*, *maitrī* and *karuṇā*. This is the path that we, as Buddhists, have to follow, and if we follow it, we shall become like the Buddha, we shall gain Enlightenment. And Sangha means the spiritual family of all those who are following the Dhamma, all those who are trying to follow the path taught by the Buddha. That is to say, all of us here. A Buddhist is not someone who merely repeats the *tisaraṇa* and the *pañcasīla*. The only true Buddhist is a practising Buddhist.

Anyway, I am not going to give the same lecture that Lokamitra gave when he came here last. I'm not really going to speak about the Three Jewels. I just wanted to refresh your memories. Tonight I am going to speak about the Buddha, or rather, I'm going to speak about the *image* of the Buddha. Here in Maharashtra you have many ancient Buddha images, most of them found in the Buddhist caves. Some of them are very big, much bigger than human size, and some are quite small. Some of these images are sitting cross-legged, some of them are sitting European fashion, as though on a chair, and some are even lying down. Now when we look at these Buddhas, we notice something else about them. We notice that their hands are held in different positions. These positions of the hands are called *mudrās*. There are many different *mudrās*, but five of them are the most important, so tonight I want to say something about these five. Each of them has a definite meaning and in some cases this meaning is associated with a particular episode in the Buddha's life.

1. First, there is the *bhūmisparśa mudrā*. This is the *mudrā* of touching the earth. Here the Buddha is shown seated cross-legged. His left hand is resting in his lap and his right hand hangs down over his right knee, palm inwards, the tips of the fingers just touching the earth. But why is the Buddha touching the earth? To understand this we have to refer to ancient accounts of the Buddha's life. As you know, he left home at the age of twenty-nine and for six years he practised self-mortification or self-torture in the jungle. But he found that this path of self-mortification did not lead him to Enlightenment, so he gave up that path. He decided to follow the middle way between the extremes of self-mortification on the one hand and self-indulgence on the other. He decided to practise meditation. So he came to Bodh Gaya and sat down beneath the bodhi tree, on what is called the *vajrāsana*. This is the very spot where, according to Buddhist tradition, many other Buddhas had gained Enlightenment hundreds of thousands of years before Gautama the Buddha.

But at the very moment Gautama sat down on the *vajrāsana*, Māra appeared. Māra is the sort of Satan or Devil of Buddhism, the personification of what we call the *kleśas*, the personification of all unskilful mental states. So Māra appeared and he asked the Buddha a very direct question: 'What right have you to sit on this spot?' And in reply the Buddha said, 'I'm going to gain Enlightenment, so I have a right to sit on this spot.' So then Māra asked another question: 'How do you know that you are going to gain Enlightenment?' And the Buddha replied, 'I know because I have practised the six *pāramitās* – *dāna* and *śīla, kṣānti* and *vīrya, samādhi,* and *prajñā* – not just for one lifetime, but for hundreds of lifetimes. I know that I'm ready to gain Enlightenment because I've prepared myself by this practice of the six *pāramitās*.' But Māra wasn't convinced. He asked yet another question: 'What is your proof that you have practised the six *pāramitās* for all these lifetimes? Who is your witness?' So the Buddha replied, 'The earth itself is my witness. I have practised the *pāramitās* for hundreds of lifetimes on this earth, and the earth has seen me practising them all. The earth is my witness.' As he said these words, he touched the earth with the tips of his fingers, and as he did this, a voice came from the earth, saying, 'What he says is true. He has indeed practised the *pāramitās* for hundreds of lifetimes. I have seen it all, I bear witness.' So Māra had to go away and the Buddha proceeded to gain Enlightenment.[336] This is what ancient accounts of the Buddha's life tell us, and this is the explanation of the *bhūmisparśa mudrā*.

2. The second *mudrā* is the *dhyāna mudrā*. Here also the Buddha is shown sitting cross-legged, but this time both his hands are resting on his lap, one on top of the other. Here the Buddha is still seated under the bodhi tree. Māra has gone away and the Buddha is practising meditation. He is just about to gain Enlightenment. His eyes are half closed, his lips are gently smiling, and his whole figure is absolutely still, absolutely firm, absolutely steady, just like a great mountain. At the same time his figure is not stiff or rigid but flexible and gently poised. Images of the Buddha in *dhyāna mudrā* are very popular all over the Buddhist world, and they're very popular with Western Buddhists too. In our shrine-room in our centre in London we have a large image of the Buddha in *dhyāna mudrā* made by one of our own members. It is much bigger than life-size and of a beautiful golden colour, and the Buddha is seated on an enormous golden lotus throne. People who see this image are often very deeply impressed. Even non-Buddhists are impressed! It's as though the Buddha is actually sitting there in the shrine-room, meditating.

Different people learn to appreciate the Dhamma in different ways. Some learn to appreciate the Dhamma by reading books. This was my own experience. When I was sixteen years old I read two Buddhist *sūtras*, the *Vajracchedīka Sūtra* and the *Sūtra of Wei Lang*. The first was translated into English from Buddhist Sanskrit and the second was translated from Chinese. The first *sūtra* dealt mainly with *prajñā* and the second dealt mainly with *dhyāna* and *samādhi*. When I read those two *sūtras* I knew that I was a Buddhist. (I had realized that I was not a Christian two years earlier when I was fourteen.) So this was my own experience. Some people, however, learn to appreciate the Dhamma by listening to lectures, and perhaps that's true for many of you. Other people learn to appreciate the Dhamma simply by looking at an image of the Buddha, especially the image of the Buddha in *dhyāna mudrā*. In the West many people are interested in art, so they find it easy to appreciate Buddhism in this way. That is why so many people from the West come to Maharashtra to see the cave paintings of Ajanta. We should not think that we can learn to appreciate Buddhism only through books and lectures. We can also appreciate the Dhamma through Buddhist art. Art involves the emotions and this is very important. If we really learn to appreciate Buddhist art, we will learn to appreciate Buddhism itself, and this is especially so if we appreciate the image of the Buddha in *dhyāna mudrā*.

3. Thirdly, we come to the *dharmacakra-pravartana mudrā*. Here the Buddha is shown teaching the Dhamma. Having gained Enlightenment, he has left Bodh Gaya and come to Sarnath, near Benares, to the deer park where he has met the five monks who were his disciples when he was practising self-mortification. He is teaching them the Dhamma, and his gesture expresses this: his hands are held level with his chest and the thumb and index finger of his right hand are gently touching the thumb and index finger of his left hand. The Buddha stayed there in the deer park and taught the five monks for three or four months – that is, for the whole of the rainy season. We could say that this was the first ever *Dhamma-shibir*, led by the Buddha and attended by the five monks. So how was the *shibir* organized? The Pāli texts tell us that the monks took it in turns to go and collect food from the nearest village. One day, two of the monks would go and collect food for the other three monks and the Buddha, and while they were away the Buddha would teach the remaining three. The next day three of them would go and collect food and while they were away, the Buddha taught the remaining two. The Buddha himself did not go out collecting food. He spent his whole time teaching. So this was the first *Dhamma-shibir*, and by the end of it all five monks had become Enlightened.[337] So this is how powerful the effect of *Dhamma-shibir* can be.

Now we have seen that the *dharmacakra-pravartana mudrā* represents the Buddha's teaching of the Dhamma, not only at Sarnath in the deer park, but also on other occasions. But where does it get its name? Why is the Buddha's teaching, especially his first teaching, referred to as the turning of the wheel of the Dhamma? Why is the Dhamma compared to a wheel? The Dhamma is compared to a wheel because a wheel goes rolling on and on. There is some background to the symbolism of the wheel in ancient Indian legend, but I won't go into that now. The Dhamma is a great wheel that can go in any direction, north, south, east, or west. After the Buddha's very first teaching at Sarnath, the devas gathered around said that nobody could stop this wheel, not even Mārā together with Brahmā.[338] In other words, even Satan could not stop the wheel of the Dhamma from rolling, and neither could God, if God existed.

We find that the wheel of the Dhamma went rolling throughout Asia. It went to Burma and Thailand, to China and Japan, to Tibet, and to many other countries. And wherever the Dhamma went, it brought peace, education, and a higher standard of culture, gave birth to wonderful works of art and systems of Buddhist philosophy, and produced many Enlightened teachers. Now the wheel of the Dhamma has started rolling across Europe and America. Unfortunately, while the wheel of the Dhamma was rolling across Asia it came to a standstill in India for hundreds of years. Not only did it come to a standstill; it got covered over with rubbish. Nobody even knew that it was there any more. Now the *dhammacakka* did not stop because of some outside force. That in any case is impossible, as we have seen. It came to a standstill because Buddhists themselves stopped practising the Dhamma. But towards the end of the nineteenth century a Buddhist came from Sri Lanka and started removing the rubbish that covered the *dhammacakka*. His name was Anagārika Dharmapala. Having removed quite a lot of rubbish, he tried to give the *dhammacakka* a push and get it moving again. But he did not succeed. Some of the people working with him were Hindus, and while he was pushing the *dhammacakka* in one direction they were pushing it in another, so it did not move. Now, however, the *dhammacakka* is moving. It's rolling through Maharashtra, through India, faster and faster every day. So who has given it a push? Who has got it moving? Well, you know that it was Dr Babasaheb Ambedkar. He set it moving again on 14 October 1956. On that occasion he gave it a tremendous push. He pushed it with all his strength. Nobody in India could have given it such a push. Nobody else could have set it moving again. Now the *dhammacakka* is rolling through the hearts and minds of millions of people. So this is what Dr Ambedkar has achieved. This is why we honour his memory. This is why statues of him are going up all over Maharashtra. Dr Ambedkar turned the wheel of the Dhamma after it had been at a standstill here in India for hundreds of years. So we think especially of Dr Ambedkar when we see the image of the Buddha with the *dharmacakra-pravartana mudrā*.

4. Fourthly, we have the *abhaya mudrā*. Here the Buddha is sometimes shown sitting, sometimes standing. When sitting, his left hand rests in his lap and the right hand is raised palm outwards. So this is the *abhaya mudrā*, the gesture of fearlessness. The Buddha is saying: 'Fear not!' This *mudrā* is not usually associated with any particular incident in the Buddha's life, but fearlessness is a very important quality. Without it we cannot work for the Dhamma or achieve anything in the spiritual life. In fact, without fearlessness we cannot even succeed in worldly life. It's very important that Buddhists should practise fearlessness. Many Buddhists are still afraid of people of higher castes, but they shouldn't be afraid. You are men and women, and the people of higher castes also are simply men and women. There is no need for you to feel afraid of them, and no need for them to feel afraid of you. So Buddhists should meditate on this image of the Buddha in *abhaya mudrā*.

5. Fifthly and lastly, the *varada mudrā*. '*Vara*' means highest, or best; '*da*' means giving. Now this term *varada* occurs in the *Ratana Sutta* of the Pāli canon, which says that the Buddha himself is *vara*, the Buddha himself is the highest, or best.[339] He is the highest or best human being because he has gained Enlightenment. Then the *sutta* says the Buddha is *varaññū*. That is to say the Buddha is the knower, the one who knows. He is the highest and best knower of *Nibbāna*, the highest and best knower of the Dhamma. Then the *sutta* says that the Buddha is *varado*, the giver of the highest and the best, the giver of the Dhamma. Finally, the *sutta* says that he is *varāharo*. That is to say, he is the bringer of the highest and the best, the bringer, of course, of the Dhamma. So the *varada mudrā* is the *mudrā* of giving the highest and the best, the *mudrā* of giving the Dhamma. It is the *mudrā* of giving the teachings of *śīla*, *samādhi*, and *prajñā*. It is the *mudrā* of giving the teachings of *maitrī* and *karuṇā* – in other words, giving the teaching that helps the individual to grow as a human being. The *mudrā* of giving the teaching not only helps the individual to grow and to develop, but also helps society to progress.

We can also connect the image of the Buddha in *varada mudrā* with Dr Ambedkar. Dr Ambedkar gave his followers the highest and the best. He gave them, in fact, the Three Jewels, the three most precious things there are: the Buddha, the Dhamma, and the Sangha. He advised them to go for Refuge to the Buddha, the Dhamma, and the Sangha. So remember what Anāgārika Lokamitra told you last time he was here. Remember what I've said tonight. Think about the Buddha in the *bhūmisparśa mudrā*, the *mudrā* of touching the earth, of calling the earth to witness. Think of the Buddha in the *dhyāna mudrā*, the *mudrā* of peace of mind, of concentration, of Enlightenment. Think of the Buddha in the *dharmacakra-pravartana mudrā*, the *mudrā* of turning the wheel of the Dhamma, the *mudrā* of teaching the Dhamma. Think of the Buddha in the *abhaya mudrā*, the *mudrā* of fearlessness and courage. Think of the Buddha in *varada mudrā*, the *mudrā* of giving the highest and best, giving the gift of the Dhamma. Think of the noble example of Dr Ambedkar, the man who gave you the Dhamma, who gave you back the Three Jewels when you had lost them. Remember that you are Buddhists. Resolve that you will become Buddhas, that you will gain Enlightenment. Resolve to practise the Dhamma more and more. Resolve to live in love and friendship with other members of the Mahāsaṅgha. And for my part, I shall resolve to try to come back and see you again one day. Meanwhile I'm very glad indeed to have been able to see you tonight and to have been able to speak to you about the Dhamma. May you all be happy!

23

WHY BUDDHISM DISAPPEARED FROM INDIA AND HOW IT CAN BE PREVENTED FROM DISAPPEARING AGAIN

Nanded,[340] *29 January 1982*

Mr Chairman, Brothers and Sisters in the Dhamma: In the course of the last year I have been quite busy. This time last year I was in Greece, a country situated in the southern part of Europe, just staying there quietly for a while, thinking about Dhamma work. In fact, I was *planning* Dhamma work, because it's no use our working for the Dhamma in a haphazard, unsystematic fashion. We have to work in an organized, systematic way. After staying in Greece for a while I spent several months in England, where I was occupied mainly with literary work, especially with the writing of the second volume of my memoirs. In this volume I am dealing with my experiences here in India from the year 1953 to 1957, particularly with the various meetings with Dr Babasaheb Ambedkar. After that I spent three months in Italy, another country in the southern part of Europe, where I led a *Dhamma-shibir*. This particular *shibir* lasted for three whole months, and at the end of it twenty people became *dasa sīla upāsakas*, that is to say, became Dhammacharis, full-time workers for the Dhamma. Now I am spending three months here in India, mainly in Maharashtra. After all, Maharashtra is the main centre for our Buddhist activities here in India, the main centre of the work of Dr Babasaheb Ambedkar. During the last two or three weeks I have been on tour in Marathwada. I have visited many places, met many people, and given many lectures.

Now tonight I am here in Nanded, and I am very glad indeed to have arrived here, and to see so many people sitting and listening to the

Dhamma. Before coming here I heard quite a lot about the Buddhist people of Nanded from Anagārika Lokamitra, who has given several lectures here and knows some of you very well. Lokamitra told me that the people of Nanded are very interested in the Dhamma, and want to hear more about it. In fact, he told me that here in Nanded I would have the biggest and best programme of my whole tour of Marathwada – maybe of my whole tour of Maharashtra. Well, it looks as though he was right. I'm very glad to see the fine arrangements that have been made, very glad to see the beautiful decorations. I'm very glad to see that so many people have come. You've all come because you're interested in the Dhamma and want to hear the Dhamma. You've not come for a cinema show, or because you're looking for a job. You've come just for the sake of the Dhamma, and therefore I'm very glad to see you all. Buddhists are all like brothers and sisters. It is very good that we should all meet together from time to time. It is very good that we should get to know one another, and that we should all work together for the Dhamma. People want to hear the Dhamma all over Marathwada, all over Maharashtra, even all over India. Perhaps not quite so many people in the rest of India want to hear the Dhamma as in Maharashtra, but still, there are people in Madhya Pradesh, in Uttar Pradesh, in Gujarat, in Punjab, and in Karnataka, who all want to hear the teaching of the Buddha.

It wasn't like when I first came to India in 1944. At that time you could travel all the way from Delhi to Calcutta and not meet a single Buddhist in the course of your journey. But since then a great change has taken place. We can now find *lakhs* of Buddhists, even *crores* of Buddhists, all over India, especially in Maharashtra.[341] So what has brought about this change? *Who* has brought about this change? As we know very well, it was Dr Babasaheb Ambedkar who brought it about. On 14 October 1956 he took *Dhammadiksha* at Nagpur. *Lakhs* of his followers took it with him, and *lakhs* of them took it afterwards. So it was this great Dhamma Revolution of Dr Ambedkar's that brought about the great change. It was this that brought Buddhism back to India. In bringing Buddhism back to India Dr Ambedkar brought about a revolution in the personal lives of millions of people – a revolution in the whole society. Buddhism had been dead in India for hundreds of years. People had forgotten the very name of Buddhism. They had forgotten even the name of the Buddha. Before that, Buddhism had flourished in

India for 1,500 years – had spread from India all over Asia. But then it disappeared from the country of its birth until Dr Ambedkar brought it back twenty-five years ago.

At this point a very big question arises. Why did Buddhism disappear from India? Some people say that it disappeared because of the Muslim invasion. Others say that it disappeared because of Shankaracharya.[342] So tonight I want to go into this question of why Buddhism disappeared from India. It is not only a very big question, but a very important one. It is important because if Buddhism disappeared from India once, it could disappear from India again. We must therefore try to understand why it disappeared; then we shall be in a position to prevent the same thing happening again.

Buddhism disappeared from India for many reasons. It didn't disappear *simply* because of the Muslim invasion, or *simply* because of Shankaracharya, although these factors may have played a part. According to Buddhist philosophy, for the production of any phenomenon at least two causes must cooperate.[343] One cause is not enough. This is one of the reasons why Buddhism does not believe in the creation of the world by a single all-powerful God. Thus there are a number of different reasons for the disappearance of Buddhism from India. Tonight I am going to mention five or six of the most important reasons. All these reasons are interconnected, of course. Sometimes, in fact, it is difficult to separate one from another. We shall then see what we must do in order to prevent the same thing happening in the future.

1. The first reason for the disappearance of Buddhism from India was that the Buddhist *bhikkhus* became separated from the Buddhist lay people. Originally the Going for Refuge was the most important thing in Buddhism. That is to say, the *Dhammadiksha* was the most important thing. Going for Refuge to the Buddha, to the Dhamma, and to the Sangha, was the most important thing. It didn't matter so very much whether you were a monk, wandering from place to place, or a householder living at home with your family. What was important was that you should practise the Dhamma, that is to say practise *śīla, samādhi,* and *prajñā,* practise *maitrī* and *karuṇā*. It may be easier for the monk to practise the Dhamma, because he has more time, but the layman can practise the Dhamma too if he is sufficiently determined. A layman can become a Stream Entrant. A layman, in fact,

can become Enlightened. Many examples of this are mentioned in the Pāli scriptures.[344]

But some centuries after the time of the Buddha, a change took place. People started thinking that becoming a monk, i.e. shaving the head and wearing a yellow robe, was the most important thing. Maybe some people thought that monks had an easy life. In this way, the *Dhammadiksha* became less important. Going for Refuge became less important. Some people started thinking that only the monk really took *Dhammadiksha*. They even thought that only the monk was the real Buddhist. Other people were *not* real Buddhists. *Their* duty was simply to feed and support the monks. This was the first reason for the disappearance of Buddhism from India: that the *bhikkhus* became separated from the lay people. We shall see what the consequences of this development were later on.

2. The second reason for the disappearance of Buddhism from India was that the monks started living in bigger and bigger viharas. At first, during the lifetime of the Buddha, viharas were very small, just *kuṭis* with one or two rooms. But gradually viharas became very large indeed. Sometimes there were hundreds of *bhikkhus* living together in the same vihara, or even thousands, as at Nālandā, Vikramaśilā and Odantapuri.[345] According to the Chinese pilgrim Xuanzang, Nālandā had 12,000 to 14,000 monk students and 1,000 monk professors.[346] It was just like a modern university. This was very good from an academic point of view, but not so good from a social point of view, or from the point of view of the propagation of the Dhamma. Since the monks lived together in big monasteries, they lost contact with ordinary people. They even lost interest in ordinary people. Being neglected in this way, ordinary people started thinking that Buddhism had nothing to do with them but was just the concern of the monks in the big monasteries.

3. The third reason for Buddhism's disappearance from India was that the monks started depending exclusively on the patronage of Buddhist kings or kings sympathetic to Buddhism. The big viharas with their thousands of monks were of course very expensive to maintain. Only the king, or a very rich merchant, could do it. In the early days of Buddhism the monks used to go out begging. Two or three *bhikkhus* went to this village for food, two or three *bhikkhus* went to that village. But later everything changed. The monks stayed in the big monasteries and were

supported by the king. They didn't go to the village begging, so in this way too they lost contact with ordinary people. Not only that. The present king might be a Buddhist, but the next king might be a Hindu, even a Brahmin, and a Hindu king probably wouldn't want to support big Buddhist viharas. He would want to celebrate big *yajñas*, or feed thousands of Brahmins. So whenever a Hindu king succeeded to the throne Buddhism was weakened.

4. The fourth reason for Buddhism's disappearance was that the lay people came increasingly under the influence of Hinduism and the Brahmins. The monks were mostly staying in the big viharas, and the lay people were neglected because the monks were not taking the trouble to teach the Dhamma to them. The lay people started feeling that the Buddha-Dhamma was not for them, but only for the monks, and the result was that they came under the influence of Hinduism, which meant under the influence of the Brahmins, who of course had been there all the time. Thus there was no Buddhist lay community in existence any more. There were only monks in the big monasteries, and lay people who had fallen under the influence of the Brahmins – in some cases under the influence of Shankaracharya. This did not happen all at once, of course. The lay people became first of all seventy-five-percent Buddhist, then fifty-percent, then twenty-percent. In the end they weren't even five-percent Buddhist.

5. The fifth reason for Buddhism's disappearance was that the monks in the monasteries became one-sidedly intellectual. Monks were the educated people among the Buddhists, and they gradually came to be occupied with questions of a purely intellectual nature, questions with which the Buddha himself had not been concerned, and that had nothing to do with the attainment of Enlightenment or with the development of the individual human being. The monks became just scholars. There's nothing wrong with being a scholar, of course, but it's not good to be just a scholar. One must also practise the Dhamma. As a result of their becoming one-sidedly intellectual, the monks not only lost contact with people but also lost real contact with the Dhamma itself. Perhaps the two things are connected.

6. The sixth reason for Buddhism's disappearance from India was the Muslim invasion. Muslims are very much against the practice of making images, and when they see them, they can even become quite upset and want to smash them. It was therefore not surprising that the

Muslim invaders of India should have destroyed many images. They also destroyed many viharas, and killed many monks. Other monks fled to Tibet and other places. What, then, was left? There were no Buddhist viharas; they had been destroyed. There were no Buddhist monks; they had been killed, or had gone away. Only the lay people were left, and they were under the influence of the Brahmins. They were only twenty-percent Buddhist, or even less. Consequently, after the Muslim invasion was over, the viharas were not rebuilt. People did not become monks any more. Some of the images of the Buddha were turned into Hindu images or given Hindu names.

No doubt there were other reasons why Buddhism disappeared from India, but these are the six most important reasons. Now, as I said at the beginning, it is important that we should understand why Buddhism disappeared from India, because we shall then be in a position to prevent the same thing happening again. So let us look at each of these reasons in turn, very briefly, and see how we can do this. We shall then make quite sure that the Buddhist movement in India will continue to grow, and that Dr Ambedkar's work is not destroyed.

First of all, Buddhism disappeared from India because the *bhikkhus* became separated from the lay people. So we mustn't allow this to happen. We must realize that all Buddhists, whether monastic or lay, have gone for Refuge to the Buddha, to the Dhamma, and to the Sangha. This is the important thing. It doesn't matter so much whether we are living as a *bhikkhu*, or whether we are living as a lay person. What is important is that we have all taken the *Dhammadiksha* and that we all practise the Dhamma. On 14 October 1956, Dr Ambedkar simply gave his followers the *Dhammadiksha*, i.e. gave them the *tisaraṇa* and *pañcasīla*. He didn't say anything at all about their becoming *bhikkhus*. In fact, Dr Ambedkar criticized the *bhikkhus*. He said we need a new kind of *bhikkhu*, a new kind of Buddhist worker and teacher, and this is what we have tried to produce with our Trailokya Bauddha Mahasangha. TBM consists of *dasa sīla upāsakas*, including *anagārikas*, and Dhammacharis. Most of them are working full time for the Dhamma. They are giving lectures, leading Dhamma study classes and *Dhamma-shibirs*, writing books, editing magazines, teaching meditation, etc. These Dhammacharis are not separate from the rest of the Buddhist community. They are part of it. They are in close contact with it. In this way we keep the Mahāsaṅgha – in the sense of the wider community of all Buddhists – united, and prevent Buddhism from disappearing from India.

Secondly, Buddhism disappeared from India because the monks started living in bigger and bigger viharas. This sort of thing will not happen with the new kind of Buddhist workers. It will not happen with the Dhammacharis and Dhammacharinis. They will not live in just a few big centres, but in many small centres. They will live in the midst of ordinary people, and in close contact with them. Moreover, there will not only be many small centres, but these centres will be spread over as wide an area as possible. They will be spread not only all over Marathwada, not only all over Maharashtra, but all over India – even all over the world. As Dr Ambedkar said, we need a world Buddhist mission. So we must have just one Buddhist community, not a community of lay people and a separate community of *bhikkhus*. We must have one *Dhammadiksha*, one going for Refuge. If we have one Buddhist community this also will prevent Buddhism from disappearing from India again.

Thirdly, Buddhism disappeared from India because of lack of royal patronage. It is very dangerous for a religious movement to depend for its support on just one person, whether that person be a king or a very rich man. We should depend for our support on many people. In fact, we should depend on everybody's support. Everybody in the Buddhist community is Buddhist, so everybody has responsibility for supporting Buddhism. We should support it with time and energy, support it with thought, support it with money. Anagārika Lokamitra tells me that in Maharashtra people like giving money to the speaker after a Dhamma meeting. This is very good. First of all, it shows that people *have* money, and they also have the feeling to give. But Anagārika Lokamitra tells me that he is not quite happy that people should give *dāna* just to him personally after a lecture. He says that he would rather people spent the money on the Dhamma – for instance that they bought the TBM publications, especially the quarterly *Buddhayan*. In this way you would help yourselves and at the same time help Dhamma activities, because *everybody* has responsibility for supporting Buddhism. In any case, there's no Buddhist king in India any more. India is a secular state. And there is no very rich Buddhist industrialist – no Buddhist Birla or Tata. But this is a very good thing. It means that everybody has to support Buddhism, and if everybody supports Buddhism then Buddhism will not disappear from India again.

Fourthly, Buddhism disappeared from India because the lay people came under the influence of Hinduism. If the *anagārikas* and the *dasa sīla upāsakas* keep in touch with the lay people, then this will not happen. In fact there will not be any lay people in the old sense, i.e. people who call themselves Buddhists, but are simply supporting the monks. All will be full-time Buddhists, one-hundred-percent Buddhists. All will practise the Dhamma. There will be no separate lay Buddhist community under the influence of Hinduism. Dr Ambedkar saw this danger very clearly. That is why he gave his followers not only the *tisaraṇa* and *pañcasīla*, but also the twenty-two *pratijñās* or vows, because the observance of these twenty-two *pratijñās* would prevent Buddhists from coming under the influence of Hinduism.

I remember that originally, just after the great *Dhammadiksha* of 14 October 1956, certain *bhikkhus* were very much against the twenty-two *pratijñās* because they were not given by the Buddha. It is true that they were not given by the Buddha, but nevertheless the twenty-two *pratijñās* are still very, very important. In fact they are absolutely necessary. If we observe the twenty-two *pratijñās* then this will prevent Buddhism from disappearing from India again.

Fifthly, Buddhism disappeared from India because the monks became one-sidedly intellectual. Nowadays many people are one-sidedly intellectual, especially people who are highly educated. We find this tendency even among educated Buddhists. They read Dr Ambedkar's writings, especially *The Buddha and His Dhamma*, but they don't like to practise Buddhism. They just want to discuss various controversial points. In this way they lose contact with Buddhists who are less highly educated, or who do not have such high positions in government service as they perhaps do. They may even think that they are better than those Buddhists, whereas they are not really Buddhists at all but just highly educated people who talk about Buddhism. So we must keep Buddhism practical, keep it simple, keep it, as we say, 'down to earth'. If we keep Buddhism practical then this, also, will prevent Buddhism from disappearing from India again.

Sixthly and lastly, Buddhism disappeared from India because of the Muslim invasion. Today India is a secular state. There is no danger of any Muslim invasion. Everybody is free to practise his own religion, and the government does not favour any particular religion. We therefore have no difficulty in carrying on our Buddhist activities, no difficulty in spreading the Dhamma. All that we have to do is to take the initiative ourselves. We don't need anybody else's permission. We don't have to wait for someone else to take the initiative – not even the *anagārikas* or the *dasa sīla upāsakas*. I was very glad to learn that this programme was organized by the Bauddha Mitra Mandal, that is to say, organized by the *Dhammasahayaks* of the TBMSG. I am very glad that they have taken the initiative in this way. Maybe this is one of the reasons why tonight's programme has been so successful – why so many of you have come, and why everything is so beautifully organized.

If everybody takes the initiative then the Dhamma will continue to spread in Marathwada, in Maharashtra, and throughout India. If everybody takes the initiative then Buddhism will be prevented from disappearing from India again. So, we must have one Buddhist community, the community of all those who take the *Dhammadiksha*, all those who go for Refuge. We must have a new kind of *bhikkhu*, that is to say, we must have Dhammacharis and Dhammacharinis. We must not have just a few big Buddhist centres but many small ones, all over India, and all over the world. We must realize that Buddhism depends for its support on everybody, not just on a few rich people. We must not mix Buddhism with Hinduism. We must observe the twenty-two *pratijñās*. We must keep Buddhism practical, and not allow it to become merely a subject for intellectual discussion. Finally we must all learn to take the initiative in spreading Buddhism, in organizing programmes, just as the Bauddha Mitra Mandal has done tonight. If you can do all these things, then Buddhism will not disappear from India again. If you can do all these things, Buddhism will be more and more firmly established here in Nanded, more and more firmly established in Marathwada, in Maharashtra, and in India, and it will never disappear again. You yourselves will lead happier and ever happier lives and Dr Ambedkar's great dream will be fulfilled.

24

ASPECTS OF THE MIDDLE WAY

Latur, 30 January 1982

Brothers and Sisters in the Dhamma: For the last six weeks I have been giving lectures in different parts of Maharashtra, and for the last two or three weeks I have been on tour in Marathwada. I am very glad to be here and wherever I have gone I have been given a wonderful reception. I have seen people's enthusiasm for the Dhamma and I have seen statues of Dr Ambedkar. Last night I was in Nanded where we had a really magnificent programme that was very well organized indeed. The night before that I was in Parbhani, the night before that in Ambad, and the night before that in Aurangabad where we had many meetings especially at Milind College. Tonight I am here in Latur[347] and I am very glad to see you all and to see the fine arrangements you have made for this meeting. Buddhists everywhere are brothers and sisters; we all belong to one great spiritual family and therefore we should all help one another and work together for the Dhamma.

Although this is my first visit to Latur, Anagārika Lokamitra has been here before and given several lectures. He has told me that the people of Latur are full of energy for Dhamma work and I was very glad to hear this. Buddhists need energy because without energy we cannot practise or propagate the Dhamma. Energy or *vīrya* is one of what Buddhists call the five *indriyas* or five spiritual faculties, the others being *śraddhā* or faith, *prajñā* or wisdom, *samādhi* or meditation and *smṛti* or mindfulness.[348] When these five faculties are well developed it is possible for us to gain Enlightenment. *Vīrya* is also the fourth *pāramitā*, the others being *dāna* or generosity, *śīla* or morality, *kṣānti* or patience and tolerance, *samādhi* or meditation, and *prajñā* or wisdom. These six *paramitās* have to be practised by the bodhisattva, that is, by the Buddhist who wishes to gain Enlightenment for the sake of all living beings. Thus *vīrya* or energy is of great importance and I am therefore glad to hear that the Buddhists of Latur have plenty of it. However, tonight, I shall not be talking about energy because here there is no need for me to speak on that subject. Instead, I shall be talking about something else that is also of great importance: the Middle Way.

The Buddha's teaching of the Middle Way is one of the most important teachings in the whole field of Buddhism, but people don't always understand it properly. Usually they understand it very superficially, thinking it means, on the one hand, not giving yourself a very difficult time and, on the other hand, not giving yourself a very easy time. But it means much more than that. In fact, the Middle Way can be understood on a number of different levels, and tonight I am going to look at just some of these. I am going to look at the Middle Way in philosophy, in psychology, in ethics, in social life, and in the Buddhist movement itself. I will deal with the Middle Way in philosophy, psychology, and ethics rather more briefly since these aspects of it are rather more difficult to understand. Nonetheless, I want to say at least something about them. We can't always be dealing with the elementary teachings of Buddhism. From time to time we should learn something new and more advanced that will deepen our understanding of Buddhism and enable us to practise it more effectively. With the Middle Way in social life and in the Buddhist movement itself I shall deal at greater length since these aspects of the Middle Way are of more general interest. Under the heading of the Middle Way in social life I want to say something about the role of women as well as something about food, which is, of course, a subject that is of interest to everybody!

1. THE MIDDLE WAY IN PHILOSOPHY

Here we have to understand something about the nature of thinking, as well as something about the nature of speech. When we talk about things we usually talk about them in terms of their being this or not being that. We talk about their existence or non-existence in a particular respect or under certain conditions of time and space. We say, for instance, that motor cars did not exist a hundred years ago but they do now, or that mangoes grow in India but not in England. This is the way we talk, and we think in the same way, in terms of existence and non-existence. This is all right when we are talking about worldly things, because they are limited, that is to say, they arise in dependence on causes and conditions. But we cannot speak in the same way about what we call ultimate reality. Ultimate reality is not limited in any way and it does not arise in dependence on causes and conditions. It is beyond space and time; to use the Buddhist term, it is *lokuttara*. We cannot say that it exists and we cannot say that it does not exist (in the worldly sense), and therefore we cannot say anything about it at all. According to the Buddha it is *atakkāvacara* or beyond thought and therefore we can only be silent about it. It is something to be realized in our own personal experience, especially in our experience of meditation. It is something to be realized through the development of *samādhi* and *prajñā*.

Thus there is a Middle Way between the two extreme concepts of existence and non-existence, neither of which can be applied to ultimate reality. In fact there is no concept at all that can be applied to ultimate reality. It is empty of all concepts, empty of all limitations, and therefore we call it *śūnyatā*. This is the Middle Way in philosophy.

2. THE MIDDLE WAY IN PSYCHOLOGY

Here also there are two extreme views. According to one extreme, man has an eternal, unchanging *ātman*, and according to the other, he does not have an *ātman* at all. One extreme maintains that man consists of a changing body and unchanging *ātman*, while the other maintains that man consists only of a changing body. Here also Buddhism follows a Middle Way. According to Buddhism a human being consists of a changing body and a changing *ātman*. However, Buddhism does not actually use the word *ātman*. In India it is dangerous to use that word, because people invariably think it means something eternal and unchanging. Instead Buddhism uses the term *manas* or *citta* and sometimes it uses the term *vijñāna*.

Thus, according to Buddhism, as human beings we consist of a changing body and a changing mind. The mind in fact changes more rapidly than the body. We cannot actually see the body changing – we have to observe it over a long period of time – but we can see the mind changing every minute. Not only that. The mind can change in two different ways. It can change for the better; it can become more and more *kuśala*, as we say, more and more full of *maitrī, karuṇā,* and *prajñā*. On the other hand, it can change for the worse; it can become more and more *akuśala*, more and more full of greed, hatred, and delusion. It can come closer and closer to Nirvāṇa or Enlightenment, or it can move further and further away from it. If it was not possible for the mind to change then we could not gain Enlightenment. We could not change for the better.

The Buddha saw that there was no permanent unchanging *ātman*. Buddhists therefore follow a Middle Way according to which human beings consist of a changing body and a changing mind – a mind that is capable of changing for the better. Because the mind is capable of changing for the better it is possible to gain Enlightenment and it is possible to be a Buddhist. This is the Middle Way in psychology.

3. THE MIDDLE WAY IN ETHICS

This aspect of the Middle Way is closely connected with the life and experience of the Buddha. The Buddha was born into a wealthy Śākya family. His father was a king and as a young man he had every comfort and luxury: three beautiful palaces, many dancing girls, and a wife and child. Moreover, he had no work and no responsibility, so that all he had to do was enjoy himself as much as he could. This was one extreme – the extreme of self-indulgence. But at the age of twenty-nine the Buddha gave up that life. He just grew tired of it. He wanted something more than that, something better. So he left his palaces and his dancing girls, left his father and his wife and child, left everything he had and went off alone into the jungle. In the jungle he went to the opposite extreme, the extreme of self-mortification, because that was the fashion in India at that time, and people thought that if you tortured yourself sufficiently you would be sure to gain Enlightenment. So the Buddha stopped wearing clothes, reduced his food to the absolute minimum of two or three grains of rice a day, and he did not wash or bathe. But he found that self-mortification did not lead to Enlightenment either, so he gave up this extreme too, and decided to follow a Middle Way between self-indulgence on the one hand and self-mortification on the other. As a result of this decision he started eating properly again. He accepted the offering of *kheer* or milk-rice from Sujātā and, having strengthened himself in this way, he sat down at the foot of the bodhi tree, meditated, and gained Enlightenment.[349] This is the Middle Way in ethics.

The Buddha did not say that it was wrong to have a decent standard of living with sufficient food and clothing.[350] As Dr Ambedkar once pointed out, Buddhism does not sanctify poverty. Poverty is a curse and riches can be a blessing but only if they are used in the right way. So let us have proper food, clothing, and shelter and a decent standard of living but let us not make these things the principal objects in our lives. On the contrary, let us devote our energies to the Dhamma. Let us be like the Buddha and eat milk-rice by all means but let us also meditate; we will then be following the Middle Way in ethics.

4. THE MIDDLE WAY IN SOCIAL LIFE

Social life is a very complex thing and there are many aspects of the Middle Way that could be considered in this connection. But as I said earlier, today I will consider two: the role of women; and food.

i. There are many women here tonight and I have seen this all over Maharashtra wherever there are Dhamma meetings. Sometimes there are more women than men. Women are very interested in the Dhamma and they are very generous and give a lot of money for the Dhamma. In fact, without the support of women, Dhamma activities probably could not be carried on. Although the women may not be sitting up on the platform and speaking from the microphone, nonetheless they are very important. They are present in large numbers at every Dhamma meeting. Everywhere I have gone on my tour, the women have always greeted me on arrival with garlands and trays of lighted candles. In some places I have been greeted by hundreds of women in white saris. Wherever I have gone, in fact, the women have shown great enthusiasm and devotion, and I am very glad to see this.

At the same time, I am not quite satisfied, because I would like to see the women taking a more active part in Dhamma work. Now I know this is difficult because women have to cook, look after the children, and sometimes go out to work as well. But still I think they could do more for the Dhamma, especially if they were encouraged more by the men. They may not all be able to give lectures or organize big programmes, but there are other things they could do. They could work more among themselves and with their children. They could study the Dhamma and read *Buddhayan*. Women who can read should read *Buddhayan* out loud to women who cannot read. They should teach the Dhamma and Buddhist manners and customs to their own children, and to other children as well. In Poona we have two women – two *Dhammamitras* – who are doing this. Every week they hold Dhamma classes for forty or fifty children, and that is very good. Women also must work for the Dhamma and for society, and they can do that without losing their womanly modesty and dignity. We don't want to shut women up in the zenana as some communities do and we don't want them to hide their faces behind a veil or to be afraid to talk to people outside their own family. That would be one extreme. But on the other hand we don't want them to behave in the shameless and indecent manner in which some modern Western women behave. That would be the other extreme. Buddhist women should take their proper place in Buddhist society. They should take an active part in Dhamma work and I hope to see more of this in the future. Women have tremendous faith and devotion and they also have great energy which should not be wasted but used for the Dhamma. This is the Middle Way in social life with regard to women.

ii. As regards the Middle Way in social life with regard to food, I am not going to talk about food itself, but the eating of food, or rather, about inviting people to your house to eat food. In India people are hospitable. Some say the Punjabis are the most hospitable, some say the Bengalis and others the Maharashtrians, but there is no doubt that all Indians are very hospitable. Anagārika Lokamitra and I have plenty of experience of this. Wherever we go people want to invite us to their houses for a meal. They want to give us food, sometimes even when we don't want it because we are ill or have more important things to do. Now we are very happy to be invited to people's homes for a meal and we very much appreciate their hospitality, but we do not regard eating as our most important activity. Eating is for the sake of the Dhamma. We eat so that we may have strength to practise and propagate the Dhamma. The Dhamma is not for the sake of eating and eating is not our Dhamma.

So we have to avoid extremes here and follow a Middle Way. One extreme is not inviting anyone to your house for a meal at all. People in India are not in danger of following this extreme and Buddhists are certainly not in danger of following it. But they are sometimes in danger of going to the other extreme. Sometimes people try to fit the whole Dhamma programme into the eating part, instead of fitting the eating part into the rest of the programme. Sometimes they even get angry if we are unable to accept their invitation, and they forget all about the Dhamma. This is what the Hindus call *tamasic bhakti*. Lokamitra and I had some experience of this on my last visit to India three years ago. It happened not in Maharashtra but in Gujarat. A certain medical doctor had invited our whole party, consisting of some eight or nine people, to his house for lunch, but when the day came I happened to be quite ill with heatstroke. I had a high temperature and was confined to bed, so I could not go to the doctor's house for lunch, and Lokamitra and the rest of the party went without me. When the doctor saw that I had not come he became very, very angry and said, 'If Bhante Sangharakshita does not come I am not going to feed anybody else.' Lokamitra tried to explain the situation but the doctor would not listen. He just went on shouting, 'If Bhante does not come to my house I am not going to feed anybody.' Lokamitra thought this behaviour was very strange indeed. He thought, 'This man is a Buddhist. He is an educated man, a medical doctor, but he does not care about Bhante's health. He does not even care if Bhante dies. He just wants to feed him.' So we must not go to this extreme either. We must follow a Middle Way. It is good to feed people and be hospitable but we must do it in accordance with the Dhamma. We must not regard it as an end in itself. This is the Middle Way in social life with regard to food.

5. THE MIDDLE WAY IN THE BUDDHIST MOVEMENT

Here I am going to be quite brief. Buddhism is, in a sense, a very old religion. It is 2,500 years old, and in the course of its existence it has undergone many developments, some of which have taken place in India and others in China, Japan, and Tibet, Sri Lanka, Burma, and Thailand. Not all of these developments may be useful to us now, but we are free, as Buddhists, simply to put to one side those developments that are not useful to us. We don't have to follow something that is traditionally part of Buddhism simply because it is old or because people have followed it for a long time. That is one extreme.

At the same time, we don't have to reject something that is traditionally part of Buddhism simply because it is old. If it is useful then we should accept it, and if it is not useful we need not accept it. This is the Middle Way in the Buddhist movement itself. Tonight I have no time to go into the matter in detail, or to give any examples. You can do this for yourselves by reading *Buddhayan* where there are many articles dealing with this very subject, some by myself, some by Anagārika Lokamitra and some by our *dasa sīla upāsakas*.

So tonight I have touched upon at least some aspects of the Middle Way. I have dealt with the Middle Way in philosophy, psychology, ethics, social life, and in the Buddhist movement itself. I am very glad to have had this opportunity of speaking to you all here in Latur tonight. I wish success to all your Buddhist activities, I congratulate the young men who organized this splendid function, and I hope we may all meet again.

25

DR AMBEDKAR'S DHAMMA REVOLUTION AND ITS IMPORTANCE IN THE SCIENTIFIC AGE OF TODAY

Sholapur,[351] *1 February 1982*

Mr Chairman, Brothers and Sisters in the Dhamma: At present I am on a three-month visit to India, but although I shall be visiting Gujarat, Rajasthan, and Delhi, I shall be spending most of my time in Maharashtra. After all, Maharashtra is the centre of the Buddhist movement in India. We have more Buddhists here than in any other part of the country. I also have a lot of personal contacts in Maharashtra, and a lot of personal friends – some of them very good ones. For the last three weeks I have been on tour in Marathwada, as well as in two or three of the adjacent districts, and I have given lectures on the Dhamma practically every day. Tonight I am very glad to be here in Sholapur and to have the opportunity of speaking to you. This happens to be my first visit to Sholapur, but the city's name is known even in England on account of its *dhurries*, which are imported from this place in large numbers. (I am sure that any local businessmen sitting here will be glad to hear this.) Sholapur is also quite a big place – the fourth biggest city in Maharashtra in terms of population, my friends tell me, after Bombay, Nagpur, and Poona.

I have a close personal connection with all three of these cities. I visited Bombay for the first time in 1944. In fact, it was the first place in India that I ever saw, when I arrived there by ship from England during the war. My most important connection with Bombay is, however, a Buddhist connection, because it was there that I first met Dr Babasaheb Ambedkar.

Having been in correspondence with Dr Ambedkar since 1950, I met him in Bombay on two separate occasions, first in 1952 and then in 1955. At the time of our second meeting he was thinking very seriously about changing his religion, and had in fact already decided to become a Buddhist, but there were certain things about which he was still not quite clear. When we met in Bombay in 1955 (I think it was in the month of December) he therefore asked me a number of questions. First of all, he asked me, 'How does one become a Buddhist? If I wanted to become a Buddhist, what would I have to do?' I replied that becoming a Buddhist was, in a sense, quite a simple matter. All you had to do was to take the *tisaraṇa* and *pañcasīla* from a *bhikkhu*. Dr Ambedkar then asked me who among the *bhikkhus* could give him the *tisaraṇa* and *pañcasīla*. I replied that any *bhikkhu* could give them to him. Dr Ambedkar's next question was, 'Could *you* give them to me?' To this I replied that I certainly could, but that it would be better if he took the *tisaraṇa* and *pañcasīla* from the oldest and most senior *bhikkhu* in India, who at that time was U Chandramani of Kusinara, whom I knew quite well, since it was from him that I had received my *śrāmaṇera* ordination in 1949. And in due course, on 14 October 1956, at Nagpur, Dr Ambedkar took the *Dhammadiksha* from U Chandramani and in turn gave it to *lakhs* of his followers. At the end of our second meeting in Bombay Dr Ambedkar asked me if I would address a gathering of his followers and explain to them the significance of conversion to Buddhism. Naturally I agreed, and a meeting was arranged. It took place in Worli, late at night, and was attended by several thousand people. In the course of my lecture I explained the meaning of going for Refuge to the Buddha, Dhamma, and Sangha, as well as the significance of the *pañcasīla*. Thus I have a very strong Buddhist connection with Bombay.[352]

I also have a very strong Buddhist connection with Nagpur. I happened to be there on the very day that Dr Ambedkar died. In fact, I arrived there that morning, having been invited to give a lecture on the Dhamma in Nagpur on my way back to Calcutta. On my arrival at the station I found 2,000 people waiting on the platform to receive me, and was escorted to the house of a friend. I was still resting, and beginning to think about my lecture, when there came the dreadful news that Dr Ambedkar was dead. Like Buddhists all over Maharashtra, indeed all over India, the Buddhists of Nagpur were absolutely stunned. They didn't know what to do, didn't know what to think. They didn't know what would happen to them, or to the movement of mass conversion that Dr Ambedkar had started. Thousands of them started coming to the house where I was staying (I was the only *bhikkhu* in Nagpur at that time), and the friends who had arranged my Dhamma lecture asked me to say something to them. Since it was difficult for me to address so many people without a microphone and loudspeakers I asked them to arrange a condolence meeting in Kasturchand Park that same night. That meeting was attended by about one *lakh* of people, and it was one of the most impressive sights I have ever seen. People came in procession from all over Nagpur. They came in silence, and everyone carried a lighted candle in his hand. One could see tens of thousands of lighted candles converging on Kasturchand Park from all directions. When everybody had arrived, the meeting began. There was a microphone and loudspeakers, but since there had been no time to put up a stage I had to speak standing on the seat of an old-fashioned hand rickshaw. Other people also spoke, or rather tried to speak, but when they stood up they were unable to say anything. They opened their mouths, but no words would come. All that they could do was weep, so that I had to do all the speaking. At one point the entire crowd were weeping as though they had lost their own mother and father, and even more than that. They had lost their best friend, their saviour. They felt orphaned. They felt that their own life had come to an end and they didn't know what was going to happen to the movement of mass conversion. When I spoke to them I therefore said, 'Dr Ambedkar may be dead, but his work is not dead. His work will go on. It will never die. In fact, Dr Ambedkar himself will never die. People will always remember him. They will be inspired by his great example. Dr Ambedkar will live on in you and in your work for the Dhamma.' In this way I spoke to that crowd of people, and after hearing my words they felt a little comforted and started feeling that there was some hope. After the meeting I stayed on in Nagpur for four more days, in the course of which I gave thirty-five lectures in the different parts of the city. I think I spoke to everybody in Nagpur, to all the Buddhists, as well as to some non-Buddhists. This is why I have a very strong Buddhist connection with Nagpur, which I have visited many times since 1956.

I also have a very strong Buddhist connection with Poona. I have given more Dhamma lectures there than in any other place in India. Probably I have given over 200 lectures there, most of them between

1957 and 1967. In Poona we also started our first Indian centre of the FWBO/TBMSG – the new Buddhist movement that I started in England in 1967. This is now the biggest and most active Buddhist movement in Europe, with flourishing centres in eight different countries, including India. In Poona the TBMSG is run by Anagārika Lokamitra and the rest of the *dasa sīla upāsakas* or Dhammacharis. Between them they carry on the various activities, such as giving lectures on the Dhamma, conducting Dhamma study classes, organizing *Dhamma-shibirs*, and bringing out publications on the Dhamma in Marathi and English, including our quarterly Buddhist magazine *Buddhayan*. These activities are being carried on not only in Poona, but in many other parts of Maharashtra. Thus my Buddhist connection with Poona, too, is a very strong one.

Since I already have a strong Buddhist connection with Bombay, Nagpur, and Poona, the three biggest cities in Maharashtra, it seems only right that I should also develop a strong Buddhist connection with Sholapur. I therefore hope that I will be able to develop this connection with you all in the future, and that I can make a start on it tonight.

I am aware that some of you wanted me to talk tonight about Dr Ambedkar's conversion. In fact, yesterday I was shown the big blue and white poster that has been put up all over Sholapur announcing tonight's meeting. This poster said (in Marathi, of course) that I was going to speak on 'Dr Ambedkar's Conversion and its Importance in the Scientific Age of Today'. Now, this came as rather a surprise to me. I felt a bit like Dr Ambedkar felt in Kathmandu in 1956, when he was unexpectedly asked to address a meeting on the subject of Buddhism and communism. 'Conversion' is a very big subject in itself, as is 'the Scientific Age', and it is quite impossible for me to do justice to them in one brief lecture. However, I don't want to disappoint you, especially those of you who have come to hear me speak on the subject as announced. So I will make just a few remarks on it. However, I want to make just one small change. Instead of speaking on 'Dr Ambedkar's Conversion and its Importance in the Scientific Age of Today' I am going to speak on 'Dr Ambedkar's Dhamma Revolution and its Importance in the Scientific Age of Today'.

This at once raises the question of what difference there is between conversion to the Dhamma and Dhamma Revolution. In a sense, they are the same thing. The difference is mainly one of emphasis, or of emotional feeling. I don't know how it is in Marathi, but in English

'Dhamma Revolution' is a much stronger term than 'conversion'. This is because 'revolution' is itself a much stronger term than 'change'. Nowadays, of course, revolution is a very popular term all over the world, at least in some circles. Basically, it is a political term. It refers to a complete, radical change in the political life and institutions of a whole nation, a whole state. Political changes are usually accompanied by social and economic changes, even by intellectual changes. Moreover, revolutions usually take place suddenly and dramatically, even though the build-up to them may have been going on for quite a long time. Revolutions in the ordinary sense are also accompanied, usually, by violence. In fact they are usually brought about by violence.

In modern times four great political revolutions have taken place in four different countries. First of all, there was the English Revolution, also known as the Puritan Revolution, which took place about 350 years ago, in the middle of the seventeenth century. The religious and political party of the Puritans executed the king for offences against the people, and for twelve years England was a republic. The long-term effect of the revolution was to transform England from an absolute monarchy into a limited or constitutional monarchy. Political power passed first to the big landowners, and then to the merchant class.

Next, came the American Revolution. This took place just over 200 years ago, when the British colonies in North America broke away from the rule of the British crown. They wanted to be independent and to govern themselves. Their motto was 'No taxation without representation', and they set up a republic which fifty states eventually joined. Thus we have the name 'United States of America'. After becoming independent, America developed very rapidly and became the richest country in the world.

Thirdly, there was the French Revolution. This took place almost exactly 200 years ago, when the French people executed *their* king and proclaimed a republic. However, under Napoleon this republic soon became a dictatorship, and Napoleon crowned himself emperor. The motto of the French Revolution was 'Liberty, Equality, and Fraternity'. Dr Ambedkar, who made a close study of the French Revolution, was deeply impressed by this motto and often referred to it in his speeches and writings. In fact he believed that liberty, equality, and fraternity for all beings was the Buddha's teaching also, and this was one of the reasons why he embraced Buddhism rather than any other religion.

Fourthly and lastly, there was the Russian Revolution. This took place in 1918 when, under the leadership of Lenin, the Russian communist Party seized political power in Russia. Overthrowing the government of the czar, they set up a socialist state in which the means of production belonged to, and were controlled by, not just a privileged minority but the whole people. In practice, however, the means of production were controlled by the Communist Party acting on behalf of, or in the name of, the people.

These, then, are the four great revolutions of modern times: the English, the American, the French, and the Russian. All four of them had certain features in common. To begin with, they all involved millions of people, in fact the whole of the nation or country concerned. Indeed, their effects even spilled over into other countries. Secondly, they took place quite suddenly and dramatically, even though they were preceded by a long build-up. Thirdly, they all involved the total life of the people. Their influence was not simply political, in the narrow sense of the term, but also social, economic, intellectual, and cultural. We can see this particularly clearly in the case of the French Revolution and the Russian Revolution. Fourthly, all four revolutions were accompanied by violence – were in fact achieved by violence.

But the term 'revolution' is not only used in connection with politics. It is also used in connection with other areas of human life. For instance, we speak of the Industrial Revolution. This started in England about 200 years ago and was a revolution in the means of production. It consisted in a change from the production of things by hand by the individual worker, usually at home, to the mass production of things by means of machinery in a factory. It was also a change from agriculture to industry, from the village to the city. As a result of the Industrial Revolution there was an enormously increased production of consumer goods, at first of simple things like cloth and then of more complex things like cameras and television sets. Since more goods were being produced than before, and more cheaply, it was possible for more people to enjoy them. This resulted in a rise in the general standard of living. From England the Industrial Revolution spread all over the world. It was not only an economic revolution, but brought about changes in people's social and cultural life as well. We can see these changes taking place in India too.

Another kind of revolution is what we call the Green Revolution. I don't know how this translates into Marathi, but doubtless many of you are familiar with the English term. The Green Revolution is a revolution in food production brought about by the introduction of new kinds of crops and new agricultural methods, including the use of machinery, and in particular by increased water supply, especially increased irrigation. I saw something of this Green Revolution quite recently when passing through Marathwada and the adjoining districts.

Now we can also speak of a Dhamma Revolution, and from what I have said already it will be clear to you, in a general way, what Dhamma Revolution means. First of all, it involves a very large number of people, and brings about far-reaching changes in all aspects of their lives. It is also brought about suddenly, even dramatically, though as a result of a lot of previous preparation over a long time. Dr Ambedkar's Dhamma Revolution conforms to this pattern, so we can speak of it as a revolution.

First of all, it involved large numbers – in fact millions – of people, not only in Maharashtra but all over India, in almost every corner of the country. For this reason we can speak of Dr Ambedkar's Dhamma Revolution.

Secondly, the Dhamma Revolution involves a radical change in every aspect of life. This has certainly happened in the case of those who have followed Dr Ambedkar's example and taken the *Dhammadiksha*. They have given up all sorts of old, bad customs. In fact, they started giving them up even before the mass conversion of 1956. They gave up worshipping Hindu gods and goddesses and celebrating Hindu festivals. They gave up utilizing the services of Brahmin priests. They gave up performing *shraddh* and *pindadan* ceremonies.[353] They gave up giving dowries with their daughters at the time of marriage and spending more money on marriage festivities than they could afford. They even gave up drinking liquor. They gave up doing dirty work that no one else wanted to do. In short, they gave up all sorts of bad customs and bad habits. Nor was that all. They adopted all sorts of new, good customs. They started reciting the *tisaraṇa* and *pañcasīla*. Indeed, they started observing the *pañcasīla*. They started listening to the Dhamma, just as you are all doing now. They started practising meditation and attending *Dhamma-shibirs*. Their standard of living also improved. They started living in better houses, wearing better clothes, and eating better food. In other words, after taking the *Dhammadiksha* they became better and happier human beings. Radical changes took place in their lives.

They entered upon a new life. They were reborn. For this reason, also, we can speak of Dr Ambedkar's Dhamma Revolution.

Thirdly, Dr Ambedkar's Dhamma Revolution took place suddenly, even dramatically, though not without long previous preparation. It took place on 14 October 1956, at Nagpur, when together with *lakhs* of his followers Dr Ambedkar took the *Dhammadiksha*. One minute they were all Hindus; the next minute they were all Buddhists. Thus it was all very sudden and very dramatic. No wonder orthodox Hindus all over India were absolutely stunned! No wonder they did their best to misrepresent Dr Ambedkar's motives! Yet prior to the great conversion ceremony there had, in fact, been a long process of preparation. Dr Ambedkar had been thinking about changing his religion for thirty years. In 1935, at the Yeola Conference, he declared that although he had been born a Hindu he did not intend to die one. Subsequently he studied various religions. He studied Islam, Christianity, Sikhism, Buddhism, and all the religions. But in the end he decided to adopt Buddhism. Buddhism, he declared, was rational. Buddhism was not against science. Buddhism did not believe in the caste system. It believed in liberty, equality, and fraternity. Moreover, Buddhism gave importance to morality, and it did not glorify poverty. Thus we see that although the great conversion took place suddenly, even dramatically, it was preceded by a long process of preparation on the part of Dr Ambedkar. For this reason, also, we can speak of Dr Ambedkar's Dhamma Revolution.

Dr Ambedkar's Dhamma Revolution was therefore a real revolution. Like the great revolutions of history, it involved large numbers of people, it involved radical changes in all aspects of their lives, and it took place suddenly, even dramatically, though not without long previous preparation. There was one respect, however, in which Dr Ambedkar's Dhamma Revolution differed profoundly from the great revolutions of history. It took place *without violence*. Dr Ambedkar did not believe that any lasting good could come from violence. This is one of the reasons why he adopted Buddhism, which teaches non-violence, and also one of the reasons why he could not accept communism, and why he disagreed with Marxism. Not that he disagreed with Karl Marx totally. He agreed with him up to a point. He agreed that the private ownership of property resulted in the exploitation of the poor by the rich, the majority by the minority – resulted, in short, in suffering, sorrow, and poverty. He also agreed that exploitation and suffering must be brought to an end.

Dr Ambedkar in fact maintained that when the Buddha spoke of *duḥkha* he meant exploitation, at least in some contexts. He did not always use the word in the sense of rebirth or *saṃsāra*. In Dr Ambedkar's opinion, Karl Marx's idea of getting rid of private property and the Buddha's idea of getting rid of suffering amounted to much the same thing. Dr Ambedkar in fact said that the Buddha anticipated Marxism by 2,500 years.[354] Therefore, he said, Buddhists do not need Marxism, do not need communism. Dr Ambedkar also pointed out that the Buddha himself abolished private property in the *bhikkhu saṅgha*, saying that the monk should not own any private property, but only the 'eight requisites', i.e. three robes, a begging-bowl, a water strainer, a girdle or belt, a razor, and a needle.[355] Everything else, such as land, buildings, and furniture, should be the collective property of the whole *saṅgha*.

Now the Buddha – as Dr Ambedkar saw – intended the *bhikkhu saṅgha* to be the model of the ideal society. He intended it to show the pattern of what the ideal society would be like. It was therefore clear that, according to the Buddha, there should be no private property in the ideal society. But nevertheless – as Dr Ambedkar also saw – there are great differences between Buddhism and communism. These differences relate to the methods used to bring exploitation to an end, to get rid of suffering, and to abolish private property. As Dr Ambedkar saw, here lies the fundamental difference between the Buddha and Karl Marx. The Buddha believed in getting things done by non-violent means: by persuasion, by moral teaching, and by *maitrī* or love. Communists, however, believe in getting things done by violence. They believe in physically annihilating their opponents. This is the fundamental difference. Dr Ambedkar also says that communism may achieve quick results in the short term, but that in the long run Buddhism is undoubtedly the surest way of abolishing private property and removing exploitation and suffering.

Dr Ambedkar's Dhamma Revolution is, therefore, not just a revolution in the ordinary historical sense. It is a revolution in the best and highest sense. It is a revolution that goes far beyond the English and the American, the French and the Russian, revolutions. It goes beyond them because it is a non-violent revolution – a revolution based on *maitrī, karuṇā*, and *prajñā*. For the Dhamma Revolution to be based on anything other than non-violence is indeed impossible. Non-violence is an integral part of the Dhamma and we cannot, therefore, bring about the Dhamma Revolution by any other means. To try to do so would be self-defeating. Nor is that all. Non-violent revolution is the only revolution that really works. The communist type of revolution, as Dr Ambedkar pointed out, does not really work, because in the communist state, as it at present exists, many people are held down simply by force. How long, he therefore asked, can such a state of affairs continue? In his opinion communism can give no answer to this question. So in the end we have to come back to non-violence, back to persuasion and love, back to Dhamma Revolution. We have to come back to Buddhism. And this is exactly what Dr Ambedkar did.

By coming back to Buddhism Dr Ambedkar brought about the greatest revolution India had seen for hundreds of years. He brought about the Dhamma Revolution – the best and highest kind of revolution, and the only kind that really works. He brought about a radical change in the lives of millions of people. He gave millions of people a new life. For this he will be remembered as long as India exists, as long as Buddhism exists – as long as there are people in the world who love liberty, equality, and fraternity. He will be remembered as long as there are people who hate exploitation and who work for the happiness and welfare of all human beings.

Now I have said quite a lot about Dr Ambedkar's Dhamma Revolution, but I have not said anything about the scientific age of today. So let me say just a very few words about that before concluding. We are living in the age of science – or rather, in the age of technology, technology being applied science. As a result of technology we have mass production, which means many consumer goods and a higher standard of living. Technology also brings about many other results. It is responsible for greatly improved facilities of communication, such as the telegraph, the telephone, and the radio, as well as for greatly improved means of transport, such as the train, the car, and the aeroplane. We can now travel quickly and easily from one place to another, just as I have been doing in Maharashtra. We can move from the villages into the towns and cities, and we can get work – often factory work – in the cities. The cities are therefore growing, and of course life in the city is very different from life in the village. In a big city no one knows who you are. In a big city you can be independent: you can be just a human being, because no one knows your previous history. In a small village it is very difficult to be just a human being, because there everybody knows who your father was and they know, or think they know, your previous history. It is therefore not surprising that in all the big cities of Maharashtra there should be many Buddhists, and many Buddhist activities, whether in Bombay, in Nagpur, in Poona, or here in Sholapur. It is not surprising that in the big cities Dr Ambedkar's Dhamma Revolution should be particularly successful. In the big cities Dr Ambedkar's Dhamma Revolution and the scientific age of today come together. They have come together here tonight. *We* have come together here tonight. Though this is my first visit to Sholapur, I very much hope that it will not be my last. From now onwards, I hope, I will have a strong Buddhist connection with Sholapur too. May we all meet again!

26

A NEW VIHARA MEANS A NEW LIFE

Chikhalwadi, 6 February 1982

Brothers and Sisters in the Dhamma: In the course of the last twenty-five or thirty years I have paid a number of visits to Poona and its different localities, but this is the first time I have been to Chikhalwadi.[356] The nearest I have got is Kirkee, which I have visited a number of times, and where I have given several lectures. I am therefore all the more glad to be here tonight to see you all. Though I have not been here before, I have heard quite a lot about Chikhalwadi from Lokamitra. He tells me that there are quite a lot of active young men here, and a lot of devoted women, bright young children, and experienced old people, and I can see all of this with my own eyes.

I am particularly glad to have had the opportunity of dedicating your vihara and shrine. Though the vihara is not very big, so that not everybody was able to get inside, nonetheless we had a very fine dedication ceremony. I was very glad to see how beautiful the interior of the vihara was, and how beautiful the Buddha image was. Some of the young men, so I understand, built the shrine with their own hands. This I was very glad to hear. It is good that we do things ourselves, with our own two hands.

Although the vihara is new as a vihara, I understand that it is not new as a building, but is your old community meeting-house. This is very interesting. In a way, it is symbolical. It represents the change that has taken place in your whole lives. It is not just a question of changing the community house into a vihara. It is a question of changing your whole life. This is in fact what the *Dhammadiksha* means.

Twenty-five years ago Dr Ambedkar took the *Dhammadiksha* himself, and *lakhs* of people took it with him – either at the same time or shortly afterwards. The *Dhammadiksha* they took all those years ago did not represent just a change of religious beliefs. It did not mean that one day you believed in *ātmavāda* and the next day you believed in *anātmavāda*. It was much more than that. It represented the beginning of a change in the whole of life: not just a religious change, but a social, economic, and educational change – in fact, it was a change in every aspect of your life. This is what *Dhammadiksha*, or conversion, really represents.

But change is not easy, on any level of existence. Even to change the old community meeting-house into the new vihara was not easy. In this connection I remember an experience of my own, twenty or more years ago. In those days I visited many parts of Maharashtra, even the villages. Sometimes I went by bullock cart, and sometimes on foot. Lots of people used to accompany me, and we used to walk to the villages through the fields. In those days I was still comparatively young, so I would walk on ahead and everybody used to follow behind. Sometimes they would complain that I walked too fast. Nowadays there are no such complaints, because now I can't walk so very fast any more, but in those days I used to take the lead and we used to go through the fields to the villages to meet the Buddhists there.

I don't know how things are now, but in those days the conditions under which Buddhists lived were very bad indeed. They lived quite apart from the rest of the village in their own separate quarters, usually in the dirtiest part of the whole locality. I remember one village in particular that I visited which was surrounded by a thick mud wall, and the Buddhists lived just outside this wall, in the very place where the pipes of the village sewage system came through the wall, and out of the pipes there came not only dirty water but a lot of other nasty things. That was where the Buddhists had to live.

On our arrival at each village we used to meet the local Buddhists, and very often we would meet them in the old community meeting-house. Sometimes a lot of people would come, sometimes very few. Very often there would be talk about changing the old community meeting-house into a vihara. In those days that was quite a difficult thing to do. Some people did not want to do it, even though they were followers of Dr Ambedkar, and sometimes there were difficulties with the Hindus in the village, because in some cases there would be the image of some

Hindu god in the old community meeting-house, and if the building was going to be changed into a vihara this image would obviously have to be removed. Sometimes some of the Buddhists wanted to do this, but they were not free to do so, because the Hindus of the village would not allow it. Indeed, they threatened the Buddhists with very serious consequences if they dared to do such a thing. Sometimes the Buddhists compromised by installing an image of the Buddha in one corner, so that the place was half old community meeting-house and half new Buddhist vihara. That is what things were like in the old days. Even to change the old community meeting-house into a new Buddhist vihara was difficult – never mind other changes, like giving up old bad habits.

Even in Poona there were difficulties of the kind I have mentioned. Somewhere in the city – I don't remember exactly where, because it was a long time ago – there was a Radha-Krishna temple belonging to the people who had become Buddhists. They wanted to turn this temple into a Buddhist vihara, removing the Radha-Krishna images and installing an image of the Buddha in their place. But the Hindus would not allow them to do so, even though the temple belonged to the Buddhists. In the end the temple was closed down. The Buddhists would not go there because they didn't want to worship Radha-Krishna, while the Hindus did not go there because although they worshipped Radha-Krishna, they would not worship them in the same temple that was used by low-caste people. I don't know what the position is now. Maybe the temple has fallen down, or maybe it has been turned into a Buddhist vihara.

These examples illustrate how difficult it is to get rid of the old ways and the old gods. This isn't the case only in India, or only with the followers of Dr Ambedkar. English Buddhists have this sort of difficulty too. They have found it difficult to get rid of the Christian God, Jesus, the Virgin Mary, Christmas, and so on. Christmas is the birthday of Jesus Christ, and everybody celebrates this festival. Some people go to church, but most people celebrate by taking a holiday and indulging in a lot of eating and drinking. It is very difficult for English Buddhists to escape all this. If you don't join in, you are being impolite, and your family may be displeased. Consequently, English Buddhists experience a lot of difficulty at Christmas time and feel they want to run away from the festival. Recently what they have done is to hold a *Dhamma-shibir* over the holiday period, so that they can get away from Christmas and all its excesses.

The same sort of thing is now happening in Maharashtra. Here you don't have Christmas, of course, but you have other festivals, like Diwali. I understand that last Diwali Lokamitra was very clever and organized a *Dhamma-shibir* which Buddhists who didn't want to participate in the Diwali celebrations could attend. The *shibir* was held in Aurangabad, and a lot of people attended. But some people whom Lokamitra was hoping would go did not do so. When he met them after the *shibir* and asked them why they had not come they replied that they had not come because it was Diwali. Anagārika Lokamitra was very surprised to hear this, and remarked, 'I didn't know that Diwali was a Buddhist festival.'

This also shows how difficult it is to change, to give up the old things and start leading a new life. Often it seems that everybody wants to hold you back, everybody wants you to be the same person that you were before. They don't want you to be a new person; they don't want you to grow and develop. This is the general rule. Nonetheless, changes are taking place; progress is being made; people are going forward and giving up old, bad habits. The fact that you have changed your old community meeting-house into a new Buddhist vihara is a sign that this process is going on.

I don't know whether in your old community meeting-house you formerly kept the image or picture of any of the old Hindu gods. When I was in the vihara just now I certainly didn't see any sign of them. If they were there before, they must have been sent away! There wasn't even a calendar with a picture of a Hindu god on it. I was very pleased to see this. You have only the Buddha, a very beautiful image of shining brass, and this image, which is in the earth-touching gesture, the *bhūmisparśa mudrā*, is seated on a beautifully tiled plinth. On the wall behind the image, there is painted a bodhi tree. Thus you have the Buddha seated under the bodhi tree here in your own vihara. It is hardly necessary for you to go on pilgrimage to Bodh Gaya. You have the Buddha here.

But what is this Buddha? Who is it that is seated in your new vihara? This you have to understand. You shouldn't think that you have just got some new god. There is no use in getting rid of the old god and then just getting a new one. The Buddha isn't a new god. He isn't a god at all. He is an Enlightened human being, one who has attained the highest possible state of moral and spiritual perfection. The Buddha shows us what we can all become. That is why we keep an image or picture of the Buddha in the vihara. We keep it there as a reminder – not just a reminder of what the Buddha himself achieved, but a reminder of what we too can achieve. When we sit and look at the Buddha image, or when we recite the Buddha puja, or the *vandanā*, we should think, 'I can be like the Buddha. I can develop *maitrī*, *karuṇā*, and *prajñā*, just like the Buddha did.' That is why we keep the image of the Buddha in the vihara – not to answer our prayers for promotion, or success in our examinations, or more money. We don't pray to the Buddha for any of these things. We don't pray to the Buddha at all. We keep the image of the Buddha there simply as a reminder of the meaning and purpose of our life; and the meaning and purpose of our life is to become like the Buddha – to become a perfect human being.

Keeping the Buddha image in the vihara, we can feel that the Buddha himself is seated there. He is there as a guest, in a way. Consequently it is very important that we keep the vihara beautiful, clean, and tidy. Some years ago I was at Sarnath, where the Buddha gave his first discourse, and where there is now a big centre of the Maha Bodhi Society. I was staying at the Society's guest house. Sarnath, as you know, is only seven or eight miles from Benares (Varanasi) or Kāśī, which is one of the holy places of the Hindus. In Benares there are many temples, many sadhus, many widows, and many pilgrims. While I was staying at Sarnath some of the Hindu pilgrims who had been to the temples of Benares came on a visit to the place, and when they entered the Sarnath Buddhist temple they had quite a surprise. They said, 'This Buddhist temple is very different from the Hindu temples. It is so clean. There are no cow droppings on the floor, no coconut shells, no old newspapers, no old flower garlands. It's absolutely clean.'

We find in most Buddhist countries that the temples are kept clean, and they are painted in beautiful, bright colours. Hindu temples are often small and dark, but Buddhist temples are usually quite big, and they have large windows, so that they are full of light and sunshine. The reason for this, I would say, is that Buddhists have nothing to hide. I don't know if the Hindus, particularly the Brahmins, have anything to hide. The Buddha is said to have said that there are kinds of persons who love secrecy: women, Brahmins, and the holders of false doctrines.[357] Perhaps it is for this sort of reason that Hindu temples are so often small and dark. But Buddhist temples and viharas are not like that, and your vihara is certainly not like that.

Nonetheless, even Buddhists may fall back into bad habits because, as I said, it is very difficult to change. An example of this sort of thing occurred during our recent tour of Marathwada. Everywhere we went, big meetings were held at which I gave a lecture on the Dhamma. Before I could give my lecture, of course, I was given a large number of flower garlands, just as I was this evening. One woman came with a large garland wrapped in newspaper, and having unwrapped the garland, she threw the piece of newspaper down on the stage right in front of me. Then she offered me the garland. I said to myself, 'This woman is not yet one-hundred-percent Buddhist.'

We have to be very careful about such things. We mustn't throw pieces of newspaper down in the vihara. Every day we must sweep it thoroughly. We mustn't leave bits of old candle lying on the image table, or allow the place to get dusty. And of course we should use the vihara properly, i.e. use it only for Dhamma activities. When we are in the vihara we should observe the *sīlas* very strictly. Some of them, of course, are easy to observe in the vihara. In fact, it would be difficult not to observe them there. But there is one *sīla* that is very difficult to observe, even in the vihara. That is the *sīla* concerning speech. Sometimes I think that right speech is the most difficult of all the *sīlas* to observe. To do someone a real injury is quite difficult. You have to get quite angry first. To steal is difficult, because you have to think about it. To commit adultery is also very difficult. But to indulge in wrong speech is very easy. As soon as people open their mouths, usually wrong speech in one form or another comes out. We may not actually tell a lie, but we may speak roughly and harshly. I noticed this at some of our recent meetings. Sometimes the organizers would be arguing with one another in a corner, and talking very loudly and angrily, even though it was a Buddhist meeting. We should never do that sort of thing. There is also the danger that we may waste time indulging in idle, frivolous talk or gossip. Don't use the vihara for that sort of purpose. Don't use it for talking about other people. Unfortunately, when we talk about other people we usually say something bad about them.

In short, when you are in the vihara, be very careful to observe the *sīlas*, and be especially careful not to indulge in any form of wrong speech. As I have said, you should use the vihara only for Dhamma activities. If you talk in the vihara at all, talk only about the Dhamma, or maybe don't talk at all. Just sit quietly and practise meditation.

This is one of the best things you can use the vihara for. Of course, it is also good to use the vihara for Dhamma study. Don't keep any newspapers there, or magazines, and if you keep any books there, let them be Dhamma books, so that when you meet together in the vihara, you can study them. The vihara can also be used as a centre for the organization of Buddhist activities – meetings, and lectures like the one we are having tonight.

If you use the vihara in the right sort of way, its influence will extend throughout the entire neighbourhood. This is the Bodhisattva ideal: not just to change yourself for the better, but also to change the society – the neighbourhood – in the midst of which you live. This is what Dr Ambedkar did. He didn't just want a better life just for himself. He wanted a better life for all the Depressed people of India. Thus in his life he gave an example of the bodhisattva ideal.

The vihara, too, is an example of the bodhisattva ideal. It is not simply a place where people go and worship, but a place from which the entire neighbourhood is helped and transformed. When you create a vihara in a particular neighbourhood and install a Buddha image there, it means you want to change the neighbourhood. We want to make it a real Buddhist neighbourhood – not just a locality where people call themselves Buddhists. We want to make it a neighbourhood where real Buddhists live – people who are practising the Dhamma and developing as human beings. This is also the significance of the *Dhammadiksha*, the significance of Dr Ambedkar's movement of mass conversion to Buddhism. It means that we should change for the better. It means we should grow as human beings.

So I am very glad that you have this new vihara, with such a beautiful Buddha image seated in it. I am very glad that the vihara is so beautifully decorated, and so clean and tidy. As I said at the beginning, this is my first visit to Chikhalwadi, but I already have a good impression of the place and the people. It is very good indeed that you have been able to create this vihara. A lot of effort must have gone into it, and I congratulate everybody who was in any way involved. If you use the vihara properly, then this locality will surely develop into a real Buddhist neighbourhood. I don't know when I shall be coming to India again, but I hope that next time I come I shall see that your having a vihara here has made a very big difference to the entire locality, and to all your lives. Thank you for inviting me here this evening. I hope we shall meet again.

27

BUDDHISM IS THE ONLY ALTERNATIVE

Bombay,[358] *8 February 1982*

Brothers and sisters in the Dhamma: At present I am on a three-month visit to India, and in the course of these three months I am visiting as many places as possible, meeting as many people as possible, and communicating the Dhamma to as many people as possible. Nor is that all. I am trying to make sure that the communication of the Dhamma is only the beginning of our Buddhist activities, not the end of them. I am trying to make sure that there is a proper, organized follow-up. At present I am about half way through my visit. So far I have visited fourteen important towns and cities and given twenty-seven full-length lectures, besides a number of short talks. Tonight I am back in Bombay. I am very glad to be here, very glad to see you all, and very glad to be speaking under the auspices of the Mass Movement Buddhist Brotherhood.

This is my first official contact with the Mass Movement, which is a young, dynamic organization started, I believe, after my return to England in 1967. I am particularly glad to be speaking under the auspices of a movement which includes the word 'brotherhood' in its title. Brotherhood between all human beings, and in particular between all Buddhists, is an essential and integral part of Buddhism. Buddhists are all brothers and sisters. They all belong to the same great spiritual family. It is therefore only natural that they should have strong feelings of *maitrī* towards one another. If we do not have strong feelings of *maitrī* toward one another we are not really Buddhists. It does not matter that

I come from England and you come from India. What matters is that we are all human beings, all Buddhists, and all followers and admirers of Dr Babasaheb Ambedkar. We should therefore all help one another, all work together for the Dhamma. After all, we are all faced by the same kind of problems. We are all faced by human problems, that is to say, problems inseparable from the fact that we are human beings: social problems, economic problems, and political problems. We are all faced, also, by religious problems – problems within the Buddhist movement itself, and the problem of how to be a Buddhist, and work for Buddhism, here and now in the twentieth century. It is only natural, therefore, that we should try to solve all these problems together. In reality there is only one Buddhist movement in the world and we are all part of it.

Two or three days ago Lokamitra showed me a copy of the big orange and white poster that had been printed to advertise tonight's meeting. I was glad to see this poster, and to hear that copies by the hundred had been put up all over Bombay, but on reading the wording I had a bit of a surprise. I saw that although the title of my lecture had been given in English as 'Buddhism is enough of every -ism', this had been rendered into Hindi as *Buddhaka Dhamma sabko ekamatra pratyaya hai*, which I take to mean 'Buddhism is the only alternative'. As between the English version and the Hindi version I am not quite sure which I am supposed to be talking about tonight. However, it doesn't really matter. I am going to be talking about the movement of mass conversion to Buddhism inaugurated by Dr Ambedkar, and about some of the problems facing that movement. That, I believe, is what most of you would like me to talk about, and what the organizers of this meeting had in mind when they drew up their poster. I am going to deal with these topics under three headings, raising three questions about which we should all think clearly and carefully. (1) Why did Dr Ambedkar embrace Buddhism? (2) What is the significance of the movement of mass conversion to Buddhism inaugurated by Dr Ambedkar? (3) What is the root cause of the problems that are today facing that movement?

So first, why did Dr Ambedkar embrace Buddhism? This question can be broken down into four subsidiary questions: (a) Why did Dr Ambedkar give up Hinduism? (After all, that came first.) (b) Why did he choose Buddhism rather than any other religion? (c) Why did he not simply remain without any religion at all? (d) Why did he not become a Marxist?

The question of why Dr Ambedkar gave up Hinduism is easily answered. Dr Ambedkar, as we all know, was born a member of an untouchable family. As such he knew from his own bitter and terrible personal experience what it was like to be treated as an Untouchable by the caste Hindus. He also saw that his experience was not unique, but that millions of other people all over India were being treated in the same inhuman way. For many years Dr Ambedkar tried to persuade the caste Hindus to change their attitude and mend their ways, but he did not meet with any success. Eventually he came to the conclusion that, in practice at least, Hinduism and Untouchability were inseparable, and that if one wanted to free oneself from the misery of Untouchability, from the evil of the caste system, one would have to leave the Hindu fold altogether. In 1935 he therefore declared: 'Though I have been born a Hindu, I do not intend to die one'.[359] This, in short, is why Dr Ambedkar gave up Hinduism. He saw that within the Hindu fold it was impossible for one born as an Untouchable to live as a human being ought to live – that is, with decency and dignity.

As to why Dr Ambedkar chose Buddhism rather than any other religion, I want to deal with this question at somewhat greater length, though still not at the length it deserves. According to Dr Ambedkar there are four religions at present that still have a very great influence over vast numbers of people. These four religions are Buddhism, Christianity, Islam, and Hinduism, the founders of which are, respectively, the Buddha, Jesus Christ, Mohammed, and Krishna. Dr Ambedkar had something to say about each of these great founders in turn. Jesus Christ, he said, claimed to be the son of God and insisted that those who wished to enter the Kingdom of God must recognize him as such, since otherwise they could not gain salvation. Mohammed claimed to be God's last messenger on earth. As for Krishna, Dr Ambedkar said that he went a step further than either Jesus or Mohammed, and claimed to be God himself, to be the *Parameśvara*.[360]

Dr Ambedkar went on to say that the Buddha, by contrast, claimed to be no more than a human being who, by his own efforts, had gained a state of supreme moral and spiritual perfection. According to Dr Ambedkar's classification, therefore, Jesus, Mohammed, and Krishna all claimed to be *mokṣa dattas*, that is to say, givers or bringers of salvation to man, whereas the Buddha claimed only to be *mārga datta*, that is to say, only the shower of a way to salvation that every man and woman has to follow by his or her own human effort. Buddhism is therefore what we may call a humanistic religion, though it is not humanistic in the narrow, modern Western sense. Buddhism is a religion that gives importance to man, not God. In fact it gives no place to God at all. This, then, is the reason why Dr Ambedkar chose Buddhism rather than any other religion. He chose it because it is a humanistic, non-theistic religion. Whereas Jesus is the son of God, Mohammed is the messenger of God, and Krishna is God himself, the Buddha has no connection with God at all. So far as Buddhism is concerned, God simply does not exist. The word 'God' is not to be found in Buddhism's dictionary.

There is another difference between the Buddha and the three other founders of religions. Jesus, Mohammed, and Krishna all claimed that what they taught was infallible, and therefore not to be questioned. Man was obliged, even compelled, to accept it. After all, Jesus was the son of God, Mohammed the messenger of God, and Krishna God himself. What they taught therefore came, directly or indirectly, from God himself. God knows everything, so how could what they taught be wrong? The Buddha, however, did not claim to be infallible, or that what he taught came from God. What he taught was, he declared, based simply on his own reason, his own experience as a human being, and others should accept it only if they found that it agreed with their own reason and experience. In fact the Buddha went as far as to declare that his disciples should test his teaching as the goldsmith tests gold in the fire.[361] No other religious teacher has ever said such a thing. Other religious teachers, i.e. non-Buddhist religious teachers, ask you to believe in them, even today. But the Buddha never did this. The Buddha asked us to test his words for ourselves. He asked us to try the truth of his teaching in the fire of our own experience. Dr Ambedkar therefore chose Buddhism rather than any other religion.

There were several other reasons for Dr Ambedkar's choice of Buddhism. Buddhism, Dr Ambedkar said, is based on morality. By contrast, Hinduism is based not on morality, but on one's caste duty. Moreover, Buddhism is not in disagreement with science. If we find any statement in the Buddhist scriptures that conflicts with modern scientific knowledge, then, as Buddhists, we are free to reject it. Followers of other religions do not have this freedom. If a Christian, for instance, finds a statement in the Bible that conflicts with modern scientific knowledge he has to accept that statement, or else explain it away in some far-fetched, artificial manner, because the Bible cannot be wrong. The Bible is the word of God. This is why, in brief, Dr Ambedkar chose Buddhism rather than any other religion.

But why did Dr Ambedkar not simply remain without any religion at all? Today there are many people in the world without religion, especially in the West. Why did Dr Ambedkar not follow their example once he had given up Hinduism? In the first place, he was a deeply religious man and he personally felt the need for religion. In the second place, he believed that religion in the sense of morality was necessary to hold society together. He believed that society needed the sanction of morality because the sanction of law, that is to say, the sanction of force, was not enough. Society could be held together, he said, only if the majority of people accepted the sanction of religion, i.e. the sanction of morality. Religion in the sense of morality, so Dr Ambedkar maintained, was the governing principle of every society. Indeed he went further than that. He said that in order to function as the governing principle of society religion had to fulfil certain requirements. It had to be in accordance with science, or reason; it had to recognize the fundamental tenets of liberty, equality, and fraternity, and it must not sanctify or ennoble poverty.[362] According to Dr Ambedkar, Buddhism passed all these tests. In fact, according to him it was the only religion that passed all these tests. Buddhism could therefore be the governing principle of a society.

Finally, Dr Ambedkar believed that the world needed religion. In his view the modern world needed religion far more than the old world did. The new world in fact had to have religion, he said, and that religion, according to him, could only be the religion of the Buddha. Moreover, Dr Ambedkar said that the Buddha did not teach only the principle of *ahiṃsā*. He also taught the principle of freedom – social, intellectual, economic, and political freedom – as well as the principle of equality, and his teachings covered many aspects of the social life of man. The Buddha's teachings were, in fact, very modern. The Buddha's main concern was that man should win freedom in the course of his life here on earth. He did not merely promise man salvation in heaven after death. According to Dr Ambedkar, therefore, the world not only needed religion, it needed Buddhism. That is why Dr Ambedkar did not simply remain without a religion after he had given up Hinduism. He saw that religion – religion in the sense of Buddhism – was necessary to the existence of society itself, necessary for the uplift of the whole world.

But why did Dr Ambedkar not become a Marxist? He said that he agreed with Marx, but only up to a point. He agreed that there was such a thing as exploitation in the world. Indeed, he identified this exploitation with the Buddha's conception of *duḥkha*. He also agreed with Marx that the exploitation that existed in the world could be brought to an end only by the abolition of private property. But how was this to be done? Here Dr Ambedkar disagreed with Marx and agreed with the Buddha. Communists, he said, wanted to bring about the recognition of *duḥkha* and the abolition of private property by means of force and violence, whereas the Buddha's method was the method of persuasion, of moral teaching, of love. According to Dr Ambedkar, herein lay the fundamental difference between the Buddha and Karl Marx. The communists admittedly got quick results, but he had no doubt, he declared, that the Buddha's way was the surest way.[363] Therefore he did not become a Marxist. Instead, he became a Buddhist.

We have now answered our first main question: Why did Dr Ambedkar choose Buddhism? We have seen why he gave up Hinduism, why he chose Buddhism rather than any other religion, why he did not simply remain without any religion at all, and why he did not become a Marxist. Now, what is the significance of the movement of mass conversion to Buddhism inaugurated by Dr Ambedkar? Its significance is very great indeed. We have in fact hardly begun to understand how great it is. Dr Ambedkar was a very great man, and great men are like mountains. We can appreciate how great they are only from a distance, that is to say, only long after their death. This is very much the case with Dr Ambedkar. Only now are we beginning to appreciate how great his achievement was. And as with great men themselves, so with the movements, or the activities, they initiate. Such movements are like the river that rises from the foot of the mountain. At first the river is very small, a mere stream. It becomes big only after it has flowed for many miles – that is to say, in the case of a person, after many years have passed. So is it with the movement of mass conversion to Buddhism inaugurated by Dr Babasaheb Ambedkar. Only now are we beginning to realize how great the significance of that movement really is. Tonight I am going to deal with its significance under four headings: (1) the significance for Dr Ambedkar's own followers, i.e. for those who took the *Dhammadiksha* with him at Nagpur or soon afterwards; (2) its significance for the non-Buddhist people of India, especially the Hindus; (3) its significance for Buddhism itself; and (4) its significance for the world.

THE SIGNIFICANCE OF THE MOVEMENT OF MASS CONVERSION FOR DR AMBEDKAR'S OWN FOLLOWERS

This is not difficult to understand. Between 1957 and 1967 I myself visited Maharashtra a number of times, met many people, and gave many lectures. Whenever I met people I used to ask, 'How do you feel now that you have taken the *Dhammadiksha*? How do you feel now that you are a Buddhist? What difference has it made to you?' And whether the person I asked was educated or uneducated, old or young, a city-dweller or a villager, I nearly always got the same reply. People used to say, 'Now that we are Buddhists we feel free – free from the slavery of caste, free from the hell of Untouchability. We feel free to be human; free to grow, free to develop.' This, then, is the great significance of the movement of mass conversion inaugurated by Dr Ambedkar for his own followers. For them it means life. It means they are reborn. There is no need for me to say very much about this. This should be the experience of all of you who call yourselves Buddhists. If it is not your experience you should ask yourselves whether you have really taken the *Dhammadiksha*, and whether you are really practising the Dhamma.

THE SIGNIFICANCE OF THE MOVEMENT OF MASS CONVERSION FOR INDIA

The majority of people in India are Hindus. Buddhists are a comparatively small minority. Nonetheless, the movement of mass conversion inaugurated by Dr Ambedkar had a very considerable effect on the Hindu community. It gave them a great shock, and made some of them think very seriously. Nor was this all. After their conversion to Buddhism the new Buddhists refused to be treated as Untouchables any longer. They insisted on being treated as human beings. The Hindus were therefore forced to change their attitude towards them, at least to an extent. Some Hindus now even recognize that the caste system is an evil, that Untouchability is an evil. Nevertheless, they want to go on being Hindus and believing in the Hindu *śāstras*. This places them in a very difficult position, because some Hindu *śāstras* support the caste system, and even Untouchability. Logically speaking, such liberal-minded Hindus ought to reject those *śāstras* and move in the direction of Buddhism, and a few of them are beginning to realize this. Thus, the movement of mass conversion to Buddhism has significance for India as a whole. It is helping to make Indian society as a whole more humanistic and more truly secular.

THE SIGNIFICANCE OF THE MOVEMENT OF MASS CONVERSION FOR BUDDHISM ITSELF

Historically speaking, Buddhism is a very old religion, and during the 2,500 years of its existence it has undergone many vicissitudes. Sometimes it has been in a flourishing condition, sometimes in a state of serious decline. The Dhamma itself, of course, being *akāliko* or timeless, has never declined, but Buddhism as a socio-religious phenomenon has certainly declined from time to time. Six or seven hundred years ago Buddhism in fact disappeared from India, which was a terrible blow not only to the religion itself but also to the country of its origin. It also disappeared from central Asia, as well as from Java and Sumatra. More recently it has disappeared from, or been seriously weakened in, a number of other countries. Due mainly to the spread of communism, Buddhism has practically disappeared from Mongolia, and it has been seriously weakened in Tibet, Vietnam, Cambodia, and Laos. In fact, we have to admit that Buddhism has been on the decline for several hundred years, and that in the twentieth century the process has perhaps accelerated.

In only two parts of the world has Buddhism really been on the increase recently: the West, particularly England, and India, particularly Maharashtra. The increase in Maharashtra has of course been much greater than the increase in England. Thanks to the movement of mass conversion to Buddhism inaugurated by Dr Ambedkar, here in Maharashtra millions of people have become Buddhists in recent years. This fact is of significance not just for India but for the whole Buddhist world. Far from simply meaning that Buddhism has been revived in India after an absence of six or seven hundred years, it means that Buddhism is no longer on the decline in the world. The process of decline has been halted, even reversed. Buddhism has begun to flourish again. The movement of mass conversion inaugurated by Dr Ambedkar is therefore of significance for Buddhism itself, and for the whole Buddhist world. It comes, in fact, as a message of hope for the whole Buddhist world. It shows that Buddhism can be revived even after it has been dead, apparently, for hundreds of years. It can be revived in India, in Tibet – in fact, wherever it has died out or been destroyed. Though it may be revived in a somewhat different form, it will be the same Dhamma. Dr Ambedkar's movement of mass conversion therefore occupies an important place in the history of Buddhism. It marks a great turning point, the point at which the process of decline came to an end and the process of revival began, the point at which Buddhism started to flourish again, the point at which it entered upon a new phase of its historical existence – a phase that could be more glorious even than any previous one.

THE SIGNIFICANCE OF THE MOVEMENT OF MASS CONVERSION FOR THE WORLD

The movement of mass conversion to Buddhism inaugurated by Dr Ambedkar was not just a movement of religious conversion in the narrow sense, not just a change of religious belief. On the contrary, it represented a radical change in every aspect of life, whether religious, cultural, educational, intellectual, social, political, or economic. In other words, it was a change not just for the individual but for society as a whole. And it wasn't just a radical change, but a radical change for the better. It represented an all-round improvement, an all-round development. Hence we speak not just of Dr Ambedkar's movement of conversion to Buddhism but of his Dhamma Revolution.

In many parts of the world people today want a change for the better in every aspect of their lives, but they do not know the right way to go about it. Some try to bring about the change by means of violence, others by means of money, or science and technology, or education. They do not succeed very well. Sometimes they do not succeed at all, or even make matters worse. Dr Ambedkar's movement of mass conversion to Buddhism gives the world the example of a revolution that has succeeded. It gives the example of a Dhamma revolution, that is, a revolution brought about entirely by peaceful means. When I say that the Dhamma Revolution has succeeded, I do not mean that it has succeeded entirely. That is obviously not the case. But it has succeeded sufficiently to change the lives of millions of people entirely by peaceful means, entirely by means of the Dhamma. Thus the movement of mass conversion to Buddhism inaugurated by Dr Ambedkar is of tremendous significance for the whole world. It points the whole world in the right direction.

WHAT IS THE ROOT CAUSE OF THE PROBLEMS TODAY FACING THE MOVEMENT OF MASS CONVERSION?

These problems are of various kinds – problems of disunity, of lack of enthusiasm, of partial failure – but the root cause of all of them is threefold. They are due to: (1) lack of a clear understanding of why Dr Ambedkar chose Buddhism; (2) failure to understand the significance of the movement of mass conversion; (3) failure to discover a right way of working.

Lack of a clear understanding of why Dr Ambedkar chose Buddhism

If we do not have a clear idea of why Dr Ambedkar chose Buddhism (i.e. why he gave up Hinduism, why he chose Buddhism rather than any other religion, why he did not simply remain without any religion at all, and why he did not become a Marxist), then we will probably not understand why we ourselves have chosen Buddhism, or why we should choose it if we have not already done so. Instead, we will just have a vague, general idea that Buddhism is a good thing and that therefore conversion to Buddhism must be a good thing.

Failure to understand the significance of the movement of mass conversion

Though we may understand the significance of the movement of mass conversion to Buddhism for ourselves, at least to a limited extent, and may even understand its significance for India, probably we do not understand its significance for Buddhism, or for the world. In other words, we do not take a broad enough view of the movement. For this reason we do not feel inspired, we do not have the feeling of being involved in something much greater than ourselves, and therefore do not think in terms of working for the Dhamma Revolution. Instead, taking a very narrow view, we remain preoccupied with our personal concerns, at best thinking in terms of our own locality or our own town.

Failure to discover a right way of working

That we have not yet found the right way of working means that we have not yet found a new way of working. We are still trying to do things in the old way. The change brought about by Dr Ambedkar was a Dhamma Revolution, and we can work for the Dhamma only by means that are in accordance with the Dhamma. Political experience is of little use here. We can work for the Dhamma Revolution only if we know and practise the Dhamma, and are ourselves part of that revolution, and embody it in our lives. In other words, we can work for the Dhamma Revolution only if we ourselves have changed since conversion. We can work for it only if there has been a complete change, a revolution, in every aspect of our own lives – only if we have been reborn and are leading a new life. Simply to repeat the Three Refuges and the Five Precepts and say that you are a loyal follower of Dr Ambedkar is not enough. In other words, we do not merely have to find a new way of working for the Dhamma Revolution; we have to find a new kind of Buddhist worker. Dr Ambedkar saw this very clearly, and it was for this reason that he said that the *bhikkhu saṅgha*, in its present condition, was of no use for the spread of Buddhism. What Dr Ambedkar said, in effect, was that we need a new kind of *bhikkhu*.

Not that the new kind of Buddhist worker need actually be called a *bhikkhu*. He can be called anything you like. But whatever he is called, he must be one-hundred-percent Buddhist, not seventy-five-percent Buddhist and twenty-five-percent Hindu, or even ninety-nine-percent Buddhist and one-percent Hindu. He must think like a Buddhist, speak like a Buddhist, and act like a Buddhist. He should even look like a Buddhist, by which I do not mean that he should wear a special kind of outfit, or appear outwardly different from other people, but simply that he should look like a man who has been reborn, a man who is leading a new kind of life. If someone was to give you ten *lakhs* of rupees you would certainly look very different from how you look now. You would look different because you would feel different. It is the same with our new kind of Buddhist worker. Having been given something much more precious than ten *lakhs* of rupees, the Three Jewels of the Buddha, the Dhamma, and the Sangha, he should look different. He should look like a Buddhist.

Moreover, the new kind of Buddhist worker should be wholly committed to the Three Jewels. These should be the most important things in his life: more important than job, than wife and family, than worldly success, than ease and comfort – more important than life itself. Wherever possible, therefore, the new kind of Buddhist worker will be a full-time worker, giving all his time and energy to the Dhamma Revolution. The new kind of Buddhist worker will have good knowledge of the Dhamma, and will practise the Dhamma. He will observe the precepts, particularly the ten precepts, i.e. the *dasa kusala dhammas*, and practise meditation. He will also work hard, if necessary with his own two hands. He will not be a mere leader, just telling other people what to do. He will himself set an example. But above all, the new kind of Buddhist worker will work for the Dhamma Revolution in a way that is in accordance with the Dhamma itself. He will work for it by means of *maitrī* (love), *karuṇā* (compassion), and *prajñā* (wisdom). In addition to that, the new kind of Buddhist worker will work in cooperation with others. They will work as a team, and this team will form a Mahasangha, or great spiritual community, which will work not only in India but in many different countries all over the world. It will work for the happiness and welfare of all living beings. If we have this kind of Mahāsaṅgha all the problems facing the movement of mass conversion inaugurated by Dr Ambedkar will be finally solved, because we will have found a new way of working together for the Dhamma Revolution.

You will be happy to hear that in England we already have this kind of Mahāsaṅgha, started by me in 1967, and now Buddhism is beginning to flourish in England. In England this Mahāsaṅgha is known as the Western Buddhist Order, while in India it is known as Trailokya Bauddha Mahāsaṅgha. At present its members are running centres and regular activities in eight different countries of the world, including India. This *sangha* consists exclusively of one-hundred-percent Buddhists, of people who have committed themselves to the Buddha, the Dhamma, and the Sangha, and who observe the ten precepts.

There is a lot more that I should like to say to you on this subject, and perhaps there is a lot more that you would like to hear, but I am afraid there is no time tonight. I am very glad to have had the opportunity of placing some of my thoughts before you. I hope you now have a clearer idea of why Dr Ambedkar inaugurated the great movement of mass conversion to Buddhism, as well as a clearer understanding of the tremendous significance of that movement and of the root cause of the various problems at present facing it. I hope you can see for yourselves that Buddhism is the only alternative: the only alternative to Hinduism, the only alternative to suffering, the only alternative to exploitation – not only for India, but for the whole world. It is my hope that the Dhamma Revolution started by Dr Babasaheb Ambedkar will continue to spread, that the Trailokya Bauddha Mahasangha will continue to grow, and that the work of the Mass Movement Buddhist Brotherhood will continue to be successful. May we all cooperate for the good of the Dhamma.

28

BUDDHISM AND EDUCATION

Siddharth College, Bombay, 9 February 1982

Mr Chairman and friends old and new: I am glad to be back in Bombay, a city which for all its faults has a secure place in my affections. For quite a number of years I came here every winter, and it is with feelings of great pleasure that I am here again, this time to speak to you here at Siddharth College this morning.

Let me begin by telling you about the work that I have been doing over the last few years. I know that some of my friends have wondered what I have been doing in England and why I have been absent from India for such a long time. What I have been trying to do in England is to create a new kind of Buddhist order – an order, one might say, of Buddhist workers, consisting of people who are one-hundred-percent dedicated to the Buddha, the Dhamma, and the Sangha and who try to propagate Buddhism in various ways and by means of all kinds of activities.

I had come to the conclusion that a new Buddhist order was necessary as a result of my experience in India over a period of about twenty years, and in England itself for about two years. I saw that the old way of doing things would not work any more. We needed to work in a new way, and we needed a new kind of Buddhist worker. We needed, in fact, a new kind of Buddhist order, or Buddhist brotherhood, made up of people working for the Dhamma under the rather difficult and demanding conditions imposed upon us by life – especially city life – in the twentieth century.

I originally started this new Buddhist order (known in the West as the Western Buddhist Order, and in India as the Trailokya Bauddha Mahasangha)[364] with just twelve people. Over the years it has grown so that there are now 163 Order members, as they are called, the majority of whom are working full-time for Buddhism. At present there are Order members living in eight different countries, including India, though most of them live in England.

Order members work primarily through what are called Buddhist centres. It is quite difficult for me to convey to you what is meant by a Buddhist centre. It is not really a vihara; one can only say that it is a centre of Buddhist activities. I myself started the first of these centres, a very small one, in London at the beginning of 1967. Out of it our whole new Buddhist movement has grown, in the same way that Dr Ambedkar's educational work, starting from very small beginnings, has also grown and flourished, in a way that would perhaps have surprised even Dr Ambedkar himself. This first centre was situated in a small underground room beneath a shop in central London. The centre grew and we soon had to move to larger premises in North London, and then in 1975 we moved from there to an even bigger building in East London.

We now have about sixteen centres in England and abroad,[365] and at these centres many different activities take place every day. We have lectures and classes – meditation classes, classes in the study of the Dhamma, yoga classes, and karate classes; we also have massage courses, communication courses, film shows, and even poetry readings. A centre, then, is a very intensive situation, with many friends and members of the public attending every day. The activities do not even stop for public holidays; in fact, we try to have extra Buddhist activities then, because people have time to spare.

Originally, our only form of activity was through the Buddhist centres, but then a development took place. People started to feel that attending a centre, even for a whole day, was not enough. They wanted to participate in Buddhist activities for a week or even longer, and in a quieter, more ideal situation. And so we began to hold retreats in the countryside. These retreats often lasted for several weeks, and during this time we would live in a completely Buddhist fashion, meditating, studying, and practising the Dhamma, listening to lectures and working and talking with one another. We now regularly hold a pre-ordination course lasting for three whole months in a very beautiful place in northern Italy. All that people have to do there is practise and become ever more deeply immersed in the Dhamma.

The next step in our activities took place as a result of these early retreats. At the end of a retreat, after two or three weeks of living just with and for the Dhamma, people would often not want to return to their jobs and families; they just wanted the retreat to continue indefinitely. Sometimes people would be so sad that the retreat had come to an end that they would start crying. After discussing this problem, some of our friends decided that they could continue to live a Buddhist life by setting up what we now call a community. About ten of them started living together in a large house, meditating together every morning, performing a puja together every evening, and studying the Dhamma together at weekends. They felt that this was a better situation for a Buddhist to live in than ordinary home life. In this way Buddhist communities arose.

Once people had started living in communities, they often found that there was a considerable difference between the conditions in a community and the conditions under which they were working to earn their living. This created a tension, and they felt that to continue working in this way would be wrong. Some of them even felt that their work was not 'right livelihood', which is the fifth step of the Buddha's Noble Eightfold Path. As a result, some of our friends decided to set up businesses together and earn their living in accordance with right livelihood. Various kinds of businesses were therefore established on a cooperative basis. These cooperatives enabled people to earn their livelihood, to work together as Buddhists, and to provide money to help run the Buddhist movement.

So in the beginning there was just the Order, which then started to function, firstly through centres, then through retreats, then through communities, and finally through cooperatives. At the centres people can learn about Buddhism, and on retreats they can experience Buddhism more intensively. In the communities they can live together, and in the cooperatives they can work together as Buddhists.

With all these activities taking place, you will not be surprised to hear that the majority of our friends and Order members are young; in fact, the average age is probably somewhere between twenty and thirty years old. Some of our friends, even some of our Order members, are still in their teens though we do have a few older friends and Order members. In India, it is mostly older people who take an interest in the Dhamma, but in England, the majority of our friends and Order members are not only young, but also unmarried; whereas in India, of course, it is very difficult not to get married at an early age.

I was recently reading the life of Mahatma Jyotirao Phooley,[366] and I discovered that he was very concerned with this question of early marriage. In his time, in the nineteenth century, it was very common in India to get married at about ten years old. Dr Ambedkar himself got married at a very early age, and some of the older people here may well also have done so. Even twenty years ago, people would often be surprised if a girl was not married by the age of thirteen. Nowadays, though, people tend not to get married so young. This means that young men can finish their education and then, if they want to, get married. In the past, a young married man might have had to give up his education in order to support his wife and his growing family. (In those days there was also no family planning.) In England, this process has advanced even further. Many people are still not married when they are thirty years old, and some are still unmarried at forty. Unlike in India, parents do not put pressure on their children to get married. Most Order members in England are unmarried and free of domestic responsibilities, so, without being *bhikkhus* or *bhikkhunīs*, they can devote all their time and energies to Buddhism.

However, I must not give a one-sided impression of things. We have an increasing number of Order members and friends who are married with children. Many of them live with their families near Norwich, the capital city of Norfolk, which is an agricultural county about 100 miles from London. We have a Buddhist centre and a community in Norwich, and I myself live in a community near there with a few friends and Order members who help me with my work.

A few years ago, some of these married friends and Order members decided they were not very happy about sending their children to state schools, feeling that the education given there was not compatible with living a Buddhist life. It was not Christianity that they were concerned about, because that is not taught in schools to any great extent. They were more concerned about the materialistic, career-oriented approach to education that one finds in these schools. As a result, some of them thought that we should set up our own Buddhist schools. They began to discuss the possible nature of these schools, and the type of education that students would receive there, and they also asked me to think about this question of Buddhism and education.

This, then, is what I am going to talk about this morning. I have not come to any systematic conclusions, but I do have some definite ideas on the subject, especially about the purpose of education. I also think it is a very appropriate subject for me to lecture on, as most of you are Buddhists, and nearly all of you are involved with the educational process in one way or another. Let me begin with a summary of what I see as the threefold purpose of education. The first purpose of education is to enable the individual to take his place as a functioning, responsible member of the wider society to which he belongs; the second purpose of education is to give him the knowledge and skills that will enable him to earn his living; and the third purpose of education is to help him to develop as an individual human being. All three of these are interconnected, and it is of course the third purpose which is the most important from a Buddhist point of view, and with which I shall be dealing at the greatest length.

The first purpose of education, then, is to enable the individual to take his place as a functioning, responsible member of the wider society to which he belongs. We know very well that we cannot live for any length of time without other people. In fact, in a city like Bombay we are continually surrounded by other people, and so we have to learn to live with them. The process of learning to live with others starts when you are a baby. Babies and small children are very egoistic. They only consider their own needs and desires, and hardly recognize the existence of other people. (In the West small children, particularly babies, used to be idealized into little angels, but now people, especially child psychologists, are beginning to realize that they are little egoists, even little demons.) We have, then, to instil into the small child the awareness that there are other people living in the world who have the same feelings as he or she does, and that these feelings must be respected. The child has to learn the process of 'give and take' or 'do as you would be done by'.

There is a story to this effect in the Buddhist scriptures. It is said that the Buddha came upon a group of small boys who had caught a crow, tied it by the legs and started to torment it with sticks. The Buddha said to them, 'What are you doing? Would you like someone to do this to you?' To which the boys replied 'No'. 'In that case,' said the Buddha, 'don't do it to another living being. You must treat others in the same way that you would wish them to treat you.'[367]

It is very important in teaching children this lesson to follow a middle way. If you are too easy-going, the child will never grow up out of its basic raw egotism. If, on the other hand, you are too strict and always punish the child, you will crush its individuality, even its emotional life, and the child will grow up into a completely subservient person, devoid of energy and initiative. The child should be allowed to express its own individuality, but at the same time must learn to respect the needs, feelings, and rights of other people. Only if a middle way is followed will the child eventually be able to take his or her place as a proper, responsible member of society. In the West there has been far too much of a swing in the direction of egoism. In particular, I have heard that it has made family life in the United States very difficult. Under the influence of incorrect educational theories, American children have been allowed to do whatever they like, and consequently they are often rude and inconsiderate to their parents and even to guests. It is all perhaps a reaction to the old Victorian strictness, and people are beginning to regret it. This kind of education should start at home with small children, and should be continued at school, when as students the children start to learn about their rights and duties as citizens belonging to a particular political and social community. The process should continue through college and university. Eventually, the students should even start thinking in terms of world citizenship and of the environment.

It is very important that people realize their responsibilities towards the environment, especially in India. In Bombay, because too many people are egoistic the environment has become polluted. Owners of factories, for example, often do not think about the consequences of discharging chemical waste into the environment. The government may ask them to take certain precautions, but they do not do so, because that would mean spending money, and that would mean reducing their profits. These factory owners do not have a social conscience, because they are still children who think only of themselves and not of the convenience of society as a whole. There needs to be more emphasis in the educational process on training people to be responsible members of society.

The second purpose of education is to give people the knowledge and skills that will enable them to earn their living in the world. An important point here is that people should not all be given the same education regardless of their individual talents and preferences. Some should be encouraged to go into law, others into medicine, and so on according to their inclinations and abilities. I think it is significant that under the auspices of the People's Education Society, you have the Colleges of Art, Science, Commerce, and Law. This gives different opportunities to many different people. People's choice of profession must also take into account the needs of society; the educational process must be related to the wider social and economic situation.

The most important consideration, from a Buddhist point of view, is that people should be equipped with the knowledge and skills that will enable them to earn their living in accordance with the principles of right livelihood. According to the Buddha, right livelihood means firstly that we should earn our living in a way that does no harm to ourselves physically, emotionally, or mentally. People often engage in work that is harmful to them. I will give you two examples. When I was in the train yesterday, travelling from Poona to Bombay, I could not help noticing a certain gentleman sitting in the same compartment as me. He was behaving in rather an odd way, darting about, twitching and jumping, and looking around rapidly. Clearly his mind was not at ease. I could see that he was an educated man, and I therefore guessed that he was probably in computer programming or a related profession, because that kind of work can tend to make one a bit neurotic. A simpler example is the case of the rickshaw pullers whom I encountered on my first visit to India in 1943. In this country, rickshaws used to be pulled by human beings. (This unfortunately still happens, I am told, in Calcutta.) These rickshaw pullers used to start working when they were fifteen years old, and very often they did not live for more than another ten years, because their work was so bad for them physically. This is a very clear example of wrong livelihood.

Not only should one's means of livelihood not harm oneself, it should also do no harm to other people. Nor should one work for so many hours that no time is left for the Dhamma or other cultural activities. In an unethical society, it is very difficult for the individual to practise right livelihood; economic circumstances often force him to work otherwise. A fair and just society would not compel anyone to earn their living in such a manner. We therefore have to work to create such a society.

The third purpose of education, which is the most important from the Buddhist point of view, is to help the individual develop his potential. This development should be all round, involving every aspect of the personality; it should not include some aspects and exclude others. It should not, for example, include the intellect, but exclude the body.

The first aspect I want to consider is physical development, making the body strong and healthy by means of sports, games, and other physical activities. I recently read that in Bombay less than eighteen percent of students engage in any form of exercise. I do not know the reasons for this, but it is very sad that the physical side of education is neglected in this way. Physical health is the basis for all other activities in life. You may be highly educated, and you may have a good job, but if you are physically unhealthy you will not be able to make the best of your life and work.

Some years ago, many of our friends in England were under the impression that Buddhism and physical exercise were incompatible. They thought that being a Buddhist meant becoming very 'ethereal' or 'up in the air', and that you should try to avoid anything physical. But then things started to change. People began to take up yoga, karate, and other forms of exercise, and they found it had a beneficial effect, not only on the body, but also on the mind.

It is very important to remember that you are not just a disembodied brain. You also have a body that needs exercise. If you are really concerned about your development as an individual, you will give some attention to this aspect of education. In fact, it is shameful to be physically weak and unhealthy, especially if you are young. This applies to women as well as to men. Women should be physically healthy, even though it is not traditional in India for them to take much exercise. In England, it is quite common for women to take up yoga, and to play sports and games. Some women have even taken up football and all-in wrestling, though I am not suggesting that they should go to these extremes in India. They should follow a middle way. When I was a young monk, nobody gave me this advice, and so I did not take much exercise. I think that if I had taken more, I would be in better health now, and able to do even more for the Dhamma.

The second aspect of the all-round development of the individual is the education of the intellect. This does not simply mean cramming. When I was in India twenty years ago, people often thought that learning about a subject meant knowing the textbook off by heart, and this used to horrify me. For example, you would see a boy with a textbook in front of him repeat 'Battle of Hastings 1066' four or five times. He would then move on to the next sentence, which again he would repeat four or five times. In this way he would commit the whole book to memory, so that in an examination he could answer the questions by just reproducing passages from the textbook. I think there is still an element of this in Indian education today. The educational process, though, should teach you to think for yourself. You must of course learn the facts, but you should also think and reflect on them, and try to understand the subject you are studying. You can then answer examination questions out of that understanding, instead of just regurgitating facts from memory.

Learning to think for ourselves is important not only in connection with our formal education, but in everyday life. For example, in the West, especially in the cities, we are bombarded with advertisements. In India, the advertisements are very simple, but in the West they are very subtle indeed, and are designed by some of our cleverest people. They are aimed at persuading you to buy all sorts of consumer goods, and if you are not careful, you can easily be influenced into buying them. You therefore have to think for yourself, and not just respond automatically to the appeal of the advertisement. This also applies to political articles in newspapers. You cannot simply believe whatever you read. You have to consider, for instance, the political beliefs of the person who has written the article, and of the person who owns and controls the newspaper. If you cannot think for yourself, you will probably not be able to survive as a real human individual in the modern world. The educational process should therefore encourage you to think about the subjects you are studying, and come to your own independent understanding of them. This will stand you in good stead in later life.

The third aspect of the all-round development of the individual is the education of the emotions. This aspect of one's education is usually left to look after itself. Official attention is normally given to it only when something goes wrong, when someone becomes mentally or emotionally upset to such an extreme degree that they have to see a psychiatrist. One of the most important ways in which the emotions are developed is through ordinary human friendship. Friendship is one of the most important aspects of college life, even though it does not appear on the curriculum. At college, people sometimes develop friendships that last for many years, even for the rest of their lives. In these friendships there is the possibility of communication. I was recently reading in a book on psychology that if you are deprived of communication, if there is no one to whom you can speak your mind, you may become emotionally ill. With a friend, you can speak about anything you like – anything that interests you, or is troubling you. Whether you are happy or sad, you can share your feelings, so they do not become bottled up within you. In this way emotional warmth, and thus friendship, develops. If our emotions are not properly looked after then they will remain uneducated. It is because people have uneducated emotions that there is so much violence and hooliganism in big cities. Education of the emotions, then, is very important indeed.

The fourth aspect of education as all-round development is that of aesthetic and artistic education, which is closely connected with emotional education. In the course of our education, we should learn to appreciate the fine arts, which include painting and sculpture as well as poetry, literature, and music. This means that we should visit the art galleries and museums, as well as reading poetry and listening to music. All this helps us to develop our aesthetic sense and so become more all-round, fully developed human beings. In the course of our education we should learn to enjoy classical music, both Eastern and Western, and poetry. Unlike crude, popular film music, classical music is refined and beautiful, so helps educate our emotions. Great poetry, in fact great literature in general, can also have this effect. We should therefore ensure that we regularly enjoy both classical music and poetry. I would be very suspicious of a system of education that did not include them at some point.

An important practical point here is that there has to be external, visible beauty in our lives. D. H. Lawrence makes this point very strongly in one of his essays.[368] It is not enough to have food, clothing, shelter, and work. It is not even enough to listen to music and visit art galleries. It is also very important that we keep our surroundings clean and beautiful. If they are dirty and ugly, it will affect our minds. This point applies especially to Bombay. When I first came to know the city thirty years ago, it was a very beautiful place, and many people were public-spirited and tried to keep it beautiful. But unfortunately, Bombay has since become more and more dirty and ugly, and this must have a strong influence on its citizens. I know that there are economic reasons for this, that money is needed for other projects, but the beauty of the city should be given more importance. The buildings, parks, and streets should be kept not only clean and tidy, but also beautiful and inspiring. Beautiful surroundings are absolutely necessary to human life. Without them, we cannot develop properly as human beings. As part of our education, then, we should learn to appreciate beauty, and develop a sense of responsibility for it in our surroundings.

Fifthly, there is the ethical aspect of education. I have already mentioned this aspect, which primarily involves developing a respect for the feelings and the convenience of other people. I must observe here that although I experience tremendous friendliness and hospitality wherever I go in India, I also experience a great deal of inconsiderateness. Even if I am busy and it is quite clear that I want to concentrate, people will interrupt me. This shows a lack of awareness of others. We must be careful not to trouble people or interfere with their lives, and nor must we take their time or waste their energy.

Truthfulness is also an important part of our ethical education. This means more than just not telling lies. It also means being direct, open, and honest in our communication with other people. It can sometimes be very difficult, especially in India, to get a clear answer from someone. For example, if you visit someone's house and ask if a particular person is at home, you will be told that he is. However, after enquiring further, it will often transpire that the person is not actually there at present, but will be at some other time. People are not precise; they often say whatever enters their heads, or something that they think will please you. Even educated people do not usually listen to what is being said, with the result that they give inappropriate and vague replies that are not at all useful. We have to be very careful that we listen to people, take note of what is being said to us, and, having understood, give a straightforward, direct, and honest reply.

We must also learn to be responsible for our surroundings and not just wait for other people to do things. I will give an example of this from the communist countries. I have many criticisms of some of these countries, but they do seem, from what I have heard, to encourage this sense of responsibility. If in a communist country you get off a bus and drop your ticket on the ground, someone will approach you and ask you to pick it up and put it in the wastepaper bin. It is illegal in these countries (and also in some Western countries) to throw litter on the ground; you can be fined for this sort of behaviour. In India, by contrast, there is so much litter dropped on the ground that the government's financial problems would be solved if they were to fine people for it. People are often unaware of their surroundings and need to learn to take responsibility for them in the course of their education. It is of little use being very learned if you still drop litter on the ground; your education has not helped you to develop as a human being. Your education should also teach you to take initiative. If you see that something needs doing, then you should do it, and encourage others to follow your example. You should not just tell someone else to do it.

Sixthly and lastly, we come to spiritual development. This arises naturally out of ethical development. By spiritual development I do not mean the actual teaching of a particular religion. I do not mean, for instance, learning the facts about the life of the Buddha and the various doctrines that he taught. That is not really learning about the Dhamma; it is at most only a basis for it. In fact, to be paradoxical, one could say that religion cannot be taught, it can only be caught. You have to catch the spirit of religion, and you do this through the influence of other people.

This brings me to the subject of what is known in Buddhism as *kalyāṇa mitratā* or spiritual friendship. This is a crucial part of the educational process. In a sense, everything else depends on it. A spiritual friendship is friendship that takes place with someone who is more experienced and mature than you are. I do not mean someone who just knows more than you do, who has read more books and who has a degree. I mean someone who is more developed than you *as a human being*.

I will tell you about an experience of mine which influenced my thinking on this subject. In 1970 I had my first real taste of academic life when I went as a visiting professor in philosophy to Yale University which, along with Harvard, is one of the most prestigious universities in the United States. I was taking what was called a 'Hall Seminar' in Buddhism, which simply involved delivering one lecture a week. This seminar was very popular, so I was allowed to have twenty-five students instead of the usual maximum of fifteen. After my weekly lecture, I used to hold a question-and-answer session, and when it had finished, I used to tell the students that if there was anything that was still unclear, or if there was anything else that they wanted to talk to me about, they could come and see me in my room in college. To begin with, it really surprised the students, both that I was living in college, and that I was willing to meet them outside of the lecture hall. I later discovered that though there were many professors at Yale, they normally had hardly any contact with the students apart from lectures. The students themselves did not feel free to approach the professors about their studies, or about any problems they might be having. Moreover, the professors usually lived away from the university, only visiting to give lectures, so they were not available to the students anyway. Every day many students came to see me, both those I taught and those I did not. They asked me questions, not only about Buddhism, but about many other things as well, and I discovered that they suffered very much through not having anybody older and more experienced than themselves to whom they could talk.

It is very important, then, that there is a good relationship between teachers and students. Education in the full sense of the term is not just learning about subjects. It must also involve real human contact between the student and the teacher, between the student and someone who is more experienced, even more developed, than himself or herself. There must be friendship and true communication. If you are a student, you should not be afraid to approach your teachers with any personal problems you might have. You should get to know your teachers, be able to talk things over with them, and benefit from their greater experience at the very least. You should not benefit just from their better understanding of the subject that you are studying. It is also important that students should have free access to experienced members of the Buddhist *sangha*, who can also provide the element of *kalyāṇa mitratā* which students need in order to grow, not only within the educational process but outside it as well.

This brings me to the question of the relations between students and parents. I recently read that even in India there is beginning to be a 'generation gap'. I was very sad to read this, because in England the generation gap has very bad consequences and results in many psychological difficulties for young people. Many of our friends in England were not on friendly terms with their parents when they first attended a Buddhist centre, whether or not they had left home. In some cases, there was such a gulf of difference that they even hated their parents. The generation gap, then, causes both children and parents to suffer. I am not suggesting that you should compromise on what you believe, or that you should always do what your parents tell you. In the modern world, things are changing so quickly that sometimes parents themselves are confused and are not sure what to tell their children. You should try to understand this, and make your communication with your parents as positive as possible. If, however, you find that they don't give you the kind of mature contact you need, then try to develop it with your teachers at college, and with your religious leaders – in the case of Buddhists, with experienced members of your *saṅgha*.

It is a terrible thing to be left without any contact with someone more experienced and developed than yourself. Without this contact you will not develop and grow as well or as quickly as a human being can. *Kalyāṇa mitratā*, or spiritual friendship, is therefore an absolutely essential and integral part of the whole educational process. I very much hope that it is found, to some extent at least, in this particular group of colleges run by the People's Education Society. From a Buddhist point of view the present educational system, in both East and West, is very often one-sidedly intellectual. There is too much emphasis on passing examinations and obtaining a job afterwards. The all-round development of the individual needs to be stressed in the educational process very much more than at present. I hope this will happen at Siddharth College. I am very grateful to the People's Education Society for arranging this meeting this morning, and for giving me the opportunity to share with you all some of the ideas I have had on Buddhism and education.

29
ENTERING THE STREAM OF
THE DHAMMA

Jyoti Hall, Ahmedabad, 12 February 1982

Brothers and Sisters in the Dhamma: At present I am on a three-month visit to India, and I have already spent quite a lot of time in the state of Maharashtra, where I visited a number of towns and cities, gave a number of lectures, and met many people. Now I have come to Gujarat, and I am spending a few days in Ahmedabad and Gandhinagar. I am very glad indeed to be here tonight, and very glad to be speaking to you. This is not my first visit to Ahmedabad. My connections with the state in fact go back quite a long way – back as far as April and May 1947.[369] I came here at that time to attend the meetings of the All-India Dharma Parishad, a gathering of representatives of all the different religions extant in India. There were representatives of Hinduism, of Jainism, of Sikhism, of Islam, and of Christianity. There were even representatives of the Bahá'í faith, and there was one representative of Buddhism: myself. So there I was, sitting on the platform surrounded by dozens and dozens of Dharma gurus and Dharma *ācāryas*, all in their different shades of yellow, saffron, orange, and red. Among them there was even one Shankaracharya, the Shankaracharya of Puri, or I should say one of the *two* Shankaracharyas of Puri, because there were two of them at that time, and they were fighting for possession of the *gaddi*.[370]

  I was then only twenty-two years old, but I was the only representative of Buddhism at that gathering. In fact I think I was probably the only

Buddhist in Ahmedabad – perhaps in the whole of Gujarat. Buddhism, I gathered, was not considered of much importance in that part of the world. The Dharma Parishad lasted for a number of days, and there were representatives of Hinduism by the dozen. There were followers of the Shiva cult, there were Vaishnavas,[371] there were followers of Swami Narayan,[372] followers of Shri Ramakrishna,[373] followers of Vallabh Acharya.[374] There were representatives of so many types of Hinduism, and they all gave very long speeches – speeches that sometimes lasted for one or even two hours, and were in Gujarati, of which I didn't understand a word. And even though there was only one representative of Buddhism, myself, I was told I could speak only for twenty minutes. This shows how much importance they attached to Buddhism! As I got up to speak, the voice of one of the organizers hissed in my ear, 'Only twenty minutes!' But nevertheless, I spoke for at least half an hour.

After the Dharma Parishad was over I stayed on in Ahmedabad until the Vaiśākha Pūrṇimā or Buddha Jayanti Day, as we also call it. The people of Ahmedabad at that time were not in the habit of celebrating the Buddha Jayanti, and on discovering this I spoke to some of my Hindu friends about the matter. There was one man in particular, a dealer in coal called Patel, who was very helpful to me. Anyway, I spoke to these friends and told them we ought to celebrate the Buddha Jayanti here in Ahmedabad. It would be a great disgrace, I told them, if the Buddha Jayanti wasn't celebrated in their city. According to Pandit Nehru the Buddha was the greatest man that India has ever produced,[375] and they should certainly celebrate his spiritual birthday, the day of his great Enlightenment. A celebration was therefore organized. It was held in the Premabhai Hall, I think, and I gave a lecture. This was the first time that the Buddha Jayanti had been celebrated in Ahmedabad in modern times, perhaps the first time that it ever had been celebrated there, and I am very happy that I could be associated with that historic event.

After that first time I visited Ahmedabad on a number of occasions over a period of nearly thirty years, and each time I came here I saw that changes had taken place. Progress had been made – that is, progress in Buddhism, progress in the Dhamma – and that progress is still continuing. In 1947 there was only one Buddhist in Ahmedabad, and he was here only for a few weeks; but today, I believe, there are several thousand Buddhists living in Ahmedabad. You also have an active Buddhist organization, and a number of young men working for Buddhism.

So what is the reason for this change? How has it come about? No doubt there are a number of different reasons, but one reason is clearly the most important of all: Dr Babasaheb Ambedkar's conversion to Buddhism on 14 October 1956 in Nagpur. On that occasion he did not embrace Buddhism alone, but along with *lakhs* of his followers. Since then there has been a great revival of Buddhism all over India. The centre of that revival is, of course, Maharashtra, where there are now more than thirty *lakhs* of Buddhists, and many *lakhs* of sympathizers. In Maharashtra there is a lot of enthusiasm for the Dhamma, and a lot of Buddhist activities are going on there. I saw this for myself in the course of my recent tour. Everywhere I went people wanted to hear the Dhamma and learn how to practise it. But the revival of Buddhism is also taking place in many other parts of India: in Uttar Pradesh, in Punjab, in Karnataka, in Tamil Nadu, and here in Gujarat and in Ahmedabad. That is why we are gathered together here tonight.

In a way my talk here tonight is three years late. When I last visited Ahmedabad three years ago, I was supposed to speak to you on Buddhism and social change, but unfortunately I fell ill, and at short notice Lokamitra kindly took my place. So tonight I am going to give the talk I could not give then. But what is it that brings about social change? So far as Buddhism is concerned, it is the Dhamma itself that brings it about. When we take the *Dhammadiksha*, everything changes. When we enter the stream of the Dhamma, everything changes. So that's what I'm going to talk about tonight. I'm going to talk to you about 'Entering the Stream of the Dhamma', and I am going to deal with the subject under four main headings: (1) Seeing the stream of the Dhamma; (2) Dipping in the stream of the Dhamma; (3) Plunging in the stream of the Dhamma; and (4) Abandoning oneself to the stream of the Dhamma.

Before doing this, however, I want to raise just one question. Why do we compare the Dhamma to a stream? In what respect does the Dhamma resemble a stream? It resembles a stream in several different ways. First of all, it has a source. Just as a stream comes from the great snow mountains, so the stream of the Dhamma comes from the Buddha. Its source is the Buddha's reason and experience, the Buddha's *bodhi*, as we call it. The Dhamma does not come from God, for Buddhism does not believe in any God. Neither does the Dhamma come from any unenlightened human being – from any worldly philosopher, for example. It comes from an Enlightened human being, that is, from the Buddha. It comes from the Buddha's *mahāprajñā* and *mahākaruṇā*. This is the source of the Dhamma.

Now the Dhamma has not only a source, but a goal. Just as the goal of the stream is the ocean, so the goal of the Dhamma is Nirvāṇa or *bodhi*. This *bodhi* is a state of the highest moral and spiritual perfection. It is a state of supreme *prajñā* or wisdom, of unlimited *maitrī* and *karuṇā*, or love and compassion, and of absolute *viśuddhi* or purity. This, then, is the goal of every Buddhist, the goal of everyone who takes *Dhammadiksha*.

The Dhamma resembles a stream, or a river, in other ways. The river is always moving, always flowing in the direction of the ocean, not stopping even for a single instant. Similarly, the Dhamma is always flowing, always progressing – progressing in the direction of Nirvāṇa, of *bodhi*. If it is not progressing in the direction of *bodhi* it is not the Dhamma, just as if the river stops flowing it is not a river any more but just a swamp, or even a puddle. Because the Dhamma is always progressing in the direction of *bodhi*, someone who really enters the stream of the Dhamma will always be progressing in the direction of *bodhi* too. He will not be able to stand still. If he is standing still, he has not really entered the stream of the Dhamma. He hasn't really taken the *Dhammadiksha*.

The water of which the river consists changes all the time, but the river remains the same river. In the same way, the Dhamma changes all the time. In the course of its historical development it has assumed various forms, for example Theravāda, Mahāyāna, Chan or Zen, and Tibetan Buddhism. But despite such historical development, despite the fact that it assumes all these different forms, it remains the same Dhamma. It continues to proclaim the same basic teachings.

The Dhamma resembles a stream or a river in yet another important respect. The stream or the river consists of water, and water purifies us and washes us perfectly clean. In the same way the Dhamma also purifies us. It purifies our body, our speech, our mind, our whole being – but only if we practise it, only if we actually enter the stream of the Dhamma. Simply reciting the *tisaraṇa* and *pañcasīla* is not enough. Simply saying that we are Buddhists, or that we are followers of Dr Ambedkar, is not enough.

Water not only purifies and cleanses; it also quenches our thirst. The Dhamma is also like that. It quenches our thirst for Truth, our thirst for the good life. Nor is that all. Water helps living things to grow. Without water, in fact, nothing can grow. Trees cannot grow without water, and neither can flowers or crops. It is the same with the Dhamma. Without the water of the Dhamma, human beings cannot grow as human beings – cannot become better, cannot progress, cannot move in the direction of *bodhi*. The Dhamma is therefore not only compared to a stream or river but also to a great rain cloud. The Buddha says it's like a great rain cloud suddenly appearing in the midst of the sky. First of all there's a lot of thunder and lightning. The sky becomes very dark, and then the rain falls. It goes on falling and falling, and as it falls, all the plants and trees and shrubs grow. In the same way, when the rain of the Dhamma falls – when the Dhamma is taught by the Buddha – all living beings grow. They all develop spiritually. They are all able to follow the path of *śīla, samādhi,* and *prajñā*. They are all able to attain Nirvāṇa, to attain *bodhi* – provided they make the effort, of course.[376]

Thus the Dhamma can be compared to a stream or a river in all these different ways. Like the river, the Dhamma has a source. Its source is the Buddha's *bodhi*. Like the river the Dhamma has a goal. Its goal is Nirvāṇa. Like a river the Dhamma is always moving. It is always moving in the direction of Nirvāṇa. And although the Dhamma constantly changes, assuming many historical forms, it remains the same Dhamma. Like the water of a stream or river, Dhamma purifies, it quenches our thirst, and it helps us to grow and develop as human beings.

I. SEEING THE STREAM OF THE DHAMMA

Life, we may say, is like a desert. We are wandering in that desert with our wives or husbands and children and possessions, and with other people with their families and possessions, and together we all form a sort of caravan. We don't know where we are going. We don't have any proper guide. We just go on and on. Sometimes, in fact, we go round and round in circles, and we get very tired, hot, and thirsty. Then one day we see something shining in the distance, like a thread of silver, and as we come closer, we see that it is a great river – the river of the Dhamma. When we see the river of the Dhamma we feel very happy, and we start moving towards it, thinking that our thirst will soon be quenched.

So how do we come to see this river of the Dhamma there in the distance? Well, we can see it in various ways. We can see it just by reading books. This was my own experience. When I was sixteen I read two Buddhist *sūtras*, and when I read them I knew at once that this was the Truth. I knew that this was what I believed. I knew that I was a Buddhist. In this way I saw the river of the Dhamma shining in the distance. But we can see this river of the Dhamma in other ways. We can see it by listening to a lecture, just as you are doing now. We can see it when a friend talks to us about the Dhamma. We can see it even by just looking at the image of the Buddha. We can see the Dhamma reflected in the Buddha's smile of wisdom and compassion. That is why it is important that we should have beautiful images of the Buddha – images that really inspire people.

When we see the river of the Dhamma we naturally want to move towards it and come in contact with it – taste it, drink it, bathe in it. Nor is that all. We want other people to move towards it too. But sometimes other people are not interested in the river; they would rather go on wandering in the desert. They may even say that there isn't any river there at all, and that if we are crazy enough to think we can see it, we are just experiencing delusions. When that happens, we sometimes have to move towards the stream of the Dhamma alone, leaving behind our family, our friends and companions. Then, as we move towards the stream of the Dhamma, we see it more and more clearly. We see how beautiful it is. We start hearing the sound of the water, the cries of the wild birds, and the laughter of the people bathing. So we move towards the river more and more quickly, and eventually we reach the bank and see the water of the Dhamma flowing past our feet.

2. DIPPING IN THE STREAM OF THE DHAMMA

Dipping in the stream of the Dhamma means just going a little way into the water and then quickly coming out again. At this stage we are afraid of going too deeply into the stream, afraid of losing contact with the bank, so we just have a little dip, and then come out again very quickly. In other words, we practise the Dhamma just a little bit, and then go back to worldly life for a while. We spend a few minutes in the water, and then a few hours on the bank, because we feel much safer on the bank. We may even go back into the desert for a while, and that is quite a dangerous thing to do. We may forget all about the river, or think it was all just a dream. If this doesn't happen, however, we start spending more and more time in the water. We start thinking that this river of the Dhamma isn't really so dangerous after all, and start taking quite long dips.

3. PLUNGING INTO THE STREAM OF THE DHAMMA.

Plunging into the stream means jumping right into the stream of the Dhamma, forgetting all about the bank. It means allowing the water to cover you completely, practising the Dhamma for a long while without having any contact with worldly things, that is to say, worldly mental states. We plunge into the Dhamma when we meditate deeply and also when we go on a *Dhamma-shibir*. I may be saying a little more about this later on.

4. ABANDONING ONESELF TO THE STREAM OF THE DHAMMA.

In the previous stage, we were completely covered by the water, swimming about in it, going further and further out, and the water was becoming deeper and deeper. So then what happens? As we start getting near the very middle of the river, near the deepest part, we start feeling the current of the river, and it starts pulling us very strongly in the direction of the ocean. When this happens we usually start feeling afraid. We feel that we are going to lose ourselves, that we are going to die. Of course we don't want to die, so we resist the current; we hold back and don't abandon ourselves to the stream of the Dhamma. But after this has happened two or three times, or four or five times, or maybe more, we may start losing our fear and stop resisting. We may allow the current to carry us away completely in the direction of the ocean. When this happens we enter the fourth stage, the stage of abandoning oneself to the stream of the Dhamma. There is now no danger of us spending too much time on the bank or going back to the desert. Having become one with the stream of the Dhamma, we are sure of reaching the ocean one day, sure of attaining Nirvāṇa.

This stage of abandoning oneself to the stream of the Dhamma is what is usually called in Buddhism simply Stream Entry, and one who has abandoned himself in this way is called a Stream Entrant or *sotāpanna*. The Stream Entrant cannot fall back into lower states of existence. He can only progress. The Stream Entrant can never forsake the Dhamma, because he has *become* the Dhamma, is at one with the Dhamma. He may live at home with his wife and family, or he may go and live in a cave in the Himalayas. It doesn't make any difference; he will continue to progress. Only the Stream Entrant is the real Buddhist – apart from those, of course, who have attained even higher levels. Only the Stream Entrant has really gone for Refuge; only the Stream Entrant has really taken the *Dhammadiksha*. All Buddhists should therefore aim at abandoning themselves to the stream of the Dhamma. They shouldn't be satisfied with just dipping in it, or even with plunging into it. They should be satisfied only when they have abandoned themselves to it.

But what is it that prevents us from doing this? What is it that makes us resist the pull of the current? What makes one hold back? One is prevented from abandoning oneself to the stream of the Dhamma by what Buddhism calls the three fetters or *saṃyojanas*. In Pāli the names of these three fetters are *sakkāya-diṭṭhi*, *vicikicchā*, and *sīlabbata-parāmāsa*. *Sakkāya-diṭṭhi* is the wrong view about self, the view that one's 'self' is a permanent, unchanging entity. *Vicikicchā* is doubt, uncertainty, and indecision. It is inability to make up one's mind, even unwillingness to make up one's mind, especially about the Dhamma. *Sīlabbata-parāmāsa* is reliance on moral rules and religious observances to help one gain salvation, without developing the corresponding mental qualities and attitudes.

So how do these three fetters hold one back? How do they prevent one from abandoning oneself to the stream of the Dhamma? This is explained in Buddhism in great detail. Tonight I'm going to explain it quite simply. The first fetter consists in our keeping hold of a big rope. This rope is very long and thick. It is the rope of our own 'self'. One end of the rope is fastened to the bank, while the other end we hold very tightly in our hand. So, holding one end of the rope, we go out into the middle of the river. There we feel the current pulling us very strongly in the direction of the ocean. But although we allow ourselves to feel the current, we are very careful not to let go of the rope, and this prevents us from abandoning ourselves to the stream of the Dhamma. The first fetter is like that. The second fetter consists in our wondering whether to let go of the rope or not. Sometimes we think we should, sometimes we think we shouldn't. Sometimes we think it would be a good thing to let go, and sometimes we think it would be a very bad thing, even a dangerous thing. We can't really decide; perhaps we don't want to decide. So we continue to hold on to the rope. This also prevents us from abandoning ourselves to the stream of the Dhamma. The second fetter is like that. And the third fetter consists in our pretending to let go of the rope – that is to say, we just go through the motions of letting go. Though we pretend that we are trying very hard to let go, actually we are not trying to let go at all. This also prevents us from abandoning ourselves to the stream of the Dhamma. The third fetter is like that.

We have now seen what entering the stream of the Dhamma means. So, if you think of yourself as a Buddhist, if you have taken the *Dhammadiksha*, you should ask yourselves where you stand. What sort of Buddhist are you? To which of the four stages of progress do you belong? Have you merely seen the stream of the Dhamma, without approaching very near? Have you actually dipped yourself in it at least once? Or have you plunged right in, or even abandoned yourself to it entirely?

Nowadays it is not so difficult to see the stream of the Dhamma. You are all seeing it tonight, at this very moment. Dipping oneself in the stream of the Dhamma is a little more difficult. Some people never get as far as that, even though they have seen the stream. They sit down on the bank, look at the river and say, 'What a beautiful river!', but they never actually take a dip in it. They may even write a book about the river, giving a vivid description of it and telling you how long it is, how broad it is, and how very, very deep. They may even give you detailed instructions about how to take a dip, or even about how to swim. They may have a certificate stating that they have abandoned themselves to the stream, but all the while they have not even dipped into it. In fact, the certificate may have been given by someone who has not dipped into it either. Thus, dipping into the river is a little more difficult than seeing it.

Plunging into the stream of the Dhamma is more difficult still, but it is certainly not impossible. So what is the best way of doing this? For most people the best way is by going on a *Dhamma-shibir* for three days, or a week, or maybe longer. If you go on a *Dhamma-shibir* you will plunge yourself into the stream of the Dhamma. You will have a concentrated experience of the Dhamma – an experience of meditation, puja, Dhamma study and discussion, *maitri*, fellowship in the Dhamma.

And for three days, or a week, you will have this and nothing but this. You will be thinking about the Dhamma, talking about the Dhamma, eating the Dhamma, drinking the Dhamma. In this way you will be plunged right into the Dhamma.

Fortunately, it is now much easier to enter the stream of the Dhamma than it used to be. Formerly it was difficult even to see the stream of the Dhamma. No one knew where it was. It was hidden by piles of sand, and its name had been erased from the map. But now it is quite easy to find, and it is not very difficult at least to take a dip, because now there is a magnificent new ghat leading down to the river of the Dhamma. This ghat is very broad; it has hundreds of steps, and *lakhs* of people can go down to the river at the same time, to bathe in the water and refresh themselves. And who has built this magnificent new ghat? Well, we all know that very well. It was Dr Babasaheb Ambedkar. The name of the ghat is the movement of mass conversion to Buddhism; it is the ghat of the *Dhammadiksha*. And there is a date on the ghat: 14 October 1956. This is why it is now easier to enter the stream of the Dhamma than it used to be. Tonight we are all sitting on the steps of that great ghat, and I hope that as many of you as possible will dip yourselves in the stream, plunge into it, even abandon yourselves to it. I hope that as many of you as possible will enter the stream of the Dhamma. The ghat is for all. The Dhamma is for all. Buddhism is for all. The stream will not ask you what your colour is, or what your caste is. It will not want to know your nationality. It will wash away all those distinctions. The stream of the Dhamma is a stream of *maitrī*, a stream of *karuṇā*, a stream of *prajñā*. The stream of the Dhamma has as its source the Buddha, while its goal is the ocean of Nirvāṇa. Let us all therefore enter the stream of the Dhamma. Let us all purify ourselves. Let us all quench our thirst. Let us all grow as human beings. Let us all gain supreme wisdom or *prajñā*, limitless *maitrī* and *karuṇā*, and absolute *visuddhi* or purity. Our lives will then be fulfilled.

30

THE MEANING OF THE BUDDHA PUJA
AND THE FUNCTION OF A VIHARA

Bapunagar, Ahmedabad, 14 February 1982

Brothers and Sisters: At present I am on a short visit to Ahmedabad, and since I am staying for only a week or so I am very busy giving lectures in various localities, after which there will be a *Dhamma-shibir* in Gandhinagar. This morning I am glad to be here with you in Bapunagar, and to have the opportunity of dedicating your new vihara. Over the years I have dedicated many viharas in India, especially in Maharashtra. Some of them were quite small, others quite big, but I think I can say that this is the biggest vihara I have so far dedicated, with the biggest and most beautiful image. I must therefore congratulate all those who had anything to do with the construction of the vihara and the image. A day or two ago I was told that formerly the vihara and the image were both quite small, but that you have reconstructed them on a much bigger scale, and made them more beautiful. I am very glad that this is the case; it is highly significant, because just as the vihara has become bigger, so have the Dhamma activities here increased and become more extensive.

Dhamma activities have increased not only in this place but elsewhere. These days I live in England, where Buddhist activities are spreading, just as they are here in India, especially in Maharashtra. On my recent tour there, everywhere I went meetings were organized, attended by thousands of people, all eager to hear the Dhamma, and the same sort of thing appears to be happening in Ahmedabad, even though not on quite so big a scale. Here also Buddhism is spreading and becoming stronger, and that is why you have built this new vihara. But though it is good to have such a big vihara, with such a beautiful image, we have to ask ourselves what the function of a vihara is. Why do we have a vihara at all? Why do we have an image of the Buddha? We must understand these things.

The literal meaning of the word vihara is 'dwelling place', but it is a special kind of dwelling place. In the Buddha's day it was the place where the Buddha stayed, or where the *bhikkhus* stayed. Usually this place was very small, consisting of just one or two small rooms. Sometimes it was a cave, or even a hollow tree. All these places were called viharas. In Buddhist countries the word vihara still has this meaning today. It is the place where the *bhikkhus* stay, or where they live. It is what in India is usually called an ashram.

But the word vihara has another meaning. It is not just where the Buddha stayed in the past, or where the *bhikkhus* live today, it is also the place where the Buddha image is kept. Physically speaking, the Buddha is no longer with us. The Buddha lived 2,500 years ago, and although we still have his teaching we do not have the Buddha himself. He cannot himself come and sit here with us, so we keep the Buddha image to remind us of him. When we keep the Buddha image here it is as though the Buddha himself was sitting here. The image helps to remind us about the life of the Buddha. That is why we also have pictures of various incidents in the life of the Buddha on the walls of the vihara. They remind us how the Buddha was born, how he grew up, how he led a life of luxury, how he left it all and went off into the jungle, how he practised self-mortification, how he found the Middle Way and, most important of all, how he gained Enlightenment. We keep the image to remind us of all these things.

But that is not our only reason for keeping the image of the Buddha. We also keep it in order to remind us of Enlightenment itself. Enlightenment is the goal of every Buddhist. The Buddha gained Enlightenment under the bodhi tree at Bodh Gaya, at the age of thirty-five, by his own human efforts, without the help of any god. Since the Buddha was a human being like ourselves, what the Buddha attained we also can attain. If we follow the path of the Dhamma, we also can gain Enlightenment. Keeping the image of the Buddha reminds us of this too. It reminds us that Enlightenment is the ideal for every human being, and that the way to Enlightenment is to follow the path of the Dhamma. Thus the image reminds us not only of the Buddha, but also of the Dhamma.

Although we keep the image of the Buddha here in the vihara we don't worship it in the Hindu way. We don't come here and pray to the

Buddha for worldly things. We don't ask the Buddha to help us pass our examinations, or to help us get promotion, or to give us a son. When we come before the image we think only of the Enlightenment of the Buddha, and of the Dhamma, which is the path leading to that Enlightenment. Thus a Buddhist vihara is not like a Hindu temple, and the significance of keeping the Buddha image there is quite different from the significance of keeping a Hindu image in a Hindu temple. The Buddha image does not possess any magic powers, or work any miracles. We keep the Buddha image simply to remind us of the Buddha because, if you are a Buddhist, you must never forget the Buddha. You must think about him every minute, even. In the same way, if you are a Buddhist, you must think about Enlightenment as your goal. You must think about the Dhamma, because the Dhamma is the way to Enlightenment.

Although we don't worship the Buddha in the Hindu way, we do make certain offerings, and we have to understand the significance of this. You will have noticed that after completing the installation of the image we lit candles, and offered flowers and lighted incense-sticks. These are the only things that Buddhists usually offer. We offer flowers because although today they are very beautiful, both in colour and scent, tomorrow they will be withered and ill-smelling. We have to reflect that all worldly things are like that. We ourselves are like that. Today we may look young and fresh and beautiful, especially when we are wearing our nice new clothes, but what will we look like in a few years time?[377] In a few years we will have no teeth, we won't be able to see very well, our body will be crooked and bent, and we will be able to walk only with the aid of a stick. We therefore have to ask ourselves, what is the meaning and purpose of human life? Why are we here on this earth? What is the best way of using this life of ours? How can we grow and develop? Offering flowers reminds us of all these things. It reminds us that all worldly things are impermanent, and that it is only the Dhamma that lasts. We need to involve ourselves in worldly things to some extent – we should have good food, good clothing, good housing, and education – but at the same time, we must always think of the Dhamma. The Dhamma is the most important thing. This is what we remember when we offer flowers.

When we offer lighted candles we reflect that light, also, is very beautiful. However dark it may be, if we light even one candle, at once the whole place becomes bright. The candle is like the Buddha's teaching, the light of which shines in the midst of the darkness of the world. The world is indeed very dark. It is full of all sorts of bad things, such as greed, conflict, and exploitation. In the world there is the caste system, there is Untouchability. All these bad things exist in the world. But the Buddha's teaching is just like the candle. When you light a candle the darkness goes, not only from the world, but from your own mind. When you practise the Dhamma, the darkness in your mind disappears, and your mind becomes full of *maitrī*, full of *karuṇā*, full of *prajñā*. When you offer a lighted candle you therefore think, 'May I light the lamp of *prajñā* in the world, and in my own mind! May the light of the Buddha's teaching shine on the whole world!'

The third offering is incense. Lighted incense-sticks smell very sweet; even if you light only a very small stick of incense, it can be smelt dozens of yards away. Similarly, if you practise the Dhamma, even just a little, it will exert a positive influence over a wide area. It will influence all the people in your family, all the people in the locality. You yourself will be like an incense-stick. So when you offer an incense-stick you must reflect, 'May I be like this incense-stick! May I practise the Dhamma so sincerely that it affects the whole community!'

Such then are the reasons we offer flowers, candles, and incense-sticks before the image of the Buddha. These things all remind us of the Dhamma, and offering them reminds us to practise the Dhamma. We don't give the flowers, the lights, and the incense to the Buddha as a sort of bribe, so that he will give us what we want. The Buddha does not need anything. He certainly does not need our flowers, our candles, or our incense. So we don't offer these things for the sake of the Buddha. We offer them for our own sake, because giving them reminds us of the Dhamma, and if we remember the Dhamma we can practise it.

Thus, the vihara is the place where we remember the Dhamma. At home it is sometimes difficult to remember the Dhamma. There is a lot of work to be done. There are children to look after, meals to cook, clothes to wash. There is sweeping and cleaning, and going to the bazaar. So much work is there to be done that there is no time to remember the Dhamma. Similarly, men have to go off to work, and are very busy at the office. They too have no time to remember the Dhamma. The vihara is the place where you can remember the Dhamma. I am not saying you need not remember it at home. If you can remember it at home too, that is very good. But if you cannot remember it at home, at least you can remember the Dhamma when you come to the vihara.

The vihara is also the place where you can practise the Dhamma. Again, I am not saying you cannot practise the Dhamma at home. You can indeed practise it at home, but when you come to the vihara you can practise it more intensively. When you come to the vihara, you can take a dip in the stream of the Dhamma. Or, to change the image, we can say that the Dhamma is like an oasis, a small body of water in the midst of a great desert. The vihara exists in the midst of the vast desert of the world, and when you come to the vihara you can obtain the water – in fact the nectar (*amṛta*) – of the Dhamma.

The vihara should therefore be kept strictly for the purposes of the Dhamma, for spiritual purposes. You should not hold political meetings or conduct any kind of worldly activity there. Moreover, you must keep the vihara clean and beautiful and nicely decorated. You must repair it every year. You must keep it really clean and really beautiful all the time.

Basically the vihara is for the practice of four things.

1. THE VIHARA IS FOR THE PRACTICE OF *ŚĪLA*

This place is called the Pancasila Vihara, which is a reminder that here you can not only practise the *pañcasīla*, but practise them fully. You all know what the five *sīlas* are: (a) to refrain from injuring any living being, (b) to refrain from taking what has not been given, (c) to refrain from sexual misconduct, i.e. adultery, (d) to refrain from false speech, and (e) to refrain from intoxicating drinks and drugs. You should of course observe the five *sīlas* at home, but they are much easier to observe when you come to the vihara. Or at least, four out of the five *sīlas* are much easier to practise here. But there is one *sīla* that is very difficult to observe even when you come to the vihara. Which one is that? It is the fourth *sīla*, to refrain from false speech. When we examine this precept, we find that it can be divided into four. It is not just a matter of refraining from telling lies. It is much more than that. It consists in (i) refraining from speech that is actually false, (ii) refraining from harsh or abusive speech, (iii) refraining from idle and useless talk, and (iv) refraining from slander and backbiting. The fourth *sīla* includes all those things. When you come to the vihara you certainly won't injure any living being, or steal anything, or commit adultery, or take intoxicating drinks or drugs.

All these *sīlas* are quite easy to practise here. But you may not find the fourth *sīla* quite so easy to keep when you come to the vihara. Even though you may not actually tell any lies, you might start indulging in idle and useless talk about the family and the home, about shops, about the prices of goods. You might talk very loudly, or start arguing. You might shout at your children. All these things are a breach of the fourth *sīla*. In the vihara you should practise all five *sīlas*, including this fourth one. The vihara is supposed to be a very quiet and peaceful place. If it is not quiet and peaceful you won't be able to remember the Dhamma. If it is not quiet and peaceful it will be just like home. We should be careful about this when we come to the vihara.

Ladies, especially, should be careful. I don't know why it is, but ladies very much like to gossip. At all our recent meetings in Maharashtra the organizers had to shout at the ladies every now and then and tell them to be quiet. I don't know why this should be necessary. The men also talk sometimes – I am not saying that the men don't ever make a noise. Sometimes they make it on the platform itself. Sometimes they even have big arguments on the platform about how to run the meeting. This sort of thing also we should not do. The vihara must be completely peaceful. As soon as you enter the vihara, you should feel more quiet and peaceful within yourself.

2. THE VIHARA IS FOR THE PRACTICE OF MEDITATION

The vihara is the place where we can at least sit quietly. Usually we can't do this at home, because there is so much work to be done, but when we come to the vihara we can sit quietly and not do anything for a while. By this I don't mean we should have a rest, or go to sleep. In some places I have seen people come to the vihara in the afternoon and have a little sleep, but the vihara is not meant for this. You should just sit here quietly, wide awake, and, if you can, practise a little meditation, or recite some *pūjā gāthas*. Whatever you do, make sure your mind becomes very quiet, very peaceful. If you know the *ānāpānasati* practice you can do that, or you can do the *mettā bhāvanā*. If a lot of you meditate here regularly, there will be a good atmosphere in the place. If you see someone sitting and meditating as you enter the vihara, be sure to enter quietly and don't start talking. Perhaps there could be a rule that you don't talk in the vihara, or that you talk only about the Dhamma.

3. THE VIHARA IS FOR THE STUDY OF THE DHAMMA

The vihara is the place for the study of Buddhist books – not just reading them in a mechanical way but really trying to understand them. You should study books like the *Dhammapada* and the *Udāna*, or like Dr Ambedkar's *The Buddha and His Dhamma*. You should meet regularly in small groups for the study of the Dhamma, and of course you should study it in your own language, whether Gujarati, Marathi, or whatever. Not only should you read, but you should discuss what you read among yourselves. If possible, get an experienced Order member to lead the discussion, or even to take a regular class. In this way you will come to understand something about the Dhamma. It is disgraceful to be a Buddhist and not know anything about the Dhamma. If you don't understand the Dhamma, then you won't be able to practise it. You will be a Buddhist in name only. So use the vihara for the study of the Dhamma. Have Dhamma study classes here regularly, every week. In this way your understanding of the Dhamma will grow. You will know what the Dhamma is, you will be able to answer the questions of non-Buddhists, you will be able to practise the Dhamma, and you will feel happier in your own mind.

4. THE VIHARA IS FOR CELEBRATING BUDDHIST FESTIVALS

Festivals like Buddha Jayanti, and Dr Ambedkar's birthday, should all be celebrated on a grand scale and very beautifully. There should be lectures on the Dhamma, and maybe Buddhist dramas, as well as devotional songs in praise of the Buddha and Dr Ambedkar. Perhaps all the different Purnima days could be celebrated in this way.

Thus the vihara is the place where we practise the five *sīlas* more intensively than usual, where we practise meditation, where we study the Dhamma, and where we celebrate Buddhist festivals. It is a place that reminds us of the Buddha, reminds us of the Dhamma. I hope you will use your big new vihara in the way I have described. No doubt you are doing that to some extent already. If you can use your vihara in this way you will be real Buddhists. You will develop as human beings, you will lead happier lives, and you will progress towards Enlightenment.

31
WHY CHOOSE BUDDHISM?

Majuragaon, Ahmedabad, 13 February 1982

Sisters and brothers: As many of you know, I've been to Ahmedabad on quite a number of occasions before, but this is the first time that I've come to this locality. I am glad to have been welcomed by you all this evening, and especially glad to have heard the music. Music always draws people. According to ancient Indian mythology the deer could be trapped by playing music, and sometimes human beings also can be drawn by music. And if they're drawn by music so that then they can listen to the Dhamma, that's very good. But if you want to listen to the Dhamma, if you want to be able to hear, you must be quiet. I don't want to have to shout, and I don't think the translator wants to shout either. It isn't really possible to teach the Dhamma by shouting. So please listen very carefully and very quietly.

Since I haven't seen you before and many of you haven't seen me before, I'm going to start by saying a few words about myself. As you can guess, I wasn't born in India. I was born in London. My family wasn't very strongly Christian – in fact, my parents only went to church about once every few years – so Christianity didn't have much influence on me when I was young, but I was very interested in different religions and philosophies and I read translations of the scriptures of many religions, including the Upanishads, the *Bhagavad Gītā*, the Bible, and the Koran. Then, when I was sixteen I happened to read two Buddhist *sūtras*, and when I read these two *sūtras*, in translation of course, I had a very strong experience. I at once felt that this was the Truth. Indeed,

I at once felt that this was what I already believed. I realized that I was a Buddhist.

For two years after that I was completely on my own as a Buddhist. At that time in England there were very few Buddhists – maybe only two or three dozen, and even they weren't one-hundred-percent Buddhist. But when I was eighteen I came into contact with the London Buddhist Society and I used to go along to their meetings every now and then. At the meetings there were never more than a dozen people. We used to have a lecture on Buddhism and then meditate for few minutes and that was all. This was in about 1942, during the war.

Then, when I was nineteen, I was sent to India in connection with the war. I thought, 'India is the country of the Buddha. This is where the Buddha was born and gained Enlightenment, and taught the Dhamma. India is a very holy place.' So I was very happy to come here, because I thought that here I could learn about Buddhism. Eventually I spent twenty years in this country, from 1944 to 1964. First I spent about two years in South India, wandering from place to place. At that time I was living like a sadhu, like an *anagārika*, and I walked from place to place visiting different Hindu teachers, because in South India there were no Buddhist teachers at all. Sometimes I stayed in caves and meditated, and sometimes I stayed in ashrams. Once I stayed in Mysore state (the present day Karnataka) in an old ruined temple on top of a hill, many miles away from any village. The friends who took me there left with me some rice and some dhal and that was what I ate every day. In the night I heard strange sounds coming from the roof of the temple, and I eventually realized that it was the sound of leopards snarling, but they never did me any harm. So in this way I spent two years in South India, and then I felt that I wanted some contact with Buddhism, so I came to Sarnath.

There I met the Maha Bodhi Society *bhikkhus* and asked them to make me a *sāmaṇera*, but these *bhikkhus*, who were from Sri Lanka, were quite suspicious of me, mainly because I had no money. Thinking that it was one of the monastic rules, for two years I had not touched money, but the Sri Lanka *bhikkhus* thought this very strange. In their opinion a modern monk ought to have money, and because I had none they were unwilling to make me a *sāmaṇera*.

From Sarnath I walked to Kusinara, the place where the Lord Buddha attained *parinirvāṇa*. Here I was more fortunate. I met U Chandramani

Maha Thera, of whom I am sure you have heard, because it was he who gave the Three Refuges and the Five Precepts to Dr Ambedkar in Nagpur in 1956. A week after my arrival he gave me the *sāmaṇera* ordination. Although I didn't know it at the time, this gave me a sort of connection with Dr Ambedkar, because U Chandramani was now my guru and he was afterwards to become the guru of Dr Ambedkar.

Having become a *sāmaṇera*, I went on foot up into Nepal. I visited Lumbini, the birthplace of the Buddha, as well as Butaol and Tansen, where I gave lectures on Buddhism to the local Buddhists. From Nepal I came down to Benares and stayed at the Hindu University, there studying Pāli and Abhidhamma with a famous Indian *bhikkhu*, Jagdish Kashyap. When I had been with him for nearly a year, Kashyapji took me up to Kalimpong, a small town in the eastern Himalayas, in the Darjeeling District of West Bengal, not far from Tibet. Here he left me, saying, 'Stay here and work for the good of Buddhism.'

In this way I was left on my own in Kalimpong, while Kashyapji returned to Benares. I was then twenty-five years old. Since I had been told to work for the good of Buddhism I started a Buddhist organization, and later on a Buddhist magazine. At the same time I made my first contact with Dr Ambedkar. An article he wrote for the May 1950 issue of the *Maha Bodhi* journal entitled 'Buddha and the Future of His Religion' impressed me very much, so I wrote to Dr Ambedkar telling him what I was doing in Kalimpong, and adding that I liked his article. He replied saying that he was glad to hear what I was doing and that *bhikkhus* must be more active than ever. This was in 1950.

Every winter I used to come down to the plains: to Calcutta, to Bombay, and sometimes to Ahmedabad. I met Dr Babasaheb Ambedkar twice in Bombay, shortly before the great mass conversion, so in this way I established good contact with him and with his followers. As you know, Dr Ambedkar unfortunately died only seven weeks after the great mass conversion in Nagpur, and on that very day I arrived in Nagpur. His followers there were dreadfully distressed at his death. It seemed like the end of the world. They didn't know what was going to happen to them, or to the movement of *Dhammadiksha*. So I stayed in Nagpur and gave many lectures in all the different localities. I spoke to many thousands of people and I told them that the movement of *Dhammadiksha* must go on. In this way I developed a very close connection with the Buddhist people of Nagpur – in fact with Buddhists throughout Maharashtra, as well as with those of Gujarat and other places. I continued coming down every winter, giving lectures and sometimes taking *Dhammadiksha* ceremonies. I remember one ceremony I took here in Ahmedabad, when five young men took the *Dhammadiksha*. It's mainly those five young men who have been carrying on the Buddhist activities here ever since.

I carried on this way of life until 1964, when I went back to England. It was the first time I had visited England and my family and friends there for twenty years, and they were all very glad to see me. I stayed there for two years, working for Buddhism – but I wasn't quite satisfied with the Buddhist movement in England at that time. It wasn't Buddhist enough. It wasn't one-hundred-percent Buddhist; it was a bit mixed with Christianity. I realized we needed a new Buddhist movement in the West, so in 1967 I started what we call in English the Friends of the Western Buddhist Order and in Hindi, as well as in Marathi and Gujarati, the Trailokya Bauddha Mahasangha Sahayak Gana. This is now the biggest and most active Buddhist movement in Europe, and runs activities in eight different countries in the world, including India.

You may wonder why it is that so many people in the West nowadays are attracted to Buddhism. There are various reasons, and tonight I am going to give you just a few of the more important ones. The first reason may surprise some of you, if you have got old-fashioned ideas about religion, and especially it may surprise some of our Hindu friends. The main reason why people in the West are attracted to Buddhism is that in Buddhism there is no God. In Buddhism there is no supreme being who has created the universe and is governing it. In the West, when people learned that in Buddhism there is no God, at first they were very surprised because in the West, due to the influence of Christianity, people usually think that if you believe in religion, you must believe in God. And once they had got over their surprise that in Buddhism there is no God, they were often very relieved. In the West there are many people who want to follow some religion, but they don't find it possible to believe in God so they are very glad to hear that in Buddhism we have to depend on our own efforts for salvation. In Buddhism man has to save himself, to purify himself. It's no use praying to God; you have to do it yourself. This idea appeals very much to people in the West.

Secondly, people in the West are attracted to Buddhism because it shows them a practical path of human development. Buddhism shows us how to improve towards perfection; it gives us a path we can follow, a path of *śīla* or ethics, *samādhi* or meditation, and *prajñā* or higher wisdom. Nowadays in the West, many people are interested in meditation, and Buddhism is very rich in methods of meditation. For instance there is what we call the *ānāpānasati*, the mindfulness of breathing. In this practice you count the breaths as you breathe in and out. You don't try to control your breathing; you just watch and count. In this way the mind becomes concentrated, steady, and clear, and with this clear, concentrated mind you can understand the Dhamma much better than before. Buddhism also teaches the *mettā bhāvanā* meditation, through which we can develop *mettā* or *maitrī*, friendliness, to other living beings – especially other human beings. The meditation has five stages. First we develop *maitrī* towards ourselves, then towards a near and dear friend, then towards a neutral person, then even towards an enemy, and then we start developing *mettā* or *maitrī* towards all the people in the world. First of all we send *mettā* to all the people in our own house, then all the people in the locality – all the people in the town – all the people in the state – the whole country, and the whole world. I've explained this very briefly, but when we practise we spend ten minutes over each of these five stages, so the whole practice takes about fifty minutes or one hour. And as a result of doing the practice we develop a strong feeling of *mettā* towards other living beings.

This is one of the things that shows how practical Buddhism is. All the religions say that you must love other people. The Christian Bible says that you should love your neighbour as yourself. But how are you to do this? The Bible doesn't tell you. It's not easy to love your neighbour. Sometimes it's not even easy to love your friends and relations – sometimes you may not even love your own mother and father – so how are you to develop love? Christianity doesn't tell you, Hinduism doesn't tell you, Islam doesn't tell you, but Buddhism gives you a step by step method. So in this way Buddhism is very practical. It works, and this is why so many people in the West are attracted to it.

People in the West are also attracted to Buddhism because of its emphasis on one's own personal experience. In Buddhism there is no blind faith, no requirement to believe anything without evidence. In the Buddhist scriptures there is a very important text called the *Kālāma Sutta*,[378] which tells the story of how the Buddha was once wandering among some people called Kālāmas who came from a place near what is now Delhi. These Kālāma people were very worried because many religious teachers had come to them and some teachers had said one thing and some had said another, so the Kālāmas did not know who to believe. They were very puzzled, very confused, so they came to the Buddha.

You might be confused in the same sort of way. After all, in Ahmedabad there are so many religions, so many places of worship. There are Hindu temples, Muslim mosques, Jain temples, Sikh gurdwaras – so which one should you go to? Most people don't even think about it. They just go to the one their father or grandfather or grandmother went to. But the Kālāmas weren't like that. They listened to all these different religious teachers, but they didn't know which one to follow, because each teacher said that all the others were wrong. So the Kālāmas came to the Buddha, and he said it wasn't surprising that they were confused. His advice to them was that one should test what all the different religious teachers say in one's own experience, with one's own reason. You shouldn't follow something just because it is very old, or because it's your family tradition, or because some big guru tells you to do so. You shouldn't follow it just out of blind faith. But if you practise a certain teaching and if you find it is in accordance with your reason and your own experience, if you find it does you good, then accept it.

On another occasion, he went even further than that. He said, 'Don't simply believe what I tell you. Test my words, just like a goldsmith tests gold.'[379] So why does the goldsmith test gold? He tests it to find out whether it's really gold, because there are many imitations. Similarly with religious teachings, there are many imitations, so you should test them all. The Buddha says that we should even test *his* words. If we have to test the Buddha's words, how much more important it is to test the words of others. So in Buddhism, we have this emphasis on one's own personal experience. Test everything with your own experience and your own reason, and only then follow it. The Buddha is the only great religious teacher who has said this sort of thing. Other teachers tend to say, 'Believe in me, and I will save you.' Nowadays many teachers come from India to England saying this sort of thing, and some foolish people do follow them. But wise people test the words of those people just like a goldsmith tests gold, and usually they find it's not real gold but only imitation. The Buddhist emphasis on personal experience, not blind faith, is another reason why many people in the West are attracted to Buddhism.

Another characteristic of Buddhism is that it is very tolerant. It leaves people free to follow their own path; it never tries to force anybody to follow it. We know that hundreds of years ago Buddhism spread from India all over Asia, a very large area, but it spread quite peacefully. Buddhist teachers went from India on foot or by sea, and wherever they went they just talked about the Dhamma and persuaded people of its truth. They never used any force. People in the West are very impressed by the tolerance of Buddhism and the peaceful way in which it spread.

The history of Buddhism in this respect is very different from the history of Christianity. Of course the early Christians went on their individual missions, but once kings and rulers became interested in it, Christianity began to be spread by force. Sometimes a king would become Christian and would tell his subjects that they had to be Christian too; otherwise he would kill them. In this way Christianity spread very quickly in Europe. It was the same with Islam; it was spread by people with the Koran in one hand and a sword in the other. But Buddhism did not spread like that. Buddhism was spread by the *bhikṣu* with his begging-bowl. In Europe, in the past, there were many wars of religion. There were wars between Christians and Muslims called the Crusades, and there were wars between Catholics and Protestants in Germany, in France, in Italy, in Netherlands and in Holland. Even nowadays in Northern Ireland there is a religious war going on between Catholics and Protestants.[380] For many people in the West, religion means fighting, and they are very surprised when they find a religion like Buddhism, which has always spread peacefully.

Here in India, many people are attracted to Buddhism for much the same reasons. Dr Babasaheb Ambedkar was attracted to Buddhism for reasons like these. But at the same time there is quite a big difference between the reasons why people in the West are attracted to Buddhism and the reasons why people in India are attracted to it. One of the reasons why people in India are so attracted to Buddhism is because Buddhism is against the caste system. In the West there is no caste system, so this aspect of Buddhism does not concern people there, but in India it is very important.

Some people in India find it very difficult to believe that there isn't any caste system in other countries. When I was in South India all those years ago, I met many orthodox Hindu people, and their first question was always 'What is your caste?' This was more than thirty years ago, and maybe things aren't so bad now, but at that time I would be walking peacefully in the street when some man would come up to me, someone I hadn't seen before, and he would stand in front of me, look me up and down, and say: 'What is your caste?' I used to say, 'I don't have any caste', but he would say, 'That's impossible. You must have a caste. Everybody has a caste.' So I said, 'No, I don't have any caste, for two reasons. First of all, I come from England, where there is no caste system. And secondly, I am a Buddhist, and there is no caste system in Buddhism. So I am doubly without caste.' But the person would always repeat, 'No, that's impossible,' clearly thinking that I must be from such a low caste that I was ashamed of saying what it was. In India people always want to know your caste, and usually they can tell what it is just by looking at you, especially in the small villages.

But Buddhism doesn't agree with this. Buddhism is against this system because according to the Buddha human beings should be regarded and treated just as human beings, not as members of a particular caste. Buddhism does not recognize caste in any way. The Buddha said that when someone joins the *saṅgha*, when he becomes a *bhikṣu*, he loses his previous caste.[381] He said it's just like all the rivers flowing into the ocean. When the Ganga flows into the ocean, it's not called Ganga any more, it just becomes ocean, and it's the same with the Yamuna and the Indus: they lose their names and become just ocean. In the same way, when you come into the *saṅgha*, you lose your old caste and you become just a Buddhist, just *śākyaputra*. There's no need even to say you're a Buddhist; you can say you're a human being. You are just a human being and you see and treat other people as human beings. That's what it really means to be a Buddhist. Many people in India are attracted to Buddhism, and some of them have actually become Buddhist, because Buddhism does not believe in caste. Buddhism believes in the human being. Especially in Maharashtra many people have become Buddhists, mainly as a result of the movement of mass conversion started by Dr Babasaheb Ambedkar.

Just recently I spent six or seven weeks in Maharashtra – especially in that part of the state called Marathwada. In the course of those weeks, I visited many cities and towns giving lectures, and wherever I went I found great enthusiasm for the Dhamma. Some of the meetings were very big. It was quite usual to have a crowd of two or three thousand people, and sometimes there were as many as eight thousand. All these people wanted to hear the Dhamma, and they listened very carefully, taking it all in. Wherever I went throughout Marathwada I saw this tremendous enthusiasm. Not only that. I saw that since my last visit many years ago there has been a great change in the ordinary life of the Buddhist people. Their economic condition was much better, they were much better dressed than before, they had better houses, many were living in housing colonies, and they were sending their children to school. Culturally, also, they had improved; they were producing their own writers, their own poets, their own musicians, their own professors. They even had big educational institutions. All this has happened in such a short time, due mainly to the inspiration provided by the conversion, by the *Dhammadiksha*.

So what does *Dhammadiksha* mean? What does conversion mean? Well, it's the same in the East and the West. It means simply Going for Refuge to the Buddha, Dhamma, and Sangha. But it's not enough just to recite the words; we have to understand them as well. So what do we mean, what do we understand, when we chant the Three Refuges?

First, when we say *Buddhaṃ saraṇaṃ gacchāmi*, how do we see the Buddha? We see him as our teacher, as the shower of the way. We don't see him as God, or as the *avatāra* of God or the messenger of God. We see him as a human being who by his own efforts gained Enlightenment. Because he gained Enlightenment himself, he can show us the way to Enlightenment.

He shows us the way to Enlightenment through his teaching of the Dhamma. The Dhamma is the way. The Dhamma shows us how to grow, how to develop as a human being. Once the Buddha's aunt and foster mother Mahāpajāpatī came to him and asked, 'How can we know what is really your teaching?' and the Buddha gave her a very short and simple reply. In effect he said, 'Whatever helps you to grow, whatever helps you to develop, whatever makes you a better human being, that is my teaching.'[382] So the Dhamma is the way – it's the way of human development, the way of gaining Enlightenment, for all human beings to follow.

And then, what about the Sangha? The Sangha is the community of all those who have gone for Refuge to the Buddha and the Dhamma, all those who are trying to be like the Buddha, all those who are practising the Dhamma. The Sangha doesn't just consist of the *bhikṣus*. It consists of all those who have taken the *Dhammadiksha*. This is what we call the Mahāsaṅgha. Within this Mahāsaṅgha, some are more experienced than others, some know more about the Dhamma than others, and those who have less experience of the Dhamma receive help from those who have more experience. Those who have more experience of the Dhamma than us are just like our elder brothers. They are not gurus in the usual sense. They just help us. They are just our good friends, our *kalyāna mitras*, to use the traditional Buddhist expression.

When we go for Refuge to the Buddha, Dhamma, and Sangha, we also take the five precepts, the *pañcasīla*. We promise not to injure living beings, not to take what is not given, not to commit adultery, not to indulge in false speech and not to take intoxicating drinks and drugs. This *pañcasīla* is the first step in our practice of the Dhamma. Afterwards we can practise all the other steps, and as we do so, we can become better and better human beings, and eventually we can attain Enlightenment.

I am very glad to have had this opportunity this evening to speak to you all about these things. I could of course go on, but perhaps you've heard enough for now. I hope it will be possible for us to meet again on some future occasion, and meanwhile I hope that you will keep in touch with the *anagārikas* and *upāsakas*. They are your friends. They are like your elder brothers. They will tell you whatever you want to know about the Dhamma, and they will help you to practise it – that is to say, they will help you to practise it if you want to. They can't *make* you practise it. They can't force you. You must want to practise it yourself. In English, we have a proverb which says 'You can lead a horse to water, but you can't make it drink.' Now, I don't want to compare you to horses, but the Dhamma can certainly be compared with water, and it's certainly good for us to drink that water. In fact, the Dhamma isn't just water. The Dhamma is *amrta*, nectar. I've tried to give you just a few drops of that *amrta* tonight, and if you want, you can get many more drops of *amrta* from the *anagārikas* and *upāsakas*. But even though it is *amrta*, they can't make you drink it. You must want to drink it. You have to make the choice. In Buddhism we are all free. No one is going to force you to follow the Dhamma. You have to listen very carefully, then decide yourself whether you are going to follow it or not, just as the Buddha says in the *Dhammapada*: 'You yourself must make the effort. The Buddha only shows the way.'[383] I've shown you just a little of the way this evening, but you must make the effort to follow it yourself – if you want to.

32
WORDS AND MEANINGS

Ganpatnagar, Ahmedabad, 15 February 1982

Brothers and Sisters in the Dhamma: When I left England two months ago, it was very cold and the snow was two or three feet deep, but here in India it is very hot and dry and there is a lot of dust in the air. Some of that dust has got into my throat and that is why I am coughing. Anyway, I shall speak for as long as I can. Most of my time during the last two months has been spent in Maharashtra, where our Buddhist movement is flourishing. For quite a few weeks I travelled from place to place, and everywhere I went I delivered lectures on the Dhamma and people gave me a very enthusiastic reception. In this way I visited Bombay, Poona, Aurangabad, Ahmednagar, Nanded, Sholapur, Latur, Manmad, Kannad, and many other places, and thousands of people attended the meetings. I was very glad to see what enthusiasm the people of Maharashtra have for the Dhamma and how faithful they still are to the memory of Dr Babasaheb Ambedkar.

After all those weeks in Maharashtra I have come to Ahmedabad and here too I have been quite busy giving lectures and meeting people. Just before I left for this meeting, a reporter from the *Gujerat Samachar* came and interviewed me. He wanted to know my impressions of Ahmedabad and whether I can see any changes in the place since my visit some years ago. I said, 'Yes, I have seen many changes, but there is one change in particular that I would like to mention.' I then told him that I visited Ahmedabad for the first time in 1947 and stayed for only a few weeks. At that time, so far as I know, there was only one Buddhist in Ahmedabad: myself. But now there are thousands of Buddhists in

Ahmedabad. This is the biggest change that I have seen. I am very glad to see that change and I hope that there will be more and more people in Ahmedabad, and more and more people in Gujarat, taking the *Dhammadiksha* and becoming Buddhists.

Now tonight I am very glad to be here in Ganpatnagar. I am grateful to you for the reception you have given me. I am glad to see the place so beautifully decorated with coloured lights and glad to see the young men with their music and dancing. I am also glad to find that here there are many followers of Dr Ambedkar. Without Dr Ambedkar there would be no Buddhist movement in India today, so we must remember him with gratitude and follow his example. Formerly he was known only in India, but now he is beginning to be known in the wider world. Buddhists in England know the name of Dr Ambedkar very well, and they are very impressed by the work that is being done in India, especially in Maharashtra, in his name.

During the last few days I have visited several localities in Ahmedabad, as a result of which I have begun to get some idea about the Buddhist movement here. Compared with places like Bombay and Poona, the Buddhist movement in Ahmedabad is still quite small, but even so, it is in a very healthy condition. There is a lot of life here and a lot of energy. People have a lot of interest in the Dhamma. They want to do something for the Dhamma. Only yesterday I was in Bapunagar, where they have built a big new vihara with a fine image of the Buddha. Not even in Maharashtra have I seen such a grand vihara. So, even though the Buddhist movement here in Ahmedabad is small, it is in a healthy condition and I am sure it will continue to grow. You could say that in the course of the last thirty years there has been a 3,000 or a 4,000 percent increase in the number of Buddhists. At that rate there will soon be *lakhs* of Buddhists in Gujarat.

Even though I have been busy with meetings and lectures over the last week, I have still had a little time for sightseeing. Among the sights of Ahmedabad there are a number of places of historical interest, and yesterday I went to see Sarkhej Roza. Though I had read about the place, I had never seen it, so yesterday I decided to go there. As you probably know, it is a place of some importance for Muslims, but there is nothing of Buddhist or Hindu interest there. However, the architecture of the buildings, which is very fine and very famous, was the main reason I wanted to go there.

On my arrival at Sarkhej Roza I found that the principal objects of interest there were four tombs. Three of these tombs belonged to Muslim sultans or kings of Ahmedabad who lived some 500 years ago. The remaining tomb belonged to a *pir*, a Muslim saint or holy man. There was also a big tank, round which stood the ruins of various royal palaces. All these buildings were about 500 years old and I noticed one thing about them which was of great interest to me. I noticed that whereas the royal palaces were all in ruins, some of them being almost completely destroyed, the tombs were all very well kept, especially the tomb of the *pir*. Inside the tomb there were many people praying and some were offering baskets of roses. Reflecting on the ruined palaces and the well-kept tombs, I was reminded that worldly things pass away, and people lose interest in them and forget them, but spiritual things do not pass away, because people remember them and continue to derive inspiration from them.

This is very much the case with Buddhism. In the time of the Buddha there were a number of rich and powerful kings in India, who lived in magnificent palaces with hundreds of wives and hundreds of dancing-girls. But now the palaces are all in ruins or don't even exist, and in any case, people aren't interested in them any more. Even where there are ruins, no one wants to visit them. Even the names of those great kings of the Buddha's time have been forgotten, except those that are mentioned in the Buddhist books. We remember the name of King Bimbisāra because he came to see the Buddha; otherwise we would never have heard of him, because his name isn't preserved anywhere else.[384]

But although the palaces of those kings and the kings themselves have been forgotten, the places associated with the name of the Buddha are still carefully preserved and people still visit them. They visit Bodh Gaya where the Buddha gained Supreme Enlightenment, and Sarnath, where he taught his first five disciples. They visit Kusinara, the place where the Buddha attained *parinirvāṇa*, as well as many other places associated with the Buddha in Bihar and Uttar Pradesh. In fact, in recent years some of these places have been made more beautiful than they used to be. Many new viharas, temples, and rest houses have been built and gardens have been laid out. So the people of India, indeed the people of the world, have not forgotten the Buddha, even though he lived 2,500 years ago. The Buddha was not a great king, nor a rich man. He was just a poor wanderer who went from place to place teaching people.

Whether they were rich or poor, of high caste or low caste, didn't matter to him. He didn't recognize any difference between one person and another. He taught everyone the Dhamma. So here again we see that worldly things pass away, and people forget them, but spiritual things do not pass away. People remember them and continue to derive inspiration from them.

This is a very wonderful thing. The Buddha lived 2,500 years ago but here we are tonight, in Ganpatnagar, remembering him. Nor is that all. People are remembering him in Maharashtra and in other parts of Asia. They are remembering him in the West. Our own Buddhist organization, the Trailokya Bauddha Mahasangha Sahayak Gana, has a number of centres in the West, and some of these centres have big golden images of the Buddha, much larger than life. So in all these different parts of the world, people remember the Buddha, because of his great spiritual attainments, and of course because they remember the Buddha, they also remember the Dhamma, the Buddha's teaching.

The Dhamma has been preserved for 2,500 years. This is also wonderful. It has been preserved by means of words, and it is words I want to talk about tonight – because words are very important. Confucius, an ancient Chinese teacher who lived at about the same time as the Buddha, was once asked by one of his disciples, 'What is the first thing that must be attended to if you want to reform society?' Confucius replied, 'The rectification of terms'. In other words, we must give words their right meaning. If you give words their right meaning you will think clearly, and if you think clearly you will be able to bring about changes in society.

The newspapers have announced the subject of tonight's lecture as 'Buddhism and social change'. The rectification of terms, that is, giving words their right meaning, is naturally of great significance to this topic, so I am going to talk about words. The Buddha taught by means of words – at least, he usually did. Sometimes he remained silent, and sometimes he refused to answer people's questions because he considered them unanswerable;[385] but usually he taught by means of words. When he gained Enlightenment under the bodhi tree at Bodh Gaya, he saw the supreme, ultimate truth, and after his Enlightenment, he communicated that truth to other people. But it is not always easy to communicate the truth. People don't always want to hear it. They are interested in other things. So at first the Buddha hesitated to teach the truth that he had discovered, because it was very deep and he thought it would be too difficult for people to understand. But after thinking the matter over he saw that some people would understand, and so he started communicating the truth.[386]

He didn't invent a new language of his own but used the words that people were using already, the language of the people. He did not speak in Sanskrit because that was the language only of the learned. Some years later some of his disciples asked for permission to put his teaching into Sanskrit verses, but the Buddha refused to allow them to do this. He wanted everybody to learn the Dhamma in their own language.[387] But here a difficulty arose. The Buddha had to use the old words in order to express the new truth he had discovered, but when the Buddha used them, the old words took on a new meaning. The word 'Buddha' itself is an example of this. Originally it meant simply a wise man in the ordinary, even worldly, sense. But the Buddha himself used the word 'Buddha' in a new, different sense, to refer to a human being who, by his own efforts, has realized the highest truth for the benefit of all living beings. This was the new meaning that the Buddha gave to the old word 'Buddha'. It was the same with the word 'arahant'. Originally this meant simply a person worthy of respect, but as the Buddha used it, it has a quite different meaning. In the Buddha's teaching, as preserved in both Pāli and Sanskrit, it means a disciple of the Buddha who has realized Nirvāṇa by following the path shown by the Buddha.

The Buddha's teaching has come down to us in Pāli, a language based on a dialect spoken in India at the time of the Buddha or shortly afterwards. Some of that teaching has also come down to us in what is called Buddhist Hybrid Sanskrit. Here a very important point arises. Many of the words that are used in the Buddha's teaching, as preserved in both Pāli and Sanskrit, are also used today in modern Indian languages, languages of North India, such as Hindi, Marathi, Gujarati, and Bengali. This is true not only of ordinary words but of religious terms, and this creates a difficulty for us, because Buddhists talking about Buddhism in one of the modern Indian languages sometimes use the same words as Hindus use to talk about Hinduism, but for Buddhists the words have a quite different meaning.

Let me give you an example. Last night there was a meeting in another locality and Anagārika Purna gave a lecture after which one of the questions he was asked was 'Why is the Buddha called "Bhagwan"

Buddha? "Bhagwan" means God and the Buddha is not God, so what is the meaning of this?' I don't know how Anāgārika Purna answered this question, but it is based on a misunderstanding. In Buddhism, whether in Pāli or Sanskrit, *bhagavan* does not mean God. Originally the word meant simply 'lucky' but then later it came to mean a human being who possessed noble qualities, even spiritual qualities. Since the Buddha possesses these qualities we call him Bhagavan Buddha. So here *bhagavan* has nothing to do with God. In Hinduism, of course, *bhagavan* is used in the sense of God but in Buddhism the word is never used in this sense. It simply means a human being possessed of eminent spiritual qualities. Thus we can call the Buddha 'Bhagavan' Buddha but we must understand what we mean by the word *bhagavan* when we use it in this way.

Another word that is used by both Buddhists and Hindus is 'puja'. For Hindus, puja means going to a temple, making an offering and asking the god for something. But in Buddhism the word simply means showing respect to the Buddha on account of his outstanding spiritual qualities – qualities that we also can develop. We don't ask the Buddha for anything, whether for promotion or money or success in examinations or a son. We don't ask the Buddha for anything at all. Thus the Buddhist puja is quite different from the Hindu puja. When Buddhists perform puja they do it to show their love and respect for the Buddha and their appreciation of his lofty spiritual qualities. They want to give to the Buddha rather than take from him.

There is yet another word the meaning of which is very ambiguous because it is used by Buddhists and Hindus in different ways. This is the word 'Dhamma' or 'Dharma'. In Hinduism your *dharma* is your duty as a member of a particular caste. If you are born as a Brahmin your duty is to teach, to take *dakṣiṇi*,[388] and to eat a lot. If you are born as a Kshatriya your *dharma* is to fight, even to kill. If you are born a Vaishya i.e. born into a Baniya family, your *dharma* is to make money. Even if you cheat a little, it doesn't matter. That is your *dharma*. You are just being a good Baniya. Similarly, if you are born into a Shudra family, your *dharma* is to serve. You must be very humble. You must work for people of higher caste, taking from them only cast-off clothes and the leavings of their meals. You should have no money and no property except the donkey and the dog. That is your *dharma*, according to Hinduism. If you happen to be born in a family of thieves, then your *dharma* is to steal. That path also leads to God, so Hinduism maintains. So this is the meaning of the word '*dharma*' in Hinduism. It is your caste duty as determined by your birth into a certain social group.

In South India more than a thousand years ago there was a great Brahmin scholar named Kumārila Bhaṭṭa who wrote a book called *Ślokavārttika*. In this book he criticizes the Buddha very severely.[389] He says that although the Buddha was born in a Kshatriya family, he abandoned his own *dharma*, i.e. fighting, and took up the *dharma* of a Brahmin, i.e. teaching. In this way, Kumārila Bhaṭṭa says, the Buddha committed a great sin and his teaching, though good, should therefore not be followed because it comes from the wrong source. Milk cannot be taken from a bag made from the skin of a dog, which is an impure creature, even though there is nothing wrong with the milk. In the same way, religious teaching cannot be accepted from a Kshatriya but only from a Brahmin. This is what Kumārila Bhaṭṭa says. In the words of another Hindu text, the *Bhagavad Gītā*, 'There is fear in the *dharma* of another.' Here again this refers to *dharma* in the Hindu sense, your duty as a member of the caste into which you were born.

But in Buddhism the meaning of the word 'Dharma' is quite different. In Hinduism there is a different *dharma* for everybody, according to their caste, but in Buddhism the Dharma is the same for all because all are human beings and the Dharma is meant for human beings simply as human beings. In Buddhism, the Dharma is a path and as a path it is the same for everybody. It is the path of *śīla*, *samādhi*, and *prajñā* and you follow this path simply as a human being. It has nothing to do with caste. You may be born into any kind of family but you all follow the same spiritual path. There isn't one path for a man of one caste and another path for a man of another caste. We have to be very clear about this. Hindus and Buddhists both use the word '*dharma*' but Hindus use it in one sense and Buddhists in another quite different sense. This is why here in India we usually use the Pāli version of the word, 'Dhamma', to show that we are using the word in a distinctively Buddhist way. (In the West, where the word is completely new to most people, we tend to use the Sanskrit form, Dharma.)

It is just the same with the word '*saṅgha*'. This too is used in different senses. Nowadays in India *saṅgha* usually means just an association, a society, and it can be applied to any kind of organization. Even political organizations are sometimes called *saṅghas*. But in Buddhism the word 'saṅgha' has a very special meaning. It doesn't even mean just a Buddhist organization. It means all those who have gone for Refuge to the Buddha, the Dhamma, and the Sangha. 'Saṅgha' means all those who have taken the *Dhammadiksha*, whether they are *bhikkhus* and wandering from place to place or *upāsakas* staying at home with their families. If they have taken the *Dhammadiksha*, they are all members of the *saṅgha*. They are all members of the Mahāsaṅgha, because they have all gone for Refuge to the Buddha, the Dhamma, and the Sangha.

There are four different levels of going for Refuge or four different levels of *Dhammadiksha*. On the first level we simply repeat the words of the *tisaraṇa* and *pañcasīla*. We repeat them because other people repeat them, perhaps our parents repeat them, but we don't understand the meaning of the words. In fact, we never think about their meaning. We just go on repeating them. This kind of going for Refuge is very common in some Buddhist countries. At the second level, you take the Refuges and Precepts, the *Dhammadiksha*, very genuinely and sincerely, and you take them as an individual, not just because other people take them. You try to understand the *tisaraṇa* and the *pañcasīla*. You try to practise *sīla* and you try to practise meditation. You also try to study the Dhamma of the Buddha. This brings us to the third level. One reaches this level when one 'enters the stream' and becomes what we call a *sotāpanna* or 'Stream Entrant'. Your faith in the Buddha is now unshakeable. There is no falling back into lower states, no falling away from the path of the Buddha, because you have had at least a glimpse of the truth. The fourth and last level of going for Refuge is when the person going for Refuge and the object of his Refuge are the same. Here the Buddha goes for Refuge to the Buddha. You go for Refuge to yourself because you are Enlightened. You have become Buddha and don't need to go for Refuge to anyone beside yourself.

So we can understand how important it is to give words their correct meaning. We have to understand that the same word can be understood in very different senses, otherwise we shall understand Buddhist terms in the Hindu sense, and in this way we shall misunderstand Buddhism. We have this difficulty in England too. In England we generally translate Pāli terms into English, but sometimes the English words we use have the wrong kind of meaning. For instance, there is the Pāli word *mettā* (Sanskrit *maitrī*). This used to be translated into English by the word 'love' but this is misleading, because when you use the word 'love' in

English, usually people start thinking of the kind of love that is the theme of cinema films, so it isn't a very suitable translation of *mettā* or *maitrī*. To solve this problem, English Buddhists often just use the word *mettā*. Though they may be talking in English, they use the Pāli word, so in effect *mettā* has become an English word. But in India you can't use a word from a quite different language, as the English do. You have to use the same words in Marathi or Gujarati that your Hindu friends use, so it is important for you to understand that, although you may use the same words as Hindus, the meaning is different when you use them as Buddhists.

In the modern Indian languages spoken by Buddhists there are three kinds of religious terms. First of all, there are words that are used by Hindus but never by Buddhists – for instance, words like *iśvara* and *avatāra*. Secondly, there are words used by Buddhists, but not by Hindus. For example there is the term *pratītya samutpāda*. You will never find any Hindu using this term; even many Buddhists do not know it. Other exclusively Buddhist words include *anātma* and *śūnyatā*. Thirdly, there are words that are used by both Buddhists and Hindus but in different senses – words like *bhagavan, puja, dharma, saṅgha, brāhmaṇa, karma, nirvāṇa, vijñāna*. All these words are used by both Hindus and Buddhists but Hindus use them in one sense and Buddhists in another. It is very important to understand this, otherwise there will be confusion. If we understand Buddhist words in the Hindu way, then we will not understand the Buddha's teaching.

As I said a little while ago, the Buddha's teaching or Dhamma has been preserved by means of words. In a sense it consists of words and it is therefore important to understand the meaning of the words correctly. But we cannot really understand the Buddha's teaching only by knowing the meaning of the words. It is no use simply looking in the dictionary. In order to understand the Dhamma, we must practise it. We must have some spiritual experience, especially through meditation in the Buddhist sense, *samathā-bhāvanā*. Book knowledge is not enough. There are a lot of people who have read a lot of books on Buddhism but even so they don't understand the Dhamma at all. They only understand the words. Sometimes they don't even understand the words properly, because they have not practised the Dhamma. So we must understand the usefulness of words but we must also understand their limitations. The Dhamma cannot be preserved without words but it cannot be preserved only by means of words. It is truly preserved only when people actually practise it.

We are very lucky. We have the opportunity of understanding the Dhamma, and we also have the opportunity of practising it. I hope you will all take full advantage of both. I hope you will understand the Dhamma, practise it, and experience the benefit. I am very glad to have had this opportunity of speaking to you tonight and I hope you have been able to understand what I said. It may have been a little more difficult than what you are accustomed to hearing but that isn't a bad thing. Students of any subject cannot be learning just ABC all their lives. Sooner or later you have to start learning more advanced, more difficult things. May you be able to put into practice whatever you might have learned here tonight. May we meet again. I am very happy to have had the opportunity of coming to this place and meeting you all. I thank all those who have been sitting and listening so quietly and so patiently all this time.

33

WHY PEOPLE IN THE WEST HAVE BECOME BUDDHISTS

Ajmer, Rajasthan, 22 February 1982

Brothers and Sisters: First of all let me say how happy I am to be here with you this evening. It is always a joy to meet those who are interested in the Dhamma.

At present I am on a three-month visit to India. I have already visited many places in Maharashtra, and have given a number of lectures there, and I have also visited Gujarat. Now I am on my way to Delhi, and I couldn't go there without spending a little time here in Ajmer, especially as I wanted to see my old friend Rahul Suman Chhawara and to visit this vihara. This is not my first visit to Ajmer. I came once many years ago, and though I cannot remember exactly when it was (it must have been about twenty-five years ago) I remember my first sight of this picturesque old city very well. I also remember going to see the famous Hindu pilgrimage centre of Pushkar, and of course I remember my contact with Rahulji. But although this is only my second visit to Ajmer, I have been to India many times. In fact, a long time ago I spent many years in India. Perhaps I should tell you something about how I originally came to this country, as well as something about how I became a Buddhist.

As you probably realize, I was not born a Buddhist. Of course, *nobody* can really be 'born a Buddhist'. What I mean is that I was not born into a Buddhist family. I was born into a Christian family, though one that was not very strongly Christian. Nowadays many people in the West are only five-percent or ten-percent Christian, and my family was rather like that. My parents only went to church once every two or three years, but all the same they considered themselves Christians.

When I was eight years old I fell ill, so ill that for several years I was confined to bed. I was not allowed to run about, or to play football, or to do any of the things that boys usually do. I just had to stay in bed. The only thing I was allowed to do was read, so I spent the whole day reading. I read everything that I could get hold of – books, magazines, and so on. Somebody gave me a complete encyclopaedia, in twelve volumes, and I read it right through. In this way I came to know something about the various countries of the world, and about their culture and their religion. One of the countries about which I read was India, on which the encyclopaedia contained several articles. In fact I must have read something about this area, because one of the articles was entitled 'India, the Land of Princes', and Rajasthan means, of course, 'Land of Princes'. The article was illustrated, I remember, by pictures of palaces just like the ones I have seen on my present visit.

It was through reading that I came to know something about the religions of India. In fact, I became very interested in religion and philosophy generally, and started reading all the books I could on both these subjects. I read the Hindu Upanishads and *Bhagavad Gītā*, the Muslim Koran, the Christian Bible, and many other books of these and other religions. And eventually I started reading about Buddhism. First I read the life of the Buddha, which appealed to me very strongly, and then, when I was sixteen (by which time I had recovered from my illness and was able to explore the bookshops of London), I came across two Buddhist *sūtras*. These teachings impressed me very deeply indeed. In fact, I realized not only that what the Buddha taught in these *sūtras* was the Truth, but also that this truth was what I myself had believed even before reading the *sūtras*. From that time onwards I therefore considered myself to be a Buddhist. I had not met any other Buddhists. No one came along and converted me to Buddhism. I converted myself, or perhaps I should say that the *sūtras* converted me.

When I had been a solitary Buddhist for two years I came into contact with other Buddhists in London. There were then only twelve or fourteen of them, and their leader was the famous lawyer Christmas Humphreys, who subsequently became a judge. He is, in fact, still alive today, and we are still in contact.[390] Anyway, I met him for the first time during the war, when I was eighteen, and a year later I came to

India. The war was of course a very bad thing, but for me it was a good thing in at least one respect. It resulted in my coming to India in 1944. I had always wanted to visit India, the land of the Buddha, the land where Buddhism began, and I was overjoyed to get the opportunity of coming here.

On my arrival in Delhi I did my best to meet the local Buddhists, but without any success. There was a Buddhist vihara, but when I went there I found that the place had closed. I therefore left for Sri Lanka, where I spent a year and where I came in contact with Sinhalese Buddhists. From Sri Lanka I went to Calcutta, and from Calcutta to Singapore, where I also spent a year. In Singapore I came in contact with Chinese Buddhists, and started giving lectures on Buddhism. At that time I was twenty-one and had been writing articles on Buddhism for several years.

By that time the war had ended, and I had to decide whether to go back to England or to stay on in the East. Realizing that it might be difficult for me to visit India again if I went back to England, I decided to stay here. Giving up all worldly ties, I became an *anagārika* and wandered about from place to place. At first I wandered in South India, often on foot, and visited famous Hindu holy places like Wadura, Kanya Kumari, and Tiruvannamalai. I also met some of the famous Hindu religious teachers who were then living in South India, such as Swami Ramdas and Ramana Maharshi, with both of whom I stayed for a while. Sometimes I meditated in ashrams or caves. Once I spent ten days in an ancient, half-ruined Shiva temple in Mysore State. This temple was situated in the hills, and nobody went there except the *pujari*, who came once a week. At night I used to hear strange sounds and I eventually realized that they were the snarls of leopards on the roof, but they never tried to harm me.

After two years in the south I decided to go to North India, visit the Buddhist holy places, and get proper ordination as a Buddhist monk. First of all I went to Sarnath, but I couldn't get ordination there, so I walked from Benares up to Kusinara. It was the month of May and the weather was very hot indeed, so I used to start walking very early in the morning. During the hottest part of the day I would take shelter somewhere, and then carry on walking again in the evening. In this way I walked all the way from Benares to Kusinara.

In Kusinara I met U Chandramani Mahathera, a famous Burmese monk who had lived there for about fifty years. From him I took ordination as a *śrāmaṇera* or novice monk. After I had stayed with him for a short while he asked me to go up into Nepal and preach the Dhamma to his disciples there. I therefore walked to Lumbini, the Buddha's birthplace, and from Lumbini I penetrated further into Nepal, where I spent some time preaching the Dhamma to the Nepalese Buddhists.

After that I went to Benares, where I spent a year at the Hindu University with Bhikkhu Jagdish Kashyap studying Pāli, Abhidhamma, and Logic. At that time Kashyapji was getting quite fed up with the university, which was a very caste-ridden Brahmin-dominated sort of place, so he suggested that we should have a holiday and visit the holy places of Bihar, such as Rajgir and Nālandā. From Bihar he took me up into the eastern Himalayas, to a place called Kalimpong, which is situated in the state of West Bengal, not far from Darjeeling. When we had been there for two or three weeks Kashyapji left me saying, 'You stay here and work for the good of Buddhism.' So I stayed in Kalimpong for fourteen years, working for the good of Buddhism.

I started up Buddhist activities in Kalimpong, and in 1950 I took ordination as a *bhikkhu* or full Buddhist monk. It was at that time that I came in contact with Rahul Suman Chhawara. Kashyapji had visited him in Ajmer, and told him about me. He wrote to me, and I wrote back, and in this way we formed a connection – a connection that now goes back thirty-two years. During the fourteen years I lived in Kalimpong I used to spend most of my time studying, writing about Buddhism, and practising meditation, but in the winter I would come down to the plains, sometimes to Calcutta, sometimes to Bombay, and sometimes to Delhi, and in all of those places I would give lectures on the Dhamma. It was during this period that I paid my first visit to Ajmer. In the early fifties I came in contact with Dr Ambedkar, first through the medium of correspondence and then personally. After Dr Ambedkar's untimely death in 1956 I came in closer and closer contact with his followers in Maharashtra. Each year I used to go down to Maharashtra every winter and travel around giving lectures and doing whatever I could to help the great movement of mass conversion started by Dr Ambedkar.

This brings us to 1964, by which time I had been in India for twenty years. In 1962 I had received a letter from London, where there was a small Buddhist movement, inviting me to go back there for a while. Since I hadn't been to England, and hadn't seen my friends and relations there, for twenty years, I decided to accept the invitation, and went back to spend two years working for the Dhamma in England. As a result of this experience, I realized that England was a good place for Buddhist activities, but I felt that a new kind of Buddhist movement was needed in England. I wasn't satisfied with the way things were going. At that time there may have been several hundred English Buddhists, mostly in London, but they were part-timers. They would just go along to the Buddhist Society once a week, perhaps do a little meditation, and then go home. In all other respects they lived just like other English people. Most of them still ate meat and drank alcohol. So I wasn't happy about that. I thought that a new Buddhist movement was needed, a movement of full-time Buddhists.

In 1967, after paying a short visit to India, I therefore started up a new Buddhist movement which we called the Friends of the Western Buddhist Order. (In India this movement is known as Trailokya Bauddha Mahasangha Sahayak Gana.) We started our new Buddhist movement in London, and at that time I was, in reality, on my own. Nobody understood what I meant when I said that we needed a new kind of Buddhist movement. Moreover, I had no money, since I was a *bhikkhu*, but anyway, I was determined, so we started Buddhist activities on a very small scale. We hired a basement room in central London, where rents are very high (a room like the one in which I am now speaking might cost as much as a *lakh* of rupees a month), and in that room we held meetings once a week. But we didn't start with lectures. We started with meditation. At 7 o'clock every Thursday evening we had a meditation class, and a few people used to come. We used to do the *mettā bhāvanā* and the mindfulness of breathing, which some of you may also be doing. These practices are very simple, but very effective. If you do them regularly, you will find that your mind begins to change. At first eight or ten people used to come to the meditation classes, then twelve or fourteen, then fifteen or twenty or more. After a while I had to start a second weekly class. I also started giving lectures, for which we hired a small hall. As a result of this, more and more people came to us. We then started holding *Dhamma-shibirs*, first for one week, then for two. We would go away to some beautiful place in the country and there we would devote our whole time to the Dhamma. We would spend the whole day meditating, listening to lectures on the Dhamma, and so on.

In this way our activities expanded. Even though we had no money, things were growing. Eventually we had to start looking for a bigger centre. We also started having more and more *Dhamma-shibirs*. People used to enjoy these very much indeed, so much that at the end they didn't want to leave. They thought, 'How wonderful it would be if we could live like this all the time!' Some of them therefore decided that they wanted to live with other Buddhists, so they could practise the Dhamma together every day. So they found a big house, and five or six of them moved in. (In England everybody expects to have a room of their own, and there must be separate rooms for cooking, eating, etc.) Later on, ten or twelve people moved into an even bigger house. In this way we started having what we call Buddhist communities. At first we had communities for both men and women together but this did not work very well, so we started having separate communities for men and women.

After five or six years, we had not only Buddhist centres but also communities. People used to come regularly to the nearest centre, and they also lived in a community. But after a while they started thinking that even that was not enough. Even those who were living in communities still had to go outside to work, and sometimes what they were doing was not in accordance with the principle of Buddhism. Realizing that *samyag-ājīva* or right livelihood was a very important part of Buddhism, they wanted to practise that too, so they started setting up Buddhist cooperative businesses. There are many advantages in having such businesses. First of all, Buddhists work together, so you have contact with other Buddhists even when you are working. Secondly, you work in accordance with the principles of right livelihood. For instance, we have Buddhist vegetarian restaurants – not little 'hotels' such as you see here but quite big, beautiful places. In this way we propagate vegetarianism, which is an application of the first precept, the precept of abstaining from injury to living beings. At the same time, through our vegetarian restaurants and our other cooperative businesses, we make money for Dhamma activities. We don't like to take money for this purpose from the general public. This is, in fact, one of the principles that we have developed. We believe that a Buddhist movement should be self-supporting. It is not good that a religious movement should depend on the support of a few very rich people. During my twenty years in India I saw a lot of this sort of thing. A rich man donates a large sum of money to a temple or an ashram, but then he wants his name to be inscribed over the door in big letters and he wants to exercise control over it, which is not a good thing. So we do not approach the general public for donations. (If our own members and friends donate money of their own accord that is another matter.) We get most of the money for our Dhamma work from our cooperative businesses. This system is of great benefit to us. It means that our members can practise right livelihood, they can work on a cooperative basis, they can support themselves and their families, and they can also contribute something to Buddhist activities.

So this is the pattern we have developed in England. There are public centres where Buddhist activities are carried on every day; there are the communities, and there are the cooperative businesses. This is the threefold structure of our new Buddhist movement in England, both in and outside of London. In East London, for instance, we have a big, five-storey building which houses both a public centre and a large men's community. In the area round about are located various businesses and various other communities. It is like a Buddhist colony. Elsewhere in England we have the same pattern of activities in a number of different places, though on a smaller scale. Our new Buddhist movement has also spread to other countries. We have centres, communities, and businesses in places like Finland, Sweden, the United States of America, Australia, and New Zealand, and we are also beginning to have activities here in India. We also hold *Dhamma-shibirs* in different parts of Europe where we do not have centres. This should give you an idea of what has been built up in the West in the space of some fourteen years. It should also serve to explain why I was so busy in the West, and why I could not come to India for such a long time.

Now you may be wondering who is carrying on all these activities in the West. It is not just me. In fact, it would not be possible for me to do all that work single-handed. We have created a team. One of our principles is the principle of teamwork. We don't believe that one person should be prominent. It is just like a football team. In the football team you have eleven people, all of whom have different responsibilities. Similarly we have built up a Dhamma team, a team of what we call *dasa sīla upāsakas*. They are not *bhikkhus*, but at the same time they are not ordinary laymen. They are a bit like our Rahulji here – they have got one foot in the family camp and one foot in the spiritual camp. But we find that people of this kind work very well in the West. In the West, if people see you wearing a yellow robe such as I am wearing now they will be a little suspicious. They will be happier if you look like an ordinary person.

The members of our team look like ordinary people, but actually they are deeply committed to the Dhamma. They go for Refuge to the Buddha, the Dhamma, and the Sangha, and they observe ten *sīlas*. Usually Buddhists observe only five *sīlas*. Ten is more than the ordinary Buddhist observes, but not so many as the *bhikkhu* observes, so our *dasa sīla upāsakas* follow a middle path, you could say. Thus we have this team of dedicated people, most of whom give their whole time to the Dhamma. Even though they are not *bhikkhus*, they are full-time workers. At present we have 165 of them.[391] Together they make up a real *sangha*, a real Order. They run the centres, direct the businesses, and lead the communities, in eight different countries in the world.

Some of you may be wondering why it is that people in the West are becoming interested in Buddhism. All of you are interested in Buddhism, but that is understandable, because Buddhism originated in India, and so it is only natural that people in this country should take an interest in it, at least as part of their culture. But in the West Buddhism is not part of people's history. The West is Christian. So why is it that people are becoming interested in Buddhism? One very obvious reason is that they have lost interest in Christianity. They are born into Christian families, but for some reason or other they don't take to Christianity; they don't like it. Perhaps the main reason for this is that in Christianity one of the basic things is belief in a personal God. According to Christian teaching God has created the world, and governs it by his providence. Many people in the West find it very difficult, nowadays, to believe in God. I am not going to go into the reasons for that now, but the fact is that many people in the West are no longer able to believe in a personal God. Broadly speaking, they feel that such a belief is not rational. But according to Christianity you must believe in God. Not only that. In the West people usually think that religion *means* believing in a personal God. If you don't believe in a personal God, you can have no religion – that's what people think. Many people in the West want to follow a religion of some kind. The difficulty is that they can't believe in God, so they think that there is no place in religion for them, but at the same time, they are not happy with this state of affairs, because they really do want to follow a religion of some kind.

When people of this sort come in contact with Buddhism they learn that although Buddhism is a religion, there is no such thing in Buddhism as belief in a personal God. They are very pleased to learn this. Moreover, in Buddhism you are not asked to have blind faith. Buddhism emphasizes the importance of your own rational thought and your own experience. Again, this is very different from Christianity. Christians usually say that you must believe what they tell you because it is written in the Bible. The Bible is the Word of God, and God cannot be wrong. Similarly, orthodox Hindus say that if something is written in the Vedas it cannot be questioned. But Buddhism isn't that kind of religion. According to Buddhism you are perfectly free to question everything. Indeed, according to Buddhism you *must* question everything. The Buddha himself said, 'Test my words as the goldsmith tests the gold in the fire.'[392] Christ never said, 'Test my words.' He said, 'Believe in me.' The freedom to question is found only in Buddhism. This is one of the reasons why people in the West like Buddhism. When you become a Buddhist you do not have to throw away your reason. Buddhism encourages you to think for yourself. It encourages you to rely on your own rational thought and your own experience.

Also, Buddhism shows you how to develop into a truly human being. It shows you how to change yourself for the better. This again is very different from Christianity. Christianity says, 'Love your neighbour.' This is what children are told at Sunday school, and Christian preachers always say, 'You must love other people.' But nobody ever explains how to do this. They never give you any instructions. You are just given the order, 'Love your neighbour,' and since it is God who gives the order you will go to hell when you die if you disobey. But it can be very difficult to love your neighbour. Sometimes you feel ill will towards your own brother, or your own father, or your own wife, or your own husband, at least for a while. There is a lot of hatred in the human heart. How are you going to get rid of this hatred and replace it by love? Christianity doesn't help you. It just gives you an order. Buddhism isn't like that. Buddhism tells you how, step by step, you can replace hatred by love. Buddhism teaches *mettā bhāvanā*, or the development of universal loving-kindness. This is a meditation in which first you develop love towards yourself, then towards a near and dear friend, then towards a neutral person, then towards an enemy. Step by step, you develop love towards everybody in the locality, in the town, in the state, in the whole country and eventually the whole world. You develop it without making any distinction between young and old, male and female, and so on. Whether they belong to the same country or to another country, whether they are Buddhist or non-Buddhist, doesn't make any difference. Buddhism shows you how to develop a feeling of *mettā* towards all living beings, both human beings and animals, in this way.

People in the West therefore find that Buddhism actually works. They find that you really can get rid of your anger and hatred in this way. You really can develop *mettā* if you try. Buddhism is a very practical religion, a very practical path. Everything about Buddhism is practical. If you follow the path of Buddhism, you can change your own life. You can become a better and happier human being. In the end you can even become Enlightened. Buddhism teaches that whatever the Buddha achieved, you too can achieve. The Buddha was not a god. He started off just as an ordinary human being. We also are human beings. What the Buddha achieved, we too can achieve.

This is very encouraging. In the West, in Christianity, people are always being told, 'You are a sinner. You are very bad. You were born bad. Only Jesus can save you.' I was told this as a small child, and so were most of my friends, and it is not very encouraging. We know that if you are always telling a small boy, 'You are a bad boy,' it doesn't help him. When he grows up he will probably become bad. Similarly, it doesn't help if your religion is always telling you that you are a sinner. A lot of people in the West feel very unhappy because of the effect of Christianity. Such people are pleased to find that Buddhism is, on the contrary, very encouraging. Buddhism doesn't say that you are bad. It doesn't say that you are good either. It says that you can be either the one or the other. It is a matter of your own free choice. You can be good if you want to be. You can become like the Buddha. In this way Buddhism is very encouraging, very optimistic. This is one of the things that people in the West like about Buddhism. It always encourages us as human beings to think we can become better if we try.

Another thing that people in the West like about Buddhism is its tolerance. In the West, if you talk about religion, a lot of people at once start thinking about fighting. If you read the history of Europe you find a great many religious wars. There were the Crusades, in which the Christians fought with the Muslims. Then there were the wars which the Christians fought with one another. Catholic fought with Protestant, and Protestant fought with Catholic. The history of Europe is full of this sort of thing. When we read the history of Europe, therefore, we feel very sad. We reflect that religion is supposed to make people happy, but here we find it creating so much misery. Similarly, in the West the different churches have been very intolerant. One form of Christianity refuses to tolerate another. In the Europe of a few hundred years ago, if you started thinking for yourself, and if you did not agree with the teaching of the Church, you could be burnt alive as a heretic. This tendency towards violence and intolerance is another of the reasons why a lot of people in the West have turned against religion.

When such people come in contact with Buddhism they are very pleased and very surprised. If they read the history of Buddhism, they find that it spread entirely by peaceful means. From India Buddhism spread all over the East. It spread to Sri Lanka, Burma, and Thailand, as well as to China, Japan, Indonesia, Tibet, and Nepal. But in the case of every one of these countries, all you had to begin with was one *bhikkhu* who started walking. According to legend some *bhikkhus* went flying through the air, but I don't know about that. Most *bhikkhus* must have walked. Anyway, they went to these new countries, they learned the local languages and they talked with people, just as I am talking with you. They didn't go with an army, or a lot of money. They just went with their begging-bowl and talked with people about the life of the Buddha, and about the Dhamma. Thus people became interested, accepted the Buddha's teaching, and said *Buddhaṃ saraṇaṃ gacchāmi*. In this way Buddhism spread all over the East. Of course, the early Christian missionaries also travelled on foot and spread their message personally, but once Christianity had attracted the attention of emperors and kings, it became caught up with power and conflict. When people in the West read how Buddhism spread by such peaceful means they are therefore very much impressed to learn how tolerant Buddhism is, and how it allows you to think for yourself.

The last point I want to make concerns the Buddhist teaching of brotherhood. According to Buddhism, all human beings are brothers and sisters. We belong to the same human family. Essentially, none are high and none are low. For this reason, Buddhism does not believe in the caste system. It believes that all are fundamentally the same. Regardless of whether you come from the East or the West, regardless of colour, regardless of language, and even regardless of religion, we are all human beings. We must therefore see one another and treat one another just as human beings.

This message of Buddhism, too, is liked very much by people in the West. In recent years there have been some very terrible wars. These two world wars, as they are called, started in Europe, so people in the West are extremely worried about this question of war, realizing that if there is another war it may be the last. Many years ago the famous scientist Albert Einstein was asked, 'If there is another war, with what weapons will people fight it?' Einstein replied, 'I don't know. But I can tell you with what weapons they will fight the war after the next one. They will fight it with sticks.' What he meant was that the next war will wipe out civilization. People are now thinking that if there is another war, it won't be possible after that even to fight with sticks. There won't be anybody left to hold the sticks. Such is the threat of nuclear weapons.

The question of war and peace is very important. People definitely see Buddhism as a religion of peace, and for this reason many people in the West are attracted to Buddhism, and want to learn more about it. They, too, repeat *Buddhaṃ saraṇaṃ gacchāmi*. All over the world, more and more people are going for Refuge in this way. I don't want to exaggerate, but it is clear that, in the course of the last twenty or thirty years there has been a great revival of Buddhism in many parts of the world.

There has been quite a big revival of Buddhism in India, mainly in Maharashtra. Lokamitra will be telling you something about that, but before he does so I must correct something that Rahulji said, because it involves giving me credit which I do not deserve. Buddhist activities in Poona were started not by me, but by Lokamitra. Of course it is true that I spent some time in Poona many years ago, and that I have many friends there, including Dharmarakshita.[393] I have also given many lectures in Poona. But I never started any regular activities there. That was done by Lokamitra.

Thus the Dhamma is spreading, and I am very happy to see that it is now flourishing here in Ajmer. When I last came here there was only Rahulji working for the Dhamma, helped by his old father. Later on, of course, there was Mrs Chhawara to help, and gradually more and more people have become involved. This evening we have quite a good audience for this talk on the Dhamma, even though it is Shivaratri. This means that at least some people are more interested in hearing a serious talk on the Dhamma than in watching the Shivaratri celebrations, and I am very glad to see this.

Since my last visit to Ajmer very little has changed. The old city looks very much the same as it did. There has been no modern development in the form of big blocks of flats and offices, I'm glad to say. London has been spoiled by modern development, and so has Bombay. The developers haven't succeeded in spoiling Ahmedabad, because the modern development has been put twenty miles away, in the form of the new city of Gandhinagar. Bombay used to be a very beautiful city, but now there is so much pollution, so much overcrowding, so much noise, that it has lost its beauty. But here everything is the same as it was. Ajmer is still a very beautiful city, and I am very glad to see this. The only difference is that the Dhamma is now flourishing here more than it did before. There are more Buddhist activities. Last time I came there was only Rahulji's house, and everything had to be carried on there, but now there is a separate place for Buddhist activities. Just as we did in London you started things on a small scale and they have grown. It is indeed very encouraging to see this sort of thing.

I cannot conclude this lecture without congratulating Rahulji and Mrs Chhawara, together with all their friends and helpers, on what has been achieved here over the years. It gives me great pleasure to have had this opportunity of speaking to you. I hope we will be able to keep up friendly connections, and that we shall all meet again.

34

BUDDHISM IN INDIA AND
BUDDHISM IN ENGLAND –
A PARALLEL

Delhi BAMCEF *Programme,*[394] *27 February 1982*

Mr Kanshi Ram, Sisters and Brothers: Mr Kanshi Ram has reminded you that I'm from England, and that English people are, or are supposed to be, very punctual. This reminds me of something that happened when I returned to England after spending twenty years here in India. I was invited to give a lecture by the London Buddhist Society, whose president is a famous lawyer and judge called Mr Christmas Humphreys. When I turned up for the meeting Mr Humphreys was waiting outside the door of the lecture room, and when I arrived he looked at his watch and said, 'You are two minutes late.' So I said, 'That must be because I've spent twenty years in India.' He asked me, 'Don't you have a watch?' and I said, 'No. All the time that I was in India I never kept a watch.' So he said, 'Alright, I shall buy you a watch.' He did – I made him buy me a very good one – and I'm still wearing it. That incident made me think that now I was back in England, I had become the prisoner of time.

At present I'm in India on a three-month visit. I arrived in Bombay, went to Poona and then began a quite intensive lecture tour of Maharashtra. I've been to so many different towns and cities that I'm learning the geography of Maharashtra very well. Then, after spending about two months in Maharashtra I went to Ahmedabad, then Ajmer, and now I've come to Delhi for a few days. Tomorrow I go back to Poona, and then I will be returning to England. So I'm very glad to be in Delhi tonight and to have this opportunity of addressing you all, especially in connection with your Buddhist Research Centre.

This is not my first visit to Delhi. My first visit here was in 1943, during the war that, in fact, brought me to India. Of course I was very interested to have some contact with other Buddhists, so I tried to find some Buddhist centre in Delhi. After a lot of difficulty I found the Maha Bodhi Society's Buddha vihara, which was in what was then called Reading Road. (Now of course it's called Mandir Marg.) I found a small building and on the grass outside there was a yellow robe spread out to dry so I thought perhaps there was some *bhikkhu* in residence. But the windows were closed, and there was no sound. Thinking that perhaps everyone was asleep, I knocked at the door, but no one came. I waited for some time, then knocked again, but still nobody came, so I went away, and that was the extent of my contact with Buddhism in Delhi. I was a bit disappointed.

At that time, I was already a Buddhist. I was only nineteen, but I had become a Buddhist about three years before. Perhaps I'd better say a few words about that. I happened to be born in London, and of course I was born into a Christian family, though my family was not at all strongly Christian. When I was quite young, I became ill and I had to stay in bed for several years. I wasn't allowed to move. I couldn't walk. I couldn't even stand up. I just had to lie in bed. The only thing that I was allowed to do was to read. So I read many books, and eventually I became very interested in reading about religion and philosophy. I read all about the different religions of the world: Christianity, Islam, Sufism, Hinduism, Jainism, and Confucianism. And then one day – later on, when I had recovered and was able to go out and about among the bookshops of London – I happened to come across two Buddhist *sūtras*, and when I read these two texts I at once had a very strong experience. I thought, 'Here is the Truth. What these *sūtras* say is true. What the Buddha says is true.' Not only that. I realized that this was what I had always really believed. In this way I realized that I was a Buddhist. I was sixteen. Nobody came and converted me. I converted myself, or rather, those books converted me.

For two years, I was completely on my own as a Buddhist. I never even spoke to another Buddhist. But I knew that I was a Buddhist. After two years, I came in contact with the London Buddhist Society and with Christmas Humphreys, and in 1941 and 1942 I used to go along to meetings of the Society. Then, when I was nineteen, I came to India. I had always wanted to come to the land where the Buddha was born, so I was very happy to get the chance. I didn't stay in Delhi very long, only about a month, and then I went to Sri Lanka, where I stayed for one year. But I didn't make much contact with Buddhism there either. I met a few *bhikkhus* but they didn't know any English. There is a big Buddhist temple in Kandy where they keep what is believed to be a tooth of the Buddha. So I saw the tooth of the Buddha, and I was quite pleased to see it, but this was not enough for me. I wanted the Dhamma. I wanted to have contact with Buddhists. After a while I left Sri Lanka and went to Singapore, and there I had better contact. I met some very sincere Chinese Buddhists and, at the age of twenty-one, I started giving public lectures on Buddhism.

By that time the war had come to an end, so I came back to India and decided that I wanted to stay. I wrote to my parents and told them that I wasn't going back to England and that I was going to become a Buddhist monk. They wrote back and said, 'Your life is your own. You must do whatever you think best.' Reflecting that to become a Buddhist monk is very difficult, I decided that I had to test myself first. So I spent two years in South India and I became an *anagārika* – not a proper *bhikkhu*, just an *anagārika*, living like a *bhikkhu* but without the *bhikkhu* ordination. I wandered from place to place, sometimes on foot. I stayed in different ashrams and sometimes I stayed in a cave. I was meditating, studying Buddhism, reading Buddhist books and following the Buddhist *śīla*. In this way I spent two years in different parts of South India, and after those two years I thought, 'Yes, I can become a Buddhist *bhikkhu*, I can lead this life.' So I went up to North India, to the Buddhist holy places, where I hoped I could be ordained as a monk. I went to Sarnath and met the Maha Bodhi Society *bhikkhus* there, but they didn't want to give me ordination. So I went to Kusinara, and there I met U Chandramani Mahathera, who later gave *Dhammadiksha* to Dr Babasaheb Ambedkar. So U Chandramani gave me the *śrāmaṇera dīkṣā*, and then he sent me up into Nepal. I went there for some time and gave lectures on the Dhamma, and then I went to Benares, where I studied with Jagdish Kashyap, a famous *bhikkhu* with whom I studied Pāli, Abhidhamma, Logic, and other things.

Kashyapji one day took me up to Kalimpong, which is a town near Darjeeling in West Bengal, for a little holiday. But after we'd been there just for a few weeks Kashyapji said to me, 'Stay here and work for the good of Buddhism.' So I stayed in Kalimpong, and I lived there altogether for fourteen years. In 1950 I received the ordination, the *dīksā*, as a *bhikkhu*, and I started Buddhist activities in Kalimpong. It was at that time that I had my first contact with Dr Babasaheb Ambedkar. In Kalimpong I started up the Young Men's Buddhist Association and a Buddhist magazine, and I wrote to Dr Ambedkar to tell him what I was doing. I got back from him a very encouraging letter. He was very pleased to hear that I was carrying on Buddhist activities in Kalimpong. So that was the beginning of our contact. Then in 1952 I happened to be in Bombay and went to visit Dr Ambedkar in his house, Rajagriha. At that time I had some connection with the Maha Bodhi Society in Calcutta. I was helping to edit their magazine, the *Maha Bodhi* journal. Dr Ambedkar knew this, so when we met he asked me a question. Dr Ambedkar was a very strong man, and he used to speak very strongly, so he put his question in quite a strong way. The question was, 'How is it that in your Maha Bodhi Society you have a Bengali Brahmin for the president?' The president at that time was indeed a Brahmin, a man called Shyama Prasad Mukherjee. So I said to Dr Ambedkar, 'I am also not happy about this. I also don't think that a non-Buddhist should be the president of a Buddhist organization. But there's nothing I can do about it.' So Dr Ambedkar and I agreed about this matter, and some time later a Buddhist was elected as the president of the Maha Bodhi Society, the Maharaj Kumar of Sikkhim, who died just a few weeks ago.

So this was my first meeting with Dr Ambedkar. While we were talking, many people were coming to see him and putting garlands around his neck. I saw that Dr Ambedkar did not like that, and he spoke to them roughly, saying, 'Why are you bringing these things? I don't want them.' But I also saw that the more Dr Ambedkar grumbled at them, the happier his followers were. They clearly had a very great love and devotion for him.

The next time that I met Dr Ambedkar, it was in 1955, also in Bombay, at 'Buddha Bhavan' in Siddharth College. At that time he was thinking very seriously about conversion to Buddhism, so we had a long discussion on this matter. Dr Ambedkar said, 'How does one become a Buddhist? What is the procedure?' And I told him, 'It's very simple. You just repeat the *tisaraṇa* and the *pañcasīla*. You repeat them after a *bhikkhu*.' So he said, 'Can you give me the *Dhammadiksha*?' And I said, 'Yes, I could. But it would be better if you took the *Dhammadiksha* from the oldest and most senior *bhikkhu* in India, U Chandramani

Maha Sthavira, who lives in Kusinara.' Dr Ambedkar accepted this suggestion, and as you know, it was from U Chandramani that he took the *Dhammadiksha* in Nagpur, in October 1956.

My next – and last – meeting with Dr Ambedkar was at his residence here in Delhi. This was after the conversion in Nagpur. At that time Dr Ambedkar was extremely ill. I went along to see him and took some Buddhist friends with me, and when I saw that Dr Ambedkar was ill, I said, 'I'm very sorry that we have disturbed you. Please allow us to go.' But Dr Ambedkar said, 'No, no, you must not go; we need to talk about Buddhism.' So we talked about Buddhism for two hours. Dr Ambedkar was so ill that I felt quite uncomfortable keeping him talking for so long. Every half an hour or so I would say, 'Please allow me to go', but he would say, 'No, no, we must talk some more.' So we talked in this way for most of the afternoon. I could tell that Dr Ambedkar was very worried about the future of the Buddhist movement that he had started. He knew that there was a lot of very difficult work to be done. As he had said earlier, 'Buddhism is a difficult religion to practise.' He knew that his followers had to be educated about Buddhism. So he was telling me about all these worries of his.

Then, only a few days later, Dr Ambedkar died. On the very day he died, I was in Nagpur. I had been invited there by the new Buddhists to give some lectures. When I arrived at Nagpur station at about 10 or 11 o'clock in the morning, there were about 2,000 people waiting on the station platform to receive me, and they took me in procession to the place where I was to stay. I had something to eat there, I had a little rest, and then at about 3 o'clock I heard some disturbance outside. Then someone came into the room and said, 'We've just heard some terrible news. Babasaheb has died.' By this time there were thousands of people outside the house where I was staying, wanting me to speak to them. So I said, 'It's very difficult to speak to so many people without a microphone. Let there be a meeting at 7 o'clock tonight.'

So at 7 o'clock that same night a big meeting was held in Kasturchand Park, and about one *lakh* of people were there. Everybody was very, very upset, thinking, 'What will happen to us now? We have taken *Dhammadiksha* out of our faith in Dr Ambedkar. But Dr Ambedkar is no longer here to lead us.' Some people were afraid that the movement of conversion would come to an end, and they were very sad, and very quiet. I remember this occasion very well. There had been no time to make a stage, so I had to speak to the people standing on a rickshaw. I could see coming from all parts of Nagpur these thousands and thousands of people, all very quiet, and every single person had a lighted candle in his hand. You know that in India it's very difficult for people to be quiet, but on that occasion everybody was absolutely silent. At the meeting, some of the local leaders tried to speak, but they couldn't say anything. As soon as they opened their mouths, they started weeping, so they had to step down. In the end I stood up to speak, and I told the people, 'We mustn't think that Dr Ambedkar is dead. Dr Ambedkar will live on in his work. The movement of conversion will continue.' In the course of the next four or five days I gave about thirty-five lectures in different parts of Nagpur, and in every lecture I said the same thing: 'The movement of *Dhammadiksha* must not come to an end. It must be carried on.' In that way, people began to feel some hope, and I established a strong connection with the Buddhist people of Nagpur.

That was at the end of 1956, and after that I went to Maharashtra each winter, travelling all around the state giving lectures. I did that practically every year until 1964, when I went back to England after spending twenty years in India. Originally I went just for a short visit, but after arriving in England I saw that it was a very good field for our Buddhist work, so I stayed on there and established a new Buddhist movement. I saw the need to establish a new Buddhist movement because I was not satisfied with the old one. The existing Buddhist movement was very small and some of the people involved in it were not one-hundred-percent Buddhist, but half-Buddhist and half-Christian. There weren't many activities either – just a lecture or class once a week. So I stayed in England for fourteen years, and I established a new Buddhist movement. In English we call this the Friends of the Western Buddhist Order, and in India we call it the Trailokya Bauddha Mahasangha Sahayak Gana.

We have established three different kinds of institutions. First of all, we have Buddhist centres, buildings in which we run all sorts of Buddhist activities. We have lectures on the Dhamma, and we have classes in meditation, in hatha yoga, in the study of Buddhist scriptures, and in human communication. We also run courses and *Dhamma-shibirs*. In all our centres, activities go on every day, not just once or twice a week or once or twice a month. Sometimes different activities go on in different parts of the building at the same time. Many people are coming to these centres, and in England we've got eight of them, the biggest of which is in London. It's a big five-storey building with sixty rooms including two big shrines and meeting rooms. And in seven other countries also we have centres of this kind.

In addition to the centres we have communities, which are the places where our full-time workers live. We've got communities for men and communities for women where people live together and work together for the Dhamma. They meditate together, and they have a good friendly relationship with one another. In England alone we have twenty of these communities, and some of them accommodate ten or twelve people, or even more. We also have these communities in other countries in the West.

Then we have got a third kind of institutional organization. This is what we call team-based right livelihood businesses. I must say a few words of explanation about these. One of our principles in our movement in England is that we should not ask the non-Buddhist public for donations. So where is the money to come from? We have to earn it ourselves. So we've set up a number of different businesses. We've set up vegetarian restaurants and building and decorating businesses. We've got a press, a design studio, and a gardening service. We've got a candle factory. All these different businesses are run by Buddhists on a cooperative basis. There's no division of 'boss' and 'workers'. They work cooperatively together, happy to be working with other Buddhists, and they make enough money to support themselves and their families. They also make a profit, some of which goes to support the running of Buddhist activities. This is something quite new. No other Buddhist movement in the West is doing this, and through it we are making a very good impression on the public. In England people don't think that it is a good thing just to ask for donations. They are more impressed if you earn the money for your activities yourself. So this is what we are doing. We've got centres, communities, and co-ops in each place where we're functioning, and we think of this as the nucleus of the New Society. It took about fourteen years for these things to develop in this way; I think that's about the same length of time as it's taken to establish your own organizations.

From my personal experience of Buddhist work in India as well as in England and other places in the West, I've noticed that Buddhist activities in the East and in the West, and especially in England and in India, have got certain features in common. So I want to mention just some of these qualities or characteristics which are common to our Buddhist movement in England and our Buddhist movement in India. First of all, we're all new Buddhists. We were not born Buddhist. We've taken to Buddhism because we want to. It's our own individual decision. Of course you can't really be a 'born Buddhist'. Sometimes I meet Buddhists from Sri Lanka or Thailand and they say, 'Buddhism is in my blood.' But that is not possible. You can't be born Buddhist. You can become Buddhist only as a result of deciding to do so. If you say that you are born a Buddhist it's just like saying you are born a Brahmin, and we don't want anything like Brahmanism in Buddhism. There's only one way of being Buddhist, and that is to understand Buddhism for yourself and to accept it and follow it because you understand it. This is the case in England. People are not born Buddhist. They *become* Buddhist. They make themselves Buddhist. And it's the same here in India. Dr Ambedkar was not born Buddhist. His followers were not born Buddhist. They chose Buddhism because they could see that it was the right path. So they are new Buddhists.

I remember that after the *Dhammadiksha* in 1956 some of the Hindu newspapers started referring to the new Buddhists as *narva bolta* or 'neo-Buddhists.' They did this because they thought that it was a bad thing to be a new Buddhist. For some reason or other they thought that it was good to be an old Buddhist but not good to be a new Buddhist. But this is a great mistake. There's only one kind of Buddhist: a new Buddhist. You can't be an old Buddhist. You can't be a born Buddhist. So this is one of the things that Buddhists in England and Buddhists in India have in common.

After the mass conversion in Nagpur some of our Hindu friends asked the new Buddhists, 'Have you become converted to Mahāyāna Buddhism or Hīnayāna Buddhism?' Some of the new Buddhists didn't know what to say to that, so they used to come and ask me, and I used to say, 'You have not become Mahāyāna Buddhists or Hīnayāna Buddhists. You have become simply Buddhists. When people ask you whether you are Mahāyāna or Hīnayāna they are just trying to divide the Buddhist movement. So you must not allow yourselves to be divided. You're all just Buddhist. You've taken the *Dhammadiksha* – not Mahāyāna *Dīkṣā* or Hīnayāna *Dīkṣā*, but simply *Dhammadiksha*. So you are just Buddhist. And you're all the same.' People in England think the same thing. They don't think that they follow the Mahāyāna, or the Hīnayāna. These are all differences that have arisen in the course of the historical development of Buddhism in the East, and they don't concern us now. We're all just Buddhist.

There's another point of similarity. In England too, people want to follow what the Buddha really taught. They don't just want to follow the manners and customs of the present-day Buddhist countries. A lot of *bhikkhus* and lamas and so on come to England from Buddhist countries, and very often they want Buddhists in England to follow the Tibetan custom, or the Thai custom, or the Sinhalese custom or whatever it is. But English Buddhists are not interested in this. They don't want to follow the cultural customs of any particular Buddhist country. They just want to follow the Dhamma. It's the same in India. If you become Buddhist it doesn't mean that you have to become like a Sinhalese or a Thai. You remain Indian.

To give an example, sometimes *bhikkhus* come from Sri Lanka or Thailand, and in those countries it's the custom that lay people bow down in front of *bhikkhus*. So when Sinhalese or Thai *bhikkhus* come to England they tell the English Buddhists, 'This is what you must do. You've got to do the *panchanga panang*.' But the English Buddhists don't like this. They say, 'This is nothing to do with Buddhism. It's just your Sinhalese custom.' So when they meet a *bhikkhu* they don't bow down. They may well offer to shake hands instead. The *bhikkhu* may be very shocked and think that English Buddhists have no *śraddhā*, no faith, but it's not that. It's just that English Buddhists don't want to follow Sinhalese or Thai customs. They don't just want to follow something because it is old. So English Buddhists and Indian Buddhists have this in common too.

Some years ago I was in Bombay, in the area called Worli, and I met some Indian Buddhists chanting '*namu myōhō renge kyō*.' I asked them the meaning of what they were chanting, and they said, 'We don't know.' When I asked them where they'd got it from, they said, 'A Japanese *bhikkhu* taught it to us. We recite it every day and bang the drum. He didn't explain what it meant.' So there they were, Indian Buddhists reciting something in Japanese which they didn't understand. The same sort of thing happened in England, where the Japanese Buddhists have built a big stupa. It's very beautiful, as I saw myself when I went to see it a few months ago, but I was very surprised to see that round the stupa there are various notices all written in Japanese. There's not one word in English, so even though the stupa is in England, English people can't understand what is written around it. This is quite useless, and it's another example of the sort of thing I'm talking about. We have to learn the Dhamma in our own language and follow it in accordance with our own national culture.

There's another point of resemblance between English and Indian Buddhists. In England, in our own Buddhist movement, there's a very strong emphasis on the social aspect of Buddhism. Some years ago, English people who said that they were Buddhist lived in every respect just like everybody else. Some of them didn't even observe right livelihood. But now Buddhists in England are very conscious of the social aspect of Buddhism. They want to change society, to make a new society. And it's the same in India. Dr Ambedkar was not interested just in changing his religion in a narrow sense. He wanted that the change of religion should bring about a change in every aspect of society, should change economic, social, cultural, and spiritual life. Taking the *Dhammadiksha* means, in fact, a Dhamma Revolution. Simple conversion is not enough.

Dr Ambedkar had this great vision. He was, as you know, a very great man, but people are only beginning to understand what he was really trying to do. He saw that people were suffering in all sorts of ways, he wanted to uplift them, and he saw that Buddhism was the way to do this, because Buddhism gives people self-respect and energy. If you've got self-respect and energy, you can do anything. Just after the great *Dhammadiksha*, I was going round Maharashtra and meeting all sorts of people, young and old, educated and uneducated. When I asked them, 'Now that you've taken the *Dhammadiksha*, now that you've become Buddhist, how do you feel?' they all said the same thing. They said, 'Now that we've become Buddhist we feel free.' If you have that feeling of freedom, you can do anything.

You can't achieve very much simply by material means, or by means of violence. This is where Dr Ambedkar differed from Marxism. This is a big subject, and I can't go into it this evening, but briefly, Dr Ambedkar said he agreed with Marx up to a point. He agreed that there was suffering and exploitation, and that private property should be abolished. But he did not agree with Marx about the method. Marx believed in violence, but Dr Ambedkar believed in non-violence. Dr Ambedkar believed that the great Dhamma Revolution, new life for the individual and a new kind of society, should be brought about entirely by peaceful means. By means of the *Dhammadiksha* Dr Ambedkar did principally three things: he uplifted millions of oppressed people; he gave a challenge to traditional Buddhism; and he showed a model of a non-violent, social revolution. His work is therefore of world significance. We shouldn't think that Dr Ambedkar is just the leader of a particular community. He is the leader of all those who want to bring about a worldwide Dhamma Revolution.

The original conversion, the *Dhammadiksha* in Nagpur, took place twenty-five years ago. So what has happened since then? I want to touch very briefly upon that and then I must conclude. Twenty-five years is a long time, but some people are disappointed that not much has been achieved. The spreading of the Dhamma has not been as successful as they hoped. So why is this? I want to mention just a few of the reasons.

The main reason is of course that people did not know the right way to go about it. In the years after the original *Dhammadiksha* a lot of political leaders thought they could spread the Dhamma, but they found they could not do so. They might have been quite good people, and quite good politicians, but to spread the Dhamma you need quite different qualifications. You have both to understand and also to practise the Dhamma. The efforts of the politicians to spread the Dhamma were completely unsuccessful because they knew very little about it and they didn't practise it. Sometimes in their personal lives they were going right against the Dhamma, so what could they do to spread it? Then again, some people thought that in order to spread the Dhamma you've got to go to university and take a course in Buddhist studies. You've got to learn Pāli and Sanskrit, and do a PhD. But this also doesn't work. Purely academic, intellectual knowledge is not enough for spreading the Dhamma. Then again, some people thought if you build lots of viharas, Buddhism will spread. So lots of viharas have been built. Some are big and some are small, but not much is happening in them. The buildings are there, but there's no Dhamma activity. Then some people thought, 'We must bring big Buddhist leaders from foreign countries.' And many of them have come, including some quite famous people. Heads of big monasteries, Buddhist prime ministers, even Buddhist kings, have all come. People have given them big receptions, they've given speeches, and then they've gone away, and nothing has happened as a result. So this method doesn't work either. And then again, some people have thought that the best way is to ordain a lot of *bhikkhus*. Nowadays in Maharashtra there are about 200 *bhikkhus*, but some of them at least are not real *bhikkhus*. They don't know much about the Dhamma so they can't say much about it. They can sit on a platform and give *tisaraṇa pañcasīla*, but that's about all. So this also hasn't proved very successful.

These are just some of the reasons why there hasn't been more progress in the Dhamma movement in the last twenty-five years. The main wrong idea is that you can spread Buddhism even though you're not practising it. So the progress of the Dhamma movement has been slowed down. But though it has been slowed down it certainly has not been stopped altogether. We can see some progress. I have seen it myself quite recently during the last few weeks on my lecture tour of Maharashtra. Everywhere I went, people were very enthusiastic. In some places four or five hundred people gathered, in some places there were two or three thousand, and in some places eight or nine thousand came, not for politics or for any material gain, but just for the sake of the Dhamma. And they wanted to know more. They wanted to understand the Dhamma, and learn how to practise it. But there was no one to teach them, to guide their energy in the right channels.

So this is the great problem. We need a new kind of Buddhist worker, a new kind of Buddhist teacher. Dr Ambedkar himself said that the present-day *bhikkhus* are useless.[395] That's a very strong thing to say, but Dr Ambedkar spoke strongly. He said what he really thought. People have not yet started taking these words of his really seriously, but in England we've been taking them very seriously. In England we've produced a new kind of Buddhist worker, a new kind of Buddhist teacher. I was going to say quite a lot about this, but I'm afraid there isn't time. Just to say a very few words about it, we've got a group of people who are observing what we call the *dasa sīlas*, the *dasa kusala dhammas*, and they're working full time for Buddhism. They give all their time, all their energy, to Buddhist activities. They study the Dhamma, they practise meditation, and they teach. It's these people who are running all our Buddhist activities. They run the centres, the businesses, and the communities. It's because we've created this body of new Buddhist workers that we've been able to do so much in Britain and other countries in the West. These people aren't *bhikkhus* in the old sense or *upāsakas* in the old sense. They're something in between. We call them Dhammacharis and Dhammacharinis. Some of them have families, but most of them are single, and most of them are quite young, in their middle or late twenties. We accept these people into this Western Buddhist Order, or, as we call it in India, Trailokya Bauddha Mahasangha, only after a period of training and testing. To train one person usually takes about two years, but sometimes it takes three or four years, and in some cases seven or eight. We're very strict about this. If you go to one of the Buddhist countries you can become a *bhikkhu* the day after you arrive. It's as easy as that. But it's not easy to join our Order. It's quite difficult, because we want real workers, real teachers, people who are really committed to the Buddha, the Dhamma, and the Sangha. I hope that it will be possible to introduce this sort of system into India. This is what Dr Ambedkar wanted. I can see quite clearly that in India there is a tremendous potential for Buddhism. I'm not in the least pessimistic. I'm full of optimism about the future of Buddhism in India, especially after my recent tour. I'm quite sure that Buddhism can be revived here in India, and that when Buddhism has been revived throughout the whole of India, it will spread more and more throughout the world. I hope that all of us can work together to this end.

I'm very grateful to you for having invited me to speak to you this evening. I'm very happy to have met you all, and to be in Delhi once again. Delhi, after all, is the capital of a very great country, and people come here from all over India, and from all over the world. It's an international city, with a lot of cultural activity and spiritual interest. I'm sure that Delhi has a very important part to play in the Buddhist movement in India and in the world, so the Buddhists of Delhi have a very important part to play. I hope that all of you will be able to do something. I know that you're all inspired by Dr Ambedkar and you're all trying to follow his great example. But what was the greatest example that Dr Ambedkar gave? It was the example of the *Dhammadiksha*. I hope that you will all take that very seriously. I hope that you will all understand what the implications of *Dhammadiksha* are. I hope that you will all understand that *Dhammadiksha* means Dhamma Revolution. It means a change in the life of every individual human being and in the whole of society. It means a better life for everybody. This is what Dr Ambedkar wanted to bring about, not just in India, but in the whole world. So let us all work together to achieve this great objective.

Buddhists are all brothers and sisters. It doesn't matter whether we're born in England or in India. We all follow the same Dhamma, we've all taken the same *Dhammadiksha*, and we should work together like brothers and sisters and help one another. In that way the objective that we share will be achieved all the more quickly. So thank you once again for giving me a quiet and patient hearing. Thank you for inviting me to address you. I hope that we may all meet again.

35
QUESTIONS AND ANSWERS IN BOMBAY

Bombay, 7 March 1982

Order members, Mitras, and Friends: This is the second time in the course of my present trip that we have had a session of Questions and Answers. The first was at Milind College, Aurangabad, when many of the questions were naturally rather intellectual, or even theoretical. The questions that have been handed in this evening seem to be mainly practical – maybe because this is a *Dhamma-shibir*. I have arranged the questions in four categories, and propose to deal with the questions belonging to each category all together. The four categories in which I have arranged the questions are: (1) questions to do with meditation and other practices, (2) questions to do with *śīla*, (3) questions to do with organizational matters, (4) questions of a philosophical nature.

Before I start dealing with the questions, a word of warning. As I pointed out at Milind College, asking questions about the Dhamma is not like asking questions about history or geography, questions about matters of fact. Questions about the Dhamma are concerned with spiritual values, which have to be actually experienced. Since different people experience them in different ways, or at least under different conditions and in different circumstances, it is not always possible to give a straightforward factual answer to a question about the Dhamma. The Dhamma itself is not of that nature, and one should not expect factual answers to questions which are not really of a factual nature. In any case, if you ask a question about the Dhamma it means that you have been thinking, and the answer should help you think still more, not stop you thinking in the way that the answer to a factual question does. People often ask questions because they don't want to think for themselves, but answers to questions about the Dhamma force you to think.

I. QUESTIONS TO DO WITH MEDITATION AND OTHER PRACTICES

Q: *(a) What is the exact meaning of 'awareness'? Could you kindly explain with examples. (b) What is the difference between awareness and consciousness?*
Sangharakshita: There may be a little confusion here between English and Marathi. Since the person asking these questions clearly knows English, let me first of all say something about what in English is called 'consciousness', since this usually signifies something simpler than awareness – something more basic, more elementary. When you see something with the eye, a tree for example, you are said to be conscious of that sight. When you hear a sound with the ear you are said to be conscious of the sound, and so on for the rest of the physical senses. The same is the case when you think about something with the mind. Thoughts or ideas are the objects of the mind or 'mental sense' in the same way that sights, sounds, etc. are the objects of the physical senses. There is a particular relationship between the senses on the one hand and the sense objects on the other, and the word which is generally used in English to describe the quality of that relationship is consciousness. All human beings are conscious, at least when awake, and even in sleep there is a certain amount of subconscious mental activity in the form of dreams. Animals are also conscious – conscious of such things as other animals, and heat and cold.

'Awareness' is a more highly developed form of consciousness. As generally used, the term implies, in addition to consciousness, a kind of knowledge or understanding. It implies a more comprehensive view. Suppose you happen to be eating. You are conscious of the food, conscious of its agreeable taste, conscious of yourself eating, conscious of your stomach becoming full, conscious of your hunger abating. All this is consciousness. Awareness begins where consciousness leaves off, so to speak. In addition to being conscious of eating, you know why you are eating. You are aware that you are eating to maintain health and strength and aware that you are trying to maintain health and strength so that you can practise the Dhamma. In other words, there is a wider frame of reference. This is what we call awareness. This is why we don't say to people, 'Be conscious!' – they are conscious already – but 'Be aware!' because they are not aware – that is, they do not really know what they are doing. They need to pass from consciousness to awareness. In Pāli *viññāna* corresponds to consciousness and awareness to *sati-sampajañña*. Just to make things more difficult, in English the word consciousness is sometimes used in the sense of awareness and the word awareness is sometimes used in the sense of consciousness. It doesn't matter which word you use for the lower form and which for the higher, provided the distinction between the higher and the lower form is made.

Q: *(a) What exactly does openness mean? Could you kindly explain with illustrations. (b) What is receptivity? Please explain with illustrations.*
S: These two also are very closely connected. Openness is like keeping the door open. Receptivity is like allowing someone to come through the door. Thus openness and receptivity are psychological terms, though I must admit that as currently used in English their meaning is rather vague. For instance, with regard to the term openness one has to ask, 'Openness to what?' Usually the term openness is held to signify a positive psychological quality, but of course it is not good to be open to everything. What, then, is openness when used in a positive sense? What is it that openness is open to? It must be some good thing. Openness really means a willingness to consider something new, something you have not seen, or heard of, or experienced before. Most people get into the habit of thinking in a certain way, especially as they get older. They are not very open to new ideas, because if they were open to them they would have to start thinking, and even changing. Thus openness really means a willingness to give serious consideration to some new idea or new experience, and not closing yourself off from it.

Receptivity goes further than that. Receptivity is not just willingness to give serious consideration to the new idea or experience, but willingness to accept it and make it a part of yourself if, upon examination, you find it to be a worthwhile idea or a worthwhile experience. If we want to change and to develop as human beings, both openness and receptivity are necessary. As for illustrations, I've already given the example of the door, but there are lots of others that one could give. Suppose someone criticizes you for something that you have done, saying that you were wrong to do it. That may be a new idea to you, because it never occurred to you that what you were doing was wrong. Openness and receptivity consists in being able to listen to that person, thinking, 'Yes, maybe what I did was wrong. Maybe I should change.' This is why we think of openness and receptivity very much in connection with *kalyāṇa mitratā*. Your *kalyāṇa mitra* may see something in you that is not so good, maybe something that you haven't seen yourself, and he may point it out to you. You have to be open to that. You have to be receptive. You have to think about what your *kalyāṇa mitra* says. This doesn't mean that your *kalyāṇa mitra* is always right and you are always wrong. You are free to disagree, but you must listen very carefully and very sincerely. You must not just 'react', as we say.

Q: *What is the use of practising the mindfulness of breathing? Was this taught by the Buddha himself?*
S: The answer to the first part of the question is very simple. Mindfulness is the antidote to a particular mental poison, the poison of distraction. We know from our own experience that the mind is never still, even for a minute. It turns this way and that, thinking now of one thing and now of another. The mindfulness of breathing is a very good practice for counteracting this tendency. Since most people suffer from distraction to some extent, the mindfulness of breathing is useful for most people. For those whose minds are very, very distracted, it is particularly useful, but I don't suppose there is anybody whose mind is so free from distraction as not to be in need of the practice at all. As for the second part of the question, so far as we can tell from the Pāli scriptures the practice was definitely taught by the Buddha himself.[396] Quite a number of Pāli *suttas* mention the mindfulness of breathing, though they don't give any details about the actual method of counting the breaths. Those details are found in the *Visuddhimagga* of Acharya Buddhaghosa[397] and other works.

Q: *What are the benefits of the* mettā bhāvanā? *Has anybody been benefited by this practice, and if so, in what way? Did the Buddha teach this practice himself?*
S: The main benefit of the *mettā bhāvanā* is obvious. You get rid of anger and hatred. Just as the mindfulness of breathing is the antidote to the

poison of distraction, in the same way the *mettā bhāvanā* is the antidote to the poison of anger and hatred. Has anybody benefited from this practice? I would say that millions of people must have benefited from it, but maybe the question is referring to people within our own movement, among our own friends. Here also the answer is yes. Many people within the Movement have benefited, in that they have got rid of anger and hatred, which is surely a good thing. To be constantly subject to anger is unpleasant and even painful, not only for yourself but for other people. In the *Mettānisaṃsa Sutta*[398] the Buddha enumerates eleven advantages which are to be expected from the practice of the *mettā bhāvanā*. One of these advantages is that you will sleep well. Maybe you sleep well already, but there are many people who do not. They sleep badly, tossing from this side to that, and talking – even crying out – in their sleep. But according to the Buddha, if you practise the *mettā bhāvanā* you will sleep well. Another advantage is that you will not have bad dreams. If you dream at all, the dreams will be happy ones, and you will wake up feeling refreshed. As for whether the Buddha taught this practice himself, from what has been said already it will be obvious that he did. There are many passages in the Pāli scriptures where the Buddha is represented as teaching his disciples to extend their *mettā* to beings in all the different directions of space.[399]

Q: *Don't we strengthen the power of our enemies by doing the* mettā bhāvanā *for them and thereby put ourselves in danger?*
S: If you really do the *mettā bhāvanā* for your enemies you won't strengthen them; you will weaken them. If your *mettā* is very weak it won't have any effect on the enemy, and it won't change your attitude towards them either. But there is something you must be careful to bear in mind here. We don't develop *mettā* towards our enemies simply to stop them harming us. We develop *mettā* because this is part of our own personal development. If it also neutralizes the enemy's enmity, so much the better; but we shouldn't think that we've failed as regards the practice of the *mettā bhāvanā* if we don't succeed in stopping other people doing what we don't want them to do. We must be careful not to use the *mettā bhāvanā* with an un-*mettā*-like attitude – just to get things done in the way that we would like. Of course, the more people practise the *mettā bhāvanā* the better. Eventually we will want to teach the *mettā bhāvanā* even to our enemies, because if they also were to do

the *mettā bhāvanā* they wouldn't be our enemies any more, but that may take a long time. In the meantime we just have to get on with our own practice of the *mettā bhāvanā*.

Q: *What are the benefits of communication exercises? Have they been proved to be useful? Did the Buddha teach them?*
S: The main benefit of the exercises is obvious; as a result of them, you can communicate better. In England, in fact in the West generally, we have made extensive use of them and found them very helpful. A lot of people in England don't find it very easy to communicate. They don't find it very easy to talk to new people, or to people that they don't know very well. The communication exercises have been extremely useful in this connection, because they help stir up people's energies, as a result of which blockages to communication are removed.

I well remember the first time I used the communication exercises on a *Dhamma-shibir*. It must have been in 1967 or 1968, and it was on the second *Dhamma-shibir* to be held under the auspices of the FWBO/TBMSG. The *shibir* was held, of course, in England. At that time our movement was very young, and we had a lot of new people. Moreover, there were as yet no Order members: there was only me. Everybody on this *Dhamma-shibir* seemed very dull. They did not seem to have any life. To be honest, they seemed to be half dead, and I wondered what to do about it. Lectures did not seem to be helping them very much, and neither did meditation. Suddenly I remembered these communication exercises, which I had learned some years before. I therefore told everybody that we were going to do them, and gave the necessary instructions, after which we did the exercises in exactly the same way that you would do them here in India. The results were very surprising. Everybody became very lively, very happy, and very friendly. They started talking to one another and enjoying the *shibir*. So yes, these communication exercises are very useful, and ever since that time we have been making use of them in our movement.

With regard to the question as to whether the Buddha taught these communication exercises, the answer is that he did not, at least not in this particular form. In the Buddha's time there was communication, but there were no communication exercises. Apparently people didn't need them. But we must not forget what the Buddha said to Mahāpajāpatī Gotami, to the effect that whatever helps us to develop spiritually is to be considered as part of his Dhamma.[400] It doesn't matter that the Buddha didn't personally teach these communication exercises in this particular form. If they help us to develop they are part of the Dhamma.

Q: *Why do we observe silence? Is it not something that Hindus do, especially Vinoba Bhave? We attend the* Dhamma-shibir *with the hope of being able to learn a lot from more experienced people, but if we observe silence, we cannot communicate with such people and therefore we waste useful time.*

S: In answering some questions you have to try and see what the underlying assumptions are. Underlying this question there is the assumption that you cannot learn anything when you are being silent. But is this really so? Actually, we can learn a lot when we are being silent. For one thing, when we are silent we can think. In the course of the *shibir* you will hear a lot of useful things in the form of Dhamma teachings; but it is important that you don't just hear them. It is important that you think about them, because if you don't think about them you won't really understand them. During the period of silence you should therefore think about what you have heard in the study group, or in the lectures. Otherwise, you will very quickly forget it. When you are silent you can also study the workings of your own mind. Usually we give expression to whatever idea comes into our head, but when we are observing silence we cannot do that. The idea comes, and since we can't give expression to it we have to watch it, and ask ourselves why we wanted to give expression to it. In this way we can understand ourselves better and maybe understand the way in which our mind works.

I remember a *Dhamma-shibir* that was held on my last visit to India. Lokamitra would ring the bell for the silent period, but after a few minutes of silence everybody would be talking. The women would say, 'Of course it's a silent period, but that doesn't mean we can't talk while we are cooking.' Similarly, the men would say, 'Of course it's a silent period, but that doesn't mean we can't have a little chat when we go for a walk with a friend.' Thus everybody would find some excuse for talking, so that Lokamitra had to go round saying, 'Be quiet, be quiet!' People found it very difficult to practise self-control in respect of speech. When you observe silence you therefore learn awareness. Some people don't even know that they are talking, but if you observe silence, you become more aware of what you are doing. Sometimes people find it almost impossible to stop talking. On one of our earlier *Dhamma-shibirs* in England I noticed that, though people were not talking to one another, they were always talking to the cat. I heard one woman say to the cat, 'Hello pussy, what's your name?' In this way she held a sort of conversation with the cat for five or ten minutes. She was just in the habit of talking. I don't think she realized that she was talking to the cat.

So these are the reasons why we observe silence. By observing silence we can learn a great deal about ourselves. We don't learn just from books. We also learn from our own experience. There is another point. The questioner asks, 'Is it not something that Hindus do, especially Vinoba Bhave?' Again there is an assumption, the assumption in this case being that if Vinoba Bhave does something we should not do it. But Vinoba Bhave also gives lectures. He also writes books. Surely this doesn't mean that we cannot do these things, just because he does them. We have to see whether the thing itself is good or bad, regardless of who does it. Silence is something that certainly does help us very much, in many different ways. In Buddhism no one is allowed to take a vow of silence, because then you will not be able to teach the Dhamma.[401] But to observe silence from time to time is very useful.

Q: *What is the meaning of* oṃ maṇi padme hūṃ *and* oṃ muni muni mahā muni śākyamuni svāhā?
S: It's not easy to give an explanation in just a few minutes, but broadly speaking, *oṃ maṇi padme hūṃ* is a reminder of our own potentiality as a human being. *Padma* means lotus, and stands for the lotus of our own heart. *Maṇi* means jewel, and represents Buddhahood. When we recite *oṃ maṇi padme hūṃ* we remind ourselves that Buddhahood is something to be realized in the depths of our own heart. As for *oṃ muni muni mahā muni śākyamuni svāhā*, this is the mantra of Śākyamuni. When we recite it we remind ourselves of the Buddha's qualities of wisdom and compassion. Concentrating on those qualities in this way helps us to develop them within ourselves.

Q: *Whilst practising mindfulness of breathing it sometimes happens that one's breathing processes are obstructed due to a cold, so that one has to breathe through the mouth. Is it best not to continue the practice?*
S: When your nose is completely blocked, you can't do the mindfulness of breathing as ordinarily practised. You could, of course, change to

the *mettā bhāvanā* for the time being, but if you don't want to do that you can concentrate the attention not on the sensation produced by the breath in the nostrils but on the diaphragm as it rises and falls. That is not quite so good as concentration on the sensation produced by the breath in the nostrils, since the object is bigger and grosser and does not, therefore, allow you to develop such a subtle concentration, but it is certainly good enough – at least for a few days. So if your nose is blocked, concentrate on the rise and fall of the diaphragm.

Q: *In our practice of* mettā bhāvanā *we direct our* mettā *towards our enemy. But if such enemies assault us, how are we to defend ourselves?*
S: No hard and fast rule can be laid down. If we practise the *mettā bhāvanā* we naturally become full of *mettā*. Should someone then attack us how will we, being full of *mettā*, defend ourselves? That is the question. But we can't really say how we would defend ourselves. It depends how much *mettā* you have been able to develop. It is not possible for me to say that in such circumstances you will do this or do that, or that you will not do this or not do that. You will act according to the degree of *mettā* you have developed, and according to the situation. It seems to be assumed that *mettā* will make you weak, but this is not the case. *Mettā* makes you stronger. *Mettā* makes you fearless. It may even be said that if you are fearless you are in a better position to defend yourself. If you get angry and lose your temper, you may not be able to defend yourself so well as when you are in a positive state due to the development of *mettā*. So practise the *mettā bhāvanā*. Don't think it will make you weak. If someone attacks you, you will know what to do.

Q: *Bhikkhu Jagdish Kashyap's* mettā bhāvanā *was tested standing face to face with a deadly cobra. Is it true that we must test our* mettā bhāvanā *like this?*
S: I stayed with Kashyapji for about a year, but I don't remember his *mettā bhāvanā* being tested in that way. Perhaps the incident happened afterwards. In any case, when a deadly cobra sees a human being it usually tries to escape, because it knows that the human being is more dangerous. We don't have to worry. It's the cobra who has to worry. As for whether we should test our *mettā*, there is no need for us to do this. Life is testing us all the time. If you are a married person your wife – or your husband – will test you. If you are an employee your boss will test

you. In life there are so many things that are constantly testing our *mettā bhāvanā*. You don't have to go off into the jungle looking for a cobra. There are cobras around us all the time. So we get quite enough tests – and this is a good thing, because it enables us to know whether we have actually succeeded in developing *mettā* or not.

There is a story to this effect in the Pāli scriptures. A certain rich woman of Sāvatthi – her name was Vedehikā – had the reputation of being very meek and gentle. This woman had a servant girl named Kālī, who was not only clever but a very good worker. One day Kālī decided to test her mistress and find out whether she was really meek and gentle, or whether she only appeared to be so because she had a hard-working servant who never did anything to displease her. The next morning, therefore, Kālī got up late, and she did this for several mornings running. Each day her mistress became more annoyed, and in the end she became so angry with Kālī that she hit her over the head with a rolling pin. She hit her so hard, in fact, that her head was broken and blood streamed down her face. In this way Kālī came to know that her mistress was meek and gentle only as long as things went well, but that when difficulties arose she lost her temper.[402]

It is therefore good that we should sometimes be tested. Anyone can be full of *mettā* when things are going well. When difficulties arise, that is the test. But life itself gives us that test. There is no need to go looking for deadly cobras.

Q: *How does one know that one has attained higher states of meditation?*
S: Well, one sign is that when you have attained to higher states of meditation you no longer wonder whether you have attained to those states! If such a question arises in your mind it means you are still thinking, and if you are still thinking you have not gone very far in the *dhyānas*. If you have really gone higher – or deeper – into meditation you won't have such thoughts at all. You will just want to get more and more into your meditation.

2. QUESTIONS TO DO WITH *ŚĪLA*

Q: *When ploughing and driving a bullock cart the farmer has to beat his bullocks. How can the farmer practise the Buddha's teachings, practise the mettā bhāvanā, and still continue to beat his animals for his work?*

S: The whole question revolves around what we mean by beating. You can give just a little tap with a stick, or you can use a lot of force. If you beat the bullocks really badly, so as to give them real pain, or if you twist their tails, that is breaking the first precept, the precept of refraining from harming living beings. Obviously you can't do that and practise the *mettā bhāvanā*. So you shouldn't beat them in that way. But if you give them just a little tap with a stick, that's all right. It is the same with children. Parents may love their children dearly, but all the same they may sometimes have to give them a little slap. Of course they should never really beat their children. They should never inflict any real pain or suffering, whether physical or mental.

Q: *In villages the Hindus cut goats for meat, but they don't sell the meat to the Buddhists, so the Buddhists also cut goats for meat. Is this in accordance with the teaching of* ahiṃsā?
S: No, it is certainly not in accordance with the teaching of *ahiṃsā*, so it looks as though the Buddhists in the villages will have to give up eating meat. If you observe the *śīlas*, and if you practise meditation, you can't kill animals. Your mind becomes too sensitive. You feel the suffering of the animal and so, whether it is a goat, or a chicken, or whatever, you can't hurt it. The answer to the question therefore is that if you are really practising the teaching of *ahiṃsā* you won't kill goats for meat.

Q: *Buddhist students call themselves Hindu, Mahar, or whatever caste name they may be at the time of getting jobs reserved for Scheduled Caste people. On all other occasions they call themselves Buddhists. Is that not a breach of the fourth* śīla, *abstention from false speech?*
S: This is a very complicated issue. When you say you belong to a certain caste, what does that mean? Does it mean that you belong to that caste now or that you were born into that caste? If you say that you were born into that caste you are not telling a lie because so far as society is concerned, you were born into it, even though now you are a Buddhist by religion. Therefore you could, in a sense, say 'I was born into such-and-such caste but now I am a Buddhist.' The difficulty is that you don't, of course, make this statement all at once. You make the first half of it when you fill in the form applying for the reserved job, and the second when you recite the *tisaraṇa* and *pañcasīla*. It is therefore difficult to lay down a hard and fast rule in this matter.

Let me quote a parallel case. In order to travel from the United Kingdom to India I had to have a passport. This passport states that I am by nationality a citizen of the United Kingdom. In other words, I am not American, or Indian, or Chinese; I am English. But personally I don't believe that. I may have been born in England, but I don't think of myself as English. So far as I am concerned, I am just a human being. Yet if I want to get a passport, and be free to travel abroad, I have to accept the fact of my nationality. I have to allow people to treat me as though I really was English and not anything else. On arrival in India I have to show my British passport, and the people in the Immigration Department treat me as though I was simply English. I am English, but again in a sense I am just a human being – just a Buddhist. Sometimes we have to go along with social conventions even though we do not believe in them. What is important is that we should be quite clear in our own minds as to what we are doing. We must never actually tell a lie. If necessary, we can make it clear that we are filling in the form under protest, since we do not agree with the underlying principle. But if we don't fill in the form we shall not be free to do what we want to do in the way of obtaining employment, earning money, and supporting ourselves and our families.

After the mass conversions of 1956 there was a big discussion about this particular issue. Some people thought that they should not say even that they were born as Scheduled Caste Hindus. They thought that they should simply say that they were Buddhists. Others thought differently. Both parties were sincere in their convictions, and as yet the Indian Buddhist community has not been able to arrive at a consensus of opinion on the subject. For what it's worth, let me tell you about an incident which occurred during my recent visit to Delhi. In the course of conversation with a Punjabi Buddhist, I asked him what was the condition of the Buddhists in Uttar Pradesh and in the Punjab. He said that it was not very good – not as good as that of the Buddhists of Maharashtra. When I asked him to explain, he said, 'After their conversion to Buddhism the Buddhists of Uttar Pradesh and the Punjab all gave up their reservations. The result is that they don't have many jobs, or much in the way of money. Neither do they have much enthusiasm for the Dhamma. The Buddhists of Maharashtra do things differently. They have a lot of enthusiasm for the Dhamma, but they also hang on to their reservations!'

As I said, the issue is a complicated one. Everybody must make up his own mind about it and do what he thinks best. But certainly you must never tell a direct lie.

Q: *If an unmarried girl, because of ugliness, or maybe because of a difficult situation, finds it hard to get married, and if she therefore happens to marry someone deceitfully, would it be against the practice of the* śīlas?
S: I'm not sure what is meant by marrying someone deceitfully. It's not really possible for a girl to marry a man without him knowing that she is marrying him. Men may be stupid, but they are not as stupid as that! Perhaps it refers to the description of herself that the girl gives in reply to a matrimonial advertisement. She may write saying she is beautiful when in fact she is not. Obviously that would not be a very ethical thing to do and in any case sooner or later she would be found out. Or, perhaps the question is asking whether if a girl cannot get married, for this or that reason, she should marry someone deceitfully in the sense of marrying him without the knowledge of her parents? From the Buddhist point of view there is no objection to her doing this, provided that she is of the age of consent, and it does not involve the actual telling of lies. In any case, the girl will sooner or later have to tell her parents what she has done, presumably.

3. QUESTIONS TO DO WITH ORGANIZATIONAL MATTERS

Q: *Dr Babasaheb Ambedkar said, 'Buddhism is a social revolution.' Please elaborate and explain.*
S: There is no time for an elaborate answer. In any case, I have already given a couple of lectures on the subject, and in due course you will be able to read these lectures in *Buddhayan*. Briefly, Buddhism is a social revolution in the sense that if you practise the Dhamma correctly, fully, and thoroughly it will bring about a complete change in society. Some people think that becoming a Buddhist means changing your religion in a very narrow sense. They think that it means becoming a Buddhist in your own mind while contriving to lead exactly the same kind of social life as before. But it is not like that at all. If you really practise the Buddha's teaching there will be a change in every aspect of your life, and you will also start changing your environment. You will start

changing the society in which you live. In this way you will bring about a social revolution. The more people become Buddhist and really try to practise, the more society will be changed and the bigger the social revolution will be.

Q: *In his speech of 1950 in Kathmandu, Dr Babasaheb Ambedkar said that it is not sufficient that one should become a Buddhist, but that it is the duty of every Buddhist to spread the Dhamma. In addition he vowed that he would make India 'Buddhamaya', or full of Buddhism. What are the measures for the revival and spread of Buddhism?*
S: I will say just one thing – something I have said in several lectures in the course of the last few weeks. If you want to spread Buddhism, you must practise Buddhism. A lot of people seem to think you can spread Buddhism by purely organizational means, i.e. without practising it yourself, but this is quite impossible. You may have any amount of money, but you can't revive or spread Buddhism just with money. You may have a big organization with many workers, but if your workers don't practise Buddhism then the size and numerical strength of your organization will avail you nothing. Unless you practise Buddhism you cannot revive it or spread it.

Q: *What do you think about the future of the Bharatiya Bauddha Mahasabha founded by Dr Ambedkar?*
S: Not being an astrologer, I can't say.

Q: *What relations can be established between Bharatiya Bauddha Mahasabha and* TBMSG?
S: There is only one relation that can be established, and that is a Dhamma relation. If they practise the Dhamma and if we practise the Dhamma, we must come together: there will naturally be a relation. But there can't be a purely organizational relation. That has no meaning. Once again the emphasis must be on the practice of the Dhamma.

Q: *Will you kindly give your comment on* BAMCEF *in relation to your Delhi meeting?*
S: The Delhi meeting was not, strictly speaking, a BAMCEF affair. BAMCEF has three labels, the other two being DS4 and the Buddhist Research Centre. As the office-bearers were careful to explain to me, the three are

organizationally distinct. Since I gave my lecture under the auspices of the Buddhist Research Centre I can't really say anything about BAMCEF or DS4 – though the people are the same. My lecture came at the end of a two-day session of DS4, for which some 500 activists had come from all over India. As soon as the proceedings were over the banners were changed, the meeting became a meeting of the Buddhist Research Centre, and I gave my lecture. Mr Kanshi Ram remained in the chair, and from being chairman of DS4 became chairman of the Buddhist Research Centre.[403]

I was very glad to have an opportunity of speaking to these 500 youngish people from all over India. Since I had not had any previous contact with them I gave a general talk, telling them about my own life, about my earlier experiences in India, about my meetings with Dr Ambedkar, about my work in Maharashtra, and about my work in England. I also explained why it was that people in England took to Buddhism, besides telling them all about TBMSG and about my recent tour. People seemed to enjoy my lecture very much, even though they had already had two days of talks and discussions and were very tired. In fact I think my lecture made a pleasant change for them. Shortly before I spoke they had the last DS4 speaker, and from a distance I could hear him shouting into the microphone and trying without much success to stir people up. But when I spoke I met with a good response – so much so, in fact, that after the meeting a number of young men crowded round me asking for my autograph.

This is all I can say. I don't know enough about BAMCEF to be able to make any general comments. They seem to be active, and they seem to have some good ideas, and I was therefore glad to be in contact with them and glad to have the opportunity of speaking under the auspices of the Buddhist Research Centre.

4. QUESTIONS OF A PHILOSOPHICAL NATURE

Q: *The Lord Buddha said that the whole world is changing and nothing is permanent. If that is so, how are we to understand Nirvāṇa as a permanent place of bliss, peace, and calmness?*
S: The Buddha distinguished between what he called *saṃskṛta-dharmas* and *asaṃskṛta-dharmas*, i.e. between those things that were 'put together' and those things that were 'not put together'. When he said that the

whole universe was constantly changing and nothing was permanent he was speaking of the *saṃskṛta-dharmas*, and when he spoke of Nirvāṇa as a place of permanent peace, bliss, and calmness he was referring to the *asaṃskṛta-dharmas*. So there is no contradiction. In the *Ariyapariyesanā Sutta* of the *Majjhima-Nikāya* the Buddha distinguishes between what he calls the *ariyapariyesanā* and what he calls the *anariyapariyesanā*.[404] The *anariyapariyesanā* is when, you yourself being subject to change, you pursue those things which are also changing. The *ariyapariyesanā* is when, you yourself being subject to change, you pursue that which does not change, i.e. Nirvāṇa. Thus we have to understand what the Buddha is actually talking about – whether about *saṃskṛta-dharmas* or about *asaṃskṛta-dharmas*.

Q: *Does Dr Ambedkar's book* The Buddha and His Dhamma *fulfil the need for the Buddhist Bible needed for the revival of Buddhism?*
S: Here we have to ask 'Whose need?' Need is not an objective thing, but a subjective thing. If people feel the need of such a Bible, then Dr Ambedkar's book certainly meets their need. If you yourself feel the need for a Buddhist Bible, then read Dr Ambedkar's book. But if you don't feel any such need then, so far as you are concerned, it is not needed. It depends on you.

Q: *If Enlightenment is an increase in the level of awareness, does the touch of a teacher increase the level of awareness? If not, why not?*
S: According to Buddhism the touch of a teacher cannot increase the level of awareness – unless he gives you a good slap, maybe! Sometimes, of course, one person can influence the mind of another person, but that doesn't have any great significance from the spiritual point of view. It is only those mental states which you generate yourself, as a result of your own free choice, that have any real spiritual significance. A teacher can, of course, help you by creating a more positive and inspiring attitude, or environment, or atmosphere, but he can't do much more than that.

Q: *Some students of Buddhism and the scientific process think this is a subject for research. Many arguments of Buddhism give a different view however. Can you explain?*
S: The Buddha gained Enlightenment through *prajñā*. By scientific process one means verification for oneself, i.e. if you want to verify

something you have to verify it in your own personal experience. Now *prajñā* is developed with the help of *samādhi*. If you want to verify this for yourself then you must be ready to take up the practice of meditation so as to experience *samādhi* personally. That is the real scientific attitude.

36
QUESTIONS AND ANSWERS
WITH ORDER MEMBERS

Bombay, 10 March 1982

Only part of the transcription from this Order gathering with Sangha-rakshita could be found. We join the assembly in the middle of a session.

Sangharakshita: We need more and more preparation before the ordinations – though of course, if the new Order members are so very well trained, the old Order members have to work very hard to keep up with them! We have this difficulty in England too.

Q: *How should we spend our time?*
S: We have very limited time and energy, so we have to sort out our priorities. The most important thing is to teach the Dhamma and encourage people to practise it. We need to practise the Dhamma more and more strongly. If we don't do this, other problems will not be solved. We have to be careful, therefore, not to use too much energy on purely social and economic questions. We want to solve these problems also, but they can only really be solved on the basis of the Dhamma, so we must make the Dhamma strong first and then gradually we can come to these other questions. If any individual Order member feels strongly about doing some sort of social work, he is free to do this, but he has to do it in his personal capacity. If any Order member does anything in the name of TBMSG, he should do it only after reaching agreement with all the other Order members.

Q: *What does one do about buzzing in the ears?*
S: This is quite a strange question. It may be due to some physical cause or to a mental one. If the cause is physical, some treatment may be required, but if the cause is mental, meditation will put it right in the end. Just dropping meditation may be all right as a short-term measure, but not as a long-term one. In the meantime, before getting back into meditation, if you find you have a lot of energy, you can do more chanting. Chanting takes a lot of energy if it is done properly and mindfully. When one is chanting the various *suttas* and *gāthas*, this is also a spiritual practice. It has an effect on the mind even if you're not consciously thinking of the meaning all the time.

Q: *What should we do if we don't have a job?*
S: As regards work, the situation here is different from that in the West. In the West, people aren't usually worried about not working, at least from an economic point of view, because there is state support for the unemployed. But in India it's not like that. Here, if you haven't got a job, the government won't look after you. So here, if we're going to ask people to give up their jobs and work in a right livelihood business, we must be very sure that the business is going to be successful. This idea of cooperative businesses could potentially be developed even more in India than in England. Eventually we could start our own housing societies, not only with houses, but also with cottage industries, so that people living in the housing society have their work in the co-op. There would be a vihara too, so you would have a whole Buddhist village. This could be done in India if we plan it very carefully. I think we could also get money from the government. Unfortunately most of our friends don't have any business experience, so we do need a few people with business experience.

Q: *What do the strings of the* kesa *represent?*
S: The strings of the *kesa* represent an endless knot, as there is no actual end, but only a loop. The endless knot is explained in Tibetan Buddhism as being like a bodhisattva going from *saṃsāra* to Nirvāṇa, and then returning back to *saṃsāra*. There's no break, it's endless. So it represents wisdom and compassion. Through *prajñā* you leave *saṃsāra* and go to Nirvāṇa; through compassion you come back again into *saṃsāra*.

Q: *Should we read newspapers, and concern ourselves with politics?*
S: Newspapers are very discouraging sometimes. I read them to keep in touch with what's going on. In the past I wondered if there might be some way we could do something in the political field, but I came to the conclusion that you can only get into politics by sacrificing your Buddhist principles and joining a political party. In England you can't do anything politically just as an individual, even if you get into Parliament. I disagree with the two major parties and I don't feel happy with the smaller parties either, as they are all based on wrong principles. So it's impossible to do anything in the political field. The only way to do anything is through the Buddhist field. We get impatient sometimes, and we want to do something big, but it's quite difficult. Nowadays one of the most effective ways to get publicity is to do something violent, as everyone is interested in this: it's news. If you just do something good, no one is interested. Give a lecture on Buddhism, and it's not news; the papers aren't interested. My conclusion therefore is that the only thing to do is to work for the Dhamma, concentrate all our energy there. Dhamma work is very slow, and there are no big results quickly, but it's very sure – we know we're doing good. In politics you never know if you're doing good or evil, even if your intentions are good to start with. So if we're concerned about the state of the country or the world, the best thing to do is work for the Dhamma. If it's spread widely enough, the problems will be solved.

Q: *Does being a Buddhist mean giving up my caste?*
S: When you say that you belong to a particular caste, what does that mean? Does it mean simply that you were born into a certain family that is regarded as such-and-such caste by society as a whole? You can say, 'I am Buddhist, I don't believe in the caste system. But I was born into a certain community and according to society that's what I belong to. I've got to accept that, that's what society says.' You have to be clear in your own mind. I gave an example of this a few days ago. In order to get a passport, I have to fill in an application form, and give some proof that I was born in England, and that means that the government then regards me as being of English nationality. So yes, it's a fact that I was born in England, so in that sense I'm English. But I don't identify myself with being English, I just regard myself as a human being. So in the same way, if you were born into a Mahar family, from a social point of view you are Mahar; but actually

you don't believe in the caste system, you are Buddhist. Just be clear in your own mind about it. I show my English passport, but it doesn't mean that I think I'm English in a nationalistic way. In the same way you can say, 'Yes, I was born into a Mahar family, but it doesn't mean anything any more. If the government wants to know that, all right, let it know it.' From the government point of view, the conversion doesn't alter the fact of the original community. If the father is Mahar, even though he believes in Buddhism, the son is also Mahar. The main thing I want to emphasize is that you should be clear in your own thinking. You may be forced to recognize certain social realities, but in your own mind you must be clear that you do not accept this. We don't agree that it's good for the world to be divided into separate states, but if we want to travel from country to country, we have to accept that we will have to declare our nationality if we are to get a passport and a visa.

If you feel very strongly that you just want to say you're Buddhist, you don't want to say you're Mahar, you can do that, but certain consequences will follow which you will have to accept. Under the existing system you can't have it both ways. You have to decide, and in order to decide, you must first think clearly about the alternatives and the issues. If, even though you are a Buddhist, nonetheless you write 'Mahar', to give that information to the government, I will not say that you are wrong. I'm not advising you to do it, but I will not say you are wrong.

Q: *But shouldn't you just tell the truth?*
S: One of the points I'm making is that if, even though you're a Buddhist, you declare yourself as a Mahar, you are not telling a lie, because that is a fact of your social history, even though you don't accept the caste system. Twenty-five years ago, people were asking me these same questions. I never said that you should either do this or do that. If someone says, no, I will not write that I am a Mahar, I'm a Buddhist – that's fine. But if someone does write that he is Mahar, I am not saying he is wrong, even though he has declared himself a Buddhist.

Q: *What about getting community concessions?*
S: People must think clearly and make up their minds one way or the other. If they say they are Buddhist and they are not going to say they belong to a particular caste, that's good. I'm not saying that that is

wrong. But if someone says that they used to belong to a particular community, they were born into that community, and therefore they have a right to a certain concession, I'm not going to say that that is wrong, because it's a fact that they were born into that community even though they don't accept that particular social system. You see the distinction.

When I was in Delhi, in a conversation with some of the leading Buddhists there, I asked about the position of the Buddhist movement in Uttar Pradesh, Punjab, and other places, and I was told that it's not very good, not as good as Maharashtra, so I asked why. They told me that many people in these places were converted, and after they'd converted, they declared themselves as Buddhists – they did not say that they belonged to a particular community – so they didn't get any concessions. So for twenty-five years now they've not been getting those concessions, and because of that, Dhamma activities also are not going very well. By contrast, I was told, the Maharashtrians did things in their own way, so now they are flourishing. Whether this is the real explanation I cannot say, but this is what I was told.

Q: *Does becoming a Buddhist help you materially?*
S: In Marathwada, comparing it with the situation twenty-five years ago, I noticed that people were more prosperous. Formerly, when I gave lectures, many people came, not exactly in rags, but in very poor clothes. This time I hardly saw anything like that. Nearly everywhere, people were wearing quite good clothes. In many places, ladies were wearing new saris – we didn't see this twenty-five years ago. At the same time, I noticed that there is more interest in the Dhamma than before. These two things seem to go together, to some extent. If you're starving, you can't have much enthusiasm for the Dhamma. So we have to give some importance to material improvement. From that point of view it's very important and maybe even indispensable that these people get concessions and are therefore able to improve materially and in other ways as well.

Q: *Do I have to leave home to go for Refuge?*
S: I don't want to lay down a hard and fast rule that you're not really going for Refuge unless you leave your home: that would be saying too much. But if you go for Refuge, there must be some external change. That change may involve physically leaving home, or it may not, but

some external change must be there. In Buddhist countries there are many *bhikkhus*, but they haven't left home in any real sense, because the vihara has become a second home for them. So we have to be very clear about what leaving home really means. I would suggest that for Order members in India, one very good thing to help them leave home externally is to spend some time in another part of India. Even when you come on the *Dhamma-shibir*, that's a good experience, don't you feel? If Gujarati Order members come on *shibir* in Maharashtra, that's good, and if the Maharashtrian Order members go to Gujarat for *shibir*, that's good. It's a different cultural environment; things are not quite the same in the two states. If you get the opportunity to go to England for a few months, that will be very much a Going Forth.

To come back to the point that Bodhidhamma was making about Indian Order members leaving home, I think that's quite a good idea. Obviously they have to do it after their children are educated and married and after some arrangement is made for their wife. Then they can give all their time and energy to Dhamma work, especially if they're on a pension. Maybe they can go home and see their family just one night a week, but really they will have left home, because their hearts will be in the vihara, not in the house. People must do this only when they themselves feel really ready for it; there is no compulsion. But to come back to the original issue, if you really go for Refuge, there will be, sooner or later, whether quickly or slowly, some big change in your external life. Sometimes I ask the question – who is the *bhikkhu* and who is the householder? If you go, say, to Sri Lanka or Thailand, you might well find a *bhikkhu* who is a professor in the university and drawing a salary for his academic work. So who has left home and who has not? We mustn't be misled by appearances. If we see someone wearing a yellow robe, it doesn't necessarily mean that he has really left home. Some of our *bhikkhu* friends from Sri Lanka told me that when they became *bhikkhus*, they stayed in the vihara in their own village just a few doors away from their own house, and every day their mother would bring food for them. So have they really left home? It's just the same with the householder who is spending all his time teaching meditation. He isn't a *śrāmaṇera*, but actually he has left home. So we have to see the realities of things.

There are different levels of leaving home. You can't classify people into two mutually exclusive groups – these have left home, these haven't left home – it's not so simple as that. Some people are one-hundred-percent at home, some fifty-percent. Very few people have left home one-hundred-percent. In most people, however sincere, there's some little attachment to the home, to the family. I've known many *bhikkhus* who are so attached to their families that they even earn money for them or arrange the marriages of their nieces. So they haven't really left home. But the idea is to go for Refuge, to go forth with body, speech, and mind.

Q: *Do you think there's no need for* bhikkhus *any more?*
S: It's not that I think that *bhikkhus* in the real sense are out of date, but they must be *real bhikkhus*, and one doesn't often meet real *bhikkhus*. I would say that the *anagārikas* we have in our own Order are much more like the *bhikkhus* in the Buddha's day than are the present-day *bhikkhus* in Buddhist countries. If we use the word *bhikkhu*, it creates some confusion, but we've certainly got people who are living in the sort of way *bhikkhus* lived in the Buddha's time. It may be that it's confusing to use the word *bhikkhu*, because it has a different meaning nowadays. Nowadays most parts of the Buddhist world believe that if you've undergone a certain ceremony, you're a *bhikkhu*. But we want real *bhikkhus*.

Q: *What do the three coloured jewels of the* kesa *stand for?*
S: The yellow jewel stands for the Buddha – because yellow, or gold, is mainly associated with Enlightenment. Then the blue jewel is the Dhamma, because blue is associated with the sky. It is also associated with Truth, and the Dhamma is the Truth. And red is associated with Sangha because red is the colour of *mettā*, of love, and this should be the characteristic of the Sangha.

Q: *Can you explain the meaning of 'commitment'?*
S: It's not easy to understand this word commitment; it needs some explanation. Some time ago I started speaking in terms of committing yourself to the Buddha, Dhamma, and Sangha, instead of saying 'going for Refuge'. 'Going for Refuge' doesn't always have a very positive connotation. To some people it suggests running away, hiding yourself, as in the word 'refugee'. Committing yourself simply means giving yourself completely, wholeheartedly, seriously – holding fast to something, not giving up.

Q: *What is the difference between* maitrī *and* karuṇā?
S: Strictly speaking, according to Buddhist tradition, *maitrī* and *karuṇā* are really the same thing, the same emotion. *Maitrī* is more basic; it's the emotion you have to develop first, which is why it's the first of the four *brahma vihāras*. When *maitrī* contacts suffering people, the *maitrī* becomes *karuṇā*. So you can say that *karuṇā* is a further development of *maitrī* or *mettā*.

Q: *Can you explain the meaning of* brahma vihāra?
S: Buddhaghosa gives an explanation of this.[405] *Brahma* means 'high, noble, lofty' and *vihāra* means 'dwelling', so *brahma vihāra* refers to those dwelling in high, noble, lofty states of mind. *Brahma* in Pāli often has this sort of meaning. For example, *brahmadaṇḍa* has nothing to do with the god Brahmā. It means chief energy or chief punishment.

Q: *Can one translate* brāhmaṇa *as Brahmin?*
S: This raises the problem of translation. Sometimes you can make a literal translation, but sometimes you can bring out the real meaning better by means of a freer translation. The Buddha used many terms which were also being used by the people of his time, and Brahmin is one of these. He said the Brahmin is made by deeds, not by birth. For some time, people accepted this, but after a while they started believing again that one is a Brahmin by birth and not by deeds. It was made easier for them because the word Brahmin was still being used by Buddhism in a good sense. So the attempt to give a Buddhist meaning to non-Buddhist words was not very successful. I think therefore that in India we should probably not translate the word *brāhmaṇa* by 'Brahmin'. This can only create misunderstanding, because then Hindus can say that the Buddha isn't against Brahmanism. I think we should therefore use some other word when we translate '*brāhmaṇa*'. We could translate it as something like 'religious person', or 'sincere person'. If we use the word Brahmin, whatever meaning we give to the word as Buddhists, the Hindus are sure to give their own meaning to it.

It's similar with the word *Dharma*. Buddhists use the word in a completely different way from Hindus. That's why we use the Pāli word *Dhamma* instead of the Sanskrit *Dharma*, just to make some difference. It's difficult to avoid these misunderstandings. If you use completely different terms all the time, people won't know what you're talking about. In England many people don't like the word religion because it's associated with belief in God, so many English Buddhists prefer to use the word *Dharma*, which for them has only the Buddhist meaning and never the Hindu one. We have to be sensitive to people's reactions to words. To give another example, people in the West often don't like the idea of a Buddhist 'Bible', because of its Christian connotations; it's the equivalent of saying in India that we need a Buddhist *Veda*, or a Buddhist *Bhagavad Gītā*! We have to consider local conditions. People in India shouldn't be surprised if people in the West aren't so enthusiastic about *The Buddha and His Dhamma* by Dr Ambedkar. They may be put off because its numbered passages make it look like the Bible!

Q: *Couldn't we simply use the word* Dhamma *all the time?*
S: Using *Dhamma* instead of *Dharma* doesn't completely solve the problem, because all the Mahāyāna Sanskrit texts use the word *Dharma* in the Buddhist sense. When referring to Pāli texts, I use the word *Dhamma*, and I speak of *Dharma* when referring to Sanskrit texts. It might be a solution to make a new word or spelling. We could have D-H-A-R-M-M-A! – and we could use this for both scriptures. In England we could use this word instead of 'religion' and in India we could use it instead of '*Dharma*'. But it isn't so easy to introduce new words. For example, Mrs Rhys Davids tried to introduce the word 'Norm' to replace *Dharma*, but this hasn't been generally accepted.

Q: *Can one look forward to a time when one will be pure?*
S: Purification is a process, and a process takes place in time. Within time you can think 'Before, I was impure, but now I am pure.' But if you go out of time, as when you are Enlightened, or gain Nirvāṇa, in the state of Nirvāṇa you are pure, but there's no time. So you can't think, in that state, that 'before', you were impure. It's as if you were always pure. Not that you think that 'before, I was always pure'. There's no past, present, or future. You just experience your own purity, which has nothing to do with time.

Q: *The mantra* oṃ *has Hindu associations for me. Can you suggest an alternative?*
S: If you find that when you repeat *oṃ* all sorts of Hindu associations come up, it's better to drop it. If you like you can say *namo buddhāya*,

then repeat the mantra, or you can just repeat the mantra without the *oṃ*, though that may affect the rhythm. Maybe to complete the rhythm you need to put something like *namo buddhāya* before the mantra. If you can't get on with the *oṃ*, and if you want to chant the mantra of the Buddha, you can chant *namo tassa bhagavato arahato sammāsambuddhassa*, because this has no Hindu associations at all.

Q: *By mokṣa, do Hindus understand the same thing as Nirvāṇa?*
S: All Hindus don't understand the word *mokṣa* in the same way – there is no one Hindu meaning. Therefore when we use words like Nirvāṇa, which are also used by Hindus, we must add some explanation. If we use the word *mokṣa*, for instance, we can add 'freedom from all past conditioning'. This makes it clear in what sense we are using that word. If we can't include the explanation in the text of a book, we must put a footnote giving the explanation.

Q: *Does the Order in India have any shortcomings?*
S: I can't see any shortcomings that are special to the Order here and not elsewhere. There are some shortcomings in the Order everywhere. Even so, it's better than anything else we have in the Buddhist world. More Order members in India need to take more initiative and responsibility – this is one thing I have noticed. Obviously the full-timers will have more time, but nonetheless all have equal responsibility, and all must think how to improve the Movement, how to start up new activities and so on. Otherwise you fall back into the system of *bhikkhus* and *upāsakas* in the old sense. In England, I don't spend all my time telling people what to do – they get on with it by themselves, unless it's something very important.

Q: *Shall we proceed to use the word* Dhammachari?
S: If you all decide to use the word Dhammachari, I have no objection. I think it's a good idea, but people should be happy with it. The *dasa sīla upāsaka* ordination remains the same, but the title can be changed from *upāsaka* to Dhammachari.

Appendix
DR AMBEDKAR'S TWENTY-TWO CONVERSION VOWS

1. I shall not consider Brahma, Vishnu, and Mahesh as gods, nor shall I worship them.
2. I shall not consider Rama and Krishna as gods, nor shall I worship them.
3. I shall not believe in 'Gauri', Ganapati, and any other gods and goddesses of Hinduism, nor shall I worship them.
4. I do not believe that god has incarnated.
5. I do not and shall not believe that Lord Buddha was the incarnation of Vishnu. I believe this to be sheer madness and false propaganda.
6. I shall not perform 'shraddha' nor shall I give 'pind-dan'.
7. I shall not act in a manner violating the principles and teachings of the Buddha.
8. I shall not get Brahmins to perform any ceremonies.
9. I believe that all human beings are equal.
10. I shall endeavour to establish equality.
11. I shall live according to the Noble Eightfold Path taught by the Buddha.
12. I shall practise the Ten Paramitas taught by the Buddha.
13. I shall be compassionate towards all living beings and nourish and protect them.
14. I shall not steal.
15. I shall not tell lies.

16. I shall not commit sexual misconduct.
17. I shall not drink alcohol.
18. I shall lead my life bringing together the three Buddhist principles of wisdom, morality, and compassion.
19. I renounce Hinduism, which is detrimental to the fulfilment of human beings, and which considers human beings as unequal and degraded, and I embrace the Buddha Dhamma.
20. I firmly believe the Dhamma of the Buddha is the *saddhamma*.
21. I believe that I am taking a new birth.
22. Thus I vow to lead my life according to the Buddha's teachings.

Translated from Marathi by
Mangesh Dahiwale and Dhammachari Lokamitra

GLOSSARY

anagārika

Lit. 'not having a house or home'. In the Triratna Buddhist Order this denotes one who has taken a vow of celibacy and is committed to a life without a career and with minimum possessions. *Anagārikas* wear a golden rather than a white *kesa*, giving public recognition to the vow taken. (The golden *kesa* does not indicate a 'higher' ordination.) Lokamitra was an *anagārika* during the early years of his work in India.

ānāpānasati

The mindfulness (*sati*) of inhalation and exhalation (*ānāpāna*), in other words the Mindfulness of Breathing meditation practice. See p. 203 and p. 375. It is explained by the Buddha in the *Majjhima Nikāya, sutta* 118, and is the basis for one of the two main meditation practices taught at all Triratna centres (the other being the *mettā bhāvanā* or development of loving-kindness).

bhikkhu (m.), *bhikkhunī* (f.) (Pāli); *bhikṣu* (m.), *bhikṣunī* (f.) (Sanskrit)

Lit. 'one who begs for almsfood'. In the Buddha's day it was the term used to refer to all those followers of the Buddha who had 'gone forth from the home life into homelessness' and joined the mendicant *saṅgha*, following the Vinaya or disciplinary rules laid down by the Buddha. In the course of time the wanderers became settled monastics, which is what they are today, but they have continued to follow the Vinaya in various recensions. In general the Pāli form is used to refer to followers of the Theravāda tradition, whereas *bhikṣu* or *bhikṣunī* refers to those ordained within the Mahāyāna traditions.

Buddhayan

The Marathi quarterly journal of TBMSG in which many of the talks included in this volume were first published.

caste *dharma*

According to Hindu belief, everyone is born into a particular caste that requires them to take up certain duties of work or '*dharma*'. This can be anything from the priestly duties of the Brahmin to the 'work' of being a thief. Since you are born into a caste, you cannot avoid or change your caste *dharma*. In Buddhism, *dharma* has a very different meaning, see below.

dalit

Sometimes used as an alternative to 'untouchable' (and to 'Harijan' or 'Children of God' – the term adopted by Gandhi). It means 'oppressed' and was probably first used by Jyotirao Phooley in the nineteenth century. Though Untouchability was made illegal in India through article 17 of the constitution – a constitution drafted by Dr Ambedkar and adopted by India's Constituent Assembly in 1949 – the practice continues in the attitudes of many caste Hindus, particularly in rural areas. Naturally no one wishes to be reminded that they have been or may still be considered 'untouchable' and different terms have been adopted by people from these communities. For example, some people continue to use the term 'scheduled caste' coined by the Government of India in 1936, a term also used by Ambedkar. Though 'dalit' has been quite widely used, not all Buddhists favour the term. As Buddhists practising the Buddha's Dhamma they no longer wish to see themselves as oppressed.

dasa sīla

Daśa (Sanskrit) means 'ten' and '*śīla*' here means ethical precept. The ten precepts are equivalent to the ten *kusala-dhammas* (see below).

dasa sīla upāsaka

Lit. an *upasāka* (layman) who practises the ten precepts. In the early years this was the designation of someone ordained within the Western Buddhist Order or Trailokya Bauddha Mahasangha (later the Triratna Buddhist Order). The nomenclature was soon to change to make it clear that the new Buddhist order that Sangharakshita had founded was based on the principle that commitment is primary and lifestyle secondary, though not unimportant. Order members were not lay practitioners, even though most were not living a monastic life, so they became known as Dhammacharis and Dhammacharinis. See 'Notes from the Editors', p. 165.

dhammachari (m.); dhammacharini (f.)

Lit. 'one who fares in the Dhamma', the title of a member of the Triratna Buddhist Order (see 'Notes from the Editors', p. 165). The Pāli *dhammacāri* or *dhammacārinī* is preferred in India to avoid misunderstandings associated with the Hindu '*dharma*' (see below), whereas in the rest of the world the Sanskrit forms *dharmacāri* and *dharmacārinī* are generally used.

Dhammadiksha

Dīkṣā is a Sanskrit word meaning a religious ceremony, used in the

Buddhist world to mean commitment to the Three Jewels. Dr Ambedkar's *Dhammadiksha* took place on 14 October 1956 in Nagpur when he 'took' the Three Refuges and Five Precepts from U Chandramani, and recited twenty-two vows that he had formulated himself. This was followed by the *Dhammadiksha* of hundreds of thousands of his followers. In this case one might translate the term as 'conversion'. '*Dīkṣā*' is also used in the Triratna movement in India to mean ordination within the Triratna Buddhist Order.

Dhammamitra
This is explained in Lecture 14, p. 308. '*Mitra*' means 'friend'. In India the term 'Dhamma' is added to make the Buddhist association clear. At the time the talks in this volume were given, there were four criteria that had to be fulfilled in order to become a Mitra of the FWBO/ TBMSG. Today (2016) there are three guidelines that someone who wishes to become a Mitra should follow: they should consider themselves to be a Buddhist, should be practising the five precepts, and should consider Triratna to be their spiritual home. Becoming a Mitra is marked by a simple but significant ceremony that usually takes place during a sevenfold puja, often on a festival day, in which those becoming Mitras make the traditional threefold offering of flower, candle, and incense, and recite the five precepts before a shrine.

Dhammasahayak
Sahāyak means 'helper' and *Dhammasahayak* indicates anyone

involved with the Triratna movement (sometimes called a Friend in the West).

Dhamma-shibir
Shibir literally means a camp. A *Dhamma-shibir* is a retreat. Sangharakshita often exhorted his audience to go on retreat for the spiritual benefits of the experience – see for example Lecture 21, p. 377.

dharma
In Hindu India this is taken to refer to caste *dharma* (see above). In Buddhism the word has many meanings, a chief one being the teaching of the Buddha. In Buddhist India, to avoid the confusion with caste *dharma*, the Buddha's teaching is usually referred to using the Pāli word *Dhamma*.

dīkṣā
See *Dhammadiksha*.

FWBO
The Friends of the Western Buddhist Order is the original name of the Triratna Buddhist Community, founded by Sangharakshita on 6 April 1967 (see *Moving Against the Stream*, at the end of chapter 53 (*Complete Works*, vol. 23). In India the Movement was known as Trailokya Bauddha Mahasangha Sahayak Gana (TBMSG). See 'Notes from the Editors', p. 165.

kalyaṇā mitratā
Spiritual friendship, one of the 'six distinctive emphases' of the Triratna tradition. Sangharakshita has drawn particular attention to the Buddha's

teaching that '*kalyaṇā mitratā* is the whole of the spiritual life',[406] pointing out the spiritual benefits of *kalyaṇā mitratā* both in its horizontal form (i.e. between peers) and in its vertical form (friendship with those more or less experienced than oneself). See *What is the Sangha?* (*Complete Works*, vol. 3.)

kesa
Members of the Triratna Buddhist Order (Triratna Bauddha Sangha) wear a *kesa* on religious or public occasions. It is a strip of white cloth worn around the neck on which are emblazoned the Three Jewels.

kusala dhamma
Kusala (Pāli) means 'clever, skilful, or expert in the sense of knowing how to act in a way that is beneficial … securing, both for oneself and others, the best possible results in terms of happiness, knowledge, and freedom.' *Dhamma* may be rendered here 'item of training'. More specifically it refers to the basic principles of ethics. See Sangharakshita, *The Ten Pillars of Buddhism*, part 1, especially section 4, 'The Ten Precepts as Principles of Ethics' (*Complete Works*, vol. 2.) The ten *kusala dhammas* are synonymous with the *dasa sīla* (see above).

lakh
A unit of 100,000 in the Indian numbering system.

mettā; mettā bhāvanā
Mettā (Pāli) or *maitrī* (Sanskrit) means loving-kindness. The Buddha is recorded as extolling the virtues of loving-kindness in different places e.g. in the *Karaniya Mettā Sutta* of the *Sutta Nipāta* where he shows how *mettā* developed to its fullest extent is equivalent to Enlightenment itself. The *mettā bhāvanā* meditation is one of the two main meditation practices taught at all Triratna centres. Its form is based on that explained by Buddhaghosa in his *Visuddhimagga*. See Lectures 21, p. 375 and 33, p. 494.

Mindfulness of Breathing
See *ānāpānasati* above.

Mitra
See *Dhammamitra*.

pañcasīla
Pañca means 'five' and *sīla* (Pāli) is 'item of training' or precept. The five precepts are universally recognized in the Buddhist world as constituting basic ethical practice. One who takes up the practice of the *pañcasīla* undertakes to abstain from harming life, taking the not-given, sexual misconduct, false speech, and taking intoxicants; and to practise actions that express loving-kindness, generosity, contentment, truthfulness, and mindfulness. See Lecture 5, p. 215.

parivrājaka
A wanderer, one who has gone forth from the household life. In the time of the Buddha there were many such mendicants. By extension it can mean one who has experienced a fundamental change in life, or conversion. See Lecture 3, p. 191.

pratijñā
This is a Sanskrit word meaning 'vow' or 'promise'. Here it refers to the twenty-two vows Dr Ambedkar devised and recited immediately after his conversion to Buddhism, which he then administered to his followers as part of their conversion. (See p. 129 and appendix p. 541) They remain an important part of the conversion ceremony for Buddhists in India from a Hindu background.

sāmaṇera (Pāli); *śrāmaṇera* (Sanskrit)
Sāmaṇa means a renunciant. At the time of the Buddha there were many homeless wanderers known as *sāmaṇas*. The lower monastic Buddhist ordination became known as *sāmaṇera* ordination which is followed some time later by a higher or *bhikkhu* ordination. Sangharakshita describes his own *sāmaṇera* ordination (which took place at Kusinara in 1949) in *The Rainbow Road*, chapter 49 (*Complete Works*, vol. 20.); and his higher or *bhikkhu* ordination (which took place at Sarnath in 1950), in *Facing Mount Kanchenjunga* chapter 6 (*Complete Works*, vol. 21).

TBM
Trailokya Bauddha Mahasangha – the Indian wing of the Western Buddhist Order, now known as Triratna Bauddha Sangha (see 'Notes from the Editors', p. 165).

TBMSG
Trailokya Bauddha Mahasangha Sahayak Gana – the Indian wing of the Friends of the Western Buddhist Order/Triratna Buddhist Community – now known as Triratna Bauddha Mahasangha (see 'Notes from the Editors', p. 165)

tisaraṇa (Pāli); *triśaraṇa* (Sanskrit)
The Three Refuges: Buddha, Dhamma, and Sangha, which are to Buddhists the highest of all values.

Triratna Grantha Mala
The publishing house of TBMSG / Triratna which published a number of the talks in this volume.

upāsaka (m.) upāsikā (f.)
A term used to refer to householder followers of the Buddha (as distinct from bhikkhus and bhikkhunīs or monastic followers). In the context of these talks *dasa sīla upāsaka* indicates members of the Order (see above).

NOTES

FOREWORD

1 In Dr Ambedkar's speech
'What Path Salvation' delivered
to the Mahar conference
in Bombay, May 1936, see
Bhagwan Das (ed.), *Thus Spoke
Ambedkar*, vol. iv, Ambedkar
Sahithya Prakashana,
Bangalore c.1980, p. 60.

2 Dr B. R. Ambedkar: speech
on All-India Radio, 3 October
1954.

3 See p. 21.

4 He is reported to have
said that there were only
two *bhikṣus* his followers
should trust: Bhantes
Anand Kausalyayan and
Sangharakshita.

5 Available for free download
from www.sangharakshita.org/
online_books.html.

6 Lecture 27 below, p. 431.

AMBEDKAR AND BUDDHISM

7 Edward Carpenter (1844–1929),
Towards Democracy, GMP
Publishers, London 1985, p. 219.

CHAPTER I

8 B. R. Ambedkar, *The Evolution
of Provincial Finance in British
India: A Study in the Provincial
Decentralization of Imperial*
Finance, P. S. King, London
1925.

9 Dr Babasaheb Ambedkar,
Writings and Speeches, vol. i,
Education Department,
Government of Maharashtra,
Bombay 1979, pp. 3–22.

10 B. R. Ambedkar, *The Problem
of the Rupee: Its Origin*

and its Solution, P. S. King, London 1923.

11 Dhananjay Keer, *Dr Ambedkar: Life and Mission*, third edition, Popular Prakashan, Bombay 1971, p. 201.

12 380,000 was Ambedkar's own figure, as given in his letter to Devapriya Valisinha dated 30 October 1956 and published in the May 1957 edition of the *Maha Bodhi*, vol. 65, Maha Bodhi Society, Calcutta, p. 226.

13 'Buddha or Karl Marx' in *Dr Babsaheb Ambedkar, Writings and Speeches*, vol. iii, Education Department, Government of Maharashtra, Bombay 1987, pp. 441–62.

CHAPTER 2

14 Sangharakshita writes about this period of his life in his first volume of memoirs, *The Rainbow Road*, Windhorse Publications, Birmingham 1997 (*Complete Works*, vol. 20).

15 Sangharakshita, *Anagarika Dharmapala: A Biographical Sketch and Other Maha Bodhi Writings*, Ibis Publications, Ledbury 2013 (*Complete Works*, vol. 8).

16 These events are recorded in Sangharakshita, *Facing Mount Kanchenjunga*, Windhorse Publications, Glasgow 1991, chs. 18–20 (*Complete Works*, vol. 21).

17 For a brief history of the Maha Bodhi Society and how it came to have Brahmins running its affairs, see Sangharakshita, *Beating the Drum*, Ibis Publications, Birmingham 2012, Introduction (especially pp. 62–5) (*Complete Works*, vol. 8).

18 This first meeting with Ambedkar is also recorded in Sangharakshita, *Facing Mount Kanchenjunga*, Windhorse Publications, Glasgow 1991, pp. 449–51 (*Complete Works*, vol. 21). See also Sangharakshita, *In the Sign of the Golden Wheel*, Windhorse Publications, Birmingham 1996, pp. 59–60 & 272 (*Complete Works*, vol. 22).

19 Sangharakshita returned to Siddharth College in 1982 to give a talk on *Buddhism and Education*; see p. 435 et. seq.

20 This second meeting with Ambedkar is also recorded in *In the Sign of the Golden Wheel*, Windhorse Publications, Birmingham 1996, pp. 273–5 (*Complete Works*, vol. 22).

21 Sangharakshita returned to Worli to give talks there in both 1982 (see p. 260 et. seq.) and 1983.

22 This third meeting is also recorded in *In the Sign of the Golden Wheel*, Windhorse Publications, Birmingham 1996, p. 331 (*Complete Works*, vol. 22).

CHAPTER 3

23 See Book 3, Champai 36
    in A. G. Atkins (ed.), *The
    Ramayana of Tulsidas*,
    vol. ii, Birla Academy of
    Art and Culture, Calcutta
    1966, p. 573 (alternative
    translation).

24 B. R. Ambedkar, *Annihilation
    of Caste*, Bheem Patrika
    Publications, Jalandhar 1982,
    p. 83. Also Dr Babasaheb
    Ambedkar, *Writings and
    Speeches*, vol. i, Education
    Department, Government of
    Maharashtra, Bombay 1979,
    p. 52.

25 Quoted in Dhananjay Keer,
    *Mahatma Jotirao Phooley:
    Father of the Indian Social
    Revolution*, second edition,
    Popular Prakashan, Bombay
    1974, p. 115.

26 Dr B. R. Ambedkar, *The
    Untouchables*, Bharatiya
    Buddha Shiksa Parishad,
    Balrampur 1977, third edition,
    p. 27. Also Dr Babasaheb
    Ambedkar, *Writings and
    Speeches*, vol. vii, Education
    Department, Government of
    Maharashtra, Bombay 1990,
    p. 266.

27 Quoted in B. R. Ambedkar,
    Who Were the Shudras?
    Thacker & Co. Ltd., Bombay
    1946, reprinted 1970,
    pp. 38–9. Also Dr Babasaheb
    Ambedkar, *Writings and
    Speeches*, vol. vii, ibid., p. 49.

28 Valmiki, *Ramayana*, book 7
    (*Uttarakanda*), sargas 73–6.

29 B. R. Ambedkar, *Annihilation
    of Caste*, Bheem Patrika

Publications, Jalandhar 1982,
p. 93. Also Dr Babasaheb
Ambedkar, *Writings and
Speeches*, vol. i, Education
Department, Government of
Maharashtra, Bombay 1979,
p. 57.

30 This is the nineteenth of the
    twenty-two *pratijñās* or vows
    composed by Ambedkar (see
    Appendix, p. 541).

31 Dr B. R. Ambedkar, *The
    Untouchables*, third edition,
    Bharatiya Buddha Shiksa
    Parishad, Balrampur 1977,
    p. 26. Also Dr Babasaheb
    Ambedkar, *Writings and
    Speeches*, vol. vii, Education
    Department, Government of
    Maharashtra, Bombay 1990,
    p. 265.

32 Dhananjay Keer, *Mahatma
    Jotirao Phooley: Father of
    the Indian Social Revolution*,
    second edition, Popular
    Prakashan, Bombay 1974,
    p. 41.

33 Bhagwan Das (ed.), *Thus
    Spoke Ambedkar*, vol. iv,
    Ambedkar Memorial
    Society, Bangalore n. d.,
    pp. 67–8. These incidents
    are also described in B. R.
    Ambedkar, *Waiting for a
    Visa, Reminiscences*, Siddarth
    Publication, Bombay 1990,
    and Dr Babasaheb Ambedkar,
    Writings and Speeches,
    Education Department.,
    Government of Maharashtra,
    Bombay 1993, vol. xii,
    pp. 666–70.

34 Bhagwan Das (ed.), *Thus
    Spoke Ambedkar*, vol. iv,

Ambedkar Memorial Society, Bangalore n. d., p. 69.

CHAPTER 4

35 Dr Babasaheb Ambedkar, *Writings and Speeches,* vol. i, Education Department, Government of Maharashtra, Bombay 1979, p. 485.
36 Ibid., p. 487.
37 Ibid.
38 Dhananjay Keer, *Dr Ambedkar: Life and Mission,* third edition, Popular Prakashan, Bombay 1971, p. 100.
39 Ibid., p. 106.
40 Ibid., p. 71.
41 Sangharakshita, *The Ten Pillars of Buddhism,* fourth edition, Windhorse Publications, Birmingham 1996, p. 34 (*Complete Works,* vol. 2).
42 Referred in Dhananjay Keer, *Dr Ambedkar: Life and Mission,* third edition, Popular Prakashan, Bombay 1971, p. 253.
43 Ibid., p. 255.
44 Bhagwan Das (ed.), *Thus Spoke Ambedkar,* vol. iv, Ambedkar Memorial Society, Bangalore n. d., p. 257, quoting the *Times of India,* June 1935.
45 Ibid., p. 110.
46 Ibid., p. 111.
47 Ibid., pp. 112–13.
48 Ibid., p. 113.
49 Ibid., p. 111, quoting the *Times of India,* 17 January 1935.
50 Ibid., pp. 71–2.

51 T. W. and C. A. F. Rhys Davids (trans.), *Dialogues of the Buddha,* part 2 (*Dīgha Nikāya* ii.100), fifth edition, Pali Text Society, London 1966, pp. 107–8.
52 Bhagwan Das (ed.), *Thus Spoke Ambedkar,* vol. iv, Ambedkar Memorial Society, Bangalore n. d., p. 65.
53 During his 1981–2 tour, Sangharakshita gave a lecture to the students of Siddharth College on 'Buddhism and Education'; see p. 435.
54 Bhagwan Das (ed.), *Rare Prefaces Written by Dr Baba Saheb B. R. Ambedkar,* Bheem Patrika Publications, Jullundur 1980, p. 20.
55 D. C. Ahir (ed.), *Dr Ambedkar on Buddhism,* Siddharth Publications, Bombay 1982, p. 97.
56 B. G. Kunte (comp.), *Source Material on Dr Baba Saheb Ambedkar and the Movement of Untouchables,* vol. i, Education Department, Government of Maharashtra, Bombay 1982, p. 366.
57 Ibid., p. 368.
58 B. R. Ambedkar, *Buddha and the Future of His Religion,* third edition, Bheem Patrika Publications, Jullundur 1980, p. 12; also in Dr Babasaheb Ambedkar, *Writings and Speeches,* vol. xvii (part 2), Education Department, Government of Maharashtra, Bombay 2003, p.105; available at www.mea.gov.in/images/attach/amb/

volume_17_02.pdf (April 2016).

When checking quotations from Dr Ambedkar's works during the preparation of 'Ambedkar and Buddhism' for publication, we have generally used the version given in the *Writings and Speeches* where the two versions differed. This occurred most notably with the terms *bhikkhu* and *bhikshu*. Since at the time of going to press we were unable to find a printed copy of volume 17 (part 2) of the *Writings and Speeches*, we have had to rely on the very useful PDF version available on the internet. We have also supplied the page reference of the small pamphlet which was Sangharakshita's own source for this essay.

59 B. G. Kunte (comp.), *Source Material on Dr Baba Saheb Ambedkar and the Movement of Untouchables*, vol. i, Education Department, Government of Maharashtra, Bombay 1982, p. 372.

60 Ibid., p. 372.

61 Ibid., p. 374.

62 D. C. Ahir (ed.), *Dr Ambedkar on Buddhism*, Siddharth Publications, Bombay 1982, pp. 14–15.

63 The theory of the division of society into four classes: Brahmins (priests), Kshatriyas (warriors), Vaishyas (traders), and Shudras (menials).

64 D. C. Ahir (ed.), *Dr Ambedkar on Buddhism*, Siddharth Publications, Bombay 1982, p. 73.

65 B. G. Kunte (comp.), *Source Material on Dr Baba Saheb Ambedkar and the Movement of Untouchables*, vol. i, Education Department, Government of Maharashtra, Bombay 1982, p. 406.

66 The Lok Sabha (House of the People) is the lower house in the Indian Parliament with over 500 members elected by universal suffrage. The Rajya Sabha (Council of States) is the upper house whose members are elected by state legislative assemblies.

67 Dhananjay Keer, *Dr Ambedkar: Life and Mission*, third edition, Popular Prakashan, Bombay 1971, p. 459.

68 D. C. Ahir, *The Legacy of Dr Ambedkar (Bharat Ratna)*, B. R. Publishing Corporation, Delhi 1990, p. 156.

69 D. C. Ahir, *Dr Ambedkar on Buddhism*, Siddharth Publications, Bombay 1982, p. 17.

70 Ibid., p. 55.

71 Dhananjay Keer, *Dr Ambedkar: Life and Mission*, third edition, Popular Prakashan, Bombay 1971, p. 496.

72 See Appendix, p. 541.

CHAPTER 5

73 B. G. Kunte (comp.), *Source Material on Dr Baba Saheb Ambedkar and the Movement*

of Untouchables, vol. i,
Education Department,
Government of Maharashtra,
Bombay 1982, p. 171.

74 Ibid., p. 212.

75 'Who Were the Shudras?' in
Dr Babasaheb Ambedkar,
Writings and Speeches, vol. vii,
Education Department,
Government of Maharashtra,
Bombay 1990, p. 9.

76 Ibid., p. 12.

77 Sangharakshita notes:
'Curiously enough, in the
Hindu law books a Shudra is
termed a graveyard.'

78 'The Untouchables' in
Dr Babasaheb Ambedkar,
Writings and Speeches,
vol. vii, Education
Department, Government of
Maharashtra, Bombay 1990,
p. 243.

79 Ibid., p. 244.

80 Ibid., p. 280.

81 Frederic Seebohm, *The Tribal
System in Wales*, Longmans,
Green & Co., London 1895.

82 'The Untouchables' in
Dr Babasaheb Ambedkar,
Writings and Speeches,
vol. vii, Education
Department, Government of
Maharashtra, Bombay 1990,
p. 317.

83 Ibid., p. 320.

84 Ibid., pp. 346–7.

85 Ibid., p. 355.

86 Ibid., p. 379.

CHAPTER 6

87 Bhimrao Ambedkar,
*Buddha and the Future
of His Religion*, third

edition, Bheem Patrika
Publications, Jullundur 1980,
p. 3, and 'Buddha and the
Future of His Religion', in
Dr Babasaheb Ambedkar,
Writings and Speeches,
vol. xvii (part 2), Education
Department, Government of
Maharashtra, Bombay 2003,
p. 97.

88 Ibid., pp. 3–4 / p. 97.

89 Ibid., p. 4 / p. 97.

90 Ibid.

91 T. W. and C. A. F. Rhys
Davids (trans.), *Dialogues of
the Buddha*, part 2 (*Dīgha
Nikāya* ii.154), fourth
edition, London 1959, p. 171.

92 T. W. Rhys Davids (trans.),
*The Questions of King
Milinda*, Sacred Books of
the East, vol. 35, Motilal
Banarsidass, Delhi 1988,
p. 202.

93 Bhimrao Ambedkar,
*Buddha and the Future
of His Religion*, third
edition, Bheem Patrika
Publications, Jullundur 1980,
p. 4, and 'Buddha and the
Future of His Religion', in
Dr Babasaheb Ambedkar,
Writings and Speeches,
vol. xvii (part 2), Education
Department, Government of
Maharashtra, Bombay 2003,
p. 98.

94 Ibid.

95 Ibid., p. 5 / p. 98.

96 Ibid.

97 Ibid., p. 5 / p. 99.

98 Ibid., pp. 5–6 / p. 99.

99 Ibid., p. 6 / p. 99.

100 Ibid., p. 7 / p. 100.

101 Ibid.
102 'Annihilation of Caste', in Dr Babasaheb Ambedkar, *Writings and Speeches,* vol. i, Education Department, Government of Maharashtra, Bombay 1979, p. 58.
103 Bhimrao Ambedkar, *Buddha and the Future of His Religion*, third edition, Bheem Patrika Publications, Jullundur 1980, p. 6, and 'Buddha and the Future of His Religion', in Dr Babasaheb Ambedkar, *Writings and Speeches*, vol. xvii (part 2), Education Department, Government of Maharashtra, Bombay 2003, p. 99.
104 Ibid., p. 7 / p. 100.
105 Ibid., p. 8 / p. 101.
106 Ibid., p. 10 / p. 103.
107 Ibid., p. 11 / p. 103.
108 Ibid.
109 Ibid., p. 11 / p. 104.
110 Ibid., p. 12 / p. 104.
111 Ibid.
112 Ibid.
113 Dr Babasaheb Ambedkar, *Writings and Speeches,* vol. i, Education Department, Government of Maharashtra, Bombay 1979, p. 57.
114 Ibid., p. 57.
115 Bhimrao Ambedkar, *Buddha and the Future of His Religion*, third edition, Bheem Patrika Publications, Jullundur 1980, p. 12, and 'Buddha and the Future of His Religion', in Dr Babasaheb Ambedkar, *Writings and Speeches*, vol. xvii (part 2), Education Department, Government of Maharashtra, Bombay 2003, p. 104.
116 Ibid.
117 Ibid.
118 Ibid., p. 13 / p. 105.
119 Ibid.
120 Ibid.
121 Ibid.
122 Ibid.
123 Ibid.
124 Ibid.
125 Ibid.
126 Ibid., p. 14 / p. 106.
127 Ibid.
128 Ibid., p. 15 / p. 106.
129 Ibid.
130 Ibid., p. 15 / p. 107.
131 From Francis Bacon's essay, 'Of Marriage and Single Life' (1612).
132 Bhimrao Ambedkar, *Buddha and the Future of His Religion*, third edition, Bheem Patrika Publications, Jullundur 1980, p. 15, and 'Buddha and the Future of His Religion', in Dr Babasaheb Ambedkar, *Writings and Speeches*, vol. xvii (part 2), Education Department, Government of Maharashtra, Bombay 2003, p. 107.
133 Ibid.
134 Ibid.
135 James Hastings (ed.), *Encyclopaedia of Religion and Ethics*, T. & T. Clark, Edinburgh 1914, vol. vii, p. 501b.
136 Ibid., p. 502a.

137 Bhimrao Ambedkar,
*Buddha and the Future of
His Religion*, third edition,
Bheem Patrika Publications,
Jullundur 1980, p. 15–16,
and 'Buddha and the
Future of His Religion', in
Dr Babasaheb Ambedkar,
Writings and Speeches,
vol. xvii (part 2), Education
Department, Government of
Maharashtra, Bombay 2003,
p. 107.
138 Ibid., p. 16 / p. 107.
139 Ibid.
140 Ibid.
141 Ibid., p. 16 / p. 108.
142 Ibid.

CHAPTER 7
143 Bhagwan Das (ed.), *Thus
Spoke Ambedkar* vol. ii,
Bheem Patrika Publications,
Jullundur n. d., pp. 141–2.
144 Dhananjay Keer,
*Dr Ambedkar: Life and
Mission*, third edition,
Popular Prakashan, Bombay
1971, p. 498.
145 Ibid.
146 *Chinthes* are mythical,
lion-like creatures, set as
guardians at the entrance to
Burmese temples.
147 Bhagwan Das (ed.), *Thus
Spoke Ambedkar*, vol. iv,
Ambedkar Memorial Society,
Bangalore n. d., pp. 272–4.
148 Bhagwan Das (ed.), *Thus
Spoke Ambedkar*, vol. ii,
Bheem Patrika Publications,
Jullundur n. d., p. 147.
149 Ibid., p. 148.
150 Ibid., p. 150.

CHAPTER 8
151 Bhagwan Das (ed.), *Rare
Prefaces Written by
Dr Ambedkar*, Bheem Patrika
Publications, Jullundur 1980,
pp. 28–9.
152 Ibid., p. 29.
153 B. R. Ambedkar, *The Buddha
and His Dhamma*, People's
Education Society, Bombay
1991, p. 80.
154 Ibid.
155 Ibid., p. xlii.
156 Ibid., p. 91.
157 Ibid., p. 80.
158 Ibid., p. 159.
159 Ibid., p. 232.
160 Ibid., p. 231.
161 Ibid.
162 Ibid.
163 Ibid.
164 Ibid., p. 234.
165 Ibid., p. 309.
166 Ibid., p. 310.
167 Ibid., p. 401.
168 Ibid., p. 331.
169 Ibid., p. 319.
170 Ibid., p. 330.
171 Ibid., p. 328.
172 Ibid., p. 425.

CHAPTER 9
173 Shri Sankarananda Shastri,
'A Report on the Conversion
Movement' in the April 1957
edition of the *Maha Bodhi*,
Maha Bodhi Society, Calcutta,
vol. 65, pp. 128–30.
174 S. N. Shastri, 'Revival of
Buddhism in India' in the
March–April 1959 edition
of the *Maha Bodhi*, vol. 67,
Maha Bodhi Society,
Calcutta, p. 67.

LECTURE TOUR IN INDIA
December 1981–March 1982

NOTES FROM THE EDITORS
175   No.10: *Dr Ambedkar's
       Dhamma Revolution*
       (October 1982); no. 11:
       *Religion and the Secular
       State* (January 1983); no. 12:
       Going for Refuge (also
       published by Windhorse
       Publications in 1986);
       no. 14: *Questions and
       Answers at Milind College*
       (October 1983); no. 17: *My
       Life and Mission and the
       Teaching of Dr Ambedkar*
       (July 1984); no. 22:
       Buddhism and Education
       (October 1985); no. 23:
       *Dr Ambedkar's True
       Greatness* (n.d.).
176   Terry Pilchick, *Jai Bhim!
       Dispatches from a Peaceful
       Revolution*, Windhorse
       Publications, Glasgow 1988.

CHAPTER 1
177   The Ambedkar Housing
       Society was established in
       Pune by Buddhists. The
       first TBMSG centre was
       located in a building there.
       Naturally it was here that
       Sangharakshita's tour began.
178   Sudarshan, one of the first
       Indian Order members, was
       ordained in June 1979. For
       some years he was Indian
       Order Convenor. He died in
       2009.

179   Sangharakshita first visited
       the newly-founded TBMSG in
       1979 when he gave a number
       of talks and performed the
       first TBM ordinations in India.
180   Lokamitra arrived in India
       from the UK in 1978 and
       began working there to
       establish the TBMSG. It was
       he who organized the entire
       1981–2 tour.
181   6 December 1981.
182   Paraphrase of 'The Song of
       Good Companions' in Karma
       C. C. Chang (trans.), *The
       Hundred Thousand Songs
       of Milarepa*, Shambhala
       Publications, Boston 1999,
       pp. 653–4.
183   'Buddha and the Future of
       His Religion' in Dr Babasaheb
       Ambedkar, *Writings and
       Speeches*, vol. xvii (part
       2), Education Department,
       Government of Maharashtra
       2003, pp. 97–108.
184   Ibid., p. 103.
185   See 'Notes from the Editors'
       p. 165.
186   Published as *Facing Mount
       Kanchenjunga*, Windhorse
       Publications, Glasgow 1991
       (*Complete Works*, vol. 21).
187   Ibid., ch. 8, pp. 182–3.
188   This was the Dharmodaya
       Vihara. These experiences
       are related in chs. 4 and 6 in
       Facing Mount Kanchenjunga,

Windhorse Publications,
Glasgow 1991 (*Complete
Works*, vol. 21).

189 Shok Sabh means
'condolence meeting'.

CHAPTER 2

190 This is the first of three talks
on the Buddha's threefold
way (*śīla, samādhi, prajñā*)
held in the grounds of the
Ahilya Ashram, a school in
central Pune run by Dalits.

191 See 'Waiting for a Visa' in
Dr Babasaheb Ambedkar,
Writings and Speeches,
vol. xii, Education
Department, Government of
Maharashtra, Bombay 1993,
pp. 661–91.

192 Satara is the name of both a
city and a district of modern
day Maharashtra.

193 A suburb of Bombay.

194 Baroda State existed 1721–
1949, ruled by a Maharaja
for the Gaekwad dynasty. It
was located in what is now
Gujarat.

195 Subtitled 'The Great
Renunciation', *The Light
of Asia* was composed by
Sir Edwin Arnold and first
published in London in
1879.

196 'Buddha and the Future
of His Religion' in
Dr Babasaheb Ambedkar,
Writings and Speeches,
vol. xvii (part 2), Education
Department, Government of
Maharashtra 2003, p. 104.

197 Ibid., p. 98.

198 Ibid., p. 104.

199 This is the sixth of the eight
qualities of the great ocean
described by the Buddha in
Udāna 5.5 (the *Uposatha
Sutta*); see for example John
D. Ireland (trans.), *The
Udāna and the Itivuttaka*,
Buddhist Publication Society,
Kandy 2007, p. 68; see also
Sangharakshita's talk 'The
Taste of Freedom' (*Complete
Works*, vol. 11).

200 Pope Pius IX in his encyclical
'Quanta Cura' (1864),
following his predecessor
Gregory XVI, declared
erroneous – and fatal to the
Roman Catholic Church
– the idea that 'liberty of
conscience and worship is
each man's personal right'.

201 Kumārila Bhaṭṭa lived in the
seventh century CE, and was a
contemporary of the Buddhist
philosopher Dharmakīrti;
Bhaṭṭa is widely believed to
have exercised an influence
on his younger contem-
porary Śaṅkara (fl. *c.* 710).
The legendary account of his
life says that he studied at
the Buddhist monastic university at Nālandā, then in its
prime, and used the know-
ledge gained to try to counter
Buddhist philosophical
positions. His *Ślokavārttika*
is the first of a three-part
treatise on the *Mīmāṃsa
Sūtra* composed by the third-
century BCE Vedic philo-
sopher Jaimini. Kumārila
Bhaṭṭa is regarded as the
founder of one of the

six orthodox (*āstika*) philosophical schools of Hinduism.

202 *Ariyapariyesanā Sutta, Majjhima Nikāya* (i.169), Bhikkhu Ñāṇamoli and Bhikkhu Bodhi (trans.), *The Middle Length Discourses of the Buddha*, Wisdom Publications, Boston 1995, pp. 261–2.

203 I. B. Horner (trans.), *The Book of the Discipline (Vināya)*, part 4, *Mahāvagga* I, Pali Text Society, Oxford 1996, p. 28.

204 A name for someone of no or low caste; an Untouchable.

CHAPTER 3

205 Pimpri is a suburb of Pune.

206 Presumably indicating the *kesas* worn by Order members standing on the speakers' platform.

207 'Buddha and the Future of His Religion' in Dr Babasaheb Ambedkar, *Writings and Speeches,* vol. xvii (part 2), Education Department, Government of Maharashtra 2003, p. 107.

208 See Glossary for the meaning of *dasa sīla upāsaka*. The Order (now known as the Triratna Buddhist Order) has over 2,000 members as of 2016.

209 14 October 1981.

210 See 'Three Meetings', p. 13 et. seq.

211 The story of this incident is told in Aśvaghoṣa's *Buddhacarita* or *Acts of the Buddha*, a long poem written in the second century CE which gives a legendary account of the Buddha's life; see Aśvaghoṣa, *The Buddhacarita*, trans. E. H. Johnston, Motilal Banarsidass, Delhi 1984, pp. 89–90.

212 The *Gadrabha Sutta* is *sutta* 82 of the *Aṅguttara Nikāya*; see Bhikkhu Bodhi (trans.), *The Numerical Discourses of the Buddha*, Wisdom Publications, Boston 2012, p. 315; or F. L. Woodward (trans.), *Gradual Sayings*, vol. i, Pali Text Society, Oxford 1995, p. 209.

213 The ten fetters are enumerated, for instance, in *Saṃyutta Nikāya* 45.179 and 45.180; see Bhikkhu Bodhi (trans.), *The Connected Discourses of the Buddha*, Wisdom Publications, Boston 2000, pp. 1565–6; see also F. L. Woodward (trans.), *Kindred Sayings*, part 5, Pali Text Society, Oxford 1979, p. 224.

214 *Ekādaśī* or the eleventh day of the lunar cycle is regarded by Hindus as a day of prayer and fasting.

215 I. B. Horner (trans.), *The Book of the Discipline (Vinaya)*, part 4, *Mahāvagga* I, Pali Text Society, Oxford 1996, pp. 431–4.

216 Mahars and Chamars are two 'untouchable' communities. Dr Ambedkar came from the Mahar community.

CHAPTER 4

217 See *Aṅguttara Nikāya,*
Book of the Eights, sutta
53, in E. M. Hare (trans.),
Gradual Sayings, vol. iv,
Pali Text Society, Oxford
1995, pp. 186–7; and
Bhikkhu Bodhi (trans.),
*The Numerical Discourses
of the Buddha*, Wisdom
Publications, Boston 2012,
p. 1193.

218 Bhabra Rock Edict,
N. A. Nikam and R. McKeon
(trans.), *The Edicts of
Ashoka*, Asia Publishing
House, Bombay 1959, p. 61.

219 *Adhyasayasaṃcodana
Sūtra.* Quoted by Śāntideva;
see Cecil Bendall and
W. H. D. Rouse (trans.),
*Compendium of Teachings
(Śikṣā-samuccaya)*, London
1922, p. 17.

220 Bhagwan Das (ed.), *Thus
Spoke Ambedkar*, vol. ii,
second edition, Bheem
Patrika Publications,
Jullundur n. d., pp. 148–9.

221 Ibid., p. 148.

222 These five factors are
enumerated by the Buddha
in the *Anupada Sutta,
Majjhima Nikāya* (i.25–9);
see Bhikkhu Ñāṇamoli and
Bhikkhu Bodhi (trans.), *The
Middle Length Discourses
of the Buddha*, Wisdom
Publications, Boston 1995,
p. 899, or I. B. Horner
(trans.), *Middle Length
Sayings*, vol. iii, Pali Text
Society, London 1959, p. 78.

223 This is in Buddhaghosa's
*Visuddhimagga (The Path
of Purification)*, ch. 4,
paragraph 91. In Bhikkhu
Ñāṇamoli's translation
(fourth edition, Buddhist
Publication Society, Colombo
2010, p. 137) the description
is: 'applied thought is like the
hand that grips firmly and
sustained thought is like the
hand that rubs, when one
grips a tarnished metal dish
firmly with one hand and
rubs it with powder and oil
and a woollen pad with the
other hand.'

224 The four *dhyānas* (Pāli
jhānas) are described in
the *Mahā-Assapura Sutta,
Majjhima Nikāya* (i.276–8),
see Bhikkhu Ñāṇamoli and
Bhikkhu Bodhi (trans.), *The
Middle Length Discourses of
the Buddha*, pp. 367–9.

CHAPTER 5

225 Panchgani is a hill station
about 100 kilometres south
of Pune in the Satara district
of Maharashtra.

226 *Facing Mount Kanchenjunga*,
Windhorse Publications,
Glasgow 1991, p. 97
(*Complete Works*, vol. 21).

227 For more on the Maha
Bodhi Society and
Anagārika Dharmapala see
Sangharakshita, *Beating the
Drum*, Ibis Publications,
Ledbury 2012 and *Anagarika
Dharmapala: A Biographical
Sketch*, Ibis Publications,

Ledbury 2013 (*Complete Works*, vol. 8).

228 For an account of how Devapriya Valisinha, General Secretary of the Maha Bodhi Society, managed to ensure a Buddhist was elected president, see *Beating the Drum*, Ibis Publications, Ledbury 2012, p. 63 (*Complete Works*, vol. 8).

229 For an account of this tour and the meeting with Dr Ambedkar see *In the Sign of the Golden Wheel*, Windhorse Publications, Birmingham 1996, ch. 22 (*Complete Works*, vol. 22).

230 Recounted in a letter to his friend, Dinoo Dubash, dated 15 December 1956; see *Dear Dinoo: Letters to a Friend*, Ibis Publications, Birmingham 2011, pp.53–4 (*Complete Works*, vol. 21).

231 See *Facing Mount Kanchenjunga*, Windhorse Publications, Glasgow 1991, pp. 218–22 (*Complete Works*, vol. 21).

232 *Indriya* is usually translated 'spiritual faculty'. In the *Aṅguttara Nikāya* (*Book of the Sixes*, sutta 55), the Buddha advises Soṇa to attune the pitch of the five spiritual faculties as one would tune the strings of a lute; see Bhikkhu Bodhi (trans.), *The Numerical Discourses of the Buddha*, Wisdom Publications, Boston 2012, p. 933 and E. M. Hare (trans.),

Gradual Sayings, vol. iii, Pali Text Society, Oxford 1995, p. 267. The idea of a balance between pairs is introduced in Buddhaghosa's *Visuddhimagga*, ch. 4; see Pe Maung Tin (trans.), *The Path of Purity*, Pali Text Society, Oxford 1975, p. 151.

233 *Bodhicaryāvatāra*, ch. 7, verse 2. 'Energy in pursuit of the good' is Sangharakshita's favoured translation.

234 *Shraddh* and *Pindadan* are traditional Hindu after-death ceremonies.

235 A *talwa pūjā* is a ceremony for getting rid of one's enemies; from *talwar*, a type of sabre.

CHAPTER 6

236 Mahad is situated 175 kilometres south of Mumbai.

237 The Buddha described the great lengths he went to in practising austerities in the *Mahāsaccaka Sutta*, *Majjhima Nikāya* (i.242–6); see Bhikkhu Ñāṇamoli and Bhikkhu Bodhi (trans.), *The Middle Length Discourses of the Buddha*, Wisdom Publications, Boston 1995, pp. 337–40, or *Middle Length Sayings*, vol. i, I. B. Horner (trans.), Pali Text Society, London 1967, pp. 297–301.

238 I. B. Horner (trans.), *The Book of the Discipline* (*Vināya*), part 4, *Mahāvagga I*, Pali Text Society, Oxford 1996, p. 28.

239 *'Satyāgraha'* is literally 'holding on to truth'. The term was popularized by Gandhi and was used to mean a non-violent campaign to establish certain rights. A *satyāgrahi* is one who takes part in such a campaign.

240 For an account of the conference speech see Dhananjay Keer, *Dr Ambedkar: Life and Mission*, Popular Prakashan, Bombay 1981, p. 253.

241 'Buddha and the Future of His Religion' in Dr Babasaheb Ambedkar, *Writings and Speeches*, vol. xvii (part 2), Education Department, Government of Maharashtra 2003, p. 105.

CHAPTER 7

242 *Udāna* 6.4 (*Paṭhamanānātitthiya Sutta*), in John D. Ireland (trans.), *The Udāna and the Itivuttaka*, Buddhist Publication Society, Kandy 2007, pp. 81–4.

243 *Mundaka Upanishad* 1.1.7.

244 These are listed in, for example, the *Sangiti Sutta*, *Dīgha Nikāya* (iii.219); see M. Walshe (trans.), *The Long Discourses of the Buddha*, Wisdom Publications, Boston 1995, section 1.10, point 43. p. 486.

245 Paraphrasing from B. R. Ambedkar, *The Buddha and His Dhamma*, People's Education Society, fourth edition, Bombay 1991, book 3, part 4, 7: 'Reading Books of Dhamma is Not-Dhamma', no. 3.

246 The three *laksaṇas* or characteristics of conditioned existence are enumerated by the Buddha in, for example, *Dhammapada* verses 277–9.

247 See *Saṃyutta Nikāya*, section 6, *Brahmasamyutta* 1 (1) in Bhikkhu Bodhi (trans.), *The Connected Discourses of the Buddha*, Wisdom Publications, Boston 2000, p. 233; and also C. A. F. Rhys Davids (trans.), *Kindred Sayings*, part 1, Pali Text Society, Oxford 1979, p. 174.

248 C. A. F. Rhys Davids (trans.), *Poems of Early Buddhist Nuns (Therīgāthā)*, Pali Text Society, Oxford 1989, canto x, pp. 88–91.

CHAPTER 8

249 Currey Road, along with Worli, were massive housing developments in Bombay known as *chawls*. The blocks were four storeys high with twenty rooms per floor, each room housing at this time two to four families.

250 A rendering of Vinaya, *Mahāvagga Khandaka* 1.11 – see I. B. Horner (trans.), *The Book of the Discipline*, part 4, *Mahāvagga* I, Pali Text Society, Oxford 1996, p. 28.

251 Dadar railway station is in a neighbourhood at the centre of Mumbai about three kilometres north of Currey

Road where this talk was given.

252 Nagabodhi afterwards wrote about this tour in *Jai Bhim! Dispatches from a Peaceful Revolution*, Windhorse Publications, Glasgow 1988.

CHAPTER 9

253 Theosophy Hall was the headquarters of the Bombay branch of the United Lodge of Theosophists founded by B. P. Wadia. In the audience were not just Theosophists but people from diverse backgrounds including local Buddhists, Parsis, liberal Hindus, and Christians.

254 Madame Sophia Wadia was born in 1902 in Colombia, but lived in India after her marriage to B. P. Wadia. In 1954 the Wadias invited Sangharakshita to Bangalore, where he gave four talks at their Indian Institute of World Culture. (The first three talks were subsequently written up as *A Survey of Buddhism* and the fourth as *Paradox and Poetry in the Voice of the Silence*.) Mme Wadia was a well-known litterateur, editor of *The Aryan Path* and *The India Pen*. (Sangharakshita dedicated a poem to her for her sixtieth birthday.) On the death of her husband in 1958, she succeeded him as head of the United Lodge of Theosophists until her death in 1986.

255 To take one of many examples, in the *Mahāvagga* of the *Sutta Nipāta*, the Brahmin Sundarikabhāradvāja makes this very exclamation; see K. R. Norman (trans.), *The Rhinoceros Horn and Other Early Buddhist Poems*, Pali Text Society, London 1985, p. 79.

256 Alfred Lord Tennyson's *Idylls of the King: Guinevere*.

257 *Aṅguttara Nikāya, Book of the Eights, sutta* 53, in E. M. Hare (trans.), *Gradual Sayings*, vol. iv, Pali Text Society, Oxford 1995, pp. 186–7; and Bhikkhu Bodhi (trans.), *The Numerical Sayings of the Buddha*, Wisdom Publications, Somerville 2012, p. 1193.

258 'Buddha and the Future of His Religion' in Dr Babasaheb Ambedkar, *Writings and Speeches*, vol. xvii (part 2), Education Department, Government of Maharashtra 2003, p. 107.

CHAPTER 10

259 The Worli *chawls* were built by the British in the 1920s as low cost housing. Many of Dr Ambedkar's followers lived there.

260 See 'Three Meetings', p. 13 et. seq.

261 *The Sūtra of the Lotus Flower of the Wonderful Law* in B. Katō et al (trans.), *The Threefold Lotus*

Sūtra, Kosei Publishing, Tokyo 1957, p. 177. See also Sangharakshita's commentary in *The Drama of Cosmic Enlightenment*, ch. 7 (*Complete Works*, vol. 17).

262 This story is told in Tale XVII of *The Gulistan (The Rose Garden)*, by the thirteenth-century Persian poet Saadi of Shiraz.

263 A subcaste of the Vaishya caste, Banias are merchants, bankers, and money-lenders.

CHAPTER 11

264 Ulhasnagar is in the Thane district of Maharashtra, 50 kilometres north-east of central Mumbai. During the partition of India and Pakistan, many people seeking refuge from the calamities of those days, including many from Dalit communities, came there from the Sind, this influx giving rise to sprawling slum developments, home to many who came to Sangharakshita's talk.

265 The talk was given in the open air. A strong wind was blowing at the time.

266 This Thai version of the Pāli canon was published between 1925 and 1928.

267 The *Gadrabha Sutta* is *sutta* 82 of the *Aṅguttara Nikāya*; see Bhikkhu Bodhi (trans.), *The Numerical Discourses of the Buddha*, Wisdom Publications, Boston 2012, p. 315; or F. L. Woodward

(trans.), *Gradual Sayings*, vol. i, Pali Text Society, Oxford 1995, p. 209.

CHAPTER 12

268 A city 80 kilometres east of Pune.

269 See *The Rainbow Road*, Windhorse Publications, Birmingham 1997, pp. 56–7 (*Complete Works*, vol. 20).

270 Ibid. p. 80.

271 Ibid, pp. 96–7.

272 The following episodes from his life are described in greater detail in his memoirs, volumes 20–3 of the *Complete Works*.

273 Now known in both countries as Triratna, i.e. the Triratna Buddhist Community.

274 B. R. Ambedkar, *The Buddha and His Dhamma*, People's Education Society, fourth edition, Bombay 1991, pp. 160–73.

275 The *FWBO Newsletter*.

CHAPTER 13

276 Manmad is a city some 200 kilometres north of Daund in the Nasik District of Maharashtra. It is famous as a major railway junction.

277 See p. 50.

278 Founded by Dr Ambedkar; see p. 8.

279 Dhananjay Keer, *Dr Ambedkar: Life and Mission*, Popular Prakashan, Bombay 1981, p. 253.

280 This organization (in English the Buddhist Society of

India) was founded by Dr Ambedkar in 1955, developing branches all over Maharashtra. Though it became largely non-functioning, it continued to organize programmes of talks, Buddhist ceremonies, and festivals.

281 The seven *bodhyaṅgas* are enumerated in, for example, the *Mahāsatipaṭṭhana Sutta*, *Dīgha Nikāya* (ii.303–4), see M. Walshe (trans.), *The Long Discourses of the Buddha*, Wisdom Publications, Boston 1995, p. 343; and the *Ānāpānasati Sutta*, *Majjhima Nikāya* (iii.85–7), see Bhikkhu Ñāṇamoli and Bhikkhu Bodhi (trans.), *The Middle Length Discourses of the Buddha*, Wisdom Publications, Boston 1995, pp. 946–8, or I. B. Horner (trans.), *Middle Length Sayings*, vol. iii, Pali Text Society, London 1967, pp. 128–9.

282 This story is about Tenno, a disciple of Nan-in. He had become a teacher when Nan-in asked him this question, after which he went back to being a pupil. The story is told in Paul Reps (comp.), *Zen Flesh, Zen Bones*, Penguin Books, Middlesex 1971, p. 43.

283 Śāntideva, *Bodhicaryāvatāra*, ch. 7 verse 2. 'Energy in pursuit of the good' is Sangharakshita's favoured translation.

284 Śāntideva, *Bodhicaryāvatāra*, ch. 7, verse 65.

285 Buddhaghosa, *Visuddhimagga* (iv.94–8), in Pe Maung Tin (trans.), *The Path of Purity*, Pali Text Society, Oxford 1975, p. 167.

286 *Dīgha Nikāya* (ii.130); see M. Walshe (trans.), *The Long Discourses of the Buddha*, Wisdom Publications, Boston 1995, p. 258, or T. W. Rhys Davids (trans.), *Dialogues of the Buddha*, part 2, Pali Text Society, London 1971, pp.141–2. It is in fact a story told to the Buddha by Pukkusa the Malla about his teacher Āḷāra Kālāma.

287 The meeting was held only a few hundred yards from Manmad Junction, one of the busiest railway stations in Maharashtra.

288 *Alagaddūpama Sutta*, *Majjhima Nikāya* (i.135), Bhikkhu Ñāṇamoli and Bhikkhu Bodhi (trans.), *The Middle Length Discourses of the Buddha*, Wisdom Publications, Boston 1995, pp. 228–9.

289 See Glossary, p. 543

290 The *FWBO Newsletter* of which Nagabodhi was the editor.

CHAPTER 14

291 The historic city of Aurangabad with its Mughal architecture is situated some 100 kilometres to the south and east of Manmad.

The Milind Mahavidyalaya
or College was named
after the famous second-
century BCE Bactrian King
Milinda whose questions
to the Buddhist teacher
Nāgasena are recorded
in the *Milindapañha*. The
College was founded by
Dr Ambedkar in 1950 and in
1958 became affiliated to the
newly founded Marathwada
University. In 1994 the
university was renamed
Dr Babasaheb Ambedkar
Marathwada University.
This was a public talk. The
following day Sangharakshita
spoke to the college students.

292 Vinaya ii. 188.

293 This conversation
is recounted in the
Mahāparinibbāna Sutta,
Dīgha Nikāya (ii.101);
see M. Walshe (trans.),
*The Long Discourses
of the Buddha*, Wisdom
Publications, Boston 1995,
p. 245; or T. W. Rhys
Davids (trans.), *Dialogues
of the Buddha*, part 2, Pali
Text Society, London 1971,
p. 107.

294 *Mahāparinibbāna Sutta*,
Dīgha Nikāya (ii.102);
see M. Walshe (trans.),
*The Long Discourses
of the Buddha*, Wisdom
Publications, Boston 1995,
p. 245, or T. W. Rhys Davids
(trans.), *Dialogues of the
Buddha*, part 2, Pali Text
Society, London 1971,
p. 108.

295 This famous incident is
recounted in *sutta* 45, the
Maggasaṃyutta, in the
Mahāvagga of the *Saṃyutta
Nikāya*; see Bhikkhu Bodhi
(trans.), *The Connected
Discourses of the Buddha*,
Wisdom Publications, Boston
2000, pp. 1524–5; also F. L.
Woodward (trans.), *Kindred
Sayings*, part 5, Pali Text
Society, London 1979, p. 2.

CHAPTER 15

296 M. B. Chitnis, who had
been a close associate of
Dr Ambedkar, was vice-
president of the People's
Education Society as well as
Principal of Milind College.

297 *Dhammapada*, verse 5.

298 *Puṇyabhūmi* means 'sacred-
earth', i.e. the land sacred to
the Hindus.

299 Literally 'black sea'. A Hindu
taboo meant that crossing the
sea would bring about loss of
one's caste.

300 *Gaṅgāpāṇi* is water from
the Ganges, regarded by
orthodox Hindus as holy and
capable of purifying what
has become polluted.

301 The *ticīvara* are the three
robes of a monk, the inner or
lower, upper, and outer robes.

302 'Buddha and the Future
of His Religion' in
Dr Babasaheb Ambedkar,
Writings and Speeches,
vol. xvii (part 2), Education
Department, Government of
Maharashtra 2003, p. 107.

CHAPTER 16

303 Vaijapur, on the Narangi
River, is a city some
70 kilometres west of
Aurangabad.

CHAPTER 17

304 The *āryamārga*, 'noble path',
generally refers to the Noble
Eightfold Path, the *ārya-
aṣṭāṅgika-mārga*, which
is said to have been the
Buddha's first ever teaching,
given to the five disciples at
Sarnath. The story is told
in the first section of the
Mahāvagga of the Vinaya
Piṭaka; for the teaching of
the Noble Eightfold Path,
see I. B. Horner (trans.), *The
Book of the Discipline*, part
4, Pali Text Society, Oxford
1996, p. 15. The teaching is
also found in the *Saṃyutta
Nikāya*; see Bhikkhu Bodhi
(trans.), *The Connected
Discourses of the Buddha*,
Wisdom Publications,
Boston 2000, p. 1844; also
F. L. Woodward (trans.),
Kindred Sayings, part 5, Pali
Text Society, London 1979,
p. 357.

305 See Sangharakshita, *Precious
Teachers*, Windhorse
Publications, Birmingham
2007, p. 170 (*Complete
Works*, vol. 22).

306 An editorial for the October
1961 edition of the *Maha
Bodhi* is addressed to the
WFB before their sixth
conference. See *Beating the
Drum*, Ibis Publications,

Ledbury 2012, p. 247
(*Complete Works*, vol. 8).

307 Child's naming ceremony.

308 Wedding ceremony.

309 The seven steps taken around
the sacred fire by the couple,
a rite central to a Hindu
wedding.

310 Death ceremony.

311 Detailed information
regarding the marriage
rituals etc. that can be
performed by Buddhists will
be found in Marathi puja
books published by Triratna
Grantha Mala.

312 There are many examples
of this in the Pāli canon,
for example, the *Kūṭadanta
Sutta, Dīgha Nikāya* (i.134)
describes a company of
people approaching the
Buddha: some of the
Brahmins and householders of
Khānumata made obeisance
to the Lord, some exchanged
courtesies with him, some
saluted him with joined
palms, some announced
their name and clan, and
some sat down to one side
in silence; see M. Walshe
(trans.), *The Long Discourses
of the Buddha*, Wisdom
Publications, Boston 1995,
pp. 134–5.

313 A full-length prostration.

314 Hermann Oldenberg,
*Buddha: His Life, His
Doctrine, His Order*,
first published in 1882
by Williams of London.
A typical example of the
outdated view of Buddhism

expressed in the book: 'According to Buddhist dogmatic, a Buddha can be born only as a Brahmin or as a noble: in this we have it clearly indicated, that the distinctions of caste have by no means vanished or become worthless to the Buddhist consciousness.'

315   See talk given at Panchgani p. 207 et. seq.

CHAPTER 18

316   Vishwa Hindu Parishad is a right-wing Hindu organization founded in 1964 and a member of the Rashtriya Swayamsevak Sangh (RSS), renowned for being both anti-Muslim and anti-Dalit. There were those members of the VHP of a more open mind who were interested to hear what Sangharakshita might have to say on this highly important topic, i.e. Religion and the Secular State. What he did have to say deeply challenged their own ideologies.

317   Meetings with all these figures are related in *The Rainbow Road*, Sangharakshita's first volume of memoirs (*Complete Works*, vol. 20).

318   A ceremonial sword or knife worn by some Sikh men.

319   The monk was Mahaprajna, and Sangharakshita knew him as a layman in Kalimpong. The Prime Minister concerned was Mohan Shamser Jang Bahadur Rane.

CHAPTER 19

320   A *jap-māla* is a string of 108 beads used for counting when reciting a mantra. It is used in India by Hindus, Jains, and Sikhs, as well as Buddhists.

321   The parable is addressed to Śāriputra; see B. Katō et al (trans.), *The Threefold Lotus Sūtra*, Kosei Publishing, Tokyo 1975, ch. 3, pp. 85–7; also Sangharakshita, *The Drama of Cosmic Enlightenment*, ch. 3 (*Complete Works*, vol. 16).

CHAPTER 20

322   Jaikwadi lies on the Godavari river some 60 kilometres south of Aurangabad. It is famous for its huge dam.

323   *Dhammapada*, verse 320.

324   *Dhammapada*, verse 29.

325   Cited in Dhananjay Keer, *Dr Ambedkar: Life and Mission*, third edition, Popular Prakashan, Bombay 1971, p. 201.

CHAPTER 21

326   Ambad is a city in the Jalna district of Maharashtra about 200 kilometres south of Aurangabad.

327   It seems the night of 26 January was spent in Aurangabad.

328   An armed robber.

329   *Aṅgulimāla* means 'garland of fingers' or 'finger necklace'.

330 *Aṅgulimāla Sutta, Majjhima
     Nikāya* (ii.98–105); see
     Bhikkhu Ñāṇamoli and
     Bhikkhu Bodhi (trans.), *The
     Middle Length Discourses
     of the Buddha*, Wisdom
     Publications, Boston 1995,
     pp. 710–17, or I. B. Horner
     (trans.), *Middle Length
     Sayings*, vol. ii, Pali Text
     Society, London 1959, p. 284.

331 *Alagaddūpama Sutta,
     Majjhima Nikāya* (i.134–5);
     see Bhikkhu Ñāṇamoli and
     Bhikkhu Bodhi (trans.), *The
     Middle Length Discourses
     of the Buddha*, Wisdom
     Publications, Boston 1995,
     pp. 228–9.

332 Throughout this section
     Sangharakshita uses 'he' and
     'him' when clearly the person
     could be either a man or a
     woman. Thus the pronoun
     should be taken generically,
     i.e. as referring to both men
     and women. The friend who
     is chosen for the second stage
     is usually someone of the
     same sex as the meditator;
     the neutral person and enemy
     may be of either sex.

333 *Ariyapariyesanā Sutta,
     Majjhima Nikāya* (i.169);
     see Bhikkhu Ñāṇamoli and
     Bhikkhu Bodhi (trans.), *The
     Middle Length Discourses
     of the Buddha*, Wisdom
     Publications, Boston 1995,
     pp. 261–2.

CHAPTER 22

334 Marathwada is one of the
     five regions of Maharashtra,
     located in the central and
     eastern parts of the state. Its
     largest city is Aurangabad.

335 Parbhani is one of the largest
     cities in the Marathwada
     region of Maharashtra. It is
     230 kilometres north-east of
     Ambad.

336 The story of the Buddha,
     Māra, and the earth
     goddess seems first to have
     been introduced to the
     accounts of the Buddha's
     journey to Enlightenment
     in the Mahāyāna tradition's
     Lalitavistara Sūtra. For a
     translation, see Gwendolyn
     Bays (trans.), *The Voice of
     the Buddha*, vol. ii, Dharma
     Publishing, Berkeley 1983,
     pp. 481–2.

337 The story of the Buddha's
     first teaching at Sarnath
     is told in the first section
     of the *Mahāvagga* of the
     Vinaya Piṭaka; see I. B.
     Horner (trans.), *The Book
     of the Discipline*, part 4, Pali
     Text Society, Oxford 1996,
     pp. 13–21.

338 Vinaya Piṭaka, *Mahāvagga*;
     see I. B. Horner (trans.),
     The Book of the Discipline,
     part 4, Pali Text Society,
     Oxford 1996, p.18, also
     Bhikkhu Bodhi (trans.),
     *The Connected Discourses
     of the Buddha*, Wisdom
     Publications, Boston
     2000, p. 1846; and F. L.
     Woodward (trans.), *Kindred
     Sayings*, part 5, Pali Text
     Society, London 1979,
     p. 359.

339   The *Ratana Sutta* is to be found in the *Sutta Nipāta*, published as K. R. Norman (trans.), *The Rhinoceros Horn and Other Early Poems*, Pali Text Society, London; see p. 37, verse 224.

CHAPTER 23

340   Nanded is the second largest city of the Marathwada region of Maharashtra, situated on the Godavari River. It is some 75 kilometres east of Parbhani.

341   A lakh is 100,000. A crore is 10,000,000.

342   Shankara, also called Shankaracharya, was an Indian philosopher and theologian of the eighth century CE, and a renowned exponent of the Advaita Vedanta school of philosophy, from whose doctrines the main currents of modern Indian thought are derived. He wrote commentaries on the *Brahma-sūtra*, the principal *Upaniṣads*, and the *Bhagavad Gītā*, affirming his belief in one eternal unchanging reality (*brahman*) and the illusion of plurality and differentiation.

343   This is one way of describing the process of *pratītya-samutpāda*, which Edward Conze translated as 'conditioned co-production', and which is fundamental to the Buddha's teaching. For a detailed account, see

Sangharakshita, *A Survey of Buddhism*, especially ch. 1, section 11, 'The Essence of Enlightenment' (*Complete Works*, vol. 1).

344   To give one of many examples, in the *Mahāvacchagotta Sutta*, *Majjhima Nikāya* (i.491), the Buddha is represented as stating that far more than five hundred of his men and women lay followers will 'reappear spontaneously (in the Pure Abodes) and there attain final Nibbāna without ever returning from that world'; see Bhikkhu Ñāṇamoli and Bhikkhu Bodhi (trans.), *The Middle Length Discourses of the Buddha*, Wisdom Publications, Boston 1995, p. 597.

345   These were three of the most famous Buddhist Mahaviharas of the eighth century CE, all in the area of India now called Bihar.

346   The narrative of Xuanzang's pilgrimage is available as Li Rongxi (trans.), *The Records of the Western Regions Visited During the Great Tang Dynasty*, Numata Center for Buddhist Translation and Research, Berkeley 1996.

CHAPTER 24

347   Latur is some 130 kilometres south-west of Nanded.

348   *Indriya* is usually translated 'spiritual faculty'. In the

Aṅguttara Nikāya (Book of the Sixes, sutta 55), the Buddha advises Soṇa to attune the pitch of the five spiritual faculties as one would tune the strings of a lute; see Bhikkhu Bodhi (trans.), *The Numerical Discourses of the Buddha*, Wisdom Publications, Boston 2012, p. 933 and E. M. Hare (trans.), *Gradual Sayings*, vol. iii, Pali Text Society, Oxford 1995, p. 267. The idea of a balance between pairs is introduced in Buddhaghosa's *Visuddhimagga*, ch. 4; see Pe Maung Tin (trans.), *The Path of Purity*, Pali Text Society, Oxford 1975, p. 151.

349   See, for example, Gwendolyn Bays (trans.), *The Voice of the Buddha*, Dharma Publishing, Berkeley 1983, pp. 411–12.

350   The Buddha certainly spoke approvingly of voluntary poverty, i.e. that of the monk. He did not criticize poverty in the modern sense for the simple reason that such poverty did not exist in ancient India. The general trend of his teaching to the laity would suggest that he accepted a decent standard of living as the normal state of affairs. In the *Sigālovāda Sutta*, for example (*Dīgha Nikāya* iii.191), masters are exhorted to treat their servants well.

CHAPTER 25

351   From Latur, Sangharakshita went to Osmanabad before travelling on to Sholapur in the south-west of Maharashtra.

352   This is recounted in *In the Sign of the Golden Wheel*, ch. 19 (*Complete Works*, vol. 22).

353   *Shraddh* and *Pindadan* are traditional Hindu after-death ceremonies.

354   'Buddha or Karl Marx', in *Dr Babasaheb Ambedkar, Writings and Speeches*, vol. iii, Education Department, Government of Maharashtra 1987, pp. 441–62.

355   Ibid., p. 446.

CHAPTER 26

356   Chikhalwadi is a village in the Sangli District of Maharashtra, some 240 kilometres south-west of Sholapur.

357   'Monks, there are these three things which are practised in secret, not openly. What are they? The ways of womenfolk are secret, not open. Brahmins practise their chants in secret, not openly. Those of perverse views hold their views secretly, not openly. These are the three things.... Monks, there are these three things which shine forth for all to see, which are not hidden. Which three? The disc of the moon shines for all to see; it is not

hidden. The disc of the sun does likewise. The Dhamma-Discipline of a Tathāgata [Buddha] shines for all to see; it is not hidden. These are the three things.' *Aṅguttara Nikāya, Book of the Threes,* no. 129, 'Secret'; see F. L. Woodward (trans.), *Gradual Sayings,* vol. i, Pali Text Society, Oxford 1995, p. 261; see also Bhikkhu Bodhi (trans.), *The Numerical Discourses of the Buddha,* Wisdom Publications, Boston 2012, p. 361.

CHAPTER 27

358 Venue unknown.
359 For an account of the speech at the Yeola conference in which Dr Ambedkar made this momentous statement see Dhananjay Keer, *Dr Ambedkar: Life and Mission,* Popular Prakashan, Bombay 1981, p. 253.
360 'Buddha and the Future of His Religion' in Dr Babasaheb Ambedkar, *Writings and Speeches,* vol. xvii (part 2), Education Department, Government of Maharashtra 2003, p. 97.
361 'O Bhikṣus, my words should be accepted by the wise, not out of regard for me, but after due investigation – just as gold is accepted as true only after heating, cutting, and rubbing.' Ganganatha Jha (trans.), *The Tattvasaṅgraha of Shāntarakṣita,* Motilal

Banarsidass, Delhi 1986, vol. ii, p. 1558, text 3588.
362 'Buddha and the Future of His Religion' in Dr Babasaheb Ambedkar, *Writings and Speeches,* vol. xvii (part 2), Education Department, Government of Maharashtra 2003, p. 104.
363 'Buddha or Karl Marx', in Dr Babasaheb Ambedkar, *Writings and Speeches,* vol. iii, Education Department, Government of Maharashtra 1987, pp. 441–62.

CHAPTER 28

364 In 2010 the Order and Movement were renamed so that they would have the same names worldwide: the Triratna Buddhist Order and Triratna Buddhist Community. See 'Notes from the Editors', p. 165.
365 As of 2016 there are more than 90 urban centres and rural retreat centres in over twenty countries.
366 Jyotirao Phooley (1827–1890) was one of the prominent social reformers of nineteenth-century India. Born into a low caste, he was influenced by an experience of being insulted by higher caste people for daring to take part in a wedding celebration and by reading Thomas Paine's *The Rights of Man.* He led the movement against the prevailing caste restrictions

in India and campaigned for the rights of peasants and other low-caste people, and also for the rights of women.

367 In *Udāna* 5.4, the Buddha tells this story and draws from it exactly this moral, though in the story the boys are tormenting fish, not a crow; see *The Udāna and the Itivuttaka*, trans John D. Ireland, Buddhist Publication Society 2007, p. 66.

368 D. H. Lawrence makes this point in his essay 'Art and the Individual: a Paper for Socialists', published in the collection *Study of Thomas Hardy and other Essays*, Grafton, Cambridge 1986. He says, apparently quoting someone else: 'Men, women and children want food and raiment now; we also need our Beauty – in our streets, in our crafts, in our paintings.'

CHAPTER 29

369 Recounted in *The Rainbow Road*, ch. 18 (*Complete Works*, vol. 20).

370 Sangharakshita became acquainted with this Shankaracharya and corresponded with him for a time. A second meeting took place two years later at the ashram of Ramana Marharshi (see *The Rainbow Road* ch. 39). The *gaddi* was a sort of cushion-throne, part of the Shankaracharya's paraphernalia.

371 i.e. devotees of the god Vishnu.

372 Swami Narayan 1781–1830, the central figure of a modern Hindu sect.

373 Ramakrishna (1836–1886) and his disciple Swami Vivekananda were the inspiration for the Ramakrishna Mission. His teachings were broadly Advaita Vedanta.

374 Vallabha Acharya (1479–1531), founder of the Pushti sect.

375 In *The Discovery of India*, Nehru wrote, 'Ashoka's pillars of stone with their inscriptions would speak to me in their magnificent language and tell me of a man who, though an emperor, was greater than any king or emperor.'

376 This is a story from the *Lotus Sūtra*, the Parable of the Herbs, to give its title in Bunnō Katō et al. (trans.), *The Threefold Lotus Sūtra*, Kōsei Publishing Company, Tokyo 1995, pp. 126–34.

CHAPTER 30

377 Sangharakshita noted at the time, 'The vihara on this occasion was entirely filled with women, so that the men had to look in through the windows and doors. Organizers of meetings should avoid this kind of arrangement, as women are often talkative and do not pay attention to the lecture.'

CHAPTER 31

378 The *Kalāma* or *Kesaputtiya Sutta* is found in the *Aṅguttara Nikāya*; see F. L. Woodward (trans.), *Gradual Sayings*, vol. i, Pali Text Society, Oxford 1995, pp. 170–5, or Bhikkhu Bodhi (trans.), *The Numerical Discourses of the Buddha*, Wisdom Publications, Boston 2012, pp. 279–83.

379 'O Bhiksus, my words should be accepted by the wise, not out of regard for me, but after due investigation – just as gold is accepted as true only after heating, cutting, and rubbing.' Ganganatha Jha (trans.), *The Tattvasaṅgraha of Shāntarakṣita*, Motilal Banarsidass, Delhi 1986, vol. ii, p. 1558. text 3588.

380 Both sides eventually signed the Good Friday Agreement on 10 April 1998, which enabled a peaceful resolution to the dispute.

381 This is one of the eight wonderful qualities of the great ocean described by the Buddha and recorded in the *Pahārāda Sutta, Book of the Eights, sutta* 19 in the *Aṅguttara Nikāya*; see E. M. Hare (trans.), *Gradual Sayings*, vol. i, Pali Text Society, Oxford 1995, p. 136; or Bhikkhu Bodhi (trans.), *The Numerical Discourses of the Buddha*, Wisdom Publications, Boston 2012, p. 1142; also *Udāna* 5.5, in John D. Ireland (trans.), *The Udāna and the Itivuttaka*, Buddhist Publication Society 2007, pp. 68–70.

382 See *Aṅguttara Nikāya, Book of the Eights, sutta* 53, in E. M. Hare (trans.), *Gradual Sayings*, vol. iv, Pali Text Society, Oxford 1995, pp. 186–7; and Bhikkhu Bodhi (trans.), *The Numerical Discourses of the Buddha*, Wisdom Publications, Boston 2012, p. 1193.

383 *Dhammapada*, verse 276.

CHAPTER 32

384 The story of King Bimbisāra's first meeting with the Buddha is told in the *Pabbajā Sutta* of the *Saṃyutta Nikāya*; the king saw the Buddha (who was not yet Enlightened) through his palace window, and Siddhattha promised to visit him once he had gained Enlightenment. This he did, and King Bimbisāra became one of the Buddha's chief lay supporters. There are many reference to him in the *Jātaka* stories, including the tale of how the king came to a sad end at the hands of his son, Prince Ajātasattu.

385 For example, in *Saṃyutta Nikāya* (44.10), Vacchagotta the wanderer asks the Buddha whether there is a self, but the Buddha does not answer. After Vacchagotta has left, Ānanda asks the Buddha why he gave no

answer to the question, and the Buddha explains that any answer to such a question would imply the extreme of either eternalism or nihilism, and furthermore that the result of any answer would be that 'the bewildered Vacchagotta would become even more bewildered'; see Bhikkhu Bodhi (trans.), *The Connected Discourses of the Buddha*, Wisdom Publications, Somerville 2000, pp. 1393–4; or F. L. Woodward (trans.), *Kindred Sayings*, part 4, Pali Text Society, London 1980, pp. 278–9.

386 The story is told in various places in the scriptures, for example in the *Ariyapariyesana Sutta, Majjihma Nikāya* (i.167–70); see Bhikkhu Ñāṇamoli and Bhikkhu Bodhi (trans.), *The Middle Length Discourses of the Buddha*, Wisdom Publications, Boston 1995, pp. 260–2, or I. B. Horner (trans.), *Middle Length Sayings*, vol.i, Pali Text Society, London 1967, pp. 211–3.

387 Vinaya, *Cullavagga V*, 33.1; see I. B. Horner (trans.), *The Book of the Discipline*, part 5, Pali Text Society, Oxford 1992, pp. 193–4.

388 In the Vedic system, *dakṣiṇi* is the gift from a student to his teacher at the end of his studies. In early times the gift was often a number of cows.

389 Kumārila Bhaṭṭa lived in the seventh century CE, contemporaneous with the Buddhist philosopher Dharmakīrti, and is widely taken to have exercised an influence on his younger contemporary Śaṅkara (fl. c. 710). The legendary account of his life says that he studied at the Buddhist monastic university at Nālandā, then in its prime, and used the knowledge gained to try to counter Buddhist philosophical positions.

CHAPTER 33

390 Christmas Humphreys died in 1983, aged 82 years.

391 The Triratna Buddhist Order has over 2,000 members as of 2016.

392 'O Bhikṣus, my words should be accepted by the wise, not out of regard for me, but after due investigation – just as gold is accepted as true only after heating, cutting, and rubbing.' Ganganatha Jha (trans.), *The Tattvasaṅgraha of Shāntarakṣita*, Motilal Banarsidass, Delhi 1986, vol. ii, p. 1558. text 3588.

393 Dhammachari Dharmarakshita accompanied Sangharakshita to Ajmer, and translated this.

CHAPTER 34

394 BAMCEF is the All India Backward And Minority Communities Employees

Federation. The organization was founded in 1971 with the aim of changing India's social (caste) system.

395 'Buddha and the Future of His Religion' in Dr Babasaheb Ambedkar, *Writings and Speeches,* vol. xvii (part 2), Education Department, Government of Maharashtra 2003, p. 107.

CHAPTER 35

396 See, for example, the *Ānāpānasati Sutta, Majjhima Nikāya* (iii.82–5) in Bhikkhu Ñāṇamoli and Bhikkhu Bodhi (trans.), *The Middle Length Discourses of the Buddha*, Wisdom Publications, Boston 1995, pp. 943–6, or I. B. Horner (trans.), *Middle Length Sayings*, vol.iii, Pali Text Society, London 1967, pp. 124–6. See also the *Satipaṭṭhāna Sutta, Majjhima Nikāya* (i.55–6) in Bhikkhu Ñāṇamoli and Bhikkhu Bodhi (trans.), *The Middle Length Discourses of the Buddha*, Wisdom Publications, Boston 1995, pp. 145–6, or I. B. Horner (trans.), *Middle Length Sayings*, vol.i, Pali Text Society, London 1967, pp. 71–2. See also the *Mahāsatipaṭṭhāna Sutta, Dīgha Nikāya* (ii.291), in M. Walshe (trans.), *The Long Discourses of the Buddha*, Wisdom Publications, Boston 1995,

pp. 335–6, or T. W. Rhys Davids (trans.), *Dialogues of the Buddha,* part 2, Pali Text Society, London 1971, p. 328. See also *Saṃyutta Nikāya* ch. 10, no. 54 (*Ānāpānasaṃyutta*) in Bhikkhu Bodhi (trans.), *The Connected Discourses of the Buddha*, Wisdom Publications, Somerville 2000, pp. 1765–6, or F. L. Woodward (trans.), *Kindred Sayings*, part 5, Pali Text Society, London 1979, pp. 275–80.

397 Buddhaghosa, *Visuddhimagga* (278–80), in Te Maung Tin (trans.), *The Path of Purity*, Pali Text Society, Oxford 1975, ch. 8, pp. 319–21. This is a commentary by Buddhaghosa on the Buddha's words in the *Satipaṭṭhāna Sutta.*

398 The *Mettānisaṃsa Sutta* is in the *Book of the Elevens* of the *Aṅguttara Nikāya;* see F. L. Woodward (trans.), *Gradual Sayings*, vol. v, Pali Text Society, Oxford 1996, p. 219, or Bhikkhu Bodhi (trans.), *The Numerical Discourses of the Buddha*, Wisdom Publications, Boston 2012, p. 1573.

399 The Buddha speaks of extending *mettā* in all directions in verse 150 of the *Karaniya Mettā Sutta, Sutta Nipāta* 1.8; see K. R. Norman (trans.), *The Rhinoceros Horn and Other Early Buddhist Poems*, Pali

Text Society, London 1985, p. 24, and in verse 76 of the *Tevijja Sutta, Dīgha Nikāya* (i.250–1); see M. Walshe (trans.), *The Long Discourses of the Buddha,* Wisdom Publications, Boston 1995, p. 194, or T. W. Rhys Davids (trans.), *Dialogues of the Buddha,* part 1, Pali Text Society, London 1973, pp. 317–8.

400 See *Aṅguttara Nikāya, Book of the Eights, sutta* 53, in E. M. Hare (trans.), *Gradual Sayings,* vol. iv, Pali Text Society, Oxford 1995, pp. 186–7; and Bhikkhu Bodhi (trans.), *The Numerical Discourses of the Buddha,* Wisdom Publications, Boston 2012, p. 1193.

401 For example, see the second section of the *Mahāvagga* of the Vinaya Piṭaka, in which a group of monks who are sitting down in silence are criticized by some people who want to hear the Dhamma and say, 'How can these recluses … sit in silence, like dumb pigs?' Hearing about this, the Buddha says, 'I allow you, monks, having assembled together … to speak *dhamma*.' See I. B. Horner (trans.), *Mahāvagga II, Book of the Discipline,* part 4, Pali Text Society, Oxford 1996, p. 131.

402 This story is told in the *Kakacūpama Sutta, Majjhima*

Nikāya (i.125–6); see Bhikkhu Ñāṇamoli and Bhikkhu Bodhi (trans.), *The Middle Length Discourses of the Buddha,* Wisdom Publications, Boston 1995, pp. 219–20; or I. B. Horner (trans.), *Middle Length Sayings,* vol. i, Pali Text Society, London 1967, p. 162.

403 BAMCEF is the All India Backward And Minority Communities Employees Federation. The organization was founded in 1971 with the aim of changing India's social (caste) system. DS4 is short for Dalit Shoshit Samaj Sangharsh Samiti, an organization formed in 1981 and later dissolved by Mr Kanshi Ram, who formed a purely political party, the Bahujan Samaj Party.

404 *Ariyapariyesanā Sutta, Majjhima Nikāya* (i.161–3). For the 'noble search' and the 'ignoble search', see Bhikkhu Ñāṇamoli and Bhikkhu Bodhi (trans.), *The Middle Length Discourses of the Buddha,* Wisdom Publications, Boston 1995, pp. 254–6; or I. B. Horner (trans.), *Middle Length Sayings,* vol.i, Pali Text Society, London 1967, pp. 205–6.

CHAPTER 36

405 'They [the *brahma vihāras*] are to be understood as

divine in the sense of 'best' (or highest), and by their faultless natures. For these states are best as constituting the right mode of conduct towards other beings.' Buddhaghosa, *The Path of Purity*, Pe Maung Tin (trans.), Pali Text Society 1975, p. 369.

406 GLOSSARY *Maggasaṃyutta*, in the *Mahāvagga* of the *Saṃyutta Nikāya*; see Bhikkhu Bodhi (trans.), *The Connected Discourses of the Buddha*, Wisdom Publications, Boston 2000, pp. 1524–5; also F. L. Woodward (trans.), *Kindred Sayings*, part 5, Pali Text Society, London 1979, p. 2.

INDEX

Introductory note

References such as '178–9' indicate (not necessarily continuous) discussion of a topic across a range of pages. Wherever possible in the case of topics with many references, these have either been divided into sub-topics or only the most significant discussions of the topic are listed. Because the entire work is about 'Dr Ambedkar' and 'Buddhism', the use of these terms (and certain others which occur constantly throughout the book) as entry points has been restricted. Information will be found under the corresponding detailed topics.

abhaya mudrā 367, 385–6
Abhidhamma 281, 468, 489
abstention 19, 51, 259, 523
abuses 51, 57, 347, 354–5, 366, 368
adultery 265, 420, 463, 475
advancement 36, 58, 60, 129, 153
Agra 19, 150–1
ahiṃsā 68, 108, 364, 426, 523
Ahmedabad 157–8, 279, 449–51, 459, 466, 468–9, 471, 476–8
Ahmednagar 176, 292, 370, 476
aids to change 370–8
Ajanta caves 313, 363, 383
Ajmer 158, 486, 489, 497–9
akāliko 314, 316–17, 320
All-India Dharma Parishad 279, 449

Ambedkar, Bhimrao, *see also*
  Introductory Note
Buddha and His Dhamma, The 11–12, 63–4, 72, 130, 135–59, 360–1, 528, 538
conversion xvi, 37, 163, 407
  milestones on road to 45–73
death 76, 92, 107, 157, 330
Dhamma Revolution 407, 410–14
followers 18, 21–3, 123–4, 150, 154, 158–9, 208, 217
meetings with author 13–24
reason and emotion in spiritual life 321–6
search for roots 74–91
significance 3–12
thinking about Buddhism 92–119

Ambedkar (*cont.*)
    turning points in life 219–25
    young 4, 40–2, 45, 179–80
Ambedkar Housing Society Welcoming
    Programme 169–77
anagārikas 259, 279, 308, 318–19,
    394–5, 475, 501, 543
Ānanda 61, 98, 194, 215, 298, 306,
    309, 356
ānāpānasati 203–4, 308, 342, 375, 464,
    470, 543
anariyapariyesanā 528
anger 58, 495, 516–17
animals 89, 186, 221–2, 264–5, 323,
    364–7, 514, 522–3
    four animals of Aśoka 363–9
    sacrifice 76, 89, 100, 143, 236
Annihilation of Caste 101, 106
anthropology 4, 27, 173, 230
ariyapariyesanā 528
army 13, 39–40, 115, 179, 278–9, 496
Aryans 77, 84, 121
Āryasaṅgha xiv, 129, 250
asaṃskṛta-dharmas 527–8
Aśoka 12, 363–4, 367, 369
    four animals of 363–9
Aśvaghoṣa 111, 139–40
ātman 232, 343–4, 398
atrocities 58, 158
Aurangabad 169, 302–3, 305, 312,
    327, 329, 356, 370
Australia 171–2, 189, 492
Avarnas 28–9
avatāras 18, 248, 265, 304, 310, 365,
    474, 484
awareness 86, 214, 216, 294–5, 439,
    445, 514–15, 519

bad habits 371, 410, 418, 420
Bahá'í faith 348, 449
Bamcef 526–7
barbers 39–40, 142, 179
Baroda 4, 42–5, 180
basic principles 66, 156, 249, 546
beef-eating 87–90
belief 66, 68, 113, 120, 143, 228–9,
    283, 493–4

Benares 11, 13, 141, 281, 365, 419,
    468, 488–9
Bengali Brahmins 15–16, 93, 174, 208,
    502
Bhagavad Gītā 95, 102, 266, 466, 482,
    487
bhāvanā 204, 231, 234, 374–5, 521
bhāvanā, mettā 203–5, 375, 490, 494,
    516–18, 521–3, 543, 546
bhikkhu saṅgha 115–16, 172–3, 190,
    194–5, 224–5, 305–6, 317–19,
    339–40
bhikkhunīs 101, 165, 198, 438, 543,
    547
bhikkhus 146–7, 173–4, 194–5, 318,
    337–40, 392–4, 500–502, 535–6
    new kind of 318, 392, 395, 432
    senior 209, 359, 405, 502
bhikṣu saṅgha xiii–xiv, 64, 108, 112–
    18, 128, 131, 318
bhikṣunīs 131
bhikṣus xiv, 89–90, 112–17, 127–8,
    131, 472–4, 543
bhūmisparśa mudrā 381–2, 386, 418
Bible 109–11, 136, 426, 466, 470, 487,
    494, 538
Bihar 66, 175, 478, 489
Bimbisāra, King 54, 142, 478
birth 1, 4, 46, 140, 143, 257, 353–4,
    364–5
blind faith 213, 218, 303, 342, 470–1,
    494
blood 81, 83, 185, 522
Bodh Gaya 202, 208, 220, 235, 237,
    381, 418, 478–9
bodhi 294, 324, 451–3
bodhisattvas 60, 89, 115, 140, 149,
    249, 254–5, 421
bodhyaṅgas 291–301
body 51, 150–1, 187, 233, 273–4,
    287–8, 398, 442
Bombay 62–4, 150, 153–5, 208–10,
    244–5, 277–8, 404–5, 439–42
Brahmanism 52, 63, 86, 88–90, 120,
    257, 319, 364
Brahman
    Nirguṇa 228
    Saguṇa 228

Brahmin 16, 26, 28–30, 30, 52, 76–7,
    84–90, 184–6, 236–7, 257, 391,
    537
  Bengali 15–16, 93, 174, 208, 502
  by birth 257, 537
  liberal-minded 45, 52
breath 203–4, 375, 470, 516, 520–1
breathing, mindfulness of 470, 490,
    516, 520
Broken Men 81–3, 85–8, 90, 121, 132
brotherhood 144, 290, 422, 496
Buddha, turning points in life 219–25
Buddha and His Dhamma, The 11–12,
    63–4, 72, 130, 135–59, 360–1, 528,
    538
Buddha images 128, 367, 415, 419,
    421, 460–1
Buddha Jayanti 19, 21, 133, 169, 187,
    335, 450, 465
Buddha puja 323, 419
Buddhacarita 111, 139–40
Buddha-Dhamma xii, 380, 391
Buddhaghosa, Acharya 200, 297, 516,
    537, 546
Buddhahood 213, 248–50, 252, 378,
    520
Buddha's death 98, 254, 271
Buddha's life 110, 139–40, 220, 381–2,
    385
Buddha's teaching xv, xvii, 142–3, 383–
    4, 461–2, 479–80, 484, 545–6
Buddhayan 164, 170–1, 218, 268, 300,
    309, 401, 525
Buddhism
  disappearance from India 387–95
  and education 435–48
  in India and in England 499–512
  as morality 178–88
  as only alternative 422–34
  propagation 69–70, 108, 112, 117,
    119, 121, 172, 223–4
  reasons for choice 466–75
Buddhist activities 312, 421–2, 436,
    490, 492, 498, 504–5, 510
Buddhist Bible 108, 110–11, 136–8,
    172, 223–4, 317, 528
Buddhist ceremonies 66, 110, 119,
    335–6

Buddhist community xviii, 56, 113,
    163, 166, 189, 339–40, 392–5
Buddhist countries 66, 112, 118–19,
    173, 256–7, 332, 507, 535–6
Buddhist movements xiii–xiv, 158–9,
    211–12, 238–42, 245, 281–2,
    490–2, 503–6
Buddhist organizations 153, 208, 212,
    281, 293, 307–8, 479, 483
Buddhist philosophy 13, 245, 338–9,
    384, 389
Buddhist scriptures 51, 64, 145, 174,
    198, 247, 251, 271
Buddhist sūtras 278, 356–62, 382, 454,
    466, 487, 500
Buddhist teachers 170, 173–4, 213,
    320, 467, 472, 510
Buddhist temples 159, 363, 419, 501
Buddhist tradition 200, 251, 259, 291,
    362, 381, 537
Buddhist viharas, *see* viharas
Buddhist worker, new kind of 173–4,
    224, 258, 392–3, 432–3, 435, 510
Buddhist world xiii, 128, 133, 300–301,
    430, 536, 539, 545–6
Buddhists
  Chinese 279, 488, 501
  ex-Untouchable 24, 151, 154
  Hīnayāna 361, 506
  Indian 139, 163, 242, 261, 286, 336,
    361, 507–8
  Japanese 197, 261, 295, 362, 507
  local 166, 280, 416, 468, 488
  Mahāyāna 255, 361, 506
  new xiii, 171, 317, 428, 503, 506
  newly converted 21, 152–3, 155–8,
    335
  one-hundred-percent 211–12, 239–
    40, 242, 268–9, 281, 307–8, 341,
    432–3
  Sinhalese 16, 56, 72, 133, 151, 197,
    488, 507
  Theravāda 183, 254, 316, 338
  Tibetan 171, 197
  true and false distinguished 270–6
  Western 336–7, 357, 382
bullock carts 40–1, 43–4, 122, 180,
    238, 298, 358–9, 416

bullocks 89, 358, 522–3
Burma xiii, 11, 56, 69–71, 119, 133, 174, 197
businesses, cooperative 202, 241, 259, 267, 320, 491–2, 531

Calcutta 14, 19, 21, 166, 171, 237–9, 279, 488–9
candles, lighted 22, 177, 246, 292, 324–5, 400, 406, 461–2
caste Hindus 5–7, 28–9, 31–5, 37–8, 48–50, 52–4, 57–9, 221–2
caste system 25–44, 53–4, 175, 240, 349–50, 353–5, 472–3, 532–3
castes 27–31, 174–5, 184–6, 280, 349–50, 353–5, 473, 481–2
  hell of caste xii, 25, 36–7
  high 52, 270, 315, 479
  low 52, 175, 240, 270, 280, 473, 479
  Scheduled Castes 10, 31, 64–5, 68–9, 71, 104, 153, 155
  untouchable 26, 38
cave temples 236, 363
caves 214, 279, 313, 316, 363, 456, 460, 467
ceremonies 73, 122, 126–7, 129, 131, 150–1, 209, 541
  Buddhist 66, 110, 119, 335–6
  conversion, see conversion ceremonies
Ceylon, see Sri Lanka
change
  aids to 370–8
  radical 93, 108, 111, 408, 410–11, 413, 430
Chinese Buddhists 279, 488, 501
Constitution, Indian xii, 3, 6, 8–9, 12, 32, 112, 544
conversion xi–xiii, xvi–xviii, 17, 59–62, 140–2, 430–2, 502–4, 545–7
  ceremonies 21–2, 122, 126, 128, 130–1, 134, 150–2, 155
  mass 151, 155, 170, 190, 199, 201, 223
  meaning of 260–1
  milestones on road to 45–73

movement xiii–xvii, 151–4, 158, 177, 242, 335, 503–4
cooperative businesses 202, 241, 259, 267, 320, 491–2, 531
corruptions 347, 354–5
courage xviii, 98–9, 118, 154, 172, 367–9, 386
cows 26, 76, 84, 88–90, 192–3, 221, 273, 374
craving 143, 213, 259, 287–8, 310, 345
crowds 21, 23, 48, 127, 176, 406, 473

Dadar 14, 16, 18, 54, 60, 150, 208, 238
dāna 216, 249, 267, 345, 361, 367, 393, 397
danger 216, 221, 240, 313, 357–8, 394, 401–2, 420
darkness 41, 46, 120, 248, 324, 462
dasa sīla upāsakas 246, 308–11, 392, 394–5, 403, 492–3, 544, 547
dasa sīlas 510, 544, 546
Daund 277, 289, 292, 370
dead wood 98, 108, 124, 128
deaths
  Ambedkar 76, 92, 107, 157, 330
  Buddha 98, 254, 271
debt 217, 265
degradation 30, 53, 78, 104, 130, 367
Delhi 11–12, 19, 150, 209–10, 278–9, 488–9, 499–501, 511
delusions 97, 143, 183, 187, 345, 358, 380, 399
demarcation 28–9
democracy xii, xviii, 106
dependants 39, 284, 357
Depressed Classes 5–7, 31, 53–6, 58–9, 62, 69, 75, 77
Depressed Classes Conference 7, 10
development 198, 231–2, 251–2, 333–4, 375, 377–8, 402, 442
  all-round 241, 258, 430, 442–4, 448
  human 199–200, 212, 355, 469, 474
devotion xiv, 15, 181, 267, 302, 400–401, 502
Dhamma, working together for 302–11
Dhamma activities 208, 287, 326, 331, 373–4, 378, 420, 459

Dhamma Revolution 200–202, 292, 407–8, 410–14, 430–4, 508–9, 511
  failure or not 235–43
  and scientific age 404–14
  seed of, see *samādhi*
Dhamma study 173, 189, 242, 268, 308, 376–7, 457, 465
Dhamma work 201–2, 296–7, 330–1, 387, 396, 400–401, 532, 535
dhammacakka 355, 364, 384
Dhammacharinis 165, 393, 395, 511, 544
Dhammacharis 165, 308–9, 387, 392–3, 395, 407, 539, 544
Dhammadiksha 360–1, 388–90, 392–5, 415–16, 483, 501–3, 506–9, 511–12
Dhamma-indriyas 213–14, 216
Dhammamitras 165, 169, 201, 302, 308–11, 401, 545–6
Dhammapada xv, 72, 110, 271–2, 314–15, 366–7, 465, 475
Dhammasahayaks 169, 302, 308, 310–11, 395, 545
Dhamma-shibirs 282, 377–8, 383, 417–18, 457, 490–2, 518–20, 545
Dharma Eye 251–3, 255–6
dharma-cakṣus 251
Dharmapala, Anagārika 14, 93, 208, 211, 237, 239, 318, 384
dhyāna 200, 204, 206, 231, 236, 382, 522
dīkṣā 191, 502, 544–5
disabilities 32, 36–8, 53, 55, 77
  religious 33, 35
disappearance of Buddhism from India 387–95
disciples xiv–xv, 53, 157–8, 163, 197, 235–6, 356, 479–80
dispassion 198, 249
distance 26, 44, 61, 122, 172, 191, 321, 453–4
doctrines 93, 101–2, 108, 146, 338, 446
donkeys 192–3, 273–4, 481
doubt 252, 258, 278, 392, 401, 451, 456, 465
dowry system 192, 217, 265

Dravidians 84
dreams 53, 364, 455, 514, 517
drugs 19, 129, 216, 265, 374, 463, 475
duḥkha 213, 232, 412, 427
duty 119, 185, 212, 215, 262, 266, 481–2, 544
Dvijas 29

East India Company 39
economic condition 6, 125, 286, 474
economics 4–5, 125, 173, 230, 322
education 3, 6, 42–3, 45, 224, 320, 354, 372–4
  and Buddhism 435–48
  first purpose 439
  formal 4, 338–9, 443
  higher 105, 173
  second purpose 439–40
  third purpose 439, 442
educational process 439–41, 443, 446–8
Eightfold Path, Noble 18, 141, 147, 213, 248, 377, 437, 541
Ekajas 29
ekayāna 359, 361–2
elections 10, 125–6, 128, 151, 153, 155
elephants 15, 38, 49, 227–8, 297, 364, 366–7, 369
emancipation 54, 60
emotions 22, 110, 130, 322–3, 325, 383, 443–4, 537
enemies 52, 86, 146, 204–5, 366, 376, 517–18, 521
energy 194–6, 198, 213–14, 296–8, 366–9, 396–7, 508, 530–2
England 238–41, 267–8, 280–6, 289–91, 329–31, 370–3, 488–92, 504–8
  friends in 175–6, 205, 241, 285, 442, 447
English Buddhists 242, 301, 330, 361–2, 380, 417, 484, 507
Enlightenment 18, 234–5, 247–8, 254–5, 314–15, 399–400, 460–1, 474–5
  attainment 45, 140, 378, 391
  Buddha's 198, 258
  Supreme 115, 149, 202, 226, 270, 478

enmity 121, 145, 271, 310, 314–15, 364, 376

enthusiasm 134–5, 199–203, 205–6, 292, 297, 474, 476, 524
  lack of xvi, 118, 134, 199, 201, 431

equality 68, 101–2, 105–8, 143–4, 183–7, 354–5, 408, 426
  standing for 101–2

ethics 58, 397, 400, 403, 470, 546

Europe 8, 380, 384, 387, 469, 472, 492, 495–7

evidence 5, 82–3, 85, 89, 93, 96, 159, 470
  direct 82, 85

evil 35, 75, 103, 198, 249, 424, 429, 532

exclusion of Untouchables from Hindu temples 6–7

existence 80–1, 227, 229, 343–4, 347, 397–8, 427, 429
  conditioned 232
  true nature of 227–9, 231–5

exogamy 27

experience 96–8, 206, 256, 343, 424–5, 445–7, 471, 475
  personal 4, 40, 229, 373, 398, 424, 470–1, 505

exploitation 411–12, 427, 434, 462, 508

ex-Untouchable Buddhists 24, 151, 154

Eye of Truth 251

faculties, spiritual 207–18

faith xiii, xv, 110–11, 159, 171–2, 181, 213–14, 342–3
  blind 213, 218, 303, 342, 470–1, 494

false speech 19, 129, 154, 216, 259, 310, 374, 463

families 40, 42, 179, 437–8, 453–4, 456, 481–3, 535–6

fearlessness 367–9, 385–6, 521

festivals 61, 70, 120, 410, 417–18, 465

fetters xv, 193, 252–3, 257, 456
  first 252, 456
  second 252, 456–7
  third 253, 457

five precepts 17–19, 73, 130, 132–3, 141, 150–1, 216, 545–6

flowers 72, 195, 208, 292, 298, 324–5, 453, 461–2

followers 97–9, 120–2, 130–3, 140–2, 221–3, 348, 361–2, 450–2
  true 154, 218, 301, 369, 378

food 38–9, 41–2, 81, 216, 262–5, 288, 383, 399–402

football 304, 307–8, 310–11, 442, 487, 492

force 3, 103, 105, 107, 120, 426–7, 472, 475

formal education 4, 338–9, 443

founders of religions 94–5, 97, 99, 138, 424–5

four animals of Aśoka 363–9

fraternity 105–7, 144, 183, 185–7, 192, 194, 408, 411

freedom 33, 65, 99, 183, 198, 426, 539, 546
  political 108, 426
  social 70, 108

French Revolution xii, 70, 106, 373, 408–9

friendliness 24, 204, 215, 312, 375, 445, 470

friends
  in England 175–6, 205, 241, 285, 442, 447
  Hindu 205, 338, 347, 361, 450, 469, 506
  near and dear 204–5, 375–6, 470, 494

friendship 377, 386, 443–4, 446–7, 546
  spiritual 446, 448, 545

fundamental principles 105, 109, 183, 186

fundamental unity 131, 133, 141, 147

FWBO 163, 165, 241, 245–6, 250, 254, 407, 518

Gandhi, Mahatma xi, 5–9, 31, 53, 57–9, 75–6, 111, 125

garlands 15, 273, 292, 325, 373, 400, 420, 502

Germany 1, 5, 8, 319, 372–3, 472

ghettoes 32–3, 38–40, 123

God 95–7, 99–102, 228–9, 283, 344–5, 424–5, 469, 481–2

existence of 342, 344–5
messenger of 18, 94–7, 109, 248,
425, 474
son of 94, 96, 424–5
word of 97, 109, 426, 494
goddesses 33, 129–30, 239, 410, 541
gods, Hindu 89, 130, 192, 217, 239,
264, 360, 418
going for Refuge 17, 128, 244–59, 340,
483, 536
levels of 256–7, 483
gold xv, 33, 62, 93, 425, 471, 494, 536
Goregaon 40–1, 179–80
gospels 69, 94–7, 103, 109–11, 141
gossip 273–4, 310, 420, 464
Gotamī, Kisā 233–4
Gotami, Mahāpājapatī 142, 198, 518
Government 3, 19, 38–9, 47–9, 68–9,
153–4, 284, 531–3
graded inequality 28, 30, 77, 353–4
Gujarat 331, 371, 402, 404, 449–51,
469, 477, 486
gurus 30, 250, 280, 295, 304, 468,
475

habits, bad 371, 410, 418, 420
hair 40, 43–4, 179, 274, 279
happiness 185–6, 200, 204, 206, 234,
236, 266, 342
hardships 32, 53–4
Harijans, *see* Untouchables
health 9, 67, 232, 377, 514
hell of caste xii, 25, 36–7
hereditary principle 354–5
higher states of consciousness 116, 183,
232, 522
Hīnayāna 73, 123–4, 137, 255, 361,
506–7
Hindu community 33–4, 50, 55, 57, 65,
132, 428
Hindu friends 205, 338, 347, 361, 450,
469, 506
Hindu gods 89, 130, 192, 217, 239,
264, 360, 418
Hindu society 28, 32, 68, 75, 101, 103,
353–5, 360
Hindu temples 6–7, 33, 339, 419, 461,
471

Hinduism 53–5, 57–9, 61, 99–104,
181–2, 184, 423–7, 480–2
renunciation 40, 43–4, 53–4, 56–7,
59, 73, 124, 154
Hindus 84–5, 103–4, 174–5, 351–3,
416–19, 480–2, 484, 537–9
caste 5–7, 28–9, 31–5, 37–8, 48–50,
52–4, 57–9, 221–2
non-caste 28–9, 49
orthodox 18, 48, 50, 54, 56, 208,
211, 221
history 79, 83, 173, 222–3, 321–2, 411,
413–14, 495–6
holy places 419, 467, 489
Buddhist 210, 488, 501
Hindu 488
horses 186, 264, 273–5, 364–7, 369,
475
householders 145–6, 389, 535
houses 43, 58, 210, 233, 357–8, 401–2,
405–6, 535
human beings 185–6, 351–5, 377–8,
380, 421–5, 473–4, 480–2, 494–7
human development 199–200, 212,
355, 469, 474
humanity 36, 72, 96, 101, 106, 129,
148, 232–3
husbands 17, 146, 192, 216, 259, 453,
494, 521

ideal society 106, 113, 115, 412
ideals 23, 47, 113, 115, 173, 194, 243,
255
ignorance 36, 179, 226, 324, 343
images 71, 323–4, 380–3, 385–6, 391–
2, 416–19, 454, 459–63
imagination 78, 110–11, 171
impermanence 143, 232, 251–3, 288–9,
358, 461
impurities 80, 143, 145, 271
incense 246, 324–5, 462, 545
Indian Buddhist Society 11, 21, 23, 68,
123, 128, 151, 156
Indian Buddhists 139, 163, 238, 242,
261, 286, 336, 507–8
Indian Constitution xii, 3, 6, 8–9, 12,
32, 112, 544
Indian Dhammapada 109–10

indriyas 213–14, 396
inequality 52, 58, 99, 101–3, 106, 129,
    135, 353–4
  graded 28, 30, 77, 353–4
infallible scriptures 99–100
initiation 77, 101, 110, 112, 133
initiative, taking 302–6, 311, 366, 395,
    440, 446, 539
injustice 51, 135, 179, 222, 322
inspiration 134–5, 200–202, 205–6,
    267, 275, 279, 474, 478–9
intoxicating drinks 19, 129, 216, 463,
    475
Islam 54–5, 57, 348, 350, 353, 355,
    470, 472
Italy 170, 173–4, 189–90, 370, 387,
    472

Jabalpur 24, 157
Jaikwadi 363, 369–70
Japan 69, 197, 236–7, 301, 357, 360,
    379, 384
Japanese Buddhists 197, 261, 295, 362,
    507
Jesuits 116–17, 318–19
Jesus 94–7, 99, 211, 315, 417, 424–5,
    495
Jewel of the Dhamma, losing and finding
    260–9
jewels 135, 262–4, 275–6, 300, 380,
    386, 536, 545–6
jungle 202, 219, 280, 366, 374, 381,
    399, 460
justice xii, 78, 145, 147, 407
  social 105

Kālāmas 470–1
Kalimpong 13, 157, 207–8, 210, 281,
    468, 489, 501–2
kalyāṇa mitras 317, 320, 376, 475,
    516
kalyāṇa mitratā 246, 309, 446–8, 516,
    545–6
karma 100, 102, 143–4, 278, 289, 484
karuṇā 231, 233–4, 323, 342, 358,
    360–1, 380, 537
Kashyapji, Jagdish 281, 468, 489, 501,
    521

Kasturchand Park 22–3, 176, 406, 503
Kathmandu 11, 21, 407, 526
Kavitha 58–9
Keluskar, Krishnaji Arjun 45
kesas 190, 311, 531, 536, 546
kings 227–8, 350, 365, 390–1, 393,
    408, 472, 478
knowledge 4, 43–4, 92, 94, 237–9, 322,
    372–3, 439–41
Krishna 10, 64, 94–7, 99, 102–3,
    424–5, 541
Kshatriyas 28–30, 77–8, 84, 101, 184–
    5, 191, 195, 481–2
kusala dhammas 225, 287, 309–10,
    332, 360, 546
Kusinara 11, 17, 19, 73, 478, 488, 501,
    503

lack of enthusiasm xvi, 118, 134, 199,
    201, 431
ladies 171, 221, 292, 296, 302, 316,
    464, 534
lagna-vidhi 335–6
language 36, 111, 166, 170, 251–2,
    316–17, 331, 480
last messenger of God 95–6
law 62, 76–7, 104, 181, 289, 349–51,
    354, 441
laymen 19, 114, 129–31, 254–5, 348,
    389–90, 544
laywomen 129, 131
leaders 15, 46, 52, 54, 56, 303–6, 330,
    509
  great 12, 65, 72, 123, 126, 128, 130,
    135
lecture tour in India 161–3
lectures 157–9, 174, 260–2, 299–300,
    404–7, 446–7, 503–4, 525–7
letters 40, 92, 174, 179, 208–9, 312,
    314, 317
levels of going for Refuge 256–7, 483
liberal-minded Brahmins 45, 52
liberty 98, 105–8, 144, 183–4, 186–7,
    192, 194, 408
life
  changing 189–96
  spiritual 47, 96, 114, 246, 253, 309,
    385, 508

lighted candles 22, 177, 246, 292, 324–5, 400, 406, 461–2
lions 186, 364–5, 367, 369
liquor 192, 216–17, 335, 360, 410
litter 445–6
localities 415–16, 421, 459, 462, 466, 468, 470, 477
Lok Sabha 10, 69, 126
Lokamitra, Anagārika 164, 286, 292–3, 388, 393, 401–3, 418, 497
London 4–6, 230, 241, 277–8, 282–3, 299, 489–90, 498
lotuses 128, 130, 185, 313, 364, 378, 520
loudspeakers xv, 22, 130, 164, 176, 406
love 143–4, 204, 212–13, 215, 267, 470, 483–4, 494
Lumbini 19, 237, 280, 468, 489

magazines 93, 202, 208, 241, 290, 320, 349, 421
Maha Bodhi 14, 65, 68, 93, 119, 171, 190, 208
Maha Bodhi Society 14–16, 56–7, 155, 208–9, 211, 239, 279–80, 501–2
Mahad 6, 48–9, 52, 176, 219–20, 225, 286, 292
Maharashtra 151–4, 169–72, 223–5, 370–1, 379–81, 387–8, 404–5, 476–7
Mahars 37–40, 42, 45, 60–1, 82–3, 151–2, 154, 532–3
Mahāsaṅgha 194–5, 379, 386, 392, 433, 474, 483
Mahāyāna 73, 123–4, 137, 231, 254–5, 257, 361, 506–7
Mahāyāna sūtras 60, 89, 137, 139, 148, 198, 345, 361
Mahāyāna traditions 142, 255, 543
maitrī 186–7, 192, 323, 362, 374–6, 380, 470, 537
Malaysia 301, 350
Manmad 176, 291, 293, 300–301, 370, 476
Manusmṛti 6, 50–1, 54, 68, 220–3, 225, 292, 368

Marathi 4–5, 170, 407, 409, 465, 469, 480, 542–3
Marathwada 158, 387–8, 393, 395–6, 404, 410, 473–4, 534
marriage 9, 27, 68, 110, 265, 336, 410, 536
  ceremonies 217, 335–6
Marx, Karl 11, 69, 411–12, 427, 508
mass conversion 120–35, 179, 181, 238, 423, 427, 429–31, 468
  ceremony 151, 155, 170, 190, 223
  movement 149–50, 152, 329, 406, 421, 423, 427–31, 433
meaning of conversion 260–1
meanings, and words 476–85
meditation 201–3, 242, 295, 297–8, 374–8, 470, 522–3, 531
  classes 189, 201–3, 245, 282, 297, 308, 436, 490
  experience of 231, 246, 398, 457
meetings between author and Ambedkar 13–24
memoirs xvi, 174–5, 387
mental energies 267, 297, 375
mental states 187, 296, 528
  skilful 187, 375
  unskilful 296, 333, 381
messenger of God 18, 94–7, 109, 248, 425, 474
mettā 186, 204–5, 375–6, 470, 517, 521–2, 536–7, 546
  developing 470, 522
mettā bhāvanā 203–5, 375, 490, 494, 516–18, 521–3, 543, 546
Mettānisaṃsa Sutta 517
microphones 22, 176, 210, 228, 305, 400, 406, 503
Middle Way 141, 396–403, 460
Milarepa 107, 109, 170
Milind College 169, 287, 302–3, 312–13, 327–46, 396, 513
milk 49, 185, 229, 482
mindfulness 145, 203–4, 214, 216, 267, 294–5, 543, 546
  of breathing 470, 490, 516, 520
Minister for Law 8, 62, 67, 76
miracles 23, 95–6, 146, 345, 461
miraculous cures 344–5

mitras 165, 245-6, 513, 545-6
mitras, kalyāṇa 317, 320, 376, 475, 516
Mohammed 10, 94-9, 424-5
monasteries, big 390-1, 509
Monastic Order 112, 129, 131-2, 146
money 118-19, 201-2, 216-17, 265-6, 286, 393, 481, 490-2
monks 17-18, 131-3, 254-6, 258-9, 261, 383, 389-94, 501
moral rules 193, 253, 456
morality 99-100, 102-4, 144-5, 249, 284, 287, 333-4, 425-6
  Buddhism as 178-88
  sanction of 104, 172, 181, 334, 426
  sense of 104, 181, 426
mothers 194-5, 198, 205, 210, 215, 260, 263, 301
mountains 172, 299, 321, 427
movement xiii, xvii-xviii, 166, 202-3, 258-9, 422-3, 427-8, 517-18
movement of mass conversion 149-50, 152, 329, 406, 421, 423, 427-31, 433
mudrās 379-86, 418
Mukherjee, Shyama Prasad 208-9, 502
music 170, 444, 466, 477
Muslim invasion 66, 236, 389, 391-2, 394
Muslims 7, 9, 180, 184, 236, 238, 350-3, 472
Mysore State 467, 488

Nagpur 21-4, 120-3, 126-8, 176-7, 209-10, 404-7, 468, 503-4
Nālandā 390, 489
Nanded 387-8, 395-6, 476
nationalities 205, 260, 319, 360, 377, 458, 524, 532-3
near and dear friends 204-5, 375-6, 470, 494
necessities 6, 50, 98, 108, 110, 112
  social 99, 182
nectar 298, 463, 475
Nehru, Pandit 8, 10, 68, 75, 450
Nepal 175, 280, 347, 349-50, 468, 489, 496, 501

new kind of Buddhist worker 173-4, 224, 258, 392-3, 432-3, 435, 510
New Zealand 301, 336, 492
newly converted Buddhists 21, 152-3, 155-8, 335
Nibbāna, *see* Nirvāṇa
Nirvāṇa 143, 145, 287-8, 344-5, 452-3, 527-8, 531, 538-9
Noble Eightfold Path 18, 141, 147, 213, 248, 377, 437, 541
non-Buddhists 141, 267, 323, 340, 344, 495, 502, 505
non-caste Hindus 28-9, 49
non-violence 100, 108, 411-13, 508
non-violent revolution 412-13
North India 26, 480, 488, 501
nuns 19, 129, 131

objections 59, 87, 101, 106, 126, 525, 539
objects 26, 60, 62, 66, 86, 89, 112, 514
observances 18, 79, 100, 102, 155, 253, 259, 394
  religious 61, 193, 253, 456
occupations 26, 84, 102-3, 115
  unclean 26
ocean 183, 195, 372, 452, 455-6, 458, 473
offerings 34, 324-5, 461
old Hindu gods 192, 217, 239, 264, 360, 418
oṃ maṇi padme hūṃ 520
oṃ muni muni mahā muni śākyamuni svāhā 520
one-hundred-percent Buddhists 211-12, 239-40, 242, 268-9, 281, 307-8, 341, 432-3
openness 515-16
Order members 165, 436-8, 513, 518, 530, 535, 539, 544
origin of Untouchability 75-6, 79, 84-5, 87, 230
orthodox Hindus 18, 48, 50, 54, 56, 208, 211, 221
outcastes 4, 31, 53-4

Paganism 104
palaces 38, 191, 202, 365, 399, 478, 487

Pāli 137–8, 229–31, 294, 297–9, 316,
    357, 480–2, 546–7
  scriptures 52, 137, 183, 227, 385,
    390, 516–17, 522
  studying 13, 156, 281, 468, 489
pañcasīla 192–3, 215–16, 299, 324,
    405, 410, 475, 483, *see also* five
    precepts
pantheism 228–9
paramitas 141, 147, 249, 287, 361,
    366, 381–2
parents 26–7, 153, 353, 438, 440,
    447–8, 523, 525
Parsis 43–4, 180, 348
People's Education Society 8, 286,
    292–3, 302, 312, 320, 441, 448
perfections 143, 147, 249, 287, 470
personal experience 4, 40, 229, 373,
    398, 424, 470–1, 505
philosophy 4, 42, 46–7, 70, 75, 241,
    397–8, 403
  Buddhist 13, 245, 338–9, 384, 389
poetry 181, 198, 270, 278, 359, 444
political career 10, 62, 69
political freedom 108, 426
political power 7, 35, 57, 184, 353,
    359, 408–9
political science 4, 70, 173, 322
political slavery 34–5, 50
politicians 14, 128, 151, 155, 157,
    201–2, 509
politics 4, 122, 125–6, 134, 284–5, 330,
    332–3, 532
Poona 11, 17, 24, 32, 39, 59, 157–8,
    169–71, 176, 178, 197, 201–11,
    226, 286, 406–7, 417, 497
positive emotional responses 248, 323,
    342
possessions 26, 263, 449, 453
poverty 53, 105–7, 179, 222, 400, 411,
    426
power, political 7, 35, 57, 184, 353,
    359, 408–9
prajñā 143, 226–34, 324–6, 342,
    358–9, 361, 380–2, 396–9, *see also*
    pañcasīla
precepts 131, 187, 193–4, 216, 259,
    433, 544, 546

five 17–19, 73, 130, 132–3, 141,
    150–1, 216, 545–6
private property 49, 221, 412, 427, 508
property 3, 47, 106, 112, 114, 354,
    411, 481
  private 49, 221, 412, 427, 508
psychology 99, 397, 399, 403, 444
publicity 201, 245, 532
puja 217, 323–5, 437, 457, 481, 484,
    545
punishment 34, 62, 76, 86, 146
purification 49, 51–2, 287, 538
purity 67, 141, 143, 232, 275, 287,
    452, 458
Purna, Anagārika 480–1

quarrels 63, 103, 192, 195, 205, 359,
    364

radical change 93, 108, 111, 408, 410–
    11, 413, 430
Rajagriha 54, 150, 190, 502
Rajasthan 371, 404, 486–7
Rajbhoj, P.N. 64–5
Rajya Sabha 10–11, 69
Ramakrishna Mission 23, 115–17, 211
real Buddhists 131–2, 192–3, 239, 242,
    374, 378, 390, 456
rebirth 12, 73, 144, 149, 343–4, 411–
    12, 428, 432
receptivity 515–16
recollection 267, 294–5, 313
red lotus throne 275
Refuge 17–18, 128–33, 212, 214–18,
    246–59, 267–8, 483, 534–6
religion
  as morality 178–88
  and secular state 347–55
religions, founders of 94–5, 97, 99,
    138, 424–5
religious observances 61, 193, 253, 456
religious wars 184, 472, 495
responsibility 60–1, 241, 246, 303–5,
    366–7, 393, 440, 445–6
retreats 159, 169, 173, 189, 203, 245,
    436–7, 545
revival 14, 17, 67, 70, 130, 451, 526,
    528

revolution 63, 76, 388, 408–10, 412–
13, 431–2, 469
French xii, 70, 106, 373, 408–9
social 1, 289, 509, 525–6
rice 193, 264, 296, 399, 467
right action, see śīla
right livelihood 267–8, 283, 377–8,
437, 441, 491–2, 508
righteousness 120, 141, 143, 145, 257
rights 22, 30, 35, 64, 82–3, 184, 349, 440
rivers 195, 298, 300, 374, 427, 452–8,
473
robes 18, 20, 114, 128, 261, 293, 316,
319
Roman Catholic Church 116, 184,
318–19, 349, 352–3
roots 70, 106, 144
search for 74–91
ruins 52–3, 178, 478
rules, moral 193, 253, 456
rūpa-dhyānas 200–201

sacrifices 66, 89, 100, 122, 125, 134,
143, 217
animal 76, 89, 100, 143, 236
Saddharma Puṇḍarīka Sūtra 261, 357,
359, 362
salvation 1, 94, 97, 108, 425–6, 469
samādhi 197–206, 213–14, 231, 298–9,
342, 358–9, 380–2, 396–8
sāmaṇeras 280, 338, 467–8, 547
saṃsāra 193, 358, 412, 527–8, 531
sanantana-dhamma 312–20
sangha xiii–xiv, 17–18, 128–9, 212–16,
250, 256–9, 473–5, 482–4
saṅgha
bhikkhu 115–16, 172–3, 190, 194–5,
224–5, 305–6, 317–19, 339–40
bhikṣu xiii–xiv, 64, 108, 112–18,
128, 131, 318
new kind of xiv, xvii, 224, 258, 318–
19
Sangharakshita xii–xvii, 2, 163–6, 175,
327, 335, 530, 544–7
and teaching of Dr Ambedkar 277–
90
Sanskrit 36, 137–8, 229–31, 357, 361,
480–1, 543–4, 546–7

Śāntideva 109, 137, 213, 297
Sarkhej Roza 477–8
Sarnath 19, 56, 280, 383–4, 419, 467,
478, 488
Satara 40, 42, 179
sati 203, 214, 216, 267, 543; see also
mindfulness
satkāya-dṛṣṭi 193, 252
Scheduled Caste Federation 8, 18, 63,
69, 128
Scheduled Castes 10, 31, 64–5, 68–9,
71, 104, 153, 155
scholarship 4, 43, 45, 78, 153, 180
schools 35, 42, 58, 171, 173, 197, 278,
438–40
science 105, 107, 110, 116–17, 365,
411, 413, 425–6
political 4, 70, 173, 322
scriptures 29–30, 32–4, 50, 100, 247,
271, 309, 466
Buddhist 51, 64, 145, 174, 198, 247,
251, 271
infallible 99–100
Pāli 52, 137, 183, 227, 385, 390,
516–17, 522
search for roots 74–91
secular state 133, 393–4
and religion 347–55
self, unchanging 232
self-abnegation 94, 97, 99
self-confidence xviii, 303
self-mortification 219–20, 381, 399, 460
self-respect 50, 55, 134, 508
self-view 252
Shankaracharya 348, 389, 391, 449
shelter 81, 263, 400, 444, 488
shibir 282–3, 308, 378, 383, 418,
518–19, 535, 545
Sholapur 62, 176, 404, 407, 414, 476
Shudras 26, 28–32, 34, 76–8, 82, 84,
101, 184–5
Siddharth College 16, 63, 190, 209,
260, 435, 448, 502
significance of Ambdekar 3–12
Sikhism 7, 44, 55–7, 86, 348, 411, 449
Sikkim 19, 174, 209
śīla 143, 186–7, 231, 309–10, 332–4,
374, 420, 463–5

śīlavrata-parāmarśa 193, 253
silence 19, 125, 226, 406, 519–20
Singapore 13, 279, 347, 488, 501
Sinhalese Buddhists 16, 56, 72, 133,
    151, 197, 488, 507
skilful mental states 187, 375
skills 78, 439–41
slavery 1, 4, 34–5, 74, 222, 360, 428
    political 34–5, 50
smṛti 294–5
social change 178–9, 451, 479
social freedom 70, 108
social justice 105
social life 104, 108, 397, 400–403, 426,
    525
    fundamental principles of 102, 105–
    6, 183, 186
social necessities 99, 182
social revolution 1, 289, 509, 525–6
society 104, 113–15, 178–9, 181, 208–
    9, 284–5, 426–7, 439–41
    ideal 106, 113, 115, 412
    new 182, 186–8, 194, 218, 241, 243,
    505, 508
    New Society 505
son of God 94, 96, 424–5
South India 13, 279–80, 314–15, 467,
    472, 482, 488, 501
speeches 23, 43–4, 51, 57, 64, 67–8,
    179, 187
spiritual community 118, 124, 129,
    131–3, 141, 147, 250, 258–9
spiritual faculties 207–18
spiritual family 195, 225, 277, 301,
    360, 379–80, 396, 422
spiritual friendship 446, 448, 545
spiritual life 47, 96, 114, 246, 253, 309,
    385, 508
śraddhā 323, 325–6, 337–8, 342, 507
Sri Lanka 10, 65–7, 70–1, 119, 230,
    279–80, 501, 506–7
statues 3, 9, 159, 321, 380, 385, 396
stories 3, 138, 140, 226–7, 262–3, 288,
    295, 357–61
    little 288, 294–5, 314
Stream Entrants 250, 252, 390, 455–6,
    483
Stream Entry xiii–xiv, 252–7, 449–58

strength 43, 262, 268, 297, 362, 366–7,
    369, 514–15
students 90, 93, 153–4, 171, 175,
    439–40, 442, 446–7
stupas 14, 88, 508
śūnyatā 338, 345–6, 398, 484
sūtras 182, 261, 278, 357, 359, 382,
    466, 487
    Buddhist 278, 356–62, 382, 454,
    466, 487, 500
    Mahāyāna 60, 89, 137, 139, 148,
    198, 345, 361
Sweden 171–2, 189, 319, 492

TBMSG (Trailokya Bauddha Mahasangha
    Sahayak Gana) 164–6, 239, 245,
    305–10, 407, 526–7, 545, 547
teachers xi, 29, 36, 42, 447–8, 471,
    474, 528
    Buddhist 170, 173–4, 213, 320, 467,
    472, 510
teachings 96–9, 108–10, 137–8, 197–8,
    262, 356–8, 361, 385–6
temples 33, 272, 417, 419, 478, 481,
    488, 492
    Buddhist 159, 363, 419, 501
    cave 236, 363
    Hindu 6–7, 33, 339, 419, 461, 471
Thailand 156, 197, 309, 317, 350, 355,
    496, 506–7
Theravāda Buddhism 112, 183, 254,
    316, 338
Tibet 56, 66, 174, 236–8, 384, 392,
    402, 429–30
Tibetan 109, 137–8, 170, 507
Tibetan Buddhism 171, 197, 244, 361,
    452, 531
tisaraṇa 192–3, 216, 266–7, 378, 380,
    392, 405, 483
tolerance 148, 183, 350, 366–7, 369,
    397, 472, 495
tradition 34, 98, 125, 130–1, 141–2,
    247, 348, 365
Trailokya Bauddha Mahasangha 165–6,
    201, 203, 205, 286–7, 433–4, 436,
    544
Trailokya Bauddha Mahasangha
    Sahayak Gana, *see* TBMSG

transformation 81, 191, 251–2
transitoriness 251, 288
trees 228, 264, 294, 453, 514
Tripiṭaka 271, 344
Triratna Buddhist Order and
    Community xiii–xviii, 165–6,
    543–7
true Buddhists 194, 206, 234, 367, 380
    and false distinguished 270–6
true nature of existence 226–34
truth 61, 213, 219–20, 235, 247–8,
    251, 267, 479–80

U Chandramani 17, 73, 127–9, 131,
    209, 280, 467–8, 501–3
unchanging self 232
understanding xvi–xvii, 18, 20, 256–7,
    266–7, 325, 338–9, 372–3
United States 351, 373, 440, 446, 492
unity 131, 133, 141, 147, 192, 332,
    336, 362
unskilful mental states 296, 333, 381
Untouchability 31–2, 36–7, 75–6, 79–
    80, 82–3, 86–8, 90, 428–9
    origin 75–6, 79, 84–5, 87, 230
untouchable castes 26, 38
untouchable communities 33, 37, 55,
    59, 62, 82, 151–2
Untouchables 1, 4–12, 25–7, 29–39,
    48–50, 54–60, 73–80, 82–8
upāsakas 131, 141, 146–7, 165, 173–4,
    338–40, 475, 539
upāsikās 131, 165, 201, 310, 379, 547

Vaishyas 28–30, 77–8, 84, 101, 184–5,
    195, 481
Vajracchedīka Sūtra 278, 382
Valisinha, Devapriya 71, 73, 127–8
vandanā 313, 419
Varnas 28–9, 31, 77–8, 103
Vedas 26, 29, 33–6, 63, 68, 100, 143,
    184–5
viharas 157, 175, 279, 283, 390–2,
    415–21, 459–65, 535
    Buddhist 157, 237, 279, 391–2,
    417–18, 461, 488

function 459–65
    new 415–21, 459, 478
villages 31–3, 58, 80, 82–3, 155–6,
    158–9, 370–2, 416–17
vimutti 183
Vinaya 112–13, 146, 148, 198, 249,
    543
violence xviii, 47, 221, 408–9, 411–12,
    427, 430, 508
vīrya 47, 249, 275, 287, 296–7, 361,
    367, 396–7
Vishnu 18, 46, 129, 265, 310, 365, 541
vows 73, 117, 129–33, 141, 148–9,
    216, 542–3, 547

walls 82, 275, 313, 363, 416, 418, 460
war 47, 363–4, 467, 472, 487–8, 495,
    497, 500–501
    religious 184, 472, 495
water 30, 41, 48–50, 180, 221, 378,
    452–5, 475
Western Buddhist Order xiii–xiv, 166,
    239, 245, 433, 436, 544–5, 547
western India 24, 38, 122, 151, 155
Westerners, reasons for becoming
    Buddhists 486–98
wheel 11, 22, 364, 384–6
White Lotus Sūtra 261–3
winter 158–9, 163, 210, 238, 244, 281,
    468–9, 489
wisdom 96, 143, 145, 212–14, 249,
    251, 396–7, 452
women xiii–xv, 122–3, 186, 325–6,
    400–401, 419–20, 442, 519–20
word of God 97, 109, 426, 494
words and meanings 476–85
World Fellowship of Buddhists 10–11,
    21, 65–6, 70, 119, 332
Worli 18, 67, 260–1, 405, 507

yellow robes 206, 254, 266, 271, 279,
    293, 493, 500
Yeola conference 54, 56, 58, 60, 222–3,
    292, 370, 411
yoga 245, 442

A GUIDE TO THE COMPLETE
WORKS OF SANGHARAKSHITA

Gathered together in these twenty-seven volumes are talks and stories, commentaries on the Buddhist scriptures, poems, memoirs, reviews, and other writings. The genres are many, and the subject matter covered is wide, but it all has – its whole purpose is to convey – that taste of freedom which the Buddha declared to be the hallmark of his Dharma. Another traditional description of the Buddha's Dharma is that it is *ehipassiko*, 'come and see'. Sangharakshita calls to us, his readers, to come and see how the Dharma can fundamentally change the way we see things, change the way we live for the better, and change the society we belong to, wherever in the world we live.

Sangharakshita's very first published piece, *The Unity of Buddhism* (found in volume 7 of this collection), appeared in 1944 when he was eighteen years old, and it introduced themes that continued to resound throughout his work: the basis of Buddhist ethics, the compassion of the bodhisattva, and the transcendental unity of Buddhism. Over the course of the following seven decades not only did numerous other works flow from his pen; he gave hundreds of talks (some now lost). In gathering all we could find of this vast output, we have sought to arrange it in a way that brings a sense of coherence, communicating something essential about Sangharakshita, his life and teaching. Recalling the three 'baskets' among which an early tradition divided the Buddha's teachings, we have divided Sangharakshita's creative output into six 'baskets' or groups: foundation texts; works originating in India; teachings originally given in the West; commentaries on the Buddhist scriptures; personal writings; and poetry, aphorisms, and works on the arts. The 27th volume, a concordance, brings together all the terms and themes of the whole collection. If you want to find a particular story or teaching, look at a traditional term from different points of view or in different contexts, or track down one of the thousands of canonical references to be found in these volumes, the concordance will be your guide.

1. FOUNDATION

What is the foundation of a Buddhist life? How do we understand and then follow the Buddha's path of Ethics, Meditation, and Wisdom? What is really meant by 'Going for Refuge to the Three Jewels', described by Sangharakshita as the essential act of a Buddhist life? And what is the Bodhisattva ideal, which he has called 'one of the sublimest ideals mankind has ever seen'? In the 'Foundation' group you will find teachings on all these themes. It includes the author's *magnum opus, A Survey of Buddhism*, a collection of teachings on *The Purpose and Practice of Buddhist Meditation*, and the anthology, *The Essential Sangharakshita*, an eminently helpful distillation of the entire corpus.

2. INDIA

From 1950 to 1964 Sangharakshita, based in Kalimpong in the eastern Himalayas, poured his energy into trying to revive Buddhism in the land of its birth and to revitalize and bring reform to the existing Asian Buddhist world. The articles and book reviews from this period are gathered in volumes 7 and 8, as well as his biographical sketch of the great Sinhalese Dharmaduta, Anagarika Dharmapala. In 1954 Sangharakshita took on the editing of the *Maha Bodhi*, a journal for which he wrote a monthly editorial, and which, under his editorship, published the work of many of the leading Buddhist writers of the time. It was also during these years in India that a vital connection was forged with Dr B. R. Ambedkar, renowned Indian statesman and leader of the Buddhist mass conversion of 1956. Sangharakshita became closely involved with the new Buddhists and, after Dr Ambedkar's untimely death, visited them regularly on extensive teaching tours.

From 1979, when an Indian wing of the Triratna Buddhist Community was founded (then known as TBMSG), Sangharakshita returned several times to undertake further teaching tours. The talks from these tours are collected in volumes 9 and 10 along with a unique work on Ambedkar and his life which draws out the significance of his conversion to Buddhism.

3. THE WEST

Sangharakshita founded the Triratna Buddhist Community (then called the Friends of the Western Buddhist Order) on 6 April 1967. On 7 April the following year he performed the first ordinations of men and women within the Triratna Buddhist Order (then the Western Buddhist Order). At that time Buddhism was not widely known in the West and for the following two decades or so he taught intensively, finding new ways to communicate the ancient truths of Buddhism, drawing on the whole Buddhist tradition to do so, as well as making connections with what was best in existing Western culture. Sometimes his sword flashed as he critiqued ideas and views inimical to the Dharma. It is these teachings and writings that are gathered together in this third group.

4. COMMENTARY

Throughout Sangharakshita's works are threaded references to the Buddhist canon of literature – Pāli, Mahāyāna, and Vajrayāna – from which he drew his inspiration. In the early days of the new movement he often taught by means of seminars in which, prompted by the questions of his students, he sought to pass on the inspiration and wisdom of the Buddhist tradition. Each seminar was based around a different text, the seminars were recorded and transcribed, and in due course many of the transcriptions were edited and turned into books, all carefully checked by Sangharakshita. The commentaries compiled in this way constitute the fourth group. In some ways this is the heart of the collection. Sangharakshita often told the story of how it was that, reading two *sūtras* at the age of sixteen, he realized that he was a Buddhist, and he has never tired of showing others how they too could see and realize the value of the '*sūtra*-treasure'.

Who is Sangharakshita? What sort of life did he live? Whom did he meet? What did he feel? Why did he found a new Buddhist movement? In these volumes of memoirs and letters Sangharakshita shares with his readers much about himself and his life as he himself has experienced it, giving us a sense of its breadth and depth, humour and pathos.

6. POETRY, APHORISMS, AND THE ARTS

Sangharakshita describes reading *Paradise Lost* at the age of twelve as one of the greatest poetic experiences of his life. His realization of the value of the higher arts to spiritual development is one of his distinctive contributions to our understanding of what Buddhist life is, and he has expressed it in a number of essays and articles. Throughout his life he has written poetry which he says can be regarded as a kind of spiritual autobiography. It is here, perhaps, that we come closest to the heart of Sangharakshita. He has also written a few short stories and composed some startling aphorisms. Through book reviews he has engaged with the experiences, ideas, and opinions of modern writers. All these are collected in this sixth group.

In the preface to *A Survey of Buddhism* (volume 1 in this collection), Sangharakshita wrote of his approach to the Buddha's teachings:

> Why did the Buddha (or Nāgārjuna, or Buddhaghosa) teach this particular doctrine? What bearing does it have on the spiritual life? How does it help the individual Buddhist actually to follow the spiritual path?... I found myself asking such questions again and again, for only in this way, I found, could I make sense – spiritual sense – of Buddhism.

Although this collection contains so many words, they are all intent, directly or indirectly, on these same questions. And all these words are not in the end about their writer, but about his great subject, the Buddha and his teaching, and about you, the reader, for whose benefit they are solely intended. These pages are full of the reverence that Sangharakshita has always felt, which is expressed in an early poem, 'Taking Refuge in the Buddha', whose refrain is 'My place is at thy feet'. He has devoted his life to communicating the Buddha's Dharma in its depth and in its breadth, to men and women from all backgrounds and walks of life, from all countries, of all races, of all ages. These collected works are the fruit of that devotion.

We are very pleased to be able to include some previously unpublished work in this collection, but most of what appears in these volumes has been published before. We have made very few changes, though we have added extra notes where we thought they would be useful. We have had the pleasure of researching the notes in the Sangharakshita Library at 'Adhisthana', Triratna's centre in Herefordshire, UK, which houses his own collection of books. It has been of great value to be able to search among the very copies of the *suttas*, *sūtras* and commentaries that have provided the basis of his teachings over the last seventy years.

The publication of these volumes owes much to the work of transcribers, editors, indexers, designers, and publishers over many years – those who brought out the original editions of many of the works included here, and those who have contributed in all sorts of ways to this *Complete Works* project, including all those who contributed to funds given in celebration of Sangharakshita's ninetieth birthday in August 2015. Many thanks to everyone who has helped; may the merit gained in our acting thus go to the alleviation of the suffering of all beings.

Vidyadevi and Kalyanaprabha
Editors

THE COMPLETE WORKS OF
SANGHARAKSHITA

TITLE AND CONTENTS

I FOUNDATION

VOLUME I A SURVEY OF BUDDHISM / THE BUDDHA'S NOBLE EIGHTFOLD PATH
A Survey of Buddhism
The Buddha's Noble Eightfold Path

2 THE THREE JEWELS I
The Three Jewels
Going for Refuge
The Ten Pillars of Buddhism
The History of My Going for Refuge
Was the Buddha a Bhikkhu?
Forty-Three Years Ago
My Relation to the Order
Extending the Hand of Fellowship
The Meaning of Conversion in Buddhism

3 THE THREE JEWELS II
Who is the Buddha?
What is the Dharma?
What is the Sangha?

4 THE BODHISATTVA IDEAL
The Bodhisattva Ideal
The Bodhisattva Principle
The Endlessly Fascinating Cry

5 THE PURPOSE AND PRACTICE OF BUDDHIST MEDITATION
The Purpose and Practice of Buddhist Meditation

6 THE ESSENTIAL SANGHARAKSHITA
The Essential Sangharakshita

TITLE AND CONTENTS

II INDIA

VOLUME 7   CROSSING THE STREAM: INDIA WRITINGS I
           Early Writings 1944–1954
           Crossing the Stream
           Buddhism in the Modern World
           Ordination and Initiation in the Three Yānas
           Buddhism in India Today
           A Bird's Eye View of Indian Buddhism
           The Meaning of Orthodoxy in Buddhism

        8 BEATING THE DHARMA DRUM: INDIA WRITINGS II
           Anagarika Dharmapala and Other 'Maha Bodhi' Writings
           Dharmapala: The Spiritual Dimension
           Beating the Drum: Maha Bodhi Editorials
           Book Reviews

        9 DR AMBEDKAR AND THE REVIVAL OF BUDDHISM I
           Ambedkar and Buddhism
           Lecture Tour in India, December 1981– March 1982

       10 DR AMBEDKAR AND THE REVIVAL OF BUDDHISM II
           Lecture Tours in India 1979 & 1983–1992

       III THE WEST

       11 A NEW BUDDHIST MOVEMENT I
           The Buddha's Victory
           The Taste of Freedom
           Buddha Mind
           Human Enlightenment
           New Currents in Western Buddhism
           Buddhism for Today – and Tomorrow
           Ritual and Devotion in Buddhism
           Great Buddhists of the Twentieth Century
           Articles and Interviews

VOLUME 12   A NEW BUDDHIST MOVEMENT II
Previously Unpublished Talks

13   EASTERN AND WESTERN TRADITIONS
Buddhism and the West
The FWBO and 'Protestant Buddhism'
Buddhism, World Peace, and Nuclear War
From Genesis to the Diamond Sūtra
Dialogue between Buddhism and Christianity
Aspects of Buddhist Morality
Buddhism and Blasphemy
Buddhism and the Bishop of Woolwich
Buddhism and the New Reformation
Alternative Traditions
Creative Symbols of Tantric Buddhism
Tibetan Buddhism
The Essence of Zen

IV COMMENTARY

14   THE ETERNAL LEGACY / WISDOM BEYOND WORDS
The Eternal Legacy
The Glory of the Literary World
Wisdom Beyond Words

15   PALI CANON TEACHINGS AND TRANSLATIONS
Dhammapada (translation)
Karaniya Metta Sutta (translation)
Living with Kindness
Living with Awareness
Mangala Sutta (translation)
Auspicious Signs (seminar)
Tiratana Vandanā (translation)
Salutation to the Three Jewels (seminar)
The Threefold Refuge (seminar)
Further Pāli Sutta Commentaries

TITLE AND CONTENTS

VOLUME 16   MAHĀYĀNA MYTHS AND STORIES
The Drama of Cosmic Enlightenment
The Priceless Jewel (essay)
Transforming Self and World
The Inconceivable Emancipation

17   WISDOM TEACHINGS OF THE MAHĀYĀNA
Know Your Mind
Living Ethically
Living Wisely
The Way to Wisdom (seminar)

18   MILAREPA AND THE ART OF DISCIPLESHIP I
Milarepa and Rechungpa Seminars

19   MILAREPA AND THE ART OF DISCIPLESHIP II
Milarepa and Rechungpa seminars
The Yogi's Joy

V MEMOIRS

20   THE RAINBOW ROAD FROM TOOTING BROADWAY TO KALIMPONG
The Rainbow Road from Tooting Broadway to Kalimpong

21   FACING MOUNT KANCHENJUNGA
Facing Mount Kanchenjunga
Dear Dinoo: Letters to a Friend

22   IN THE SIGN OF THE GOLDEN WHEEL
In the Sign of the Golden Wheel
Precious Teachers
With Allen Ginsberg in Kalimpong 1962 (essay)

23   MOVING AGAINST THE STREAM
Moving Against the Stream
1970: A Retrospective
Moseley Miscellany Writings

TITLE AND CONTENTS

VOLUME 24   THROUGH BUDDHIST EYES
              Travel Letters
              Through Buddhist Eyes

              VI POETRY AND THE ARTS

        25   POEMS AND STORIES
              Complete Poems 1941–1994
              The Call of the Forest
              Moseley Miscellany Poems
              Adhisthana Poems
              How Buddhism Disappeared from India: A Satire
              The Cave
              The Artist's Dream
              The Talking Buddha
              The Antique Dealer
              The White Lotus
              The Two Roses
              The Healer

        26   APHORISMS AND THE ARTS
              Peace is a Fire
              A Stream of Stars
              The Religion of Art
              In the Realm of the Lotus
              The Journey to Il Convento
              St Jerome Revisited
              A Note on the Burial of Count Orgaz
              Criticism East and West
              Book reviews
              Urthona articles and interviews

        27   CONCORDANCE AND APPENDICES